THE S. MARK TAPER FOUNDATION

IMPRINT IN JEWISH STUDIES

BY THIS ENDOWMENT
THE S. MARK TAPER FOUNDATION SUPPORTS
THE APPRECIATION AND UNDERSTANDING
OF THE RICHNESS AND DIVERSITY OF
JEWISH LIFE AND CULTURE

The publisher and the University of California Press Foundation gratefully acknowledge the generous support of the S. Mark Taper Foundation Imprint in Jewish Studies.

How to Read the Mishnah and Midrash

How to Read the Mishnah and Midrash

An Introduction to Early Rabbinic Literature

ISHAY ROSEN-ZVI

Translated by   DANIEL TABAK

UNIVERSITY OF CALIFORNIA PRESS

University of California Press
Oakland, California

© 2026 by The Regents of the University of California.

Original Hebrew language title: *Between Mishna and Midrash: The Birth of Rabbinic Literature*, by Prof Ishay Rosen-Zvi © 2020 by The Open University of Israel.

Library of Congress Cataloging-in-Publication Data

Names: Rosen-Zvi, Ishay, author. | Tabak, Daniel, translator.
Title: How to read the Mishnah and Midrash : an introduction to early Rabbinic literature / Ishay Rosen-Zvi ; translated by Daniel Tabak.
Description: Oakland, California : University of California Press, [2025] | Includes bibliographical references and index.
Identifiers: LCCN 2025017594 (print) | LCCN 2025017595 (ebook) | ISBN 9780520389830 (hardback) | ISBN 9780520389847 (paperback) | ISBN 9780520389854 (ebook)
Subjects: LCSH: Rabbinical literature—History and criticism.
Classification: LCC BM496.6 .R663 2025 (print) | LCC BM496.6 (ebook) | DDC 296.1/2306—dc23/eng/20251114
LC record available at https://lccn.loc.gov/2025017594
LC ebook record available at https://lccn.loc.gov/2025017595

GPSR Authorized Representative: Easy Access System Europe, Mustamäe tee 50, 10621 Tallinn, Estonia, gpsr.requests@easproject.com

35 34 33 32 31 30 29 28 27 26
10 9 8 7 6 5 4 3 2 1

CONTENTS

Preface   vii

PART I Mishnah

Introduction: The Emergence of Halakhic Literature   3

1. The Form of the Mishnah   17
2. The Mishnah's Sources and Layers   34
3. The Mishnah's Legal Sources   52
4. The Editing of the Mishnah   75
5. The Mishnah as a Composition   94
6. Aggadah and Halakhah in the Mishnah   112
7. The Transmission and Textual History of the Mishnah   137
8. The Tosefta and the Mishnah   155

Epilogue: The Mishnah and Future Scholarship   176

PART II Midrash

Introduction: Understanding Midrash   183

9. Biblical Interpretation in Second Temple Literature   197
10. The Schools of Rabbi Akiva and Rabbi Yishmael   218
11. The Motivations of Midrash   238
12. Midrash's Conception of the Biblical Text   267
13. The Self-Awareness and Didacticism of Midrash   290
14. Aggadah in the Midrash   310
15. The Midrash and the Mishnah   332
16. The Editing and Transmission of the Midrash   348

Epilogue: The Midrash and Future Scholarship   367

Notes   369
Bibliography   417
General Index   447
Index of Primary Sources   450

PREFACE

The early rabbinic period saw the formation of two major literary corpora: the Mishnah and the Midrash. These have remained the two main pillars of Jewish textual engagement ever since: the former for the thematic study of Halakhah (Jewish law), and the latter for the systematic study of Scripture. In a sense, all subsequent rabbinic literature is cut from the cloth of the Mishnah and the Midrash.

Each work is revolutionary in its own way, representing a dramatic shift from the works and genres that precede it. The Mishnah presents for the first time in history a comprehensive Jewish legal system independent of the Bible. It includes a strikingly wide range of legal topics, encompassing everything from ritual law and marital status to monetary damages and capital punishment. Some of these laws have biblical precedents, others date from earlier postbiblical traditions, and still others are entirely new. The Mishnah assimilates and organizes these all into a coherent and comprehensive legal system. But why does the Mishnah essentially fashion a new Torah instead of building upon the existing one? And why does it not, at least formally, preserve a connection to Scripture?

The Midrash is another riddle. Anyone who learns it is taken aback by the gap between the biblical verses and the midrashic conclusions. Why does the Midrash reject or diverge from more straightforward readings of the text? Are its farfetched ideas genuine interpretations intended to explicate the text, or might they be independent teachings masked as exegesis to acquire biblical authority? What rabbinic conception of the Torah's text allows for such radical manipulations of the biblical text?

How to Read the Mishnah and Midrash endeavors to address these two puzzles in turn, focusing first on the Mishnah as a new Torah and then on the innovative hermeneutics of the Midrash. As it proceeds, it also tries to solve a third puzzle: the relationship between these two works. Could the same study houses have produced such utterly different legal compositions, the one an independent juristic project, and the other a line-by-line engagement with Scripture?

In its exploration of the uniqueness of these two foundational works of Jewish law and thought, the book before you constitutes an alternative introduction to early rabbinic literature in English. Its main goal is to examine the Mishnah and the Midrash as intellectual projects, whose logic and goals ought to be understood non-reductively, that is, on their own terms. This sets it apart from new scholarly trends that contextualize the two in terms of sociopolitical history or comparative literature and law, although these (and others) contexts are discussed when pertinent.

This book aims to deeply familiarize readers with the language and logic of the Midrash and the Mishnah. These texts, however, are locked in Hebrew from the mishnaic period. While it was possible to introduce readers of Hebrew to these texts, with relatively minimal mediation, in the Hebrew edition titled *Bein Mishnah le-Midrash* (Open University, 2020), for an English readership the challenge is of a different scale. There are existing translations, which were consulted by the translator along the way, but in their production of an elegant English translation, the contours of the original are often lost. Linguistic affinities and wordplay disappear in the paraphrastic renderings of standard editions. Since much of Midrash reworks or plays with the biblical text, even using a standard Bible translation obscures its workings. The translation therefore strives to create a text that retains the feel of the original; it deliberately does not smooth out irregularities or rephrase odd-sounding locutions since they are part of the character of these texts. We have consulted existing translations, but adapted them so as to keep them as close to the original as possible. An apparatus accompanies every quotation in order to facilitate understanding.

In addition to a new translation of and commentary on the sources, the Hebrew book has been intensively revised and reworked to improve its organization, streamline its argumentation, and update the discussion with scholarship that has appeared since its publication. I hope that the care and effort poured into this work resonate through the final text before you.

I would like to express my wholehearted gratitude to Daniel Tabak, a superb translator who skillfully navigated the delicate balance between preserving my precise meaning and applying his professional judgment on what would and would not work. My research assistant, Yaakov Kroizer, provided invaluable support in diligently and skillfully preparing the text for print.

I am grateful to the UCP editors who guided this project—Eric Schmidt, Margo Irvin, Jyoti Arvey, Cindy Fulton, Jessica Moll, and Robert Demke—whose professionalism and genuine menschlichkeit were evident throughout the process.

I am deeply indebted to Mira Balberg, Daniel Boyarin, David Lambert, Moulie Vidas, and Azzan Yadin, whose insightful feedback played a crucial role in refining the text.

The project that led to this book was funded by the Israeli Science Foundation (no. 202/23).

PART ONE

MISHNAH

Introduction

The Emergence of Halakhic Literature

The Mishnah is a comprehensive code of Halakhah, Jewish law, which summarizes the many fields developed in rabbinic academies from the end of the first century to the beginning of the third century CE. Its reach far exceeds the jurisdiction of modern law, including nearly every conceivable aspect of ancient Jewish life. Beyond the more familiar civil and criminal law, the Mishnah governs everything from daily prayers to dietary restrictions, festival celebrations to sacrificial libations, agricultural practices to ritual purifications.

There is no better way to get a sense of what the Mishnah is all about than to dive right in and read it:

> A sukkah[a] that is taller than twenty cubits[b] is invalid,[c] but R. Yehudah validates it. One that is not taller than ten handbreadths, or does not have three walls, or has more sun than shade[d] is invalid. (*Sukkah*, 1:1)[1]

סוכה שהיא גבוהה מעשרים אמה—פסולה, ור׳ יהודה מכשיר.

ושאינה גבוהה עשרה טפחים, ושאין לה שלוש דפנות, ושחמתה מרובה מצילתה—פסולה.

This mishnah exemplifies many of the Mishnah's characteristics.[2] First, the law of sitting in a sukkah has its origins in the Bible, yet one finds no mention of it here. In fact, there is no

---

   a The booth for the holiday of Sukkot; see Leviticus 23:40–43.
   b The span from the elbow to the tip of the fingers, about 1.5 feet (0.5 meters).
   c Unfit for discharging one's obligation to dwell in a sukkah.
   d The proportion of the sukkah exposed to the sun is greater than that shaded by the vegetative covering.

justification or sourcing whatsoever, which is true of most of the Mishnah.[3] Second, the subject matter is concrete as opposed to abstract. This mishnah opens Tractate *Sukkah*, so one might have expected it to first articulate general principles and then move to their practical applications, but it instead begins with detailed quantification. This focus on defining sizes and minimum and maximum amounts (and, elsewhere, timing) is characteristic of the Mishnah.[4] Finally, the Mishnah's main voice is anonymous, but it sometimes includes dissenting voices attributed to specific rabbis (here, Rabbi Yehudah), and in these latter instances no final ruling decides between them.[5] The Mishnah is clearly no legal code in the conventional sense, but it is also not a jurisprudential textbook that presents the rules and principles of the law.

What is the Mishnah, then? This question will occupy us for the next few chapters, but first we need to become better acquainted with the roots of the Mishnah and its historical formation.

As noted, the Mishnah presents itself as an independent, standalone body of law. In its time, the Mishnah was innovative in this regard (and in many other respects to be detailed throughout the book), but it did not mark the beginning of postbiblical legal development. Though the word "Halakhah" might have been a rabbinic coinage,[6] it was applied to an interpretive phenomenon long in existence. For hundreds of years biblical passages had been elaborated and expanded upon to derive new legal rules, details, and applications. When the rabbis of the mishnaic period (second century CE), known as the Tannaim (literally, "repeaters" or "reciters"), debated different areas of Halakhah, they were relying on long-standing precedent and engaging in conversation with a wide range of existing interpretive traditions.

This chapter explores the broader context in which the Mishnah came into being. It begins by surveying the major trends of halakhic production that preceded the Mishnah and then notes several historical realities of Judaea and the Galilee in the second century CE, which are critical to our understanding of the world in which the rabbis lived.

THE DEVELOPMENT OF BIBLICAL LAW

To properly understand the rabbinic legal activity that culminated in the Mishnah it is necessary to trace its formative precedents: centuries of active engagement with the Bible and the transmission of traditions.

The Bible itself contains several considerable tracts of law: the Covenant Code in Exodus (Ex. 20–23), the Priestly Code in Leviticus and Numbers, and the Deuteronomic Code in Deuteronomy (Deut. 12–26). These collections were composed in different periods and contexts. Their very composition teaches us that the biblical laws were formed and joined together through a lengthy and complex process, and that the formation of legal texts was ongoing, even into the Second Temple period.

As the Pentateuch underwent canonization, its treatment changed accordingly.[7] This can be seen in the use of the Hebrew term *torah*. In certain biblical verses, especially Priestly ones, *torah* refers to a specific law or set of laws (e.g., Lev. 6:18, 12:7). Elsewhere, it has a much broader sense of "instruction" (e.g., Prov. 1:8). Only in time would it come to mean

> THE SECOND TEMPLE PERIOD
>
> The Second Temple stood for about six hundred years, from the end of the sixth century BCE until its destruction in 70 CE. During this period the area called by Jews "the Land of Israel" changed hands many times. The Persian Empire was in control from the fifth to fourth centuries BCE, and Hellenistic rule of Judea followed (the Ptolemies in the third century and the Seleucids in the beginning of the second century BCE). After the Maccabean revolt, the Hasmoneans held on to political control until the Roman conquest in 63 BCE. Rome ruled directly or through local proxy kings (like Herod and Agrippa I) until the destruction of the Second Temple.

"the Torah," reflecting the existence of a nascent canon, with everything that entails for interpretative activity.

After the Pentateuch became *the* Torah in the Persian period (fifth–fourth centuries BCE), the revision and creation of laws continued, but a new interpretive dimension arose. At this point the story becomes rather complicated, because distinct groups engaged in this interpretative activity, but our historical knowledge of them is hazy and uncertain. Since the historical identification of these groups and their chronological order are the subject of endless academic debate, and since the purpose here is merely to acquaint the reader with the Mishnah's precursors, no attempt is made to tell their story linearly or to delineate clear lines of influence between them. Instead, I describe the main features and trends that characterize the pre-mishnaic development of Halakhah by examining three groups: the priesthood, the scribes, and, finally, the various sects of the Second Temple period.

A. The Priests in the Temple as the Source of Law

In late biblical texts, the keeper of the law is often the priest. The prophet Malachi, writing at the beginning of the Second Temple period, describes the priests as teachers of wisdom: "For the lips of a priest guard knowledge *(da'at)*, and they should seek instruction *(torah)* from his mouth, for he is the messenger of the Lord of Hosts" (Malachi 2:7).[8] The priest is God's messenger or representative who guides the people of Israel in His path. In this context, *torah* is clearly being used in its general sense of "instruction."[9] At this early date, then, the priest is a guide to and guardian of God's instruction, but he is nowhere described as an interpreter of a canonized Bible or as a source of new law.

During the Second Temple period, the Temple served as the home of the priests, its cultic functionaries. The priestly elite zealously policed the Temple precincts to ensure adherence to the demanding norms of ritual purity and cultic ritual, and presented themselves as the repository of tradition and legal knowledge. This is reflected in an episode involving the prophet Haggai. Not long after the Second Temple has been finished, Haggai describes a halakhic question that God charged him to ask the priests:

> Thus said the Lord of hosts: Ask the priests for a ruling *(torah)*: If a man carries consecrated meat in the skirt of his garment, and with his skirt touches bread, or stew,

or wine, or oil, or any kind of food, does it become holy? The priests answered, "No." Then Haggai said, "If someone rendered impure by a corpse touches any of these, does it become impure?" The priests answered, "It becomes impure." So Haggai spoke up and said, "So is this people and so is this nation before Me, said the Lord, and so is all their handiwork and what they offer there—it is impure." (Haggai 2:11–14)

Haggai asks the priests for a ruling, a *torah*, about the transmission of holiness when one food ("consecrated meat") touches another ("bread . . . or any kind of food"). The priests respond that ritual impurity is transmissible but holiness is not. Now, the continuation makes clear that the purpose of this question-and-answer session is not to convey the halakhic rulings themselves, but to send a symbolic message to the nation. Nevertheless, one can assume that this episode captures a historical reality: people regularly approached the priests with their questions, since they were the authorities on Temple law, sacrificial law, and purity law. Note that the priests here do not rely on any written text to produce or justify their specific answer (which is far from obvious in light of other biblical texts).[10] They are teachers of the law, not interpreters of text.

A shift can be detected when the Bible introduces Ezra the Scribe. Ezra came from Babylonia to live in Jerusalem in the fifth century BCE, a few decades after the Temple was rebuilt. This great leader and teacher of the law was also a priest, and the book of Ezra takes great pains to trace his priestly lineage all the way back to Aaron, the first priest (Ezra 7:1–5). The books of Ezra and Nehemiah (which are actually two parts of one edited book) credit Ezra with placing the Pentateuch at the forefront of communal gathering in Jerusalem (Neh. 8:8) and stressing its centrality for Judean identity, which gradually transformed it into a book from which ever new laws and instructions could be deduced.

The priests continued to legislate and make halakhic rulings throughout the Second Temple era, and they did not confine themselves to matters of Temple ritual or purity. Thus, in the middle of the Maccabean Revolt against the Seleucid Greeks (167–164 BCE), Mattathias, the founder of the Hasmonean priestly dynasty, ruled that the fight with the enemy had to continue even on Shabbat, as it was a matter of life and death.[11]

Still, most of the extant evidence of priestly legal activity surrounds the Temple. Here is an example from the *end* of the Second Temple period that is described in the Mishnah. The fact that a Sage from the second century CE cited a legal ruling from Temple times as a proof for the correct law sheds light on the continuity between the Temple and the Mishnah's process of halakhic decision making:

Rabbi Yehudah said, "Ben Kuvari testified[a] in Yavneh that any priest who pays the shekel[b] commits no sin."[c]

 a Gave testimony about practices in the Temple from when it was still standing.
 b Who pays the half-shekel tax for the purchase of the public offerings brought in the Temple.
 c He may pay it even though he is under no obligation to do so.

Rabban Yohanan ben Zakkai said to him,[a] "Not so; rather, any priest who does not pay the shekel commits a sin. But the priests expound this verse for themselves:[b] 'And every meal-offering of the priest shall be wholly burnt, it shall not be eaten' (Lev. 6:16)—since the *'omer*, the two loaves, and the showbread[c] would be ours,[d] how could they be eaten?" (*Shekalim*, 1:4)

אמר ר׳ יהודה: העיד בן כוברי ביבנה שכל כהן הוא שוקל אינו חוטא.

אמר לו רבן יוחנן בן זכיי: לא כי, אלא שכל כהן שאינו שוקל חוטא, אלא שהכהנים דורשים מקרא זה לעצמן: "וכל מינחת כהן כליל תהיה לא תאכל", הואיל והעומר ושתי הלחם ולחם הפנים שלנו היאך הן נאכלים?

The half-shekel was a head tax that funded the public offerings in the Temple patterned on the biblical tax for the construction of the Tabernacle (see Ex. 30:13). The annual Temple tax probably originated with the Hasmoneans in the second century BCE.[12] The mishnah opens with two testimonies bearing on the question whether the priests were obligated to bring the half-shekel. Since some of the offerings brought to the Temple were given to them, were they exempt from this tax? According to Ben Kuvari, a priest could volunteer to contribute a half-shekel, while Rabbi Yohanan ben Zakkai countered that a priest had to contribute like everyone else. Both sages lived during the final years of the Second Temple and could have possessed firsthand information about the actual practice.

The priests maintained a third, dissenting view based on a biblical verse. According to their understanding of Leviticus 6:16, any public offerings bought with priestly money would be forbidden for consumption, so the priests were barred from contributing! The priests relied on a biblical verse to answer a question that cut to the heart of their very role and stature in Jewish society: Should priests be taxed? Are they only recipients of public funds or also part of the public itself? The textual interpretation that exempted them from the tax is marked as partisan by Rabbi Yohanan ben Zakkai: "But the priests expound this verse for themselves," that is, they used their special status as halakhic experts to benefit themselves. Of remarkable significance here is that they did not simply pronounce a ruling, but rather expounded the biblical text and thus "deduced" the conclusion they desired.[13]

The takeaway for our inquiry into the process of early halakhic development is that a subtle but all-important change was occurring in halakhic reasoning. Previously, Halakhah had been produced by the priests in the Temple on account of their very authority there. The Bible was only one source of inspiration for them. Other sources were traditions of old and decrees of more recent mintage. The mishnah, though, explicitly notes the role of biblical

---

a To Ben Kuvari.
b For their own benefit.
c Different types of meal-offerings eaten by the priests.
d If we, the priests, were to give the half-shekel, we would be partial owners of the public offerings purchased with it.

interpretation, which in time would be developed into a full-fledged hermeneutical system. While the Mishnah's placement of biblical interpretation at the heart of halakhic legislation in the Second Temple period is probably anachronistic, it does show the growing centrality of the Torah as a source of Halakhah. It also provides a snapshot of the twilight years of the Second Temple period, when three sources of religious authority—priestly ruling, tradition ("testimony"), and biblical interpretation—existed side by side. The evolving relationships between these sources, between priests and sages and between tradition and a canonical text, will be examined in depth below.

B. The Scribes and Biblical Interpretation

The priests in the Temple did not enjoy a monopoly on the production of Halakhah. Authority was also vested in the scribes, who served as clerks and copyists in the halls of government and apparently were also teachers of literacy. They might have even been authors in their own right, not just copyists of existing literary and legal compositions. Part of carrying out their various jobs involved interpretation of the Bible.[14] Ezra "the Scribe" is so called because he is portrayed not just as a priest but also as "a scribe deft in the Torah of Moses" (Ezra 7:6) and "a scribe of the words of the Lord's commandments and laws upon Israel" (7:11). The word "scribe" *(sofer)* here is certainly not intended in the limited sense of a scrivener, but in the broader sense of someone who has great familiarity with a text—an expert, a scholar. Ezra was a priest, a scribe, and a teacher of Torah, embodying every kind of Torah teacher of his era.

The verses from Haggai demonstrated above that in the early Persian period the priests formed and taught *torah*, in the sense of individual rulings. But by Ezra's time, the word *torah* had taken on the new meaning it retains to this day: the five books of Moses known as the Torah. When Ezra is described as a "scribe of the Torah of Moses," it means that he was an expert in the written book of the Mosaic Torah. To dispel any doubt about this, "the Torah of Moses" is also called "the book of (the Torah of) Moses" throughout Ezra and Nehemiah, and is presented as a composition that one could read consecutively (Neh. 8:18). This new conception of *torah* as *the* Torah would reorient Jewish society around a text, making it possible—indeed mandatory—to interpret and reinterpret it and on that basis render new halakhic rulings.

The books of Ezra and Nehemiah contain a lot of halakhic material, including several innovative interpretations of earlier biblical laws. A clear example is the issue of exogamy, intermarriage between Israelites and non-Israelites. The rejection of marriage with foreigners has roots in the Torah, but it first appears as a general prohibition here, regarding the exiles who returned to Second-Temple Jerusalem. While the book of Nehemiah is likely the actual source of the general ban on intermarriage, it presents this law as a straightforward reading of an earlier biblical one:

> On that day they read aloud to the people from the book of Moses, and it was *found written* in it that no Ammonite or Moabite may ever enter the assembly of God, because they did not meet the Israelites with bread and water, and hired Balaam against them to curse them, though our God turned the curse into a blessing.

> When they heard the Torah, they separated from Israel all the mixed multitude.
> (Neh. 13:1–3, emphasis mine)

In this scene, a public reading of the Torah caused an unexpected encounter with an unfamiliar law in what the Israelites considered the divine Book or books, resulting in its immediate application. What is obscured here, though, is that the earlier text does not speak for itself. The verses quoted from the Torah (Deut. 23:4–7) are specifically about Ammonites and Moabites, singled out on account of their historical mistreatment of the Israelites. In fact, immediately afterward the Torah instructs, "Do not eschew the Edomite. . . . do not eschew the Egyptian" (Deut. 23:8). Nehemiah's reading expands the prohibition to include any outsider who has insinuated themselves into "the assembly of God."[15] All foreigners, not only the Moabites and Ammonites, are prohibited from marrying a Judean. This expansive interpretation arguably contradicts the earlier law, which does not have a sweeping ban on (or even a clear concept of) intermarriage!

This act of interpretation is quite radical, but it is not the only one in Ezra and Nehemiah. In a scene that unfolds almost identically to the previous one, the details of a vague biblical commandment are filled in:

> And they found it written in the Torah, which the Lord had commanded via Moses, that the Israelites should live in sukkot (booths) during the festival of the seventh month, and that they should announce and proclaim in all their towns and in Jerusalem as follows, "Go out to the hill country and bring back branches of olive, oil tree, myrtle, palm, and [other] leafy trees to make sukkot, as it is written." So the people went out and brought them, and they made themselves sukkot on their roofs, in their courtyards, in the courtyards of the House of God, in the square of the Water Gate and in the square of the Ephraim Gate. (Neh. 8:14–17)

Here, too, the "reading" of the Torah led to the immediate fulfillment of the law written in it, with the people relying on the authority of Holy Writ ("as it is written"). But let us compare this account with what is in fact written earlier in the Bible about the Festival of Sukkot (Tabernacles or the Festival of Booths):

> On the first day you shall take for yourselves the fruit of beautiful trees, branches of palm trees, boughs of leafy trees, and willows of the brook; and you shall rejoice before the Lord your God for seven days. You shall celebrate it as a festival of the Lord seven days a year; you shall celebrate it in the seventh month as a law for all time, for your generations. You shall live in sukkot for seven days; all citizens in Israel shall live in sukkot. (Lev. 23:40–43)

These verses raise some basic questions: What should one do with the species taken on the first day? How does one rejoice with them for seven days? Is the final verse about living in sukkot a separate command or a summation of what precedes it? In Nehemiah, the answer

> **PHARISEES, SADDUCEES, AND ESSENES**
>
> In his *Antiquities of the Jews* (10:12–20), Flavius Josephus described the difference between these groups in both sociological and philosophical terms. Sociologically, the Sadducees comprised the priestly elite, the Pharisees were the party of the people, and the Essenes lived as an isolated community. Philosophically, the Sadducees completely denied the existence of an afterlife, the Essenes believed only in the eternity of the soul, and the Pharisees had faith in the full resurrection of the dead, restored in both body and soul.

to all these creatively ties them all together: the species are collected in order to build the sukkot! This is a logical interpretation of the verses in Leviticus; if the species are used to build the booths that are lived in for seven days, then it follows that the people are rejoicing with these species for that same length of time.[16] This interpretation is still followed and put into practice by the small Samaritan community today. The reader might be more familiar with the widespread Jewish practice, however, based on the rabbinic reading that discerns two distinct obligations: taking the four species in hand and waving them, and living in sukkot constructed out of any plant material.

The actual relationship between the scribes' activity and the development of biblical interpretation into Midrash, the topic of the second half of this book, is the subject of great scholarly debate.[17] The scribes are seldom mentioned in the sources and might not have even formed a cohesive group. What we don't know about them far outweighs what we do know. But it is clear that the scribe depicted in Ezra and Nehemiah marks an important turning point in halakhic history, with regard to both the authority of the Torah itself as a source of law and the authority of those leaders who expound and expand on it. The written text is read, explained, and used as justification and motivation for halakhic innovation and application.

C. Sectarian Struggles

The development of Halakhah and biblical interpretation was further stimulated by internal competition in Judea later in the Second Temple period. In the second century BCE, Jewish society was riven by sectarian splits. Flavius Josephus, a Jerusalemite priest and historian living at the end of the Second Temple period, wrote of three main groups: the Pharisees, the Sadducees, and the Essenes (these are their anglicized names from the Greek).[18] As with the scribes, the historical record is not as clear as one would like, and some have even argued that these sects existed only on the margins or were relatively small.[19] Even if true, there is no denying that sectarian strife had an outsized influence on halakhic development.

A number of elements divided these groups, but their conflicts over Halakhah are of greatest relevance here. The divisiveness and the plurality of halakhic opinions in this period are indicative of earlier halakhic developments that were further catalyzed by the sectarian polemics. One can see this playing out in some of the Dead Sea Scrolls, which include the writings of the Qumran sect, conventionally identified with Josephus's Essenes.[20]

> **THE DEAD SEA SCROLLS**
>
> In the mid-twentieth century, many ancient scrolls were found in the hard-to-reach Qumran caves near the Dead Sea. Although nearly two millennia old, the scrolls were preserved in good condition because the aridity of the region prevented their decay. Among the many astonishing finds were scrolls belonging to the eponymous Qumran sect. That group's identification with the Essenes has been conjectured on the basis of, among other things, their communal structure, strictures regarding ritual purity, and religious beliefs. The scrolls have been digitized and are viewable online (http://dss.collections.imj.org.il/).

One such composition that combines Halakhah and polemics is known as the Halakhic Letter (its scholarly designation being 4QMMT), from which the following example is illustrative (see figure 1):

Also with regard to poured streams *(ha-mutzakot)* we say that there is no purity in them. Neither can poured streams separate impure from pure, for the liquid of the poured stream and that of the vessel which receives it are a single liquid.[21] (4Q394 f8iv:5–8)[22]

[ו]אף על המוצקות אנחנו אומר[ים] שהם שאין בהם [ט]הרה.
ואף המוצקות אינמ מבדילות בין הטמא [ל]טהור.
כי לחת המוצקות והמקבל מהמה כהמ לחה אחת.

This passage is about the transmissibility of ritual impurity via the stream of liquid that connects two vessels during pouring. According to the sectarian Halakhah, if there is an impure vessel involved, then "there is no purity" in any of the vessels or the liquid—everything becomes impure. Even if the lower, receiving vessel is impure, the impurity is passed against the direction of the flow and gravity to the higher, pouring vessel. The connection created by the poured liquid, however temporary, means that all elements in this closed system must have the same status.

A careful reading of the Qumran text reveals that it is engaging in a halakhic polemic. The sect is staking out its own position—"we say"—against another one and countering an objection about the transfer of impurity back up to the pouring vessel. The unidentified group espousing the contrary halakhic opinion did not deem the liquid connection strong enough to work against the direction of flow and gravity. A mishnah in Tractate *Yadayim*, which deals primarily with the ritual purity of food and drink, helps us identify this "other group" as the Pharisees:

The Sadducees say, We complain against you, Pharisees, for you deem the poured stream *(ha-nitzok)* pure. (*Yadayim*, 4:7)

אומרים צדוקין: קובלין אנו עליכם פרושים שאתם מטהרים את הנצוק.

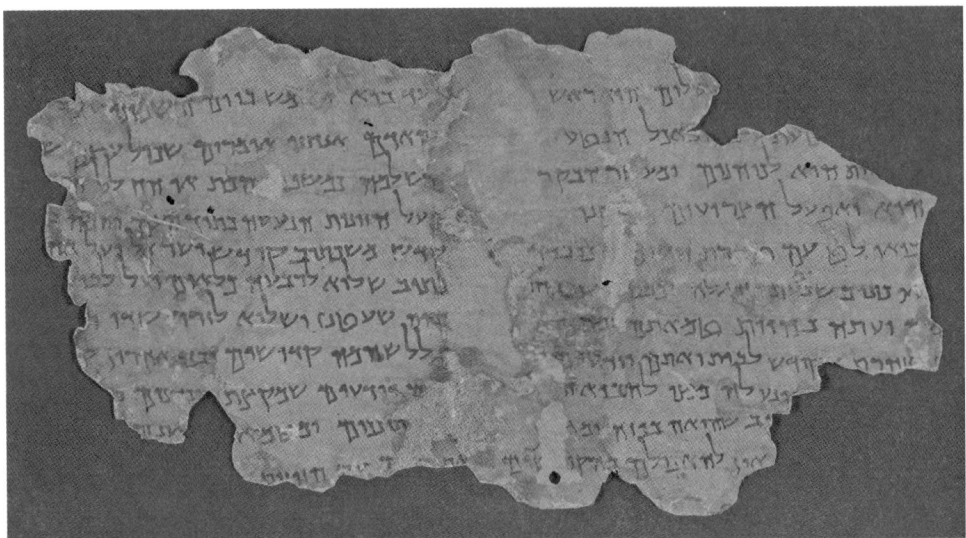

FIGURE 1. The Halakhic Letter (4Q394 –4Q Cal. Doc. D, B-474167). By courtesy of The Leon Levy Dead Sea Scrolls Digital Library. Photographer: Shai Halevi.

Since the disagreement recorded in the Mishnah is already attested in the earlier Halakhic Letter from Qumran, the halakhic difference between Qumranic and mishnaic law does not reflect a historical development in this case, but a debate originating in Temple times.[23] One may well wonder why this minute detail of esoteric law warranted a denunciation of the Pharisees, and why the rabbis turned it into a matter of record. But recall that this law had real implications for everyday living: you would have to be careful about how you filled your cup, poured olive oil into a frying pan, and drizzled honey into a hot drink. In this way, how a given community ruled on this issue (and others relating to the purity of foodstuffs) crystallized its identity and dictated the parameters of permissible contact with outsiders. The strict position of the Qumran sect on the poured stream limited social contact.[24]

Sectarian polemics of this kind spawned from what must have been a hothouse of halakhic creativity during the late Second Temple period. These polemics acted as a feedback loop, as polemics tend to do, that intensified the development of Halakhah. To win over the greatest number of skeptics or those undecided to one's side demands persuasiveness, which can actually generate robuster discourse, deeper attention to details, and more sophisticated justifications.[25]

Another series of texts from the Second Temple period that can help us reconstruct sectarian halakhic debates is the Jewish Apocrypha, particularly the book of Jubilees. It retells the story cycles of Genesis and Exodus, beginning with creation and ending with the giving of the Torah at Mount Sinai. In the course of its retelling, Jubilees fills gaps and solves problems in the biblical narrative, as we shall see in part 2 when we discuss the roots of Midrash. But the major innovation of the book is its integration of law into the narrative of Genesis, backdating it to the very foundation of the world.[26] Although the dating of Jubilees is not settled, its laws and ideology seem pretty close to those of the Dead Sea Scrolls attributed to the Essenes.[27]

> **JEWISH APOCRYPHA**
>
> An assortment of Hebrew books written largely by Jews during the Second Temple period that did not find their way into the Hebrew Bible, the Tanakh, and so the Hebrew originals were lost. Some were included in the Septuagint, the canon of Alexandrian Jewry, which became holy for early Christianity; others were only included in the canons of specific Christian communities. The book of Jubilees, for example, is extant in its entirety only in Ge'ez, the ancient language of Ethiopia, where it was revered as part of the biblical canon. Only in the twentieth century were fragments of the Hebrew original found at Qumran.

Here is an example of a polemic in the book of Jubilees about the fulfillment of the biblical commandment of circumcision:

> This law is (valid) for all history forever. There is no circumcising of days, nor omitting any day of the eight days because it is an eternal ordinance ordained and written on the heavenly tablets. Anyone who is born, the flesh of whose private parts has not been circumcised by the eighth day, does not belong to the people of the pact that the Lord made with Abraham, but to the people (meant for) destruction. [. . .] Now you command the Israelites to keep the sign of this covenant throughout their history as an eternal ordinance so that they may not be uprooted from the earth, because the command has been ordained as a covenant, so that they should keep it forever on all the Israelites.
>
> For the Lord did not draw near to Himself either Ishmael, his sons, his brothers, or Esau. He did not choose them (simply) because they were among Abraham's children, for He knew them. But He chose Israel to be His people. He sanctified them and gathered (them) from all humanity. [. . .]
>
> I am now telling you that the Israelites will prove false to this ordinance. They will not circumcise their sons in accord with this entire law because they will leave some of the flesh of their circumcision when they circumcise their sons. All the people of Belial will leave their sons uncircumcised just as they were born. (Jubilees 15:25–33)[28]

The polemical tone of this passage unmistakable, but its barbs seem aimed at two separate targets. The first is Abraham's firstborn son, Ishmael, whose progeny is identified here, for the first time in recorded history, with the people of Arabia. Although Ishmael was circumcised together with Abraham, he is not considered by the author to be part of God's covenant, since he was thirteen years old at the time of his circumcision (Gen. 17:25). Jubilees stresses that whoever is not circumcised "by the eighth day" is not a member of the divine covenant. A clear distinction is drawn between the Israelites, who ritually circumcise on the eighth day, and everyone else, whether or not they practice circumcision. Jubilees takes pains to reject a plausible understanding of Genesis according to which Ishmael is also included in the circumcision covenant.[29]

But then a second attack is launched, and this time it is directed internally: "I am now telling you that the Israelites will prove false to this ordinance." The author couches his criticism of contemporaries in the guise of a prophecy, but which of his coreligionists does he have in mind? Hellenized Jews, who came under the sway of Greek culture and did not circumcise their children, seem an obvious option. But some scholars argue that the stress is laid not on "they will not circumcise their sons," but on "in accord with this entire law," on the all-important timing of the eighth day.[30] In other words, the author is writing out of the covenant not those who turned their back on Halakhah entirely, but those who subscribed to an alternative halakhic practice of circumcision. Fortunately, the Mishnah preserves just such a tradition of flexibility in carrying out the circumcision of a newborn:

> A child is circumcised on the eighth,[a] the ninth, the tenth, the eleventh, and the twelfth—no more and no less.[b] (*Shabbat*, 19:5)

> קטן נימול לשמונה, לתשעה, ולעשרה, ולאחד עשר, ולשנים עשר—לא פחות ולא יותר.

In the continuation, the mishnah specifies the circumstances under which the circumcision is delayed: for example, if there is uncertainty about when exactly the baby was born, that impacts whether Shabbat is to be counted as the eighth day. When reading this mishnah with the critical "prophecy" of Jubilees in mind, one can speculate that these or similar traditions are its intended target.

The two examples analyzed above, one from the Qumran sect and the other from the Jewish Apocrypha, concern individual laws or legal details. But the Dead Sea Scrolls also furnish us with entire halakhic compositions that can be productively compared with the Mishnah. The Damascus Document, which dates to the early history (or even prehistory) of the Qumran sect, consists of two parts: an extended exhortation and a legal code. The latter devotes an entire section to laying out the laws of Shabbat in detail, which begins as follows:

> Concerning the Sa[bba]th, to observe it in accordance with its regulation. No one should do work on the sixth day, from the moment when the Sun's disc is at a distance of its diameter from the gate, for this is what he said, "Observe the Sabbath day to keep it holy" (Deut. 5:12).
>
> And on the day of the Sabbath, no one should say a useless or stupid word.
>
> He is not to lend anything to his fellow.
>
> He is not to take decisions with regard to riches or gain.
>
> He is not to speak about matters of work or of the task to be carried out on the following day.[31]

a The eighth day after birth, and so on and so forth.
b No earlier and no later.

על הש[ב]ת לשמרה כמשפטה. [] [[ ]] אל יעש איש ביום הששי מלאכה מן העת אשר יהיה גלגל השמש רחוק
מן השער מלואו. כי הוא אשר אמר שמור את יום השבת לקדשו. וביום השבת אל ידבר איש דבר נבל ורק.
אל ישה ברעהו כל. אל ישפוט על הון ובצע. אל ידבר בדברי המלאכה והעבודה לעשות למשכים

These laws have been discussed extensively in academic scholarship, and particular attention has been paid to their similarity to mishnaic laws about Shabbat.[32] But for our purpose the structure is even more important than the content. The Damascus Document contains a thematically organized collection of laws that prevent the profanation of Shabbat. A single biblical verse anchors the opening law, and another one (not included in the citation above) appears later for the closing law, providing a literary frame for the passage as a whole. Most of the laws, however, are not accompanied by any biblical prooftext, nor does their order track anything in Scripture. This thematic organization and independence from the biblical text parallels what we find in the Mishnah.

Beside these works, there is a sizable literature from the Second Temple period replete with halakhic treatments and references, including the allegorical interpretations of Philo, the theological treatments of the New Testament, and the historical records of Josephus.[33] It is beyond the scope of this introduction to delve more deeply into halakhic material from the end of this period. The limited sources explored above suffice to show that the Mishnah did not materialize out of thin air, and that its Halakhah was to a large degree a continuation and outgrowth of the legal material and biblical interpretation that preceded it. Nevertheless, as the next few chapters will show in detail, the Mishnah is, in many respects, in a category of its own.

THE WORLD OF THE RABBIS: A VERY SHORT INTRODUCTION

The rabbinic academies of Judea and the Galilee coalesced under the direct rule of the Roman Empire. A sizable portion of mishnaic law had no practical application in the lifetime of these Sages. Nearly a third of the Mishnah—*Seder Kodashim* about the sacrificial cult of the Temple and much of *Seder Teharot* about the related requirements of ritual purity—was obsolete, because the Second Temple had lain in ruins for decades before its compilation. For the vast majority of Sages quoted in the Mishnah, the Temple that had loomed so large in Jewish life existed only in texts. Even seemingly practical laws, unrelated to the Temple's existence, remained merely theoretical. For instance, the Mishnah's procedural laws for running a trial could not be implemented, because Roman governance disallowed Jewish judicial autonomy.

At the same time, many of the laws set forth in the Mishnah do align with what we know about the Jewish experience in this period. The Mishnah begins with the agricultural laws of *Seder Zera'im*, a fitting choice given that many Galilean Jews earned their living from the soil, as either landowners, sharecroppers, or laborers.[34] The laws of ritual purity detailed in *Seder Teharot* were largely necessitated by the sanctity of the Temple and its offerings, yet strong evidence suggests that they continued to be practiced after its destruction. Texts that attest to the long afterlife of such purity practices well into the second century are corroborated by

> **THE LAND OF ISRAEL**
>
> The territory in which the rabbis of the Mishnah lived had several names. They called it *Eretz Yisra'el*, "the Land of Israel," a name intended to convey both its continuity with the promised land of the Bible and its special halakhic status vis-à-vis certain commandments. They lived mainly in two areas: Judea in the south and the Galilee in the north. The coastal areas and the inland region of Samaria were occupied chiefly by Greek speakers of various ethnicities.
>
> When the Romans occupied this territory, they eventually incorporated it into their empire as a province. It was initially called "Judaea," but after the Bar Kokhba Revolt it was renamed "Syria-Palaestina." Therefore, scholars often refer to this area as "Roman Palestine."
>
> When discussing halakhic issues, this territory will be referred to here by its rabbinic, halakhic designation: "the Land of Israel." For more on the names of the land and their political and religious significance, see Ben-Eliyahu, *Identity and Territory*, 86–109.

archeological findings of many mikvahs (ritual baths) and stone vessels (that are halakhically immune from impurity) from this period.[35]

The types of cities and villages where Jews lived and their demographic makeup are also relevant to understanding rabbinic legal and literary production. Some settled in mostly homogenous Jewish villages, but others took up residence in cities with mixed populations, where daily contact with a variety of other ethnic and cultural groups (Romans, Greeks, Syrians) and religious adherents (Pagans, Christians, Samaritans) was the norm.

The Sages of the Mishnah formed a small, relatively uniform elite. They were not political leaders of the entire Jewish population in Judea and the Galilee by any stretch of the imagination,[36] but they did variously serve as halakhic decisors and religious functionaries for the commonfolk.[37] Furthermore, they constituted the "Great Court," a centralized legislative body that, at least in the early tannaitic period,[38] produced a consensus on communal issues, such as the annual determination of the lunisolar calendar.[39]

The period in question is split in half by the failed Bar Kokhba Revolt (132–135 CE), when the Jews of Judea took up arms against their Roman overlords. This war ended with the destruction of Jewish life in Judea and its permanent relocation to the Galilee. Among those swelling the numbers of the Galilean Jewish population were rabbinic scholars from the city of Yavneh, who resettled in Usha and reconstituted their study houses there. During this period the economic fortunes of the Jews declined rapidly and many landed Jews lost their ancestral estates. By the end of the tannaitic era, though, the Jewish economy was in an upswing, and one can even speak of relative prosperity. Rabbi Yehuda ha-Nasi (early third century) was not only the editor of the Mishnah, but the first chief representative of the Jewish people to be officially recognized by Rome.

Limitations on political authority and legal autonomy, losses of halakhic moorings, tensions from living among non-rabbinic Jews as well as pagans—all these provide crucial context for understanding the rabbis and their literary and legal projects. Strikingly, the Mishnah rarely addresses these important issues explicitly. We will discuss this silence in the chapters to come.

ONE

The Form of the Mishnah

The Mishnah is essentially different from the legal material and collections surveyed in the previous chapter. It presents itself as a standalone body of law, and its sheer ambition to encompass the totality of Jewish law makes it far larger and more extensive than all the earlier halakhic corpora combined. Owing to its vastness, and the fact that it was formed and transformed orally, the Mishnah needed to devise an intricate system of organization for its legal material, which is the subject of the first part of this chapter. The subsequent two parts examine the text of the Mishnah, introducing the reader to its language and style.

A. ORDER AND ORGANIZATION

Unlike the Midrash (the subject of the second half of this book), which tracks the general order of biblical verses, the Mishnah is organized thematically. Each of its six major divisions known as *sedarim* (sg. *seder*) exhibits overall thematic coherence, with some notable exceptions.

The standard, accepted arrangement of the six *sedarim* shown below was presented by Rabbi Shimon ben Lakish, a third-century Galilean sage. Living a century later, Rabbi Tanhuma offered an alternative order: *Nashim, Zera'im, Teharot, Mo'ed, Kodashim,* and *Nezikin*.[1] Menahem Kahana has shown that the organizing principle behind both arrangements is formal. If one divides the six into two groups of three, in both cases each triad contains thirty tractates.[2] The two arrangements were probably influenced by additional considerations, though. The conventional order reasonably places Tractate *Berakhot*, with its treatment of everyday rituals and the liturgy, at the head of the Mishnah. The alternative order puts

> THE SIX *SEDARIM* OF THE MISHNAH
>
> 1. *Seder Zera'im* (Seeds)—Agriculture; as well as prayers and blessings (Tractate *Berakhot*)
> 2. *Seder Mo'ed* (Appointed Time)—Shabbat and the Festivals
> 3. *Seder Nashim* (Women)—Marriage and divorce; as well as vows in general and the Nazirite vow in particular (Tractates *Nedarim* and *Nazir*)
> 4. *Seder Nezikin* (Damages)—Torts, commerce, and courts; as well as idolatry (Tractate *'Avodah Zarah*), halakhic traditions (Tractate *'Eduyyot*), and ethical maxims (Tractate *Avot*)
> 5. *Seder Kodashim* (Holies)—Sacrifices, ritual slaughter, and other Temple-related topics
> 6. *Seder Teharot* (Purities)—Ritual purity

Tractates *Avot* and *Horayot*—on the transmission of tradition and the authority of rabbinic courts—at the very end.

Each *seder* is divided into tractates, of which there are sixty in total.[3] *Seder Zera'im*, for example, comprises eleven tractates, of which all aside from the first tractate fall squarely under the heading of agricultural law.

One can quibble about where to put those tractates that seem to fall outside the thematic scope of a *seder*, but there is a thematic logic to their placement, and it is difficult to conceive of a superior alternative. Tractate *Berakhot* is not overtly agricultural, but its inclusion in *Seder Zera'im* can be easily explained. Jews were mostly farmers in this period, and the laws of *Seder Zera'im* governed their daily life. In similar fashion, the blessings and prayers of Tractate *Berakhot* are rituals that punctuate everyday life. Additionally, many of the blessings are recited before consuming the end products of agriculture.

The other outliers also have underlying thematic connections to their *sedarim*. Tractate *Nedarim* about vows and Tracate *Nazir* about the Nazirite seem out of place in *Seder Nashim*, which mainly covers marriage and divorce law. The Bible provides the solution. Numbers 30 discusses a case in which a wife takes a vow and grants her husband the right to annul it, thereby bringing together the laws of marriage and the laws of vows (Tractate *Nedarim*). As for Tractate *Nazir*, it is logical that it should immediately follow Tractate *Nedarim*, since the Nazirite takes a special kind of vow.[4]

The lion's share of *Seder Nezikin* is about financial relationships and obligations. It therefore includes Tractate *'Avodah Zarah*, because the tractate is more about commercial dealings with idolaters than about the practice of idolatry per se. The ethical maxims of Tractate *Avot* that deal with interpersonal relationships are also a good fit for this *seder*. What about the testimonies about halakhic traditions in Tractate *'Eduyyot*? They fall under the smaller portion of *Seder Nezikin* that covers legal procedure, because testimony *('edut)* is given in a bet din (rabbinical court). In each of the six *sedarim*, then, one observes thematic cohesion being more or less preserved across all of the tractates.

As for the order of tractates within each *seder*, length is the determining factor: the longest are first and the shortest are last. *Seder Mo'ed* begins with Tractate *Shabbat* (twenty-four

> **SEDER ZERA'IM**
>
> Tractate *Berakhot*—Blessings and prayers
> Tractate *Pe'ah*—Agricultural gifts to the poor
> Tractate *Demai*—Produce of doubtful tithed status
> Tractate *Kil'ayim*—Prohibited mixtures
> Tractate *Shevi'it*—The sabbatical year
> Tractate *Terumot*—The tithe given to the Kohen (a male of priestly lineage)
> Tractate *Ma'asrot*—The tithe given to the Levite
> Tractate *Ma'aser Sheni*—The tithe eaten by the owner
> Tractate *Ḥallah*—The tithe taken from dough
> Tractate *'Orlah*—The first three years of tree fruit
> Tractate *Bikkurim*—The first fruits

chapters) and ends with Tractate *Ḥagigah* (three chapters). The only *seder* that defies such an explanation is *Seder Zera'im*.[5]

Theme reemerges as an organizing principle when we move from the organization of tractates within *sedarim* to the organization of material within tractates. This is self-evident in the few tractates that revolve around a single halakhic issue. Tractate *Ma'asrot*, for instance, centers on what exactly triggers the obligation to separate tithes from crops grown or produce purchased. Most of the time, though, a tractate encompasses multiple legal topics, and their connectedness varies. Tractate *Kiddushin* is about halakhic betrothal, in which a man "acquires" a woman in marriage. Accordingly, chapter 1 details the multiple means of halakhic acquisition.[6] Chapters 2 and 3 discuss how the betrothal is actually performed (e.g., via an agent). Chapter 4 treats lineage and status, crucial considerations in matchmaking. Furthermore, this final chapter brings the tractate to a close because it is a marriage's consummation that can result in illegitimacy, impacting the marital prospects of one's offspring. Distinct thematic rationales bind the material together into a full tractate.

But it does not always work out so neatly. Tractate *Sotah* can be roughly divided into two disparate parts. The first (chs. 1–6) is about the eponymous *sotah*, a woman suspected of adultery who must undergo a rite of drinking to establish her innocence.[7] The second part (chs. 7–9) discusses a range of rituals that involve speaking, such as the rousing speech given to the troops before battle by the specially appointed priest. The thin line connecting these two parts is the fact that the *sotah*'s drinking ritual includes a declaration. None of the other subject matter in the second part of the tractate has anything to do with the laws of the *sotah*.[8]

Tractates are formally divided into chapters, each of which takes its title from its opening words. The chapter divisions were made quite early, as the two Talmuds already mention some of them by name. Chapters generally form minor thematic units that can serve the major thematic thrust of a tractate or a part thereof.

When dealing with calendrical mitzvot, the Mishnah's order is usually temporal. The former include Shabbat, the Festivals, and the sabbatical year in Tractates *Shevi'it*, *Shabbat*, *Pesaḥim*, and *Shekalim*, which begin with preparations for these sacred occasions and then discuss the laws for the relevant period of time. This is also the Mishnah's approach to

> **THE TWO TALMUDS**
>
> As the foundational text of the Oral Torah, the Mishnah merited two lengthy commentaries: the Talmuds.
>
> The Palestinian Talmud (Talmud Yerushalmi) was composed in the Galilee in a dialect of Western Aramaic called Jewish Palestinian Aramaic. Its editing was finished by the end of the fourth century.
>
> The Babylonian Talmud (Talmud Bavli) was composed in Babylonia in a dialect of Eastern Aramaic called Jewish Babylonian Aramaic. It was probably completed sometime in the sixth century. In comparison to the Palestinian Talmud, it possesses a broader scope, includes more developed debates, and features more Aggadah.
>
> The two Talmuds share many interpretive and other traditions. These include *baraitot* (lit. "external ones"), that is, tannaitic traditions studied in the bet midrash (study hall) that were not incorporated into the Mishnah.

highly regulated rituals, such as the order of service on Yom Kippur and the procedure of the daily burnt offering in Tractates *Yoma* and *Tamid*, which move through the rites in sequence. Let us take Tractate *Shabbat* as an illustration. The first mishnah lays out the prohibition against moving items on Shabbat from private to public domains and within the public domain itself. It then abruptly shifts to preparations made for Shabbat on Friday, progressively moving toward Shabbat's onset. It lists what activities one may not begin on Friday afternoon (the rest of ch. 1), how to light the obligatory Shabbat candles before Shabbat (ch. 2), and, because one may not kindle a flame on Shabbat, how to prepare a fired oven (ch. 3) and keep food warm (ch. 4). Only in the fifth chapter does the Mishnah return to the subject matter of the very first mishnah.

Also at an early date, chapters were broken down into their smallest constituent unit: the *halakhah* (pl. *halakhot*).[9] Today we simply call this unit a mishnah (*pl.* mishnayot). Note that the division and numbering of the mishnayot in the standard printed editions of the Mishnah are the handiwork of copyists and printers—they do not reflect the original division into *halakhot*.

Halakhic units of law often have aggadic (non-halakhic) material appended to their tail end. The first chapter of Tractate *Sotah* ends with a few mishnayot about measure-for-measure punishment, a principle that the Mishnah sees at work in the *sotah* ritual. The mishnayot at the end of the tractate cite a string of dicta about the gradual decline of the generations: "When the Sanhedrin ceased functioning, the song of the banquet halls ceased. . . . When the early prophets died, the Urim and Thummim ceased to exist. [. . .] When Rabban Yohanan ben Zakkai died, the splendor of wisdom was gone."[10]

The thoroughgoing thematic structuring of the larger and smaller units of the Mishnah is not only a sensible way of ordering a welter of source material. Since the Mishnah was learned exclusively orally, topical groupings were conducive to forming and navigating a mental map.[11] Sometimes, though, the Mishnah put memorization front and center, and eschewed thematics for accessibility, giving rise to more formal methods of arrangement.

The fifth chapter of Tractate *Avot* groups diverse dicta based on number alone and places them in descending order: "The world was created through ten utterances," "Seven types of punishment enter the world," "There are four temperaments." The goal of facilitating memorization could not be more transparent here. For the same reason, the Mishnah regularly collates laws on the same topic under a numerical header. This is especially true at the beginning of tractates: "Five may not take *terumah*" (*Terumot* 1:1); "Thirteen statements about the carcass of a pure bird" (*Teharot* 1:1); "There are thirty-six cases of *karet* in the Torah" (*Keritot* 1:1).[12] The tendency to begin a tractate in this manner is very strong. Recall that the first four chapters of Tractate *Shabbat* are about Shabbat preparations, yet the opening mishnah is not. Instead, it bears this same kind of numerical categorization: "Regarding going out [of domains] on Shabbat, there are two kinds which are really four inside, and two kinds which are really four outside" (*Shabbat* 1:1).

The Mishnah also brings together laws from different fields via a shared principle or locution. "Even if there is no proof for it, there is a hint to it" (*Shabbat*, ch. 9); "for the betterment of the world" (*Gittin*, ch. 4); "for the promotion of peace" (*Gittin*, ch. 5), "On that very day he expounded" (*Sotah*, ch. 5). More formulaic are: "X does not restrict Y" (*Menahot*, ch. 4); "There is no difference between X and Y except . . ." (*Megillah*, ch. 1); "Every X is Y but not every Y is X" (*Niddah*, ch. 6). Here is a condensed example:

Valuations[a] have [cases of] leniency and stringency;[b] the ancestral field[c] has leniency and stringency; the forewarned ox that killed a slave[d] has leniency and stringency; the rapist, seducer, and slanderer[e] have leniency and stringency. (*'Arakhin*, 3:1)

יש בערכים להקל ולהחמיר, ובשדה אחוזה להקל ולהחמיר, בשור המועד שהמית את העבד להקל ולהחמיר, באונס ובמפתה ובמוציא שם רע להקל ולהחמיר.

Only the first member of the series, "valuations" (*'arakhin*), belongs in Tractate *'Arakhin*. The other items are grouped together under the title "[cases of] leniency and stringency" to assist memory. The Mishnah included the mnemonic list as a whole, placing it where its first item, "valuations," thematically belongs.

---

a The value of a person dedicated to the Temple treasury; see Leviticus 27:1–8.
b A fixed sum must be paid in all cases, without regard for specific circumstances, generating cases of leniency and cases of stringency.
c A field that the owner or his relatives want to redeem after it was sold; see Leviticus 25:25–28.
d An ox that had already gored and the owner was forewarned about it; see Exodus 21:29–32.
e The first two violate a pubescent virgin and the last falsely accuses his new bride of infidelity during the betrothal period; see, respectively, Exodus 22:15, Deuteronomy 22:28–29, and Deuteronomy 22:13–22.

> ### HILLEL, SHAMMAI, AND THEIR ACADEMIES
>
> Hillel and Shammai were rough contemporaries of Jesus. It is hard to extract reliable biographical data from the various legends (e.g. it is said that Hillel was originally from Babylonia), but the mishnaic debates reveal two Sages who disagreed about almost everything—Shammai generally being stringent and Hillel lenient. Each figure had disciples who formed respective academies, called Bet Hillel (the House of Hillel) and Bet Shammai (the House of Shammai), who were active from the mid-first century until the destruction of the Second Temple.
>
> The Mishnah systematically collects the disputes between the masters and between the academies in Tractate ʿEduyyot and in other smaller clusters of mishnayot. The Tosefta declared that "the Halakhah is always like Bet Hillel," but added that to follow Bet Shammai's rulings, as some Tannaim did, is also legitimate (Tosefta, *Sukkah*, 2:3 and *Yevamot*, 1:13).

At times, the Mishnah creates a potent aide-mémoire by combining thematic arrangement with repeat phrases. Tractate *Bava Metzi'a* does this to great effect, where batches of mishnayot begin with identical wording: "If one hired" (6:1–6), "If one borrowed a cow" (8:1–3), "If one rented out a house to his fellow" (8:6–9); "If one received a field from his fellow" (9:1–10).

While these phrases can turn out to be additions of the Mishnah's editor, they aren't always.[13] We know that by the end of the first century CE early Sages were using numerical formulas to transmit the halakhic disputes of Bet Hillel and Bet Shammai: "Rabbi X says: On [number] matters Bet Shammai are lenient and Bet Hillel stringent."

Halakhic material was also chunked to optimize memorization. Rabbi Akiva reportedly did this with everything he learned:

> To what can Rabbi Akiva be compared? To a worker who takes his basket and goes out. He finds wheat, he puts it in; he finds barley, he puts it in; he finds spelt, he puts it in; he finds lentils, he puts them in. When he comes home, he cleans the wheat by itself, the barley by itself, the beans by themselves, the lentils by themselves. Thus did Rabbi Akiva do, sorting the entire Torah like coins. (*Avot de-Rabbi Natan*, version A, ch. 18)

While this text has often been read as a description of the compilation of tannaitic texts, with Rabbi Akiva weighing the value of each tradition, Shlomo Naeh has shown that it actually describes his method of study and memorization. When he studied at his masters' feet, Rabbi Akiva would categorize the many halakhic traditions and opinions to keep them straight in his head and learn them by heart.[14] We would be wise not to draw too sharp a distinction between learning strategies and editorial practices, though, because the exclusively oral existence of the Mishnah means that the former would have shaped the latter. A well-edited composition would have been one that made committing it to and retrieving it from memory as easy as possible.

> **AVOT DE-RABBI NATAN**
>
> A commentary on Tractate *Avot* edited between the seventh and ninth century that nonetheless contains earlier tannaitic and amoraic material. It exists in two quite different recensions. Solomon Schechter produced a synoptic edition in 1886 (the first critical edition of a rabbinic text) and called them version A and version B.

B. LANGUAGE

The language of the Mishnah is simple, unadorned Hebrew. It does not imitate the Hebrew of the Bible, as some of the Dead Sea Scrolls do. Scholars once believed that the idiom of the Mishnah, known as mishnaic Hebrew, is an artificial literary language, due to the absence of any attestation outside rabbinic literature. This idea was laid to rest with the discovery of the Bar Kokhba letters, some of which were written in vernacular Hebrew between 132–135 CE, when the Tannaim of the Mishnah were very much alive. In a brief letter, Simon Ben Koseba, better known by the nom de guerre Bar Kokhba, warns a subordinate commander of the Herodion garrison to keep watch over the Galileans in his unit. (See figure 2.) His words reflect the spoken Hebrew of the time:

> From Shimon ben Koseba to Yesha ben Galgula and the men of the fortress *(kerakh)*—Greetings. I call the heavens over me as witness *(me'id ani alai ta-shamayim)*: Should harm come to any of the Galileans *(Gelila'im)* who are with you, I will put fetters *(ta-kevalim)* to your feet as I did to Ben Aflul.[15]

> משמעון בן כוסבה לישע בן גלגלה ולאנשי הכרך, שלום. מעיד אני עלי תשמים (שאם) יפסד מן הגללאים שאצלכם כל אדם—שאני נתן תכבלים ברגלכם, כמה שעסתן[י] לבן עפלול.

The Hebrew of this letter is cut from the same cloth as the Mishnah's. The transliterated words and phrases read like sentences Tannaim could have uttered. There is one salient difference, though, because this epistolary Hebrew reflects the language as it was spoken *(ta-shamayim, ta-kevalim)*.[16] The Mishnah represents an elevated register of the spoken idiom that insists on grammatical correctness. In a way, it can be likened to the first literary expressions of the vernacular Romance languages in the Late Middle Ages.[17]

The language of the Bar Kokhba letters demonstrates that mishnaic Hebrew was a living language and not one acquired solely from texts.[18] Nevertheless, for everyday affairs it took a back seat to Aramaic. The majority of the Bar Kokhba letters themselves were penned in Aramaic,[19] and the Bible was commonly translated into Aramaic in the synagogue, indicating that the commonfolk were not expected to understand the Bible in the original Hebrew.[20] The financial documents and letters written in Hebrew, which were preserved in the dry air of the Judaean Desert, mostly date to the tumultuous years of the Great Revolt and of the Bar Kokhba

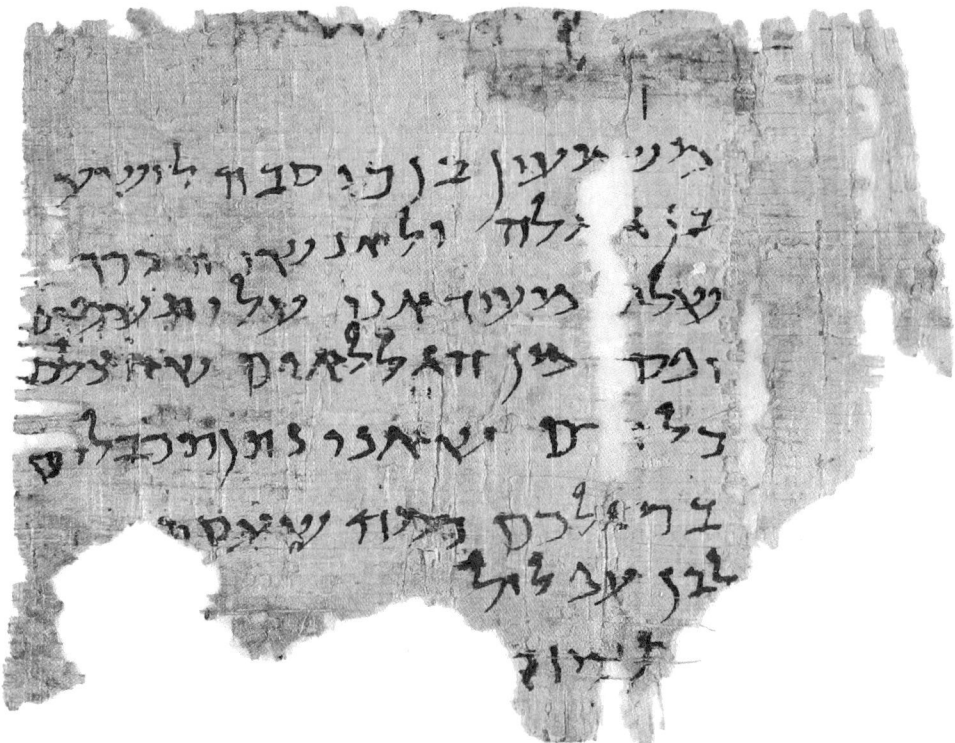

FIGURE 2. Letter from Simon Ben Koseba (MUR43, B-482962). By courtesy of The Leon Levy Dead Sea Scrolls Digital Library. Photographer: Shai Halevi.

Revolt, when Hebrew enjoyed temporary revivals for nationalistic reasons.[21] The Hebrew correspondence consequently teaches us that the Mishnah could be composed in Hebrew because it was still spoken, and that it was chosen over Aramaic partly for reasons of ideology.[22]

Now let us examine a characteristic feature of the Mishnah's Hebrew that generates normative ambiguity and poses an enduring difficulty for translation. It generally expresses its legal instructions using a singular or plural active participle (e.g., *ma'akhil, madlikin*), without an accompanying subject pronoun.[23] The meaning of the participle, though, is quite tricky to pin down, as the following will show. The Mishnah asks rhetorically about lighting the Shabbat candles: "With what *madlikin*?" (*Shabbat*, 2:1). The most literal rendering into English would be: "With what does one light?" On its own, the participle does not necessarily signal any kind of normative obligation. One cannot tell if lighting Shabbat candles is an absolute requirement, a matter of propriety, or simply common practice.[24]

But the Mishnah uses the exact same participle all over to indicate absolute halakhic duties. For example, the second chapter of *Bava Batra* lists the necessary precautions one *must* take to avoid damaging someone else's property. The first mishnah in that chapter requires someone to stop digging on their property once they are three handbreadths away from their neighbor's wall, and it also demands that a person keep any noxious and injurious material in their yard at the same distance. The first is formulated as a negative imperative, "one may not dig" *(lo yaḥpor)*, and the second is phrased as a participle, most literally, "one distances" *(marḥikin)*. Since there is no indication that there has been a drop in normativity from one sentence to the next, a proper translation must convey an obligation: "one *must* distance."[25]

But the Mishnah uses the same participial construction even when discussing activities that are optional or permitted. The translator must therefore weigh other auxiliary verbs as potential candidates, too. For example, the Mishnah states: "the bride turns *(hofekhet)* her head and eats" *(Pesaḥim,* 7:13). The context is the Pesach (Passover) Seder, at which a bride joins her new husband's family to dine on the paschal lamb. The translation above as a description doesn't sound right, but neither does a prescription—"the bride *must* turn her head"—make much sense. According to the two Talmuds, she is being given halakhic license to eat semi-privately until she feels at home in this new household, thus: "the bride *may* turn her head."[26]

Now we can return to the clause from Tractate *Shabbat* and better evaluate the possibilities: "With what *madlikin?"* On its own, this can still be read as a description of how people light Shabbat candles: "With what does one light?" But given the framework of the Mishnah, where the participle regularly carries normative implications, the translation needs to be something like: "With what *may* one light?"

The fact that the participle can bear so many shades of meaning likely reflects a feature of the Hebrew spoken by the Tannaim,[27] and they were well aware of its ambiguity. In certain cases, they even offered a clarification:

All substitute *(memirim),*[a] both men and women alike.

Not that anyone *may* substitute, but that if one did so it is substituted[b] and one receives forty.[c] *(Temurah,* 1:1, emphasis mine)

הכל ממירים—אחד אנשים ואחד נשים. לא שאדם רשיי להמיר אלא אם המיר מומר וסופג את הארבעים.

The second statement seems to be an addition that is meant to clarify that the participle, *memirim,* is intended to convey ability rather than permission (the Torah is abundantly clear that it is prohibited). Accordingly, one should translate the first line with yet another auxiliary verb: "all *can* substitute."[28]

Another mishnah contains a similar disambiguation about two events on Yom Kippur:

---

a All have the legal power to substitute an animal consecrated to be a sacrifice with another animal; see Leviticus 27:33.
b The new animal is considered consecrated.
c Lashes.

Whoever sees the Kohen Gadol (High Priest) reading does not see *(ro'eh)* the burnt bull and he-goat. . . .[a]

Not because one is not permitted,[b] but because it was far away and both were carried out at once. (*Yoma*, 7:2)

הרואה כהן גדול שהוא קורא אינו רואה פר ושעיר הנישרפים. . . . לא מפני שאינו רשאי, אלא שהייתה דרך רחוקה ומלאכת שניהם היתה כאחת.

Here, too, the Mishnah prevents potential misunderstanding of the participle with a clarification: not impermissibility but impossibility. The mishnah means to say, "Whoever sees the Kohen Gadol reading *cannot* see the burnt bull and he-goat." One cannot be in two places at once.

In addition, the participle serves a rhetorical function. Mishnaic Hebrew, unlike biblical Hebrew, has a tense system, in which the participle marks the present tense. In the above example, when the mishnah says, "whoever sees . . . cannot see," it has the effect of drawing the learner into the action like an eyewitness.[29]

C. LEGAL STYLE

The Mishnah combines two distinct legal styles. Sometimes it takes a more direct approach, "one may not do X," and at other times it presents a hypothetical, "if one did X." These phraseologies of the law appear already in the Bible, and scholars call the first "apodictic" (from Greek *apodeiktikos*, "being demonstrably true") and the second "casuistic" (from *casus* in Latin, "being case-based"). The Torah rules apodictically, "Do not steal" (Ex. 20:12), but also frames the law casuistically, "If someone steals . . ." (Ex. 21:37).

These two styles can mingle in the Mishnah's treatment of a single topic. Tractate Ḥullin, chiefly about ritual slaughter and kashrut (kosher diet), dictates the following:

[8] If one slaughters for the sake of[c] mountains, hills, lakes, rivers, wildernesses, his slaughter is invalid.[d] [. . .]

[9] One may not slaughter[e] into lakes nor into rivers. . . . (*Ḥullin*, 2:8–9)

[8] השוחט לשם הרים, לשם גבעות, לשם ימים, לשם נהרות, לשם מדברות—שחיטתו פסולה. [. . .]

[9] אין שוחטין לא לתוך ימים ולא לתוך נהרות. . . .

  a The sin-offerings brought on Yom Kippur that were ultimately burnt; see Leviticus 16:11, 15.
  b To observe both activities.
  c In order to worship these natural features or the entities that govern or inhabit them.
  d And the animal may not be eaten.
  e Even if one does not have intent to worship, because it looks like one is acting with such intent.

It is possible that these mishnayot are based on more than one source, which would account for the shift in style. Indeed, in some places where the Mishnah formulates its laws casuistically, other tannaitic sources preserve apodictic versions of the same laws.[30] About the obligation to read the three passages of the Shema (Deut. 6:4–9, 11:13–21, and Num. 15:37–41) in the morning, the Mishnah says: "One who was reading the Torah and the time of recitation arrived—if he had intention, he fulfilled his obligation, if he did not, he did not fulfill it" (*Berakhot*, 2:1). Compare this to the direct language preserved in a parallel: "One who reads the Shema must have intention."[31]

Nevertheless, there are numerous cases where the Mishnah shifts seamlessly between styles within a single mishnah, making a plurality of sources an unlikely explanation.[32] Here is one example:

One may cover a sukkah with beams—the words of Rabbi Yehudah. Rabbi Meir forbids it.

If one placed a beam on it that is four handsbreadths wide it is valid, provided one does not sleep under it. (*Sukkah*, 1:6)

מסככים בנסרים—דברי רבי יהודה. רבי מאיר אוסר. נתן עליה נסר שהוא רחב ארבעה טפחים כשירה, ובלבד שלא יישן תחתיו.

Since the Mishnah's stylistic switching follows no predictable pattern, one can surmise that a desire for variety, more than anything else, drives these shifts in style.

The casuistic style of the Mishnah tends to train its focus on details instead of generalities. Tractate *Bava Metzi'a* begins with a fight over ownership of a find:

[1] If two people are holding a garment, this one says "I found it" and that one says "I found it"; this one says "It's all mine" and that one says "It's all mine"—this one swears that he has no less than half of it and that one swears that he has no less than half[a] of it and they split it. [. . .]

[2] If two people were riding on an animal, or one was riding and the other leading, this one says "It's all mine" and that one says "It's all mine"—this one swears that he has no less than half of it and that one swears that he has no less than half of it and they split it. [. . .] (*Bava Metzi'a*, 1:1–2)

---

a They do not swear to ownership of the entire object in question so that their oaths are not of necessity contradictory; see BT *Bava Metzi'a* 2b.

[1] שנים אוחזים בטלית, זה אומר 'אני מצאתיה' וזה אומר 'אני מצאתיה', זה אומר 'כולה שלי' וזה
אומר 'כולה שלי'—זה יישבע שאין לו בה פחות מחציה וזה ישבע שאין לו בה פחות מחציה, ויחלוקו. [. . .]

[2] היו שנים רכובים על גבי בהמה, או שהיה אחד רכוב ואחד מהלך, זה אומר 'כולה שלי' וזה אומר
'כולה שלי'—זה ישבע שאין לו בה פחות מחצייה וזה ישבע שאין לו בה פחות מחציה, ויחלוקו. [. . .]

The two mishnayot are similar in both the circumstances and the ruling, and the nearly identical language bears this out.[33] Yet, the Mishnah does not endeavor to distill the essential, shared features of these two cases into a broader ruling. Instead, it lets the common denominator emerge from the student's comparison of the two separate treatments. In the absence of a rule with explicit parameters, the Talmuds have their work cut out for them. They must determine how similar is similar enough to warrant applying the same ruling to other cases. For example, does the swear-and-split solution also apply to real estate?

The casuistic formulation in the Mishnah is sometimes indebted to related passages of biblical law.[34] Note how the two mishnayot above give one example of finding a garment and another of finding an animal. Biblical law about the different kinds of bailees, into whose hands property is entrusted, includes a similar presentation:

> If a man gives his fellow money or goods for safekeeping and they are stolen from the man's house . . .
>
> If a man gives his fellow a donkey or an ox or a sheep or any beast for safekeeping and it dies, is maimed, or is carried off . . . (Exodus 22:6, 9)

Although the mishnayot are not about this exact law, they share with it separate treatments for inanimate objects and for living, breathing animals.

Every once in a while, the Mishnah does offer a rule. Yet even then it does not forgo the details. After the rule comes a concrete instantiation of it, introduced by "How so?"

> Which finds belong to a person[a] and which must one announce?
>
> These finds belong to a person: If one found scattered fruit, scattered money, bundles[b] in the public domain, cakes of pressed figs, baker's loaves, strings of fish, pieces of cut meat, wool shearings that come from their region,[c] flax stalks, and strips of purple wool—these belong to them.

a The finder.
b Of grain.
c They have come from wherever they were shorn and not from the dyer, so they bear no identifying mark.

Rabbi Yehudah says, Anything that has a change[a] one must announce. How so? If one found a cake containing a potsherd, a loaf containing money.

Rabbi Shimon ben Elazar says, Any merchant's wares[b] one need not announce. (*Bava Metzi'a*, 2:1)

אלו מציאות שלו ואלו חייב להכריז?

אלו מציאות שלו: מצא פירות מפוזרים, מעות מפוזרות, כריכות ברשות הרבים, עיגולי דבילה, ככרות שלנחתום, ומחרוזות של דגים, וחתיכות שלבשר, וגיזי צמר הבאות ממדינתן, ואניצי פשתן, ולשונות שלארגמן—הרי אילו שלו.

רבי יהודה אומר: כל דבר שיש בו שינוי חייב להכריז. כיצד? מצא עיגול ובתוכו חרס, ככר ובתוכו מעות.

רבי שמעון בן אלעזר אומר: כל כלי אנפוריא אינו חייב להכריז.

The mishnah records three opinions about found items, all of which consider the same issue: whether an item possesses an unusual feature that sets it apart from similar ones in the public domain. The unnamed first Tanna, known as the *tanna kamma*, compiles a long list of indistinguishable items that includes coins, produce, and raw materials.[35] While homemade bread has a personal touch, the baker forms identical loaves. Rabbi Shimon ben Elazar concurs and adds mass-produced tools and utensils. Rabbi Yehudah makes a qualification: even a generic item needs to be announced if there's something remarkable about it. One can see how the Mishnah moves freely between details and abstractions. The *tanna kamma*'s enumeration of everyday items is followed by two generalizations ("Anything..." and "Any...") made by Rabbi Yehudah and Rabbi Shimon ben Elazar, but only the former's is then concretized ("How so?") with two examples.

At other times, the order of the rule and its application is reversed. The specific case culminates in a rule, usually prefaced explicitly by "this is the rule." The following example from Tractate *Berakhot* concerns the proper blessing to recite on a food that is typically eaten together with another food:

If someone was first served a salty dish accompanied by bread, they should make a blessing over the salty dish and exempt the bread,[c] as the bread is an adjunct to it.[d]

This is the rule: Whenever there is a principal accompanied by an adjunct, one blesses on the principal and exempts the adjunct. (*Berakhot* 6:7)

a Has been visibly changed in some way, so as to constitute proof of ownership recognizable to its owner.
b Hebrew *kelei anpurya*, from Greek ἐμπορία (*emporia*), referring to mass-produced items with no individual marks of ownership.
c From requiring a blessing before its consumption.
d It is not considered an independent food that requires its own blessing.

The Form of the Mishnah

הביאו לו מליח בתחילה ופת עמו—מברך על המליח ופוטר את הפת, שהפת טפילה לו.

זה הכלל: כל שהוא עיקר ועימו טפילה—מברך על העיקר ופוטר את הטפילה.

The Mishnah leads with a specific case and then states the general rule. But these cases are exceptional. Usually, the Mishnah does not care to formulate rules at all. It falls to the student to extract the legal principles from their casing of specificity. The first mishnah of Tractate *Shabbat* serves us yet again as a good example. After the initial mnemonic categorization noted above, the mishnah goes on to discuss situations in which it is prohibited to transfer objects from one domain to another:

The pauper stands outside and the homeowner[a] inside.[b]

If the pauper extends his hand inside and transfers into the hand of the homeowner, or if he takes from it and brings it outside, then the pauper is liable and the homeowner exempt.

If the homeowner extends his hand outside and transfers into the hand of the pauper, or if he takes from it and brings it inside, then the homeowner is liable and the pauper exempt.

If the pauper extends his hand inside and the homeowner takes from it, or if he transfers into it and brings it outside, both are exempt.

If the homeowner extends his hand outside and the pauper takes from it, or if he transfers into it and brings it inside, both are exempt. (*Shabbat*, 1:1)

העני עומד בחוץ ובעל הבית בפנים.

פשט העני את ידו לפנים ונתן לתוך ידו שלבעל הבית, או שנטל מתוכה והוציא—העני חייב ובעל הבית פטור.

פשט בעל הבית את ידו לחוץ ונתן לתוך ידו שלעני, או שנטל מתוכה והכניס—בעל הבית חייב והעני פטור.

פשט העני את ידו לפנים ונטל בעל הבית מתוכה, או שנתן לתוכה והוציא—שניהם פטורים.

פשט בעל הבית את ידו לחוץ ונטל העני מתוכה, או שנתן לתוכה והכניס—שניהם פטורין.

The Mishnah could have boiled down all these cases to one concise rule: One violates the prohibition of transferring between domains on Shabbat only if one removes something from its state of rest in one domain *and* sets it down in another domain. This is precisely what Maimonides did a millennium later in his code of law: "One who transfers from one domain to another ... is only liable if he removes it from a place that is four handbreadths

---

a This is simply an example of two people who would be in separate domains; the laws apply equally to any two people in separate domains.

b The house.

square or more and places it in a place that is four [handbreadths] square."³⁶ The difference in formulation is glaring. The Mishnah, like the Bible, preferred to lay out all the permutations, whereas Maimonides, a rationalist jurist, sought to bring conceptual order and clarity to the law.

The continuation of the same chapter in Tractate *Shabbat* quotes a series of disputes between Bet Hillel and Bet Shammai, the two great early schools of Halakhah. Here too, the Mishnah reports the narrow disputes without attempting to put its finger on the broader point of contention:

[5] Bet Shammai say, One may not soak ink, dyes, or vetch unless they can soak[a] while it is still day.[b] Bet Hillel permit it.

[6] Bet Shammai say, One may not place bundles of flax in the oven unless they can steam while it is still day, or wool into the kettle[c] unless it can absorb the color. Bet Hillel permit it.

Bet Shammai say, One may not set traps for animals, fowl, or fish unless they can be trapped while it is still day. Bet Hillel permit it.

[7] Bet Shammai say, One may not sell to a gentile, or pack a load with him,[d] nor hoist onto him,[e] unless he can arrive at a nearby place.[f] Bet Hillel permit it.

[8] Bet Shammai say, One may not give hides to a tanner or clothing to a gentile launderer unless they can be done[g] while it is still day. But Bet Hillel permit all of them with the sun.[h] (*Shabbat*, 1:5–8)

[5]בית שמיי אומרים: אין שורין דיו סממנים וכרשינים אלא כדי שישורו מבעוד יום. בית הלל מתירין.

[6]בית שמיי אומרים: אין נותנין אונין שלפשתן בתוך התנור אלא כדי שיהבילו מבעוד יום, לא את הצמר ליורה אלא כדי שיקלוט את העין. בית הלל מתירין.

בית שמיי אומרים: אין פורשין מצודות חייה ועופות ודגים אלא כדי שיצודו מבעוד יום. בית הלל מתירין.

[7]בית שמיי אומרים: אין מוכרין לנכרי ולא טוענין עמו ולא מגביהין עליו אלא כדי שיגיע למקום קרוב. בית הלל מתירין.

[8]בית שמיי אומרים: אין נותנין עורות לעובדן ולא כלים לכובס נכרי אלא כדי שיעשו מבעוד יום, וכולם בית הלל מתירין עם השמש.

a Sufficiently.
b Before Shabbat's onset with the sunset.
c The dyer's kettle for dyeing the wool.
d Help place a load on a beast of burden.
e Something heavy or unwieldy to carry.
f Before Shabbat.
g The tanning and laundering.
h So long as the sun has not set they may be begun.

This series of disagreements revolves around a single concept that the Mishnah never articulates, but that the Babylonian Talmud terms *shevitat kelim*, letting one's tools "rest" from their "work" on Shabbat.[37] That is, one may not perform labor on Shabbat, but may one's utensils (an oven, a kettle, a trap) be involved in prohibited labor on the holy day? Bet Shammai say no, Bet Hillel say yes.

Much of the Babylonian Talmud (and, to a lesser extent, the Palestinian Talmud) is devoted to stripping down and conceptualizing the Mishnah's fleshed-out, real-world cases. But why does the Mishnah present its law in this manner? Why does it not just set forth its legal logic? Some theorize that it comes from a lack of self-reflection that is the mark of an immature legal system. A high degree of abstraction is only achieved at a later stage.[38] Chapter 5 will look at other explanations, rhetorical and didactic, of this phenomenon.

In the same way that the Mishnah does not provide rules, it is sparing in the explanation of its laws.[39] Tannaitic parallels, especially in the Tosefta, are useful for filling in such gaps.[40] For example, part of the degrading *sotah* ritual involves the Kohen exposing the accused wife's bosom in the Temple. Rabbi Yehudah adds a qualification in the Mishnah: "If her bosom was attractive he would not uncover it" (*Sotah*, 1:5). The reasoning only appears in the Tosefta (1:5): "on account of the adolescent Kohanim." Rabbi Yehudah is worried that an act intended to be degrading might end up being arousing, so he recommends skipping it when young men are present.[41]

On occasion, the Mishnah does explain its laws. In six places the Mishnah excludes from certain mitzvot the threesome of "the deaf-mute, the mentally incompetent, and the minor," but only in one context, ritual slaughter, does it make the grounds of exclusion explicit: "lest they ruin their slaughter."[42] When it does give a rationale, the Mishnah may appeal to biblical prooftexts (introduced by "as it says") or to logic and common sense. In the following instance, the Mishnah relies on both:

> A wayward and rebellious son[a]—at what point does he become a wayward and rebellious son? From when he produces two hairs[b] until he has a beard around[c]—the lower and not the upper one. [. . .][d] As it says, "When a man has a son" (Deut. 21:18)—not a daughter; "a son"—not a man. A minor is exempt since he does not come within the scope of the commandments. (*Sanhedrin*, 8:1)

בן סורר ומורה מאימתי הוא נעשה בן סורר ומורה? משיביא שתי סערות עד שיקיף זקן—התחתון, לא את העליון. [. . .] שנאמר "כי יהיה לאיש בן"—לא בת, "בן"—לא איש. הקטן פטור שלא בא לכלל המצות.

    a A delinquent who does not listen to his parents; see Deuteronomy 21:18–21.
    b In the pubic region, indicating the onset of sexual maturation.
    c The completion of sexual maturation.
    d A later layer added this clarification that the mishnah here refers to the pubis rather than the face.

This mishnah excludes from the definition of the wayward and rebellious son both a young man who has reached sexual maturity and a boy who is still a minor. The former is excluded by a biblical derivation from the relevant passage, while the latter is excluded by a general rule, excluding minors from the commandments. Taken together, these exclusions limit the law, whose penalty is stoning to death, to a relatively brief, intermediate stage of pubescence.[43]

One sees another repeating feature of the Mishnah here: the introduction of material, especially about rituals, with a rhetorical question. For example, the chapter dedicated to the location of the slaughter and offering of the Temple sacrifices begins with the question, "Where was the location of the sacrifices?" (*Zevaḥim*, 5:1). In this vein we find, "How would they light the torches?" (*Rosh ha-Shanah*, 2:3), "How was the water libation done?" (*Sukkah*, 4:9), and so on. This brings the Mishnah's concise, laconic language somewhat to life, adding vividness and a sense of dialogue.

D. THE MISHNAH IN BRIEF

Our examination of the Mishnah's organization, language, and style reveals an interplay between constancy and mutability. The Mishnah can be casuistic or apodictic in its presentation of Halakhah. It tends to be detail-oriented and parsimonious in its explanations, but in some places it zooms out to supply rules and is more generous with its rationales. One is hard-pressed to find any obvious pattern to this alternation, and it likely stems, ultimately, from the different sources stitched together by R. Yehudah ha-Nasi, the editor of the Mishnah, whose conservative editing policy will be discussed in chapter 4.

Underneath this variability, though, one discerns unchanging features. First, the Mishnah is not a massive jumble of assorted laws. It is the product of meticulous editing, which combined thematic, formal, and linguistic principles to create an elegant, balanced work that facilitated its memorization. Second, the Mishnah is a corpus of specific rulings with precious few broad principles. This explains the Talmuds' massive discursive undertaking of extrapolating those principles that will apply to other cases. Finally, the Mishnah considers itself an independent halakhic work. Its thematic arrangement does not follow any biblical sequence; its laws are not constantly interlaced with scriptural prooftexts. This is critical to understanding what the Mishnah is and purports to be, a point that will be revisited in the coming chapters.

TWO

The Mishnah's Sources and Layers

The discussion in the previous chapter about the organization, language, and style of the Mishnah treated it as what it purports to be: a uniform composition. But the Mishnah is not the handiwork of a single author. It features four primary, successive generations of Sages who transmitted traditions, stated opinions, and offered explanations. Careful analysis reveals unattributed, earlier material as well. The Mishnah was clearly a long time in the making.

Scholarly convention refers to mishnaic source material from different periods and generations as layers. In theory, one should be able to identify these layers and excavate them to reach the earliest source material; in practice, this is both difficult and controversial because the Mishnah smooths over shifts between them. Even the early material that is recoverable is usually not preserved intact. It was already tampered with in antiquity.

This chapter will investigate how far back the Mishnah's sources go and present methods for isolating and teasing apart the Mishnah's many layers. The editorial process that gave the Mishnah its final cast will be the subject of chapter 4.

A. THE ORIGINS OF THE MISHNAH

Several rabbinic sources assert that the Oral Torah, with its dizzying amount of detail, was transmitted by God to Moses fully formed during the revelation at Mount Sinai.[1]

In many places, however, rabbinic literature departs from this ideological tenet and demonstrates an awareness of halakhic development and its partial dependency on historical conditions. Thus, in more than twenty places the Mishnah distinguishes between the law of old (*ba-rishonah*, "originally") and the subsequent rabbinic decree that replaced it.[2] Both of these views take the classical rabbinic form of brief dicta.

> ### THE ORAL TORAH
>
> The Oral Torah *(torah she-be-'al peh)* is the name given by the rabbis to the body of halakhic interpretations, traditions, and practices first embodied in the Mishnah. Since it is clearly at variance with laws in the Written Torah *(torah she-bi-khetav)*, some Sages developed a theory of two complementary Torahs. (See Sifra, Beḥukkotai, 2:7; Sifrei Deuteronomy, §351.) It held that alongside the Pentateuch dictated by God to Moses was a parallel, unwritten Torah that was passed down orally from generation to generation. This second Torah was supposed to explicate the Written Torah and also add new halakhic themes. Decrees and institutions of rabbinic origin were consciously added to the Oral Torah along the way. Throughout Jewish history, schisms have repeatedly been created by groups (such as the Samaritans, Sadducees, Karaites) rejecting this oral legacy or denying its antiquity.

> ### THE GEONIM
>
> The Geonim headed the major rabbinic academies in the Land of Israel and Babylonia in the post-talmudic period, from the seventh to eleventh centuries. They are called Geonim because the central academy over which they presided was called *Ge'on Ya'akov*, "the pride of Jacob." They were the leaders of the Rabbanites, adherents of the Oral Torah transmitted by the rabbis, and waged ideological battles against the Karaites, scripturalists who rejected the Oral Torah.
>
> The Geonim who left a significant literary legacy mostly lived toward the end of the Geonic period, in the tenth to eleventh centuries. These include Saadia, Sherira, and Hayya. Of many earlier Geonim we know nothing aside from their names.
>
> By the eleventh century, the Geonim were losing influence as the gravity of Torah scholarship shifted to the nascent centers of North Africa and Europe.

Many centuries would pass until the first attempt was made to provide a substantive historical account of the Oral Torah. Saadia Gaon wrote in the early tenth century, toward the end of the Geonic period: "the forefathers began the composition of the Mishnah 40 years after [the construction of] the Second Temple until 150 years after its destruction."[3]

That is, the Oral Torah grew over many centuries, beginning with the Men of the Great Assembly in the early Second Temple period and ending with its consolidation after the Temple's destruction in the academies of the Tannaim.

But one cannot ignore the fact that this account arose in a polemical context. When Saadia Gaon wrote that the Mishnah began with the Men of the Great Assembly, he was polemicizing against Karaites, who denied the existence of an ancient Oral Torah.[4] This history served as a kind of foundation myth, around which the Rabbanite identity could crystallize in the face of the Karaite threat. Nearly a millennium later, when practitioners of *Wissenschaft des Judentums* adopted and propounded this historical account, they too were in the midst of an ideological war against those criticizing the antiquity and value of rabbinic traditions.[5]

> **WISSENSCHAFT DES JUDENTUMS**
>
> Literally, "the science of Judaism," this intellectual movement arose in nineteenth-century Germany and spread from there to other European countries. Its mission was to study Jewish tradition according to the historical and philological standards of the day, with the same rigor that universities were applying to classical and Christian texts. These maskilim, members of Jewish Enlightenment, wanted to show that Judaism was just as rich, profound, and worthy of study as other religions and peoples. Leading figures were Leopold Zunz, Abraham Geiger, and Heinrich Graetz.

Historically speaking, there is little to substantiate the Geonic origin story of the Oral Torah. We know nothing about the Men of the Great Assembly, who appear only in this context, as links in the chain of transmission from Sinai, and our data about oral traditions during the Persian period (fifth–fourth centuries BCE) is no better. In the absence of corroboration, the Geonic account must be regarded as speculation in the service of polemics.

Another thorny issue of relevance here is the relationship between the Mishnah and Midrash. It was commonly maintained in earlier scholarship that the Mishnah was an outgrowth of the intensive halakhic exegesis of Scripture that began in the early Second Temple period, perhaps even during the time of Ezra the Scribe.[6] The Mishnah would therefore represent the distilled halakhic bottom line reordered by theme.[7] In a seminal article, Ephraim Elimelech Urbach challenged this theory and argued that the Oral Torah was the product not of scriptural exegesis but of the development of ancient traditions. The Pharisees, the spiritual forbears of the Tannaim,[8] were jurists who debated and developed their received traditions, and it was their drawing of comparisons and analogies, their filling of perceived halakhic lacunae, that expanded the Halakhah. Urbach argued that Midrash belonged to the world of the scribes and postdated the Pharisees' traditions.[9] Midrash, then, was a revolutionary innovation, while the Oral Torah had been transmitted independent of Scripture since time immemorial.

Urbach's contention about the antiquity of mishnaic law and its independence from Midrash has received unexpected support from recent studies of the Dead Sea Scrolls. Various scholars have shown that the sect behind these scrolls, which was hostile to the Pharisees and rejected their ancient traditions, developed Midrash as means of undermining and supplanting Pharisaic Halakhah. Since the two vied with each other for the crown of halakhic authority, it is clear that the Oral Torah was not simply an outgrowth of Midrash.[10]

The fact that the Mishnah itself attributes many laws to Second Temple Sages, and the fact that, as shown in the introduction, the Dead Sea Scrolls and other literature exhibit a shared halakhic heritage, demonstrate that the Mishnah has its roots in this same period. The earliest laws in the Mishnah do in fact date from the Hellenistic period, the era in which the *Zugot* were purportedly active.

> **THE *ZUGOT***
>
> Literally, "pairs," who according to the Mishnah were the co-leaders of the rabbinic establishment from the second to first centuries BCE. The Mishnah enumerates five "pairs," the last being Shammai and Hillel. The first chapter of *Avot* records sayings attributed to them. According to another mishnah (*Ḥagigah*, 2:2), in each pair the first person listed is the president and the second is the head of the bet din (religious court). The historicity of the institution of the *Zugot*, however, remains doubtful. See Schürer, *History of the Jewish People*, 2:361

The earliest law attributed to a Sage is reported in the name of Yose ben Yo'ezer, who together with Yose ben Yohanan formed the first "pair."

Rabbi Yose ben Yo'ezer of Zeredah testified that the <u>ayyal kamtzayyah[a] is pure</u>;[b] the liquid in <u>the butchery</u>[c] is pure; and that <u>one who touches the dead is impure</u>.[d]

<u>They called him Permissive Yose.</u>[e] (*'Eduyyot*, 8:4)

העיד ר' יוסה בן יועזר איש צרידה על אייל קמיצייה—דכי. ועל משקה בית מטבחייה—דכיין. ודי יקרב למיתה—מסאב.

וקרון ליה יוסה שרייא.

The Mishnah attributes three leniencies to a very early Sage, but should we believe this attribution? In this case, there are multiple indicators of this mishnah's early provenance. First, the underlined sections are in Aramaic; later Sages transmitted their traditions and opinions in Hebrew. Second, the rulings are laconic in the extreme, another mark of antiquity. Finally, these three laws all deal with ritual purity and the Temple, pointing to a time when they were still applicable. This would date the earliest attributed material in the Mishnah to the second century BCE.

Even if this is historically accurate, similar mishnayot are few and far between. To find out more about the earliest sources of the Mishnah, we must look for other markers of antiquity in it.

   a A type of locust or perhaps locust broth. The latter possibility was proposed to me by Dr. Yakov Z. Mayer. If correct, this mishnah would parallel *'Eduyyot*, 7:2 and *Terumot*, 10:9.
   b Permitted for consumption. The use of purity terminology to label permitted and forbidden food has roots in the Bible (e.g., Lev. 11:8).
   c The Temple precinct where sacrifices were slaughtered.
   d For purposes of ritual purity. The meaning of this seemingly obvious law is disputed. See the summary in Noam, *From Qumran to the Rabbinic Revolution*, 255–264.
   e Due to these lenient rulings.

B. *MISHNAH RISHONAH*

One seemingly fruitful line of investigation is the Mishnah's own awareness of halakhic change. In some instances, the Mishnah refers to the earlier law that has been changed as *mishnah ha-rishonah*, "the former mishnah." Here the term "mishnah" means an oral teaching and does not necessarily imply the existence of an edited body of such teachings. For example:

> A virgin[a] is given twelve months to furnish[b] herself from the time her husband claims her.[c] [. . .]
>
> If their time came and they did not wed, or their husbands died—they eat from what is his[d] and they[e] eat *terumah*.[f] [. . .]
>
> This was the *mishnah rishonah*. A succeeding bet din (rabbinic court) said, A wife does not eat *terumah* until she enters the wedding canopy. (*Ketubbot*, 5:2–3)

נותנין לבתולה שנים עשר חודש משתבע לה הבעל לפרנס את עצמה. [. . .]

הגיע זמנם ולא נישאו או שמתו בעליהן—אוכלות משלו ואוכלת בתרומה. [. . .]

זו משנה הראשונה. בית דין שלאחריהם אמרו: אין האשה אוכלת בתרומה עד שתיכנס לחופה.

According to the *mishnah rishonah*, once a year has passed since the betrothal, a fiancée is to be supported by her fiancé, to the point that she, a non-priest, can even eat *terumah*. A later authority struck this down, ruling that only actual marriage—and not time—can initiate a husband's obligation to support his wife.[11]

Although the Mishnah's awareness of chronological development seems a promising portal to older halakhic traditions, the use of the term *mishnah rishonah* is infrequent in the Mishnah and, more importantly, only establishes a relative chronology. The Mishnah is merely noting a change in mishnaic law without necessarily labeling the outdated law as ancient. The distinction between "former" and "latter" is not of much help in establishing absolute dates.[12]

Undiscouraged by this, scholars have coopted the term *mishnah rishonah* to refer to those mishnayot, chapters, or even entire tractates that date to the Second Temple period.[13] The identification of this *mishnah rishonah* mostly began with Nachman Krochmal, an early pro-

---

a As opposed to a widow or divorcée.
b To accumulate property for a dowry.
c From the time her intended husband seeks her hand in marriage.
d Because a husband is obligated to feed his wife.
e The switch to the plural is on account of other omitted cases, represented by the points of ellipsis.
f The priestly tithe or heave-offering that may only be eaten by a priest and his household. This includes wives who are not of priestly descent. (On the various tithes, see below, section E.)

ponent of *Wissenschaft,* and was adopted by most of his successors, especially David Zvi Hoffmann, who wrote a book incorporating the term into its title: *Die erste Mischna und die Controversen der Tannaim* (The First Mishnah and the Controversies of the Tannaim). In his *Introduction to Tannaitic Literature,* Jacob Nahum Epstein dedicated much of the introduction to the Mishnah's tractates to identifying collections of this *mishnah rishonah.*[14] The only classic scholar of rabbinics to disagree with this approach was Hanoch Albeck. He was of the opinion that there were only scattered traditions, and that no edited units of Mishnah existed until the generation of Yavneh.[15]

There is no question, though, that the Mishnah does contain entire sections that are considerably earlier than the rest, even from the time of the Second Temple or thereabouts. Like the brief laws attributed to Yose ben Yo'ezer, their character gives them away. Tractate *Tamid,* which details the ritual of the daily Temple sacrifice, offers a stark example of this. The language is archaic, no Sages are named,[16] and other tractates *(Middot* and *Yoma)* incorporate material from it.[17] In addition, the two Talmuds attribute the editing of this tractate to Rabbi Shimon of Mitzpah, a scholar who lived while the Temple still stood. Scholars today put its composition toward the end of the first century CE, not long after the destruction of the Second Temple.[18]

The problem is that the identification of early material in the Mishnah has all too often relied not on sound linguistic evidence,[19] but on content alone. This may seem reasonable enough for laws pertaining to the Temple and its service, but scholars have been increasingly discovering that what were once taken as ancient, authentic records of Temple practices are really the imaginative output of later study halls.[20] It turns out that there is no reason to assume that descriptions of the Temple cult are earlier than anything else.

The mishnaic account of the bringing of the *bikkurim,* the first fruits to ripen, is a perfect example of why readers must be cautious. The Bible requires the farmer to annually bring the first fruits to the priest in the Temple (Deut. 26:2). Philo and Flavius Josephus described the *bikkurim* as an individual's gift to the Temple, whereas the Mishnah describes it as a communal celebration with much fanfare:[21]

> [2] How does one bring the *bikkurim*? All of the towns of the *ma'amad*[a] gather in the city of the *ma'amad,*[b] and lodge in the city square. They would not enter any homes. In the morn, the appointed official would exclaim, "Arise so that we may ascend Zion, to the Lord our God" (Jer. 31:5).
>
> [3] The near bring fresh figs and grapes; the far[c] bring dried figs and raisins. The ox proceeds with them, its horns gilded and an olive wreath on its head. The flute plays

---

a The Land of Israel was divided into twenty-four districts, each of which would send priests to the Temple two weeks a year (see *Ta'anit,* 4:2). While the priests were away, the Israelites would form their own *ma'amad,* or "assembly." Here *ma'amad* stands for one of the twenty-four administrative districts.

b The main city in the district; such a division is found nowhere else in tannaitic literature.

c Those living near and far from Jerusalem.

before them until they reach the outskirts of Jerusalem. Once they reached the outskirts of Jerusalem, they sent ahead of them[a] and adorned[b] their *bikkurim*. The rulers *(paḥot)*, chiefs *(seganim)*, and treasurers *(gizbarim)*[c] go out to meet them. They would go out according to the honor of the entrants. All the artisans of Jerusalem stand before them and inquire after their welfare: "Our brothers of such-and-such place, have you arrived in peace?"

[4] The flute plays before them until they reach the Temple Mount. Once they have reached the Temple Mount, even King Agrippas takes the basket[d] on his shoulder and enters until he reaches the Temple court. Once one reached the Temple court, the Levites intoned in song, "I will extol You, Lord, for You have raised me up, and you have not allowed my enemies to rejoice over me" (Ps. 30:2). [. . .]

[6] With the basket yet on his shoulder, he recites from[e] "I acknowledge this day to the Lord, your God" (Deut. 26:3) until he finishes the entire passage.[f] Rabbi Yehudah says, Until "My father was a wandering Aramean" (Deut. 26:5). Once he reached "My father was a wandering Aramean," he takes down the basket from his shoulder and holds it by its rim. The priest places his hand under it, waves it,[g] and recites from "My father was a wandering Aramean," until he finishes the entire passage. He placed it beside the altar, prostrated himself, and left. (*Bikkurim*, 3:2–4, 6)

[ב] כיצד מעלין את הביכורים? כל העיירות שבמעמד מיתכנסות לעירו שלמעמד, ולנים ברחובה שלעיר. לא היו נכנסים לבתים. ולמשכים היה הממונה אומר "קומו וְנַעֲלֶה צִיּוֹן אֶל יי אֱלֹהֵינוּ" (ירמיה לא, ה).

[ג] הקרובים מביאים תאינים וענבים. הרחוקים מביאים גרוגרות וצימוקים. והשור הולך עימהן וקרניו מצופות זהב ועטרה שלזית בראשו. והחליל מכה לפניהן עד שמגיעין קרוב לירושלם. הגיעו קרוב לירושלם. שלחו לפניהם ועיטרו את ביכוריהם. הפחות והסגנים והגיזברים יוצאין לקראתם. לפי כבוד הנכנסים היו יוצאין. כל בעלי אמניות שבירושלם עומדים בפניהם ושואלים בשלומם: אחינו אנשי מקום פלוני באתם בשלום.

[ד] החליל מכה לפניהם עד שמגיעין להר-הבית. הגיעו להר-הבית אפילו אגריפס המלך נוטל את הסל על כתיפו ונכנס עד שהוא מגיע לעזרה. הגיע לעזרה ודיברו הלוים בשיר "אֲרוֹמִמְךָ יי כִּי דְלִיתָנִי וְלֹא-שִׂמַּחְתָּ אֹיְבַי לִי" (תהלים ל, ב). [. . .]

  a A messenger heralding their arrival.
  b The Mishnah shifts from the participle into the perfect tense here (this recurs in mishnayot 4 and 6). The dominant tense throughout the description, however, is the present. See the end of this section.
  c The Temple officials.
  d Holding the *bikkurim*.
  e According to the following mishnah unit, the offerer recited from a written text. Contrast Philo, *On Laws*, 2:216.
  f Deuteronomy 26:3–10.
  g In all of the cardinal directions, as with a sacrifice; see Leviticus 7:30 and *Menaḥot*, 5:6.

[ו] ועודיהו הסל על כתיפו וקורא מ"הִגַּ֤דְתִּי הַיּוֹם֙ לַיי אֱלֹהֶ֔יךָ" (דברים כו, ג) עד שהוא גומר את כל הפרשה. ר' יהודה אומר עד "אֲרַמִּי֙ אֹבֵ֣ד אָבִ֔י" (דברים כו, ה). הגיע ל"אֲרַמִּי֙ אֹבֵ֣ד אָבִ֔י" מוריד את הסל מכתיפו ואוחזו בשפתותיו. וכהן מניח את ידו תחתיו ומניפו וקורא מ"אֲרַמִּי֙ אֹבֵ֣ד אָבִ֔י" עד שהוא גומר את כל הפרשה. הניחו בצד המזבח והשתחווה ויצא.

The Mishnah displays this celebratory procession to the Temple and each offeror's conduct within it in very high resolution. When is it from? Based on the content, David Zvi Hoffmann claimed it for the *mishnah rishonah*, the most ancient of the Mishnah's layers. To narrow it down even more, given the reference to "King Agrippas," he thought it should be dated to the reign of Agrippas I in the 40s of the first century CE. Jacob Nahum Epstein held a similar view, although he thought the king in question was Agrippas II, who ruled briefly in the 60s. For Epstein, archaisms helped substantiate the dating: "in the morn" *(ve-la-mashkim)*, "the Levites intoned *(ve-dibberu)* in song," and "with the basket yet *('odehu)* on his shoulder."

Neither of these claims withstands criticism. First, does mention of a known historical personality prove that the text dates from their lifetime? It would be quite natural for an author living after the collapse of the monarchy to reach for one of the most recent kings as an example. Note that the Mishnah is not descriptively recollecting an episode where a King Agrippas stooped to shoulder the burden of fruit, but prescriptively stating that even royal status does not release a monarch from this minor exertion. Second, is archaic language proof positive of genuine age? A late author could have specifically selected these words of yore to evoke the halcyon era of the Temple, much the same way archaic English was chosen for the King James Bible to, rather successfully, lend the text gravitas and underscore its antiquity.[22]

The problem posed by language comes to the fore in another way as well. Like other scholars, Saul Lieberman argued for the authenticity of the Mishnah's description, but on the strength of its extra-scriptural elements. The gilt and garlanded ox, the music, the grand spectacle—all these imitate Hellenistic celebrations, Lieberman argued.[23] But how does this square with the use of Persian loanwords from Late Bible Hebrew to denote Jerusalem's notables—the *paḥot*, *seganim*, and *gizbarim*—when some of these positions no longer existed in any form by the Hellenistic period?[24]

These irreconcilable inconsistencies invite a literary analysis. The Mishnah borrows three biblical terms for officials in order to archaize the ceremony, imbuing it with the luster of the past. Instead of reading the Mishnah's account of the *bikkurim* procession as documenting history, it can be read as a literary re-creation intended to persuade its audience. Perhaps the rhetorical effect was to generate a sense of fraternity—the pilgrims spend the night in the city square, the king has the same obligation as the commoner, "brothers" inquire after the welfare of one another.[25]

This is an important point with broader implications. When the Mishnah depicts rituals, it tends to call forth a reality that seems older than the one that emerges from the relevant laws. This does not mean that the depictions are actually older than the laws, but that they are rhetorically meant to give that impression. The rituals are supposed to conjure a perfect world centered on the Temple, for Jews living in a harsh, imperfect reality. The use of the participial—"the ox proceeds *(holekh)* . . . the flute plays *(makkeh)*"—instead of the past tense may also hint that the Mishnah is not reporting a past memory but presenting an ideal reality.[26]

The *mishnah rishonah*, the Mishnah's earliest source material, is elusive and the object of contested speculation. Dwelling on expressions from times past or the vivid depictions of Temple rites can lead to the wrong historical conclusions, as things in the Mishnah are not always as they appear. Instead of trying to isolate the oldest material in absolute terms, it proves more profitable to map the various layers of the Mishnah's sources in relative ones.

C. MAPPING THE LAYERS

The Mishnah's many layers record statements by named (and unnamed) Sages of different generations. When it comes to attributions of opinions to particular Sages, the operative assumption of this book is that they are more or less accurate unless there are compelling reasons to doubt them. The remarkable stability of attributed opinions across tannaitic corpora, which were never edited as a whole to produce uniformity of any kind, argues strongly in favor of their accuracy and reliability.[27]

The easiest way to get a general sense of a given mishnah's layers is to look for signs of a shift between them. The presence of an explanation following a law is an excellent indicator of this. The opening mishnah of Tractate *Kiddushin* exemplifies explanatory nesting of multiple layers, where an earlier law is elaborated, and then that elaboration is further explained:

> A wife is acquired[a] in three ways and acquires herself[b] in two ways. She is acquired with money, a contract,[c] or intercourse.
>
> With money—Bet Shammai say, With a *dinar*[d] or the value thereof;[e] Bet Hillel say, With a *perutah*[f] or the value thereof.
>
> How much is a *perutah*? One-eighth of an Italian *issar*.[g] (*Kiddushin*, 1:1)

> האישה נקנית בשלוש דרכים, וקונה את עצמה בשתי דרכים. נקנית בכסף, ובשטר, ובביאה.
>
> בכסף—בית שמאי אומרין, בדינר ובשווה דינר; ובית הלל אומרין, בפרוטה ובשווה פרוטה.
>
> כמה היא פרוטה, אחד משמונה באיסר האיטלקי.

    a Betrothed for marriage.
    b Is released from marriage (by divorce or her husband's death).
    c Given by the husband to the wife in which he formalizes the betrothal.
    d A *denarius*, a Roman silver coin.
    e An object with the value of a *dinar*.
    f A copper coin of minimal value.
    g An *assarius*, a Roman copper coin.

This mishnah has three distinguishable layers. First, there is the early law that a woman can be acquired in three ways and an enumeration thereof. Second, the schools of Bet Shammai and Bet Hillel debate the minimum amount that qualifies as "money" for this purpose. Third, the precise parameters of Bet Hillel's definition of "money" are defined. It should be pointed out that these explanations are not merely academic. From the fact that the Mishnah asks, "How much is a *perutah*?" but does not also wonder "How much is a *dinar*?" one can deduce that Bet Hillel's opinion was the accepted one, a deduction supported by *Kiddushin*, 2:1.

Scores of laws are attributed to Hillel and Shammai and their academies in the Mishnah. Given the fact that they were active in the waning years of the Second Temple, their laws are among the earliest in the Mishnah. Working backward, since their opinions make up the second layer here, the previous layer is even earlier. Simply paying close attention to the way a mishnah is structured can expose earlier source material that is not attributed to any particular Sage.[28]

Stock phrases often introduce explanations, which signal that the mishnah is jumping forward in time. These include questions ("about what did they disagree?" and "why did they say it?") and observations ("because they said," "even though they said," "we learn from their words"). The fact that such phrases are frequently encountered in the Tosefta, where they are undoubtedly interpretations of and additions to the Mishnah, indicates their origin and purpose in the Mishnah.[29]

The beginning of Tractate *Niddah*, which is about the menses that renders a woman ritually impure, illustrates this. There, there is a debate between Hillel, Shammai, and the Sages about the possibility that a woman who sees menstrual blood actually began bleeding earlier but has only noticed it now. In the opening mishnah a rule is stated: "Any woman who has a menstrual cycle—her time is enough" (1:1), meaning that impurity is only assumed from the moment of observation and not retroactively. A string of questions and qualifications appears in subsequent mishnayot: "In what respect is 'her time enough'?" (1:2); "About what did they say 'her time is enough'?" (1:6); "Even though they said 'her time is enough' . . ." (1:7). One mishnah has later Sages listing women whose "time is enough" (1:3). One cannot but conclude that the entire chapter is essentially an elaboration of this concise, early law.[30] Although one cannot pinpoint its exact date, the fact that Shammai and Hillel are involved implies that it at least preceded them. This would put it not long after the turn of the Common Era, in the lifetimes of Philo and Jesus.

Sometimes the Mishnah presents a list followed by a later elucidation. Yet again, the beginning of a tractate, this time *Terumot*, serves as an example:

> [1] Five may not take *terumah* (the priestly tithe), and if they took *terumah* it is not valid: the deaf, the mentally incompetent, the minor, and one who takes *terumah* from what is not his. If a gentile takes *terumah* for a Jew, even with permission it is not valid.
>
> [2] A deaf person who can speak may not take *terumah*, but if he took *terumah* it is valid. The deaf spoken of by the Sages everywhere is a deaf-mute. (*Terumot*, 1:1–2)

[א] חמשה לא יתרומו ואם תרמו—אין תרומתן תרומה: החרש, והשוטה, והקטן, והתורם את שאינו שלו. נכרי שתרם את שלישראל אפילו ברשות—אין תרומתו תרומה.

[ב] חרש המדבר ואינו שומע לא יתרום. אם תרם תרומתו תרומה. חרש שדיברו חכמים בכל מקום—שאינו לא שומע ולא מדבר.

Although the last sentence sounds like a general point ("everywhere"), coming on the heels of the previous mishnah it is clearly a gloss on "the deaf" listed there. The phrase "spoken of by the Sages" is thus a reference to the preceding mishnah (similar to the way we use "aforementioned" or "above"). The Mishnah adopts different strategies for internal references and for explanatory additions to earlier material.

If the Mishnah is composed of layers, explanation and elaboration deepen the lines between them and render them visible. Unfortunately, most mishnayot are virtually seamless, necessitating painstaking analysis of language, parallels, contradictions, and more to pry apart the layers. Most of the philological work of modern scholars of the Mishnah consists of precisely this. For example, a sizable portion of Epstein's *Introduction to Tannaitic Literature* endeavors to identify the Sages and academies responsible for the principal layer in each tractate. This will be discussed at length in chapter 8 on the relationship between the Mishnah and the Tosefta, because the latter often enables us to reconstruct how the former's source material was combined and reworked into its current form. For now, one example must suffice:

> If one found [. . .] piles of fruit, <u>piles of coins, three coins on top of one another</u> [. . .] one must announce it. (*Bava Metzi'a* 2:2)

מצא [. . .] ציבורי פירות, ציבורי מעות, שלשה מטבעות זה על גבי זה [. . .] חייב להכריז.

What is the relation between the underlined items, "piles of coins *(ma'ot)*" and "three coins *(matbe'ot)* one atop the other"? Diction and phraseology notwithstanding, aren't these conceptually identical? If so, why do both appear in a single mishnah? The parallel tosefta provides the answer:

> If one found *coins (ma'ot) made into stacks*, one must announce it; scattered, one need not announce it. Partly stacked and partly not, one must announce it.
>
> How much is a stack? *Three coins (matbe'ot) on top of one another.* (Tosefta, *Bava Metzi'a*, 2:7)

מצא מעות עשויות מגדלות חייב להכריז, מפוזרות אינו חייב להכריז. מקצתן מגדלין ומקצתן אין מגדלין חייב להכריז.

וכמה הוא מגדל? שלשה מטבעות זה על גבי זה.

In this tosefta, the three coins are not a separate type of find but a later clarification of what counts as a pile or stack of coins. In the mishnah, the line separating the source from its interpretation was eroded, such that the original can only be recovered through comparative analysis of parallels.[31]

D. FOUR GENERATIONS OF MISHNAIC SAGES

The anonymous, old material discussed in the previous section is a tiny fraction of the Mishnah. This brings us to the bulk of the Mishnah that consists of four primary layers, which are associated with distinct generations of Sages known after their principal urban residence:[32]

1. The end of the Second Temple period and shortly after: Bet Hillel and Bet Shammai and their disciples who lived through and after the Destruction, such as Rabban Yohanan ben Zakkai. This early layer has the smallest scope. It is worth noting that disputes between Bet Hillel and Bet Shammai often appear at the beginning of tractates. This may imply an editorial policy that systematically begins tractates with the "founding fathers" of the Mishnah.[33]

2. The first generation of Yavneh, from the end of the first century CE through the beginning of the second: Rabban Gamaliel, Rabbi Eliezer, Rabbi Yehoshua, and their colleagues.

3. The second generation of Yavneh, which ended with the Bar Kokhba Revolt in the 130s: Rabbi Tarfon, Rabbi Elazar ben Azariah, Rabbi Akiva, Rabbi Yishmael, Rabbi Yose ha-Gelili, and their colleagues.

4. The generation of Usha, spanning the second half of the second century: Rabbi Meir, Rabbi Yehudah, Rabbi Shimon, Rabbi Yose, and their colleagues. This layer constitutes the bulk of the Mishnah.[34]

Notably missing from the Mishnah is the fifth generation of Rabbi Yehudah ha-Nasi and his colleagues. They are present in the Tosefta, however, which, as chapter 8 will show, was edited later.[35]

Dissent in the Mishnah is usually confined to a single generation. Bet Hillel argue with Bet Shammai, the Sages of Yavneh disagree with one another, the Sages of Usha dispute their colleagues.[36] The absence of intergenerational disputes should be taken as evidence of fundamental historical accuracy, even if it does not extend to the exact formulation of opinions.[37]

Outliers do exist though. In the example below, the Mishnah records a dispute that spanned several generations, with later scholars (Rabbi Akiva and Rabbi Papyas) openly discussing the merits of their predecessors' opinions (Rabbi Eliezer and Rabbi Yehoshua):

If someone consecrates their possessions,[a] among which was an animal fit for the altar,[b] then for males and females[c]—

Rabbi Eliezer says, Males should be sold to those in need of burnt offerings, females should be sold to those in need of peace offerings, and the proceeds should go with the rest of the possessions toward the upkeep of the Temple.

Rabbi Yehoshua says, Males should be brought as burnt offerings[d] themselves; females should be sold[e] to those in need of peace offerings and one should bring burnt offerings with the proceeds. The rest of the possessions should go toward the upkeep of the Temple.

Rabbi Akiva said, I prefer[f] Rabbi Eliezer's opinion to Rabbi Yehoshua's, because Rabbi Eliezer applied his principle equally,[g] whereas Rabbi Yehoshua made a distinction.

Rabbi Papyas said, I recognize the merits[h] of both opinions. One who consecrates explicitly[i] is like the opinion of Rabbi Eliezer, and one who consecrates without specifying is like the opinion of Rabbi Yehoshua. (*Shekalim*, 4:7)

המקדיש נכסיו, והיתה בהן בהמה ראויה על גבי המזבח, זכרים ונקיבות –

ר׳ אליעזר אומר: זכרים ימכרו לצריכי עולות, ונקיבות ימכרו לצריכי זבחי שלמים. ודמיהן יפלו עם שאר נכסים לבדק הבית.

ר׳ יהושע אומר: זכרים עצמן יקרבו עולות, ונקיבות ימכרו לצריכי זבחי שלמים, ויביא בדמיהן עולות. ושאר נכסים יפלו לבדק הבית.

אמר ר׳ עקיבה: רואה אני את דברי ר׳ אליעזר מדברי ר׳ יהושע, שר׳ אליעזר השווה את מידתו ור׳ יהושע חלק.

אמר ר׳ פפייס: שמעתי דברי שניהם: המקדיש בפירוש—כדברי ר׳ אליעזר, והמקדיש סתם—כדברי ר׳ יהושע.

On the face of it, this debate is about minutiae, but in reality it hinges on a fundamental issue: May the daily burnt offerings be brought from private pockets? Rabbi Eliezer rules that no privately consecrated animal can be offered as a public sacrifice. They must all be

a Donates them to the Temple.
b A kosher, unblemished animal.
c The sex of an animal determines the kinds of sacrifices for which it can be offered.
d The public sacrifice brought every day in the early morning and late afternoon.
e Because only males can be bought as public burnt offerings.
f *ro'eh ani*, literally, "I see."
g To both males and females.
h *shama'ti*, literally, "I have heard."
i That the consecration is entirely for the upkeep of the Temple.

> **TITHES**
>
> Agricultural produce must be tithed a number of times.
>
> *Terumah*, which is separated first (after *bikkurim* when applicable), is holy and given to a priest to eat in purity.
>
> *Ma'aser rishon*, the first 10 percent tithe, is not holy and is given to a Levite. (The Levite must himself give *terumat ma'aser, terumah* from the *ma'aser* he has received, to a Kohen.)
>
> *Ma'aser sheni*, the second 10 percent tithe, is holy but according to tannaitic Halakhah is not given to a Kohen (as it was in the Second Temple period). Instead, it must be brought by its owner to Jerusalem and eaten there in a state of purity. If the owner lives far from Jerusalem or the produce is highly perishable, its holiness can be transferred to coins in a ritual known as "redemption." These coins are then used to purchase foodstuffs in Jerusalem. Once *ma'aser sheni* produce enters Jerusalem, this transfer can no longer be effected. *Ma'aser sheni* is only separated in the first, second, fourth, and fifth years of the sabbatical cycle. In years three and six, *ma'aser 'ani*, a 10 percent tithe for the poor that is not holy, is separated.

sold. Rabbi Yehoshua dissents and rules that male animals can themselves be offered as a communal sacrifice.[38] This controversy spills over into the next generation, with Rabbi Akiva and Rabbi Papyas debating who got it right. Rabbi Akiva prefers the consistent approach, while Rabbi Papyas finds a compromise.

This rare description opens a window onto the tannaitic bet midrash, from which we glimpse later scholars spiritedly evaluating the rulings of previous generations. Although this surely took place regularly, the Mishnah by and large restricts disputes to a single generation, without surveying previous developments or appending later commentary. The history of a law can therefore only be reconstructed—partially at best—only through a detailed comparison of the available sources. When such meticulous work is done, the curtain is pulled back on the study hall, so that one can get a glimpse at the Tannaim adapting, interpreting, and reinterpreting earlier material.

E. TRANSMISSION AND INTERFERENCE

Determining the layers of the Mishnah does more than allow us to trace lines of halakhic development from the earliest traditions to their later, expansive forms. The careful reader can also learn from them how the Mishnah took shape. It is true that the Mishnah generally keeps the generations separate in debates; later Sages did reach across those generational lines to rework the traditions they received. Though they did this without demarcating where the source ends and their input begins, this can sometimes be recovered through comparison to parallel sources.

In Tractate *Ma'aser Sheni*, the Mishnah presents a dispute between Bet Hillel and Bet Shammai about eating *ma'aser sheni* (second tithe) in buildings that are only partly within the municipal boundary of Jerusalem:

Regarding olive presses whose entrances are inside and interior[a] outside,[b] or their entrances are outside and interior inside—

Bet Shammai say, All of it is considered inside.

Bet Hillel say, What is in line with the wall and inward is considered inside, what is in line with the wall and outward is considered outside. (*Ma'aser Sheni*, 3:7)

בתי הבדים שפיתחיהן לפנים וחללן לחוץ או פיתחיהן לחוץ וחללן לפנים –

בית שמי אומרין: הכל כלפנים.

בית הלל אומרין: מכנגד החומה ולפנים—כלפנים, מכנגד החומה ולחוץ—כלחוץ.

According to the Mishnah, Bet Shammai consider these structures to be entirely within the city, regardless of where their entrance is situated. If olives are brought in, their holiness can no longer be transferred onto coins and they must be eaten in a state of ritual purity. Bet Hillel are willing to draw an imaginary continuation of the city wall through the structure, so that the limitations only apply to areas that fall within this extension of the wall.

The toseftan parallel, however, preserves what seems to be the original version of this disagreement, which reduces the daylight between the two academies:

Rabbi Yose said, This is the mishnah of Rabbi Akiva. The *mishnah rishonah* is:

Bet Shammai say, One may not redeem[c] *ma'aser sheni* in them, as if they are inside, and one may not eat lesser sacrifices[d] in them, as if they are outside.

But Bet Hillel say, They are like the chambers:[e] Whatever has its opening inside is considered inside, and whatever has its opening outside is considered outside. (Tosefta, *Ma'aser Sheni*, 2:12)

אמר רבי יוסי: זו משנת רבי עקיבא.

משנת ראשונה: בית שמאי אומרים: אין פודין בהן מעשר שני כאלו הן מבפנים, ואין אוכלין בהן קדשים קלים כאלו הן מבחוץ.

ובית הלל אומרים: הרי הן כלשכות—את שפיתחה לפנים כלפנים, ואת שפתחה לחוץ כלחוץ.

a The *ma'aser sheni* olives are being brought through the entrance, so its location seems pivotal.
b The wall of Jerusalem.
c Transfer the tithe's holiness onto coins.
d In the sense that the limitations on consumption are more relaxed, such as peace-offerings that may be eaten anywhere in Jerusalem.
e Of the Temple; see the description thereof in *Middot*, ch. 2.

According to this tosefta, the *mishnah rishonah* (in the original rabbinic sense and not the modern scholarly one) transmitted the dispute between academies in one way, until Rabbi Akiva taught it differently. Originally, Bet Shammai's was the more stringent opinion. Since the status of the olive-press straddling the boundary is doubtful, the strictures of both possible locations are applied. One loses the ability to transfer the sanctity onto coins in case it's part of Jerusalem, and one is forbidden from eating lesser sacrifices in case it's not. This fits with Bet Shammai's general tendency toward stringency throughout rabbinic literature. Bet Hillel's position in the *mishnah rishonah* is also different. The status of the structure depends on a single factor: the location of the primary access point.[39]

Both opinions in the Tosefta differ from those in Rabbi Akiva's version in the Mishnah. While one can speculate as to how and why Rabbi Akiva came to teach a different version,[40] the important point here for understanding the Mishnah's formation is that the Tosefta reveals the reshaping or reinterpretation of earlier traditions in the Mishnah. Rabbi Yose clarifies that this is not a case of competing traditions; rather, there is one older tradition, the *mishnah rishonah*, which was deliberately adapted by a later, authoritative Sage. According to Rabbi Akiva's own disciple, he reworked earlier material to accord with his own halakhic tradition, and, in so doing, consciously obscured the reported tradition of previous generations.

The "Mishnah of Rabbi Akiva" is the new face of an older tradition, which was refashioned in Rabbi Akiva's study hall. The corpus of such mishnayot together constituted a Mishnah, with a capital M, a body of teachings that his disciples transmitted, taught, and edited. While we do not know the precise contours or contents of Rabbi Akiva's Mishnah, and how fixed and fashioned it was, we can deduce that it revised older traditions and that its text was fairly set, enough so that Sages could compare it to other versions and pick out minute differences. Rabbi Akiva's Mishnah ultimately became *the* Mishnah of Rabbi Yehudah ha-Nasi, who gave it its final form.[41] One of the many proofs for this comes from the example above, where the Tosefta reveals that the Mishnah adopted and anonymized Rabbi Akiva's version of an earlier dispute, thereby making it authoritative.

The implication of this insight for reconstructing older layers from the edited Mishnah is enormous. Disputes between Bet Hillel and Bet Shammai or between early Yavneh Sages are presented in the Mishnah according to the particular tradition of Usha, where Rabbi Akiva was the towering figure. Halakhic positions attributed to the first two generations of named Sages in the Mishnah have been filtered through the minds, sensibilities, and principles of later scholars. Even if the Mishnah can be trusted when it says that a debate occurred in such-and-such generation between Rabbi X and Rabbi Y, the historical accuracy of the reported opinions cannot be taken for granted. When the Mishnah provides no accompanying information, such as the names of the tradents transmitting its version or disputes over the correct version, one must look to the Tosefta to, it is hoped, get the fuller story.[42]

On occasion, one can actually see Rabbi Akiva's construal of matters being rejected by the Mishnah.

If one rubs a hide[a] with oil from the seventh (sabbatical) year,[b] Rabbi Eliezer says, It should be burnt.[c] [. . .]

They said in front of Rabbi Akiva: "Rabbi Eliezer used to say, If one rubs a hide with oil from the sabbatical year, it should be burnt."

He said to them, "Silence! I won't tell you what Rabbi Eliezer says about it." (*Shevi'it*, 8:9)

עור שסכו בשמן שלשביעית רבי אליעזר אומר ידלק [. . .].

אמרו לפני רבי עקיבה: אומר היה רבי אליעזר, עור שסכו בשמן של שביעית ידלק.

אמר להם: שתקו! לא אומר לכם מה שרבי אליעזר אומר בו.

In this case, Rabbi Akiva is said to have possessed a different version of Rabbi Eliezer's halakhic opinion that he was unwilling to share publicly, perhaps because he felt it was too lenient. In contrast to the previous example, Rabbi Akiva's version was not the one incorporated into the Mishnah, for the very obvious reason that he refused to reveal it. This seems to be the exception, though. The transmission of earlier mishnaic sources met with interference of some kind in later academies, such that the cruxes of debate, let alone their precise wording, are in doubt.

F. WHY THE SECOND CENTURY?

Various halakhic traditions were in circulation, then, by the end of the Second Temple period or shortly thereafter, and it was the Sages of the second century, first in Yavneh and then in Usha, who were responsible for collecting, adapting, and editing these traditions. But why did this period specifically see intensive, lively debate about received traditions and their consolidation and formulation as mishnayot? Jewish tradition itself has reflected on this. Medieval rabbis viewed the destruction of the Second Temple as a calamity that ushered in dark times for the Jewish people. Persecution galvanized them to collect and systematize the teachings of the Oral Torah. Sherira Gaon wrote:

> After they had settled down from the destruction of the Temple came an important time, when they gathered to preserve the laws that were almost lost in the chaos of the destruction and persecution, and through the dissent between Bet Shammai and Bet Hillel.[43]

---

a The tanner uses the oil to work the hide, as is his practice.
b Oil produced from olives grown during the sabbatical year is holy, and can therefore only be used for consumption or rubbing on human skin.
c On account of the oil that cannot be used in such a fashion.

Generally speaking, though, the centrality of the second century CE to the Mishnah's formation did not vex medievals all that much because for them the Mishnah had been gradually growing from the beginning of the Second Temple period.[44] They focused instead on why the mishnaic corpus was edited and closed in the era of Rabbi Yehudah ha-Nasi, a question that will be addressed in chapter 4. Since scholars today view the Mishnah primarily as the product of the second century, its formation at precisely that time demands explanation.

No scholarly consensus exists on this, and a range of theories have been aired. One very broad approach attributes it to internal factors. Sherira Gaon's view, that the chaotic aftermath of the Temple's destruction drove home the need to preserve earlier traditions, has not completely fallen out of favor.[45] Some pin it on the loss of the Temple as a watershed moment: it either necessitated a comprehensive vision for a "restored, Torah-perfected, 'messianic' world,"[46] or precipitated a massive turn inward, to the safe study hall where an ideal textual world could replace a catastrophic reality.[47] Still others view it as an attempt to create a unified Halakhah, to repair the sectarian schism of the Second Temple period.[48]

A different tack locates the possible answer in the wider religious or cultural environment. In one interpretation, the formation of the Mishnah should be situated within the context of early Jewish-Christian relations, where it substantiated the antiquity of the Oral Law to dismissive Christians.[49] Another school of thought submits that it should be read as part of the legalistic culture of the Roman Empire and the marked growth of legal activity and writing in the provinces during the second century.[50]

Finally, it might simply be part of the natural cycle of creativity and codification, when the sheer number and variety of laws and practices demand that they be put in some semblance of order.[51]

All these explanations are highly speculative. It is impossible, and perhaps unnecessary, to decide which best fits the data, as each one illuminates a different facet of the Mishnah. What is certain is that the Mishnah as we know it is the product of the tannaitic academies dotting Judea and the Galilee in the second century CE.

THREE

The Mishnah's Legal Sources

The previous chapter looked at the sources and layers of the Mishnah through a diachronic lens. That is, it gave a historical accounting of the gradual formation of the Mishnah, from the earliest known traditions to the textual recasting of Rabbi Akiva and his students. It answered the question of where the Mishnah's halakhic rulings and traditions came from in the personal and institutional sense, and employed a kind of literary archaeology to separate out the activity of various generations of Sages. This chapter complements that discussion by investigating the Mishnah's halakhic sources with a synchronic gaze. It endeavors to answer a related but distinct question: When looking at the Mishnah as a whole, what counts within it as an authoritative legal source? The Sages of the Mishnah listed in the previous chapter transmitted laws that they had received from their teachers, but law does not spring from a vacuum, even if its sources and precedents are not apparent.

In American law, for example, federal and state statutes are enacted by their respective legislatures and recorded in the relevant codes, but the source of legal inspiration for the lawmakers (common law, continental law, local colonial regulations) is not supplied. In the same way, the Mishnah takes the form of a code stating the law, and rarely reveals the sources on which its rulings are based. Consequently, some of its sources evade scholarly detection, while others are recoverable through comparative studies.

Shaye Cohen compared the contents of mishnaic law with other corpora and drew up the following list of sources: the Torah; Mesopotamian and Greco-Roman legal traditions; common practice; Temple realia; priestly traditions; and the laws of pietists and sectarians.[1] While Cohen's comparative work is crucial, I will focus on the manner in which the various sources appear in the Mishnah itself and on the Mishnah's handling of them. Does it treat all these traditions equally?

> BIBLELESS TRACTATES
>
> 1. *Seder Zera'im:* The blessings and prayers of Tractate *Berakhot;* the produce of doubtful tithing in Tractate *Demai.*
>
> 2. *Seder Mo'ed:* The eruv that allows the carrying of objects on Shabbat and the eruv that enables one to leave the Shabbat boundary in Tractates *Shabbat* and *'Eruvin;* the half-shekel tax of Tractate *Shekalim;* the laws of publicly reading the megillah (book of Esther) and the Torah in Tractate *Megillah;* the laws of mourning and *ḥol ha-mo'ed* (intermediate days of the Festival) in Tractate *Mo'ed Katan.*
>
> 3. *Seder Nezikin:* The judicial system and capital punishments of Tractate *Sanhedrin;* the types of oaths taken in God's name in both religious and judicial contexts in Tractate *Shevu'ot;* the ethical maxims of Tractate *Avot;* the collections of testimony about halakhic traditions in Tractate *'Eduyyot.*
>
> 4. *Seder Kodashim:* The rules for slaughtering an animal in Tractate *Ḥullin.*
>
> 5. *Seder Teharot:* The *mikveh* (ritual bath) that effects ritual purification in Tractate *Mikva'ot;* the laws concerning someone who immersed in a *mikveh* but must wait until nightfall for full purification in Tractate *Tevul Yom;* the ritual impurity transmitted by the hands in Tractate *Yadayim;* the potential for plant material attached to fruit to transmit impurity in Tractate *'Uktzin.*

The investigation begins with the Mishnah's erratic relationship with the Torah and then examines two other explicit sources: "testimonies," i.e., oral traditions regarding the Temple, and the *ma'aseh*, a story or event with halakhic ramifications. The next section considers the place of external legal sources in the Mishnah, especially Hellenistic and Roman ones.[2] The chapter concludes with examining debates and discussions in the tannaitic academies, which simultaneously produced its own laws and consolidated all the material from other sources into mishnaic law.

A. THE PENTATEUCH

The first port of call in determining the rabbinic legal position on anything is the Bible, and first and foremost the Pentateuch. From holidays to purity to tort law, tannaitic Halakhah in all its vastness is first and foremost an elaboration and interpretation of the Written Torah. Yet, we have seen that the Mishnah largely does not follow the order of the Torah and represents itself as an independent legal work.[3] What, in fact, is the level of the Mishnah's halakhic dependence on the Torah?

For some tractates, the answer is none at all, because their subject matter is absent from the Torah. Tractate *Ta'anit*, for example, deals extensively with the laws governing public fasts if rain fails to fall by a certain date in the Land of Israel or in response to other calamities. The Torah provides no legal kernel for this. Tractate *Ketubbot* is about the ketubah, the marriage contract signed and witnessed at the time of marriage. This, too, appears nowhere in Scripture, and the first certain evidence of it comes from the second century CE, from the period of the Mishnah itself.[4] There are tractates in all six *sedarim* that have little to no biblical foundation, because their halakhic concerns arose after the Bible's canonization.

Notably, the *sedarim* that contain the most post-biblical material are those that deal with a person's daily routine or weekly ritual observances: *Mo'ed* and *Teharot*.[5]

Even those tractates that are anchored well enough in the Torah contain large, free-floating tracts.

Chapters 10 and 11 of Tractate *Nedarim* discuss the ability of a husband to annul the vows of his wife and of a father to annul those of his daughter. This is based on an extensive passage in the Torah about vows (Num. 30). Chapter 9, though, discusses the capacity of a sage to undo anyone's vows, which has no foundation in Scripture whatsoever. The Mishnah itself admits that "the dissolution of vows" by a scholar "hovers in the air and has nothing on which to rely" (Ḥagigah, 1:8), meaning that the Torah offers no support for this allowance.[6]

But the bulk of mishnaic law does have some basis in Scripture. Does that mean the Mishnah cites the relevant verses? It's complicated. There are times when the Mishnah explicitly cites its biblical source, typically introducing it with the word *she-ne'emar*, "as it says." Of the hundreds of scriptural citations, some are further followed by an exegetical comment or homily. The Mishnah even has a number of sophisticated exegeses that span an entire chapter, like the law of the wayward and rebellious son (Deut. 21:18–22) interpreted in chapter 8 of Tractate *Sanhedrin*.[7] Exegesis tends to be more concentrated in certain tractates, like *Nezikin*, which has a rich scriptural foundation, compared to others.[8]

The vast majority of the Mishnah's laws, though, are presented without any scriptural support, even when it's ready to hand, as in the case of sacrifices, tithes, or the Festivals. Parallels found in other rabbinic corpora frequently reveal that a given mishnah is actually an unmarked or disguised interpretation of a biblical verse. Consider the opening mishnah of Tractate Ḥagigah, which enumerates those exempt from making the triannual pilgrimage to the Temple for each of the three Festivals:

> All are obligated in appearing,[a] except for the deaf-mute, the mentally incompetent, and minors; the *tumtum*[b] and the androgynous;[c] women and unemancipated slaves; the lame and the blind; the ill and the elderly—whoever cannot ascend[d] on their own feet.[e] (Ḥagigah, 1:1)

    a The obligation to make a pilgrimage to the Temple and bring an offering on the Festivals; see Exodus 23:17.
      b Someone with no distinguishable genitalia.
      c Someone with both male and female genitalia.
      d From Jerusalem to the Temple Mount.
      e This is a justification for the exemption of the last four individuals on the list.

הכל חייבים בראייה חוץ מחרש שוטה וקטן, וטומטום ואנדרוגינס, נשים ועבדים שאינן משוחררים, החיגר
והסומא, החולה והזקן—כל שאינו יכול לעלות ברגליו.

What are the halakhic grounds for exempting all these categories of people? The two Talmuds show that the mishnah is in fact an exposition of the verse that lays out the relevant obligation: "Three times *(pe'amim)* a year all your males shall be seen in the presence of the Master, the Lord" (Ex. 23:17).[9] "All your males" excludes those who are not categorically male; "be seen" excludes the blind; and the Hebrew word for "times" in this verse, *pe'amim*, can also mean "footfalls," excluding those who cannot make the ascent unassisted. The mishnah, for its part, never discloses this scriptural basis of its exclusions.

There is more. The mishnah continues with a disagreement between Bet Hillel and Bet Shammai about how to define the excluded minor:

Who is a minor?[a] Whoever cannot ride on his father's shoulders and ascend from Jerusalem to the Temple Mount—so the words of Bet Shammai.

But Bet Hillel say, Whoever cannot hold his father's hand and ascend[b] from Jerusalem to the Temple Mount, as it says, "three times *(regalim)*"[c] (Ex. 23:14). (Ḥagigah, 1:1)

אי זה הוא קטן? כל שאינו יכול לרכוב על כתיפו שלאביו ולעלות מירושלם להר הבית—כדברי בית שמי.
ובית הילל אומרין: כל שאינו יכול לאחוז בידו של אביו ולעלות מירושלם להר הבית, שנאמר ״שָׁלֹשׁ רְגָלִים״.

One cannot say for certain if Bet Hillel themselves supplied the prooftext or it was added later. But given the lack of proof for Bet Shammai's position and the absence of Scripture from the entire mishnah, the latter seems more likely. With each generation, the desire to link mishnaic law to the Torah grew, as we will see when we discuss the Midrash's increasing tendency to provide scriptural support for mishnaic laws.[10] Indeed, in the halakhic Midrash, we find a citation appended to Bet Shammai's opinion as well: "the words of Bet Shammai. As it says, 'your males.'"[11]

Here is another example of undeclared exegesis in the Mishnah:

If someone deposits with his fellow an animal or object for safekeeping, and it is stolen or lost:

---

a The question pertains specifically to this law and is not intended to establish a general halakhic definition.
b This minor is older than the one riding on shoulders.
c Hebrew *regalim* can also mean "feet/legs," indicating that there must be more than just the two feet of the father walking.

> If he paid and did not want to swear—since they said that an unpaid bailee may swear and be released—then if the thief is found, he pays double;[a] if he slaughtered or sold it, he pays fourfold or fivefold.[b] Whom does he pay? The one who has the deposit.
>
> If he swore and did not want to pay, then if the thief is found, he pays double; if he slaughtered or sold it, he pays fourfold or fivefold. Whom does he pay? The owner of the deposit. (*Bava Metzi'a*, 3:1)

> המפקיד אצל חבירו בהמה או כלים וניגנבו או שאבדו:
>
> שילם ולא רצה להישבע—שהרי אמרו שומר חינם נישבע ויוצא—נימצא הגנב משלם תשלומי כפל, טבח ומכר משלם תשלומי ארבעה וחמשה. למי הוא משלם? למי שהפיקדון אצלו.
>
> נשבע ולא רצה לשלם, נימצא הגנב משלם תשלומי כפל, טבח ומכר משלם תשלומי ארבעה וחמשה. למי הוא משלם? לבעל הפיקדון.

This mishnah sets forth a bailee's responsibility. If the deposit in his safekeeping is stolen or lost, he must either pay back the value of the object, or take an oath that he was not negligent in keeping watch. If the bailee chooses to pay, then the thief—if caught—makes him whole. If the oath option is exercised, exempting the bailee from repayment, then the thief pays the owner.

The structure of the mishnah looks unnecessarily complicated. Conditional statements are nested within conditional statements: "If someone deposits . . . If he paid . . . then if the thief is found." It is also longwinded: Why repeat what happens when the thief is located, if the only element that changes is the recipient of the payment? Since the Mishnah is usually direct and concise, why is it convoluted and verbose here?

Hanoch Albeck proposed, simply enough, that the mishnah is mimicking the structure of the relevant passage in Exodus:

> If a man gives his fellow money or goods for safekeeping and they are stolen from the man's house, if the thief is found, he shall pay double. [. . .] If a man gives his fellow a donkey or an ox or a sheep or any beast for safekeeping and it dies, is maimed, or is carried off, with no witness, an oath of the Lord shall be between the two of them, that he has not laid hands on his fellow's effects, and the owner shall accept and he shall not pay. [. . .] (Exodus 22:6, 9–10)

The conditional language, which the mishnah repeats in both scenarios, is lifted straight from the Torah: "If a man gives . . . if the thief is found." This is an unmarked inter-

---

a Like all cases of surreptitious theft; see Exodus 22:3, 6, 8.
b The exact amount depends on the type of animal; see Exodus 21:37.

pretation of an entire passage of biblical law, and the only hint to it lies in its peculiar phraseology.¹²

Occasionally, the Mishnah will even paraphrase scripture, as in the law of the goring ox:

> If an ox gored someone and they died, the *mu'ad*ᵃ pays the ransomᵇ and the *tam*ᶜ is exempt from it. This one and that one are liable to die.ᵈ
>
> The same for a son or daughter.
>
> If it gored a slave or maidservant, one must pay thirty *sela'*, whether they are worth one-hundred *maneh* orᵉ only one golden *dinar*.ᶠ (*Bava Kamma*, 4:5)

> שור שנגח את האדם ומת, מועד משלם את הכופר ותם פטור מן הכופר. וזה וזה חייבים מיתה. וכן בבן או בבת.
>
> נגח עבד או אמה, נותן שלושים סלע, בין שהוא יפה במאה מנה, ובין שאינו יפה אלא דינר זהב.

The presentation of the law seems needlessly drawn out and fragmented. Some of the language is unusual for the Mishnah, such as "son or daughter" in lieu of the expected "minor" *(katan)*. If one looks at the underlying passage in the Torah, one discovers that this mishnah is reworking both its form and content:

> If an ox gores a man or woman and they die, the ox shall surely be stoned and its flesh shall not be eaten, but the ox's owner shall be clear.
>
> But if the ox is a gorer and was warned about to its owner, who did not guard it, and it kills a man or a woman, the ox shall be stoned and the owner also put to death.
>
> If a ransom is set for him, then he shall give whatever has been set for him as redemption for his life.
>
> And if it gores a son or daughter, he shall be dealt with according to this law.
>
> If the ox gores a slave or maidservant, he shall give thirty shekels of silver to their owner and the ox shall be stoned. (Ex. 21:28–32)

---

    a An ox that has a history of goring three times, and the owner has been warned to keep close watch over it since it is a menace. The term comes from the biblical phrase, "was warned about *(ve-hu'ad)* to its owner" (Ex. 21:29).

    b Payment for the life of the person who was killed.

    c An ox that does not have the violent tendencies of a *mu'ad*. This term is not of biblical origin and has the general sense of "innocuous" or "harmless."

    d Both oxen are stoned to death.

    e The pecuniary penalty is a flat fee, and has nothing to do with how much a particular slave is worth at market.

    f The fixed price of thirty *sela'* (120 silver *denarii*) applies whether the slave would have fetched a cheap price or an astronomical one.

TABLE 1 Comparison of Mishnah *Bava Kamma* 4:5 and its scriptural source

Bava Kamma, 4:5	Exodus 21:28-32
If an ox gored someone and they died	If an ox gores a man or woman and they die (v. 28)
the *mu'ad*	the ox . . . was warned about *(ve-hu'ad)* to its owner (v. 29)
pays the ransom	If a ransom is set for him . . . (v. 30)
and the *tam* is exempt from it.	but the ox's owner shall be clear (v. 28)
This one and that one are liable to die.	the ox shall surely be stoned (v. 28)
The same for a son or daughter.	And if it gores a son or daughter . . . (v. 31)
If it gored a slave or maidservant . . .	If the ox gores a slave or maidservant . . . (v. 32)

Table 1 shows the progression of the mishnah compared to its biblical foundation: Some features of this mishnah derive from the Torah's presentation: The disjointed structure of the mishnah was produced by slavishly adhering to the biblical casuistry. The odd diction, such as "ransom" and "son or daughter," are the Torah's own terms. But other elements have been reworked. The Torah's separate treatments of the two oxen form the halakhic backbone of the mishnah, but it has reduced them to a brief contrast. It has translated some of the original terminology into mishnaic Hebrew: "thirty shekels of silver" becomes "thirty *sela'*," "a man or woman" becomes "someone," "shall surely be stoned" becomes "liable to die."[13] All in all, the mishnah owes much to the biblical pericope, yet this relationship is nowhere disclosed.[14]

The mishnayot dissected above turn out to be heavily indebted to the Bible in language and content. Once one is attuned to the signs of this influence, one begins to see it throughout the Mishnah. This unannounced but pervasive presence of Scripture dwarfs all the explicit citations. The halakhic language of the Mishnah turns out to be rife with biblicisms: "the heifer whose neck is broken *('eglah 'arufah),*" "the first shearing," "between the hall *(ulam)* and the altar," "the betrothed maiden," "the stoned ox."[15]

The Mishnah possesses its own organizing principles, but there are times when it is subtly following some biblical order. This can even be seen also on the larger scale of tractates. Tractate *Nezikin* (the three *Bava*s, gates) basically follows the order of Exodus 21–23, the pericope known as *Parashat Mishpatim*.[16] Tractate *Nega'im*, about dermatological and other conditions that fall under the diagnosis of *tzara'at*, proceeds according to Leviticus 13–14.[17] Tractate *Shevu'ot* covers the various kinds of oaths, yet its first two chapters delve deeply into the intricacies of purity law. Why? Probably because of Leviticus 5, where the two appear in close proximity.[18]

Not all mishnayot that draw on the Torah reveal this influence in their language or style. Many are unquestionably founded on biblical law, but one would not know it even after scrutinizing the mishnaic text. For example, the Torah requires one to take four species in hand on Sukkot: "On the first day you shall take for yourselves the fruit of beautiful trees, branches of palm trees, boughs of leafy trees, and willows of the brook" (Lev. 23:40). The exact species are not clearly identified in the Written Torah, so the Oral Torah must specify them. In doing so, the Mishnah chooses to use terms for the species from its own time period, without linking them back to their biblical designations.[19] Its halakhic treatment of the species does not follow their order in the verse; neither are any citations of the biblical text brought. It does not make even the slightest attempt to establish a connection between the Written and Oral Torahs here. Only the parallel halakhic midrash adduces the relevant scriptural exegesis.[20]

If we look at the Mishnah as a whole, a strange picture emerges. It does not go to the trouble of presenting its biblical sources in any consistent fashion, but neither does it actively try to conceal them. Appeals and allusions to Scripture in the Mishnah are patchy, perhaps primarily because it is a patchwork of distinct legal collections and diachronic layers. Whatever the root cause of this inconsistency, it is quite revealing about the Mishnah's model of halakhic authority. Whether a law is explicit in the Torah, is the product of rabbinic exegesis, or is free of any biblical basis is immaterial; all are placed on equal footing in the mishnah. What lends all of them their authority is the very fact of their inclusion in the mishnaic corpus.

In some mishnayot, this vision of equality apparently guided an editorial hand. The first mishnah in the sixth chapter of Tractate *Terumot* states: "One who eats *terumah* (the priestly tithe) unintentionally pays the principal and a fifth." That is, if a Levite or Israelite consumes the tithe intended for a priest, they must pay him the amount consumed plus a fine. The evident source for this law is Leviticus 22:14: "If a man eats the sacred donation unwittingly, he shall add a fifth of its value to it and give the sacred donation to the priest." The existence of this verse is not acknowledged in the above mishnah; the law comes with no pedigree. And yet, it would be incorrect to conclude from this that the Mishnah is deliberately obscuring the scriptural source, because the end of that same chapter presents two expositions of the verse. Why, then, does the verse not appear earlier in the chapter in the quote above, where it would be appropriate?

Between the beginning and end of the chapter there is a series of laws about eating *terumah* unintentionally, laws that have no scriptural basis. One can venture that if the chapter were to include a verse in its first mishnah, it would, in a sense, demote the non-scriptural laws that follow it. By delaying the citation until the end of the chapter where it no longer poses a "threat" to the preceding material, a sense of equality is generated. The suspension of biblical citations until the end of a chapter (and thus of a topic) is, in fact, a recurring pattern in the Mishnah, which contributes to the impression that all its laws bear identical status.[21]

The Talmuds depart radically from this view. For them, not all halakhot are equal by dint of their incorporation into the Mishnah. The Oral and Written Torahs must be closely knitted, a scriptural anchor found for every single law of the Mishnah. This endeavor began earlier with the halakhic Midrash of the Tannaim, from which it was carried over to the Palestinian Talmud and eventually the Babylonian Talmud. In the latter, citations of the Mishnah are inevitably trailed by the question "Whence do we know this?" and the answer is usually a scriptural citation. This ubiquitous question challenges the Mishnah's self-image of an authoritative halakhic corpus independent of Scripture.

The very first mishnah begins with a question, "From when may one recite the Shema in the evening?" (*Berakhot*, 1:1). The Babylonian Talmud immediately questions the question: "On what grounds does the Tanna recite, 'From when . . . ?'"[22] That is, how can the Tanna here begin the laws of reciting the Shema with a question about parameters, without first establishing the very obligation to recite the Shema?[23] The Talmud answers, "The Tanna grounded himself on a verse, as it is written, 'in your lying down and your getting up' (Deut. 6:7)." The obligation taken for granted by the mishnah rests on the bedrock of Scripture.[24]

It is fitting to conclude this section by revisiting an example cited at its beginning, this time from the talmudic vantage point. Recall that, according to the Mishnah, the dissolution of vows by a Torah scholar has no precedent in the Torah. Yet the two Talmuds cite a dissenting assertion that "it has something on which to rely," and various scriptural interpretations are offered as proof.[25] The Talmuds abhor the vacuum between mishnaic and biblical law that the Mishnah itself is quite comfortable with.[26] The idea that there can be a bibleless body of Jewish law died in the early amoraic period.

B. TRADITION

Beside the Bible, the Mishnah relies on halakhic traditions transmitted by previous generations. To move straight into an example, the second chapter of Tractate *Pe'ah* discusses various aspects of the mitzvah to leave the *pe'ah*, the corner or edge of one's field, for the poor. What if a field is sown with multiple crops, does it suffice to leave the edge of one crop for the entire field, or must one leave one edge per crop?

> It once happened that Rabbi Shimon of Mitzpah sowed in the presence of Rabban Gamaliel, and they ascended to the Chamber of Hewn Stone[a] and asked.[b]
>
> Rabbi Nahum ha-Livlar[c] said, "I have received a tradition from Rabbi Meyasha, who received it from his father, who received it from the *Zugot*, who received it from the prophets, a halakhah[d] of Moses from Sinai: Regarding someone who sows a field with two species of wheat, if he processes them at a single threshing floor then he gives one edge, two threshing floors then he gives two edges." (*Pe'ah*, 2:6)

מעשה שזרע ר' שמעון איש המצפה לפני רבן גמליאל, ועלה ללשכת הגזית ושאלו.

אמר נחום הליבלר: מקובל אני מרבי מייישא שקיבל מאבא שקיבל מן הזוגות שקיבלו מן הנביאים, הלכה למשה מסיני—הזורע את שדיהו שני מיני חיטים, אם עשאן גורן אחת נותן פיאה אחת, שתי גרנות נותן שתי פיאות.

    a According to tradition, this was where the supreme judicial and legislative body presided in the Temple; see *Sanhedrin*, 11:2.
    b What the law is in this case.
    c The title comes from Latin *librarius*, meaning "scribe" or "copyist."
    d In this context, the word means "tradition."

Note the source of this law. Rabbi Nahum ha-Livlar was a court clerk with no legislative power. He established the law solely on the basis of a tradition he personally received from his teacher, who was taught it by his father, who heard it from his teachers.[27] This chain of transmission is said to reach all the way back to Mount Sinai, where God revealed the Torah to Moses. There can be no second-guessing this law: the word of tradition is final. This mishnah disregards the status of the tradition-bearer; he can be a revered scholar or a simple secretary. What matters is only the antiquity and reliability of the tradition.

This model of an unbroken line of transmission is especially elaborate in the first two chapters of Tractate *Avot*, beginning with "Moses," who "received the Torah from Sinai and transmitted it to Joshua," through the Men of the Great Assembly, and all the way down to Rabban Yohanan ben Zakkai and his students in the bet midrash (study hall) of Yavneh. In this model, the Sages of Yavneh are but the latest link in a chain that began with God Himself.[28]

But, as noted in the previous chapter, the Mishnah does not regularly trace the Oral Torah to the revelation at Sinai.[29] In fact, in the voluminous Mishnah a law is explicitly designated "a halakhah of Moses from Sinai" only two more times.[30] Less scarce are short-range transmissions of a tradition, when a Sage will say "I have heard" (*shama'ti*) or "I have received a tradition" (*mekubbal ani*). The long-term pedigree of the law in these instances is unknown.

In one place, Rabbi Akiva asserts the superiority of tradition, when he says to his teachers: "If it's a halakhah (tradition), we will accept it, but if it is a logical deduction, there's a rebuttal" (*Keritot*, 3:7). Tradition is unimpeachable, but logic is never airtight.[31] In another place, the Mishnah explicitly presents tradition as one of the main sources of mishnaic law, alongside the Torah and later rabbinic enactments.

> New grain[a] is prohibited by the Torah everywhere;[b] *'orlah* by halakhah;[c] and *kil'ayim* by the words of the scribes.[d] (*'Orlah*, 3:9)

> החדש אסור מן התורה בכל מקום, והעורלה הלכה, והכלאים מדיברי סופרים.

The Mishnah presents three agricultural prohibitions that are extended to outside the Land of Israel by three sources of Halakhah: the Torah, tradition, and rabbinic legislation. Take note that here (and elsewhere) the tradition is unqualified. It may not be dated to the biblical assembly at Sinai, but it is also not a scribal innovation. It is an early, extra-biblical tradition.

   a The new crop may not be eaten prior to the offering of the *'omer* wave-offering on the sixteenth of Nisan; see Leviticus 23:9–14.
   b Even outside the Land of Israel; see Leviticus 23:14 and *Sifra, Emor*, 10:1 (100d).
   c The prohibition to eat tree fruit within the first three years of the tree's planting is biblical, but it is a tradition that extends it to outside the Land of Israel.
   d The prohibition on sowing two species in a single field is biblical, but only the scribes extended it to outside the Land of Israel.

If there is one tractate in which the traditions underlying mishnaic law take center stage, it is *'Eduyyot* (literally, "testimonies"). Various Sages therein attest that they have received a tradition about a practice from the Second Temple period, usually connected to the Temple cult or ritual purity. Unlike other tractates that are organized by topic, *'Eduyyot* is organized by tradent. For example, "Rabbi Hananiah Chief Deputy of the Priests attested to four things," "Akaviah ben Mehalalel attested to four things," "Rabbi Yehoshua and Rabbi Tzadok attested," and so on for the entire tractate. For example:

> Rabbi Yehudah ben Abba attested to five things: minor girls are made to exercise their right of refusal;[a] a woman may be permitted to marry by the testimony of a single witness;[b] a chicken was stoned in Jerusalem for killing a person; forty-day-old wine was poured on the altar;[c] and the daily morning sacrifice was offered at the fourth hour.[d] (*'Eduyyot*, 6:1)

ר' יהודה בן אבא העיד חמשה דברין: שממאנים את הקטנות, ושמשיאין את האשה על פי עד אחד, ושניסקל תרנגול בירושלים על שהרג את הנפש, ועל היין בן ארבעים יום שניתנסך על גבי המזבח, ועל תמיד שלשחר שקרב בארבע שעות.

These attestations truly range across Halakah, concerning marital, penal, and sacrificial law. The first two are phrased normatively using the participle *(mema'anin, massi'in)*, while the next three are cast in the passive past tense (was stoned, was poured, was offered). The common denominator is the speaker, the Sage who received all these traditions while the Temple was still standing. These testimonies may be formulated either descriptively, as accounts of past events, or normatively, as expressions of Temple law.

This accords with Flavius Josephus's characterization of the Pharisees, who considered tradition, rather than biblical exegesis or an assertion of early revelation, as a source of binding law:

> [T]the Pharisees had passed on to the people certain regulations handed down by former generations and not recorded in the Law of Moses, for which reason they are rejected by the Sadducaean group, who hold that only those regulations should be

---

a If a minor girl lost her father and was married off by her brother or mother, she may refuse the marriage when she reaches majority, and sometimes the bet din will even instruct her to do so while she is still a minor; see *Yevamot*, 13:7.

b Who says her husband is dead, even though two witnesses are typically necessary to establish a fact.

c As the libation that accompanies a sacrifice.

d The diacritics in MS Kaufmann (קָרֵב) mark the word as a participle, rather than a reference to a past event. Of the twelve variable hours into which the rabbis divide the day from sunrise to sunset, which change incrementally with the seasons.

considered valid which were written down (in Scripture), and that those which had been handed down by former generations (lit. the fathers) need not be observed.[32]

Interestingly, outside of Tractate *'Eduyyot* one scarcely encounters such attestations. Mishnaic laws are not regularly labeled as traditions, and mishnaic Sages are not in the habit of reporting their opinions in the name of anyone else.[33] Of those that are, most are duplicates of the traditions recorded in *'Eduyyot*. Hanoch Albeck was correct when he claimed that Tractate *'Eduyyot*, populated with Sages who lived in the immediate aftermath of the Temple's fall, was the original, earlier collection of traditions. As the Mishnah was being arranged thematically, this material was split up and duplicated in the thematically relevant tractates.[34] By Rabbi Akiva's generation the practice of testifying to the existence and authenticity of a tradition had already stopped.

The testimonies about tradition in Tractate *'Eduyyot* reflect a model of halakhic authority in which teachings vouchsafed from teacher to student constitute an unassailable, authoritative source of Halakhah. In Rabbi Akiva's words, "If it's a halakhah (tradition), we will accept it," and in another tannaitic formulation, "a person should not cling to their opinion where there is a tradition *(shemu'ah).*"[35] The Pharisees in their time enshrined this source of law, and for a couple of generations after the destruction of the Temple the Sages continued to draw on it, as part of their effort to keep practices from Temple times from being forgotten. As time went on, though, tradition stopped being treated as sacrosanct and determinative, as is evidenced by the few appeals to it outside of Tractate *'Eduyyot*. The simple clarity of tradition was gradually replaced by the complex and sophisticated learning of the study hall, where the law was decided.[36] The Mishnah, therefore, mostly consists of disagreements between Sages living in the same time and place, and not of traditions handed down across the ages.

C. THE *MA'ASEH*

The Mishnah has another primary source that emerges from neither text nor tradition but from action: the *ma'aseh* (pl. *ma'asim*), a story or event with halakhic ramifications. The Mishnah has over 150 *ma'asim*. Most of them are cases brought to one or more Sages for a halakhic ruling. The very first mishnah features such a case:

> From when may one recite the Shema in the evening? From the time when the Kohanim (priests) enter to eat their *terumah*[a] until the end of the first watch[b]—the words of Rabbi Eliezer.

  a If a priest becomes ritually impure, he must immerse in a *mikveh* (ritual bath) and wait until sunset, which brings full purification for the purposes of eating *terumah*. It's possible that priests who were unsure if they had contracted impurity also observed this practice, in which case this would have been a common sight.
  b The last time one may recite the Shema according to Rabbi Eliezer is at the end of the first of the three equal watches of the night; see, e.g., Judges 7:19.

But the Sages say, Until midnight.

Rabban Gamaliel says, Until dawn.

<u>It once happened (ma'aseh)</u> that his sons[a] came from the wedding hall. They said to him, "We haven't recited the Shema." He said to them, "If it is not yet dawn, you may recite it."[b] (*Berakhot*, 1:1)

מאמתי קורין את שמע בערבים? משעה שהכהנים נכנסים לאכל בתרומתן עד סוף האשמורת הראשונה — דברי רבי אליעזר.

וחכמים אומרים: עד חצות.

רבן גמליאל אומר: עד שיעלה עמוד השחר.

מעשה שבאו בניו מבית המשתה. אמרו לו: לא קרינו את שמע. אמר להם: אם לא עלה עמוד השחר, מותרין אתם ליקרות.

Would Rabban Gamaliel's sons have been unfamiliar with an explicit ruling of their father? This seems unlikely. It thus seems that the original order of the ruling and the event has been reversed. A situation arose that resulted in Rabban Gamaliel giving halakhic instruction to his sons. The Mishnah adopted this case-based ruling as the law and reformulated into its legalese. The *ma'aseh* is the basis for the halakhah!

This is even clearer in the mishnah below, which forbids a wife from presuming her husband has drowned if he has fallen overboard and not emerged from the water:

If he fell into water, whether it has an end or does not have an end[c] his wife is prohibited.[d]

Rabbi Meir said, *It once happened (ma'aseh)* that someone fell into a massive cistern and climbed out after three days. (*Yevamot*, 16:4)

נפל למים, בין שיש להן סוף ובין שאין להם סוף, הרי אשתו אסורה.

אמר רבי מאיר: מעשה באחד שנפל לבור הגדול ועלה לאחר שלושה ימים.

If someone falls into a small body of water and does not wash up on the shore dead or alive, one might suppose that he could be presumed drowned. The Mishnah, however, takes into account the remote possibility that a person can tread water or find some flotsam to cling to and survive. While Rabbi Meir appears to be buttressing this anonymous ruling, it is really

---

a Rabban Gamaliel's.
b Some texts have "you must recite it."
c Whether the water has a visible end with a shore in view.
d To remarry, out of concern that her husband emerged from the water alive.

the other way around. The parallel tosefta (14:5) identifies the anonymous voice as Rabbi Meir's, whose ruling is very clearly informed by the unusual case of the man in the cistern.

These *ma'asim* are incidents that exemplify halakhic decisions, but there are others where the actions of Sages themselves serve as exempla. In the second chapter of Tractate *Berakhot*, there is another *ma'aseh* involving Rabban Gamaliel:

> A groom is exempt from reciting the Shema on the first night through Saturday night if has not done the deed *(ma'aseh)*.[a]
>
> *It once happened (ma'aseh)* that Rabban Gamaliel got married and recited it on the night of the nuptials. They said to him, "Didn't you teach us that a groom is exempt from reciting the Shema on the first night?"
>
> He said to them, "I won't listen to you to suspend the kingdom of Heaven from over me[b] even for a moment." (*Berakhot*, 5:2)

> חתן פטור מקריית שמע בלילה הראשון ועד מוצאי שבת אם לא עשה מעשה.
>
> מעשה ברבן גמליאל שנשא וקרא בלילה שנשא. אמרו לו: לא לימדתנו שחתן פטור מקרית שמע בלילה הראשון?
>
> אמר להם: איני שומע לכם לבטל ממני מלכות שמים שעה אחת.

In this story, Rabban Gamaliel's piety is held up as an example. He was not required to recite the Shema yet did so anyway.[37] Unlike the earlier examples, where the *ma'aseh* feeds directly into the determination of the law, this *ma'aseh* injects tension into the Mishnah, between the demands of universal halakhic obligation and those of individual piety. This same tension is accentuated in the following case:

> Women, slaves, and minors are exempt from the sukkah,[c] but any minor who does not need his mother[d] is obligated in the sukkah.
>
> *It once happened (ma'aseh)* that Shammai the Elder's daughter-in-law gave birth, and on account of the minor[e] he broke through the plasterwork[f] and added a sukkah covering over the bed. (*Sukkah*, 2:8)

---

a Consummated the marriage through the mitzvah of marital relations.
b The first chapter of the Shema is about accepting the kingdom of Heaven upon oneself; see Deuteronomy 6:4.
c See Leviticus 23:40–43.
d He is independent to some extent; see the criteria proposed in BT *Sukkah* 28b.
e The newborn boy.
f Of the ceiling to expose the sky to the area underneath it.

נשים ועבדים וקטנים פטורים מן הסוכה, וכל קטן שאינו צריך לאמו חייב בסוכה.

מעשה שילדה כלתו של של שמי הזקן, ופחת את המעזיבה וסיכך על גבי המיטה בשביל הקטן.

The most acute example of disconnect between pietistic conduct and normative Halakhah is the story of Honi the Circle-Maker. Tractate *Ta'anit* lays out a series of fasts instituted by the rabbis in case of drought, but Honi circumvents this entire process by going directly to God, as it were, and demanding rain—no fasts necessary.[38]

The Babylonian Talmud takes notice of *ma'asim* that ostensibly undermine the law, and asks in thirteen different places, "Is the *ma'aseh* intended to contradict?" When *ma'asim* look to the supererogatory behavior of the rabbinic elite, they can pose a challenge to the relevant law. But these are not the norm. As we have seen above, a *ma'aseh* usually functions to shore up the law, and is itself sometimes reformulated as the law.

Other *ma'asim* involve popular practices or customs from the Second Temple period. The Mishnah records the following about binding the four species together on Sukkot:

One may only bind the lulav with its own species[a]—the words of Rabbi Yehudah.

Rabbi Meir says, Even with a cord.[b]

Rabbi Meir said, *The people of Jerusalem used to (ma'aseh)* bind their lulavs with gold bands.

They said to him, They would bind it with its own species below.[c] (*Sukkah*, 3:8)

אין אוגדים את הלולב אלא מימינו—דברי רבי יהודה.

רבי מאיר אומר: אפילו במשיחה.

אמר רבי מאיר: מעשה באנשי ירושלים שהיו אוגדים את לוליביהם בגימונות שלזהב.

This *ma'aseh* is taken as a halakhic precedent by Rabbi Meir for his opinion. It holds special importance because it describes a practice from the Second Temple period, before Jews were banished from the Holy City.

The previous two sections of this chapter stressed that the Mishnah treats two primary sources of law, the Torah and tradition, as indisputable. This mishnah in *Sukkah* shows us that the *ma'aseh*, a third legal source, enjoys no such protection. In fact, the Sages of this mishnah reimagine a practice of old to conform with their own halakhic views. Here is another example from Tractate *Sukkah* that exposes the vulnerability of the *ma'aseh* to realignment with one's bias:

   a Vegetal matter from the palm tree.
   b Of flax or some other species.
   c They would bind it with gold for decorative purposes higher up, and with palm material lower down, nearer to where it was grasped. This line does not apper in the MSS and was added to the printed editions of the Mishnah from a baraita (see Tosefta *Sukkah*, 2:10).

If most of a person and their head were in the sukkah and their table[a] was inside the house,[b] Bet Shammai invalidate it and Bet Hillel validate it.[c]

Bet Hillel said to Bet Shammai: "*It once happened (ma'aseh)* that the elders of Bet Shammai and the elders of Bet Hillel went to visit Yohanan, son of the Horonite,[d] and they found him with most of him and his head in the sukkah and the table inside the house."

Bet Shammai said to them: "That's a proof![e] They even told him,[f] 'If this has been your practice, you have never fulfilled the mitzvah of sukkah[g] in your life.'" (*Sukkah*, 2:7)

מי שהיה ראשו ורובו בסוכה ושולחנו בתוך הבית, בית שמי פוסלין ובית הלל מכשירין.

אמרו בית הלל לבית שמי: מעשה שהלכו זקני בית שמי וזקני בית הילל לבקר את יוחנן בן החרוני, ומצאוהו ראשו ורוב בסוכה ושולחנו בתוך הבית.

אמרו להם בית שמי: משם ראיה! אף הן אמרו לו, אם כך היתה נוהג, לא קיימתה מצות סוכה מימיך.

The two academies of Bet Hillel and Bet Shammai are not wrangling over the legal ramifications of the episode, but over the facts themselves.[39] Since *ma'asim* are considered legal precedents, they are open to manipulation in the bet midrash. In the same way that Rabbi Akiva reconstrued the halakhic opinions of his predecessors, the two houses imagine conversations their elders would have had. History in the Mishnah is not as solid as it feels to us moderns.

D. ROMAN LAW

In his comparative study, Shaye Cohen detected Roman law (as well as some earlier Hellenistic law) among the Mishnah's legal sources. This should not surprise us. The Sages lived under Roman rule, and the Roman Empire was famously an empire of law: it anchored its deeds in formal legislation and edicts, it developed sophisticated legal procedures and established a hierarchical judicial system, it worked out its legal thought and theory through the pens of professional jurists. The oppressive, pervasive Roman legal atmosphere quite naturally would have permeated the legal thinking and observances of its subjects, even in provinces like Judaea.[40]

---

a Which has the meal on it.
b Because the sukkah was too small to fit the table; according to BT *Sukkah* 3a, this mishnah is discussing a sukkah's minimum dimensions.
c The sukkah's ritual fitness for discharging one's obligation.
d From the Houran, in today's Syria.
e To our opinion rather than to yours. For this reading see Kahana, "On Halakhic Tolerance," note 7.
f The elders of Bet Hillel and Bet Shammai told Yohanan.
g Because your sukkah is invalid.

Let us reexamine a mishnah discussed in the previous chapter, which enumerates three means of marrying a woman:

> A wife is acquired in three ways and acquires herself in two ways. She is acquired with money, a contract, or intercourse. (*Kiddushin*, 1:1)[41]

> האישה נקנית בשלוש דרכים, וקונה את עצמה בשתי דרכים. נקנית בכסף, ובשטר, ובביאה.

Compare this to the means of acquisition set forth by Gaius, a second-century Roman jurist:

> Formerly, there used to be three methods by which they (i.e. women) fell into subordination *(manus)*: by usage *(usus)*, by sharing of bread *(confarreatio)*, and by contrived sale *(coemptio)*.[42]

In antiquity, Gaius says, one took a wife by "usage," that is, the woman lived intimately in her husband's house for a year; "sharing of bread," a religious ceremony in which the woman was transferred from her father to her husband; or "contrived sale." The similarity between this and the mishnah extends beyond the details to the language itself.[43] The very itemization of three means of effecting marriage is in and of itself telling. In a pioneering comparative study, Boaz Cohen writes about this correspondence and others that he found in additional areas of law: slave, transactional, tort, and more.[44] Other scholars have uncovered even more potential parallels.[45]

The example from marriage law highlights that Roman legal thinking penetrated far beyond the sterile world of boilerplate contracts and multinational business arrangements into the inner sanctum of Jewish life, the Jewish home. What is more, scholars have shown how the Mishnah's definition of who is a Jew is also partly patterned on non-Jewish models of identity. First, a slave that is emancipated becomes Jewish, similar to how a manumitted slave becomes a full Roman citizen. Second, the legitimacy of a child in both legal systems depends on whether the parents could have been married. In the Mishnah this litmus test is called "marriage is effective" *(yesh kiddushim)*, and in Roman law it is termed *conubium*.[46]

The imprint of Roman law runs even deeper, down to the very conceptual building blocks with which the Sages constructed their legal world. For example, the mishnaic Hebrew term *ke-illu*, "as if it were," first occurs in the Mishnah, where it is attested about fifty-five times. Its purpose is to create a legal fiction that does not accord with reality. Let us examine one usage regarding the laws of Shabbat. After Shabbat's onset, if a person is outside a city, they are forbidden to travel more than two thousand cubits from their present location. If someone is within a municipal boundary, the entire city is considered their home base, and the relevant boundary extends two thousand cubits around the city in every direction.

> ## THE ARCHIVE OF BABATHA
>
> Babatha was a wealthy matron from Zoar, located on the east side of the Jordan river. In 106 CE, the area under Nabatean rule was incorporated into the Roman province of Arabia. Babatha moved to Ein Gedi, but during the Bar Kokhba Revolt of the 130s she fled with family members to a cave in the Judaean Desert. She brought her archive with her, which contained legal correspondence on matters of marriage, inheritance, and commerce written in Aramaic, Nabatean, and Greek.
>
> The archive, discovered by Yigael Yadin in 1960, shed new light on the actual legal conduct of Jews in the region. Among other things, it showed that they followed the general Roman practice and even brought their disputes to the local Roman administrator.

Regarding someone who went out[a] with permission,[b] if they said to him, "The deed has been done,"[c] he has 2,000 cubits in every direction.[d]

If he was within the boundary,[e] it is as if *(ke-illu)* he did not leave, for whoever goes out to rescue may return to their place. (*'Eruvin*, 4:3)

מי שיצא ברשות, אמרו לו כבר נעשה המעשה, יש לו אלפים אמה לכל רוח.

אם היה בתוך התחום, **כאילו** לא יצא, שכל היוצאים להציל חוזרין למקומן.

Leib Moscovitz has illustrated the kinship between *ke-illu* and Latin *fictio*, which is so prevalent in Roman law and plays the same legal-conceptual role.[47]

When it comes to the Bible, tradition, or the *ma'aseh*, the Mishnah actively recognizes and incorporates these sources of law. How did Roman laws and legal concepts become ingrained in the Mishnah? While the typical model of gradual influence of the majority on the minority applies, perhaps there was also a conscious adoption in this case. Contracts involving Jews discovered in the Judean Desert, especially from the archive of Babatha, inform us that Jews resorted to arbitration by Roman officials and judges.

Sages would have competed with the Roman courts for cases and tried to stop Jews from appearing before Roman magistrates.[48] To retain litigants, they would have had to present Halakhah in a way that fit the familiar models of the Roman legal system. Such remodeling might also have been accelerated by the change in the status of Jews in the early third century, when all provincial residents of the Roman Empire received full citizenship under the

a Of his initial 2,000-cubit boundary.
b Of the rabbinic court.
c And there's no longer a need to go further.
d From where he was stopped.
e If the place he was stopped was within 2,000 cubits of the municipal boundary, he may return home.

> **THE *CONSTITUO ANTONINIANA***
>
> In 212 CE, Roman emperor Caracalla (Marcus Aurelius Antoninus) decreed that all free men of the Roman Empire be granted full citizenship. Scholars disagree about the impetus behind this edict, whether it was economic (more efficient tax collection) or political (to better integrate the provinces). Prior to this, Roman citizenship in the provinces, including that of Judaea and later Syria-Palaestina, was granted only to emigrants from Rome or to those with special privileges, such as local aristocrats or discharged soldiers.

Constituo Antoniniana. Contact between Jewish and Roman law would have increased as Jews now had full rights to be judged by a Roman judge, who also had to take into account local laws.

Although the contribution of Roman law and legal concepts to the Mishnah is undeniable, it must be kept in proper perspective. There is overlap in certain concepts and laws, but as legal systems the two are utterly different. In terms of form, Roman law developed through imperial edicts that turned into precedents, and the writings of jurists from this period were not binding. A compilation of Roman law that is comparable to the Mishnah in its normative authority was edited only long after the tannaitic period, in the fifth and sixth centuries CE. Even then, there is a significant difference in substance. The Mishnah has a much broader scope, encompassing rules related to Temple purity and rituals and other theoretical laws.[49] In fact, most of the Mishnah is dedicated to ritual matters that would not have been recognizable to Romans as law (or at least the type of law discussed by jurists).[50] Some even view the Mishnah as an alternative legal system intended to compete with Roman law.[51] In any case, Roman law can illuminate circumscribed areas of mishnaic law for us, but it cannot clarify much more than that.[52]

E. SCHOLARLY DEBATE

Let us return to the first mishnah in Tractate *Berakhot*. It records a debate regarding the last time the evening Shema may be recited, and the three opinions are the end of the first watch (R. Eliezer), midnight (the Sages), and dawn (Rabban Gamaliel). The sources of these times vary. The division of the night into three shifts is biblical, while the split into two (before and after midnight) is Roman.[53] The third opinion originated from a *ma'aseh*, although Rabban Gamaliel argues that it actually represents the real reasoning of the Sages. None of these opinions, though, appears in their original form; instead, they are presented as a three-way debate in the study hall. The question we must contend with is how realistic this presentation is. Is it merely a literary convention, or does it reflect the reality of the bet midrash? Additionally, what is the relationship between the conventions of the tannaitic academy and the other sources of Halakhah discussed in the preceding sections?

Over a hundred Sages are named in the Mishnah.[54] Many of them make one or two cameos and disappear, but a small cast of Sages dominate the Mishnah's stage throughout the six *sedarim*. This is especially true of Rabbi Akiva's disciples—Rabbi Yehudah, Rabbi Yose, Rabbi Meir, and Rabbi Shimon—whose opinions and disagreements are mentioned everywhere. Sometimes, the student of the Mishnah is privy to a version of the behind-the-scenes dialogue. Tractate *Pesaḥim* has a drawn-out debate about what one may do when the fourteenth of Nisan coincides with Shabbat. The paschal sacrifice is supposed to be offered in the afternoon of the fourteenth and eaten that night, the beginning of the fifteenth. In this instance, the fourteenth happens to be Shabbat, on which all labor is usually forbidden. The Mishnah allows certain types of labor for offering the sacrifices, but prohibits others:

[1] These aspects of the paschal sacrifice override Shabbat: its slaughter, the sprinkling of its blood, the cleansing of its innards, and the burning of its fats.[a] But its roasting and the washing of its innards do not override it. Shouldering it, bringing it from outside the boundary,[b] and cutting off its wart[c] do not override it. Rabbi Eliezer says, They override it.[d]

[2] Rabbi Eliezer said, "If slaughtering which is prohibited as labor[e] overrides Shabbat, shouldn't those prohibited on account of *shevut*[f] override Shabbat?"

Rabbi Yehoshua said to him, "Let Yom Tov prove it,[g] for it permits as labor but prohibits on account of *shevut*."

Rabbi Eliezer said to him, "What is this, Yehoshua? Of what proof is something optional for something commanded?"[h]

Rabbi Akiva responded, "Let sprinkling[i] prove it, for it is a mitzvah and is prohibited on account of *shevut* but does not override Shabbat. Likewise, do not be perplexed about these,[j] for even though they are a mitzvah and are prohibited on account of *shevut*, they do not override Shabbat."

a On the altar.
b Of Shabbat of 2,000 cubits.
c Which, left on, would invalidate it as a sacrifice.
d These acts are only preparatory to the actual sacrifice, so there is a disagreement whether such preparations override Shabbat.
e Which is biblical and therefore more severe. Slaughtering, for example, is one of the thirty-nine biblically forbidden types of labor on Shabbat; see *Shabbat*, 7:2.
f Rabbinically mandated "rest" that should be easier to override. For the origin of *shevut*, see Exodus 16:29: "every man remain (*shevu*) in his place."
g The law concerning the Festivals disproves the a fortiori argument, because certain labors prohibited biblically on Shabbat are completely permitted for making food on Yom Tov, while the *shevut* prohibitions remain in force.
h Food preparation and the offering of the paschal lamb, respectively.
i The waters mixed with the ash of the red heifer on someone who contracted corpse impurity; see Numbers 19.
j The shouldering, bringing from outside the boundary, and removal of the wart.

Rabbi Eliezer said to him, "But it is about this[a] that I reason: If slaughtering, which is prohibited as labor, overrides Shabbat, shouldn't sprinkling, which is prohibited on account of *shevut*, override Shabbat?"

Rabbi Akiva said to him, "The reverse! If sprinkling, which is prohibited on account of *shevut*, does not override Shabbat, then slaughtering, which is prohibited as labor, also should not override Shabbat."

Rabbi Eliezer said to him: "Akiva, you have uprooted what is written in the Torah,[b] 'in the afternoon at its appointed time'[c]—whether on a weekday or on Shabbat."

He said to him, "Cite me an appointed time for these[d] like the appointed time for the slaughtering." (*Pesaḥim*, 6:1–2)

[1] אלו דברים בפסח דוחין את השבת: שחיטתו, וזריקת דמו, ומיחוי קרביו, והקטר חלביו. אבל צלייתו והדחת קרביו אינן דוחים. הרכיבו והבאתו מחוץ לתחום וחתיכת יבלתו אינן דוחים. רבי אליעזר אומר: דוחים.

[2] אמר רבי אליעזר: מה אם שחיטה שהיא משום מלאכה דוחה את השבת, אלו שהן משום שבות לא ידחו את השבת?

אמר לו רבי יהושע: יום טוב יוכיח, שהיתיר בו משום מלאכה ואסר בו משום שבות.

אמר לו רבי אליעזר: מה זה, יהושע, ומה ראיה רשות למצוה?

השיב רבי עקיבה: הזייה תוכיח, שהיא מצוה והיא משום שבות, אינה דוחה את השבת. אף אתה אל תתמה על אלו, שאף על פי שהן מצוה והן משום שבות, לא ידחו את השבת.

אמר לו רבי אליעזר: ועליה אני דן – מה אם שחיטה שהיא משום מלאכה דוחה את השבת, הזיה שהיא משום שבות אינה דוחה את השבת?

אמר לו רבי עקיבה: חילוף! מה אם הזייה שהיא משום שבות אינה דוחה את השבת, אף שחיטה שהיא משום מלאכה לא תדחה את השבת?

אמר לו רבי אליעזר: עקיבה, עקרתה מה שכתוב, "בין הערבים במועדו"—בין בחול בין בשבת.

אמר לו: הבא לי מועד לאלו כמועד לשחיטה.

The structure, more than the particulars about the paschal sacrifice, is of direct relevance here. The first mishnah is quite typical, with a dispute between two Sages about the permissibility of certain activities. The first opinion, which the second mishnah shows to be that of Rabbi Yehoshua and his disciple Rabbi Akiva, is unattributed, because the Mishnah accepts it

a The sprinkling itself.
b By reasoning that the slaughter of the paschal sacrifice is forbidden on Shabbat, the Torah's command to slaughter in the afternoon is negated.
c "On the fourteenth day of this month in the afternoon shall you perform it, at its appointed time" (Num. 9:3).
d The preparatory activities that Rabbi Eliezer contends override Shabbat.

as the law. The second opinion is attributed to Rabbi Eliezer. What follows is an involved disputation. Rabbi Eliezer makes his case first, and Rabbi Yehoshua counters. Rabbi Eliezer points out a logical leap that Rabbi Yehoshua has made, which causes him to fall silent. So Rabbi Akiva, youngest of the disputants, steps in and advances a counterargument. Rabbis Eliezer and Akiva have at it for two rounds, until Rabbi Akiva emerges triumphant in the third.

The number of extended debates like this in the Mishnah can be counted on two hands, but they more than make up for their small quantity in their quality.[55] If only for a brief while, they lead us into the vibrant scene of the tannaitic bet midrash, where Sages pitted their breadth of knowledge and logical analysis against one another in spirited battles of wits. Those Sages whose intellects and controversies were responsible for the development of mishnaic Halakhah are generally reduced to names and barebone opinions in the Mishnah. We must look instead to the Tosefta, Midrash, and *baraitot* of the two Talmuds, which more faithfully preserve the original argumentation.[56]

Now, this appraisal of the above mishnah makes a major assumption, that the dissent in the Mishnah is a literary record of real-life disputes between flesh-and-blood scholars, that when Sages who did not live near one another are presented as disagreeing, their disputes are not the product of editorial magic, because they had ample opportunities to spar in person. They could have bumped into one another in the market: "Rabbi Akiva said, I asked Rabban Gamaliel and Rabbi Yehoshua in the fair of Emmaus when they went to buy an animal for his son's wedding feast" (*Keritot*, 3:7). They could have met when rabbis from far and wide converged for a rabbinic conference: "Rabbi Shimon ben Azzai said, I received an oral tradition from seventy-two elders on the day that they installed Rabbi Elazar ben Azariah at the council" (*Yadayim*, 3:5 and 4:2). Sages also moved around, studying in and teaching at various villages across Judea and the Galilee.[57]

Does this mean that the Mishnah is a stenographic record? Of course not. Elements of the aforecited mishnah from Tractate *Pesaḥim* indicate the use of rhetorical conceits. The argumentation proceeds in three stages, which accords precisely with the halakhic etiquette of disputation.[58] Rabbi Akiva has the last word, which cannot be a coincidence, given what we know about his centrality in the Mishnah's formation. He will always have the advantage over Rabbi Eliezer, whose opinions are almost never accepted by the Mishnah. Nevertheless, the contention here is that disputes have not been invented out of whole cloth but are probably moderately stylized.

My argument is that these minutes are merely where the lively engagement of the bet midrash manages to make it into the text, but it is everywhere present behind it. The many sources of law discussed in this chapter were debated in the bet midrash and recast in the Mishnah's characteristic discourse. This chapter has identified the major legal sources that emerge from the Mishnah itself: the Torah, tradition, *ma'asim*, and Roman law. These raw inputs entered the rabbinic academy, where they were debated, interpreted, and reconfigured, emerging in the form of characteristic mishnaic discourse. Given the vast amount of source material and the way the Mishnah dedicates space to debate, the resulting product is enormous. One can get a sense of the scope and ambition of the rabbinic project by comparing the Mishnah's treatment of the laws of Shabbat, which runs to twenty-four chapters in Tractate *Shabbat* and another ten in Tractate *'Eruvin,* with the earlier and much briefer halakhic treatments in the book of Jubilees and the Damascus Document.[59]

Despite the meager number of detailed debates in the Mishnah, we now know that they are but the tip of the proverbial iceberg. Looking only at the staid and concise codificatory language, one would not know that at one time the concise opinions were preceded by intense debate, sharp ripostes, and clever critiques, some of which can still be found in parallel sources. Controversy was the hallmark of the bet midrash. By contrast, earlier halakhic compositions from Qumran brook no dissent; the law is what it is. For the Sages, scholarly debate was not only another source of mishnaic law, but a mold that reshaped all of the other source materials.

FOUR

The Editing of the Mishnah

If you flip open a printed Mishnah to any page, you will almost certainly encounter a debate. The ubiquity of dissent, which differentiates the Mishnah from earlier halakhic compositions, is a textual manifestation of the contentious, continuous debates of the tannaitic bet midrash (study hall). But as I pointed out at the end of the previous chapter, many of the longer debates were pared down in the Mishnah and are only extant in their fuller form in the Tosefta and in the *baraitot* cited in the two Talmuds. These other tannaitic corpora also preserve scores of shorter debates that did not make it into the Mishnah. So, on that same random page of the Mishnah, you will see what has taken the place of many of these argumentative voices: a lone, anonymous, uncontested voice of authority. This voice is referred to in the Talmud as *stam*, the "unattributed" or "unmarked" opinion, the voice of the Mishnah itself. Who endowed the Mishnah with a voice of its own? To answer this question, we now turn from the sources of the Mishnah to its editing.

It is evident from the Mishnah itself that some amount of editing occurred before the final editing. Unfortunately, the extent of this early editing is impossible to estimate. This proto-editing will be noted where relevant, but the bulk of this chapter concerns the labors of the Mishnah's final and chief editor: Rabbi Yehudah ha-Nasi.

Evaluating the work of an editor should naturally begin with the stated goals and methods, but in the case of the Mishnah the editor left us nothing. Rather than proceed from principles to execution, we must begin with the finished product and extrapolate from there what his aims and goals might have been. As we will see, there is no consensus on what the Mishnah is or was intended to be, but certain proposals can be definitively ruled out.

A. RABBI YEHUDAH HA-NASI'S EDITING

Let us begin with a basic question: How do we know that Rabbi Yehuah ha-Nasi was in fact involved in editing the Mishnah?

The first generation of Amoraim, some of whom were his direct disciples, already attributed the final stage of editing to him. In several contexts, the Talmud reports, in the name of various early Amoraim, "here Rabbi recited X." His identification as the Mishnah's ultimate editor, therefore, rests on a solid foundation.[1] But—and take note that this is a very big but— we must bear in mind constantly that we know nothing about Rabbi Yehudah ha-Nasi's actual intentions. Any editorial policies and goals attributed to him below are inductively extracted from the text as we have it. Furthermore, Rabbi was certainly not the Mishnah's first or only editor, and one cannot always tell which editorial moves can be confidently ascribed to him. Therefore, as convenient as it is to associate a complex process with a known figure, the reader should bear in mind that the majority of the editorial processes attributed to Rabbi throughout the chapter are being reverse-engineered from the Mishnah's final form.

With that caveat in mind, let us now define our terms. What does it mean that the Mishnah was edited? For the modern reader, editing conjures the image of someone feverishly scribbling, drawing arrows, and crossing out words with a red pen to smooth out a text's rough edges and irregularities, thereby ensuring cogency and consistency from beginning to end. Such editing was in fact done to legal codes in late Antiquity. Most relevant here is the *Corpus Juris Civilis*, the monumental codification of Roman law undertaken in sixth-century Byzantium. The Emperor Justinian I instructed an editorial commission to compile and edit all the imperial edicts and other laws that had accumulated over the centuries. The editors were given broad license and produced a text that is stylistically uniform, free of redundancies and contradictions, and unencumbered by obsolete law. The preface states expressly that they "removed every inconsistency from the sacred constitutions, hitherto inharmonious and confused."[2]

Rabbi Yehudah ha-Nasi was working with centuries' worth of legal material, too. Thanks to Rabbi Akiva's school, many of those myriad laws had already been consolidated into small collections, and some even had a set phraseology. He adopted the "Mishnah of Rabbi Akiva" as the basis for his own,[3] but he tended to be eclectic and inclusive.[4] This inclusiveness was likely one of the secrets to the Mishnah's enduring success.[5] Rabbi Yehudah ha-Nasi did not arrogate himself the carte blanche editorial powers that Justinian granted his editors.[6] His own proclivity to include a plurality of opinions lent the Mishnah an unevenness in style and substance that he was unwilling to iron out. Consequently, the very things Justinian's men eliminated abound in the Mishnah, where obsolete or rejected laws mingle with those still in force.

Rabbi Yehudah ha-Nasi's fundamentally conservational attitude toward his source material is captured by an observation made several times by the Babylonian Talmud: "a mishnah does not budge" (e.g., *Yevamot* 30a; *Kiddushin* 25a; *'Avodah Zarah* 35b). That is, even when a law was rejected or made obsolete by later Tannaim, it was left intact in the edited Mishnah.

The Mishnah also contains redundancies. Sometimes these are laws with the same exact wording; at other times they exhibit minimal variation.[7] The Mishnah's treatment of the pro-

> ### RABBI YEHUDAH HA-NASI
>
> The editor of the Mishnah and leader of the Sages from the end of the second century through the beginning of the third century CE. Many of the biographical details given below stem from later rabbinic traditions, the reliability of which remains highly contested. For the sources, see Oppenheimer, *Rabbi Judah ha-Nasi*. For a skeptical approach to the traditional sources see Stern, "Rabbi."
>
> Rabbi Yehudah ha-Nasi was descended from a dynastic line of leaders; according to the Babylonian Talmud he was the son of Rabban Shimon ben Gamaliel and the grandson of Rabban Gamaliel, the leader of the Sages in Yavneh after the Temple's destruction. There is no evidence of any dignified lineage in tannaitic sources, however.
>
> He was the first to hold the formal leadership position of nasi on account of good relations with the Roman overlords. Various rabbinic sources say that he was close to the Roman Emperor "Antoninus," but it is not clear who they intend, as several emperors bore that name during this period.
>
> He was rich and powerful. He enacted religious decrees, and, according to his contemporary Origen, who lived in Caesarea, he possessed the authority to try capital cases.
>
> Evidence of his revered status among his Jewish brethren can be seen in the simple tannaitic honorific "Rabbi," as if he needed no further introduction. His influence and image likely helped his Mishnah beat out all others for dominance.
>
> He was active in Tzippori (Sepphoris) and died (according to a chronology supplied in the Geonic period) in 220. He is said to be buried in Bet She'arim, and there is circumstantial evidence that he was actually interred there. The position of nasi was passed on to his descendants.
>
> On the position of the nasi, see Goodblatt, *Monarchic Principle*. Yitz Landes ("Rise of the Jewish Patriarchate") has recently suggested that the editing of the Mishnah should be seen as part of the solidification of the institution of the nasi. Indeed, there are indications that R. Yehuda ha-Nasi and his bet midrash were involved in adapting tannaitic Midrashim too; see Kahana, "Foreign Bodies." On the involvement of his son R. Shimon and his grandson R. Yehudah in editing the Mishnah, see Rosenthal, "Mishna Aboda Zara," vol. 1, and below, chapter 7, section C.

hibition against eating the new cereal crop illustrates this. According to the Torah, one may not eat the new crop until the *'omer* grain offering is waved in the Temple on the sixteenth of Nisan (Lev. 23:9–16). With the destruction of the Second Temple, the offering could no longer be brought. Rabban Yohanan ben Zakkai therefore decreed that the prohibition against eating the new grain would now last throughout the entire sixteenth day of Nisan until nightfall. The mishnaic formulation is "the day of waving is prohibited in its entirety." This law appears in no fewer than three places in the Mishnah: once among the laws of the *'omer* offering where it is expected, and twice more in connection with the enactments Rabban Yohanan ben Zakkai made after the Temple's destruction.[8]

Rabbi Yehudah ha-Nasi's editing also did not resolve glaring contradictions, even factual ones. In two places the Mishnah says that the Temple has seven gates, and in two others it gives the number as thirteen. In this case the two contradictory numbers coexist within the same tractate, *Middot*.[9]

Even mishnayot in close proximity can be incongruous. The fifth chapter of Tractate *Ma'aser Sheni* covers the laws of fruit produced by trees in their fourth year. During the first three years, the fruit is forbidden for consumption; in the fourth year, the fruit is holy and must be eaten in Jerusalem in a state of ritual purity. The first three mishnayot of this chapter refer to this law as *kerem reva'i*, "the fourth-year vineyard," but the next two mishnayot call it *neta' reva'i*, "the fourth-year planting." The Palestinian Talmud reports an exchange about this shift:

> A pair of Sages asked Rabbi, "What should we recite, *kerem reva'i* or *neta' reva'i*?"
>
> He said to them, "Go ask Rabbi Yitzhak Rova, for whom I have vetted the entire Mishnah." They went and asked him.
>
> He said to them, "The first are *kerem reva'i*, and the second are *neta' reva'i*." (Palestinian Talmud *Ma'aser Sheni*, 5:5 [55d])[10]

The Talmud reveals that the change is intentional: it preserves the language of the two original sources. The first three mishnayot come from one collection, the next two belong to another. While the incongruity does not seem as severe as, say, the number of the Temple's gates, this is no mere matter of style either. *Kerem reva'i* and *neta' reva'i* are not interchangeable terms. The former restricts the holiness and its attendant rules to a vineyard alone, while the latter extends it to all fruit trees.[11] The editing evidently did not impose consistency on the sources, even when it resulted in halakhic incompatibilities.

If the texture of the Mishnah remains so coarse, one might well wonder what Rabbi Yehudah ha-Nasi's editorial achievement was. To appreciate his editorship, one must remember that unlike the written sources of Roman law, the Oral Torah existed only in the mind and on the lips. Rabbi's workstation was not littered with styluses and wax tablets. His primary editorial contribution was less copy editing and more structural editing, that is, determining how to best organize the immense source material into a coherent whole. Holding all the material in his mind, he devised an optimal arrangement of the smaller legal collections, forming coherent thematic and conceptual units, all while respecting the integrity of his predecessors' halakhic traditions. Sherira Gaon indeed claimed that the "elegant organization of the Mishnah" is what led directly to its widespread acceptance.[12]

The Mishnah resembles a massive mosaic, in which the joins between constituent parts are visible (lucky for the textual historian, who seeks to reconstruct the editorial activities). One can see, for example, that to protect the integrity of a preexisting collection, it was inserted wholesale into a tractate or chapter, even when only one of its laws was germane. Tractate *Kiddushin* is about marriage, yet it opens with a full listing of the halakhic means of acquiring property, land, slaves, and the like. Why is this list there? Because its first item is the halakhic acquisition of a wife. Rabbi Yehudah ha-Nasi could have chopped up this collection and moved each part to its relevant context, but he preserved the collection as it was transmitted to him. This does not necessarily mean that the textual unit at the beginning of Tractate *Kiddushin* was thoughtless. Rabbi Yehudah ha-Nasi could have chosen to reproduce the list elsewhere, in the context of the acquisition of movable property or land, or place it in other contexts in the same tractate. Here as elsewhere, scholars have shown that careful planning went into the combination and organization of the various sources.[13]

In an oral culture, association can be a powerful tool to aid the memory, and it was a crucial organizing principle of the orally learned Mishnah.[14] Tractate *Sotah* exemplifies the use of association—weak as it may be—to string together collections of tannaitic material. Chapter 5 contains a collection of Rabbi Akiva's exegeses, even though only the first one is relevant to the topic of discussion.[15] Chapters 7 through 9 are a sustained treatment of verbal rituals that can only be said "in the Holy Tongue" (Hebrew), as opposed to others that can be spoken "in their language" (the vernacular).[16] What has this to do with the laws of the *sotah*, the wife accused of adultery? The first item on the list happens to be the "passage of the *sotah*" recited during her ritual at the Temple. The Mishnah doesn't expand on this ritual at all, though, because it is one of those that may be recited "in their language," and the Mishnah expands only on those rituals recited "in the holy Tongue"! At the end of the tractate, there is another collection of teachings about the decline of generations. The justification for its placement is again a mere reference to the *sotah*'s trial by water: "when adulterers proliferated the bitter waters ceased." Although the connection is tenuous, the decision to end Tractate *Sotah* with this body of teachings seems to have been a thoughtful one.[17] Rabbi Yehudah ha-Nasi was clearly working with independent textual units of fixed language, and he had to decide, based on multiple considerations, where they best fit in the Mishnah.

He was conservative and cautious in his treatment of his sources, but there is evidence that he did not altogether refrain from altering them. It was precisely in the service of structural editing that he also engaged in fine-grained adjustment of texts. In this he was following in the footsteps of earlier, anonymous editors from various study houses, who emended the collections they inherited.[18] Observe, for example, the manner in which mishnayot from Tractate *Tamid*, some of the oldest in the Mishnah, were transposed to other tractates:[19]

> In three places the priests would keep watch in the Temple: in the Chamber of Avtinas, the Chamber of the Spark, and the Chamber of the Hearth. The Chamber of Avtinas [and the Chamber of the Spark] had upper stories, where the young men would keep watch. The Chamber of the Hearth was domed and a large room; it was surrounded by rows of stones. The elders of the patrilineal family[a] would sleep there with the keys to the courtyard in their hands. Each of the adolescent priests had their clothes on the ground. They would not sleep in their sacred vestments but remove, fold, and place them under their heads, and cover themselves with their own clothes.
>
> If one of them had a seminal emission, he would go out and make his way through the tunnel that goes under the *Birah*.[b] Lamps would be burning on both sides until he reached the Chamber of Immersion, where there was a fire and a bathroom of dignity.

a The clan of Kohanim serving that day.
b The Temple edifice.

This was its dignity: if one found it locked, he would know that someone was there; if open, he would know that no one was there. He would go down and immerse, and then come up, dry off, and warm himself by the fire. He would come and sit near his fellow priests until the gates were opened. He would leave and go on his way. (*Tamid*, 1:1)

בשלשה מקומות הכהנים שומרים בבית המקדש: בבית אבטינס, ובבית הניצוץ, ובית המוקד. בית אבטינס [ובית הניצוץ] היו עליות והרובים שומרים שם. בית המוקד כיפה ובית גדול; היה מוקף רובדין שלאבן, וזקני בית אב ישינים שם ומפתחות עזרה בידן. ופירחי כהונה איש כסתו בארץ. לא היו ישינים בבגדי קודש אלא פושטין, ומקפלין, ומניחין אותן תחת ראשיהן ומתכסין כסות עצמן.

אירע קרי באחד מהן יוצא והולך לו במסיבה ההולכת תחת הבירה, והנירות דולקין מיכן ומכן עד שהוא מגיע לבית הטבילה, ומדורה היתה שם ובית כסא שלכבוד. וזה הוא כבודו: מצאו נעול—יודע שיש שם אדם; פתוח—יודע שאין שם אדם. ירד וטבל, עלה ונסתפג ונתחמם כנגד המדורה. בא ויישב לו אצל אחיו הכהנים עד שהשערים נפתחים. יוצא והולך לו.

This mishnah was incorporated into the first chapter of Tractate *Middot*, but with adjustments. The first sentence about the guard posts was placed at the beginning of the chapter (1:1), while the sleeping arrangements and the procedure for a seminal emission were left for the final ones (1:8–9). In between, a discussion of the locations where the Levites kept watch and details of the Temple structure were added.[20] This is logical. Tractate *Tamid* is about the daily sacrifice offered at first light, so the activities taking place at night are a kind of preamble. Tractate *Middot*, on the other hand, is about the Temple structure itself, so the material from *Tamid* has been stretched across the chapter to better integrate it into its new context.[21] Note that in spite of the breakup of the original collection, the pieces are all contained within a single chapter. Even when applying pressure, the editor's touch is light.

While in some cases material was extended from one tractate to another, in others the opposite occurred: material was removed because fuller treatments already existed elsewhere. A closer look at the coverage of the verbal rituals in Tractate *Sotah* mentioned above is revealing in this regard:

But these[a] must be said in the Holy Tongue: the *bikkurim* recitation[b] and *ḥalitzah*;[c] blessings and curses;[d] the priestly blessing[e] and the blessings of the High Priest;[f]

---

a As opposed to the ones listed above that may be said "in their language."

b The declaration of the farmer when he brings his first fruits; see Deuteronomy 26:1–11 and *Bikkurim*, 3:6.

c The ceremony by which a woman is released from a potential levirate marriage, in which she recites a few words; see Deuteronomy 25:5–10 and *Yevamot*, 12:6.

d Which the Kohanim pronounced on Mount Gerizim and Mount Ebal when the nation entered the Land; see Deuteronomy 27 and *Sotah*, 7:5.

e That the Kohanim regularly bestow on the people; see Numbers 6:22–27 and *Sotah*, 7:6.

f Given to the people on Yom Kippur; see *Sotah*, 7:7.

the pericope of the king;[a] the pericope of the *'eglah 'arufah*;[b] and the one anointed for war[c] when he speaks to the people. (*Sotah*, 7:2)

ואלו נאמרים בלשון הקודש: מקרא הביכורים וחליצה, ברכות וקללות, ברכת כהנים וברכות כהן גדול, ופרשת המלך, ופרשת עגלה ערופה, ומשוח המלחמה בשעה שהוא מדבר אל העם.

After this list, the Mishnah elaborates at length (7:3–9:8) on each of these ceremonies and their conditions—except for the first two. The Mishnah is satisfied with establishing the biblical source for their recitation in Hebrew and adds nothing about how the rituals themselves are to be performed. Why? Because Tractate *Bikkurim* and Tractate *Yevamot* devote entire chapters to the bringing of *bikkurim* and the performance of *ḥalitzah*. In this way, the Mishnah can rely on its extensive treatments in the relevant tractates.[22]

Beside the addition and removal of duplicate material, there is the inclusion and exclusion of opinions. In this respect, the Mishnah is Rabbi Yehudah ha-Nasi's Mishnah. While he tended toward inclusivity, he simultaneously served as gatekeeper. Not every halakhic opinion voiced by a Tanna made the cut. Although it is impossible to draw up a list of opinions that Rabbi Yehudah ha-Nasi definitely knew and consciously left out, in certain cases it is reasonable to assume he was familiar with those preserved in the Tosefta, Midrash, and *baraitot*. Consider the following tosefta:

> [25] If this one poured out his wine to save someone else's honey,[d] he pays his wage[e]—the amount for [his effort] saving the lost item. But if he said to him, "On condition that I take the value of mine from yours," he must give it to him.
>
> [26] [. . .] Rabbi Yohanan ben Barokah says, It is a provision of the court[f] that this one can pour out his wine to save someone else's honey and take the value of his wine from that person's honey. . . .
>
> [27] [. . .] If a person's swarm entered someone else's garden, and the owner of the garden does not permit him entry so that he not crush his herbs, he may enter

---

a The part of the *Torah* read by the king during the Hakhel assembly every seven years; see Deuteronomy 31:10–13 and Sotah, 7:8.

b The *'eglah 'arufah* is the heifer whose neck is broken when a murder victim is found outside a city and the murderer is unknown. Part of the ceremony involves the elders of the closest city and the Kohanim reciting a ritualized formula; see Deuteronomy 21:1–9 and *Sotah*, ch. 9.

c The priest anointed to lead the war gives a rousing speech to the people, instructing certain would-be soldiers to turn back; see Deuteronomy 20:1–9 and *Sotah*, ch. 8.

d He emptied his barrel of wine so that the person whose barrel broke could transfer his honey to it, as honey is worth more than wine.

e The owner of the honey pays the wine owner for his labor but not for the value of the lost wine. On this interpretation see Lieberman, *Tosefta ki-Feshutah*, vol. 9–10, p. 127; Goldberg, *Tosefta Bava Kamma*, 206.

f It applies even if no explicit stipulation was made between the two parties.

against his will to save his swarm. And if he did damage, he pays for whatever he damaged.

Rabbi Yishmael son of Rabbi Yohanan ben Barokah says, It is a provision of the court that this one may cut down the limb[a] to save his swarm *(neḥilo)* and he takes the value,[b] for it was on this condition[c] that Joshua gave *(hinḥil)* the Land to Israel as an inheritance. (Tosefta, *Bava Kamma*, 10:25–27)

[25] שפך זה יינו והציל את דבשו של חבירו, נותן לו שכרו, דמי השב אבידה. ואם אמר לו: על מנת שאטול דמי שלי מתוך שלך, חייב ליתן לו.

[26] [. . .] רבי יוחנן בן ברוקה אומר: תניי בית דין הוא שיהא זה שופך את יינו ומציל דבשו של חבירו, ונוטל דמי יינו מתוך דבשו של חבירו . . .

[27] [. . .] הרי שירד נחילו לתוך גינתו של חבירו, ואין בעל הגינה מניחו להכנס, שלא לשבר את ירקו, הרי זה יורד על כרחו ומציל נחילו, ואם הזיק משלם מה שהזיק.

רבי ישמעאל ברבי יוחנן אומר: תניי בית דין הוא שיהא זה קוצץ את הסוכה ומציל נחילו ונוטל דמים, שעל מנת כן הנחיל יהושע לישראל את הארץ.

The Mishnah first presents the Tosefta's bee case with the opinion of Rabbi Yishmael the son of Rabbi Yohanan ben Barokah, and then the honey salvage without the dissenting opinion of Rabbi Yohanan ben Barokah himself (*Bava Kamma*, 10:2, 4). Now, Rabbi Yohanan ben Barokah and his son each give a nearly identical ruling—"it is a provision of the court"—for related cases involving the damaging of property to save other property. Are we to honestly believe that Rabbi Yehudah ha-Nasi only knew of the son's opinion and not the father's, even though they appear in succession in the Tosefta? More reasonable is that he deliberately left it out. Perhaps he felt it to be redundant once the son's position was included in the earlier mishnah (10:2). Or maybe he thought that the court provision makes less sense when a person damages their own property. One can only speculate.

As editor, Rabbi was also the final arbiter of halakhic opinion. In the same way that he imposed order on the multitude of halakhic collections, he cut through the dissent that epitomizes rabbinic learning in order to establish the law. Two literary devices, present in nearly every mishnah, communicate his halakhic decision.

The first is the voice of the Mishnah itself. More often than not, a mishnah begins with an unattributed opinion stated in a normative tone, which the Babylonian Talmud descriptively calls the *tanna kamma*, the first Tanna. Those who dissent are then named. Rabbi

---

a Not only may one do inadvertent damage to save the swarm, but one may intentionally lop off the tree limb on which the hive is located.

b The owner of the garden receives restitution for the damage. Note the pun *nehil-hinhil*.

c A legal-historical fiction, according to which the tribes agreed to a kind of social contract that allows for the abrogation of ownership rights in situations such as this.

Yehudah ha-Nasi created the illusion of the Mishnah voicing its own opinion, when really it is the opinion of a Tanna with whom he agreed, stripped of its attribution.

The omission of names is particularly striking when one mishnah presents an issue as the subject of dispute between named Tannaim, and another mishnah, sometimes nearby, states the law as if it were undisputed. For example, Bet Hillel and Bet Shammai disagree about what happens to extra money that was collected for the half-shekel tax to the Temple:

> If someone collects coins and says, "These are for my shekel"[a]—
>
> Bet Shammai say, The remainder[b] is a donation.[c] But Bet Hillel say, The remainder is unconsecrated. (*Shekalim*, 2:3)

> המכנס מעות ואמר הרי אלו שיקלי—
>
> בית שמי אומרים: מתרן נדבה, ובית הילל אומרים: מתרן חולים.

Only two mishnayot later the Mishnah states without qualification: "The remainder of shekels is unconsecrated" (*Shekalim*, 2:5). The Mishnah has characteristically adopted Bet Hillel's opinion, so it presents it as if it were the only one. By anonymizing it, Rabbi Yehuda ha-Nasi has transformed the halakhic opinion of an individual authority into *the* position of the Mishnah.[23]

The Mishnah contains many examples of this phenomenon, which have been collected and analyzed by scholars.[24] The two Talmuds already noted that Rabbi Yehudah ha-Nasi universalized those opinions he agreed with by anonymizing them.[25] Parallel sources in other collections attribute the same material to specific Sages, demonstrating that they were removed from the Mishnah.[26]

In order to better understand the power of the Mishnah's anonymous voice, it would be helpful to compare it to the method adopted by Moses Maimonides in his monumental halakhic code. Maimonides explicitly took the Mishnah as his precedent, and adopted its anonymizing approach to the law, without citing dissenting opinions, for his own. He writes to Rabbi Phineas ha-Dayyan:

> I have only followed the style of Rabbi Yehudah [ha-Nasi] here. He, too, did this before me, for every halakhah which he recorded without qualification and anonymously was originated by other scholars. . . . Indeed, it is mentioned explicitly in several places that Rabbi Yehudah adjudicated the law according to the opinion of a certain rabbi which he favored and nevertheless recorded his opinion anonymously. . . .[27]

---

a i.e., half-shekel.
b Whatever was collected that is more than one person's half-shekel.
c To the upkeep of the Temple, because the money has been consecrated.

But Maimonides attached his name to the work, so that the uncontested voice belongs to him. Those who disagree with the halakhot contained therein disagree with Maimonides the jurist. Rabbi Yehudah ha-Nasi, on the other hand, does not identify himself with the voice of the Mishnah. The lack of attachment to any single individual empowers this voice even more. The Mishnah itself commands ultimate authority, and when it speaks, its talmudic students listen.

A second device used by the Mishnah to highlight an opinion as normative is attribution to an unspecified group of "Sages" (ḥakhamim), giving the impression of a large consensus group whose opinion ought to be accepted. That this is a rhetorical device is made plain through a comparison between two mishnayot in Tractate Ḥullin.

> If someone slaughters and it is found a *terefah*,[a] slaughters for idolatry, or slaughters a heifer of purification,[b] an ox liable for stoning,[c] or an *'eglah 'arufah*—Rabbi Shimon exempts them and the Sages find them liable. (Ḥullin, 5:3)[28]

השוחט ונמצא טריפה, השוחט לעבודה זרה, השוחט פרת החטאת, ושור הנסקל, ועגלה ערופה—רבי שמעון פוטר וחכמים מחייבין.

The fifth chapter of this tractate relates to the biblical law not to slaughter an animal and its offspring on the same day (Lev. 22:28). At the heart of the mishnah above is a question: Does the prohibition apply when the slaughter is halakhically ineffective, and so does not render the meat kosher for consumption? Rabbi Shimon considers it as if no slaughter has taken place, so one could go ahead and slaughter the other animal without violating the prohibition. The Sages disagree.

Yet, in the next chapter of Tractate Ḥullin, which is about covering the blood of certain slaughtered animals, we find a reversal in the position of "the Sages":

> If someone slaughters and it is found a *terefah*, slaughters for idolatry, slaughters unconsecrated animals[d] inside or consecrated ones[e] outside,[f] or an undomesticated animal or bird to be stoned—*Rabbi Meir* finds them liable and the Sages exempt them. (Ḥullin, 6:2)

השוחט ונמצא טריפה, השוחט לעבודה זרה, השוחט חולין בפנים וקדשין בחוץ, חייה ועוף הניסקלין—רבי מאיר מחייב, וחכמים פוטרין.

  a The animal would have died anyway on account of some injury or health condition.
  b The red heifer whose ashes can remove corpse impurity; see Numbers 19.
  c On account of killing a human being; see Exodus 21:28.
  d A violation of Torah law according to the Midrash; see BT *Kiddushin* 57b.
  e A violation of Torah law; see Leviticus 17:3–9.
  f Of the Temple courtyard.

Like the earlier mishnah, this one also wants to determine whether a slaughter has taken place, requiring the blood to be covered, if the meat may not be eaten. But while there "the Sages" answer in the affirmative, here "the Sages" rule in the negative. How is such inconsistency possible? The Babylonian Talmud cites Rabbi Yohanan's explanation:

Rabbi Ḥiyya bar Abba said in the name of Rabbi Yohanan:

Rabbi agreed with Rabbi Meir's opinion about the animal and its offspring and recited it as "the Sages"; [he agreed] with Rabbi Shimon's opinion about covering the blood and recited it as "the Sages." (BT *Ḥullin* 85a)

אמר ר' חייא בר אבא אמר ר' יוחנן:

ראה רבי דבריו של ר' מאיר ב"אותו ואת בנו" ושנאן בלשון חכמים.

דבריו של ר' שמעון בכיסוי הדם ושנאן בלשון חכמים.

According to Rabbi Yohanan, one of the earliest Amoraim in the Galilee who was familiar with Rabbi Yehudah ha-Nasi's editorial methodology, this contradiction is illusory.[29] In both mishnayot, it is only Rabbi Meir versus Rabbi Shimon. In neither are "the Sages" so called on account of their number. Rabbi Yehudah ha-Nasi ruled like Rabbi Meir in one area of Halakhah and like Rabbi Shimon in another, and he signaled the normative opinion by attributing it to "the Sages." This editorial policy is at the root of the apparent contradiction.

One may encounter both of these editorial techniques within a single mishnah. In fact, the very first mishnah of the entire corpus has them:

From when may one recite the Shema in the evening? <u>From the time</u> when the Kohanim enter to eat their *terumah* until the end of the first watch—the words of Rabbi Eliezer.

<u>But the Sages say,</u> Until midnight.

Rabban Gamaliel says, Until dawn.

It once happened that his sons came from the wedding hall. They said to him, "We haven't recited the Shema." He said to them, "If it is not yet dawn, you may recite it." (*Berakhot*, 1:1)

מאימתי קורין את שמע בערבים? משעה שהכהנים נכנסים לאכל בתרומתן.

עד סוף האשמורת הראשונה—דברי רבי אליעזר.

וחכמים אומרים: עד חצות.

רבן גמליאל אומר: עד שיעלה עמוד השחר.

The Editing of the Mishnah

מעשה שבאו בניו מבית המשתה. אמרו לו: לא קרינו את שמע. אמר להם: אם לא עלה עמוד השחר, מותרין אתם ליקרות.

The specifics of this mishnah were already addressed in the discussion of the *ma'aseh* as a source of mishnaic law.[30] In the present context, let's consider its editing. On the question of the last possible time to recite the Shema, there is a three-way dispute between Rabbi Eliezer, the Sages, and Rabban Gamaliel. The attribution to "the Sages" is presumably the second rhetorical technique in action, signaling that Rabbi Yehudah ha-Nasi deems this position normative. But what is the earliest opportunity for reciting the Shema? The Mishnah states unequivocally that it is when the priests go home and eat *terumah*. Without other sources, one could conclude that there is no disagreement on the matter. A glance at parallels in the Tosefta and the two Talmuds, however, reveals additional opinions on the earliest time for the Shema. Rabbi Yehudah ha-Nasi privileged one opinion above all others and anonymized it, so that it is elevated to the voice of the Mishnah itself.

The labeling of the middle opinion as "the Sages" is the more obvious editorial intervention. One can sense the hand of the editor pointing to the correct opinion, like an invisible manicule. The anonymization at the very beginning of the mishnah and the obliteration of any trace of dissent is unnoticeable without knowledge of the parallel sources.[31]

In some cases, these two editorial techniques are applied to the selfsame law:

A day-laborer may eat[a] cucumbers even to a *dinar*[b] and dates even to a *dinar*.

Rabbi Elazar Hasama says, A day-laborer may not eat[c] more than his wages, but the Sages permit it.

However, a person should be taught not to be a glutton, closing the door in his face. (*Bava Metzi'a*, 7:5)

אוכל פועל קישות אפילו בדינר וכותבת אפילו בדינר.

רבי אלעזר חסמא אומר: לא יאכל פועל יתר על שכרו, וחכמים מתירין.

אבל מלמדים את האדם שלא יהא רועבתן ויהא סותם את הפתח לפניו.[d]

The anonymous ruling of the first line, "A day-laborer may eat," seems substantively identical to the contrastive opinion of the third line, "but the Sages permit it." Rabbi Yehudah ha-

---

a If he is performing agricultural work, he may eat the produce while working; see Deuteronomy 23:25–26.

b Even up to the value of a *denarius*, a Roman silver coin, regardless of how much the worker is being paid for the work.

c Rabbi Elazar Hasama, in contrast, tethers the food allowance to the wages, capping it at whatever the payment is.

d His being a glutton causes potential employers to avoid hiring him.

Nasi employed two complementary strategies here for underscoring that this is the law, and this is not the only instance of this. Regarding eleven additional mishnayot the Babylonian Talmud, that incisive parser of texts, wonders aloud: "Are the Sages identical to the *tanna kamma*?" The Talmud then searches out some halakhic difference that will establish the two as distinct opinions.[32] While the Talmud is always on the lookout for legal meaning in the smallest of details, it seems more reasonable to answer the Talmud's question affirmatively: Yes, "the Sages" are identical to the anonymous opinion, because both are literary creations of Rabbi Yehuda ha-Nasi intended to bolster his halakhic determination.

Of the two methods, the anonymized opinion is much more common. Being orally transmitted, the Oral Law was by definition embodied, channeled by a specific speaker. When a law's ties to any particular tradent or scholar are cut, it takes on the quality of disembodied, ideal, incontestable law. When done consistently, an authorial voice seems to emerge from the Mishnah itself, which states the law with ultimate authority. When the Talmuds, therefore, declare that "the law is according to the *stam*," the unattributed voice, they are in fact basing it on Rabbi Yehudah ha-Nasi's own editorial policy.

Broadly speaking, we have seen that the editing respected the transmitted texts with just limited intervention. One type of such intervention is the addition of editorial notes. For example, the Mishnah says about the bitter waters administered to the *sotah*:

> He[a] would bring a new earthenware *fiyali*[b] and pour into it half a *log*[c] of water from the laver. Rabbi Yehudah says, A quarter.
>
> The same way he[d] minimizes the writing[e] he also minimizes the water. (*Sotah*, 2:2)

היה מביא פיילי שלחרס חדשה ונותן לתוכה חצי לוג מים מן הכיור. רבי יהודה אומר: רביעית.

כשם שהוא ממעט בכתב כך הוא ממעט במים.

Rabbi Yehudah's disagreement here is about how much water should be used in the ritual: the *tanna kamma* says half a *log*, and Rabbi Yehudah says a fourth of a *log*. It is the Mishnah itself that adds the next comment, which draws attention to a pattern of minimalism in Rabbi Yehudah's rulings about the *sotah* ritual. Editorial comments like this are scattered across the Mishnah: "there is no difference between the words of Rabbi X and Rabbi Y except...," or "the words of these are close to the words of those."[33]

This general editorial decision to preserve source material could sometimes cause conceptual confusion. As legal thinking developed over the tannaitic period, new paradigms

---

a   The priest overseeing the ritual.
b   From Greek φιάλη (*fiale*), a broad and flat bowl.
c   A biblical liquid measure (appx. half a liter).
d   Rabbi Yehudah.
e   On the *sotah* scroll during the ritual; see *Sotah*, 2:3.

had to be layered over the old ones instead of replacing them. We have already met one mishnah in which this occurs:

> If someone deposits with his fellow an animal or object for safekeeping, and it is stolen or lost:
>
> If he paid and did not want to swear—*since they said that an unpaid bailee may swear and be released*—then if the thief is found, he pays double; if he slaughtered or sold it, he pays fourfold or fivefold. Whom does he pay? The one who has the deposit.
>
> If he swore and did not want to pay, then if the thief is found, he pays double; if he slaughtered or sold it, he pays fourfold or fivefold. Whom does he pay? The owner of the deposit. (*Bava Metzi'a*, 3:1)[34]

> המפקיד אצל חבירו בהמה או כלים וניגנבו או שאבדו:
>
> שילם ולא רצה להישבע—שהרי אמרו שומר חינם נישבע ויוצא—נימצא הגנב משלם תשלומי כפל, טבח ומכר משלם תשלומי ארבעה וחמשה. למי הוא משלם? למי שהפיקדון אצלו.
>
> נשבע ולא רצה לשלם, נימצא הגנב משלם תשלומי כפל, טבח ומכר משלם תשלומי ארבעה וחמשה. למי הוא משלם? לבעל הפיקדון.

Oddly, this mishnah refers to the bailee in two ways. It calls him "an unpaid bailee" (line 3) and "the one who has the deposit" (line 5). The second is descriptive and fits the context. The first, in contrast, sounds like a legal concept, and only appears in a parenthetical remark (underlined above). Where does it come from? The phrase "since they said" clues us into the fact that there is a shift between layers here.[35] But why is there a shift in the middle of the mishnah at all, especially when it ruins the flow?

The answer is complicated but enlightening. The core chapters of Tractate *Bava Metzi'a* imply that there are three categories of people who voluntarily take on some level of responsibility for another person's property: the bailee (ch. 3), the renter (chs. 5–7), and the borrower (ch. 8). The bailee and the borrower exist in biblical law, while the renter is a new, intermediate category.[36] An explicit typology in one mishnah, however, expressly contradicts this scheme: "There are *four* bailees: the unpaid bailee, the borrower, the wage earner, and the renter" (*Bava Metzi'a*, 7:8). David Henshke has shown that the threefold division is original and that the fourfold one, which subdivides the bailee into paid and unpaid types, is a later invention squeezed into this earlier scheme.[37] It was too late to refashion this entire area of mishnaic law, so the new had to be interpolated somehow into the old. One option was to insert this material as independent mishnayot into the seams of the existing ones, as the rules of the paid watchman are in rental law (6:6–7). Another, more intrusive option was to append it to a mishnah, in the way that the teaching about the four types of bailees was shoehorned into the middle of laws of renting and borrowing (7:8). Most obstructively, it could be inserted into the running text of a mishnah itself, like the statement above, "since they said that an unpaid bailee may swear and be released." Thus, the parenthetical comment that upsets the mishnah's symmetrical form dates from the later, fourfold categorization of bailees, and its purpose is to bridge the old and the new.

Rabbi Yehudah ha-Nasi's editorship was a reversal of the scholarly revolution of previous generations. Where the "Mishnah of Rabbi Akiva" had actively reshaped traditions, the Mishnah of Rabbi Yehudah ha-Nasi meticulously preserved them.[38] Rabbi was so careful with the traditions of his forbears that he included those that contravened his own. A clear example of this is the Mishnah's ruling that one may recite the Shema in any language, when Rabbi Yehudah ha-Nasi's own opinion is that it may be recited only in Hebrew.[39]

B. RABBI YEHUDAH HA-NASI'S OBJECTS

What were Rabbi Yehudah ha-Nasi's aims in editing the Mishnah? He never says. Unlike collections of Roman law from late Antiquity, the Mishnah has no explanatory preface. The most one can do is look for hints and form reasonable speculations.

Sherira Gaon believed that it was first and foremost an attempt to bring unity to the Oral Torah, which had fragmented among the different schools and scholars. He wrote in his epistle about Rabbi Yehuda ha-Nasi's time:

> the Sages of his day were free from all persecution, because of Antoninus's love for him. So he decided to arrange the laws, in order that the Sages learn them in a uniform recitation, and not recite their own formulation *(lashon)*.[40]

Saadia Gaon took the exact opposite position:

> the circumstance that forced them to compose it was that after the prophets were no more and they saw how scattered they were, they were worried that the tradition would be forgotten. . . . Therefore, they collected all of the preserved opinions, wrote them down, and called them "Mishnah."[41]

This reasoning was elaborated by Maimonides:

> Why did our holy Rabbi do this and not leave the matter as it had been? Seeing that students were continuously dwindling and new tribulations constantly arising, the evil empire spreading throughout the world—its might ascendant—and Israel being buffeted to far-flung places, he composed a single work that everyone could have in hand to learn it quickly so it would not be forgotten.[42]

According to Saadia and Maimonides, Rabbi Yehudah ha-Nasi was forced by necessity and his goal was preservation. The Oral Torah had become an endangered language; its surviving speakers needed to be tracked down and every last word entered into the written record.[43]

According to Sherira, by contrast, Rabbi Yehudah ha-Nasi was not compelled to act by the pressures of persecution. He was driven by an ambition to overcome the fission of the tannaitic academies and he aimed to decide and standardize the law.⁴⁴ What Rabbi Yehudah ha-Nasi's motivations and aims were—preservation, codification, or something in between—remains an open question.

The Mishnah's exact genre is elusive, and it is likely a genre-bending or crossover work. Even if one cannot describe precisely what it is, one can say confidently what it is not: a primer for beginning students.⁴⁵ The Mishnah's text is laconic and its presentation is non-linear. It begins its discussions in medias res, without having first laid the groundwork. In fact, the fundamentals are sometimes never mentioned anywhere in the Mishnah, on the assumption that the learner knows his Scripture and is familiar with the abundant traditions of the Oral Torah. Halakhic concepts and terms are not defined. Cruxes and debates are the Mishnah's focus, rather than basic, undisputed laws. The Mishnah must have been composed for scholars who had the requisite background to jump straight to the complicated edge cases. In this way, it has more in common with the casuistic law of the Torah than with later halakhic codes.

Tractate *Gittin*, for example, does not begin by defining its terms or the exact parameters for giving a get, a writ of divorce. Instead, it discusses the somewhat unusual case of a man living abroad who sends his wife a get via messenger. The specifics of this situation occupy the Mishnah until it shifts topics to a get signed by Samaritans (1:5), a get signed at night (2:2), a get written on the hand of a slave (2:3), a man with two wives bearing identical names (3:1), a husband who invalidated a get that he sent via messenger before the messenger arrived (4:1), and more. The core requirements of the get, namely, that it must be written down, signed, witnessed, and delivered into the wife's domain, are never articulated. Compare this to how Maimonides begins divorce law in his halakhic code: "A woman may only be divorced with a written instrument that reaches her, and this written instrument is called a get. Ten elements constitute divorce according to the Torah."⁴⁶ He then enumerates and discusses them, one by one.

That this is not an isolated phenomenon is confirmed by a run-through of *Seder Mo'ed*. The opening tractate, *Shabbat*, talks about the transfer of objects from four types of domains, without defining said domains. The Tosefta is forced to fill in the blanks. Tractate *Pesaḥim* begins with the search to eradicate hametz rather than with the prohibition of eating or possessing hametz. The first mishnayot in Tractate *Sukkah* specify the dimensions and materials of the sukkah (the booth for the holiday of Sukkot) but not the basic obligation to dwell in it. And so on and so forth.⁴⁷ Emblematic of this is the very first law in the entire Mishnah, which wonders about the appropriate times to recite the Shema but not the very mitzvah of its recitation.

In the same way that the basic obligations are absent from the Mishnah, so are the religious motivations behind them. In several cases, they are pushed to margins of the relevant tractates. The end of Tractate *Berakhot* discusses the theological reason behind the utterance of God's name in blessings; the end of Tractate *Gittin* gives legitimate and illegitimate causes of divorce; and the end of Tractate *Menaḥot* offers the proper motivation for bringing a sacrifice.

Of course, the Mishnah possesses a definite structure and order on the macro and micro levels, as already discussed in the book.[48] Tractate *Sukkah* covers the three major topics of Sukkot: the sukkah (chs. 1–2), the four species (ch. 3), and the holiday rituals (chs. 4–5). Tractate *Rosh ha-Shanah* begins by establishing the calendar date through the sighting of the moon (chs. 1–2), then turns to the mitzvah of blowing the shofar (ch. 3), and finally discusses the liturgy that incorporates the shofar blowing (ch. 4). Tractate *Nazir* progresses from taking the Nazirite vow (chs. 1–2), to the period of its observance (ch. 3), to the annulling of a Nazirite vow (ch. 4–5), and ends with the relevant prohibitions, presented in their biblical order, against drinking wine, cutting one's hair, and becoming impure from a corpse.[49] Other tractates are organized chronologically, like *Shabbat* and *Betzah*, which move from the time leading up to the holy day to the day itself.

The structure of these tractates is easy enough to uncover. In other tractates, scholars have identified much more sophisticated literary structures.[50] The point is that the Mishnah's organization is not inviting for beginners. The prerequisite learning assumed by the unexplained terminology and the regular appearance of highly complex cases means that it was intended for accomplished scholars and not young students.

The Mishnah capably covers the main topics of tannaitic study in the second century. It anthologizes the major opinions and often chooses between them, but in a restrained manner. This combination of preservation and tendentious editing, which has confounded modern scholars about the Mishnah's essence and purpose, is in fact one of Rabbi Yehudah ha-Nasi's crowning achievements, striking a middle note between revisionism and conservatism.

As the preceding section detailed, the edited Mishnah can be puzzling. It takes care to cite earlier halakhic collections in their entirety, to the point that the boundaries between them stick out, yet it omits opinions and explanations that are preserved elsewhere. It leaves the language of its sources mostly untouched, but considers attributions to specific scholars fair game for removal. It uses two techniques to mark one opinion as normative, yet it does not settle most disputes. The edited Mishnah is a complicated, even conflicted work, which has led to multiple theories about its purpose: halakhic code, anthology, textbook, and even philosophical composition.

The nature of the Mishnah defies neat characterization, and no scholarly proposal is free of challenges. If the Mishnah is a halakhic code, for example, how can disputes be left unresolved? If it is an anthology, why are scored of opinions omitted? If it is textbook, why isn't it arranged didactically, advancing from basic principles to hard cases in each area of law? And if it is a work of philosophy, why does it largely consist of legal discussions and rulings?[51]

The Sages of the two Talmuds venerated the Mishnah as an authoritative work of Halakhah.[52] Since the inception of modern Jewish Studies, most scholars accepted this perspective and assumed that Rabbi Yehudah ha-Nasi had intended it to be a legal code.[53] Why, then, does the Mishnah not decide the outcome of disputes in the same way the

Talmud concludes, "and the law is according to Rabbi X"? The argument goes that the Mishnah does not wish to emend its sources, so halakhic determinations are made inexplicitly. Jacob Nahum Epstein put it this way:

> Rabbi changed and added a number of things to our Mishnah, but he could not have inserted a new composition or made radical changes to the Mishnah, because the Mishnah was official and memorized by everyone ("a mishnah does not budge"). To the extent possible, Rabbi left his sources intact, but he did append additional sources to the existing ones.[54]

The gradual formation of the Mishnah, and the widespread knowledge of its component collections, made it impossible to make extreme changes. Elsewhere, Epstein added that this was also the general policy of transmission among the Tannaim, who "would sometimes teach the words of those with whom they disagreed."[55]

Hanoch Albeck, on the other hand, argued that the sheer quantity of contradictions and disputes in the Mishnah combined with its indecisiveness preclude it from being a practical legal code. He decided it was meant to be an anthology, a collection of halakhic opinions with no normative aspirations.[56] As evidence, he appealed to the fact that the Mishnah is composed of earlier collections preserved in their entirety, with no attempt to make them uniform:

> In our Mishnah, the mishnahs [i.e., earlier collections of mishnaic material] compiled according to certain rules or mnemonic devices in the tannaitic study halls have retained their character intact. They are not organized according to our Mishnah's foundational principle of thematic arrangement. This fact alone proves that the Mishnah's editor did not alter, nor transpose, nor truncate the material before him, but set it [in the Mishnah] as he had received it. [. . .] His entire aim in ordering the Mishnah was to preserve their words with precision so that they not be forgotten.[57]

In truth, there is not much daylight between Epstein and Albeck. Both agree that the Mishnah was based on traditions Rabbi Yehudah ha-Nasi inherited and that he edited them conservatively. Some scholars have staked out a position somewhere in between: the Mishnah was compiled not to be a halakhic code per se, but to serve as an authorized legal collection from which such a code could be produced.[58] Others have suggested that the Mishnah is too variegated for any single label to stick: it is at one and the same time an anthology and a code and a textbook.[59]

Yehuda Brandes has offered the interesting theory that the purpose of the Mishnah shifted over time. It began as an anthology, as Albeck proposed. But the first generation of Amoraim in the Land of Israel, headed by Rabbi Yohanan, treated it as a binding code and developed rules for extracting the normative law from it. They formulated rules like "the law is according to the *stam*," which we saw above, as well as "the law follows Rabbi Yose against his colleagues" and "the law follows Rabbi Akiva against his colleague."[60] Through consistent application of these rules, the Mishnah became—first in the Land of Israel and then in Babylonia—a binding source of Halakhah.[61]

Let me finally add my own theory about the purpose behind compiling the Mishnah. I would cautiously suggest that the Mishnah represents an effort to encompass the Oral Torah in its entirety.[62] This perspective helps explain several of the phenomena discussed: the Mishnah's unprecedented comprehensiveness, its attempt to leave no aspect of Jewish life outside its scope—a feat without precedent in Jewish tradition. This also accounts for the systematic organization, with all material arranged into six orders and sixty tractates according to thematic logic. Its unparalleled exhaustiveness is further reflected in the Mishnah's equal regard for explicit Torah commandments, deducible laws, and laws with no biblical source. Finally, this theory also clarifies a phenomenon addressed below: the Mishnah's intended status as an oral composition, maintaining its distinction from the written Torah and preventing the existence of two independent written Torahs.[63]

The full significance of the concept of Oral Torah will be explored in the next chapter, where we discuss the complex normative role of the Mishnah.

FIVE

The Mishnah as a Composition

A diachronic view of the Mishnah, like the one adopted in the preceding chapter, looks at the development of the Mishnah through the accretion of layers and stages of editing. But the Mishnah is more than the sum of its parts. Once its major sources—Scripture, tradition, *ma'asim*, rabbinic debate—were interwoven through various editorial processes, the result was a fully developed composition. It is therefore appropriate now to switch to a synchronic view of the Mishnah that regards the work as an integrated body of law.

An example should illustrate my meaning. Tractate *Berakhot* covers a whole range of mitzvot: prayers, Grace after Meals, blessings over various phenomena, and more. One could draw distinctions between these mitzvot based on phenomenology (recurring vs. incidental blessings) or historical and textual sources (dating from before or after the Temple's destruction). But it is their integration that transforms them into a full-bodied corpus of liturgical law. The meaning, importance, and authority of each element depends on the place it has been assigned or the role it plays within this composition.[1]

This chapter zooms out to allow this composite whole to fit in our analytic field of view. It investigates three aspects of the Mishnah: normativity, conceptualization, and imagination. In the end, these reveal it to be, notwithstanding its practical side, an exceptionally ambitious intellectual project.

A. THE NORMATIVITY OF MISHNAIC LAW

The composition before us is not a legal code as we tend to think of one, namely, a comprehensive set of obligations, prohibitions, and sanctions. A typical code has two characteristics absent from the Mishnah: uniformly normative laws, and detailed penalties for their breach.

The Mishnah, as we will see, has neither. First, it displays considerable variability in the normativity of its directives and in the way it expresses that normativity. Second, it hardly gives much thought to punishments, which are marginal, if they even appear at all.

The lion's share of the Mishnah indeed consists of obligations and prohibitions, but scattered throughout it are customs, descriptions of rituals, practical advice, ethical reflections, and purely theoretical laws.[2] The Mishnah may note that something is a custom, and not an absolute law, with a set formula: "in a place where the custom is to X," or "everything is according to the local practice."[3] The Mishnah's attitude toward common customs is complex; it can equally support them or criticize them. The third chapter of Tractate *Sukkah* reports two customs that receive unequal treatment:

> [9] Where would they wave?[a] During "Thank the Lord" at the beginning and end,[b] even during "Lord, please save us"[c]—the words of Bet Hillel.
>
> Bet Shammai say, Even during "Lord, please let us prosper."[d]
>
> Rabbi Akiva said, I observed that while *all of the people* would shake[e] their lulavs[f] continuously, Rabban Gamaliel and Rabbi Yehoshua would only wave[g] during "Lord, Please save us." [. . .]
>
> [13] If the first holiday of the Festival[h] occurs on Shabbat, *all of the people* bring their lulavs[i] to the synagogue.[j] Every single person recognizes their own and takes it.[k] For they said,[l] A person may not fulfill their obligation on the first holiday of the Festival with someone else's lulav, but on the rest of the days of the Festival a person may fulfill their obligation with someone else's lulav. (*Sukkah*, 3:9, 13)

---

  a The four species are waved on Sukkot during the recitation of Hallel, which comprises Psalms 113–118, so the Mishnah is inquiring at what point exactly one is to wave them.
  b The phrase appears in twice in Psalm 118, at the beginning (verse 1) and at the end (verse 29).
  c The first half of Psalms 118:25.
  d The second half of Psalms 118:25.
  e Heb. *metarefim*, a vigorous movement.
  f The closed palm frond that is the centerpiece of the four species taken in hand, though all species are held for the shaking.
  g Heb. *ni'ane'u*, a more restricted motion.
  h In mishnaic parlance, Sukkot is known simply as "the Festival" (*ḥag*).
  i The "lulav" here serves as a synecdoche for all four species.
  j Before the onset of the holiday.
  k In the holiday in order to fulfill their obligation.
  l The Sages said based on the wording of the verse, "take for yourself on the first day . . ." (Lev. 23:40).

[9] ואיכן היו מנענעים? ב"הודו לה'" תחילה וסוף, אף ב"אנא ה' הושיע נא"—כדברי בית הלל. בית שמיי אומרים: אף ב"אנא ה' הצליחה נא".

אמר ר' עקיבה: צופה הייתי ברבן גמליאל וברבי יהושע שכל העם מטרפים את לולביהם והם לא ניענעו אלא ב"אנא ה' הושיעה נא" בלבד.

[13] יום טוב הראשון של חג שחל להיות בשבת, כל העם מוליכים את לולביהם לבית הכנסת. כל אחד ואחד מכיר את שלו ונוטל. מפני שאמרו: אין אדם יוצא ידי חובתו ביום טוב הראשון שלחג בלולבו שלחבירו, ושאר כל ימות החג יוצא אדם ידי חובתו בלולבו שלחבירו.

The two mishnayot depict widespread customs relating to how "all of the people" (lines 4 and 7) took the four species on Sukkot. Yet the Mishnah adopts opposing stances. In the first case, the Mishnah finds the frenzied shaking of the people excessive and pointedly contrasts it with the more restrained, appropriate practice of two Sages. In the second, the Mishnah approves of the general practice of bringing one's lulav to the synagogue before the holiday, while trying to mitigate this by instructing people to find their own lulav. In the Mishnah, not all customs are normative.[4]

Unlike a dry, formulaic code of law, the Mishnah expresses its binding norms dynamically. The first chapter of Tractate *Sukkah* discusses the fitness of various structures for fulfilling the mitzvah of dwelling in the sukkah (booth). When a proposed sukkah does not meet the requirements, the Mishnah expresses this in various ways: "it is not a sukkah" (1:8), "it's as if one made it inside the house" (1:2), and more. Since the Babylonian Talmud wants to extract unambiguous norms from the Mishnah, it asks: "Why does one recite 'it's as if one made it inside the house'? Let one recite 'it is invalid'!"[5] We can surmise from what we have seen thus far that the colorful variations in the Mishnah likely come from the integration of distinct sources that were not editorially uniformized. As a composition, the Mishnah is not fully consistent in the presentation and formulation of norms.

Even if the Mishnah is not solely a legal code, it by all accounts purports to make normative claims. Whom does the Mishnah envision will enforce compliance with its norms? Rare are the mishnayot that address enforcement of the law, but they do exist. A mishnah in Tractate *Shekalim*, for example, says about the planting of *kil'ayim* (forbidden mixtures) and paying the half-shekel tax to the Temple:

[1] On the first of Adar they[a] would make an announcement about the shekels[b] and about *kil'ayim*.[c] On the fifteenth . . . they would even go forth for the *kil'ayim*.[d]

a Agents of the court.
b That it is time to pay the half-shekel tax to the Temple for the public sacrifices.
c That one should uproot those species which are forbidden to be planted together.
d The agents would inspect fields personally for *kil'ayim*.

[2] Rabbi Yehudah said, Originally, they would uproot[a] and toss it in front of them. Once sinners proliferated,[b] they would uproot and toss it onto the roads. They instituted[c] that they should declare an entire field ownerless.

[3] On the fifteenth, moneychangers would set up[d] in the province.[e] On the twenty-fifth, they set up in the Temple. Once they had set up in the Temple, they began taking collateral.[f] From whom did they take collateral? From Levites and Israelites, converts and freed slaves, but neither women, nor slaves, nor minors. If a father had begun paying for his minor son, he could no longer stop. But they did not take collateral from the priests, in order to promote peace.[g] (*Shekalim*, 1:3)

[1] באחד באדר משמיעים על השקלים ועל הכלאים. בחמשה עשר בו . . . וויוצאין אף על הכילאים.

[2] אמר רבי יהודה: בראשונה היו עוקרים ומשליכים לפניהם. משרבו עוברי עברה היו משליכים על הדרכים. התקינו שיהו מבקירים את כל השדה.

[3] בחמשה עשר בו שולחנות ישבו במדינה. בעשרים וחמשה ישבו במקדש. משישבו במקדש התחילו למשכן. ואת מי ממשכנים? לווים וישראלים, גרים ועבדים משוחררים, אבל לא נשים ולא עבדים ולא קטנים. וכל קטן שהתחיל אביו לשקול על ידו אינו פוסק. ואין ממשכנין את הכהנים מפני דרכי שלום.

The agents of the court and the moneychangers were empowered even to seize property, all to ensure that people were fulfilling their halakhic duties. But this system of enforcement is atypical in the Mishnah, and it seems to have been connected to robust institutions that existed before the destruction of the Temple.[6]

Much more commonly, the Mishnah leaves it to the people to police the religious observance of their fellow Jews. Consider the following mishnah:

It is a mitzvah for the oldest[h] to perform *yibbum*. If he is unwilling, they approach all the brothers. If they are unwilling, they go back to the eldest and say to him, "The mitzvah is upon you: either perform *ḥalitzah* or perform *yibbum*."

---

a The agents would uproot the plant species planted too close together.
b Who would replant what had been uprooted.
c The courts instituted that the fields of those who transgressed the prohibition of planting *kil'ayim* should be declared ownerless, presumably because tossing it onto the roads wasn't an effective deterrent.
d Literally, "sit."
e That is, outside of Jerusalem.
f Forcibly, if a person had not paid.
g Since the priests had a unique position in society, the Sages did not want to initiate conflicts with them.
h Brother of the deceased by the same father.

> ### YIBBUM AND ḤALITZAH
>
> The Torah generally forbids a man to have relations with his brother's wife (Lev. 18:16), but if his brother dies childless, the Torah instructs him to marry the widow (Deut. 25:5–6). This is called *yibbum* (rendered into English as "levirate marriage"; *levir* in Latin means "brother's husband"). Tractate *Yevamot* outlines the many conditions that must obtain in order for *yibbum* to be a mitzvah, and also discusses the procedure for when the deceased had multiple wives.
>
> Since the Torah anticipated that a brother might refuse, it details a ceremony in which the widow makes his refusal public knowledge, removes his shoe, and spits. See Deuteronomy 25:7–10 and *Yevamot*, 12:6.

If he postponed his decision until a younger one[a] reaches maturity, or until an older one[b] returns from overseas, or until a deaf-mute or mentally incompetent one[c] [is healed]—they do not listen to him. Instead, they say to him, "The mitzvah is upon you: either perform *halitzah* or perform *yibbum*." (*Yevamot*, 4:5)

מצוה בגדול ליבם. לא רצה, מהלכן על כל האחין. לא רצו, חוזרים אצל הגדול ואומרים לו: עליך מצוה, או חלוץ או ייבם.

תלה בקטון עד שיגדיל, ובגדול עד שיבוא ממדינת הים, ובחרש ובשוטה, אין שומעין לו. אלא אומרין לו: עליך מצוה, או חלוץ או ייבם.

In this mishnah, "they approach" (*mehallekhin*), "they go back" (*hozerim*), "they say" (*omerin*), "they do not listen" (*ein shome'in*).[7] Who are "they"? It could refer to Jewish authorities, such as the local court or its agents, but a similar formulation elsewhere indicates a more abstract enforcing body. On Shabbat, the Mishnah rules, a fire may not be extinguished, "but if a minor comes to extinguish it *they* do not listen (*ein shome'in*) to him because his resting [from labor] is incumbent upon them" (*Shabbat*, 16:6). In the life-or-death, split-second decision whether to extinguish a fire, no court is being convened or agents summoned. The ones refusing the minor's help are the bystanders or homeowners. In other words, the general populace carries out the Mishnah's will. The same is true in the above mishnah and elsewhere. This explains why norms involving this nonspecific authority are never accompanied by a sanction.

In most of mishnaic law, though, personal responsibility is assumed. The Mishnah recognizes that people are people, and sometimes they will do less or even more than required. Below is a list of cases, drawn from each of the six *sedarim* of the Mishnah, which indicates in some fashion that people are responsible for themselves:

  a A younger brother.
  b The implication is that the oldest here is only the oldest among the brothers who are present and approachable.
  c Perhaps they will recover and be able to perform the *yibbum*.

1. The proper time for reciting the morning Shema, according to Rabbi Yehoshua, extends until the third variable hour of the day. The Mishnah adds: "If someone recites it hereafter, they do not lose out; it is like someone reading from the Torah" (*Berakhot*, 1:2). The Mishnah recognizes that compliance rests with the individual and cannot always be expected.

2. The Mishnah says that trappers would work discreetly on ḥol ha-mo'ed, so that people would not think they were catching food for after the holidays. Rabbi Yose then adds: "they were stringent upon themselves" (*Mo'ed Katan*, 2:5). Some people go beyond the requirement of the law.

3. The Mishnah states that if a husband divorces his wife with a get (writ of divorce) that specifies that she may marry "anyone except X," the Sages prohibit her from remarrying on its basis. The Mishnah asks, "What should he do?" and then outlines a procedure (*Gittin*, 9:1). It is on him and him alone to follow the protocol. Nowhere is it implied that authorities get involved.

4. The Sages permit a day-laborer to eat more than his wages but add that "a person should be taught not to be a glutton" (*Bava Metzi'a*, 7:5). They did not take it upon themselves to institute nationwide training in portion control. A person is responsible for their own character development.

5. Tractate *Keritot* discusses the unwitting transgression of a severe prohibition, which requires the bringing of a sin-offering to the Temple. Since the sinner was unaware at the time of the violation, he or she must find out about it in order to bring the sacrifice. The Mishnah says, "If they told someone, 'You ate ḥelev (forbidden fat),' he brings a sin-offering" (*Keritot*, 3:1). The Mishnah assumes that the unwitting violator will take care of it and no follow-up is necessary.

6. In a case where operators of a winepress or olive-press are suspected of being incautious about ritual purity, Rabbi Meir maintains that if they go into the vicinity of a cave that contains a purifying *mikveh* (ritual bath), "it is sufficient for him" (*Teharot*, 10:3). One need not watch them immerse to be satisfied that they are now pure.

Even with regard to the laws of *kil'ayim*, which had institutionalized oversight in the Second Temple period, compliance was largely up to the individual. If someone buried vegetables beneath a grapevine, the Mishnah rules that "one need not be concerned about *kil'ayim*" (*Kil'ayim*, 1:9)—and not "*they* are not concerned." The address of the Mishnah is the individual. That is not to say that the Mishnah never makes enactments or penalties for transgressions, but that its guiding assumption is that those who learn the Mishnah fundamentally want to keep Halakhah, so the Mishnah need only tell them how to do so.[8]

That the Mishnah presumes a willingness to carry out its laws is buttressed by the few sanctions it imposes when someone inadvertently fails to observe or intentionally

> ### ḤOL HA-MO'ED
>
> The first and last days of Pesach (Passover, days 1 and 7) and the first and last days of Sukkot/Shemini Atzeret (days 1 and 8) are all holidays on which labor unrelated to food preparation may not be performed. The intermediate days (aside from Shabbat) are known as ḥol ha-mo'ed, literally "the profane/weekdays of the festival." One may only perform labor on ḥol ha-mo'ed if certain conditions are met: the work could not have been performed before the festival, it is not for after the festival, and failure to do it will result in an unrecoverable and significant loss of income. This topic is discussed in tractate Mo'ed Katan.

transgresses its laws. Most of the negative commandments have no sanctions whatsoever.[9] And even when the Mishnah attaches punishments like exile or lashes to some laws, it knows that they are not actionable: the Sages could not officially exile someone or administer whippings, for that was the exclusive right of their Roman overlords. Furthermore, the language used when recording the punishments is neutral legalese, with no evident exhortation or textual danger sign. The inclusion of capital punishment, lashes, exile, and even *karet* (spiritual excision) is because they are convenient halakhic categories for organizing sins by severity.

In the mishnah below, the punishment, of death no less, is merely another item on the list:

Terumah[a] and *bikkurim*—[b]

Regarding them one is liable for death[c] or a fifth;[d] they are prohibited to non-Kohanim; they are the property of the Kohen; they are neutralized[e] in one hundred and one; and they require handwashing[f] and the setting of the sun.[g] (*Bikkurim*, 2:1)[10]

התרומה והביכורין—חייבין עליהן מיתה וחומש, ואסורין לזרים, והן נכסי כהן, ועולין באחד ומאה, וטעונין רחיצת ידים והערב שמש.

   a The tithe given to the priest that has sanctity and must be eaten in ritual purity.
   b The first fruits brought to the Temple and eaten by the Kohanim.
   c If a non-Kohen eats them intentionally, they are liable for death at the hands of Heaven; see Leviticus 22:10.
   d If a non-Kohen eats them unintentionally, they must pay the value of what they ate plus a fine of a fifth; see Leviticus 22:14.
   e If they fall into a mixture, the entire mixture may not be eaten by a non-Kohen unless there are one hundred parts of *ḥullin* (unconsecrated food) for every part of *terumah* or *bikkurim*.
   f Before eating them.
   g If a Kohen was ritually impure and immersed, he must wait until sunset before eating them; see Leviticus 22:7.

Nothing identifies the enumeration of capital punishment as a deterrent; it looks the same as the other items on this list. The Mishnah includes the punishment simply because the severity of a prohibition is indexed by its accompanying punishment.[11]

The only substantive treatment of penalties and punishments is in Tractates *Sanhedrin* and *Makkot* (originally one tractate). But there is no reason to assume that it forms the basis for a genuine law enforcement that gives sanctions their teeth and turns mishnaic law into a proper legal system.[12] These tractates bear no resemblance to modern penal codes. Their sanctions completely ignore transgressions that do not result in execution or lashing, that is to say, most of the Mishnah's laws! This treatment exists because punishment is part of Jewish law, based on a biblical commandment (see Deut. 16:18). As such, *Sanhedrin* and *Makkot* are no different from tractates that cover other areas of Halakhah, say, the laws of the sukkah or of marriage. They do not imply the actual establishment of penal institutions or the implementation of punitive measures.

Further corroborating the idea that the Mishnah entrusts the individual with proper performance is the inclusion of laws that are impossible to externally enforce. There are certain cognitive frames of mind or emotional states enjoined or forbidden by the Mishnah. The second and third chapters of Tractate *Zevaḥim*, all about animal sacrifices, go into great detail about the ramifications of the officiating priest's thoughts during the sacrificial rite. If at any of the critical stages he plans ("thinks") that the other stages or the eating of the sacrifice will occur "beyond its time and place," the sacrifice becomes unfit and may not be eaten. Obviously, no one aside from the serving priest knows what is in his mind. Many other laws in the Mishnah apply to the realm of the mind—thought, intention, will—and evince no concern for gauging their observance.[13]

At times, the Mishnah adds words of encouragement or exhortation, with no normative implications. One who lowers prices "is remembered for good" (*Bava Metzi'a*, 4:12). If someone needs charity but doesn't take it, "they will not die of old age until they have supported others from their own [wealth]" (*Pe'ah*, 8:9). Such statements tend to conclude tractates, and are more aggadic than halakhic.[14]

The Mishnah's fluctuations in normativity, inclusion of extra-legal material, and fundamental assumption of compliance point to the fact that it constitutes an all-encompassing manual for serving God. Its unspoken assumption is that rabbinic Jews aspire to piety and consider its contents binding, so it need not instill fear of punishment to assure its observance.

B. LEGAL CONCEPTUALIZATION

In the same way that the Mishnah's normativity is not uniform, its legal conceptualization is uneven across the composition. In some chapters the Mishnah does not delineate its underlying principles, while in others it lays bare its high-order thinking.

The first chapter of Tractate *'Avodah Zarah* exemplifies the Mishnah's tendency to collect similar cases without distilling them to extract the essential rule.

[6] In a place where the custom is to sell small domesticated animals[a] to gentiles, one may do so; in a place where the custom is not to sell, one may not do so. [. . .]

[7] One may not sell them bears or lions or anything else that may harm the public. One may not build with them a basilica, a scaffold, a stadium, or a platform. [. . .]

[8] [. . .] One may not sell them something attached to the ground,[b] but one may sell it on condition that it be cut down. (*'Avodah Zarah*, 1:6–8)

[6] מקום שנהגו למכור בהמה דקה לגויים—מוכרין. מקום שנהגו שלא למכור—אין מוכרין. [. . .]

[7] אין מוכרין להן דובים ואריות, ולא כל דבר שיש בו נזיקה לרבים.

אין בונין עימהן בסילקי וגרדון, אסטרייה ובימה. [. . .]

[8] אין מוכרין במחובר לקרקע, אבל מוכר הוא משיקצץ.

The Mishnah does not supply a rationale for these prohibitions and exceptions; there is no "this is the rule." The two Talmuds therefore struggle to reconstruct what the Sages were thinking. Is the concern that these practices will lead a Jew to benefit from idolatry somehow? Are they considered a show of favor to idol worshippers, transgressing a biblical prohibition (Deut. 7:5)? Or perhaps the formal subject of the tractate—idolatry—is not the issue here at all. Other suggestions include the prohibition against placing a stumbling block before the blind (Lev. 19:14), abetting Roman murderousness, and keeping distance from "gentiles" more generally. The uncertainty in both Talmuds stems from the Mishnah's lack of interest in conveying its animating concerns.[15]

The third chapter of Tractate *Keritot*, on the other hand, demonstrates a high degree of halakhic conceptualization. The rule is that if a prohibition carries the penalty of *karet* for an intentional violation, then its unintentional violation necessitates the bringing of a sin-offering. Performing any of the thirty-nine categories of prohibited work on Shabbat falls under this rule. Rabbi Akiva formulated a hypothetical to cut to the conceptual heart of what exactly triggers the sin-offering obligation. He posed it to his teacher Rabbi Eliezer:

Rabbi Akiva said, I asked Rabbi Eliezer: "If one performs multiple labors of a similar type,[c] on many Shabbatot, during a single lapse of awareness[d]—what is it?[e] Must he bring one[f] for all of them or one for each and every one?" (*Keritot*, 3:10)

a Sheep and goats.
b Plants.
c A number of acts that all fall under a single category of forbidden labor on Shabbat, such as planting seeds and planting saplings.
d One forgot that there is a prohibition against performing certain types of work on Shabbat.
e What is the law?
f Sin-offering, since it was an unintentional violation.

אמר רבי עקיבה: שאלתי את רבי אליעזר, העושה מלאכות הרבה בשבתות הרבה מעין מלאכה אחת בהעלם אחד, מה הוא? חייב אחת על כולן או אחת על כל אחת ואחת?

Let us unpack the question. Is a sin-offering triggered by a prohibited action alone, so that "multiple labors" obligate the sinner in the same number of sacrifices? If so, someone who plants seeds five different times over the course of Shabbat would need to bring five sacrifices. But perhaps one cannot be held liable over and over for not knowing the same information. In that case, so long as the labor done is "of a similar type," belonging to the same halakhic category, one need only bring a single sacrifice. Not only repeated planting of seeds but also planting saplings and grafting branches would qualify as the same for this purpose. A third option is for the temporal "lapse of awareness" to be the determining factor, with the offerings corresponding to the number of discrete lapses. By inventing this hypothetical, Rabbi Akiva was trying to put his finger on the defining criterion. The ensuing back-and-forth between Rabbi Akiva and Rabbi Eliezer, the specifics of which must be left for another time, showcases the Sages' intellectual rigor and the level of conceptual precision they pursued.[16]

As Leib Moscovitz has documented, explicit conceptualization is rare in the Mishnah.[17] The Mishnah often has a rule in mind but it does not express it. Sometimes, a parallel tosefta tells us what it is. Let us revisit a mishnah from Tractate *Bava Metzi'a* discussed in chapter 1:

> If two people are holding a garment, this one says "I found it" and that one says "I found it"; this one says "It's all mine" and that one says "It's all mine"—this one swears that he has no less than half of it and that one swears that he has no less than half of it and they split it.
>
> If this one says "It's all mine" and that one says "Half of it's mine"—the one who says "It's all mine" swears that he has no less than three parts and the one who says "Half of it's mine" swears that he has no less than one-quarter. This one takes three parts and that one takes one-quarter. (*Bava Metzi'a*, 1:1)

שנים אוחזים בטלית, זה אומר 'אני מצאתיה' וזה אומר 'אני מצאתיה', זה אומר 'כולה שלי' וזה אומר 'כולה שלי'—זה יישבע שאין לו בה פחות מחציה וזה ישבע שאין לו בה פחות מחציה, ויחלוקו.

זה אומר 'כולה שלי' וזה אומר 'חצייה שלי', האומר 'כולה שלי' ישבע שאין לו בה פחות משלושה חלקים, והאומר 'חצייה שלי' ישבע שאין לו בה פחות מרביע. זה נוטל שלושה חלקים וזה נוטל רביע.

Here is the parallel tosefta:

> If this one says "It's all mine" and that one says "One-third of it's mine"—the one who says "It's all mine" swears that he has no less than five parts and the one who says "One-third of it's mine" swears that he has no less than one-sixth.

The Mishnah as a Composition

> *This is the rule:* One may only swear about half of what one claims. (Tosefta, *Bava Metzi'a,* 1:2)

> זה אומר 'כולה שלי' וזה אומר 'שלשה שלי'—האומר 'כולה שלי' ישבע שאין לו בה פחות מחמשה חלקין, האומר 'שלשה שלי' ישבע שאין לו בה פחות משתות.
>
> כללו של דבר—אין נשבע אלא על חצי מה שטוען.

The Mishnah presented two claims, all versus all and all versus half. Now, the Tosefta introduces a third case of all versus a third. The rule then stated by the Tosefta is obviously behind the Mishnah's ruling as well, albeit unstated.

Nevertheless, care must be taken when looking to the Tosefta for the Mishnah's rationale. As Moscowitz astutely points out, the Mishnah's own reasons might not be identical to the Tosefta's. For example, when Tractate *Mo'ed Katan* enumerates the kinds of work that one may perform on *ḥol ha-mo'ed,* it does not formulate the operative rule that permits these and not those exertions. It is the Tosefta that categorizes them all as "something that will be lost" *(davar ha-aved),* meaning, if one does not perform this labor now on *ḥol ha-mo'ed,* it will result in a permanent loss, since the window of opportunity will have passed. The Mishnah, however, only mentions this criterion in one specific case:

> A person may bring in their fruit[a] because of thieves and draw their flax out of the soaking pool *to prevent its loss,*[b] provided that they do not intend[c] to do this labor on the *mo'ed.*[d] Regarding all of them, if one intended to do this labor on the *mo'ed* they must be lost.[e] (*Mo'ed Katan,* 2:3)

> מכניס אדם את פירותיו מפני הגנבים, ושולה פשתנו מן המשרה בשביל שלא תאבד. ובלבד שלא יכוון את במועד. וכולם אם כיוונו את מלאכתן במועד—יאבדו.

The Tosefta appears to have generated a rule from the Mishnah's reasoning behind removing flax from the soaking pool. This sort of legal development and abstraction is common to the Talmuds, which often tease out or articulate the principles behind the Mishnah.[18]

Beyond explicit rules governing cases or the unstated principles behind laws, the Mishnah includes other, more covert forms of conceptualization. When it draws comparisons between unrelated areas of Halakhah, for example, it conceives of broader categories that can encompass aspects of both. In other situations, the Mishnah discusses an object or act with respect to numerous areas of law. Apparently, beyond the discrete details stands a

---

a From the field into the home.
b Getting spoiled from soaking for too long.
c Schedule this work before the holiday.
d On *ḥol ha-mo'ed.*
e One must forgo the fruits of this labor.

> **LOAN FORGIVENESS DURING *SHEMITTAH***
>
> According to the rabbinic understanding of Deuteronomy 15, all debts are canceled every seven years during *shemittah*, the sabbatical year. (Some scholars think the loan forgiveness might have originally been more modest, being restricted to a prohibition against collecting the debt for the duration of the sabbatical year.)
>
> According to the Mishnah, Hillel made an enactment that circumvents this biblical law "when he saw that the people refused to make loans to one another" (*Shevi'it*, 10:3). This enactment is called *prozbol*, from Greek προσβολή *(prosbolé)*, a word attested in Egyptian papyri that designates a contract between a creditor and a debtor (see Heijmans, "Greek and Latin Loanwords," 179). The Mishnah states that a *prozbol* transfers the debt to a court so that the obligation to forgive debts on *shemittah* does not apply to it. The *prozbol* would later serve as a precedent for radical rabbinic legislation that uprooted biblical laws.

single halakhic idea. The following exceptional instance of naked conceptualization in the Mishnah should give a sense of what I mean:

A beehive—

Rabbi Eliezer says, It is like land, so one may write a *prozbol* on it; it does not contract ritual impurity in its place;[a] and one who takes honey from it on Shabbat is liable.[b] (*Shevi'it*, 10:7 / *'Uktzin*, 3:10)

כוורת דבורים—רבי אליעזר אומר: הרי הוא כקרקע, וכותבין עליה פרוזבול, ואינה מקבלת טומאה במקומה, והרודה ממנה בשבת חייב.

In rabbinic thinking, there are two primary classes of objects: land and movables. To which is a beehive more similar? This mishnah makes the conceptualization explicit when it compares it to land and lists the ramifications for different areas of Halakhah. Notably, it is Rabbi Eliezer, of the generation of Yavneh, who conceptualizes the beehive in this way, so one can posit that this type of thinking was already a feature of the early rabbinic academies (compare Rabbi Akiva's question to Rabbi Eliezer about the trigger of the sin-offering above).

On a much larger scale, conceptualization serves to organize the Mishnah. In the discussion of the Mishnah's order, I detailed various principles of organization, of which theme is predominant. But thematic unity can sometimes be pretty abstract. Here is an example. The first eleven chapters of Tractate *Yevamot* are about the mitzvah of *yibbum*, and chapter 12 turns to *ḥalitzah*, which is certainly thematically connected. But what about the next chapters? Chapter 13 is about the rabbinic institution of *me'un*, a girl's right to refuse a marriage

---

a If it hasn't moved it is considered like land, which cannot become impure.

b For violating Shabbat, as it is tantamount to uprooting something from the ground, a prohibited labor on Shabbat.

arranged by her mother or brother (after her father died) upon reaching majority. (Chapter 14 is a kind of appendix to this, as it discusses marriages involving deaf people, also a rabbinic institution.) Chapters 15 and 16, which conclude the tractate, are about the *agunah*, a woman "anchored" to a marriage because her husband may be dead, and about the kind of evidence that allows a woman to remarry without fear of committing adultery and giving birth to a *mamzer*. What common thread runs through chapters 12 to 16? The release of a woman from marriage without a get. *Ḥalitzah* does not require a get from the brother-in-law; *me'un* does not necessitate a get for dissolving the marriage of the minor to her husband; and releasing an *agunah* permits her to remarry without a get because the husband is presumed dead. In this and other cases, halakhic conceptualization must be the Mishnah's basis of organization.[19]

Usually, this conceptual work is implicit and remains behind the scenes.[20] The next mishnah from Tractate *Ḥallah*, about the tithe known as *ḥallah*, which is removed from dough and given to a Kohen, has a similar structure to the mishnah about the beehive but it omits the explicit conceptualization:

Dough for dogs—[a]

If the shepherds eat from it, it is obligated in *ḥallah;* one can make an eruv and a *shittuf* wth it;[b] one must make a blessing[c] on it and one may make a *zimmun*[d] over it; it may be made on a holiday;[e] and one may fulfill one's obligation with it on Pesach.[f] (*Ḥallah*, 1:8)

עיסת הכלבים—בזמן שהרועים אוכלים ממנה חייבת בחלה, ומערבים בה ומשתתפין בה, ומברכין עליה ומזמנין עליה, ונעשת ביום טוב, ויוציא בה אדם ידי חובתו בפסח.

The common benchmark of all of these laws is that the item in question must meet the definition of food. If the shepherds are eating the food of their sheepdogs, it must be edible, even if only just so. That is enough for all of these areas of Halakhah.

The mishnayot presented in this section demonstrate the sophisticated legal thought. The discussion between Rabbi Akiva and Rabbi Eliezer about the precise trigger of the sin-offering is the acme of intellectual rigor. Looking at the bulk of the Mishnah, though, one

a Used to prepare food for sheepdogs.

b The *'eruv ḥatzerot* and *shittuf mevo'ot* join together adjacent courtyards and alleyways, in order to allow for carrying within these shared spaces on Shabbat, by designating a joint meal of bread of which anyone in these areas can partake.

c The Grace after Meals recited after eating bread.

d Three or more men convene to say Grace after Meals together and say a special formula; see *Berakhot*, chapter 7.

e Certain forbidden labors are permitted on holidays to prepare food for consumption, so this dough must be considered food.

f The dough can be used for the mitzvah of eating matzah on Passover.

wouldn't know that behind the simplistic language is razor-sharp conceptual analysis. Why is the Mishnah's thinking seldom outwardly perceivable and so rarely encountered?

Scholars have offered explanations tied to the purpose of the Mishnah as a composition,[21] but the presence or absence of conceptualization is first and foremost a reflection of the nature of the source material, which, as we have seen, the Mishah's editor left relatively untouched. Another mishnah from Tractate *Bava Metzi'a*, already discussed in chapter 1 with regard to the Mishnah's style, illustrates this well:

[1] Which finds belong to a person and which must one announce?

These finds belong to a person: If one found scattered fruit, scattered money, bundles in the public domain, cakes of pressed figs, baker's loaves, strings of fish, pieces of cut meat, wool shearings that come from their region, flax stalks, and strips of purple wool—these belong to him.

Rabbi Yehudah says, Anything that has a change one must announce. How so? If one found a cake containing a potsherd, a loaf containing money.

Rabbi Shimon ben Elazar says, Any merchant's wares one need not announce.

[2] But these one must announce: If one found fruit in a vessel or a vessel as is, coins in a wallet or a wallet as is, piles of fruit, piles of coins, three coins on top of one another, bundles in the private domain and homemade loaves, wool shearings taken from the artisan, jugs of wine or jugs of oil—one must announce it. (*Bava Metzi'a*, 2:1–2)

[1]אלו מציאות שלו ואלו חייב להכריז?

אלו מציאות שלו: מצא פירות מפוזרים, מעות מפוזרות, כריכות ברשות הרבים, עיגולי דבילה, כיכרות שלנחתום, ומחרוזות של דגים, וחתיכות שלבשר, וגיזי צמר הבאות ממדינתן, ואניצי פישתן, ולשונות שלארגמן—הרי אילו שלו.

רבי יהודה אומר: כל דבר שיש בו שינוי חייב להכריז. כיצד? מצא עיגול ובתוכו חרס, כיכר ובתוכו מעות.

רבי שמעון בן אלעזר אומר: כל כלי אנפוריא אינו חייב להכריז.

[2] ואלו חייב להכריז: מצא פירות בכלי או כלי כמות שהוא, מעות בכיס או כיס כמות שהוא, ציבורי פרות, ציבורי מעות, שלשה מטבעות זה על גבי זה, כריכות ברשות היחיד, וכיכרות שלבעל הבית, וגיזי צמר הלקוחות מבית האומן, וכדי יין וכדי שמן—חייב להכריז.

In the first mishnah, the *tanna kamma* compiles a list of items that do not need to be publicly announced. The guiding principle behind this selection is plain enough: all are generic and bear no identifying mark. The *stam* of the second mishnah bears this out, by listing nearly identical items that are differentiated by bearing some sign of ownership or stamp of individuality. Rabbi Yehudah disagrees with the *tanna kamma* and thinks that even generic items with some unique change need to be announced. He formulates a rule and clarifies it with examples. Finally, Rabbi Shimon ben Elazar states a principle alone, although it is less abstract than Rabbi Yehudah's "anything." Lists of concrete objects and abstract rules appear next to each other in a single mishnah, because traditions from schools or Sages are all being seated under the same large umbrella of the Mishnah.

Lack of conceptualization is not part of the Mishnah's ideology or goals as a composition. It results from the casuistic method of study practiced in the academies and the Mishnah's variable source material. The most important lesson to be learned is that the absence of explicit conceptualization is a superficial phenomenon, a matter of literary form and didactic format, and is not reflective about the degree of conceptual thought underlying mishnaic law.

C. REALITY AND IMAGINATION IN THE MISHNAH

We have seen that many laws of the Mishnah relate to the Temple, but only its earliest source material dates to a time when the Temple was still standing.[22] Interestingly, even laws that are not dependent on the Temple, like the separation of tithes, are taught in the Mishnah within a Temple context. In the entirety of the Mishnah, the Mishnah's destruction is only acknowledged eight times: "since the Temple was destroyed...."[23] In one such mention (*Nazir*, 5:4), the destruction seems to be deliberately compared to a trivial halakhic matter—the theft of an animal dedicated to the altar. All this is to say that, on the whole, the Mishnah makes no distinction between its own time and that of the Temple. In the Mishnah's legal imagination, the Temple is, in a sense, still standing.[24]

The Mishnah contains historical laws with no contemporary application. "What is the difference between Pesach in Egypt and Pesach for generations?" asks the Mishnah.[25] Moving forward in history, the Mishnah tells us that the blessings and curses proclaimed on Mounts Gerizim and Ebal are among those rituals whose verbalization must be in Hebrew.[26] What the Israelites did upon entering the Land of Israel with regard to *'orlah*, forbidden fruit from the first three years of a tree's planting, is the subject of another mishnah:

> At the time when our forefathers[a] came into the Land, if they found something planted, it was exempt.[b] If they planted, even though they had not conquered,[c] it was obligated. (*'Orlah*, 1:2)

עת שבאו אבותינו לארץ ומצאו נטוע—פטור. נטעו אף על פי שלא כיבשו—חייב.

The Mishnah zeroes in on a moment in time from the ancient Israelite past. While this has no practical relevance, it can serve as a kind of test case for intermediate stages, for working

---

a In the period of Joshua.
b The fruit of the tree was exempt from the law of *'orlah*; see Leviticus 19:23–25.
c The Land from the Canaanites yet, as described in the book of Joshua.

> **THE TEMPLE OF ONIAS (HONYO)**
>
> A temple built near Heliopolis, Egypt, in the second century BCE, which outlasted the Second Temple in Jerusalem. It was founded by priests from the house of Onias after the Temple in Jerusalem was desecrated by Antiochus Epiphanes in the Hanukkah story. Remains of this temple were found in archaeological digs at the beginning of the twentieth century. See further Piotrkowski, *Priests in Exile*.

out the boundaries of the law. The historical framing of Joshua's conquest allows the Mishnah to probe what kind of ownership is needed and when in order to apply the law of *'orlah*.

The Mishnah also discusses rules regarding sacrifices during the periods of the *bamot*, the open-air altars, that according to the rabbinic narrative preceded the building of the first Temple.[27] Likewise, on the list of ritually pure manifestations of the skin condition known as *tzara'at*, the Mishnah includes those that appeared on someone's skin before the giving of the Torah.[28]

This is also how we should understand the Mishnah's directive that priests who served in the Temple of Honyo should not serve in Jerusalem.[29] None of these is history for history's sake; they are hypotheticals, intermediate or marginal cases, that serve to elaborate and fill out the Halakhah. The Temple of Honyo serves as a rare case study to examine the status of Temple service outside Jerusalem that is not idolatrous, in contrast to worship at pagan temples discussed in Tractate *'Avodah Zarah*.

Legal meditations on historical episodes or circumstances belong to a pattern in the Mishnah, namely, the use of farfetched or unrealistic cases to explore the law. How often would one have to deal with the halakhic consequence of a case of "a gentile who cut the field and then converted" (*Pe'ah*, 4:6)? The Mishnah mentions the *tumtum*, someone with no discernible genitalia, and the *androginos*, possessing genitalia of both sexes, thirteen times. This is not based on prevalence, but because these categories serve as test cases for distinguishing between men and women in various areas of Halakhah.[30] The Mishnah's common concern about fifty-fifty probabilities also belongs more to the realm of legal thinking than to the actual world. In the same vein one should understand the Mishnah's disproportionate preoccupation with mixtures—of sacred and unconsecrated, of forbidden and permitted, and so on.[31] In a different kind of "mixture," the Mishnah imagines a situation in which a convicted murderer successfully blends in with innocents: "If a murderer is mixed in with others, all of them are exempt" from punishment (*Sanhedrin*, 9:3). This tests the issue of reasonable doubt in capital cases. All these borderline cases are in fact casuistic methods of probing the limits of laws.

Hypothetical cases can also be used playfully. One almost imagines the Tannaim holding a contest to see who could come up with the most violations in a single act: "Someone can plow one furrow and be liable for eight negative commandments on account of it" (*Makkot*,

The Mishnah as a Composition

3:9); "Someone in one act of eating can be liable for four sin-offerings and one guilt-offering on account of it.... Someone in one act of intercourse can be liable for six sin-offerings on account of it" (*Keritot*, 3:4–5). In the latter examples, some named Sages venture their opinion, showing that these hypotheticals were not the idle imaginings of later editors.

In connection with the *zav*, a man who has an unusual genital discharge and transmits ritual impurity, the Mishnah dreams up frankly absurd scenarios: "If one was lying on six seats—their two hands on two, their two feet on two, their head on one, and their torso on one" (*Zavim*, 4:4); "If a *zav* was on one scale of a balance and food and drink were on the second scale" (4:6); "If one was sitting on a bed and four cloaks were under the four legs of the bed" (4:7).

The Mishnah treats the practical and the theoretical the same. It does not qualify its laws or signal counterfactuality with a subjunctive mood. What is applicable in the Mishnah's day, what happened in the past, what might still happen, and what exists only in the excited minds of halakhists—all are addressed with the same seriousness. There are two complementary reasons for this. First, as we have seen elsewhere, the Mishnah embodies the discourse of the tannaitic bet midrash, where study extended beyond practical law to hypothetical and limit test cases.[32] Second, as a composition the Mishnah is a totalizing legal system, a point to which we return shortly.

One could say, then, that the Mishnah has two warring tendencies: relating to the world that is and constituting an ideal world. The Mishnah deeply concerns itself with life in this world, and no detail is too trivial for it to dilate upon: how various workers should recite the Shema while at work (*Berakhot*, 4:2), what to do when one finds sundry items in the street (*Bava Metzi'a*, ch. 2), or the laws of ritual purity regarding each and every household item (*Kelim*, ch. 24 and throughout). The laws of the Mishnah accompany a person at home and at work, in the marketplace and in the field. It is aware of difficulties in carrying out the law, around which the case story of the *ma'aseh* often revolves.[33] The Mishnah also acknowledges competing realizations of the law, as attested by formulae like "in a place where the custom is to X," "against the will of the Sages," or "the Sages did not stop them."[34]

At the very same time, we have seen equally detailed laws about a Temple-centric world that was no more, and hypothetical ones that wouldn't apply even if a future Temple were built. This is an alternative world imagined by the Mishnah to which the earthly constraints of the present one do not apply.[35]

The intellectual-legal project that is the Mishnah is preoccupied with this world, but it is not tied down by it. The result: regular observances (prayer, ritual purity, and the holidays) happily mingle with defunct practices (the Temple cult) and impracticable laws (kings and capital punishment). Laws of offering sacrifices on local altars before the Temple was built have little bearing on rabbinic Halakhah, yet they too find their place in the Mishnah. Most importantly, the Mishnah deems all of these laws equals and discusses them in a similar style and at the same length.

A clear example of this combination is found in Tractate *Nedarim* on vows. On the one hand, it is full of real-life examples and vivid stories (5:6, 9:10), and meticulous distinctions between actual places (2:4), habits (4:4, 7:3, 8:5), linguistic conventions (3:8), and political circumstances (3:3, 5:4). Indeed, scholars have noted that vows were an important part of popular religion in Roman Palestine.[36] The Mishnah provides good data on this behavior. On the other hand, the tractate is filled with utterly unrealistic cases whose purpose is to examine the operative parameters, especially the relationship between subjective intention, linguistic conventions, and rabbinic policy (3:9–10).[37] The real and the hypothetical coexist peacefully in the same text.

This is a recurring theme in the Mishnah. Whether a law is accompanied by a scriptural prooftext or explicit conceptualization does not affect its standing in the Mishnah. The same is true when it comes to applicability. Everything in the Mishnah is equal before the Law. This solidifies the Mishnah's characterization as a totalizing legal system, an empire of law produced by the tannaitic bet midrash, in which everything is fair game for halakhic analysis.

This brings us back to the question of the Mishnah's authority.[38] It comes not from the Torah, to which it only sporadically refers; nor does it stem from tradition, which is an authoritative source almost solely in Tractate *'Eduyyot*. Human reasoning, in the form of practical or theological rationales, also plays a minor supporting role in the Mishnah. The Mishnah's lack of reliance on any external authority means that it is its own authority. It is essentially a closed system, and a given law becomes authoritative by virtue of being included in this composition.

On account of its unintrusive editors, the Mishnah is not homogenized. Nevertheless, it functions as an all-embracing textual matrix into which its constituent collections gel together and form a complete system. This is genuinely a novelty vis-à-vis Midrash and the Pharisaic tradition that preceded it, and it justifies calling the Mishnah a revolutionary composition.[39] It is this novel, comprehensive system that we identified in the previous chapter as an unprecedented attempt to embody the Oral Torah as a whole.

SIX

Aggadah and Halakhah in the Mishnah

The Mishnah is a distinctly legal work, but it also contains trace amounts of material that has neither the look nor the feel of Halakhah. This material is often labeled Aggadah (literally, "a saying"),[1] which the Tannaim themselves distinguished from Halakhah as an independent discipline.[2] What is Aggadah? Conceptually it eludes precise definition,[3] but in practice it is a catch-all category broad enough to encompass anything that is not strictly legal: moral instruction, practical advice, ethical maxims, legends and stories, and more.

One of Aggadah's main characteristics is its reflexivity. By holding up a mirror to the world of the Sages, it allowed them to get a good look at themselves. This unusual perspective enriched halakhic discourse in more ways than one.

What exactly is Aggadah doing in the Mishnah? True, the halakhic Midrashim and Talmuds all feature some Aggadah, but the Mishnah is a laconic and canonical legal work. Its presence here must be deliberate and integral, which may also account for the miniscule amount of it. This chapter analyzes this aggadic material and its relationship to the immediate halakhic contexts.

A. THE ROLES OF AGGADAH

In a seminal article, Jonah Fraenkel classified the different roles of Aggadah in the Mishnah. The first role is "to explicitly add the moral-religious idea to the legal-halakhic ruling."[4] Fraenkel showed how a halakhic term in the Mishnah can take on a different shade of meaning in an aggadic context, which then enriches the halakhic usage. A mishnah in Tractate *Rosh ha-Shanah* provides an illustration of this thesis:

[7] [. . .] Likewise, if someone was passing behind the synagogue or their house was near the synagogue, and they heard the sound of the shofar or the sound of the Megillah[a]—if they directed their heart *(kivven libbo)*,[b] they fulfilled it,[c] and if not, they did not fulfill it. Even though this one heard it and that one heard it, this one directed their heart and that one did not.

[8] "It happened that whenever Moses raised his hand Israel prevailed, and whenever he let his hand down Amalek prevailed" (Ex. 17:11). Do Moses's hands make or break war? Rather, whenever Israel would look upward and direct their hearts *(mekhavvenim et libbam)* to their Father in heaven, they would prevail, and whenever they did not, they would fall.[d] (*Rosh ha-Shanah*, 3:7–8)

[. . .] וכן מי שהיה עובר אחר בית הכנסת או שהיה ביתו סמוך לבית הכנסת, שמע קול שופר או קול מגילה:

אם כיוון לבו—יצא, ואם לאו—לא יצא. אף על פי שזה שמע וזה שמע, זה כיוון לבו וזה לא כיוון.

[8]"והיה כאשר ירים משה ידו וגבר ישראל, וכאשר יניח ידו וגבר עמלק". וכי ידיו של משה עושות מלחמה או ידיו שבורות מלחמה? אלא כל זמן שהיו ישראל מסתכלים כלפי למעלן ומכוונים את לבם לאביהם שבשמים—היו מתגברים, ואם לאו—היו נופלים.

In the halakhic passage of the first mishnah, intention is determinative. The aggadic teaching in the second mishnah appears here because directing the heart is crucial to its message as well. The link between them is intentional, but Fraenkel argues that the two usages of directing the heart differ: the halakhic one is about the intention to fulfill a mitzvah, whereas the aggadic one is about a conscious connection with God that produces a miracle. Although they both fall under the category of *kavvanah*, "intention," the halakhic and aggadic usage are not the same. Their juxtaposition, though, reveals how one informs the other.[5] The intentionality Halakhah requires in fulfilling God's commandments is not merely having intention to fulfill the mitzvah, in order to exclude rote performance or accidental observance. Aggadah informs us that it is also about being conscious of one's "Father in heaven." Aggadah is Halakhah's handmaiden here, expressing the underlying logic that cannot be captured in legal language.

The second function of Aggadah, according to Fraenkel, is the opposite: instead of undergirding Halakhah, it questions its logic. For example:

a The book of Esther being read on Purim.
b Paying attention to the sound and having intention to fulfill the relevant obligation.
c Their obligation.
d In battle.

> For all seven days a person must make their sukkah[a] permanent and their house temporary.[b] If rain falls, when may one vacate it?[c] When the congealed dish is ruined.
>
> A parable is made: To what is it similar? To a servant who came to mix[d] for his master and he poured the pitcher on his face.[e] (*Sukkah*, 2:9)

> כל שבעת הימים עושה אדם את סוכתו קבע ואת ביתו עראי. ירדו גשמים, מאמתי מותר לפנות? משתיסרח המקפה.
>
> מושלים אותו משל: למה הדבר דומה? לעבד שבא למזוג לקוניו ושפך הקיתון על פניו.

The law dictates that ruinous rain grants permits leaving the "permanent" residence (the sukkah) and eating one's meal in the "temporary" one (the house). According to the aggadic parable that follows, however, the downpour signals that one *must* leave the sukkah straightaway. Halakhic permission becomes aggadic, theological imperative. Since rain is only prayed for after Sukkot ends, its early fall during Sukkot is interpreted as a sign of divine anger. In the Talmud's words, "[God] said to him: I cannot stand your service."[6] From the perspective of this aggadah, to show one's religious devotion by sticking it out through the discomfort is to blithely ignore a warning sign from God and invite His wrath. The parallel tosefta places this aggadah into a series of other signs of divine displeasure broadcast via natural phenomena: "When the luminaries are eclipsed, it is a bad sign for the world."[7] If the king throws the servant's water back in his face, the latter's decision to remain for the rest of his shift, no matter how well intentioned, places himself in mortal danger.

The analogy drawn by this aggadah may even have halakhic ramifications. Should one return to the sukkah right after the rain has passed? If it is merely a technical exemption from the mitzvah, then yes;[8] if it is a manifestation of divine anger, it would be prudent, even imperative, to wait.

Aggadah introduces a different kind of logic into halakhic discourse, one that lives in the spaces around the letters of the law.[9] Here is another example concerning holidays:

> Whoever did not bring the *ḥagigah*[f] on the first holiday of the Festival[g] may bring it for the entire Festival or on the last holiday.[h] If the Festival passed and one did not

---

a The booth for the holiday of Sukkot; see Leviticus 23:40–43.

b The sukkah must be the main residence for eating and sleeping, and the house for incidental use.

c The sukkah, on account of the rain.

d It was common practice to dilute wine with water before drinking.

e The master poured it on the servant's face.

f An animal sacrifice brought to the Temple on the Festival.

g In mishnaic parlance, Sukkot is known simply as "the Festival" (*ḥag*); see Deuteronomy 16:14.

h The *ḥagigah* sacrifice any time during Sukkot, and even on the connected Festival of the eighth day known as Shemini Atzeret.

bring the ḥagigah, one is no longer responsible for it.[a] Regarding this it is said, "The crooked cannot be made straight, and the missing cannot be counted" (Ecc. 1:15). (Ḥagigah, 1:6)

מי שלא חג ביום טוב הראשון שלחג חוגג את כל הרגל ויום טוב האחרון. עבר הרגל ולא חג, אינו חייב באחריותו. על זה נאמר "מעוות לא יוכל לתקון וחסרון לא יוכל להימנות".

In the previous example from Tractate *Sukkah*, rain absolved the person sitting in their sukkah of their obligation. Here, too, the Mishnah phrases the law as an exemption: "one is no longer responsible" to bring the sacrifice on account of the passing of time. The scriptural prooftext from Ecclesiastes, having no straightforward bearing on the bringing of sacrifices, should be considered an aggadic addition, which relays that, although technically one need not buy and bring a sacrifice any more, that does not mean that there is no theological price to pay for missing the opportunity. Aggadah complements Halakhah, adding a different dimension.

The third role enumerated by Fraenkel is Aggadah's affirmation of halakhic discourse and reinforcement of trust in the Oral Torah in general and in the Sages in particular. Beside adding a harmony or sounding a discordant note, Aggadah can sing in unison with Halakhah. The outlier tractate *Avot*, which consists entirely of ethical and religious maxims, does precisely this, as discussed toward the end of this chapter.

In Fraenkel's assessment, mishnaic Aggadah can add a "religious, almost mystical foundation to Halakhah"; articulate "religious obligations that cannot be formulated universally or normatively"; or fortify "trust in halakhic tradition and its Sages."[10] While Fraenkel conceived of these as distinct roles, the situation in the Mishnah is more complex. A single text, like the *ma'aseh*, can exhibit all of them, and it calls into question Fraenkel's conceptualization of Halakhah and Aggadah in the Mishnah as completely different.

B. THE *MA'ASEH*

The Mishnah contains various *ma'asim*, stories of halakhic consequence. Are these Aggadah or Halakhah? Fraenkel classified them as Aggadah, but our earlier analysis showed that they have an important bearing on Halakhah. In chapter 3 we saw examples where the law is plainly a restatement of the *ma'aseh* that follows it, like Rabban Gamaliel's position on the time for Shema derived from a late-night encounter with his sons.[11] To label this Aggadah gives the impression that it stands apart from Halakhah, which is untrue. Instead of saying that Aggadah introduces its own logic into Halakhah, we can imagine distinct, competing logics operating within the arena of mishnaic Halakhah itself. It is not necessarily that Aggadah and Halakhah sit in tension in the Mishnah, but that principles do not always translate cleanly into practice.

a For making restitution for the sacrifice.

The mishnah below presents an excellent test case for these two approaches:

> If someone hires day-laborers and tells them to rise early and stay late, in a place where the custom is neither to rise early nor to stay late, he may not force them. In a place where the custom is to provide food, he must provide food; to provide something sweet, he must provide it. Everything is according to the local practice.
>
> It once happened *(ma'aseh)* that Rabbi Yohanan ben Matteyah said to his son, "Go hire us day-laborers," and he stipulated to provide them meals. When he came to his father, he said to him,[a] "Even if you make them a feast like Solomon had in his time,[b] you will not have fulfilled your obligation to them, for they are the children[c] of Abraham, Isaac, and Jacob. Rather, before they start working[d] go tell them, 'On condition that you only get bread and legumes.'"
>
> Rabban Shimon ben Gamaliel says, It was unnecessary;[e] everything is according to local practice. (*Bava Metzi'a*, 7:1)

השוכר את הפועלים ואמר להן להשכים ולהעריב, מקום שנהגו שלוא להשכים ושלא להעריב—אינו יכול לכופן. מקום שנהגו לזון—יזון, לספק מתיקה—ייספיק. הכל כמנהג המדינה.

מעשה ברבי יוחנן בן מתיה שאמר לבנו: צא ושכור לנו פועלים, ופסק עמהם מזונות. וכשבא אצל אביו אמר לו: אפילו את עושה להם כסעודת שלמה בשעתו, לא יצאתה ידי חובתך עימהם, שהן בני אברהם יצחק ויעקב. אלא עד שלא יתחילו במלאכה צא ואמור להם: על מנת שאין לכם אלא פת וקטנית בלבד.

רבן שמעון בן גמליאל אומר: לא היה צריך, הכל כמנהג המדינה.

Fraenkel characterized this mishnah thus:

> The aggadah is cited here as a *ma'aseh* that . . . does not accord with the law, and Rabban Shimon ben Gamaliel, as Halakhah's representative, opposes Aggadah's supererogatory approach. Rabbi Yohanan ben Matteyah's manner of speaking is characteristically aggadic, because he advances a non-halakhic argument . . . that renders the generic "local practice" inapplicable.[12]

This posits a conflict between the halakhic norm of following the local practice and the aggadic *ma'aseh* that transcends it.

---

    a The father to the son who hired the day-laborers.
    b A grand, royal feast; see 1 Kings 5:2–3 and BT *Bava Metzi'a* 86b.
    c They are like royalty.
    d Because afterward stipulating conditions will no longer be effective.
    e To make the stipulation, because feeding workers is regulated by local custom—no more and no less.

But if we do not rush to shepherd the data into separate pens of Halakhah and Aggadah, we notice that they defy such facile compartmentalization. How does the claim that Rabbi Yohanan ben Matteyah's statement should be categorized as aggadic hold water when it is enmeshed in halakhic discourse and entrains halakhic ramifications? As unusual as his argument is, its concern is fundamentally a practical halakhic one. Furthermore, the higher standard to which the father wants to hold the son is not, in the end, upheld by anyone, because the one advocating for better treatment recommends a workaround that disadvantages the workers. Moving on to Rabbi Shimon ben Gamaliel's comment, the language indicates that it is probably the source for the *stam* opinion at the beginning of the mishnah ("Everything is according to the local practice"), a common pattern in mishnayot with a *ma'aseh*. To top it all off, the Palestinian Talmud treats the entire passage as thoroughly halakhic, and recasts Rabban Shimon ben Gamaliel's opinion as "custom negates the halakhah"—the halakhah, and not the aggadah.[13] All this is to say that the conflict here is between two halakhic opinions.[14]

A second look at Fraenkel's sample mishnayot from the previous section reveals delicate symbioses in them too. For example, in the mishnah in *Ḥagigah* about missed opportunities, the prooftext from Ecclesiastes need not be read as invoking a higher, extra-halakhic obligation. Rather, it can be understood as a warning that accompanies the exemption. The introduction of the verse with the phrase "regarding this it is said" does not bump the discussion to a separate sphere of aggadic obligation.[15] The same can be said for Fraenkel's other examples. When no dichotomy is forced on the text, an interplay between various registers within the same shared space emerges.

This dovetails with Moshe Simon-Shoshan's general finding that no dichotomy between law and narrative exists in the Mishnah.[16] The Mishnah displays a range of narrative strategies: apodictic commands, casuistic laws, real-life examples, brief stories, descriptions of ceremonies. Many of the *ma'asim*, like the one in which Rabban Gamaliel's sons come home late from a wedding, serve exclusively to exemplify the law. In that sense, the *ma'aseh* is one of the Mishnah's many formats for presenting its rulings.

There is one type of *ma'aseh*, though, that is more readily recognizable as pure Aggadah, of the kind encountered in patently rabbinic aggadic works. This is the rare and sophisticated *ma'aseh*, a product of intensive literary design on par with what we find in the Midrash and the Babylonian Talmud. Because the Mishnah itself conveys in some fashion that this *ma'aseh* is distinct, it warrants separate treatment here as an aggadic subgenre.

We will closely read two such *ma'asim* that center on the figures of Hanina ben Dosa and Honi the Circle-Maker. The two were *ḥasidim*, "pietists," individuals who held themselves rigorously to a higher standard of piety. They did not preoccupy themselves with Torah study like Sages; they were not denizens of the bet midrash. They were exemplars of piety and prayer, and both their names, coming from a Semitic root *(ḥ-n-n)* associated with compassion and mercy, reflect on their character. The masses evidently viewed them as having a hotline to God, over whom they held some sway, and as wonderworking holy men. There is a great deal of scholarship on the connection between these Jewish figures and the Christian and pagan "holy men" of late Antiquity, especially Jesus, with whom they share many qualities.[17] The analysis that follows will be restricted to the men and their deeds as portrayed in the Mishnah.

In order to understand the first *ma'aseh*, some background is required. Chapter 4 of Tractate *Berakhot* discusses technical aspects of the silent prayer known as the Amidah: timing, the number of blessings, and appropriate gestures. Chapter 5 consists of laws about the prayer experience itself, including maintaining concentration and contending with distractions. The opening mishnah of the chapter instructs:

One should not stand up to pray except with gravity.

The early *ḥasidim* would wait[a] an hour[b] and then pray, in order to direct their hearts to the Omnipresent.

And even if the king asks about one's welfare[c] one may not respond; even if a snake is coiled around one's heel one may not interrupt. (*Berakhot*, 5:1)

אין עומדין להתפלל אלא מתוך כובד ראש.

חסידים הראשונים היו שוהים שעה אחת ומתפללים, כדי שייכוונו את לבם למקום.

ואפילו המלך שואל בשלומו—לא ישיבנו, אפילו נחש כרוך על עקבו—לא יפסיק.

The *ḥasidim* would spend time mentally preparing themselves for prayer, in order to maximize their concentration and intention. While the Sages were known for their erudition and intellectual acuity, the *ḥasidim* were known for their excellence in prayer. One can reasonably speculate, then, that the directives at the end of the mishnah to ignore the king or a snake also come from the religious ethic of the pietists. For the *ḥasid*, prayer is such a crucial, ecstatic religious experience that it even requires endangering oneself.[18] The Sages, who argue that one should not endanger oneself in order to fulfill the commandments,[19] did not take very kindly to this type of extreme piety at any cost.

The parallel tosefta and discussion in the two Talmuds support the contention that the Mishnah is adopting a pietistic model of prayer here. They cite a story here about the pious Hanina ben Dosa, who was bitten by some kind of reptile, probably a snake, yet did not interrupt his prayer.[20] The last mishnah of the chapter, quoted below, features Hanina ben Dosa the pietist explicitly. Accordingly, chapter 5 of Tractate *Berakhot* begins with pietistic practices and ends with them.[21]

With this framing in mind, here is the *ma'aseh* from that concluding mishnah:

a That is, they would prepare themselves.
b This is not meant literally, but means an unspecified amount of time.
c In the middle of the Amidah prayer.

If someone praying makes a mistake,[a] it is a bad sign for him, and if he is an agent of the congregation,[b] it is a bad sign for those who sent him, because a person's agent is like themselves.

They said about Rabbi Hanina ben Dosa that when he would pray for the sick he would say,[c] "This one lives and that one dies." They said to him, "How do you know?" He said to them, "If my prayer flows[d] in my mouth, I know that he is accepted, but if not, I know that he is rejected."[e] (*Berakhot*, 5:5)

המתפלל וטעה סימן רע לו, ואם שליח צבור הוא, סימן רע לשולחיו, מפני ששלוחו שלאדם כמותו.

אמרו עליו על רבי חנינא בן דוסה שהיה מתפלל על החולין ואומר: זה חי וזה מת. אמרו לו: מנין אתה יודע? אמר להם: אם שגרה תפלתי בפי—יודע אני שהוא מקובל, ואם לאו—יודע אני שהוא מטורף.

Stumbling over the prayer is a "bad sign," but Halakhah does not typically worry about omens. This foreboding forecast sounds as if it has been beamed from the realm of Aggadah, but it may actually touch on the phenomenological core of the Amidah prayer. In the Amidah, one stands before God and entreats the King quietly with personal and national supplications. It is different from a profession of faith, like the recitation of the Shema. This conception of the Amidah has a halakhic ramification concerning the minimal standard of dress.[22] It may also explain why a prayer leader must be replaced if he makes a mistake during the public recital of the Amidah, but he only needs to start over after making a mistake in reciting the Shema.[23] If prayer is a direct encounter with God, verbal blunders may reveal that the community is not in God's good graces, and that they should expect the worst. In the Tosefta, Rabbi Akiva is reported as saying, "If someone's prayer flows in their mouth, it is a good sign for them; but if not, it is a bad sign for them."[24] And if that person happens to be leading the prayers for the entire congregation, then the assembled should view it as boding ill for all of them.

If prayer is a bridge to the heavenly realm, and faltering on its path indicates divine displeasure, then the story about Hanina fleshes this out. As a *ḥasid*, Hanina is said to have enjoyed a close link to God, and, based on the fluency of his prayer, to make deductions about the person at whose bedside he entreated God. Of course, this does not accord fully with the law that comes before it, because there is no mistake here, only a halting or stuttered prayer. The disfavor shown through the hazzan is a delicate divine body language that

---

a In saying the liturgy, because prayer was recited from memory and not from a siddur (prayerbook).

b The precentor leading the congregation in prayer.

c After reciting the prayer.

d Of its own accord, comes naturally to me. On this interpretation see Naeh, "'Creates the Fruit of Lips,'" and Walfish, "Response."

e The sick person will live or die (the grammatical gender indicates that the subject is the sick person and not the prayer).

can only be read by someone as spiritually attuned as Hanina. His sharpened senses can also pick up the exact message from God: "this one lives and that one dies."

The report about Hanina ben Dosa captures the complex interrelationship between the aggadic *ma'aseh* and its surrounding law. In general terms, this case story instantiates the law while simultaneously pushing it in the direction of extreme pietism. This friction, though, pales in comparison to the second *ma'aseh* explored here, the story of Honi the Circle-Maker. Tellingly, prayer is the religious activity here as well, it being a focal point of the pietist's spiritual life.

> The alarm is sounded[a] for every calamity that befalls the public except for an overabundance of rain.
>
> It once happened *(ma'aseh)* that they said to Honi the Circle-Maker,[b] "Pray that it should rain."
>
> He said to them, "Go bring in[c] the Pesach ovens so that they do not dissolve."[d]
>
> So he prayed, but no rain fell. He made a circle, stood in it, and declared: "Master of the World, your children have turned to me, for I am like a member of Your household. I swear by Your great name that I will not budge from here until[25] you have mercy on Your children."
>
> Rain began drizzling.
>
> He said, "That is not what I requested, but rain for cisterns, ditches, and caves."[e]
>
> Rain began falling furiously.
>
> He said, "That is not what I requested, but rain of benevolence, blessing, and generosity."
>
> It fell normally, until Israel had to ascend the Temple Mount from Jerusalem on account of the rain.

---

a The people gather in the public square and the shofar is blown.

b Hebrew *ha-ma'gal*, likely means "roofer," on account of the rolling tool *(ma'agil/ah)* used on roofs; see *Makkot*, 2:1. This epithet of Honi's is preserved in earlier sources, but because the same Hebrew root ('-g-l) is associated with circles, the Mishnah appears to be exegeting his name for its own purposes. (In the story itself, the verb and noun involving the circle-making come from the unrelated root '-w-g.) Since Honi is best known from this story, he is conventionally known as Honi the Circle-Maker. See Noam, *Megillat Ta'anit*, 309–311.

c Honi was confident that the rain would fall immediately.

d They had special clay ovens for roasting the paschal lamb, and they were outside because this episode took place right before Pesach (Passover), at the end of the what should have been the rainy season.

e Rain that will fill the large reservoirs.

They said to him, "Just as you prayed that it should fall, now pray that it should go away."

He said to them, "Go see if the Stone of the Lost[a] has washed away."[b]

Shimon ben Shetah sent to him. He said to him, "You ought to be excommunicated, but what can I do to you, when you come petulantly before the Omnipresent like a son who comes petulantly to his father and he fulfills his desire? About you does the verse say, "Let your father and your mother be glad, and let she that bore you rejoice" (Prov. 23:25). (*Ta'anit*, 3:8)

על כל צרה שתבוא על הציבור מתריעים עליה חוץ מרוב גשמים.

מעשה שאמרו לחוני המעגל התפלל שירדו גשמים. אמר להם: צאו והכניסו תנורי פסחים בשביל שלא ימקו.

והתפלל ולא ירדו גשמים. עג עוגה ועמד בתוכה ואמר: רבונו שלעולם, בניך שמו פניהם עלי שאני כבן בית לפניך. נשבע אני בשמך הגדול שאיני זז מיכן על שתרחם על בניך.

התחילו הגשמים מנטפים.

אמר: לא כך שאלתי, אלא גשמי בורות שיחים ומערות.

ירדו בזעף.

אמר: לא כך שאלתי, אלא גשמי רצון ברכה ונדבה.

ירדו כתיקנן עד שעלו ישראל מירושלים להר הבית מפני הגשמים.

אמרו לו: כשם שהתפללתה עליהם שירדו, כך היתפלל שילכו להם.

אמר להם: צאו וראו אם נימחת אבן הטועים.

שלח לו שמעון בן שטח, אמר לו: צריך אתה לנדות, אבל מה אעשה לך, ואתה מתחטא לפני המקום כבן שהוא מתחטא לאביו ועושה לו רצונו? ועליך הכתוב אומר, "ישמח אביך ואמך ותגל יולדתך."

This *ma'aseh* has received due literary analysis. Scholars have stressed the story's complex attitude toward Honi and his behavior, and examined the figure of the *ḥasid* who comes into conflict with the Sage. Moshe Simon-Shoshan has written a perceptive analysis of the story, and much of the following discussion relies on his reading.[26] He argues that if we peel back the layers, at its core the story is pietistic and presents an idealized figure. As the story progresses, this figure gets enmeshed in two dialectical webs, one with God and the other with the Sages.

The first part of the story begins with the people beseeching Honi, renowned for his piety, to pray for rain. Overconfident, Honi assures the people that the clouds are about to be emptied, but his initial prayers fail to produce even a single raindrop. This leads him to give

a The highest point in Jerusalem that served as a lost-and-found.
b The implication is that it would not be appropriate to pray for the rain to stop.

Aggadah and Halakhah in the Mishnah

God an ultimatum: either He shows mercy, or Honi doesn't budge from a circle he has drawn. God gives in to Honi's demands only reluctantly and gradually, first bringing a trickle and then a deluge. The fact that the rain is described as falling "furiously" after Honi's first demand for a correction leaves little doubt about God's mood.

When the rainfall evens out, a problem remains. The rain continues to fall at a moderate pace, threatening to submerge all of Jerusalem, and Honi refuses to intercede on behalf of its residents. Remember that the preceding law ruled explicitly that the alarm is sounded *(matri'in)* for all calamities *except* an overabundance of rain—in the unirrigated Land of Israel, it's a good problem to have. Within the logic of the story, however, one can interpret Honi's reluctance as the product of strained relations with God. Whatever the cause, Honi comes out looking much like Goethe's sorcerer's apprentice, who knows how to open the spigot but cannot manage to close it.

Now the second act begins, and with it a new conflict. The holy man must answer to the religious establishment—here represented by the rabbinic leader Shimon ben Shetah—which does not much care for his charismatic, idiosyncratic behavior. Shimon charges that Honi is not, as he has styled himself, a member of God's household, but a spoiled brat who always gets his way.[27] As a rabbinic interpreter par excellence, Shimon adduces a prooftext from Scripture. The Sage has penetrated the mystery of God's recalcitrance to make it rain normally. In this he demonstrates his superiority to Honi: the *ḥasid* may have a direct line to God, but the Sage is a master of Scripture.

Simon-Shoshan's major conceptual contribution to our understanding of this *ma'aseh* is his claim that the *ma'aseh* is a blend of two narrative genres: the exemplum and the case story *(ma'aseh)*. In the first, the actions of a figure demonstrate proper conduct—Honi refuses to pray for the rain to stop, as Halakhah requires. In the second, a problematic case is brought to the attention of the Sages and they issue a ruling—Honi's behavior is found wanting by a Sage. Based on the hybridity in this story, Honi is both role model and problem child at one and the same time.

The beginning of our mishnah states that "the alarm is not sounded" over excess rain, which is the Mishnah's way of saying that a public fast day is not proclaimed. With this as the immediate context of the story, it might seem that Honi's actions are being cited as an exemplar for this ruling. But in view of the broader context of the entire tractate, this *ma'aseh* is actually deeply subverting the law. The first three chapters of Tractate *Ta'anit* delineate the series of fasts established by the Sages during annual drought conditions, which gradually intensify the mourning rites and prayers with each unanswered public cry for rain:

[4] If the seventeenth of Marḥeshvan arrived and rain had not fallen, the *yeḥidim*[a] would begin fasting. [. . .]

---

a Literally, "individuals" or "singular ones," referring to the spiritual elite who regularly engaged in or could withstand intensive ascetic practices.

[5] If the New Moon of Kislev arrived and rain had not fallen, the court would decree three fasts on the public. [. . .]

[6] If these passed and were not answered, the court would decree another three fasts on the public. [. . .]

If these passed and were not answered, the court would decree another seven, making thirteen, on them. [. . .]

[7] If these passed unanswered, commerce, construction and planting, betrothals and marriages, and inquiring after people's welfare[a] would be minimized, like people rebuked by the Omnipresent. (*Ta'anit*, 1:4–7)

[4] הגיע שבעה עשר במרחשון ולא ירדו גשמים, התחילו היחידים מתענים. [. . .]

[5] הגיע ראש חודש כסליו ולא ירדו גשמים, בית דין גוזרין שלש תעניות על הציבור. [. . .]

[6] עברו אלו ולא נענו, בית דין גוזרים שלוש תעניות אחרות על הציבור. [. . .]

עברו אלו ולא נענו, בית די גוזרים עוד שבע שהן שלוש עשרה תעניות על הציבור. [. . .]

[7] עברו אלו ולא נענו, ממעטים במשא ובמתן, בבנין ובנטיעה, בארוסים ובנישואים, ובשאילת שלום בין אדם לחבירו, כבני אדם נזופים לפני המקום.

On account of their abilities and stature, the *yeḥidim* begin fasting before the rabbinic establishment requires it of everyone. Their fasting continues "until Nisan ends." One might think to include Honi in this group, but in the story he acts completely outside this rabbinic framework of fasting. When the people approach Honi so that he can intercede, they are all going down an alternative, unsanctioned path to securing rainfall.[28]

Underlying the series of fasts is the notion that God withholds rain as a punishment for the people's sins. During the public fast, the elder proclaims to the public:

"My brethren, it does not say about the people of Nineveh, 'God saw their sackcloth and their fast,' but 'God saw their deeds, for they had turned back from their path of wickedness'" (Jon. 3:10). (*Ta'anit*, 2:1)

אחינו, לא נאמר באנשי נינווה "וירא אלהים את שקם ואת תעניתם"

אלא "וירא אלהים את מעשיהם כי שבו מדרכם הרעה".

If God is unmoved by the people's gestures of repentance, they must be inadequate and gradually intensified. Honi, by contrast, goes full throttle from the outset. He does not

---

a Small talk.

approach God contritely, nor does he comport himself like someone "rebuked by the Omnipresent" when God refuses to cave to his demands.

One could object by invoking the fallacy of anachronism. How could Honi have been deviating from the rabbinic norm if he lived in the Second Temple period before this system of fasts was established by the rabbis? But that is beside the point. Nothing is known about Honi—whether he was a real person, whether there is any kernel of truth to this story (see below). The point is that the placement of this story at the end of the fast mandate shows it to be, according to the Mishnah's own rhetorical logic, an alternative to it. What is the student of the Mishnah supposed to make of this alternative? One is left with the Mishnah's own ambivalence. Shimon ben Shetah finds Honi liable for ostracization, yet he cannot deny that Honi came through when the fasts proved fruitless. A spiritual maverick succeeded where the rabbinic leadership failed to produce results. The story therefore holds out for consideration a theological alternative to mishnaic law, but the dialectical presentation affixes warning labels to it.

To get a better grasp of the story's literary design in the Mishnah, let us compare it to two other versions. The first appears outside of rabbinic literature in the writings of Flavius Josephus:

> Now there was a certain Onias, who being a righteous man and dear to God, had once in a rainless period prayed to God to end the drought, and God had heard his prayer and sent rain. . . . (Josephus, *Antiquities of the Jews*, 14:22)

Its similarity to the mishnaic account is notable, and both relate to the same period: the transition from Hasmonean to Roman rule circa 88–63 BCE. The two must be based on a shared tradition, but Josephus knows nothing of the rabbinic criticism of Honi. Instead, he has him tangled up in the affairs of the zealots, who seek to harness his power for political ends and eventually murder him.[29]

A second, much closer account is preserved in the parallel tosefta:

> It once happened *(ma'aseh)* that they said to a certain *ḥasid:* "Pray that it should rain." He prayed and it rained.
>
> They said to him, "Just as you prayed that it should fall, now pray that it should go away."
>
> He said to them, "Go see: If someone can stand at Keren Ofel and dip their foot in the Kidron River, we pray that rain should not fall. But we trust that the Omnipresent will not bring a flood to the world, as it says, 'and there shall not be another flood etc.' (Gen. 9:11), and it says, 'To Me, this is like the waters of Noah, about which I swore etc.' (Isa. 54:9)." (Tosefta, *Ta'anit*, 2:13)

מעשה בחסיד אחד שאמרו לו: התפלל וירדו גשמים. התפלל וירדו גשמים.

אמרו לו: כשם שהתפללת וירדו, כך התפלל וילכו להם.

אמר להם: צאו וראו—אם עומד אדם בקרן אפל ומשקשק את רגלו בנחל קדרון, אנו מתפללין שלא ירדו גשמים. אבל בטוחין שאין המקום מביא מבול לעולם, שנאמר "ולא יהיה עוד מבול וגו'" ואומר "כי מי נח זאת לי אשר נשבעתי וגו'".

Like in the Mishnah, the *ḥasid* accedes to the initial request to pray for rain to fall but balks at the later one to pray for it to cease. The toseftan version is shorter and simpler, as it is missing those elements that make the mishnaic version thematically and literarily complex: Honi's initial failure, his back-and-forth with God, Shimon ben Shetah's critical barbs. Instead of Honi is a nameless *ḥasid*. The sole goal of the Tosefta's story is to shore up the law: one does not pray for rain to stop.

Given the nature of these parallel accounts, one can speculate—and speculation is all it is—that the Mishnah began with a story much like the Tosefta's, joined it to a tradition similar to Josephus's that identifies the *ḥasid* as Honi, and reshaped it into a tale of conflicts. While in Josephus and the Tosefta the prayer works smoothly, in the Mishnah's account only Honi's ultimatum, with further demands, is ultimately effective. A vestige of the original account may be present when the people tell Honi: "Just as you prayed that it should fall, now pray that it should go away." This sounds like prayer is the key, as it is in the Tosefta. But there is another way to read these lines. Perhaps the people are not quite sure what they are witnessing and what to call it. Is Honi praying? This would underscore the dialectic within the Mishnah's portrayal.

What are the implications of this story for the relationship between Aggadah and Halakhah in the Mishnah? Does the *ma'aseh* undercut the law? Not necessarily. Although it provides an effective alternative, the very fact that the Mishnah reports it as a story and does not reformulate it in legal terms signals that it is not Halakhah but Halakhah-adjacent. This narrative strategy also allows the Mishnah to recognize pietistic phenomena with ambivalence: the *ḥasid*'s attitude toward God is a source of theological discomfort and a potential threat to the establishment, but it is not without value. The Mishnah presents Honi the *ḥasid* as a ghost of a bygone era, so that his actions do not strictly upend the current law. Nevertheless, his path is still demarcated by the Mishnah as an alternative, a problematic but not ineffective one. Seemingly, the Mishnah wants to leave things in this tension.

The stories of Hanina ben Dosa and Honi the Circle-Maker introduce into halakhic discourse theological and metaphysical considerations that are otherwise beyond the purview of pure Halakhah. The deeds of Honi present a pietistic alternative to the overall halakhic procedure of the tractate, and the fifth chapter of Tractate *Berakhot* codifies the extreme practices of *ḥasidim*. The Mishnah's attitude toward the pietism emanating from over the rabbinic horizon is not monolithic; it toggles between adoption, rejection, and tense coexistence. Yet again we see that the sharp division between Halakhah and Aggadah is too pat. The relationship turns out to be considerably more complex and richer, as the *ma'aseh* bears

> **MEASURE FOR MEASURE**
>
> The Mishnah states that "a person is measured by the measure with which they measure" (*Sotah*, 1:7). The reference is to divine recompense for a person's actions, couched in what would have been the familiar language of the market. Buyers and sellers can use generous, fair, or deceptive measuring devices. The Torah already warns of having more than one measure for buying and selling so that the person always comes out on top (Deut. 25:13-16). According to the principle of measure-for-measure reward and punishment, if a person acts generously with others, they will be judged generously in the end, and the same applies to uncharitable conduct. Such a principle is also attributed to Jesus in the Sermon on the Mount: "For the judgment you give will be the judgment you get, and the measure you give will be the measure you get" (Matt. 7:2, NRSVUE).

out. When it is not reinforcing Halakhah, Aggadah is a platform for alternative religious opinions to be aired, a space in which practices that do not belong in regular halakhic discourse—prognostication through prayer or strongarming God—can exist without judgment being expressly passed on them.

The Mishnah, therefore, is interested in preserving and presenting various opinions and options, but also in presenting the norm. The inclusion of *ma'asim* allows it to do both at once: it includes alternative religious or spiritual paths without directly subverting its mainstream halakhic ruling.

C. AGGADIC COLLECTIONS IN THE MISHNAH

In the Mishnah, Aggadah comes in many shapes and sizes. To this point, we have seen brief statements and longer stories, all of which are hooked into the surrounding Halakhah. But other aggadic passages are more isolated and form their own independent collections. These can constitute the end of a chapter, an entire chapter, or the ending of a tractate.

End of a Chapter—*Sotah*, 1:8-9

The first chapter of Tractate *Sotah* describes the ritual for assessing the "guilt" of the *sotah*, the suspected adulteress. The last two mishnayot of the chapter seem to be an independent discourse on the principle of measure-for-measure recompense in the Torah:

> [8] Samson followed his eyes;[a] therefore, the Philistines gouged out his eyes.
>
> Absalom was vain about his hair;[b] therefore, he was hanged by his hair.

---

a Lusting after Philistine women; see Judges 14:1–3.
b And he grew it out for its beauty; see 2 Samuel 25–26.

And because he had intercourse with ten of his father's concubines, therefore ten spearheads were put in him. As it says, "ten young men, bearers of Joab's arms, closed in on him etc." (2 Sam. 18:15).

And because he stole three things, the heart of his father, the heart of the court, and the heart of Israel, therefore three darts were driven into him. As it says, "He took three darts in his hand and drove them into Absalom's heart" (2 Sam. 18:14).

[9] And so it is for good:[a]

Miriam waited for Moses[b] one hour,[c] as it says, "his sister stood far away" (Ex. 2:4); therefore, Israel delayed themselves for her for seven days in the wilderness. As it says, "the people did not travel until Miriam was gathered in" (Num. 12:16).

Joseph merited burying his father, and there was none greater than he among his brothers. As it says, "Joseph went up to bury his father, and with him went up etc. Both chariots and riders went up with him; it was a very great company" (Gen. 50:7, 9). Who is greater than Joseph? For it was none other than Moses who attended to him. And Moses merited the bones of Joseph,[d] and there is none in Israel greater than he. As it says, "Moses took the bones of Joseph with him" (Ex. 13:19). And who is greater than Moses? For it was none other than the Omnipresent, blessed be He, who attended to him. As it says, "and He buried him in the valley etc." (Deut. 34:6). And they did not say this only about Moses but all of the righteous. As it says, "your righteousness shall go before you, and the glory of the Lord shall gather you in" (Isa. 58:8). (*Sotah*, 1:8–9)

[8] שמשון הלך אחרי עיניו, לפיכך ניקרו פלשתים את עיניו.

אבשלום ניתנווה בשערו, לפיכך ניתלה בשערו.

ולפי שבא על עשר פילגשי אביו, לפיכך ניתנו בו עשר לונכיות, שנאמר "ויסובו עשרה נערים נשאי כלי יואב וגו'".

ולפי שגנב שלוש גניבות, לב אביו ולב בית דין ולב אנשי ישראל, לפיכך ניתקעו בו שלשה שבטים, שנאמר "ויקח שלושה שבטים בכפו ויתקעם בלב אבשלום".

[9] וכן לעניין הטובה:

מרים המתינה למשה שעה אחת, שנאמר "ותתצב אחתו מרחוק וגו'", לפיכך נתעכבו לה ישראל שבעת ימים במדבר, שנאמר "והעם לא נסע עד האסף מרים".

---

a Measure-for-measure recompense.
b Watching over him in his basket on the Nile to make sure he was safe.
c i.e., a short time.
d To give them a proper burial in the Land of Israel.

יוסף זכה לקבור את אביו ואין באחיו גדול ממנו, שנאמר "ויעל יוסף לקבור את אביו ויעלו וגו' ויעל עמו גם רכב גם פרשים ויהי המחנה כבד מאד". מי לנו גדול מיוסף שלא נתעסק בו אלא משה, ומשה זכה בעצמות יוסף, ואין בישראל גדול ממנו, שנאמר "ויקח משה את עצמות יוסף עמו". ומי לנו גדול ממשה שלא נתעסק בו אלא המקום ברוך הוא, שנאמר "ויקבר אתו בגיא וגו'". ולא על משה בלבד אמרו אלא בכל הצדיקים, שנאמר "והלך לפניך צדקך וכבוד ייי יאספך".

A single unit, the two mishnayot illustrate the principle of measure-for-measure reward and punishment. Samson and Absalom are killed in ways that evoke their sins, and Miriam, Joseph, and Moses are rewarded in kind for their good deeds.

Why does the Mishnah go to such lengths to establish this exaction of justice throughout Scripture? According to Yitzhak Heinemann, the Sages sought to find connections between everything in our world and to unearth the deep structure beneath the chaotic surface phenomena. God is the invisible warp and woof holding all things together. This coheres into a predictable—and therefore reassuring—worldview, in which every single thing exudes meaning. In Heinemann's view, finding the hand of God in all things is the raison d'être of the rabbinic exegete.[30] But the scriptural verses in the Mishnah, introduced with the repeating formula "as it says," insist on a modification of this approach: the exegete looks for connections within Scripture and not within the wider world. Embedded in Scripture specifically is a concealed order that is invisible to the naked eye but can be seen with the exegete's lenses. By connecting like contexts or phrases with one another, the interpreter uncovers meaning. It is no accident that Samson "followed his eyes" and had them gouged out; it is no stroke of bad luck that Absalom was hanged by the hair he narcissistically grew out. God is author of both the text and the events.

This search for meaning in the biblical text is predicated on the notion that the text holds the key to understanding not just the world of biblical antiquity but the interpreter's own times. The historian Yosef Hayim Yerushalmi wrote:

> For the rabbis the Bible was not only a repository of past history, but a revealed pattern of the whole of history, and they had learned their scriptures well. [. . .] In its ensemble the biblical record seemed capable of illuminating every further historical contingency.[31]

For the rabbis, to uncover connections in the Torah is to find the cables anchoring events to one another across time, and to see God's providence and governance in action.

What does all this have to do with the Mishnah? Why are these two mishnayot on the principle of measure for measure, so emblematic of rabbinic exegesis, placed at the end of the first chapter of Tractate *Sotah*? As we have seen time and again, context provides the key. The immediately preceding mishnayot describe the humiliating ceremony and test administered by the priest to the *sotah* in the Temple:

[5] And a priest takes hold of her garments—if they were torn, they were torn, and if they were ripped at the seam, they were ripped at the seam—until he uncovers her bosom and loosens her hair.[a] [. . .]

[6] If she was dressed in white, he would dress her in black. If she was wearing jewels of gold and chains and nose rings and finger rings, they would be taken from her to deface her. Then he brings a rope of wicker and ties it above her breasts,[b] and whoever wishes to watch comes and watches. . . .

[7] A person is measured by the measure they use:

She adorned herself for transgression,[c] and the Omnipresent[d] defaced her.[e]

She uncovered herself, and the Omnipresent exposed her.[f]

The thigh[g] was first to transgress and then the belly; therefore, the thigh is struck first and then the belly,[h] and the rest of the body does not escape unharmed.[i] (*Sotah*, 1:5–7)

[5] וכהן אוחז בבגדיה—אם ניקרעו ניקרעו, ואם ניפרמו ניפרמו—עד שהוא מגלה את ליבה, וסותר את סערה. [. . .]

[6]היתה מכוסה בלבנים מכסה בשחורים. היו עליה כלי זהב קטליות נזמים וטבעות מעבירים ממנה כדי לנוולה. ואחר כך מביא חבל מצרי וקושרו למעלה מדדיה, וכל הרוצה לראות בא וראה. . . .

[7]במידה שאדם מודד בה מודדין לו:

היא קישטה את עצמה לעבירה, והמקום ניוולה.

היא גילתה את עצמה, והמקום גילה עליה.

ירך התחילה בעבירה תחילה ואחר כך הבטן, לפיכך תילקה הירך תחילה ואחר כך הבטן, ושאר כל הגוף לא פליט.

This denigrating ritual far exceeds the biblical requirement: "The priest shall stand the woman before the Lord and undo the woman's hair" (Num. 5:18). It also sticks out like a sore thumb within the rabbinic ritual landscape. Punishment in rabbinic literature generally

---

a The braids that contribute to her attractiveness.
b Which have been exposed.
c To commit adultery.
d Working through the priest administering the ritual.
e By removing her jewelry and tearing her clothes; see *Sotah*, 1:6.
f By having her clothing removed.
g A euphemism for the pudenda.
h i.e., the womb, causing miscarriage or sterility (see Numbers 5:27); the punishment thus reconstructs and inverts, the penetration of the forbidden sperm—measure for measure.
i The supernatural punishment of the bitter waters, and the woman ultimately dies; see *Sotah*, 3:4–5.

Aggadah and Halakhah in the Mishnah

avoids denigrating the body and particularly preserves the modesty of female offenders: "A man is stoned naked but a woman is not stoned naked" (*Sanhedrin*, 6:3). Even stranger here, the woman's guilt is undetermined when she suffers this humiliation. Only later, once the bitter waters have run their course, is her guilt or innocence known.

The invocation of the measure-for-measure principle of justice is meant to justify this cruel and unusual punishment. It is as if the Mishnah is saying that no aspect of the punishment is worse than what the woman herself did. As she disrobed, now she is disrobed. The fact that her guilt has not been established is moot, because, implicitly, the ritual itself reveals what she has done. In the mishnaic version of the ritual, the sin is assumed to be certain but hidden. It is not a doubt that must be resolved but a secret that must be revealed.[32]

We can now return to the two aggadic mishnayot that are tacked onto the end of the first chapter of Tractate *Sotah*. They provide a raft of examples of reward and retribution being doled out measure for measure, which reinforces the sense that the *sotah*'s treatment is fully in line with the divine workings attested throughout Scripture. The justification falls short, though. It is one thing to explain the working out of God's justice, but the Mishnah's is about the priest's actions in the Temple, which have no biblical support. The implicit argument must be that the priest is carrying out God's will, which is itself evidenced by the many biblical precedents cited. The aggadic exegesis theologically undergirds the halakhic directives here.

An Aggadic Chapter—Sanhedrin, Chapter 10

The last few chapters of Tractate *Sanhedrin*, 7 through 11, enumerate the four types of capital punishment in Halakhah: stoning, burning, beheading, and strangulation. Chapter 10 stands out because instead of continuing the theme of punishment in this world, it discusses biblical personalities and groups who have no portion in the World to Come.[33] The first five mishnayot of the chapter move chronologically from pre-Israelite history (the Flood, Sodom) through the travails of the tribes (the wandering generation, Korah's assembly). Why are they located in the middle of these other chapters? The opening mishnah may contain a hint:

> [All Israel has a portion in the World to Come, as it says, "Your people, all of them righteous, shall inherit the land forever; the shoot of My planting, My handiwork in which I glory"[a] (Isa. 60:21).]
>
> But these have no portion in the World to Come:[b] Whoever says that there is no resurrection, that the Torah is not from Heaven, and an Epicurean.[c]

a The bracketed sentence does not appear in MS Kaufmann; see chapter 7, section C, for the importance of this manuscript.

b The era that will succeed ours, when the dead will be resurrected. See Friedman, *Studies*, pt. 1, and Rosen-Zvi, *Body and Soul*, ch. 9.

c A general term for a heretic, named after the Greek philosopher Epicurus (341–270 BCE) who rejected the notions of personal divine providence and an afterlife. About such a person the Mishnah says, "Be scrupulous to learn what to respond to an Epicurean" (*Avot*, 2:14).

Rabbi Akiva says, Even someone who reads the external books, and one who whispers a charm over a wound and says, "I shall not place on you any of the sickness that I placed on Egypt, for I am the Lord, your healer" (Ex. 15:26).

Abba Shaul says, Even someone who pronounces the name according to its letters.[a] (*Sanhedrin*, 10:1)

ואילו שאין להן חלק לעולם הבא: האומר אין תחיית המתים, ואין תורה מן השמים, ואפיקורס.

רבי עקיבא אומר: אף הקורא בספרים החיצונין, והלוחש על המכה, ואומר "כל המחלה אשר שמתי במצרים לא אשים עליך כי אני יייּ רפאך".

אבא שאול אומר: אף ההוגה את השם באותיותיו.

There are two theories connecting this topic to capital punishment. The first was proposed by Jacob Nahum Epstein, who called attention to an earlier mishnah in chapter 6:

When he was at a distance of about ten cubits from the place of stoning, they would say to him, "Confess!" For it is the way of those to be executed to confess, for whoever confesses has a portion in the World to Come. (*Sanhedrin*, 6:2)

רחוק מבית סקילה עשר אמות, אומרים לו: היתודה! שכן דרך המומתים המתוודים, שכל המתוודה יש לו חלק לעולם הבא.

The execution coupled with a confession suffices to atone for the individual and secure them a place in the next life. Perhaps the entire point of the court putting sinners to death is to enable them to live on in the future.[34] Epstein's proposal is that chapter 10 of Tractate *Sanhedrin* is a continuation of this mishnah. A murderer can confess and attain their share in the World to Come, but some who profess certain heretical beliefs, as detailed in chapter 10, lose their portion.[35] The glaring delay created by this supposition—a separation of four chapters between mention and exposition—should not be counted against it, because the Mishnah is in the habit of holding off on corollary discussions until the original subject matter has been exhaustively covered.[36]

If Epstein is correct, the contrast is as follows: whoever confesses has a portion in the World to Come (6:2), but these have no portion in the world to come (10:1). What about the introduction in lines 1 through 3? It would have to be a later addition, intended to generate a new contrast when the original one was forgotten. This would explain why it is absent from the Kaufmann manuscript.[37]

Epstein's suggestion is problematic. If this excursus were merely an addendum, we would expect it to appear at the end of the whole list of those liable for capital punishment. Instead,

---

a The Tetragrammaton as it is written, as opposed to the traditional pronunciation of *adonai* ("my Lord").

it is embedded within the list of those executed by the sword, positioned between the murderer (9:1–6) and the idolatrous city (10:4–6), with the list of those sentenced to death by strangulation following (chapter 11). This placement raises the question: Is there something specific in the laws of the murderer in chapter 9 that invites this aggadic elaboration?

Hanoch Albeck proposed there is. The end of chapter 9 discusses extrajudicial, non-normative punishments, whether at the hands of religious zealots, the court, or even Heaven. Albeck claimed that the very last words of chapter 9, "at the hands of Heaven," should be identified with losing one's portion in the World to Come, which is picked up with the opening words of the next chapter.[38]

Whatever the case, these mishnah units form an aggadic expansion about the World to Come, which is mentioned by an earlier mishnah in the halakhic context of executions. Why does the Mishnah include this extended aggadic material? Because this first mishnah of the chapter illuminates the Halakhah, a pattern we have observed repeatedly. The lot of the executed discussed in the preceding chapters is not as severe as it could be: they are only purged from this world, while heretics have no place in the next one.

Here, again, we can see that the subsequent collection of Aggadah about people being refused entry into the future world was not formed in situ. The collection was already complete when introduced here to justify the death penalty as a means to live on in the World to Come. It was reproduced here in its entirety on account of its initial material, which is directly relevant. Even so, this does not necessarily preclude the existence of other factors motivating its inclusion. It may well be that the Mishnah also used this entire collection to reinforce a core belief of rabbinic identity vis-à-vis other groups. Formal and content-based editorial considerations are not mutually exclusive.

Tractate Endings—*Yoma*

Aggadah tends to close out tractates of the Mishnah, often in the form of encouragement and consolation. Tractate *Yoma*, for example, concludes with the following teaching:

> Rabbi Akiva said: How fortunate you are, Israel! Before whom are you purified, who purifies you? Your Father in heaven. As it says, "I shall sprinkle waters of purification on you so that you will be pure" (Ezek. 36:25), and it says, "the Lord is the *mikveh* of Israel" (Jer. 17:13)—just as a *mikveh*[a] purifies the impure, so does the Holy One, blessed be He, purify Israel. (*Yoma*, 8:9)

> אמר רבי עקיבה: אשריכם ישראל! לפני מי אתם מיטהרים ומי מטהר אתכם? אביכם שבשמים. שנאמר "וזרקתי עליכם מים טהורים וטהרתם וגו'". ואומר "מקוה ישראל ייי"—מה מקוה מטהר את הטמאים, אף הקב"ה מטהר את ישראל.

a In biblical Hebrew the word *mikveh* here means "hope," but Rabbi Akiva reads it as if it is the rabbinic term for a ritual bath.

This final mishnah of the tractate is strongly connected to the penultimate one:

> Thus did Rabbi Elazar ben Azariah expound, "You shall be purified[a] of all your sins before the Lord" (Lev. 16:30)—for transgressions between man and the Omnipresent, Yom Kippur atones; for transgressions between man and fellow man, Yom Kippur does not atone until one has appeased their fellow.[39] (*Yoma*, 8:8)

> את זו דרש רבי אלעזר בן עזריה: "מכל חטאותיכם לפני ייי תטהרו"—עבירות שבין אדם למקום יום הכיפורים מכפר, ושבינו לבין חבירו אין יום הכיפורים מכפר עד שירצה את חבירו.

On the face of it, Rabbi Elazar ben Azariah mentions purification on Yom Kippur, and then Rabbi Akiva describes its mechanism: a divine *mikveh*. On closer inspection, a verbal discrepancy makes this problematic. The second-to-last mishnah talks about atonement, whereas the last one focuses on purification. What is the role of the ultimate mishnah, then? Is it just to end the tractate on a positive note?

Jacob Levinger perceptively observed that Rabbi Akiva's dictum relates to the entire tractate.[40] The Torah says about Yom Kippur in the verse that Rabbi Elazar ben Azariah quotes, "You shall be purified of all your sins before the Lord." In the rabbinic interpretation, it is the High Priest who effects atonement for the people by performing an exacting ritual in the Holy of Holies. In Rabbi Akiva's metaphorical rendering, it is God who purifies the people, in the same way that a *mikveh* brings purification.[41]

Rabbi Akiva's exegesis, it turns out, is a deviation from the rest of Tractate *Yoma*. The centerpiece of the tractate is the High Priest's service on Yom Kippur. He recites a confession over the he-goat sent to Azazel, begging forgiveness for the entire people, and offers incense in the innermost sanctum. Throughout the long day, he immerses himself multiple times in a very real *mikveh* in order to secure God's atonement. Now along comes Rabbi Akiva, at the tail end of the tractate, saying that God is the sole actor in this drama and that the purificatory immersion is purely metaphorical. The rituals and ceremonies described in such minute detail throughout the tractate recede into the background. While Rabbi Akiva's statement is reminiscent of Honi's actions, which contradict the halakhic core of Tractate *Ta'anit*, it differs in a major way. This aggadah does not present an actionable alternative but a theological reconceptualization. It offers a soft alternative that does not invalidate the halakhah.

D. TRACTATE *AVOT*

There is one tractate in the Mishnah that entirely comprises collections of Aggadah: Tractate *Avot* in *Seder Nezikin*. Its unique makeup and history set it apart from all other tractates. For

---

[a] The connection to Yom Kippur itself is from the omitted beginning of this verse, which reads, "For on this day He shall atone for you to purify you."

Aggadah and Halakhah in the Mishnah

> **RABBI ELIEZER HA-KAPPAR**
>
> Rabbi Eliezer ha-Kappar was a contemporary of Rabbi Yehudah ha-Nasi, and his epithet likely derives from his occupation of making pitch (*kofer*).
>
> A stone lintel discovered in the ruins of Kefar Devorah, located in the Golan Heights, reads: "This is the bet midrash (study hall) of Rabbi Eliezer ha-Kappar." Although in most sources this Tanna's name is given as Elazar, this finding leaves no doubt that his name was Eliezer. On this inscription, see Noam, "A Glimpse."
>
> Rabbi Eliezer ha-Kappar is the only Tanna (beside Rabbi Yehudah ha-Nasi) whose existence is corroborated by external evidence. Although a number of graves found in Bet Shearim list the honorific "Rabbi" on them, their identification with famous rabbinic figures is uncertain. See Cohen, "Epigraphical Rabbis."

this reason, scholars have heaped their attention on it, and it deserves its own separate section here, too.[42]

Due to its non-halakhic character, Tractate *Avot* has fared differently from the rest of the Mishnah. It has no parallel Tosefta or tractates in either Talmud. The one exception is an unusual, late Midrash called *Avot de-Rabbi Natan*.[43] Toward the end of the first millennium, in the Geonic period, *Avot* suddenly soared in popularity, especially because it became the common practice to learn one chapter from it on Shabbat. Since this was around the time of the afternoon Minchah prayer, the tractate was incorporated into the siddur (prayerbook).[44]

The tractate can be divided into three parts: chapters 1 and 2, chapters 3 and 4, and chapter 5. Note that the tractate as we have it today ends with chapter 6, known by its opening words "Acquisition of the Torah" *(kinyan Torah)*. This was added during the Geonic period, when it became customary to study a chapter a week during the six weeks from Pesach to Shavuot, and there were otherwise not enough chapters.

Chapters 1 and 2 uncoil the long chain of transmission of the Oral Torah, beginning with Moses and ending with Rabban Yohanan ben Zakkai and his students. The Mishnah attributes nuggets of wisdom to each scholarly link in this chain. Typically, these take the form of a tripartite aphorism, addressed to budding and mature Torah scholars. The Men of the Great Assembly are according to our source the bridge between the biblical times and that of the later Sages. They reportedly said: "Be deliberate in judgment, raise many disciples, and make a fence around the Torah" *(Avot*, 1:1). In this statement, these scholars consider the role of the Sages as judges, educators, and legislators, and instruct them in properly carrying out their duties in these three spheres.[45]

Chapters 3 and 4 cite further sayings of Sages arranged in chronological order. These rabbis mostly lived after those in the preceding two chapters. The dicta begin with Sages from the final years of the Second Temple era and end with contemporaries of Rabbi Yehudah ha-Nasi, such as Rabbi Eliezer ha-Kappar.

Chapter 5 is a collection of sayings that are unrelated and unattributed. The only thing they share is their use of numbers, which the Mishnah puts in descending order: "The world was created through ten utterances," "Seven types of punishment enter the world . . .," "There are four temperaments."[46]

Tractate *Avot* revolves around the Torah, particularly the Oral Torah.[47] As noted above, since the Oral Torah is epitomized in the Mishnah, *Avot* should be seen as a reflexive justification of the Mishnah itself.[48]

In chapter 3, for example, fourteen of the eighteen mishnayot relate to the Torah or the study thereof in some respect. While concern for Torah observance crops up in this chapter, as in "tradition is a fence for the Torah," the primary focus is on its study. So much so that interrupting one's recitation of the Oral Torah is tantamount to a capital offense. Dicta about Torah study were also appended to the end of Tractate *Avot*:

5:20	Yehudah ben Tema would say:	[. . .] May it be Your will, Lord our God, . . . that you grant us our portion in Your Torah.
[5:21	He would say:	Five years old for Scripture, ten for Mishnah . . . .][49]
5:22	Ben Bagbag would say:	Delve into it and delve into it more. . . .
5:23	Ben Hehe would say:	According to the suffering [of study] is the reward.

Tractate *Avot* may not be halakhic, but it is very much about Halakhah. It is a kind of manifesto justifying and promoting the rabbinic ethos of Torah study. This solves the mystery of this tractate's inclusion in a work of Halakhah. Amram Tropper has shown that the tractate provides a justification of the Oral Torah, and by extension of the Mishnah itself, in two ways. The chain of transmission from Sinai raises the Oral Torah to the same pedestal occupied by the Written Torah,[50] and the aphorisms stress the importance of studying and preserving the Torah and promise a commensurate reward.[51]

This encapsulates perfectly the symbiotic relationship between Halakhah and Aggadah in the Mishnah. Above, we saw that *ma'asim* and aggadic additions are wired into halakhic discourse and cast it in a new light, and here a complete tractate serves the halakhic project of the Mishnah and justifies it from an aggadic perspective.

E. CONCLUSION

What is Aggadah doing in the Mishnah? There is no one answer. We have seen Aggadah exemplifying and extending Halakhah (*ma'asim*), offering a theological justification (measure for measure in Tractate *Sotah*), laying out an alternative path to the halakhic one (Honi's story and the ending of Tractate *Yoma*), justifying the entire halakhic enterprise (Tractate *Avot*). In most cases, Aggadah adds an additional moral or theological dimension to the laconic halakhic discussion without challenging the validity of the halakhic project itself. The most important finding of this chapter is that there is always a relationship, complex and conflicted as it may be, between law and narrative, Halakhah and Aggadah in the Mishnah. This is not true of tannaitic Midrash and the Talmuds, where Aggadah is included for its own sake, with no bearing on any laws. Mishnaic Aggadah purposes to serve, enrich, or otherwise challenge halakhic discourse. The Mishnah is at its core a halakhic composition, and the role of Aggadah is to be its loyal but sometimes critical handmaiden.

SEVEN

The Transmission and Textual History of the Mishnah

The Mishnah underwent its last major round of editing in the third century CE.[1] When Rabbi Yehudah ha-Nasi gave it its final form, did he write it down? To modern ears, the question sounds nonsensical. Authoritative works exist only in writing, be they weighty tomes published in ink or digital editions displayed on screens with pixels. Recall, though, that the Mishnah is part of the Oral Torah. How could Rabbi Yehudah ha-Nasi have ensured the acceptance and dissemination of his edition if he did not write it down?

This chapter shows that the Mishnah did exist for many centuries purely in oral form, looks at reasons for why this was so, and explores the implications of the Mishnah's original orality and its eventual shift to the written medium.

A. THE ORALITY OF THE MISHNAH

Today one encounters the Mishnah in a printed set of volumes. The great rabbinics scholars of the nineteenth and twentieth centuries assumed that this was always the case, that the Mishnah had been published and transmitted in writing from the beginning. How else could the Mishnah's text have remained so stable over nearly two millennia?

Jacob Nahum Epstein made a comprehensive scholarly case for this position. He claimed that the Mishnah was learned mainly orally—one cannot deny rabbinic literature's record on this—but nonetheless written mastertexts were consulted when necessary to check the exact wording and correct the oral transmission:

> They wrote "mishnayot" and "halakhot" in books and "private rolls," which could not be read in public or in the academy, but they could be consulted in

a time of need. Rabbi's Mishnah was also undoubtedly written down by his Reciter.[2]

In other words, the Mishnah edited by Rabbi Yehudah ha-Nasi always existed in writing, even if that copy was not accessible to everyone. Interestingly, in Epstein's particular theory orality and literacy combine in the very same figure: the Reciter. This was the scholarly attendant with a phenomenal memory who committed the Mishnah and other tannaitic literature to memory so that he could reproduce it on demand for the last of the Tannaim and for the generations of Amoraim.[3] Rabbi Yehudah's ha-Nasi's very own Reciter committed his Mishnah both to memory and to the page.

Saul Lieberman agreed with the assertion that the Mishnah was written down, but his conception of the interplay between the oral and the written is more sophisticated. As he imagined it, the Mishnah was "published" orally by having it drilled into the Reciters until they knew it verbatim, and they in turn would publicize the authoritative text with great precision in the various study houses:

> The authority of the college-Tanna was that of a published book. [. . .] [T]he prerequisite for making a Mishnah trustworthy is to bring it into the college and recite it there, i.e. to publish it. Evidently the Tanna was a living book [. . .] After the Mishnah was systematized, and the Tannaim knew it thoroughly by heart, they repeated it in the college in the presence of the master who supervised its recitation, corrected it, and gave it its final form. [. . .] The new Mishnah was thus published in a number of "copies" in the form of living books, which subsequently spread and multiplied.[4]

The "copies" of the Mishnah were embodied in the Reciters, whose job it was to memorize its exact formulation. They provided this text for the masters and disciples to interpret and debate in the study hall. This process is what Lieberman called oral publication, and in the Jewish canon it is unique to the Mishnah.[5]

In the shadow of the Mishnah's predominant orality was a small number of "private rolls" that Sages wrote for themselves. These were of limited extent and use according to Lieberman: "Since all of those writings had the character of private notes they had very little legal authority"; they were "put down only for the use of their writer."[6] The orally transmitted text was checked against these rolls for accuracy. Despite the variations, then, the approaches of Epstein and Lieberman are fundamentally the same.

In the other camp is Yaacov Sussmann, who argues in a monograph-length article that the Mishnah was never written down, not even informally, before the early medieval period. From its editing by Rabbi Yehudah ha-Nasi, through the talmudic period, and into the Geonic period the Mishnah was transmitted and learned exclusively orally: "we are dealing with *Oral Torah in the most literal sense*, a literature generated and transmitted for centuries exclusively orally."[7] Sussmann compellingly demonstrates that most Jewish scholars in the

Middle Ages maintained this view. One notable and influential dissenter was Rabbi Moses Maimonides. In his polemics with Karaites over the Oral Torah, he contended that the Mishnah had always been written down. Nineteenth-century *Wissenschaft* scholars, who felt themselves kindred spirits with the rationalist Maimonides, adopted his minority opinion. This went on to become the standard view of the scholarly community.[8]

Sussmann's proof for the Mishnah's exclusively oral existence is as straightforward as can be: "the simple fact that we have not found a single substantive proof for the existence of *halakhic books* even after so much hard work implies that truthfully they did not exist."[9] This is no weak argument from silence. The Sages often debate the text of the Mishnah, even down to its very letters: whether a word is spelled with an *alef* or an *'ayin*, whether a clause does or does not contain a "not" that reverses the entire binding ruling of a mishnaic law. Yet with all the brainpower in those study halls, no one thought to reach for a written copy and look up the relevant passage? The only logical conclusion, Sussmann says, is that no such copy existed. The Mishnah only existed in the minds of human beings, and not on the parchment of scrolls or the paper of codices.

How, then, was the text preserved? The Sages' entire waking existence was devoted to Torah study, a literal fulfillment of the command to "study it day and night" (Josh. 1:8). They endlessly repeated the text to themselves, so that they knew it by heart and sharpened their memory to razor-sharpness:

> The only means at their disposal for acquiring and preserving their Torah was unceasing repetition; only *girsa*—continuous review of one's studies through oral recitation—could ensure the preservation of the Oral Torah.[10]

This appeal to rabbinic culture, in which unceasing Torah study occupied the top spot on the hierarchy of values, cannot be the full answer. Torah study encompassed the entirety of the Oral Torah, yet the Mishnah merited being transmitted with far fewer textual variants than any other work of rabbinic literature. The answer is the professional Reciter. Although the Sages might have meant it derogatorily when they called the purveyors of their source material "a basket full of books," the very well preserved state of the mishnaic text testifies that they were an excellent, and perhaps even superior, substitute for books.[11] Sussmann was aware that to us, living over five hundred years after the advent of the printing press in a world where literacy is taken for granted, the notion of human beings serving as living books can sound unbelievable:

> We must change our preconceptions and presumptions and accept the simple fact that the Reciters of the amoraic academies were, in truth, the "the living libraries of the academies" who preserved the exact text of the Mishnah. In the scholarship on oral literatures, the prevalent view is that a text absolutely can be just as well-preserved in oral transmission as in books.[12]

Sussmann's proof of the Mishnah's orality is convincing. Not a single source mentions halakhic books in the tannaitic or amoraic bet midrash! But not everyone agrees that the professional Reciters of Sussmann's account, who appear primarily in the Babylonian Talmud, actually existed in the academies of the Land of Israel.[13] The question of how the orally transmitted text of the Mishnah maintained remarkable uniformity over centuries and across hundreds of miles is still a riddle.[14]

B. WHY ORAL?

Why did the Sages refuse to write down the Mishnah, leaving it to the memories of the Sages and Reciters to preserve it and pass it on? To ask it differently and more broadly, why is there an *Oral* Torah at all? Why did the Sages eschew the writing of their voluminous literature? Scholars have propounded a number of theories for this phenomenon:[15]

(1) Martin Jaffee finds the answer in the prevailing culture. In the Hellenistic world, particularly that of the Greek rhetoricians, wisdom had to be transmitted directly from master to disciple. Third-century Amoraim in the Land of Israel developed a similar model of transmitting tradition, with which books would have interfered practically and undermined theoretically. The orality of rabbinic literature is intended to privilege the living, breathing teacher over lifeless ink and paper.[16]

The parallel drawn between rabbinic and Hellenistic culture, however, is only partial and not that helpful. While both cast suspicion on writing and touted the benefits of personal instruction, the Hellenes did not outlaw writing like the Sages did.[17] What, then, prompted the Sages to take such an extreme position?

(2) Israel Jacob Yuval looks not to cultural mimicry but to religious polemic for the key. The Christians possessed the Written Torah, which they translated into Greek and reinterpreted christologically. To keep the singularity of Judaism out of Christian hands, the Jews decided to orally preserve everything aside from the Bible, and hence the Oral Torah was born.[18]

Marc Bregman has supported this theory from a midrash:

Rabbi Yehudah be-Rabbi Shalom said:

Moshe requested that the Mishnah be in writing. But God foresaw that the nations would translate the Torah,[a] read it in Greek, and say, "We are Israel."[b]

The Holy One said to him, "Moses, the nations will say, 'We are Israel! We are the children of the Omnipresent!' While Israel says, 'We are the children of the Omnipresent!' And now the scales are balanced."[c]

---

a A reference to the Septuagint, adopted by Greek-speaking Eastern Christians as canonical.
b Referring to the Christian claim that believers in Jesus are verus Israel, the "true Israel," to whom the divine promises of Scripture were made.
c Since each side makes an identical claim, the true Israel seemingly cannot be determined.

The Holy One said to the nations, "What do you say, that you are My children? I don't know. Only the one who possesses My mystery is My child."

They said to him, "And what is your mystery?"

He said to them, "It is the Mishnah." (*Pesikta Rabbati*, §5)

In this midrash, the Mishnah is the ace up God's sleeve that exposes the deception of the Christians.[19]

While this explains why not a single letter of Oral Torah should be written down, there is a problem of chronology here. *Pesikta Rabbati* is a very late Midrash. When it was composed, Christianity posed a real threat to Jewish continuity, unlike the scattered and persecuted groups of the early centuries CE. It therefore seems unlikely to accurately reflect the mindset of Jews in the time of the Mishnah.[20]

(3) Natalie Dohrmann believes the impetus was not anti-Christian but anti-Roman. Imperial Roman law existed solely in writing. Its writing and publication established its legal force and validity and made all those living in the provinces aware of it. The Tannaim created an alternative legal system suitable for the Jewish minority that could evade Roman oversight precisely because it was not written down. Dohrmann cites a midrash in which the Sages contrast Roman publication in writing with the verbal publication of the Oral Torah:

> Even though a written and sealed edict enters the city, citizens cannot be punished for it until it is publicized to them in the city square. In the same way, even though the Torah was given to Israel at Sinai, they were not punished for it until it was repeated *(nishnet)*[21] to them at the Tent of Meeting. (*Leviticus Rabbah*, 1:10)[22]

This source reflects the model of legal publication employed in the Roman Empire, in which local administrators were charged with publicizing the law. While "the law went into effect when it was given," it was only after it was publicized locally that "the administration and population in any given place were required to fulfill it."[23] The midrash draws a structurally parallel but contrastive analogy between the promulgation of the written imperial edict and the oral publication of Halakhah.

While the evasion of oversight may partly explain the insistence on oral transmission, it can hardly account for the extremeness of the prohibition. By the same token, the argument about anti-Roman sentiment animus overly general. Almost any action of the Sages can be construed as a reaction to or defiance of Roman authority. Why would they want to reject the Roman way of doing things specifically here, when written legal publication had a genuine Jewish pedigree?[24]

(4) According to David Stern, the question at hand has a flawed assumption. Asking why the Sages didn't write the Mishnah down assumes that written transmission is the default or preferred. But what if a text can be preserved faithfully *only* through oral transmission? The moment a text is channeled into written characters, it takes on a life of its own. Copies

proliferate, and the more they are copied the greater the human interference, whether through scribal errors or intentional emendations. Remember that in antiquity, copyright did not exist. Stern writes:

> [O]nce a written text was released—"published," as it were—its author effectively lost all control over it. Not only could anyone copy it; anyone could alter it as well. An oral environment of transmission was far more controlled, and controllable.[25]

This explanation is very reasonable albeit speculative, as no rabbinic source alludes to this.

(5) Yaacov Sussmann's explanation strikes me as the most straightforward: the Mishnah and other tannaitic works have an exclusively oral existence because the written word is the exclusive domain of the Bible. As Sussmann phrases it:

> [H]undreds of scholars living far from one another in different geo-cultural spheres made the conscious choice to refrain from writing down the Oral Torah, and were adamant about having only the one "*Book*," i.e., the twenty-four books of Scripture, which they constantly contemplated, revered, and treated with sanctity, and no others.[26]

To hermetically seal off the word of God from their own halakhic production, the Sages kept their own texts in oral form and preserved one and only one composition[27] in written format: the Bible, "Holy Writ."[28] The rabbinic academy recognized one book, and all others attracted their scathing criticism.[29] To underscore how unique this insistence on having only one book was at the time, one need only glance at the writing of any contemporary learned Christian, where citations of books from all genres, including historiography and scriptural interpretation, happily mingle on a single page.[30]

C. THE IMPLICATIONS OF ORAL TRANSMISSION

Regardless of the exact cause or causes, we possess no written texts of the Mishnah prior to the Middle Ages. Fragments of the Mishnah from the Cairo Genizah date from the tenth and eleventh centuries, and complete manuscripts have only come down to us from the twelfth and thirteenth centuries.[31] The better part of a millennium passed between the editing of the Mishnah and the transcription of these manuscript texts. Even if oral transmission preserved the mishnaic text with high fidelity, it was inevitable that it would undergo changes.[32] Here are some examples of the consequences.

A Second-Order Text

Given the vast amount of time that elapsed from the Mishnah's editing until the writing down of the earliest extant textual witness, even the best manuscripts preserve a second-order text. Consider the very first mishnah of Tractate *Ketubbot*:

> **MANUSCRIPTS**
>
> Until the invention of the printing press, works were copied by hand. These are known as manuscripts, from Latin *manuscriptum*, meaning "writing by hand." Having a work copied was expensive and time-consuming, and, even worse, the end product was invariably riddled with transcription errors.
>
> Christian European society had centralized *scriptoria* affiliated with certain monastic orders, where many scribes churned out copies of books on a constant basis. Jews had nothing even remotely comparable, so every copy was ordered by and made for a single wealthy individual or a community.
>
> Medieval Torah scholars regularly complained about shortages of books, even those that today are the mainstays of the Jewish library, like the Palestinian Talmud and Midrashim. Generally speaking, Jews did not have anything on the order of the massive libraries of the Greeks (e.g., the Library of Alexandria) or the nascent university libraries of medieval Christendom. For the world of Jewish manuscripts, see Beit-Arié, *Hebrew Codicology*, www.fdr.uni-hamburg.de/record/9349, and Sirat, *Hebrew Manuscripts of the Middle Ages*. On libraries, see Bar-Levav, "Libraries."

A virgin is married on Wednesday and a widow on Thursday, because courts sit[a] twice a week in the cities: on Monday and on Thursday. That way, if someone has a claim about virginity he can go early to court.[b] (*Ketubbot*, 1:1)

בתולה נישאת ביום הרביעי ואלמנה ביום החמישי, שפעמים בשבת בתי דינין יושבין בעיירות ביום השיני וביום החמישי, שאם היה לו טענת בתולים היה משכים לבית דין.

This text is universally attested in the earliest manuscripts, including the important Kaufmann manuscript from eleventh- or twelfth-century Italy (see figure 3), and the Parma and Cambridge manuscripts.[33] In both Talmuds, though, the explanatory sentence ("That way, if he had a claim . . .") is uttered by an Amora rather than the Mishnah:

Rabbi Lazar brings a reason for the Mishnah: That way, if he had a claim about virginity he could go early to court. (PT *Ketubbot* 1:1 [24d])

Rav Yehudah said in the name of Shmuel: Why did they say, "A virgin is married on Wednesday"? That way, if he had a claim about virginity he could go early to court. (BT *Ketubbot* 2a)

---

a Convene to hear cases.

b If she is married on Wednesday, he can go to court Thursday morning in the event he finds that she is not virgin (or claims as much), which would render her prohibited to him on account of adultery during the betrothal period. The following mishnayot, however, focus only on the monetary implications of this claim, since a virgin commands a higher ketubah than a non-virgin. Contrast this to the biblical text of Deuteronomy 22:17–21.

FIGURE 3. Mishna, Kaufmann manuscript, p. 94r. By courtesy of the Oriental Collection, Library of the Hungarian Academy of Sciences.

The oral text of the Mishnah that the Amoraim had, both in the Land of Israel and in Babylonia, only contained the first sentence about wedding dates. They sought to provide a rationale for this halakhic ruling and likely looked to the Tosefta, which supplies this reason.[34] At some early date, the explanation cited by the Amoraim was appended to the Mishnah's ruling as a gloss, and so ended up in as part of the mishnaic text in all our manuscripts.[35]

> **GLOSS**
>
> Ultimately from Greek γλῶσσα *(glossa)* by way of Latin, it usually refers to a word of explanation inserted into a text to explain an obscure or difficult term. The term can also be applied to a short explanation of the kind discussed here.
>
> When dealing with written texts, glosses would typically be added by copyists to the margins, and later copyists would sometimes incorporate them into the body of their copy. Since there is no physical separation between items in an oral text, presumably it is even easier for a gloss to be reanalyzed as part of the original text.

From this example and many more like it, we have to conclude that every manuscript witness preserves a text descended from a common ancestor—oral or written—that itself had already absorbed additions, glosses, and emendations. The two Talmuds can sometimes facilitate the recovery of the mishnaic text that the Amoraim were learning.[36]

The Mishnah of the Land of Israel vs. The Mishnah of Babylonia

In trying to recover the Mishnah of the Amoraim, one runs into another problem: the Mishnah recited in the Land of Israel and the Mishnah recited in Babylonia were not identical. This is evident from the extracts of each incorporated into their respective Talmuds.

Before engaging with examples of discrepant texts, it is important to clarify which mishnaic quotes in the Talmuds are helpful for this reconstructive comparison. Students of the Talmud will be familiar with its basic structure of block quotes of Mishnah followed by extensive Amoraic discourse. Nothing historically important can be derived from these quotes of the Mishnah, because they are unoriginal to the Talmud. This entire framework is an invention of copyists and scribes, who inserted quotes from the Mishnah of their own time to break up the long, free-flowing talmudic discourse. The late divergences based on our manuscripts are thus not historically relevant for the period of interest here.

Instead, meaningful differences in talmudic citations of the Mishnah must be gleaned from those that are embedded within the amoraic discourse itself. The fourth chapter of Tractate *'Avodah Zarah* offers an apt example. Halakhically speaking, a Jew may not benefit from objects associated with idolatry. If someone mutilates an idol, the stigma of idolatry and the ban on profiting from it can be eliminated, depending on who exactly that someone is:

> A gentile's idol[a] is prohibited immediately,[b] and a Jew's once it is worshipped.
>
> A gentile can annul their own idol and that of a Jew; a Jew cannot annul a gentile's idol. (*'Avodah Zarah*, 4:4)

---

a Of a god or a Caesar used in worship.
b After its formation.

עבודה זרה שלנכרי אסורה מידו, של ישראל משתעבד.

נכרי מבטל עבודה זרה שלו ושל ישראל, ישראל אינו מבטל עבודה זרה שלנכרי.

This text of the Mishnah appears in the three good manuscripts that preserve the Mishnah independent of the Talmud.[37] But the Babylonian Talmud cites a slightly different version of the Mishnah:

A gentile can annul their own idol and that of *their fellow*. (BT *Avodah* Zarah 42b)

In this instance, the Talmud fortuitously records how this divergence came about:

Rabbi Hiyyah bar Ashi said in the name of Rav:

Rabbi[a] was reciting[b] to his son Rabbi Shimon, "A gentile can annul their own idol and that of *their fellow*."

He said to him, "When you were in your prime, you recited it to me thus: 'A gentile can annul their own idol and that of *a Jew*.'"

He said to him, "No, son, an idol worshipped by a Jew can never be annulled." (PT *Avodah Zarah*, 4:4 [44a])[38]

David Rosenthal uses this text to reconstruct the origins of the Babylonian and Palestinian versions of the Mishnah.[39] In his twilight years, Rabbi Yehudah ha-Nasi recited the text of the Mishnah that we have. This was the Mishnah 2.0, which he had revised over the years to accommodate his evolving halakhic opinions. But to his displeasure, his son Rabbi Shimon dredged up the earlier version formulated with elegant symmetry: "A gentile can annul their own idol and that of a Jew; a Jew cannot annul a gentile's idol." Since Rabbi Yehudah ha-Nasi no longer accepted that an idol worshipped by a Jew could have its taint removed, the second half of the original law was struck down.

The revised Mishnah was brought by the earliest Amoraim, foremost among them Rav, to Babylonia, and that was the version they recited and learned. In the Land of Israel, however, Rabbi Yehudah ha-Nasi's son promoted the earlier version, which became the authorized one there. This led to divergent texts of the same mishnah in the two major centers of learning, both of which originated with Rabbi Yehudah ha-Nasi himself.[40]

In a strange turn of events, in this case it was not the successors of Rabbi Yehudah ha-Nasi on his home turf but the disciples who moved to faraway Babylonia who possessed the most up-to-date edition of the Mishnah. To Babylonia Rav brought the final version authorized by Rabbi Yehudah ha-Nasi, and it was treated as a closed text.[41] In the Land of Israel, the

a Yehudah ha-Nasi.
b The Mishnah.

> ### RAV
>
> The dignified sobriquet of the Babylonian Sage named Rabbi Abba, who straddled the line between the Tannaim and Amoraim, since he studied under Rabbi Yehudah ha-Nasi in the Galilee. Historians speculate that his return to Babylonia catalyzed the Mishnah's dissemination there. See Herr, "Renaissance," 74. Note, however, that the Mishnah was known in Babylonia before this time; see Lipshitz and Rosen-Zvi, "Talmud as Performance," 96n34.
>
> Once Rav resettled in Babylonia, he established the yeshiva of Sura, which was the counterpart to the yeshiva in Nehardea, headed by his colleague Shmuel. Rav is mentioned, usually in debate with Shmuel, hundreds of times throughout the Babylonian Talmud, and their opinions constitute the foundational stratum of talmudic discourse.

cradle of the Mishnah, debate over the mishnaic text continued and it took a long time for the text to fully consolidate and close.[42]

This raises two important considerations for evaluating textual variation in the Mishnah. First, distance from the original proves to be an unreliable criterion for judging the accuracy of a text. Second, the very notion of an "original" text is problematic. Variants can be traced to the time of Rabbi Yehudah ha-Nasi himself, before changes worked their way into the oral transmission, and certainly long before copyists set to work on the written text.

Independent Manuscripts vs. Talmudically Influenced Ones

Most of the textual variants found in the Mishnah, however, did not arise from the final stages of the Mishnah's editing or from the succeeding era of oral transmission. They were the handiwork, literally, of generation upon generation of copyists, each of whom made idiosyncratic mistakes and intentional emendations in their written copies. As a result, the proliferation and distribution of each change were uneven, depending on which texts were used as exemplars and where in the world the copyist was active.

Transcription mistakes, such as accidentally skipping over words, are the predictable product of human error and need not detain us here. But there is copious evidence of copyists also tampering with the text. Why did they do this? Scrutiny of these scribal interventions shows that they were by and large made on the authority of the Babylonian Talmud. This Talmud was far more popular and widespread than the Palestinian one, thanks in no small part to the Geonim of Babylonia, whose sway made it the halakhically dominant text in the Middle East, North Africa, and, later, Europe. In the Middle Ages, very few people in Europe or the Middle East learned the Mishnah independent of its interpretation in the Babylonian Talmud. The Babylonian Talmud had become the main text of study; it was copied many times and was the subject of numerous commentaries. The Mishnah ceased, for the most part, to be copied as an independent text, and was always accompanied—dwarfed really—by the surrounding discourse of the Babylonian Talmud. This means that there were very few medieval manuscripts of the Mishnah sans commentary, and that as more and more people learned and lived by the Babylonian Talmud, its interpretations of the Mishnah began to creep into the written text of the Mishnah itself.

To further complicate matters, Maimonides partly uncoupled the Mishnah from the text of the Babylonian Talmud with his very popular Judeo-Arabic commentary on the Mishnah. Beginning in the thirteenth century, the Mishnah was copied as an independent work together with Maimonides's commentary. But this did not restore the Mishnah's independence of the Babylonian Talmud; to the contrary, it deepened it. Maimonides had access to the mishnaic text found in the good manuscripts, but he emended it to conform to the authoritative Babylonian Talmud, which he believed the mishnaic text could not contradict. Therefore, the text of the Mishnah in all of these copies is a hybrid text dependent on the discussions of the Babylonian Talmud. Given the celebrity of Maimonides as a Torah scholar and leader, and the accessibility of his vernacular commentary, this text was copied time and again and increasingly accumulated glosses and emendations. When the Mishnah was finally printed in the sixteenth century, printers used this version of the mishnaic text. Following this tortuous route, additions based on the Babylonian Talmud ended up in the printed Mishnah.

Recall from the previous chapter that chapter 10 of Tractate *Sanhedrin* begins with a contrastive statement: "But these have no portion in the World to Come" (*Sanhedrin*, 10:1). According to one of the two explanations offered there, this was originally a continuation of a much earlier mishnah in chapter 6. Over time, the gap between these mishnayot led some to miss the connection and drove them to find a new contrast for the "but." This led to an insertion: "All Israel has a portion in the World to Come, as it says, 'Your people, all of them righteous, shall inherit the land forever; the shoot of My planting, My handiwork in which I glory' (Isa. 60:21)."

In what mishnaic texts does this appear exactly? To dispel confusion, I will put the stages of the Mishnah's textual history in a tentative and rough chronological order:

1. Rabbi Yehudah ha-Nasi's versions adopted in the Land of Israel and Babylonia.
2. Amoraic discourse in the two Talmuds.
3. Independent manuscripts of the Mishnah.
4. Quotes of the Mishnah added by copyists to manuscripts of the Babylonian Talmud.
5. Printed editions of the Mishnah.

The sentence under discussion seems to be late, because neither Talmud addresses it (stage 2), nor is it present in the independent manuscript witnesses of the Mishnah (stage 3).[43] The fact that it appears in a quote of the Mishnah in all manuscripts of the Babylonian Talmud (stage 4) points to a version of the Mishnah influenced by study of that Talmud. Therefore, at some point between the Babylonian Amoraim (who did not yet know this sentence) and

FIGURE 4. Mishna, Kaufmann manuscript, p. 152r. By courtesy of the Oriental Collection, Library of the Hungarian Academy of Sciences.

the extant medieval copies of the Talmud (which universally include it) this sentence was added to a quotation of the Mishnah, and thence inserted into the printed Mishnah as well (stage 5). It is impossible to determine from where this sentence was taken, but it certainly was borrowed from some existing tannaitic or liturgical source and not created as an ad hoc solution.[44]

This mishnah has another, if more subtle, addition in its continuation.

> But these have no portion in the World to Come: Whoever says that there is no resurrection [from the Torah], that the Torah is not from Heaven, and an Epicurean. (*Sanhedrin*, 10:1)

ואילו שאין להן חלק לעולם הבא: האומר אין תחיית המתים [מן התורה], ואין תורה מן השמים, ואפיקורס.

The bracketed phrase, "from the Torah," does not appear in any of the good manuscript witnesses of the Mishnah (stage 3) (see the image for MS Kaufmann, figure 4). In them, the point is the denial not of a biblical basis for resurrection but of resurrection itself; "whoever says that there is no resurrection"—period.

What is the source of the added phrase? It can be easily traced to the Babylonian Talmud, which attempts to prove that resurrection is "from the Torah" from a series of allusions. If the Talmud spends so much time trying to cast a textual anchor in the Torah that will find purchase, one can see how a medieval copyist-scholar familiar with this passage would add "from the Torah" to the text of the Mishnah (stage 4).

These three little words bear a lot more weight than is appreciable at first glance. In the mishnaic period, the very belief in resurrection was rejected or limited by some Jewish sects. For the Sages, denial of this tenet meant losing one's portion in the World to Come.[45] By the time of the Babylonian Talmud, i.e., the Amoraic period, this belief had become entrenched among rabbinic Jews, and the only question worth pursuing was how to latch it onto Scripture.[46]

The passage of time from the creation of a text to its reading hundreds of years later generates misunderstandings. Sometimes, it is because the reader misses the relevant cues, at other times it is because the cultural or religious temperature has changed so much that it exerts sufficient pressure on the reader to force a reinterpretation. The small addition of "from the Torah" speaks volumes about the changing state of rabbinic theology in late Antiquity. Paying attention to subtle textual transformations can help measure the temporal flow of ideas beyond the static letters of the text.

If the Babylonian Talmud, reflecting the beliefs held by its scholars, is the direct source for this insertion, why don't all of the independent manuscripts of the Mishnah contain the change? Every manuscript of the Mishnah postdates the existence of the Babylonian Talmud by several centuries, so how did any escape its all-pervasive influence? The answer is bound up with how the Mishnah was studied by medieval scholars. In the Jewish world, Italy and Byzantium were unique holdouts that preserved a tradition of independent study of the Mishnah.[47] All three extant manuscripts of the entire Mishnah that have been mentioned above (Kaufmann, Parma, and Cambridge) come from this region.[48] They reflect a mishnaic text that usually evaded, so to speak, the invasion of the Babylonian Talmud.

These manuscripts are important not only for recovering the unadulterated mishnaic text, but also for reconstructing mishnaic Hebrew. Yehezkel Kutscher and his students have documented how these manuscripts preserve authentic aspects of the Hebrew spoken by the Sages, whereas other manuscripts influenced by the Babylonian Talmud have been "corrected" to match later Hebrew, which was literary and not spoken, and talmudic Aramaic. Rabbi Akiva's name, for example, is conventionally spelled with a final *alef*, a marker of Aramaic influence. The spelling of Akiva attested in all of the good manuscripts is with a final *he*, which is how it would have been written in mishnaic Hebrew.

One final example bears out the difficulty in trying to draw conclusions from the textual witnesses at our disposal:

If someone found debt documents[a]

If they contain a lien,[b] then one should not return them,[c] <u>for the court will collect from them;</u>[d]

if they do not contain a lien, then one should return them, <u>because the court will not collect from them</u>—the words of rabbi Meir.

But the Sages say, In neither case should one return them, <u>because the court will collect from them.</u> (*Bava Metzi'a*, 1:6)

מצא שטרי חוב - אם יש בהם אחריות נכסים לא יחזיר <u>מפני שבית דין ניפרעים מהן</u>.

אין בהם אחריות נכסים יחזיר <u>מפני שאין בית דין ניפרעים מהן</u>, דברי ר' מאיר.

וחכמים אומרים: בין כך ובין כך לא יחזיר <u>מפני שבית דין ניפרעים מהן</u>.

Three times (in the underlined portions) this mishnah reiterates its reasoning that the court will or won't collect on the strength of the documents, a rarity for the laconic Mishnah. What does the textual evidence tell us about this oddity?

The good manuscripts of the Mishnah (stage 3) do not have the first underlined occurrence in Rabbi Meir's opinion but do have the other two. One can speculate that this was filled in later to bring balance to the whole, since the other alternatives mentioned give this reason. Going back even further in time, the Talmuds show that the text learned by the Amoraim did not have any reasoning in their Mishnah (stage 2).[49] All three explanations stem from the amoraic commentary on this mishnah in the Babylonian Talmud. Therefore, one can say with confidence that the original Mishnah had no explanations. At some point in the Middle Ages (stage 4), two explanations were added based on study of the Babylonian

---

    a Recording a loan.
    b On property, so that if the debt is not repaid it can be collected from real estate.
    c To the lender.
    d The amount of the loan from the property using this document, even though perhaps this debt was already repaid.

Talmud, and then at some later point in the medieval period a third explanation was inserted to round out the mishnah.

To reemphasize, even our best manuscripts (stage 3) preserve a second-order text that is a step down from the "pristine" original (stage 1). Even when speaking in unison, these manuscripts can deceive the textual historian. Consequently, the text of the Mishnah must be checked against the pertinent talmudic passages to see what the Amoraim had in their Mishnah (stage 2), and the Babylonian Talmud itself must be considered a powerful source of potential changes.

To summarize, the textual history of the Mishnah is quite complicated. Oral transmission of the Mishnah means that the written copies extant today date from nearly a millennium after its editing by Rabbi Yehudah ha-Nasi. Splits between textual versions occurred already during the long period of oral transmission, but they increased exponentially once the Mishnah was set in writing and the Babylonian Talmud became the primary object of study. Changes to the mishnaic text occurred in all periods and in all its forms. Sometimes, with judicious use of the two Talmuds, one can follow the trail back to their point of origin. On rare and lucky occasions, the divergence can even be located within the lifetime of Rabbi Yehudah ha-Nasi himself.

APPENDIX: A BRIEF SURVEY OF THE MISHNAH'S RECEPTION HISTORY

After the Mishnah's oral publication, scholars in the Land of Israel continued to devote time to studying it on its own, without the elaboration of the talmudic commentarial traditions.[50] This practice made its way, along with many other Palestinian traditions, to Italy, birthplace of the extant full copies of the Mishnah. From there it traveled to France, where Rabbi Samson of Sens, a leading French Tosafist of the late twelfth century, wrote commentaries on *Seder Zera'im* and *Seder Teharot*, which lack dedicated commentary in the Babylonian Talmud (aside from tractates *Berakhot* and *Niddah*). By contrast, on the Iberian Peninsula Jews continued the Babylonian-Geonic tradition of learning Mishnah only during study of the Babylonian Talmud. Even when Maimonides reestablished independent Mishnah study in the thirteenth century by prying it apart from its talmudic commentary, the Judeo-Arabic commentary he composed for it integrated the definitions and halakhic conclusions of the Babylonian Talmud. Mishnah study was still being filtered through talmudic analysis.

In the sixteenth century, two revolutionary developments, one in the wider world and the other in the Jewish one, changed Mishnah study permanently: the advent of print and the development of Safedian Kabbalah.

The entire Mishnah was first printed in Naples, Italy, by Joshua Solomon Soncino in 1492. It made the Mishnah widely available, and, as noted above, its text was based on Maimonides's hybrid Mishnah and was accompanied by his commentary. Subsequent editions comprised three volumes covering *Seder Zera'im* and *Seder Teharot*, with the commentaries of Maimonides and Samson of Sens, printed by Daniel Bomberg in Venice in the 1520s. With the

> **THEOSOPHICAL KABBALAH**
>
> One branch of Kabbalah, the esoteric traditions about God and the universe that emerged in thirteenth-century Europe, is theosophical, that is, it consists of speculation about ten aspects, dimensions, or emanations of God called *sefirot*, which together compose the Godhead. The ideas and doctrines changed over time, as did their language of expression, alternately tending toward the philosophical and the mythical. In sixteenth-century Safed, Rabbi Isaac Luria systematized and extensively elaborated this Kabbalah, and his teachings quickly conquered the Jewish world via his disciples.
>
> In this lore, the *sefirot* bridge the Infinite God with the finite universe. They are assigned various names that refer to their unique characteristics or anchor them to a scriptural verse, and they are also gendered. The lowest *sefirah* that Kabbalah conceives of as closest to the human realm is *Malkhut*, and it represents the divine feminine. All manner of things can be plotted along this divine emanatory scheme. For example, the *sefirah* known as *Tif'eret* can be symbolized by or identified with the Written Torah, and the same can be said for *Malkhut* and the Oral Torah.

printing of the Mishnah as an independent book, scholars set their hand to composing their own learned commentaries. The first popular, comprehensive commentary was written by Rabbi Obadiah of Bertinoro in Italy in the sixteenth century. It was followed in the early seventeenth century by *Tosefot Yom Tov*, composed by Rabbi Yom Tov Lippmann Heller in Central Europe. Dissemination and learning of the Mishnah grew by leaps and bounds.[51]

In sixteenth-century Safed, the Mishnah played an unusually important role in the lives and theories of its kabbalists. Aaron Ahrend writes:

> [The Mishnah] was conceived of as an embodiment of the Oral Torah, which was symbolized by the *sefirah* of *Malkhut*, representative of divine femininity. The *Shekhinah* reveals herself on account of Mishnah study, and is herself represented as the Mishnah. Kabbalists were thus known to have revelatory experiences following Mishnah study. Famously, in the context of Mishnah recitation Rabbi Joseph Caro was visited by a *maggid* (mystical guide)—*Shekhinah* herself—with which he carried on conversations.[52]

The most famous account of such mystical experiences was written by Rabbi Solomon Alkabetz. He recounted how on Shavuot of 1533 the *Shekhinah* was revealed in the guise of the Mishnah to a group of Torah scholars, including the great halakhist Caro, when they spent the night immersed in study.[53] Note that in these mystical contexts the Mishnah was being verbally recited rather than intellectually studied, ruminated on verbally rather than cognitively, and its staccato clauses and formulaic language perhaps produced a rhythm that could induce a trance and alter one's consciousness.

The Mishnah saw use in other contexts as well. The Cairo Genizah attests to this fact in liturgical poems and inventories preserved therein.[54] It is the traditional practice to study the Mishnah in a house of mourning to assist the soul of the recently deceased.[55]

Areas that remained under the cultural influence of the Land of Israel continued the ancient practice of treating the Mishnah as an independent work. The Mishnah's independent profile was raised in other parts of the Jewish world when Maimonides's Mishnah commentary conquered the Jewish world, first in the original and then in translation. But Amnon Raz-Krakotzkin argues that recognition of the Mishnah as an independent composition only fully materialized upon its printing. Interestingly, Christians had a large role to play in this. Whenever they prohibited Jews from studying the Talmud the Mishnah saw a printing surge:

> When copies of the Talmud were destroyed, the Mishnah was printed with the imprimatur of the Church. [. . .] Prohibition and permission were two sides of the same coin, a kind of "purification" and differentiation between the Mishnah, which in that period was also considered by Christian authorities to be an expression of "the truth of the Hebrews," that is, ancient authentic knowledge, and the Talmud, which was taken as evidence of the Jew's deviation from the Mosaic Torah and his adherence to a work that combined nonsense with anti-Christian vitriol.[56]

All agree that by the sixteenth century there had been a swerve in the Mishnah's reception history. The question is, was this the first time since late Antiquity that the Mishnah was universally conceived of as an independent composition? The issues are complex, involving as they do questions of methodology (what constitutes a composition? what is considered independent? who makes that call?) and factual ones. To date, there has been no comprehensive study of the Mishnah's reception, from the final redaction of the Babylonian Talmud into the era of print, that bases itself on the rich range of primary sources (manuscripts and fragments) and secondary ones (quotations by Geonim and medieval authorities and appearances in other media).

EIGHT

The Tosefta and the Mishnah

Throughout the preceding chapters, the Tosefta[1] has served as a point of comparison for discussion of the Mishnah. This chapter examines the connections between the two under a high-powered lens and discusses some of the scholarly accounts of their multifaceted relationship.[2]

The Tosefta (literally, "addition") is a tannaitic work, and it has a parallel tractate for every one of the Mishnah's except four: Tractate *Avot*, which is exceptional in nature and content,[3] and tractates *Tamid*, *Middot*, and *Kinnim*, perhaps on account of their antiquity.[4] The Tosefta's editing took place after the Mishnah's, but how much later is debated. Some scholars have pushed its editing all the way to the post-talmudic period, but most place it only a generation or two after the Mishnah's editing was completed.[5] And for good reason: the Tosefta's language is mishnaic Hebrew, its style is similar,[6] and it has the same roster of Sages, barring a handful who lived in the generation after Rabbi Yehudah ha-Nasi.[7]

What is the raison d'être of the Tosefta and how does it relate to the Mishnah? In the tenth century, Torah scholars in North Africa asked Sherira Gaon this exact question about the author-compiler of the Tosefta, identified by tradition as Rabbi Hiyya:

> Why did Rabbi Hiyya see fit to write it? If it is a supplement that clarifies matters in the Mishnah, why didn't Rabbi [Yehudah ha-Nasi] write them? After all, they are reported in the name of mishnaic Sages![8]

Sherira's answer, versions of which are accepted today in scholarship, is that Rabbi Hiyya was expansive where Rabbi Yehudah ha-Nasi was concise.[9] The length of the Tosefta far surpasses that of the Mishnah—a typical tractate has many more *halakhot*—but the additional bulk cannot be satisfactorily attributed to elaborations on concise mishnaic rulings.[10] The Tosefta has a wider embrace: it incorporates halakhic opinions, midrashic interpretations, and other material neglected by the Mishnah.

Its proportion of aggadic material is also greater than the Mishnah's and it preserves extended, unabridged collections of Aggadah.[11] A case in point is the aggadah about measure-for-measure recompense at the end of the first chapter of Tractate *Sotah* in the Mishnah, analyzed in chapter 6. Where the Mishnah's aggadah consists of two mishnayot, the Tosefta's spans nearly two chapters, adducing many additional examples from Scripture for this and similar theological principles.[12]

The Mishnah and Tosefta are intricately interrelated on multiple levels. The Mishnah itself only came into being over a long period, after which it underwent protracted editing and experienced uneven transmission. There is no reason to suppose the Tosefta had a shorter, straighter route from start to finish. That their paths would meet, cross, and overlap at many points is to be expected. The sections below endeavor to map some of this complex network of confluences.

A few words need to be said first about the text of the Tosefta being used here. The Tosefta in its entirety is preserved in only one manuscript, MS Vienna from late thirteenth-century Spain,[13] because, like the Mishnah, the Tosefta was not typically learned on its own. Learners usually encountered it through the sporadic quotations of segments of it in the Bavli. The divisions between the Tosefta's smallest constituent parts, which like the Mishnah's are termed *halakhot*, vary from manuscript to manuscript, so we will use the conventional ones found in the standard printed edition.[14] This chapter discusses the text of the Tosefta as we have it and does not dwell too much on speculative theories about its origins.[15]

A. THE TOSEFTA AS MISHNAIC COMPLEMENT

Contrary to the Mishnah, which presents itself as a standalone work, the Tosefta does not hide its dependency on the Mishnah. For example, the Tosefta asks and answers: "Why did they say 'the morning prayer is until midday'? Because the daily morning sacrifice is brought until midday" (Tosefta, *Berakhot*, 3:1). Who is "they"? The Sages of the Mishnah, as we find this exact clause there (*Berakhot*, 4:1). The Tosefta presumes that students know their Mishnah and so can present its traditions and teachings as commentary.

Any mishnaic law is fair game for exposition in the Tosefta. In one place, the Mishnah presents an abstract rule, which the Tosefta restates with an explanation:

Mishnah, *Bava Kamma*, 1:2	Tosefta, *Bava Kamma*, 1:1
I have enabled the damage of anything I am responsible to guard.	I have enabled the damage of anything I am responsible to guard—this is the ox and the pit.

The Tosefta was dissatisfied with the mishnaic abstraction ("anything"), so it concretized it ("this is").[16]

Very often, the Tosefta quotes or paraphrases the Mishnah, asks "How so?," and then explains it. Here is an example of this clarificatory format:

Mishnah, *Bava Metzi'a*, 4:1	Tosefta, *Bava Metzi'a*, 3:13
Gold acquires silver, but silver doesn't acquire gold.	"Gold acquires silver." How so? If someone gave him …
Copper acquires silver, but silver doesn't acquire copper.	"Copper acquires silver." How so? If someone gave him …

The Tosefta's clarification can be achieved by giving examples, as above, or by supplying unstated reasoning, as below:

> Rabbi Yehudah says, Even a Torah scroll, a domesticated animal, and a pearl have no price gouging. (Mishnah, *Bava Metzi'a*, 4:9)

> רבי יהודה אומר: אף ספר תורה, ובהמה, ומרגלית אין להם הוניה.

> Rabbi Yehudah says, A Torah scroll, a domesticated animal, and a pearl[a] have no price gouging.[b] A Torah scroll because it is invaluable; a domesticated animal and a pearl because one wants to pair them.[c] (Tosefta, *Bava Metzi'a*, 3:24)

> רבי יהודה אומר: ספר תורה, בהמה, ומרגלית אין להן אונאה. ספר תורה—מפני שאין לו דמים; בהמה ומרגלית—מפני שרוצה לזווגן.

The Mishnah characteristically does not reveal its reasons, even though it has them.[17] The Tosefta often steps in to fill in the obvious blank.

In the best of cases, the Tosefta announces that it is commenting on the Mishnah. "Why did they say X?" is the equivalent of providing a chapter-and-verse reference. But it is not always so explicit. Contextualizing a line in the Tosefta can require serious sleuthing. In Tractate *Berakhot*, the Tosefta includes an aggadic dictum:

> Rabbi Akiva says, If someone's prayer flows in their mouth, it is a good sign for them; but if not, it is a bad sign for them. (Tosefta, *Berakhot*, 3:3)

> רבי עקיבא אומר: אם שגורה תפלתו בפיו, סימן יפה לו, ואם לאו, סימן רע לו.

a Any precious stone.
b One does not violate a prohibition by selling them for a very high price, as there is no stable market value for such items.
c With another in their possession, and therefore is willing to pay a higher price for a specific specimen.

This has no connection to any of the surrounding material in this tosefta, so its original context must be elsewhere. The parallel mishnah has a tannaitic debate about how many blessings one must say in the Amidah. Rabbi Akiva's view is an intermediate one:

> Rabban Gamaliel says, A person must pray eighteen every day.
>
> Rabbi Yehoshua says, An abstract of eighteen.
>
> Rabbi Akiva says, If someone's prayer flows in their mouth, one prays eighteen; but if not, an abstract of eighteen. (Mishnah, *Berakhot*, 4:3)

> רבן גמליאל אומר: בכל יום אדם מתפלל שמונה עשרה. רבי יהושע אומר: מעין שמונה עשרה. רבי עקיבה אומר: אם שגרה תפילתו בפיו, מתפלל שמונה, ואם לאו, מעין שמונה עשרה.

This debate provides the context for the appearance of the aggadic dictum in the Tosefta. Rabbi Akiva's halakhic opinion hinges on the fluidity of one's prayers, so the Tosefta adds an aggadic assertion, also by Rabbi Akiva, that explains the significance of the mishnaic criterion of "prayer fluency." The Tosefta relates directly to a line in the Mishnah without indicating it in any way.

Similarly, the Tosefta at the beginning of Tractate *Berakhot* cites a dispute between Rabbi Yehudah ha-Nasi and Rabbi Natan whether the night is divided into three or four watches. As in the previous example, this debate does not relate to anything before or after it. The trigger is once again in the Mishnah. Rabbi Eliezer's opinion in the first mishnah of Tractate *Berakhot* states that one may recite the nighttime Shema until "the end of the first watch." The Tosefta (like the two Talmuds) wants to know the complete number of watches in order to determine when "the end of the first watch" occurs.

In a way, then, the Tosefta is a running commentary on the Mishnah, even though it is not always plain to see. Trying to read it straight through would be akin to reading footnotes without the body of the text.

The Tosefta complements the Mishnah in a variety of ways, including explanation and elaboration, and the addition of a dissenting opinion or an alternative tradition.[18] Examples of every type of complementarity will be illustrated using the first chapter of Tractate *Sotah* in both compendia.

Explanation

In this example of an explanatory tosefta, the parallel material is underlined for clarity. The Tosefta says:

> What is the *initial testimony*? The testimony of seclusion.[a] The *second*? The testimony of impurity.[b] (Tosefta, *Sotah*, 1:2)

    a That the *sotah*, a wife suspected of adultery, secluded herself with another man in spite of her husband's explicit "warning."

    b That the wife lay with the man her husband warned her against; for the language, see Numbers 5:13.

אי זו היא עדות הראשונה? זו עדות סתירה. שניה, זו עדות טומאה.

This is clearly commentary, but what is the original text? The relevant references are found only in chapter 6 of Tractate *Sotah*:

> [2] If one witness said, "I saw her become impure," she would not drink.[a] [. . .]
>
> [3] For it would have been logical:[b] If the *initial testimony*,[c] which does not prohibit her permanently,[d] cannot be established by fewer than two, then isn't it logical[e] that the *final testimony*,[f] which prohibits her permanently, should not be established by fewer than two? It therefore teaches: "and there is no witness against her" (Num. 5:13)—any about her.[g] (Mishnah, *Sotah*, 6:2–3)
>
> [2] אמר עד אחד: אני ראיתיה שניטמאת, לא היתה שותה. [. . .]
>
> [3] שהיה בדין: מה אם עדות הראשונה, שאינה אוסרתה אסור עולם, אינה מתקיימת בפחות משנים, עדות האחרונה, שהיא אוסרתה אסור עולם, אינו דין שלא תתקיים בפחות משנים? תלמוד לומר "ועד אין בה" — כל שיש בה.

The Tosefta is glossing select terms from the Mishnah. The Mishnah's words "initial testimony" and "final testimony" refer to the testimony of the *sotah*'s seclusion and of her adulterous sexual relations. Although the tosefta is located at the beginning of Tractate *Sotah* and this mishnah is in the middle of the tractate, it stands to reason that the Tosefta's version of the Mishnah had it at the beginning of the tractate.[19]

Elaboration

The continuation of the same tosefta appears to define and then elaborate on another term in the Mishnah: "impurity."

> How does he warn her? He says to her in front of two, "Do not speak with so-and-so." And if she spoke with him, she is still permitted to her household[h] and is permitted to eat *terumah*.[i] If she went with him into a secluded area *and stayed there long enough for impurity*,[j] then she is prohibited to her household, she is prohibited

---

a The bitter waters that determine whether she committed adultery.
b i.e., the law seems to contravene logic.
c Of her seclusion with a man.
d From her husband since the waters can acquit her of wrongdoing.
e Using a fortiori reasoning.
f That she lay with another man.
g Only when there is no testimony whatsoever about her is she submitted to the drinking test.
h She may have sexual intercourse with her husband.
i If her husband is a priest she is still fully considered his wife and may eat the priestly tithe.
j To have sexual relations.

from eating *terumah*, and if he dies, she performs ḥalitzah and not *yibbum*.[a] (Mishnah, *Sotah*, 1:2)

כיצד הוא מקנא לה? אומר לה בפני שנים: אל תדברי עם איש פלוני. ודברה עמו, אדין היא מותרת לביתה ומותרת לאכל בתרומה. ניכנסה עימו לבית הסתר ושהת כדי טומאה, אסורה לביתה, אסורה לאכל בתרומה, ואם מת, חולצת ולא מתיבמת.

The Tosefta elaborates on the minimum amount of time necessary for presuming that sexual relations took place:

How long is *impurity*? Long enough for sexual intercourse. And how long is enough for sexual intercourse? Long enough for *ha'ara'ah*.[b] And how long is enough for *ha'ara'ah*?

Rabbi [E]liezer says, Long enough to circle a palm tree.[20]

Rabbi Yehoshua says, Long enough to mix a cup.

Ben Azzai says, Long enough to mix a cup to drink it.

Rabbi Akiva says, Long enough to roast an egg.

Rabbi Yehudah ben Beterah says, Long enough to swallow three eggs in a row.

Rabbi [E]lazer ben Yirmiyah says, Long enough for a weaver to tie a fringe.

Hanan ben Pinhas says, Long enough for her to extend her finger into her mouth.

Pelimo says, Long enough for her to extend her hand and take a loaf from the basket. Even though there is no proof of it, there is an allusion to it, as it says, "The last loaf of bread is for a harlot" (Prov. 6:26). (Tosefta, *Sotah*, 1:2)

וכמה היא טומאה? כדי ביאה. וכמה היא כדי ביאה? כדי הערה. וכמה היא כדי הערה?

רבי ליעזר אומר: כדי חזרת דקל.

רבי יהושע אומר: כדי מזיגת הכוס.

בן עזיי אומר: כדי מזיגת הכוס לשתותו.

רבי עקיבא אומר: כדי לצלות ביצה.

רבי יהודה בן פתירה אומר: כדי לגמוע שלש ביצים זו אחר זו.

---

a On account of her adultery she is prohibited to her husband's brothers and may not marry one of them through *yibbum*. For the rituals of *yibbum* and ḥalitzah, see chapter 5, section A.

b The Hebrew is based on Leviticus 20:18 and refers to the first stage of sexual contact for which a person is liable for transgressing sexual relations; see Mishnah, *Yevamot*, 6:1.

רבי לעזר בן ירמיה אומר: כדי שיקשור גרדי נימה.

חנן בן פנחס אומר: כדי שתשוט אצבעה לתוך פיה.

פלימו אומר: כדי שתפשוט ידה ותטול ככר מצוך הסל. אע״פ שאין ראיה לדבר, זכר לדבר, שנאמר "כי בעד אשה זונה עד ככר לחם".

According to the Mishnah, a woman is not prohibited to her husband for merely conversing with a man he warned her not to talk to. She must be secluded with him long enough for prohibited sexual contact to be initiated: "long enough for impurity." The Tosefta endeavors to quantify this measure in a world without clocks. The time of day or longer passages of time could be judged from the sun's position in the sky or from shadow direction and length, but very short periods of time, especially those under a minute, could only be felt by comparing them to familiar activities, like preparing a drink or roasting an egg. While this sounds like a straightforward case of explanation, what justifies its categorization as an elaboration is the Tosefta's desire to comment on the prohibited act itself. On a second reading, one notices that almost every opinion uses phallic or other suggestive imagery. Pelimo's prooftext, which explicitly mentions harlotry, gives the game away. With these measurements and this imagery the Tosefta functions quasi-aggadically, adding moral overtones to the Mishnah's dry law.

In addition, the Tosefta reintroduces a dialogical dimension to the halakhah. The Mishnah omits the give-and-take from the vast majority of its disputes, and the Tosefta restores them. By doing so, it allows us to peer into, however briefly, the tannaitic bet midrash.[21]

Addition of an Alternative Tradition

> They would bring her up to the Great Court in Jerusalem and *exhort her*[a] in the same way that they exhorted witnesses in capital cases.[b] They would say to her, "My daughter, much [sin] is wrought by[c] wine, much by frivolity, much by immaturity, and much by bad neighbors. Don't cause His great name, written in holiness, to be blotted out by the water."[d] And they would tell her things that she does not deserve to hear, neither she nor any of the family of her father's household.[e] (Mishnah, *Sotah*, 1:4)

   a To confess and not be tested by the waters.
   b See *Sanhedrin*, 4:5.
   c There are many mitigating circumstances.
   d The Tetragrammaton is written out and placed in the water she is to drink, which disintegrates the ink and blots out God's name.
   e The meaning of this sentence is unclear. The Talmuds (PT *Sotah* 1:4; BT *Sotah* 7b) claim that they would give examples of biblical figures who confessed their sins, such as Reuben and Judah.

היו מעלין אותה לבית דין הגדול שבירושלים, ומאיימים עליה כדרך שהן מאיימין על עידי נפשות. ואומרים לה: ביתי, הרבה יין עושה, הרבה שחוק עושה, הרבה ילדות עושה, הרבה שכנים הרעים עושים. אל תעשי לשמו הגדול שניכתב בקדושה שימחה על המים. ואומרין לפניה דברים שאינה כדיי לשומען, היא וכל משפחת בית אביה.

Compare this to the alternative tradition recorded in the Tosefta:

> And in the same way the court would *exhort her* to recant, so they would exhort her not to recant. They would say to her: "My daughter, if it is clear to you that you are pure, remain strong and drink. For this water is like a dry powder that when placed on healthy flesh causes no damage, and only penetrates deeply when it finds a wound." (Tosefta, *Sotah*, 1:6)

וכדרך שמאיימין עליה בית דין שתחחזור בה, כך מאיימין עליה שלא תחזור בה. אומרים לה: בתי, אם ברור לך הדבר שטהורה את, עמדי על בורייך ושתי, שאין המים הללו דומין אלא לסם יבש שנתון על גבי בשר חי ואין מזיקו, ולכשמוצא שם מכה מחלחל ויורד.

In the Mishnah, the exhortation is intended to break her so that she confesses. This is the only way, the court tells her, she won't cause God's name to be erased and drink water that will kill her. This tactic seems to contradict the Torah itself, where the water vindicates the woman if she is in fact innocent: "But if the woman is not impure but pure, she shall be cleared and sown with seed" (Num. 5:28). Adding to the surprise is the explicit comparison to witnesses testifying to a capital crime. In Tractate *Sanhedrin*, the purpose of exhorting the witnesses is twofold: if they harbor any doubts about what they saw, they must not testify; if they are sure, they must not withhold their testimony. Why, in the Mishnah, does the court only try to prevent the *sotah* from drinking the water and not press her to drink it if she's innocent?

Elsewhere, I have tried to explain the Mishnah's unique reconfiguration of the ritual and why it does not seem to allow for the woman's innocence.[22] For our purposes, I merely would like to point out that the Tosefta restores what the Mishnah purposely leaves out, bringing the ritual back into balance. For that reason, the Tosefta does not need to repeat the text of the first exhortation already explicated in the Mishnah and moves straight to the second, complementary exhortation that encourages her to prove her innocence.[23]

Addition of a Dissenting Opinion

Sometimes, the Tosefta adds an opinion omitted by the Mishnah. The opening mishnah of Tractate *Sotah* records a dispute about the number of people needed to witness the husband warning his wife and to witness the seclusion that forces her to drink the bitter waters:

> Regarding one who warns his wife—

Rabbi Eliezer says, One warns by the word of two and makes drink by the word of one witness or by his own word.

Rabbi Yehoshua says, One warns by the word of two and makes drink by the word of two. (Mishnah, *Sotah*, 1:1)

המקנא לאשתו–

רבי אליעזר אומר: מקנה על פי שנים, ומשקה על פי עד אחד או על פי עצמו.

רבי יהושע אומר: מקנא על פי שנים ומשקה על פי שנים.

The very first tosefta of Tractate *Sotah* adds a dissenting opinion without reproducing the disagreement in the Mishnah:

Rabbi Yose son of Rabbi Yehudah says *in the name of name of Rabbi [E]liezer:*

One warns by the word of one witness or by his own word and makes drink by the word of two.

They responded to the words of Rabbi Yose bei Rabbi Yehudah, There is no end to the matter.[a] (Tosefta, *Sotah*, 1:1)

רבי יוסה בי רבי יהודה אומר משם רבי ליעזר: מקנה על פי עד אחד או על פי עצמו, ומשקה על פי שנים.

השיבו על דברי רבי יוסה בי רבי יהודה: אין לדבר סוף.

In the Mishnah, Rabbi Eliezer's opinion is firm: the warning requires the presence of two witnesses while the seclusion does not. But in the Tosefta a different opinion is attributed to Rabbi Eliezer, which reverses the requirement: two for the seclusion but not for the warning. Can the two versions be reconciled? One supposes that Rabbi Eliezer originally opined that only one of the two stages—warning or seclusion—requires two witnesses, in opposition to Rabbi Yehoshua, who set the higher bar for both. Rabbi Eliezer's disciples disputed which stage needs the ironclad testimony. The Mishnah cites only one of those opinions, so the Tosefta presents the other one. The Tosefta gives the fuller picture to those studying the laws of the *sotah*.

Why does the Mishnah leave out the opinion of Rabbi Yose bei Rabbi Yehudah in the first place? The principle behind mishnaic omission is often elusive, but here the answer immediately presents itself. The Sages themselves rebut his opinion: "There is no end to the matter." The Tosefta presumably includes it anyway to provide the range of opinions, even as it too preserves the Sages' rejection. This fact indicates that part of the Tosefta's mission is

---

a If the warning doesn't require a witness aside from the husband giving the warning, it is liable to result in false claims about warnings that were never given.

intellectual, even academic, in nature. Presenting the full range of opinions, including the refuted ones, illuminates the mishnaic laws.

In chapter 4 we saw that the Mishnah tends to drop dissenting opinions so that its preferred opinion becomes the authoritative voice of the anonymous *stam*. Now we see that the Tosefta regularly restores these opinions so as to paint a more complete picture. Here is an example from the very beginning of the Mishnah:

> If someone was reading the Torah and the time of recitation arrived—if they directed their heart,[a] they fulfilled it,[b] but if not, they did not.
>
> In the breaks[c] one may inquire out of respect and respond, and in the middle[d] one may inquire of out reverence and respond—the words of Rabbi Meir.
>
> Rabbi Yehudah says, In the middle one may inquire out of reverence and respond out of respect; in the breaks one may inquire out of respect and return a greeting to anyone. (Mishnah, *Berakhot*, 2:1)

> היה קורא בתורה והגיע זמן המקרא—אם כיוון את לבו, יצא, ואם לאו, לא יצא.
>
> ובפרקים שואל מפני הכובד ומשיב, ובאמצע שואל מפני היראה ומשיב—דברי רבי מאיר.
>
> רבי יהודה אומר: באמצע שואל מפני היראה ומשיב מפני הכבוד, ובפרקים שואל מפני הכבוד ומשיב שלום לכל האדם.

These two laws concern the necessity of intention and maintaining an uninterrupted recitation of the Shema's passages. The first establishes the general need for intention and the second presents a dispute about when one may interrupt it. The parallel tosefta teaches us that there was a dispute about the first law as well:

> One who recites the Shema must direct their heart. Rabbi Ahai says in the name of Rabbi Yehudah, If someone directed their heart in the first chapter, even if they do not direct their heart in the final one, they have fulfilled it. (Tosefta, *Berakhot*, 2:2)

> הקורא את שמע צריך שיכוין את לבו. רבי אחאי אומר משם רבי יהודה: אם כיון את לבו בפרק הראשון, אף על פי שלא כיון את לבו בפרק האחרון, יצא.

The Mishnah presumably leaves out this dissenting opinion in order to rule, through the usage of the *stam*, that one must have intention for the recitation of all the Shema's chapters.

---

a Had intention to fulfill their obligation.
b The obligation to recite the Shema.
c Between the chapters of the Shema.
d Of the recitation of a chapter.

The Tosefta rescues the dissenting opinion from oblivion and restores the full picture of two subsequent debates regarding intention.

Based on the foregoing, the Tosefta can be characterized as a collection of explanations, elaborations, and additions to the Mishnah. Where the Mishnah is brief and laconic, the Tosefta is expansive and inclusive.[24] It is driven not solely by halakhic or commentarial considerations, but also by a desire to widen the Mishnah's narrow view of any topic into a panoramic one for the sake of comprehensive study. From the comparisons above one can see that the Mishnah leaves out elements (half the exhortation to the *sotah*), decides between interpretations of tannaitic opinions (rejecting Rabbi Yose bei Rabbi Yehudah's version of Rabbi Eliezer), and reworks its source material (omitting the dispute about intention for the Shema). The Tosefta consistently provides the other half of the story.

Learning the Mishnah and the Tosefta together would make the Tosefta's editor very happy, because he clearly envisioned it as a kind of companion volume to the Mishnah. True, the Tosefta presents alternatives to mishnaic law and preserves sources that the Mishnah cut down and reshaped for its own purposes. But even at its most critical, when it is furthest from the Mishnah, the Tosefta remains firmly in its orbit. The Mishnah must have been regarded as authoritative by the editor of the Tosefta, but it was not yet canonical in the same way it would be in the Talmuds, where the Mishnah could only be commented on, not altered (with a few exceptions). The Tosefta therefore allows us to indirectly behold aspects of the Mishnah's consolidation, editing, and even early canonization.[25]

B. NEW-OLD TOSEFTA

Broadly speaking, the characterization of the Tosefta as a companion to the Mishnah is correct. But the Tosefta consists of individual traditions and collections, and the relationship between those and what exists in the Mishnah is a lot more complicated. Although the Tosefta was edited after the Mishnah, some of its source material actually dates from a much earlier period. The Tosefta preserves material as it was before Rabbi Yehuda Ha-Nasi edited it for his Mishnah.[26]

To draw a modern analogy: At some point in high school or college most students will have to take a class in English Literature and purchase a volume from the series Norton Critical Editions on a particular novel. These volumes include an annotated text and critical essays that often cite earlier drafts of the novel or parts the author reworked from a novella or short story, in order to elucidate the final text or tease out the author's intentions. Although these critical editions have been written and published decades or even centuries after the novel was finalized, they contain material that predates it.

This complicates the directionality of some of the cases I presented above as open and shut. When the Tosefta quotes Rabbi Yehudah's opinion about price gouging with explanations that are absent from the Mishnah, I said that the Tosefta looks to be quoting the Mishnah and adding explanations. But it is equally plausible that the directionality ought to be flipped: the material in the Tosefta is the original and the Mishnah cut away the explanation to suit its codificatory purposes.

Here's another case where one cannot be sure whether the Mishnah or the Tosefta contains the original material:

If someone sees a place where miracles were wrought for Israel, they say: "Blessed be the One who worked miracles for our ancestors in this place";

a place from which idolatry was uprooted, they say, "Blessed be the One who uprooted idolatry from our land." (Mishnah, *Berakhot*, 9:1)

הרואה מקום שנעשו בו ניסים לישראל, אומר: ברוך שעשה ניסים לאבתינו במקום הזה;

מקום שנעקרה ממנו עבודה זרה, אומר: ברוך שעקר עבודה זרה מארצינו.

With regard to idolatry, the mishnah has a single blessing that focuses on thankfulness for its eradication, placed within the context of God's miracle-working. Compare this to the lengthier parallel in the Tosefta:

If someone sees idolatry, they say: "Blessed be the Slow to Anger";

a place where idolatry was uprooted, they say: "Blessed be the One who uprooted idolatry from our land. May it be Your will, our Lord God, that idolatry be uprooted from every place in Israel, and that You turn back the heart of its worshippers[a] to worship You." (Tosefta, *Berakhot*, 6:2)

הרואה את עבודה זרה, אומר: ברוך ארך אפים;

מקום שנעקרה ממנו עבודה זרה, אומר: ברוך שעקר עבודה זרה מארצנו. יהי רצון מלפניך ה' אלינו שתעקר עבודה זרה מכל מקומות ישראל ותשיב לב עבדיה לעבדך.

The Tosefta has additional blessings about idolatry. The first praises God's patience in letting it persist, a sentiment that comports with a law stated later in the same chapter in both the Mishnah and Tosefta: "A person must make a blessing over the bad the same way they make a blessing over the good." The second is a prayer for God to extirpate idolatry from other places in the Land of Israel, and it even beseeches Him to expunge it from humankind.

In this instance of parallelism, the argument that the Mishnah is the core around which the Tosefta is built up is unconvincing. The material in the Tosefta is too organically connected as a single literary unit to have been artificially stitched together based on the Mishnah. It is more likely that the Mishnah had a source very close to the Tosefta's text, excised its middle blessing, and attached it to its blessing on miracles, thus avoiding the

---

[a] This is the version in MS Erfurt and the two Talmuds and is the original; MS Vienna's version, "Your worshippers," is probably a pious emendation.

FIGURE 5. Iron fastening bar from Pano Lefkara, Cyprus. By courtesy of Ze'ev Safrai. See *Tractate Kelim with Historical and Sociological Commentary by Ze'ev Safrai.* Kvutzat Yavne: 2020. Digital edition, p. 101.

thorny theological conundrum of the endurance of idolatry.[27] A blessing originally about idolatry thereby becomes a particularization of a blessing on miracles.

Given the copious evidence above documenting the Tosefta's role as an accompaniment to the Mishnah, one surmises that the Tosefta brought the original source in full as a supplement to the Mishnah's fragmentary adaptation of it. If so, there is no single answer to the question of which source is the earlier one: the Tosefta can, without self-contradiction, be adding material absent from the edited Mishnah, from sources in a raw state that preceded the Mishnah's alteration of them. The Tosefta's activity can postdate the Mishnah even as its sources predate it.

Another example of material that the Mishnah adapted but is preserved in a more original form in the Tosefta:

A fastening bar—[a]

Rabbi Yehoshua says, One may detach it from one door and hang it[b] on another on Shabbat.

a Which crosses the door from side to side and locks it. See figure 5.
b But the bar cannot be carried normally on Shabbat since it is not a typical implement used on Shabbat.

The Tosefta and the Mishnah   167

Rabbi Tarfon says, It is like any other utensil for him[a] and can be moved in a courtyard. (Mishnah, *Kelim*, 11:4)

קלוסטרה—

רבי יהושע אומר: שומטה מפתח זה ותולה בחבירו בשבת.

רבי טרפון אומר: הרי היא לו ככל הכלים ומטלטלת בחצר.

According to Rabbi Yehoshua, one may not move a fastening bar in the normal fashion, so he devises a workaround. The parallel tosefta, however, credits a woman named Beruriah with this ingenuity,[28] and says that Rabbi Yehoshua merely signed off on it:

Beruriah says, One may detach it from this door and hang it on another on Shabbat. When the words were said before Rabbi Yehoshua, he said, "Beruriah has spoken well." (Tosefta, *Kelim*, *Bava Metzi'a*, 1:6)

וברוריא אומרת: שומטה מן הפתח זה ותולה לחבירו בשבת. כשנאמרו דברים לפני רבי יהושע, אמר: יפה אמרה ברוריא.

It seems highly probable that the Tosefta preserves the original attribution and the Mishnah has tampered with it, because it prefers to attribute the law to a respected Sage rather than to a woman. By removing its originator, the only attribution of a law to a named woman in the Mishnah disappears.[29] Thanks to the editor of the Tosefta, the rightful author receives her due recognition.

At times, the editor of the Tosefta records an alternative to the Mishnah that is of impressive length. Chapter 4 of Tractate *Berakhot* in the Tosefta parallels chapter 6 in the Mishnah, both dealing with the blessings recited before eating. But they are quite distinct. With regard to agricultural produce, the Mishnah has two general blessings, "Creator of the fruit of the tree" and "Creator of the fruit of the earth," and two highly specific blessings over the processed staples of wine and bread. There is also a universal blessing for anything that does not grow from the ground, including water, meat, and so on. The Tosefta, on the other hand, has blessings for every halakhic species of produce: "Creator of the types of desserts . . . species of seeds . . . species of grasses . . . species of sustenance." Beyond the greater number of blessings in the Tosefta, there is also a difference of formulation: "Creator of the fruit of X" in the Mishnah versus "Creator of the species of X" in the Tosefta. There is a further discrepancy between the two corpora on the opinion of Rabbi Yehudah. The Mishnah has him ruling that vegetables require a blessing of "Creator of the species of grasses," whereas the Tosefta quotes him as saying that one recites "who makes the earth sprout with His word."

---

a The owner can use it and therefore may carry it on Shabbat.

All of this has led scholars to conclude that the network of benedictions in the Tosefta is independent of the Mishnah's and constitutes a full-fledged alternative.[30]

In light of the preceding analysis, one can submit the following. The Tannaim had two traditions concerning the blessings to be recited before partaking of food. The editor of the Mishnah chose to include only one of them. The later editor of the Tosefta decided to preserve the omitted alternative in order to complement the Mishnah's account. This explains why the material is different but follows a parallel order. This would be another case where one must distinguish between the origins of source material and its editing. The material in the Tosefta can be independent of the Mishnah and may even precede it, all while it has been edited to serve as a complement to the Mishnah.

To further complicate matters, even when the Tosefta explicitly relates to the Mishnah, one must ask which version of the Mishnah it has in mind. When the Tosefta asks, "Why did they say X?," it can be referring to earlier strata of the Mishnah. The Mishnah accreted layers over time, and later layers comment on earlier ones with precisely the same rhetorical question: "Why did they say X?"[31] In the same vein, the Tosefta could be commenting on earlier mishnayot and not the edited ones.[32] Recall that Rabbi Akiva and his disciples overhauled the Mishnah's sources and traditions, and that Rabbi Yehudah ha-Nasi himself made changes to the text in his sunset years.[33] The text was in flux until the last possible moment.

Here is the Mishnah as we currently have it about the blessings before and after the recitation of the Shema:

> In the morning one makes two blessings before it and one after,[a] and in the evening one makes two blessings before and two after. One is long and one is short. Wherever they said[b] to extend it, one may not be brief; to be brief, one may not extend it; to conclude,[c] one may not refuse to conclude, and not to conclude, one may not conclude. (Mishnah, *Berakhot*, 1:4)

בשחר מברך שתים לפניה ואחרת לאחריה, ובערב מברך שתים לפניה ושתים לאחריה. אחת ארוכה ואחת קצרה. מקום שאמרו להאריך אינו רשיי לקצר, לקצר אינו רשיי להאריך; לחתום אינו רשיי שלא לחתום, ושלא לחתום אינו רשיי לחתום.

The parallel tosefta begins with the formulaic question:

> Why did they say "one is short"? Wherever they said to extend it, one may not be brief; to be brief, one may not extend it; to conclude, one may not refuse to conclude; not to conclude, one may not conclude; to prostrate, one may not refuse to prostrate; and not to prostrate, one may not prostrate; to begin with "Blessed," one

---

a The recitation of the Shema.
b The Sages said.
c With the doxology, "Blessed are You, Lord."

may not refuse to begin with "Blessed"; and not to begin with "Blessed," one may not begin with "Blessed." (Tosefta, *Berakhot*, 1:5)

למה אמרו "אחת קצרה"? מקום שאמרו להאריך אינו רשאי לקצר, לקצר אינו רשאי להאריך; לחתום אינו רשאי שלא לחתום, לא לחתום אינו רשאי לחתום; לשוח אינו רשאי שלא לשוח, ושלא לשוח אינו רשאי לשוח; לפתוח בברוך אינו רשאי שלא לפתוח ברוך, ושלא לפתוח בברוך אינו רשאי לפתוח בברוך.

Without question, the Tosefta is relating to the Mishnah, where the precise quote, "one is short," appears. According to Saul Lieberman, the Tosefta is posing a terminological query: Why does the Mishnah choose to refer to the blessings by their relative lengths instead of by their names?[34] The Tosefta explains that the Mishnah is obliquely teaching us that benedictions must retain their required length. The problem with this explanation is that it is glaringly redundant, because the Mishnah goes on to state those laws of length outright! Of what use is this tosefta if the mishnah already spells this out?

It is only redundant if the Tosefta had the continuation in the mishnah that begins with "Wherever they said" (ll. 3–5). Let us assume that this was a later addition and that the Tosefta was working with an early mishnah which did not contain this elaboration. The Tosefta decided to clarify this early mishnah: "Why did they say 'one is short'?" The continuation came from a third source. At the same time or some later point, the Mishnah itself sought to elucidate its own early mishnah. It too drew on that same (or a similar) third source, but, in keeping with its own textual methodology, it omitted the opening question and lopped off the end of the source about prostration and use of the word "Blessed." In that way, the Mishnah papered over the seam so that its layers could blend into one another unnoticeably.[35]

If this, admittedly hypothetical, textual reconstruction rings true, then the Tosefta and the Mishnah's later stratum are both explicating an earlier mishnah. Influence in the relationship between the Tosefta and Mishnah is not unidirectional; it doubles back, it flows through other, third sources as conduits. The connections between the Tosefta and the Mishnah can be truly byzantine.

A number of methodological conclusions can be drawn from the preceding discussion. First, the question of absolute chronology ought to be separated from that of literary causality. Second, the Mishnah might have adapted earlier material that the Tosefta preserves and presents as a complement to the mishnaic presentation. Third, and more generally, the relationship between the Mishnah and the Tosefta is so complicated that every case must be scrutinized on its own. Finally, even the best-reasoned textual reconstruction is ultimately guesswork.

The knotty textual entanglement of the Mishnah and the Tosefta has spawned many approaches among scholars. In the traditional view laid out in the previous section, the Tosefta is a kind of commentary on the Mishnah. Even Saul Lieberman, one of the greatest scholars of the Tosefta, subscribed to this oversimplification. Whenever he identified parallels between the two works, his starting assumption was that the Mishnah's text chronologically precedes the Tosefta's. If the two contain identical language, the Tosefta must be quoting the Mishnah and then adding to it.[36] In the example from Tractate *Berakhot* discussed immediately above, Lieberman assumed that the overlap in material is due to the Tosefta's quotation of the Mishnah, into which it inserts the rhetorical question. He did not entertain the possibility of dynamic interaction between the corpora or the presence of shared material from a third source.[37]

In recent decades, two scholars have argued that material in the Tosefta dates from before the Mishnah. Shamma Friedman argues that there is almost no literary dependency of toseftan halakhot on earlier mishnayot. What we have are parallels, and the Tosefta usually preserves an earlier version that has undergone less textual surgery. Occasionally, there is indeed literary dependency but it goes in the other direction: the Mishnah reworks the early material preserved in the Tosefta, rather than the other way around.[38]

This gives us cause to reconsider what looked like straightforward cases of the Tosefta adding explanations to the Mishnah. The Tosefta in Tractate *Bava Metzi'a*, cited toward the beginning of this chapter, has a list of items identical to the Mishnah's but then brings explanations for them: "A Torah scroll because it is invaluable; a domesticated animal and a pearl because one wants to pair them." Is the Tosefta quoting and explaining the Mishnah, or is it quoting a source in full that the Mishnah shortened?

Here is another case where both readings can be argued equally persuasively:

If one was pressing[a] in a barrel or pressing in a bin, and the barrel broke[b] or the bin broke, one may not make an incidental meal[c] from them. Rabbi Yose permits it. (Mishnah, *Ma'asrot*, 1:8)

היה דש בחבית ומעגיל במגורה—נשברה החבת ונפחתה המגורה, לא יאכל מהן עריי. רבי יוסה מתיר.

Now for the nearly identical version in the Tosefta:

If one was pressing in a barrel or pressing in a bin, and the barrel broke or the bin opened, one may not make an incidental meal from them. Rabbi Yose permits it, because the lower ones need the upper ones.[d] (Tosefta, *Ma'asrot*, 1:11)

היה דש בחבית ומעגיל במגורה—נשברה חבית ונפתחה המגורה, לא יאכל מהן עראי. ור' יוסה מתיר מפני שהתחתונות צריכות לעליונות.

    a Figs to dry them out.
    b From the pressure.
  c One may eat an incidental meal, as opposed to a regular one, from untithed produce so long as it requires further processing. In this case, the Mishnah is debating whether the preparation of the figs is complete and the obligation to tithe has been triggered.
    d The processing is incomplete and does not trigger the tithing obligation, because the bottom figs still need the pressure of the ones on top of them.

Lieberman assumed the Tosefta is quoting the Mishnah and adding a rationale for Rabbi Yose. Friedman proposes the exact opposite: this is "an ancient law that was shortened in our Mishnah by omitting the rationale."[39] While Friedman's supposition appears correct in certain cases, in this one it is difficult or even impossible to establish directionality.[40]

Judith Hauptman has staked out an even bolder claim: the Tosefta as an edited composition is older than the Mishnah.[41] This is unsupported by any textual evidence and is, in my eyes, improbable. It is more useful to distinguish between the material preserved in the Tosefta and the actual dating of the Tosefta's consolidation and editing. This latter point brings us to editorial strategies in the Tosefta.

C. THE EDITING OF THE TOSEFTA

Although the Tosefta as a whole functions first and foremost as a textual complement to the Mishnah, it is not completely without its own order.[42] A side-by-side comparison of the last chapter of both the Tosefta and the Mishnah of Tractate *Berakhot*—presented in table 2—illustrates this visually.

To this point in the chapter, analysis of the Tosefta has preceded horizontally, that is, by comparing and contrasting parallel texts in the Mishnah and the Tosefta. This has yielded important insights, as in the case of their separate treatments of idolatry. Reading the Tosefta this way reveals how each corpus has unique approaches and perspectives and distinct thematic interests and organizational principles.

Thus, the second mishnah here records blessings over natural wonders, in the sky (lightning and thunder) or on the ground (mountains and rivers). The Tosefta injects a human element into the mix by adding blessings for human "wonders," like albinos or little people. Why does the Mishnah leave these out? While it is difficult to tell, it does seem intentional, and perhaps a clue can be found later in the third mishnah, which does relate to human affairs:

> If someone's wife was pregnant and he said, "May it be His will that my wife gives birth to a male"—this is a vain prayer.
>
> If someone arriving on the road heard cries from the city and he said, "May it be His will that they are not inside my house"—this is a vain prayer. (Mishnah, *Berakhot*, 9:3)

> היתה אשתו מעוברת, ואומר: יהי רצון שתלד אשתי זכר—הרי זו תפילת שוא.
>
> היה בא בדרך ושמע קול צווחות בעיר, ואומר: יהי רצון שלא אלו יהוא בתוך ביתי—הרי זו תפילת שוא.

The blessings and prayers in this chapter of the Mishnah relate to fortunes and misfortunes, and are framed by the requirement to bless God for the good and the bad. The whole chapter is preoccupied with this:

TABLE 2   Comparison of Mishnah and Tosefta, end of tractate *Berakhot*

Mishnah, *Berakhot*, 9:1-5	Tosefta, *Berakhot*, 6:1-25
	1. A series of exegeses that sources Grace after Meals to the Torah, followed by the same for blessings mentioned throughout this chapter[a]
1. Blessings on seeing locations connected to miracles or idolatry	2. Blessings related to seeing idolatry Blessings on throngs of people 3. Blessings on types of people 4. Blessings on beautiful people or trees
2. Blessings over natural phenomena of (or affecting) the earth Blessing on rain and good tidings 3. *She-heḥeyanu* blessing	5–6. Complementary blessings on natural phenomena of the sky Blessing on walking in a cemetery
Blessing over a misfortune A vain prayer	7. Rabbi Meir's exegesis of Deut. 5:6 (parallel to mishnah 5) A foolish prayer 9–15. Blessings over mitzvot
4. Blessing on entering a city 5. An exegesis that grounds the obligation to make a blessing over a misfortune Laws of comportment on the Temple Mount	16. Blessing on entering a city 17. Blessing on entering a bathhouse 18. Rabbi Yehudah's blessings of identity 19. Laws of comportment on the Temple Mount
Two decrees about making a blessing with God's name	20–24. Laws pertaining to decrees in the Mishnah 24–25. Two dicta of Rabbi Meir about concluding a blessing with praise The sheer abundance of blessings that surround a person

[a] On this exegesis see Rosen-Zvi, "Responsive Blessings."

[2] [. . .] On rain and good news one says, "Blessed be the One who is good and beneficent," and on bad news one says, "Blessed be the true Judge."

[3] [. . .] One makes a blessing over the bad similar to over the good and over the good similar to over the bad. [. . .]

[5] One must make a blessing over the bad just as one makes a blessing over the good. (Mishnah, *Berakhot*, 9:2–3, 5)

[2] [. . .] על הגשמים ועל בשורות טובות הוא אומר: ברוך הטוב והמטיב. ועל שמועות הרעות הוא אומר: ברוך דיין האמת.

[3][. . .] מברך על הרעה מעין על הטובה, ועל הטובה מעין על הרעה [. .].

[5] חייב לברך על הרעה כשם שהוא מברך על הטובה.

Fittingly, the example of a prayer uttered in vain pertains to the same subject matter. Contrast this with the Tosefta, which talks about a "foolish prayer." There is a subtle yet important distinction between "a foolish prayer" and "a vain prayer." This can be seen from the example given in the Tosefta:

> Some things are a foolish prayer. If one gathered in 100 *kor*[a] and said, "May it be His will that they will be 200"; if one gathered in 100 barrels and said, "May it be His will that they will be 200"—this is a vain prayer. (Tosefta, *Berakhot*, 6:7)

יש דברים שהן תפילת תיפלה. כיצד? כנס מאה כורין, אמר: יהי רצון שיהיו מאתים; כנס מאה חביות, אמר: יהי רצון שיהיו מאתים—הרי זו תפלת שוא.

In both the Mishnah and the Tosefta, the prayers concern something that has already happened, a hard reality that cannot be changed ex post facto through prayer. But whereas in the Tosefta they are attempts to increase revenue, in the Mishnah all the examples are of misfortunes. This is true for all mishnaic engagement with human affairs in this chapter.

This organizing principle can also account for why the Mishnah omits the Tosefta's blessings on the spectrum of humanity. The Tosefta looks at humankind with the same eye that it views all other natural phenomena, and without any overlaid theological lens. The Mishnah, on the other hand, posits a sharp distinction between humankind, for whom there is good and evil, and the rest of creation.[43]

This can further explain why the Tosefta has blessings on stars and constellations and the Mishnah does not. Note the Tosefta's own objection: "Rabbi Yehudah says, If someone makes a blessing on the sun, that is a different path"—i.e., idolatry (Tosefta, *Berakhot*, 6:5). The Mishnah omits blessings on celestial luminaries not only because they could be deified or otherwise worshipped,[44] but because the entire point of the chapter is to inculcate the awareness that both the good and the bad come directly from God, to the exclusion of any other entity, and must be verbally acknowledged as such.

A continuous reading of the mishnaic chapter can thus reveal the logic of its selection and the rationale used to weave together its material. I would like to propose that one can apply a similar method, to some extent, to the Tosefta. In this chapter, reading the Tosefta sequentially without referring to the Mishnah was compared to reading footnotes without the body of the text. While that is true concerning independent laws, recurring themes can still be identified when the Tosefta is read uninterruptedly. In this chapter, one such theme absent from the Mishnah is making blessings over the ritual fulfillment of the commandments. While it is concentrated in the middle of the chapter in *halakhot* 9–15, it also has a prominent place at the beginning and end of the chapter. At the beginning, there is an exegesis that grounds the various blessings in the chapter, including one "over the Torah and over the mitzvot." In a parallel tannaitic midrash, the words "over the mitzvot" are absent,

---

a A dry measure, indicating that the yield was likely grain. 100 *kor* is a typical harvest.

and they appear to have been added specifically here.[45] At the conclusion of the chapter are two exegetical comments by Rabbi Meir about the abundance of mitzvot: "There is no Israelite who does not perform one hundred mitzvot every day. . . . There is no Israelite who is not surrounded by mitzvot." There is a clear hand at work here. The editor added blessings over the mitzvot to the middle, added a relevant exegesis to the beginning, and concluded with others in the same vein. These are like pylons and cables set in place by the editor that hold up the entire span of the chapter.

How often this occurs in the Tosefta requires serious scholarly investigation.[46] Regardless, the discovery of vertical coherence in the editing of chapters or even entire tractates does not lessen the importance of horizontal reading, through which the laws of the Tosefta enlighten us about those of the Mishnah. The Tosefta is a complicated textual phenomenon, and it needs to be approached from multiple angles to comprehend its various dimensions.

Epilogue

The Mishnah and Future Scholarship

The Mishnah is a kind of textual epitome—both an embodiment and a summary—of Halakhah as it was formed and re-formed in the post-destruction rabbinic academies of the Land of Israel. While it has deep roots in the Second Temple period, as the hundreds of disputes between Hillel and Shammai's schools attest, it assumed its essential form only in the study halls of the second century, where Sages, especially Rabbi Akiva and his disciples, debated, interpreted, and expanded upon the opinions of their predecessors. In the third century, the text was officially set and closed by Rabbi Yehudah ha-Nasi, whose editorial clout flowed from his respected and powerful position in the Jewish community.

The Mishnah is unprecedented in its hungry vision of encompassing the entire sweep of Jewish law in a single composition. Its laws govern everything: from the protocols of the highest court to the dole for the poor, from semicentennial occurrences to daily observances, from Temple rituals to farming practices. In principle, the Mishnah's legal reach knows no bounds, even if in practice it does not treat every area of Jewish law equally.[1]

The audacity of this self-license is set into sharp relief by the foundational halakhic works that followed. The two Talmuds cover only those parts of the Mishnah of practical relevance. Neither includes *Seder Teharot* (aside from Tractate *Niddah* about menstruation), as the laws of ritual purity began a slow decline in observance with the loss of their cultic focal point. The Palestinian Talmud, composed by and intended for Jews living in the Land of Israel, comments on all of *Seder Zera'im*, whereas the Babylonian Talmud for the Jews of Mesopotamia does not (except for the non-agricultural tractate *Berakhot*).

By the Middle Ages, the talmudic delimitation was the norm. The only medieval halakhist to adopt the Mishnah's ambitions was Rabbi Moses Maimonides, who fittingly titled his own all-encompassing code *Mishneh Torah*, and styled himself a successor of Rabbi Yehudah ha-Nasi. The next landmark code, the fourteenth-century *Arba'ah Turim* of Rabbi Jacob ben Asher, returned to the mainstream position and concerned itself with practical law only. In the sixteenth century, Rabbi Joseph Caro took this last code, rather than *Mishneh Torah*, as the basis for his voluminous *Shulḥan 'Arukh*, so it, too, is restricted to practical halakhic matters.

What is historically fascinating is that the vision and execution of the Mishnah's totalizing legal system date from an era of profound crisis. Three revolts—the Great revolt of 70 CE, the diaspora revolt of 115, and Bar Kokhba Revolt of 132—were brutally crushed by the Romans. The Jewish population was decimated, the Land of Israel hemorrhaged its Jews to Babylonia, and Jerusalem was rebranded Aelia Capitolina, with a temple to Jupiter built on the ruins of the former Temple.

In a project of this size and scope, especially one produced by successive generations of different-minded scholars, there are bound to be warring tendencies. The Mishnah can veer from extreme practicality to hypothetical absurdity in a line. No detail is too trivial, no subject too abstruse, no case too outlandish. The Mishnah is bookended by the practical: it begins with the working of the land in *Seder Zera'im* and ends with ritual impurity in *Seder Teharot*. But in between it spends a great deal of time in areas of law that are purely theoretical: the monarchy, the Sanhedrin, capital punishment. It presents rules and regulations about ancient biblical history, never to find application again. It devotes much space to the laws of the Temple, even though it was not no longer standing and there were no prospects for its rebuilding.

The Mishnah's goal of summarizing the endless debates of the Sages also comes into conflict with the desire to present itself as a well-ordered and relatively uniform legal corpus. This has engendered a "a long-standing dispute on whether the Mishnah was intended to serve as a normative codex or corpus iuris, or as a digest or encyclopedia of sources for theoretical instruction."[2] Does the Mishnah that emerges from the preceding eight chapters resemble a codificatory enterprise?[3] The answer is yes and no. In terms of its scope and systematization, it is a code, and an unprecedented one at that. It represents the first attempt by Jewish scholars to deliberately and systematically create a standalone composition that encompasses everything. It made sense for Maimonides's to later rely on the Mishnah as a precedent for his own monumental code of Halakhah. Nevertheless, in certain respects it is dissimilar from a typical code. Our reconstruction of Rabbi Yehuda ha-Nasi's editorial techniques demonstrated that the Mishnah is not focused on the halakhic bottom line. It is a summation of the Oral Torah, of the lively learning of the tannaitic study halls. Discomfort with this lack of halakhic determination is evident in the attempts of the first Amoraim to turn the Mishnah into a practical halakhic guide by applying a set of jurisprudential rules.

The Mishnah is a multitextured weave from an array of distinctive sources, and the weavers themselves belong to distinct generations and schools. Sometimes they work in tandem and at other times they are at cross purposes. The end product is a multidimensional and multifaceted work. Each of the preceding chapters has endeavored to shine a light on one facet, while demonstrating how, as if through a crystal, the illumination is propagated to other facets as well.

Before taking leave of the Mishnah, a brief survey of recent trends in Mishnah scholarship is in order. Of note are three promising avenues of research.

The first concerns higher criticism. As shown in chapter 2, classical scholarship on the Mishnah, from Zacharias Frankel's *Darkhei ha-Mishnah* in the nineteenth century to Epstein's and Albeck's introductions to the Mishnah in the twentieth century, worked on recovering the earliest strata of the Mishnah from the final, edited text. Subsequently, source criticism fell out of favor and scholars turned to legal history and to literary analysis.[4] Studies would trace the development of specific laws, terms, or topics in the Mishnah but rarely that of the text itself. The fact that this scholarly labor is highly speculative does not sufficiently explain the loss of interest in source criticism. In academic Bible study, by comparison, source criticism is as bright a lodestar as ever, its luster undiminished by the rise of both redaction criticism and literary criticism.[5]

Perhaps what makes the Mishnah different is that there is no commensurate reward for the hard work; in the end, one is still left with irresolvable doubts. Unlike the Priestly or deuteronomic sources of the Pentateuch, the Mishnah's sources cannot be neatly categorized, attributed to schools, or reduced to a manageable number. In lieu of reconstructing discrete bodies of source material, the Mishnah scholar must be content with assigning them a relative chronology. In addition, serious methodological obstacles have been put in the way of the Mishnah's source critics. In the past, they relied on the assumption that any mishnah about Temple practices is early, which, as we have seen, is not necessarily true. Recently, scholars have returned to higher criticism, but this time with a hyper-localized focus, digging deeply into specific blocks of text. Only time will tell how productive this endeavor will be.[6]

A second line of inquiry explores the impact of Roman law on the Mishnah. No other ancient civilization accorded law such a central role as Rome did, and the Mishnah arose within that pervasively legal milieu. Some scholars have reconceived the Sages' ascendancy as part of the general rise of jurists in the second-century Roman Empire. Others protest that the jurists worked for the government and wrote in its official language, whereas the Sages generated an oral corpus in a language unintelligible to it.[7] One can even go so far as to argue that the Mishnah's very existence was predicated on the Romans having no inkling about it. It strains credulity to believe that the Roman authorities knew that the Jews of Judaea were intensively discussing laws about the political, legislative, and juridical entities that constitute a Jewish kingdom and simply let them carry on. The way forward here is to avoid sweeping generalizations and to instead isolate possible connections in specific areas, concepts, or details of the law. Since torts and other areas of financial law were not treated in earlier postbiblical Halakhah and have fascinating parallels in Roman law, they have been marked by scholars as ripe for investigation. Unexpected connections and dependencies between the legal systems also emerge with respect to personal status and marriage, as noted in chapter 3.[8]

Finally, recent years have seen more scholarly engagement with the Mishnah's reception history, especially in the early modern period. The Mishnah was first printed by the Soncino press in Naples, Italy, in 1492, and a flurry of editions with old and new commentaries soon followed. Scholars have been investigating how the printing of the Mishnah affected diverse readerships. Since the Middle Ages, Jews had studied the Mishnah primarily through the interpretations of the Babylonian Talmud; now, shorn of its accompanying talmudic commentary, the Mishnah could receive its due as a self-contained text bearing its own meaning. For non-Jewish Hebraists, whose familiarity with rabbinic Judaism came from Latin (mis)translations of select, ostensibly anti-Christian passages in the Babylonian Talmud, the printed Mishnah was a new and accessible entrée to rabbinic Judaism. With a little work, its brief rulings could be fashioned into arrowheads for polemics and missionary activity. Christian interest in the Mishnah reached its acme with the impressive, bilingual edition published by Willem Surenhuis at the turn of the eighteenth century. His is a six-volume printing of the entire Mishnah in a new Latin translation, accompanied by learned Christian commentaries. Christian interest in the Mishnah had inherent tensions: How much were Hebraists driven by scholarly humanism versus militant religiosity? Recent scholarship revisits these questions.[9]

The Mishnah reflects the intense preoccupation of the Sages with Halakhah and a mode of legal thinking that proceeds intellectually and independently, without steady reference to any other text. But this represents only one of the two overarching intellectual pursuits of the tannaitic bet midrash. The other was the systematic exegesis of Scripture, through which all kinds of meaning, especially halakhic, was extracted. This is the subject of the second half of this book. After examining firsthand the methodology and procedure of the rabbinic interpreters, we will return to the Mishnah once more, to see how the Mishnah and Midrash coexisted in the same rabbinic academies.

PART TWO

MIDRASH

Introduction

Understanding Midrash

Midrash[1] is an amplified reading of a verse in the Torah that creatively applies certain interpretive techniques in a relatively fixed format and with a set of technical terms. It often ascribes a surprising meaning to the text, which one would not expect it to bear.

This is an overly general definition, but when we try to pin Midrash down more we immediately run into problems. Is it primarily about the form or the content? Is it a distinctive interpretive method that can be distinguished from earlier or contemporary approaches? Is it unique to the Sages?

We will begin answering these questions by exploring Midrash from two angles. This introduction explores Midrash hermeneutically, as an interpretive phenomenon, and the next chapter attempts to situate it historically by surveying the preceding types of biblical interpretation. Only then will we be ready to delve into the intricacies of midrashic techniques and the ideologies behind them.

Let us begin, as always, with an example. Chapter 11 in the book of Numbers logs not one but two entries in the litany of complaints aired by the Israelites in the Sinai Desert. The second complaint is that the "riffraff" are sick of the daily manna and crave meat (Num. 11:4). The continuation describes Moses hearing "the people weeping by their families *(le-mishpeḥ otam)*, every man at the entrance to his tent" (Num. 11:10). God grows angry and sends His answer in the guise of thousands of quail and a plague that cuts down thousands of people. What are the people crying about?

R. Nehorai would say:

> It teaches that the Israelites were distressed when Moses told them to separate from forbidden sexual relations. It also teaches that a person could have married his

> **HERMENEUTICS**
>
> The study of interpretation named for the Greek God Hermes, who is said to mediate between heaven and earth and interpret the words of the gods. While reflections on interpretation date back to classical times, hermeneutics only became an independent theoretical field in the eighteenth century, with the advent of modern Bible scholarship.

sister, paternal aunt, or maternal aunt, such that when he told them to separate from (these) forbidden sexual relations, they were distressed. (*Sifrei Numbers*, §90, p. 91)[2]

היה ר׳ נהוראי אומר: מלמד שהיו ישראל מצטערין בשעה שאמר להן משה לפרוש מן העריות. ומלמד שהיה אדם נושא אחותו, ואחות אביו, ואחות אמו. בשעה שאמר להן לפרוש מן העריות היו מצטערין.

This interpretation seems to be a bizarre flight of fancy, unrelated to the biblical text in front of us, and it represents Midrash in all its glory. In fact, this weird imaginativeness is exactly what the word "Midrash" conjures for many modern readers. But Rabbi Nehorai, a disciple of Rabbi Akiva, took himself seriously, and we should too. On what basis does he read prohibited sexual relationships into this verse in Numbers, when the relevant laws appear an entire book earlier in Leviticus?

Perhaps Rabbi Nehorai was working backward from the severe punishment. Would God kill thousands for pining for the fish, melons, and garlic of Egypt? The punishment does not seem to fit the crime. The violation of a sexual taboo would explain God's wrath better. Maybe what sparked Rabbi Nehorai's imagination was the odd description of people crying by their families, the men sitting at the entrance to their tents. Why is the location of those sobbing important? If the saga centers on family matters, that might explain these peculiarities.

There is another, complementary dimension we should not forget. If the homily was delivered in public, then perhaps the homilist was simply looking for a textual opportunity to rehearse the hardship of and struggle with Halakhah's sexual restrictions.[3] These speculations are all reasonable, and it is impossible to fathom Rabbi Nehorai's mind when he gives us nothing to go on. We will return to this derashah at the end of the chapter, when we will have a third way of thinking through this conundrum.

Rabbi Nehorai's interpretation is part of the Midrash, whose individual textual unit is known in Hebrew as a derashah. The root *d-r-sh*, which underlies both terms, will be examined in the next section. This derashah is one of thousands compiled into collections that were organized according to the sequence of the Torah's verses. Like this one, most midrashic interpretations depart dramatically from the simple meaning of the biblical verses and produce stories and laws that we never would have considered possible to derive from the scriptural text.

This is the primary reason why Midrash, whether in its early tannaitic or later amoraic forms, is so puzzling. The learner is taken aback by the chasm between biblical text and midrashic conclusion. What drives Midrash to dispense with the more straightforward readings of the Torah in favor of far-out interpretations? Is the darshan, the practitioner of Midrash, aware that he has diverged from the lexical meaning of the text? What assumptions about Scripture lie at the core of the interpretive act and allow for such dramatic manipulations of the text? These questions and more drive the discussion in this chapter and those that follow.

Before such questions can be addressed, it is important to delineate the parameters of the discussion here. The subject of this book is specifically tannaitic Midrash, also known as "halakhic Midrash." These two designations are often used interchangeably: the first refers to its historical period and the second to its primary content. Tannaitic Midrash was composed in Judaea and the Galilee during the second century CE and the collections of it were edited in the third century. Given that the book of Genesis is mainly narrative and contains almost no legal content, there is no tannaitic Midrash on it. Collections of amoraic Midrash, also known as "aggadic Midrash," were only edited much later, circa the fifth century, because until that point Aggadah was not considered a genre worthy of independent compositions. Our treatment of the Mishnah showed that Aggadah played a complementary role to Halakhah in the Mishnah, and, as we will see in chapter 14, aggadic material in tannaitic Midrash functions as a kind of appendix to the legal material.[4]

The examples examined in this chapter are drawn primarily from aggadic material. This reflects a scholarly tendency to privilege the vivid and engaging world of aggadah over the drier, more austere realm of legal interpretation. Consequently, definitions of Midrash are often based on aggadic derashot, with insufficient regard for the distinctiveness of the different corpora. In the chapters that follow, we will seek to correct this bias.

A. THE TERM *MIDRASH*[5]

In the Torah, verbal forms from the Hebrew root *d-r-sh*, which also underlies the noun *midrash*,[6] mean seeking out God or His will. Such is accomplished by consulting prophets or oracles and not texts. Rebecca goes *lidrosh*—an infinitive meaning "to seek out"—God to find out why the twins are thrashing in her belly (Gen. 25:22).[7] God answers her in the form of an oracle, saying that "two nations are in your belly" (Gen. 25:23), namely, Jacob and Esau. There is neither text nor exegesis in this usage.

It is only in the Persian period (fifth–fourth centuries BCE) that the verb begins to take on the meaning "to interpret." Ezra the Scribe, leader of the returning exiles from Babylonia, is described as one who "set his heart *lidrosh* the Torah of the Lord and fulfill it, and to teach statutes and ordinances in Israel" (Ezra 7:10). For the first time, a verbal form of *d-r-sh* involves the interpretation of a written text: the Torah (which Ezra actually reads and interprets publicly in Neh. 8:2–4). From here on, the will of God can be sought out and found primarily in the divine written word.[8]

This correlates with the first appearance of the Hebrew noun *midrash* in the book of Chronicles, composed during the same period. It appears there twice: one verse mentions a *"midrash*

> **THE COMMUNITY RULE**
>
> One of the Dead Sea Scrolls discovered by Jordanian shepherds at Qumran in 1947. Titled *Seraḥ ha-Yaḥad* in Hebrew, it contains mostly non-biblical rules governing the sectarian community known as the *yaḥad* that likely lived at the site. These include laws of admission, a penal code, a hierarchy of ritual purity and its regulation among members, rules regarding temporary or permanent expulsion. Since the discovery of this text, a lot of material has been unearthed in the vicinity that paints a rich portrait of the group's communal life toward the end of the Second Temple period.

of the prophet Ido" (2 Chron. 13:23) and another a "*midrash* of the book of the kings" (2 Chron. 24:27). Both refer to specific written texts from which the author of Chronicles appears to have drawn material. While the nature of the "*midrash* of the prophet Ido" is a riddle, "the *midrash* of the book of the kings" may refer to some sort of adaption or expansion of the biblical book of Kings. If so, the Bible would be using the term *midrash* to denote one text that relates to another.[9] Combining the linguistic evidence from Ezra with Chronicles indicates that this period was likely when *midrash* took on the meaning of textual interpretation.[10]

This textual usage of *midrash* and related forms was heavily developed in the Dead Sea Scrolls found in the caves at Qumran in the mid-twentieth century.[11] Most verbal forms therein continue the biblical usages of seeking out God, but there are also many examples of the newer meaning involving textual interpretation.[12] The Community Rule Scroll (1QS), for instance, contains a description of what sounds like communal study:

> And in the place in which the Ten assemble there should not be missing a man to interpret the Torah *(doresh ba-Torah)* day and night, always, one relieving another.[13] And the Many shall be on watch together for a third of each night of the year in order to read the book, explain the regulation *(ve-lidrosh mishpat)*, and bless together. (1QS, 6:6–8)[14]

ואל ימש במקום אשר יהיו שם העשרה איש דורש בתורה יום ולילה תמיד חליפות איש לרעהו והרבים ישקודו ביחד את שלישית כול לילות השנה לקרוא בספר ולדרוש משפט ולברך ביחד.

The translation above renders *doresh* and *lidrosh*, a participle and infinitive from the same Semitic root *d-r-sh*, as "interpret" or "explain," but this is in itself an interpretive decision. In fact the connection between the reading of "the book" and the explaining of "the regulation" is unclear.[15] Nevertheless, the reference to a book and the necessity of continuous study situate the verbal forms of *d-r-sh* in a clear textual context.[16] In terms of nouns, the leader of the *yaḥad* group is called *doresh ha-Torah* in several places and the phrase *midrash ha-Torah* appears a few times in a textual setting.[17]

By this point in history, then, *midrash* is textual interpretation. But is it a specific kind of interpretation? Nothing suggests as much.[18] In the Dead Sea Scrolls, to be *doresh* retains the biblical sense of seeking out God or His will, only the means have changed—it is now through the biblical text. Those who are not part of the *yaḥad* community fail to do this: "they are not included in His covenant since they have neither sought nor examined Him *(darshuhu)* through His decrees in order to know the hidden matters in which they err" (1QS 5:11).[19] The search is still for God, but the search parameters no longer include prophets or oracles and are limited to the books of Scripture. As for specific search operators, the nouns and verbs from the root *d-r-sh* do not yet seem to denote any.

It is only in tannaitic literature that these terms gain specificity and become technical, hermeneutic ones. To be *doresh* and engage in *midrash* is to deduce Halakhah from the Torah in a specific manner. That *midrash* is distinct from other types of study in rabbinic literature is reflected in the Mishnah. The ruling in question concerns someone who has taken a vow not to derive benefit from someone else. Is being taught by the person considered a prohibited benefit? The Mishnah rules that the fellow may teach him "*midrash*, (extrabiblical) halakhot, and aggadot, but he may not teach him Scripture."[20] The former three are permitted because they are all taught in the study hall freely, so the person is not receiving any financial benefit. Basic knowledge of the Torah, however, is the province of paid schoolteachers and private tutors. To teach him his Bible would be to provide him with a benefit of monetary value. From here we can see that *midrash* refers to a discrete discipline that is part of the academic curriculum.[21]

B. DEFINING MIDRASH

The definition of Midrash in the opening line of this chapter is too vague to be useful. Some have argued that in scholarly usage, "Midrash" has become basically synonymous with "biblical interpretation," so the term ought to be avoided entirely.[22] History is no help in providing a more precise definition, because Midrash's historical emergence is the subject of wide disagreement. Some scholars claim that there is midrashic material included in the Bible itself.[23] Others push its inception to the end of the Second Temple period, but debate whether it was a widespread literary phenomenon in that era or a specifically rabbinic one.[24]

In a recent survey of Midrash scholarship, Carol Bakhos outlines several scholarly definitions of Midrash. It has been variously used to characterize a specific corpus, a literary genre with formal definitions, and a method of reading.[25] Scholars frequently combine these and other nuanced characterizations, because, as will be demonstrated below, no single definition covers this literary phenomenon adequately.

The Corpus

The simplest way to define Midrash is to focus not on method per se but on output. Midrash is a corpus of material produced in the tannaitic period that exhibits a specific kind of biblical interpretation.[26] By the Geonic period, the compositions that constitute this corpus were referred to as *midrashim*.

This definition is inadequate. After all, these compositions are the final, edited product of raw conversations and the editorial bundling of isolated viewpoints. To say that only what is included in the edited composition is in and everything else is out takes the power out of the hands of modern scholars and places it exclusively in the hands of the ancient editors. Without offering at least the contours of a descriptive definition, there is no way to compare Midrash to anything else, and, as a result, there is no possibility of discovering it anywhere outside this body of literature.

Formal Structure

Another way to define Midrash is by its structure and form.[27] Arnold Goldberg asserts that Midrash is an interpretation that unfolds according to a preset sequence. It begins with a quote from the Torah, a particular interpretive technique is then applied, and a conclusion is drawn that goes beyond the original understanding or scope of the quotation.[28] The common, seemingly natural structure of a biblical quote followed by interpretation was in fact a rarity before the rabbinic period. The norm in the Second Temple era was to rewrite the Torah in line with the interpretation, as we will see in the next chapter.[29]

To illustrate the structure being used to define Midrash, let us look at a midrashic passage concerning the Torah law that keeps a newlywed husband away from the front line of battle: "he shall be free for his household and gladden the wife whom he has taken" (Deut. 24:5):

> "When a man marries a new wife" (Deut. 24:5). I only have a virgin,[a] whence to include a widow or a *shomeret yavam*?[b] It teaches, "and gladden the wife"—under all circumstances.[c] (*Sifrei Deuteronomy*, §271, pp. 291–292)

"כִּי יִקַּח אִישׁ אִשָּׁה חֲדָשָׁה" (דברים כד, ה). אין לי אלא בתולה, מנין לרבות אלמנה ושומרת יבם? תלמוד לומר "וְשִׂמַּח אֶת אִשְׁתּוֹ"—מכל מקום.

The derashah begins with a quote from Deuteronomy 24, then it employs an exegetical principle, by which one part of a verse is reread in light of another, and it concludes with an expansion of the original law.

Throughout this book, we will see many examples that display this exact structure. While this definition of Midrash is not incorrect, it is too narrow and does not account for midrashic structures that are considerably more complex and variable. More to the point, privileging structure over substance gives us the bones with no meat to sink our teeth into. Midrash is too animate to be defined merely by its rhetorical skeleton.

---

a "New" is taken to mean that she is "new," sexually, to any man.

b A woman whose husband has died childless, and who must either be married by her *yavam*, her brother-in-law, through levirate marriage, or be released therefrom by him.

c "His wife" is absolute and thus includes women who are not virgins.

Methodology and Assumptions

A useful definition of Midrash should relate to its essential interpretive methodology. Proposed definitions focus on its departure from the simple meaning of Scripture, its consistent application of a limited set of hermeneutic principles, and its interpretive pluralism.[30]

Another possibility is to describe the assumptions that underlie its interpretive activity. James Kugel, for instance, identifies Midrash as exegesis that assumes the Torah's "omnisignificance," meaning that every word of the Torah is bursting with meaning and nothing is redundant or superfluous.[31] Such a posture is predicated on belief in the Torah as a divine text, Holy Writ.[32]

However, these definitions also suffer from being too broad. Many systems of interpretation deviate from a straight reading of Scripture, adhere to a set of principles, or allow for multiple interpretations. The rabbis weren't the only exegetes to consider the Torah an endlessly pregnant text, able to bear interpretation after interpretation. These definitional criteria are therefore too wide to catch only Midrash in their net.

This brief review of scholarly definitions demonstrates that no one has formulated a succinct one that sufficiently captures the qualities that distinguish it from similar interpretive enterprises. Each partial definition sets up artificial limits for the textual phenomenon we call Midrash.

After pointing out the challenges in properly defining Midrash, it seems imprudent to continue on the same path that has resulted in failure after failure. The approach to Midrash taken in this book is to plumb the corpus of classic halakhic works of Midrash produced by the Tannaim, and refer to Midrash inductively as the interpretive methodology found in these compositions. This methodology can then be richly compared to other forms of interpretation that existed around the same time and place, which is the subject of the next chapter.

C. MIDRASH AS INTERTEXTUAL INTERPRETATION

After having delinated the parameters of our inquiry, we can now ask a fundamental question: Is Midrash really interpretation at all? The derashah that opened the chapter reads the account of the people crying about food in Numbers 11 as tears shed over outlawed sexual relations. Is that a genuine interpretation that helps the reader understand the verse? Or is it a launch pad for the rocket of imagination, or a biblical hook on which to hang a preexisting lesson? The story it tells has little to do with the verses (that are perfectly readable without it), even if, as proposed above, it is inspired by or addresses problems in the text.

This issue has troubled great minds since the inception of Jewish Studies as a discipline. Several pioneering scholars grappled with Midrash given their own understanding of what textual interpretation is and how it works. In 1844, the masterful Abraham Geiger, who was also one of the leaders of the nascent Reform Judaism, diagnosed the Sages with "an extremely muddled exegetical sense."[33] Subsequent scholars tried their hand at explaining the interpretations that Midrash dreams up. Zacharias Frankel, whom we've met through his scholarship on the Mishnah, hypothesized that we are missing a large piece of the puzzle.[34] Isaac Hirsch Weiss reinstated a traditional explanation: the Midrash was revealed at Sinai, putting the divine logic beyond our ken.[35] Other traditionalists leaned into the weirdness and claimed that Midrash actually reveals the hidden depth of Scripture's sense.[36] Some, on the other hand, argued that Midrash is not interpretation at all, but a textual tack that fastens rabbinic ideas and stories to the biblical text.[37] What all of these explanatory forays have in common is the notion that it is ultimately impossible to understand the nature of Midrash as interpretation.

The mid-twentieth century saw a major breakthrough with the publication of Isaac Heinemann's Hebrew study *Darkhei ha-Aggadah* (The Methods of the Aggadah). Unlike some of his predecessors, Heinemann counted Midrash as interpretation, albeit a type that operates with its own principles and assumptions. He coined the term "creative philology" to express what Midrash does. It is "philological" in the sense that it pays acute attention to the original text and the nuances of its language, and it is "creative" in that it can uproot the text from its surroundings and plant it in new contexts, or water it with imagination and let it sprout new meanings.

Heinemann's major contribution was to take Midrash seriously as interpretation and to typologize its methodology. His work, though, was very much a product of a particular moment in the history of literary theory. He viewed Midrash through the lens of Romanticism, in which the space between text and interpreter collapses. This idea, popular in early twentieth-century literary theory, posited that the "creative genius" is one with his subject, as opposed to the objective scientist who examines his subject from a dispassionate distance. The darshanim of old, in Heinemann's telling, were one with the biblical text, as they attempted to convey its "lived truth."[38]

The debate over the characterization of Midrash has not abated with time. The same range of positions taken in the nineteenth century were reiterated in the late twentieth and early twenty-first centuries. At one extreme stood Joseph Dan, a celebrated scholar of Jewish mysticism, who was unwilling to count Midrash as interpretation at all.[39] At the other end were those who justify all derashot as interpretation, even when their link to the text is tenuous at best, through the resolution of implicit difficulties.[40]

It was Daniel Boyarin who broke this impasse with his *Intertextuality and the Reading of Midrash*. Boyarin's book belongs to a broader trend that picked up steam in the 1980s, in which new literary theories—structuralism and poststructuralism in particular—were applied to the study of Midrash.[41] In it, he argued that practitioners of Midrash have a common view of the Torah, in which the entirety of the biblical canon is the immediate relevant context for understanding every word of Scripture. Boyarin borrows a dichotomy from de Saussure's structuralist linguistics: the modern reader approaches the Torah as *parole*, a collection of utterances to be understood on their own terms, while the ancient darshan viewed it also as *langue*, a lexicon from which one draws and recombines phrases to say something that has never been said before.

> **STRUCTURALISM**
>
> A broad intellectual movement in the early twentieth century that analyzed its subjects as interrelated through larger structures. It owed much to the thought of Swiss linguist Ferdinand de Saussure (1857–1913), who used the terms *langue* and *parole* to account for the relationships between the constant and the variable in language.
>
> Poststructuralism is used to designate the philosophy of various thinkers from the 1980s, especially in France, who borrowed basic ideas from structuralism but rejected its basic conception of texts as having fixed meanings determined by linguistic rules. Instead, they emphasized the fundamental indeterminacy of texts.

Boyarin's explanation of why midrashic interpretation strikes us as strange is at once simple and revolutionary. Midrash doesn't well up from the profound depths of the verse's simple meaning, nor is it developed independently and then attached to it. Midrash, he says, is created at the moment different verses (or parts thereof) are joined. In the eyes of Midrash, the Torah interprets itself when its pieces are held up against one another. Midrash therefore is "a radical intertextual reading of the canon in which potentially every part refers to and is interpretable by every other part."[42]

The act of dismantling texts for their pieces and using them to build toward new conclusions is not whimsical. There are rules in construction to produce a structure that is sound, and the same is true here. Pieces can only be put together if they exhibit some affinity, as reflected through linguistic similarity, physical juxtaposition, or thematic parallels. There is a general order in which they must be placed, too. The basic assumption is that the Prophets and the Writings are a commentary on the Pentateuch, interpreting and expanding upon the narrative of the earlier books. The laconic narrative of the Torah ought to be "enriched"[43] by the more elaborate and colorful narrative of the other parts of the Bible (or, in the case of the Haggadah below, by the narrative segments of the Torah itself).

In the midrash below, this theory elucidates an otherwise cryptic text:

"And they went out into the Wilderness of Shur" (Ex. 15:22). This is the Kub Desert.[a] It is said about the Kub Desert that it was eight hundred by eight hundred parasangs, entirely filled with snakes and scorpions, as it says, "who led you through the great and terrible wilderness—snake, serpent, and scorpion" (Deut. 8:15), and it says, "A portent concerning the Desert of the Sea etc. from a terrible land" (Isa. 21:1), and it is written, "The portent of the Beasts of the Negeb. In a land of straits and stress, a lion and maned beast from among them, *ef'eh* and flying serpent" (Isa. 30:6)—*ef'eh* is nothing but the viper. It is said that when this viper sees the shadow

---

a A mythical place.

(*tzel*) of a bird in flight it is immediately spellbound and falls to pieces.[a] Even so,[b] "They did not say,[c] 'Where is the Lord who brought us up from the land of Egypt, who led us through the wilderness in a land of desert and pits, a land of parched earth and *tzalmavet*'" (Jer. 2:6). What is *tzalmavet*? A place where shadow (*tzel*) is accompanied by death (*mavet*). (*Mekhilta de-Rabbi Yishmael, Vayyassa'*, §1, pp. 153–154)

"וַיֵּצְאוּ אֶל מִדְבַּר שׁוּר" (שמות טו, כב)—זה מדבר כוב. אמרו עליו על מדבר כוב שהוא כוב שמנה מאות על שמנה מאות פרסה, כולו מלא נחשים ועקרבים, שנאמר "הַמּוֹלִיכְךָ בַּמִּדְבָּר הַגָּדֹל וְהַנּוֹרָא נָחָשׁ שָׂרָף וְעַקְרָב" (דברים ח, טו), ואומר "מַשָּׂא מִדְבַּר יָם וגו' מֵאֶרֶץ נוֹרָאָה" (ישעיהו כא, א), וכתיב "מַשָּׂא בַּהֲמוֹת נֶגֶב בְּאֶרֶץ צָרָה וְצוּקָה לָבִיא וָלַיִשׁ מֵהֶם אֶפְעֶה וְשָׂרָף מְעוֹפֵף" (ישעיהו ל, ו)—אין "אֶפְעָה" אלא עכס. אמרו שעכס זה רואה צל עוף פורח באויר מיד מתחבר ונושר איברים איברים. אף על פי כן "וְלֹא אָמְרוּ אַיֵּה ה' הַמַּעֲלֶה אֹתָנוּ מֵאֶרֶץ מִצְרָיִם הַמּוֹלִיךְ אֹתָנוּ בַּמִּדְבָּר בְּאֶרֶץ עֲרָבָה וְשׁוּחָה בְּאֶרֶץ צִיָּה וְצַלְמָוֶת" (ירמיה ב, ו). מה הוא "צַלְמָוֶת"? מקום צל ועימו מות.

At first glance, this midrash from *Mekhilta de-Rabbi Yishmael* on Exodus looks like a collection of legends artificially attached to the verses. It vividly describes creatures that populated the wilderness through which the Israelites trekked, creatures that are not present in the Torah's account. The awful Kub Desert itself is nowhere to be found in the Bible. But Boyarin points out that this midrash is transparently a patchwork of verses, indicated by the terms "as it says" and "it is written," on the terrors of the wilderness. The first act of midrashic interpretation is collecting these verses from various books of Scripture—Deuteronomy, Isaiah, and Jeremiah—on the assumption that together they fill out the laconic account in Exodus. Once they have been placed side by side, the interpretation emerges almost of its own accord. The fantastical account of the bewitching viper that downs its prey from the sky suggests itself from the unusual word *tzalmavet*. What appeared to be folklore turns out to be the imaginative product of careful textual work. The resulting midrash vivifies the people's turn into the Wilderness of Shur, and helps the reader empathize with the plight of the grumbling Israelites.[44]

Another intertextual mosaic from the *Mehkilta* focuses on the end of the very same verse: "They went three days in the wilderness and they did not find water" (Ex. 15:22). A number of Sages voice opinions on this, and we will have cause to analyze them in a later chapter, but for now we will focus on just one opinion:

Others say, Water that the Israelites took from between the parted waters[d] was finished at that time. What, then, does "they did not find" teach? Like the usage in

---

a So that the viper can eat it. This picture is based on the interpretation of Jeremiah 2:6 that follows.
b Despite the dangers and terrors of the desert.
c The Israelites.
d Of the Red Sea; see Psalms 136:13.

the following context, "And their nobles sent their lads for water. [They came to the cisterns and did not find water; their vessels returned empty]" (Jer. 14:3). (*Mekhilta de-Rabbi Yishmael, Vayyassa'*, §1, pp. 153–154)

אחרים אומרים: מים שנטלו ישראל מבין הגזרים שלמו מהן באותה שעה. הא מה תלמוד לומר "לֹא מָצָאוּ"? כענינין שנאמר "וְאַדִּרֵיהֶם שָׁלְחוּ צְעִירֵיהֶם לַמָּיִם [בָּאוּ עַל גֵּבִים לֹא מָצְאוּ מַיִם שָׁבוּ כְלֵיהֶם רֵיקָם]" (ירמיה יד, ג).

The fact that the Israelites could not find water in a desert is hardly noteworthy, so the darshan searches for other meanings of "they did not find water." In Jeremiah, he finds the only other verse in all of Scripture containing the same exact phrase. There, the failure to find water during a drought is associated with empty vessels. He reads that back into Exodus, so that "they did not find water" reports that they looked into the canteens they had filled when crossing the split sea three days earlier and found them bone dry. Thus, the terse narrative in Exodus is enriched by the theologically charged prophecy in Jeremiah, transforming the absence of water in the desert from a mere logistical detail into a parallel to the divinely sanctioned drought depicted there. Yet again, Midrash positions a verse in a way that it is refracted by another part of Scripture, yielding a new vivid image.

A third example, this one from *Sifrei Numbers*, should further sharpen our understanding of the intertextuality of Midrash. In Numbers 25, the Israelites "go astray" by worshipping other Gods and carry on sexual liaisons with Midianite women. To put an end to these brazen, forbidden unions, the zealous Phineas kills the tribal leader Zimri and the Midianite princess Cozbi. He is rewarded with a covenant of everlasting priesthood for his actions:

"In recompense for *(taḥat asher)* his acting zealously for his God" (Num. 25:13)—"in recompense for *(taḥat asher)* his exposing himself to death" (Isa. 53:12). (*Sifrei Numbers*, §131, p. 309)

"תַּחַת אֲשֶׁר קִנֵּא לֵאלֹהָיו" (במדבר כה, יג)—"תַּחַת אֲשֶׁר הֶעֱרָה לַמָּוֶת נַפְשׁוֹ" (ישעיה נג, יב).

This derashah serves its interpretation in complete silence. All it does is draw a connection, by virtue of linguistic and thematic similarity, between Isaiah's depiction of the actions of the "suffering servant" and the episode involving Phineas in Numbers. This linkage does some heavy lifting by evoking the entirety of the verse in Isaiah in connection with our verse:

Therefore I will give him shares among the many, and he shall divide the spoils with the mighty, in recompensing for exposing himself to death, and was counted among the sinners. Yet he bore the sin of the many and interceded for the sinners. (Isaiah 53:12)

Introduction: Understanding Midrash   193

The combination of these verses produces a new narrative in Numbers: Phineas receives his reward of priesthood, his "shares among the many" other priests, because he risked his life to atone for the sins of the Israelites. But it also has an effect on Isaiah. By identifying the "suffering servant" verses with a biblical figure from the Hebrew Bible, Menahem Kahana argues that the rabbis were implicitly countering the early Christian interpretation of that figure as Jesus.[45] Whatever the exact interpretation this derashah advances, the bare-bones structure of verse juxtaposed with verse exposes the essence of Midrash: intertextuality. The skill of the darshan depends on his ability to be attuned to potential linkages and to materialize them.

One of the best-known texts in which midrashic intertextuality is front-and-center is the Pesach (Passover) Haggadah read at the Seder (the ritualized night meal). The Mishnah instructs: "one must expound midrashically *(doresh)* from 'My father was a wandering Aramean' (Deut. 26:5) until one finishes the entire passage."[46] In fulfillment of this mandate, the central portion of the Haggadah is a lengthy midrash on that verse and the next four. In Deuteronomy, these are an abridged recounting of Israelite history until entry into the Land of Israel. The midrashic exposition in the Haggadah consists of linking each verse and its constituent phrases to other parts of the Torah. To choose one derashah, when Deuteronomy says that the Jewish people became "mighty and numerous" in Egypt, a derashah connects it with the exponential increase mentioned at the beginning of the book of Exodus:

> "Great, mighty *('atzum)*" (Deut. 26:5)—as it says, "and the Children of Israel were fruitful and swarmed and multiplied and grew exceedingly vast *(vayya'atzmu)*, and the land was filled with them" (Ex. 1:7).

"גָּדוֹל עָצוּם" (דברים כו, ה)—כמה שנאמר "וּבְנֵי יִשְׂרָאֵל פָּרוּ וַיִּשְׁרְצוּ וַיִּרְבּוּ וַיַּעַצְמוּ בִּמְאֹד מְאֹד וַתִּמָּלֵא הָאָרֶץ אֹתָם" (שמות א, ז).

The verses in Deuteronomy are supposed to be recited in thanksgiving upon bringing the first fruits to the Temple, so they merely recap the highlights of Israelite history. In this case, it is earlier biblical material in Exodus that enriches the retelling at the Seder.

The simplicity of these derashot has led scholars to believe that they represent the earliest type of Midrash, but David Henshke has cast serious doubt on this.[47] If other types of Midrash were available, why was this one chosen for the Haggadah? Perhaps its simplicity allows the leader of the Seder to show the participants how to create Midrash intertextually, an activity usually reserved for expert scholars in the rabbinic academies.[48] By instructing every Jew to expound these verses midrashically, the Mishnah transforms the realization of the biblical commandment to transmit the story of the Exodus to the next generation. It takes advantage of the one time in which every house becomes a small study hall in order to demonstrate the rabbinic methodology, usually the preserve of a small circle of Sages, to the broader community. Intertextuality as the essence of Midrash was already recognized in antiquity.

If Intertextuality characterizes midrashic practice, we are justified in looking for it even when it is not explicit. As promised, we now return to the derashah of Rabbi Nehorai. Recall that he radically claimed that the Israelites sobbing over the unchanging daily fare—manna—was truthfully about newly prohibited sexual relationships. The first approach says that Rabbi Nehorai sensed some kind of incongruity or difficulty in the text and intended the derashah to justify or explain it. A second possibility is that he wanted to deliver a message about sexual impropriety, and the biblical verse was but a pretext. These two approaches are antithetical, placing the derashah's full weight either on the biblical text or on the darshan's mind. A third, intertextual approach rejects this dichotomy; Rabbi Nehorai's derashah is neither the sole product of the verse nor a random imposition on it. Granted, this derashah does not make any explicit intertextual connections. But you need to pop the hood to examine the engine.

In the context of Numbers 11, the rabble "felt an intense craving" *(hit'avvu ta'avah)*, which in context is for the taste of meat. But *ta'avah*, a craving or desire, extends to other appetites in the Midrash's reading of the Torah. If the entire Torah forms a 360-degree backdrop around every word or phrase, then other occurrences of *ta'avah* can elucidate its meaning. In the Garden of Eden, the Torah says that the forbidden fruit "was a *ta'avah* for the eyes" (Gen. 3:6), which was understood by ancient readers to carry sexual undertones.[49] The guiding principle of intertextuality would have charted a path through the Torah for the darshan—and now for us following his trail—from hunger to lust.

Lastly, it is worth noting that the pervasive practice of intertextuality in Midrash likely indicates that scripture was discussed orally in the study house. As Catherine Hezser aptly observes, it is difficult to imagine, in a world where scrolls contained individual biblical books, that the rabbis would "unroll them to find the verses they wanted to comment upon," particularly when a single derasha often engages with verses from multiple biblical books, as is the case with many derashot.[50]

Let us now return to the question with which we began: Is midrash a form of interpretation? As this chapter has shown, the question is misguided, as it presupposes an objective normative standard that transcends culture and history. Instead, we should be asking what concepts of textuality, sacred text, and reading empower—indeed urge—the rabbis to engage with texts as they do. This is the inquiry that the following section of the book seeks to explore.

As noted at the beginning of the chapter, following scholarly consensus this introduction to Midrash has concentrated on aggadic passages in tannaitic Midrash. Aggadic derashot, however, comprise only a minority of it, so most of this part of the book focuses on halakhic derashot. While the approaches, definitions, and tools of this chapter will be applied to them, differences between aggadic and halakhic Midrashim will be duly noted. But before analyzing Midrash in depth, we will take a tour of Second Temple–era scriptural interpretation and Midrash's literary and exegetical antecedents.

One final caveat before we begin: Midrash is a complex and multilayered phenomenon. Throughout this study, I have not always flagged when later chapters will introduce additional perspectives that complicate earlier presentations. The chapters should therefore be read as complementary, with subsequent discussions refining and nuancing initial claims. A comprehensive understanding of the phenomenon of Midrash requires considering the following chapters together.

NINE

Biblical Interpretation in Second Temple Literature

Midrash did not spring into being out of thin air. It was nourished from a broad network of filaments reaching across time to earlier interpretive endeavors and achievements. This chapter will look at the kinds of biblical interpretation that preceded rabbinic Midrash and compare them. Such exegesis covers both biblical law and narrative, and this chapter begins with the former.

A. HALAKHIC MIDRASH IN THE BIBLE

The earliest biblical exegesis appears within the Bible itself, in its chronologically later books. These interpretations belong to a period in which Scripture had yet to be canonized, so the precise wording was not treated as sacred and immutable. There was no single, binding version of the Torah, but its contents were already considered authoritative.[1]

As noted in the introduction to part 1, new interpretations of the Torah in the time of Ezra and Nehemiah often led to innovations in halakhic practice. One such innovation is based on a sophisticated interpretive move, which may be the first documented legal midrash.[2] The historical setting is the return of a small fraction of Jews from the Babylonian exile to Judea. Upon arriving, they encounter some of their brethren who have never gone into exile, and the relationship between the two groups is fraught with tension. Part of this includes contention over who are the "real" Israelites.

In the book of Ezra, leaders of the returnees inform Ezra of supposed misconduct among the local Jewish population:

> When this was over, the officials approached me, saying, "The people of Israel, the priests, and the Levites have not separated themselves from the peoples of the lands, whose abominations are like those of the Canaanites, the Hittites, the Perizzites, the Jebusites, the Ammonites, the Moabites, the Egyptians, and the Amorites. For they have taken some of their daughters as wives for themselves and for their sons, so that the holy seed has become intermingled with the peoples of the lands." (Ezra 9:1–2)

Ezra responds:

> Now, what can we say in the face of this, our God? For we have forsaken Your commandments, which *You commanded through Your servants the prophets, saying,* "The land that you are about to possess is a land unclean through the uncleanness of the peoples of the lands with their abominations, as they have filled it from one end to the other with their uncleanness. Now, do not give your daughters to their sons or let their daughters marry your sons, and never seek their peace or prosperity, so that you may be strong and eat the bounty of the land and bequeath it to your children forever." (Ezra 9:10–12, emphasis mine)

In the italicized line, Ezra appears to signal that he is about to quote a prophetic statement found in the Torah. In reality, what follows is a pastiche of verse fragments and paraphrases drawn from texts across the Torah. The reason Ezra crafts this composite text is that no single biblical verse exists to support the claim he wants to make: that it is, and always has been, forbidden for Israelites to marry "foreign women."

Ezra begins by paraphrasing Leviticus 18:24–30 about the danger of polluting the land if the Israelites emulate the sexual practices of their Canaanite neighbors. That text never mentions marrying non-Israelites as a problem, though. The second text quoted by Ezra, Deuteronomy 7:3, does mention a marriage prohibition, but it applies only to members of the seven Canaanite nations. The final piece is based on Deuteronomy 23:7, another nuptial proscription that is very limited—this time specifically to Moabites and Ammonites. The Torah even provides a reason for their specific exclusion, that they did not offer provisions to their Israelite cousins when they skirted their lands. No law in the Torah prohibits intermarriage with Philistines (Neh. 13:23), Samaritans (Ezra 4:2), Nabateans (Neh. 4:1), or the other nations mentioned in the book of Ezra and Nehemiah. Even Egyptians, included on Ezra's list of prohibited unions, are permitted by the Torah to join the Israelite community after three generations have passed (Deut. 23:8).

The blanket prohibition on intermarriage is therefore novel. It is the practical expression of a new, idealized conception of the Israelite nation as being of "holy seed" (Ezra 9:2), which turns intermarriage into a desacralizing act. But Ezra presents this prohibition as rooted in the very birth of the nation, attested in the Torah, its foundational document. By amalgamating these distinct verses, Ezra is able to jettison the particular reasons behind the original prohibitions on marrying women of specific ethnicities or nationalities, and to generate a universal prohibition on intermarriage. Indeed, Ezra 10 is the first time the Bible uses the phrase "foreign women" as a synthetic category that encompasses women from every nation previously mentioned.[3]

B. REWRITTEN BIBLICAL LAW

The book of Jubilees, written in Hebrew circa the second century BCE, is an account of the history of the world. It claims to have been revealed to Moses on Mount Sinai by "the Angel of the Presence," who narrates the book. It retells the biblical narrative from the book of Genesis through the beginning of Exodus, while incorporating later aggadic traditions and new legal material.

Here is an example of how Jubilees adapts biblical law. It is found in the description of the paschal sacrifice toward the end of the book:

> Now you remember this day throughout all your lifetime. Celebrate it from year to year, throughout all your lifetime, once a year on its day in accord with all of its law. Then you will not pass over a day from the day or from month to month. For it is an eternal statute and it is engraved on the heavenly tablets regarding the Israelites that they are to celebrate it each and every year on its day, once a year, throughout their entire history. There is no temporal limit because it is ordained forever. The man who is pure but does not come to celebrate it on its prescribed day—to bring a sacrifice that is pleasing before the Lord and to eat and drink before the Lord on the day of his festival—that man who is pure and nearby is to be uprooted because he did not bring the Lord's sacrifice at its time. That man will bear responsibility for his own sin. (Jubilees 49:7–9)[4]

This passage demands the celebration of the biblical festival in its correct season and time, and states that someone who could bring the paschal sacrifice but didn't is "uprooted," the severe biblical punishment known as *karet*. It combines verses about the paschal sacrifice found in Exodus 12 and Numbers 9. The latter stresses the importance of bringing the sacrifice at the appointed time, and levies the punishment of *karet* for failure to do so. However, it also makes a provision for people who are unable to bring it on time due to ritual impurity or being too far away from the cultic site. If they fail to bring it on the fourteenth of Nisan, they may bring it on the fourteenth of the next month. In rabbinic literature, this makeup holiday is known as *pesaḥ sheni*, the second Pesach (Passover).

Why does Jubilees reiterate the Torah's stress on timeliness and the severity of the punishment but omits the biblically sanctioned second chance? Because according to its worldview, a mitzvah out of time is no mitzvah at all. Throughout the book, the author adheres strictly to the solar calendar, which is understood to be grounded in creation itself. As such, commandments performed in certain seasons assume cosmic significance.[5] In many of its retellings, therefore, the book attempts to bring biblical events in line with this calendar. When it comes to the paschal sacrifice, the second chance provided by the Torah one lunar cycle later does not fit a ritual life guided by the movement of the Sun alone. The book adopts the parts of Torah law that suit its worldview and leaves out those that do not.

In this example, Jubilees uses two techniques to rewrite biblical law. First, it combines Passover laws from various legal passages in the Torah, harmonizing its distinct and often contradictory parts. Second, it forces these laws into a procrustean bed of a new religious ideology. Rather subtly, the book of Jubilees remolds the Torah to fit its own worldview.

Jubilees belongs to a genre of literature in which the biblical text is retold with new details and themes by modifying the existing material. Geza Vermes has characterized this class of texts as "rewritten Bible."[6] In the Second Temple era, exegetes typically merged the biblical source text with their own interpretation and did not maintain any distinction between the two in their presentation. This is in contrast to later, rabbinic interpretation, which quotes the canonical text and then supplies the interpretation.

C. HALAKHIC MIDRASH AT QUMRAN

Many scholars have compared legal development in the texts at Qumran and in the halakhic Midrash of the Tannaim and found similarities in their respective interpretive techniques and their halakhic derivations.[7] Here is an example from the Shabbat laws of the Damascus Document, mentioned already in the introduction to part 1:

> Concerning the Sa[bba]th, to observe it in accordance with its regulation. No one should do work on the sixth day, from the moment when the Sun's disc is at a distance of its diameter from the gate, for this is what he said, "Observe the Sabbath day to keep it holy." (Deut. 5:12)[8]

> על הש[ב]ת לשמרה כמשפטה. [] [] אל יעש איש ביום הששי מלאכה מן העת אשר יהיה גלגל השמש רחוק מן השער מלואו. כי הוא אשר אמר שמור את יום השבת לקדשו.

According to this passage, one must start to observe the prohibitions of Shabbat before sunset, and not during or after it. A tannaitic midrash comes to a similar conclusion using the same verse:

> "Remember" (Ex. 20:8)—beforehand, and "observe" (Deut. 5:12)—afterward.[a] Hence they said, One should add from the mundane onto the holy.[b] (*Mekhilta de-Rabbi Yishmael, Ba-Ḥodesh*, §7, p. 229)[9]

> "זכור" מלפניו ו"שמור" מלאחריו. מכאן אמרו: מוסיפין מחול על הקדש.

a Before and after Shabbat.
b From the mundanity of Friday onto Shabbat, i.e., accept the prohibitions of Shabbat before its actual onset at nightfall.

In both the Damascus Document and the *Mekhilta*, the word "observe" in Deuteronomy (5:12) is interpreted as creating a buffer or boundary to prevent the violation of Shabbat. While one cannot discount the possibility, however remote, that these two sources generated this interpretation independently, it is far more likely that the two possessed a shared, earlier tradition. Notably, the Qumran text presents the law first and then the support from the verse ("No one should do work . . . for this is what he said. . . ."), whereas the midrash begins with the verse and then cites the extrapolation ("'Remember' . . . From here they said . . .").[10] Although this seems like a trivial difference, it is telling, and we will return to it below.

Sometimes, the biblical source for a ruling is accompanied by an explicit interpretation. For instance, in the Community Rule there is a prohibition of interacting with "sinners" outside of the sect:

No-one should eat of any of their possessions, or drink or accept anything from their hands, unless at its price, for it is written, "Shun the man whose breath is in his nostrils, for how much is he worth?" (Isa. 2:22) For all those not numbered in his covenant will be segregated, they and all that belongs to them. (1QS 5:16–18)[11]

ואשר לוא יוכל מהונם כול ולוא ישתה, ולוא יקח מידם כול מאומה אשר לוא במחיר, כאשר כתוב "חדלו לכם מן האדם אשר נשמה באפו כיא במה נחשב הואה" (ישעיהו ב, כב), כיא כול אשר לוא נחשבו בבריתו להבדיל אותם ואת כול אשר להם.

Here too the passage begins with the legal imperative and then adduces scriptural support. In this case, the author adds his interpretation: the generic worthless "man" spoken of by Isaiah is read as a reference to anyone outside of the sect who is "not numbered in his covenant." The textual justification is based on a nakedly sectarian interpretation of Scripture.

The problem with linking Qumranic literature and Midrash is that these examples are actually exceptional. The vast majority of laws in both the Damascus Document and the Community Rule are presented without any scriptural basis, so that they resemble a legal code rather than midrashic interpretation. For that reason, Steven Fraade has critiqued the scholarly presumption that links Qumran and Midrash. He writes:

Qumran writings contain a much smaller proportion of explicit scriptural exegesis than is found in early rabbinic literature. [. . .] [T]o a great degree, communal law appears to have been transmitted and taught primarily as lists of rules. While the scriptural citation is integral to the structure of the rabbinic argument, it is not required by the sectarian rule. [H]owever they regarded their laws in relation to Scripture, for the most part they were not interested in demonstrating or transmitting their exegetical interconnections, as were the rabbis. [. . .] While the early rabbinic midrashim tend to focus more on legal than narrative sections of the

> Torah, at Qumran explicit biblical exegesis tends to be employed mainly for eschatological exegesis of prophecies and hardly at all for legal exegesis.[12]

Fraade is highlighting the fact that most halakhic works from Qumran (the Damascus Document, the War Scroll, the Community Rule) are thematically organized codes similar to the Mishnah, and a few (like the Temple Scroll) take the form of rewritten Bible like the book of Jubilees. A small number of exceptions aside, if halakhic Midrash is present at all in the Qumran literature, it is at work below the surface and can only be reconstructed on the basis of later parallels in tannaitic literature.

Scholars debate what to make of this near absence of explicit Midrash in Qumran. Menachem Kister argues that it represents a historical development, from midrashic underdevelopment at Qumran to its flowering in the tannaitic collections.[13] Aharon Shemesh and Steven Fraade attribute the difference instead to genre and ideology. The Mishnah presents precious little explicit exegesis, but one would be wrong in claiming that biblical interpretation has nothing to do with its laws. The Bible is in fact a major input; it is only that the Mishnah's interpretations are typically not articulated.[14] The same can be said for sectarian Halakhah.[15]

As Fraade explains, the Qumran sect looked not only to the Torah as the source of the law but also to ongoing divine revelation. Too much emphasis on the verses and hermeneutical methodology would have obscured the sect's fundamental tenet of divine revelation to its elect, and this was one of the core beliefs that set it apart from other groups.[16] Aharon Shemesh buttresses Fraade's point by observing that the one book that does have a wealth of direct biblical quotations is the polemical Halakhic Letter. Unlike most works from Qumran, the intended readership of this book is not the members of the sectarian community but its external opponents. To persuade outsiders who do not share his beliefs, the author is forced to rely on the sole source deemed authoritative by both sides: the Torah.[17] In compositions intended for internal communal use, little use is made of Midrash so as not to in any way minimize the revelatory authority of sectarian law.[18]

One characteristic of rabbinic Midrash, which differentiates it from the Qumran literature, is the way that it rigidly separates the biblical source from its rabbinic interpretation. Let us compare the ways that the Qumran sect and the Sages treated the Torah's law about a man who has sexual relations with an unmarried virgin. The pertinent biblical passages appear in two different legal codes of the Torah:

> If a man seduces a virgin who is not betrothed and lies with her, he shall surely pay a bride-price for her as his wife. If her father utterly refuses to give her to him, he must weigh out silver according to the bride-price for virgins. (Exodus 22:15–16)

> If a man comes upon a virgin young woman who is not betrothed and he seizes her and lies with her, and they are discovered, the man lying with her shall pay the girl's father fifty [shekels of] silver, and she shall be his wife inasmuch as he abused her. He cannot send her away all his days. (Deuteronomy 22:28–29)

> **THE HALAKHIC LETTER**
>
> Also known as *Miktzat Ma'asei ha-Torah* or 4QMMT, this composition presents the Halakhah of the sect and contrasts it with that of its competitors, the Pharisees. It is written as a missive to the Sadducean High Priest in Jerusalem, requesting him to follow the correct laws. The name of the text derives from a phrase in its concluding lines: "And also we have written to you some of the works of the Torah *(miktzat ma'asei ha-Torah)* which we think are good for you and for your people, for we s[a]w that you have intellect and knowledge of the Law" (García Martínez and Tigchelaar, *Dead Sea Scrolls Study Edition*, 803).

The similarity between the two passages did not escape the notice of early exegetes, who read them in light of each other:

If a man seduces a young virgin who is not betrothed, and she is fit for him by the law and he lies with her and is discovered, then the man who lay with her shall give the girl's father fifty [shekels of] silver and she will be ‹his› wife, since he abused her; and he cannot send her away all his days. (The Temple Scroll, 11Q19 66:8–11)[19]

כי יפתה איש נערה בתולה אשר לוא אורשה, והיא רויה לו מן החוק, ושכב עמה ונמצא ונתן האיש השוכב עמה לאבי הנערה חמשים כסף, ולוא תהיה לאשה, תחת אשר ענה, לוא יוכל לשלחה כול ימיו.

"He shall surely pay a bride-price for her as his wife" (Ex. 22:15)—why is it said? Because it says, "The man lying with her shall pay" (Deut. 22:29). Could it be that in the same way one pays immediately for a seized one, one pays immediately for a seduced one? It therefore teaches, "He shall surely pay a bride-price for her as his wife," telling us that he assumes the responsibility of a bride-price, and a bride-price is nothing but a ketubah, as it says, "Ask of me however high a bride-price etc." (Gen. 24:12) [. . .]

"He must weigh out silver" (Ex. 22:16), but we have not heard how much. So I reason: It says "silver" here and it says "silver" there (Deut. 22:29). Just as there it's "fifty [shekels of] silver," so too here it's fifty [shekels of] silver. (*Mekhilta de-Rabbi Yishmael, Nezikin*, §17, p. 309)

"מָהֹר יִמְהָרֶנָּה לּוֹ לְאִשָּׁה" למה נאמר? לפי שנאמר "וְנָתַן הָאִישׁ הַשֹּׁכֵב עִמָּהּ". יכול כשם שבתפוסה נותן מיד, כך במפותה נותן מיד? תלמוד לומר "מָהֹר יִמְהָרֶנָּה לּוֹ לְאִשָּׁה"—מגיד שהוא עושה עליו מֹהַר, ואין מֹהַר אלא כתובה, שנאמר "הַרְבּוּ עָלַי מְאֹד מֹהַר וכו'" (בראשית כד, יב).

"כֶּסֶף יִשְׁקֹל" (שמות כב, טז) אבל לא שמענו כמה. הרי אני דן: נאמר כאן "כֶּסֶף" ונאמר להלן "כָּסֶף" (דברים כב, כט), מה להלן "חֲמִשִּׁים כָּסֶף", אף כאן חמשים כסף.

The Temple Scroll and the *Mekhilta* both read the case of the seducer in Exodus 22 in conjunction with the case of the rapist in Deuteronomy 22. This allows them to fill in some of the blanks present in each of the two scenarios. In Exodus, the seducer's fine is identified as a "bride-price" but no amount is specified, while in Deuteronomy, the rapist is fined an exact amount of fifty silver shekels.

No less notable than this shared methodology is the divergence. The *Mekhilta* quotes the relevant verse fragments and transparently shows its logical operations on them, whereas the Temple Scroll blends the two texts together. It chooses the case of rape in Deuteronomy 22 as the base text because it is the more detailed of the two, and incorporates the element of seduction from Exodus 22. This is the same methodology of rewritten Bible encountered in the previous section.

This profoundly distinguishes the two legal corpora. In terms of form, the Midrash shows its work, so that one can see how the two biblical passages are used to inform each other. The Temple Scroll blurs the sources by synthesizing them. In terms of content, the Midrash notes similarities and disparities in its legal sources, so that each one retains its integrity and independence.[20] The Qumran text, by contrast, melds them to the point of indistinguishability, thus leaving no room for evaluation of the legal differences between the cases of the seducer and the rapist.[21]

The Temple Scroll version contains a further requirement not found in either biblical source. Since the offender must marry his victim, the text says that she must be "fit *(r[e'] uyah)* for him by the law." The *Mekhilta* also adds this condition:

> "He shall surely pay a bride-price for her as his wife" (Ex. 22:15)—the verse is speaking about one who is fit *(re'uyah)* to be his wife, excluding a widow for a High Priest, a divorcee and a *ḥalutzah*[a] for a Kohen,[b] a *mamzeret*[c] and a *netinah*[d] for an Israelite,[e] a daughter of an Israelite for a *netin* or *mamzer*. (*Mekhilta de-Rabbi Yishmael, Nezikin*, §17, 308)

"מָהֹר יִמְהָרֶנָּה לּוֹ לְאִשָּׁה" (שמות כב, טו)—בראויה לו לאשה הכתוב מדבר, להוציא אלמנה לכהן גדול, גרושה וחלוצה לכהן הדיוט, ממזרת ונתינה לישראל, בת ישראל לנתין וממזר.

---

a A woman released from levirate marriage.
b A male of priestly descent.
c Someone born from a union forbidden by the Torah under the penalty of *karet*; see Mishnah, *Yevamot*, 4:13.
d A descendant of the Gibeonites, whose halakhic status is like that of a *mamzer*; see Mishnah, *Kiddushin*, 3:12 and 4:1.
e Neither a Levite nor a Kohen.

Both the Temple Scroll and the *Mekhilta* add this requirement to the biblical source and use the exact same language of halakhic fitness, the passive participle *re'uyah*. This makes a common tradition likely.[22] Yet again, the similarity brings the difference between the two texts into sharper relief: the Temple Scroll embeds this requirement into the sequence of verses, whereas the midrash clearly designates it an extrapolation from the verse.

A third presentation of this law, using the same language, appears in the Mishnah:

> If some promiscuity is discovered about her or she is not fit *(re'uyah)* to enter the people of Israel, he may not keep her. As it says, "and she shall be his wife" (Deut. 22:29)—a wife who is fit *(re'uyah)* for him. (Mishnah, *Ketubbot*, 3:5)

> נימצא בה דבר זמה או שאינה ראויה לבוא בישראל, אינו רשיי לקיימה, שנאמר "וְלֹא תִהְיֶה לְאִשָּׁה"—אשה שהיא ראויה לו.

This makes for a total of three ways of presenting the same law in antiquity: rewritten Bible, which integrates the law into the biblical quotation or paraphrase; Midrash, which quotes the verse and then gives the legal interpretation; and legal codification, which states the law first and then produces a prooftext. The latter two rabbinic methods make the boundary between the canonical text and the interpretation abundantly clear, whereas the former style adopted by the Qumran sect presents the Torah as observed by its members—new law mingling with the old.

D. REWRITTEN BIBLICAL NARRATIVE

Beside the exegesis of biblical law in the Second Temple era, there was extensive interpretation of biblical narrative. Here, too, one can find precursors of this in the later biblical books. The most obvious case is the book of Chronicles, which retells the narratives of the books of Samuel and Kings in a manner that suits its pro-Davidic and pietistic ideology. For example, David's testament to Solomon in 1 Kings 2 is mainly political in nature and deals with how Solomon should handle his adversaries, but its retelling in 1 Chronicles 28 turns from court politics to how God's Temple should be built.

Second Temple texts retell the biblical stories of the Patriarchs. The book of Jubilees contains many examples of this. Its account of the Binding of Isaac is almost identical to the biblical one, but there are a few significant differences. One of them concerns God's command to Abraham to stay his hand from sacrificing his son:

> And Abraham reached out his hand and took the knife to slaughter his son. And an angel of the Lord called out to him from heaven and said, "Abraham, Abraham!" and he said, "Here I am." And he said, "Do not reach out your hand against the boy nor do anything to him, for now I know that you fear God and you have not withheld your son, your only one, from Me." (Genesis 22:10–12)

Biblical Interpretation   205

Compare this to the version in Jubilees:

> Then he tied up his son Isaac, placed him on the wood that was on the altar, and reached out his hands to take the knife in order to sacrifice his son Isaac. Then I stood in front of him and in front of the prince of Mastema. The Lord said, "Tell him not to let his hand go down on the child and not to do anything to him because I have shown that he is one who fears the Lord." So I called to him from heaven and said to him, "Abraham, Abraham!" He was startled and said, "Yes?" I said to him, "Do not lay your hands on the child and do not do anything to him because I have now shown that you are one who fears the Lord. You have not refused me your son, your firstborn." The prince of Mastema was put to shame. (Jubilees 18:8–12)[23]

The narrator of the biblical account is the anonymous voice of the Torah, but in Jubilees it is the Angel of the Presence, the divine being charged with dictating the contents of Jubilees to Moses on Mount Sinai. This actually accords with the original narrative: the "angel of the Lord" referred to there in the third person is the first-person narrator here. But then Jubilees inserts another character into the scene, the "prince of Mastema," Jubilees's Satan.[24] According to this version, it is the prince of Mastema—and not God—who wants Abraham to sacrifice his son. This resolves the theological difficulty of the original narrative: Why would God ask Abraham to offer a human sacrifice—of his beloved, "only" son no less? If the blame for this sadistic command can be laid at Satan's cloven feet, it all makes sense.[25]

This desire to present God in a more positive light can account for several other discrepancies between the original Bible and the rewritten one. In the Torah, Abraham's passing of the test informs God of something He seemingly did not know before: "now I know that you fear God" (Gen. 22:11). This implies that God is not omniscient. This changes in Jubilees, where it repeats the alteration twice: "I have shown that he is one who fears the Lord" (Jub. 18:9, 11). If there are doubters of Abraham's devotion, God is not among them.

At the end of the biblical story, Abraham returns to the servants who accompanied him and they all journey to Beersheba. Jubilees alters the aftermath of the binding by characteristically bringing legal material into the narrative:[26]

> Then Abraham went to his servants. They set out and went together to Beersheba. Abraham lived at the well of the oath. He used to celebrate this festival joyfully for seven days during all the years. He named it the Festival of the Lord in accord with the seven days during which he went and returned safely. This is the way it is ordained and written on the heavenly tablets regarding Israel and his descendants: (they are) to celebrate this festival for seven days with festal happiness. (Jubilees 18:17–19)[27]

The festival referred to here is Pesach (Passover).[28] Why does the author connect the Binding of Isaac in Genesis with a holiday that will appear only in the book of Exodus? Jubilees does systematically merge biblical narratives in Genesis with the laws of later books,[29] but in this case there are more compelling thematic connections. Pesach celebrates the salvation of God's "firstborn," the nation of Israel, and here Isaac, Sarah's firstborn, is saved from slaughter. Moreover, the Israelite firstborn in Egypt are saved from "the destroyer" (Ex. 12:23), and here Isaac is saved from the destructive force of the prince of Mastema.

Satan as the driving force behind the Binding of Isaac is also found in later midrashic versions of the story, and comparing a derashah in the Babylonian Talmud with the account in Jubilees is illustrative.

> "And it came to pass after these things *(devarim)* that God tested Abraham" (Gen. 22:1). "After" what?
>
> Rabbi Yohanan said in the name of Rabbi Yose ben Zimra: After the words *(devarav)* of Satan, as it is written: "And the child grew and was weaned, and Abraham prepared a great feast on the day that Isaac was weaned" (Gen. 21:8). Satan said before the Holy One: "Master of the Universe, you favored this old man with fruit of the womb at one hundred years of age. Of the entire feast that he prepared, did he not have one dove or one pigeon to sacrifice for You?"
>
> He said to him, "Did he do anything that was not for his son? If I say to him, 'Sacrifice your son for Me, he would immediately sacrifice him.'"
>
> Immediately thereafter, "God tested Abraham." (Babylonian Talmud, *Sanhedrin* 99b)

"וַיְהִי אַחַר הַדְּבָרִים הָאֵלֶּה וְהָאֱלֹהִים נִסָּה אֶת אַבְרָהָם" (בראשית כב, א)—מאי "אַחַר"? אמר רבי יוחנן משום רבי יוסי בן זימרא: אחר דבריו של שטן, דכתיב "וַיִּגְדַּל הַיֶּלֶד וַיִּגָּמַל וגו' [וַיַּעַשׂ אַבְרָהָם מִשְׁתֶּה גָדוֹל בְּיוֹם הִגָּמֵל אֶת יִצְחָק]" (בראשית כא, ח). אמר שטן לפני הקדוש ברוך הוא: רבונו של עולם, זקן זה חננתו למאה שנה פרי בטן. מכל סעודה שעשה לא היה לו תור אחד או גוזל אחד להקריב לפניך? אמר לו: כלום עשה אלא בשביל בנו? אם אני אומר לו זבח את בנך לפני, מיד זובחו. מיד "וְהָאֱלֹהִים נִסָּה אֶת אַבְרָהָם".

Both Jubilees and the Babylonian Talmud pin the responsibility for the Binding of Isaac on Satan, relieving God of the theological pressure. There is indeed an exegetical basis for bringing Satan into the story, based on a comparison between God's testing of Abraham and his testing of Job, in which Satan is explicitly involved. But, once again, the structural difference between Midrash and Second Temple literature stands out. The midrash cites the verse as is and proceeds to interrogate its use of ambiguous *devarim* (which can mean "things," "events," or "words.") Through its exegesis, it discovers Satan lurking behind the scenes. Jubilees reworks the biblical text itself, so that the prince of Mastema is simply put on stage with the other biblical characters.

E. ALLEGORICAL INTERPRETATION

Another type of biblical interpretation used by Jews in the Second Temple period was allegory. Allegory is a Greek word that literally means "different speech," the idea being that a

> **THE SEPTUAGINT (LXX)**
>
> The title of this Greek translation of the Pentateuch derives from the legend (first told in the *Letter of Aristeas*) about seventy (or, in some versions, seventy-two) elders of Jerusalem who were sent to Alexandria to translate it. The translation dates from the third century BCE and is rather literal. Over time, the rest of the biblical books were translated into Greek and other compositions were even added to them: some of these were composed originally in Greek (most of the books of Maccabees) and some were translated from Hebrew into Greek (1 Maccabees, Ben Sira, Judith). The early Church canonized the Septuagint as its authoritative Scripture, but the exact canonical status of the various compositions included in it is a matter of debate among different Christian denominations. See further Law, *When God Spoke Greek*.

text can speak on multiple levels. On the surface, the words present a text's simple meaning; beneath the surface they function as symbols encoding profound truths. The allegorical interpretive tradition was developed in the Greek world, specifically to interpret the classical works of Homer. In the Second Temple era, Jewish interpreters applied this mode of interpretation to the Bible, and Philo of Alexandria elevated this tradition to unprecedented levels of complexity and systematization.[30]

Philo was a Hellenistic Jewish philosopher and biblical exegete who lived in Alexandria around the time of Jesus. He wrote Greek commentaries on parts of the Torah, in which he tried to show that, when read correctly, it bears the eternal truths of Greek philosophy. Although he interprets large sections of the Torah verse by verse, with the kind of close reading that we see in rabbinic Midrash, his approach differs from that of the rabbis in two critical ways. Philo bases his exegesis on the Septuagint rather than the Masoretic text, and it is by and large allegorical in nature.

Philo's allegorical interpretations depend on his being a very pedantic reader. To take one example, when the Torah states that a certain offense receives capital punishment, it often says that the offender *mot yumat*, typically translated into English as an emphatic statement: "he shall surely die." In the Greek of the Septuagint, this doubling is rendered as "by death to be put to death," which piques Philo's exegetical interest:

> Well knowing that he never puts in a superfluous word, so vast is his desire to speak plainly and clearly, I began debating with myself why he said that the intentional slayer is not to be put to death only but "by death to be put to death." "In what other way," I asked myself, "does a man who dies come to his end save by death?" So I attended the lectures of a wise woman, whose name is "Consideration" (*skepsis*), and was rid of my questioning; for she taught me that some people are dead while living, and some alive while dead. She told me that bad people, prolonging their days to extreme old age, are dead men, deprived of the life in association with virtue, while good people, even if cut off from their partnership with the body, live forever, and are granted immortality.[31]

Philo interprets the doubling as referring to two types of death: physical death, and spiritual death while still physically alive. Rabbi Akiva similarly interprets a proximate doubled phrase, *hikkaret tikkaret*, "you shall surely be cut off" (Num. 16:31): "*hikkaret*—in this world, *tikkaret*—in the World to Come."[32] The two exegetes have distinct visions of the life of the spirit,[33] but they employ a nearly identical interpretative technique grounded in a shared assumption about the biblical text. Like Philo, the rabbinic interpreters assume that no word in the Torah is superfluous.[34]

Philo's major innovation, however, lies in his allegorical interpretation, which he applies to several portions of the Torah but develops most systematically regarding the book of Genesis.[35] Genesis 3, to take one example, gives the account of the first sin in the Garden of Eden. Philo asserts that this story is not to be taken literally:

> Now these are no mythical fictions, such as poets and sophists delight in, but modes of making ideas visible, bidding us resort to allegorical interpretation guided in our renderings by what lies beneath the surface. Following a probable conjecture one would say that the serpent spoken of is a fit symbol of pleasure, because in the first place he is an animal without feet sunk prone upon his belly; secondly because he takes clods of earth as food; thirdly because he carries in his teeth the venom with which it is his nature to destroy those whom he has bitten. The lover of pleasure is exempt from none of these traits, for he is so weighted and dragged downwards that it is with difficulty that he lifts up his head, thrown down and tripped up by intemperance: he feeds not on heavenly nourishment, which wisdom by discourses and doctrines proffers to lovers of contemplation, but on that which comes up out of the earth with the revolving seasons, and which produces drunkenness, daintiness, and greediness.[36]

In Philo's sophisticated allegory, each of the characters in the biblical story stands in for an abstraction: Adam represents the mind, Eve the physical senses, the snake pleasure. The snake tries to influence Adam by way of Eve, because pleasure must work through the physical body to act on the mind. Philo didn't invent the philosophical model that underpins this reading, but rather developed a model found already in Plato's dialogues, but he systematically applied it to the Torah. Allegory enables Philo to replace the particularistic elements of biblical narrative, grounded as they are in the history and myth of the ancient Near East, with eternal truths about the nature of humanity and the world. Biblical stories transcend their literal forms to describe the human soul and its journey toward perfection. Allegorical interpretation universalizes the Torah so that it speaks to the human condition, and Philo uses it to show that the Torah is essentially a book of philosophy, of enduring wisdom, in narrative dress.

Interestingly, the above quote does not appear in one of Philo's allegorical compositions. For even in his non-allegorical commentaries, Philo occasionally turns to allegory, especially when he finds the literal sense overly simplistic, as he does in this case. Depictions of supernatural events also invite such interpretation.³⁷ In the other direction, even in his allegorical works, Philo does not wholly negate the literal sense of the text. He frequently presents side by side two interpretations that operate on two levels: one is literal, superficial, and physical; the other is allegorical, profound, and spiritual.

Philo usually refrains from relying on allegorical interpretation regarding the mitzvot, out of concern that it might lead to a weakening in the physical religious observances demanded by the text of the Torah. He writes:

> There are some who, regarding laws in their literal sense in the light of symbols of matters belonging to the intellect, are overpunctilious about the latter, while treating the former with easy-going neglect. Such men I for my part should blame for handling the matter in too easy and off-hand a manner: they ought to have given careful attention to both aims, to a more full and exact investigation of what is not seen and in what is seen to be stewards without reproach. [. . .] Nay, we should look on all these outward observances as resembling the body, and their inner meanings as resembling the soul. It follows that, exactly as we have to take thought for the body, because it is the abode of the soul, so we must pay heed to the letter of the laws. If we keep and observe these, we shall gain a clearer conception of those things of which these are the symbols.³⁸

To sharpen the abstract nature of Philo's allegorical interpretation, let us contrast it with Paul's interpretation of the biblical story of Sarah banishing Hagar in Genesis 21:

> Tell me, you who desire to be subject to the law, will you not listen to the law? For it is written that Abraham had two sons, one by an enslaved woman and the other by a free woman. One, the child of the enslaved woman, was born according to the flesh; the other, the child of the free woman, was born through the promise.
>
> Now this is an allegory: these women are two covenants. One woman, in fact, is Hagar, from Mount Sinai, bearing children for slavery. Now Hagar is Mount Sinai in Arabia and corresponds to the present Jerusalem, for she is in slavery with her children. But the other woman corresponds to the Jerusalem above; she is free, and she is our mother.
>
> For it is written: "Rejoice, you childless one, you who bear no children, burst into song and shout, you who endure no birth pangs, for the children of the desolate woman are more numerous than the children of the one who is married" (Isa. 54:1).
>
> Now you, my brothers and sisters, are children of the promise, like Isaac. But just as at that time the child who was born according to the flesh persecuted the child who was born according to the Spirit, so it is now also. But what does the scripture say? "Drive out the enslaved woman and her child, for the child of the enslaved woman

> ### PAUL
>
> Paul (from Greek Paulus; his Hebrew name was Saul) was born in Tarsus in Asia Minor and studied in Jerusalem. He was, according to his own testimony in his letters, a Pharisaic zealot who after experiencing a revelation was converted into an enthusiastic believer in Jesus. He ardently disseminated the gospel among non-Jews and laid the foundation for institutionalized Christianity.
>
> Between approximately 50 and 60 CE Paul wrote epistles to many communities that he founded in which he articulated what would later come to be Christian dogma about Jesus's life and resurrection, the necessary kind of communal life, and the expectation of Jesus's imminent return and the impending end of days.

will not share the inheritance with the child of the free woman" (Gen. 21:10). So then, brothers and sisters, we are children, not of an enslaved woman but of the free woman. (Galatians 4:21–31, NRSVUE)

In Paul's sophisticated allegory (this is the only case in which he uses explicitly the term "allegory" in his epistles), Hagar the slave, who flees to the desert, is identified with the Children of Israel, who receive the Torah in the desert and are enslaved to its law. Sarah, the free wife, represents those who have been freed from the Sinaitic covenant, meaning the non-Jews who have come to believe in Jesus, and are accepted without circumcision and the acceptance of all commandments. By means of this allegory, Paul can invert the traditional trope, according to which the Jews are Sarah and the non-Jews are Hagar and Ishmael.[39]

Paul makes an even bolder claim as he goes on. Ishmael was born naturally to Abraham and Hagar, but Isaac's birth was a manifest miracle, the result of God's promise to Abraham. The Jews, the "natural" descendants of Abraham, are just like Ishmael, and the non-Jewish Jesus believers are like Isaac, for they are party to the covenant through the fulfillment of the divine promise that Abraham will be a "father of many nations" (Gen. 17:5). In this way, Paul is able to bring his non-Jewish audience into the biblical narrative of election and salvation, while audaciously insisting that they are not merely *akin to* Abraham, but are in fact Abraham's offspring in a spiritual sense.

Even without digging deeper into this rich allegory, we can see how far it is from Philo's allegorical interpretation. Where Philo's readings contain a transposition from the concrete to the abstract, Paul's have a typological translation from past events and personalities to current ones. In other places, Paul calls this interpretation *typos*, i.e., reading the Torah as a model for the historical context of interpreter.[40]

Both Philo and Paul invoke the term "allegory," but it has a very different meaning for each. Philo's interpretive motion is vertical, as it were, moving above the arc of time, away from the physical plane of the particular and concrete to the spiritual plane of the universal and abstract. Paul, in contrast, operates on a horizontal plane through time, in which biblical occurrences and characters serve as figures for later ones, and are historically concretized by the interpreter. In this sense, Paul's writings bear a methodological similarity to the Qumranic *pesharim* discussed in the next section.[41] As Christian literature burgeoned, allegorical interpretation of the Philonic strain became increasingly dominant.[42]

There are some examples of allegorical interpretation in the Midrash, but these are few and far between. In general, it does not convert biblical details into abstract concepts, as Philo does, nor does it apply these types and forms to current events, as Paul does.[43]

F. PESHER

Pesher (pl. *pesharim*) is a genre found in the Dead Sea Scrolls that interprets biblical prophecies as referring to figures, groups, and events in the life of the Qumran sect.[44] A *pesher* commentary can appear in the form of a line-by-line commentary on prophecies (e.g., Pesher Isaiah, Pesher Habakkuk), or it can focus on a verse here or there in non-exegetical books, such as the Damascus Document and the Community Rule.[45] Usually, a verse is cited and then followed by a formulaic word, such as *pishro* or *pesher ha-davar,* introducing the interpretation. The fact that scribes left a space (designated by scholars with the word *vacat*) between the scriptural quote and the interpretation indicates that the author or copyists distinguished sharply between them. Such a distinction is exceptional in Second Temple exegesis, but becomes the rule in Midrash. Scholars have named the genre and technique after this key term *pesher,* which means "interpretation."[46]

To understand the *pesher* technique, we will look at Pesher Habakkuk. While the biblical book of Habakkuk is quite short, its running *pesher* is the lengthiest one found at Qumran.[47] The author subscribes to the basic view of the *pesher* literature that biblical prophecy is to be explicated as foretelling events from his own time. The reason that the prophecy must bear meaning for the author's lifetime is that he believes he is living on the cusp of the end of days, when a final showdown between the armies of light and darkness will occur and the persecuted Qumran sect will be vindicated.[48] These exegetes even claim that the prophets themselves did not understand the true meaning of their own utterances:

> And God told Habakkuk to write what was going to happen to the last generation, but he did not let him know the consummation of the era.
>
> And as for what he says: "So that the one who reads it may run" (Hab. 2:2). Its interpretation *(pishro)* concerns the Teacher of Righteousness, to whom God has made known all the mysteries of the words of His servants, the prophets. (Pesher Habakkuk, 7:1–5)[49]

וידבר אל <אל> חבקוק לכתוב את הבאות על הדור האחרון ואת גמר הקץ לוא הודעו.

ואשר אמר "למען ירוץ הקורא בו"—פשרו: על מורה הצדק אשר הודיעו אל את כול רזי דברי עבדיו הנביאים.

The *pesher* assumes a double revelation. There is the initial prophecy revealed to the biblical prophet, and then a secondary revelation experienced by the leader of the Qumran sect, the "Teacher of Righteousness," which teaches him how to correctly interpret the prophecies for his own historical situation. When Habakkuk mentions "the one who reads it," he is understood to be referring to the reader of his own prophecy, the Teacher of Righteousness.[50]

Habakkuk 1:5 says that people will not believe what is being related. The *pesher* construes this about the sect's enemies:

> The interpretation of the matter *(pesher ha-davar)* [concerns the trai]tors[51] in the last days. They are violator[s of the coven]ant who will not believe when they hear all that is going [to happen t]o the final generation, from the mouth of the Priest whom God has placed wi[thin him wisd]om, to foretell the fulfilment of all the words of his servants, the prophets, [by] means of whom God has declared all that is going to happen to his people Is[rael]. (Pesher Habakkuk, 2:5–10)[52]

> וכן פשר הדבר [על הבו]גדים לאחרית הימים המה עריצ[י הבר]ית אשר לוא יאמינוא בשומעם את כול
> הבא[ות על]ל [ ]הדור האחרון מפי הכוהן אשר נתן אל ב[לבו בינ]ה לפשור את כול דברי עבדיו הנביאים
> [אשר]בידם ספר אל את כול הבאות על עמו וע[ד]תו.

The *pesharim* are prophecies revealed to the Priest—the Teacher of Righteousness—and only those who believe what he says and accept his authority will merit receiving the true interpretation of the verses. The sect's opponents, who apparently broke away from the sect and became its persecutors,[53] are infidels who will not be privy to know what is about to come to pass. The events of the eschaton are revealed only during the "final generation," which is why the prophets themselves could not understand the true import of their prophecies. Only those who believe in the Teacher of Righteousness will attain that understanding, so that accepting the *pesher* is a declaration of fealty to the community of the elect.

At the heart of the interpretation in Pesher Habakkuk is the identification of words in the verse with specific referents from the interpreter's time:

> And as for what he says: "Owing to the blood of the city and the violence (done to) the country" (Hab. 2:17).[54]

> Its interpretation *(pishro)*: the city is Jerusalem in which the Wicked Priest performed repulsive acts and defiled the Sanctuary of God. The violence (done to) the country are the cities of Judah which he plundered of the possessions of the poor. (Pesher Habakkuk, 12:6–10)[55]

> ואשר אמר "מדמי קריה וחמס ארץ"—פשרו: "הקריה" היא ירושלם אשר פעל בה הכוהן הרשע מעשי
> תועבות ויטמא את מקדש אל; "וחמס ארץ" המה ערי יהודה אשר גזל הון אביונים.

In this reading, "blood" is replaced with repulsive acts, "the city" with Jerusalem, and "violence" with plundering the poor. The prophecy is connected to figures and places important to the sect, such as Jerusalem and the Wicked Priest.

Here is a second example:

"For see, I will mobilize the Chaldaeans, a cruel [and deter]mined people" (Hab. 1:6).

Its interpretation *(pishro)* concerns the Kittim, wh[o ar]e swift and powerful in battle, to slay many. (Pesher Habakkuk, 2:10–13)[56]

"כיא הנני מקים את הכדשאים הגוי המר[והנמ]הר"—פשרו: על הכתיאים א[שר המ]ה קלים וגבורים במלחמה לאבד רבים.

The Chaldaeans are the Babylonians who conquered Assyria, so the author of the *pesher* switches them with the superpower of his day: the Roman Empire under Pompey, who conquered Jerusalem in 63 CE. He calls them Kittim, who according to Numbers 24:24 and Daniel 11:30 are a people of the Mediterranean islands.

And a final example from Pesher Hosea:

"Because of this I will collect back my wheat in its time and my wine [in its season,] I will reclaim my wool and my flax so that she cannot cover [her nakedness.] Now I will uncover her disgrace in the sight of [her] love[rs and] no [one] will free her from my hand" (Hos. 2:11–12).

Its interpretation *(pishro):* he has punished them with hunger and with nakedness so they will be sham[e] and disgrace in the eyes of the nations on whom they relied. But they will not save them from their sufferings. (Pesher Hosea, 2:8–14)[57]

"לכן אשוב ולקחתי דגני בעתו ותירושי[ן] במועדו] והצלתי צמרי ופושתי מלכסות את [ערותה] ועתה אגלה את נבלותה לעיני מאה[ביה ואיש] לא יצילנה מידי"—פשר: אשר הכם ברעב ובערום להיות לקלו[ן] וחרפה לעיני הגואים אשר נשענו עליהם והמה לוא יושיעום מצרותיהם.

In the original prophecy, the "lovers" represent foreign gods as well as the other nations to whom the "wife" turns for help, when she should be looking to her legal "husband," the Israelite God. The author here has the lightest of touches, specifying the original intended referent of "lovers," the other nations. No exegetical acrobatics are needed to make the point. If one agrees with the author's assumption that the Torah speaks to the sect's historical juncture, the prophecy speaks for itself.

The bulk of the interpretation in the *pesharim* consists of such particularizations that imbue the text with immediate relevance.[58] They have the cumulative effect of making the reader or listener feel as if they are the direct address of the biblical prophecy. Importantly, they also give the sense that Scripture has a single meaning, which is now being divinely revealed with the eschaton in the offing. Because the *pesher* is itself a prophecy, each verse can have only one true meaning,[59] in stark contrast to Midrash, which is inherently multivalent.

What sets this apart from Midrash is the fact that the interpreter covers his tracks, requiring textual spadework to follow him across Scripture. The author must conceal his methods because he alone is authorized by divine revelation to endow Scripture with its true meaning. If he were to expose how he does what he does, thereby democratizing it, his exclusiveness and authority would be compromised.

Some *pesharim* are more complex than the examples above and use various interpretive techniques that we will encounter in the Midrash: making intertextual connections between scriptural verses, reading terms in a way that doesn't fit the original context, playing with the form of words.[60] In other Qumranic writings, this type of interpretation is in fact called *midrash*.[61]

Rabbinic literature also contains interpretations in the vein of the *pesharim*, but they never refer to specific events from the time of the rabbis. Instead, the Sages read their Scripture as referring to biblical events or recurring phenomena.[62] Here is an example of a *pesher*-type interpretation in the Midrash:

> "To those who love Me" (Ex. 20:5)—this is Abraham and those like him; "and to those who preserve My commandments" (Ex. 20:5)—these are the prophets and the elders.
>
> Rabbi Natan says, "To those who love Me and to those who observe My commandments" (Ex. 20:5)—these are they who live in the Land of Israel and give their life for the commandments. (*Mekhilta de-Rabbi Yishmael, Ba-Ḥodesh,* §6, p. 227)

"לְאֹהֲבַי"—זה אברהם וכיוצא בו; "וּלְשֹׁמְרֵי מִצְוֹתָי"—אילו הנביאים והזקינים.

ר' נתן אומר: "לְאֹהֲבַי וּלְשֹׁמְרֵי מִצְוֹתָי"—אילו שהן יושבין בארץ ישראל ונותנין נפשן על כל המצות.

The connection to Abraham here is based on Isaiah 41:8, where Abraham is called "the one who loves Me." While many scholars suggest that Rabbi Natan's interpretation, like other references to martyrdom made by the Sages of his generation, alludes to the harsh religious decrees issued by the Romans from 135 to 138 CE in the aftermath of the Bar Kokhba Revolt, the text betrays no such explicit indication.[63] It is generic enough that it could refer to any time from the biblical Patriarchs on or to any place of persecution in the Land of Israel. After having seen the Qumran *pesharim*, where biblical verses are linked to very specific events and individuals, the contrast in rabbinic literature could not be clearer.

G. THE DISTINCTIVENESS OF MIDRASH

The Second Temple period witnessed the development of a host of exegetical approaches and compositional styles. When Midrash came onto the scene, it had centuries' worth of prolific, rich, and diverse biblical interpretation behind it. In what ways did it choose to borrow from these other interpretive traditions or to stake out its own path?

James Kugel observes exegetical assumptions to which all ancient Jewish exegetes subscribed.[64] Chapter 12 will explore the degree to which these assumptions apply to Midrash, but right now I would like to emphasize the ways in which Midrash differs from the interpretive traditions surveyed above.

First, it systematically sets apart the biblical text from its own interpretations. The rabbinic exegete does not give himself license to insinuate his own ideas into the sacred text. In this respect, Midrash is a departure from the genre of rewritten Bible and is a more mature manifestation of this budding consciousness found in the *pesher* literature.

Second, Midrash coins new terms and uses fixed technical ones to describe its interpretive activity. This goes beyond the limited nomenclature of Philo and the sectarian texts. Furthermore, Midrash sharpens existing exegetical techniques and forges new ones, and they are all more sophisticated than anything found in Jubilees or Qumran. The coming chapters detail how Midrash developed set terms and structures that allow it to compare and contrast alternative interpretations, present a dialectical give-and-take, and reflect on different exegetical options. Its interpretive methodology is unprecedentedly reflexive and explicit.[65]

Third, for Midrash, the more opinions the merrier. Contrast this with the *pesharim* that allow one and only one interpretation. Philo gives more than one interpretation, but he plots them along a vertical axis, with some "deeper" than the others. In midrashic literature, scores of exegeses coexist peacefully in the same interpretive space. The rabbis break new ground in incorporating a plurality of voices and resist any urge to rank or privilege some over others.

Fourth, the most dramatic rabbinic innovation of all is the bifurcation of legal thinking and development into the Mishnah and the Midrash. In the writings of Philo, Josephus, the Qumran sect, and others, treatment of the law is enmeshed in biblical exegesis.[66] It is the rabbis who conceive of two methods of study that evolve into two separate bodies of literature: the topical treatment of Halakhah in the Mishnah and the running commentary on the legal portions of the Torah in the halakhic Midrash.

What motivated this new vision of Halakhah? One explanation considers the history of the Bible's canonization. By the Sages' time, the boundaries of Scripture had hardened, forcing a sharp line between the Torah and its interpretation. The destruction of the Second Temple and the rise of the ethos of Torah study could have been additional contributing factors.[67]

Another way of understanding the genesis of Midrash is as a reflection of the rabbis' uniquely democratic ideology, which encouraged students to learn how to interpret the

Torah. Unprecedented effort was made to lay out the procedure and technique of this interpretation. Learners in the study house were not merely given fish; they were taught how to fish. Recall that at Qumran, the keys to scriptural interpretation were held exclusively by the Teacher of Righteousness. His disciples were not privy to the principles of exegesis, which he claimed for himself via revelation.[68]

Finally, Midrash can also be seen as part of a much broader phenomenon. Late Antiquity saw a rise in the value of interpretive texts, which even achieved canonical status, in both the Hellenistic and the early Christian contexts. This was also when running commentaries on the classical philosophical works of Plato and Aristotle first appeared. So widespread was this phenomenon that some scholars have identified it as the key feature of this time period.[69]

We will interrogate these claims further as we explore the schools of Rabbi Akiva and Rabbi Yishmael, which produced the radically new genre of Midrash.[70]

TEN

The Schools of Rabbi Akiva and Rabbi Yishmael

The various Midrashim are attributed to two distinct schools: the school of Rabbi Akiva and the school of Rabbi Yishmael. This chapter begins with the history of this discovery and the process by which specific Midrashim have been assigned to each school. It then characterizes their fundamental exegetical and ideological approaches. It ends with the mysterious convergence of derashot from both schools in aggadic sections.

A. THE TWO MAJOR SCHOOLS AND THEIR MIDRASHIM

Until about a century ago, traditional and academic scholars possessed only one halakhic Midrash for each book of the Torah (excluding Genesis). Exodus had the *Mekhilta*, Leviticus had the *Sifra*,[1] Numbers had the *Sifrei*, and Deuteronomy also had the *Sifrei*. These titles are all in Aramaic. *Mekhilta* means "a measure," a vessel to contain something, and it is used by the two Talmuds specifically to refer to collections of halakhic material, on a par with Hebrew *massekhet*, the word for "tractate."[2] *Sifra* and *sifrei* are the singular and plural forms of "book."[3] These titles have no bearing on the content of the Midrashim; they refer only to the act of collection and compilation that turned individual midrashic units into comprehensive compositions.[4] These Midrashim are first and foremost explications of the Torah's legal passages, although they also cover some biblical narratives. This legal prominence accounts for the absence of a tannaitic Midrash on Genesis, which consists entirely of story cycles.

At the end of the nineteenth century, David Zvi Hoffmann (1843–1921), head of the Orthodox rabbinical seminary in Berlin, revolutionized our understanding of Midrash. Based on his meticulous philological work, he proposed that each book of the Torah originally had not one but two Midrashim. He further demonstrated that the two sets of four

Midrashim came from specific schools: that of Rabbi Akiva and that of Rabbi Yishmael.[5] He characterized these schools using three major criteria: terminology, rabbinic figures, and methodology.

Each school, Hoffmann showed, has a distinctive voice, a consistent way of expressing itself. This stands out when there is no difference between the midrashim contentwise and the sole difference is stylistic and terminological. After a scriptural quote, Midrashim from Rabbi Yishmael's academy often say "it relates" *(maggid)*, while those from Rabbi Akiva's say "it teaches" *(melammed)*. The former raise a possible inference or logical possibility, which is meant to be rejected, with "Do I hear . . . ?" *(shomea' ani)*, whereas the latter use an impersonal question, "Could it be . . . ?" *(yakhol)*. And so on and so forth. To the modern scholar's delight, the terminology used by each academy is usually consistent.[6]

The roster of rabbinic figures in the Midrashim of each school also differs.[7] The Midrashim of Rabbi Akiva's school feature Rabbi Akiva and his principal students, whom we've already met in the Mishnah: Rabbi Meir, Rabbi Yehudah, Rabbi Shimon, Rabbi Yose, and Rabbi Elazar. Members of Rabbi Yishmael's midrashic school, on the other hand, are mostly new to us, since they do not appear in the Mishnah that originated in Rabbi Akiva's school. Aside from Rabbi Yishmael himself are his major disciples: Rabbi Natan, Rabbi Yonatan, and Rabbi Yoshiyah.[8]

Finally, as Hoffmann demonstrated, each school has its own exegetical assumptions, principles, and techniques.[9] Broadly speaking, Rabbi Akiva's academy adopts a more atomistic approach, in which every discrete utterance of the divine word is treated as bearing meaning. Rabbi Yishmael's bet midrash, on the other hand, assumes that Scripture is instruction for human beings, and "the Torah spoke in human language." In the same way that grammar has rules, the Torah is amenable to interpretation through *middot*, exegetical principles that can be applied consistently across the entire Torah, and through comparative analysis of biblical passages. According to Rabbi Yishmael, the darshan may not strip the text entirely of its simple meaning and warn the Bible, as it were, to "keep quiet until I expound [you]."[10] Their respective hermeneutic approaches are analyzed in depth in the next section.

Awareness of the distinctiveness of the two academies waned over the centuries, to the point that only one Midrash was selected for studying each book of the Torah. Coincidentally, the works chosen alternate between schools. Exodus has *Mekhilta de-Rabbi Yishmael*, from the eponymous school, and Leviticus has the *Sifra*, a Midrash from Rabbi Akiva's school. For Numbers, the *Sifrei* comes from the school of Rabbi Yishmael, but for Deuteronomy, the *Sifrei* is the work of Rabbi Akiva's academy. The corresponding Midrashim of the other school ceased being learned and copied, and so never made it into print until the late nineteenth century.

For that we have to thank academically trained rabbinic scholars at European rabbinical seminaries, who were instrumental to recovering these Midrashim from medieval anthologies. For his edition of *Mekhilta de-Rabbi Yishmael* (Vienna, 1870), Meir Ish Shalom of the rabbinical seminary in Vienna collected medieval citations of *Mekhilta de-Rashbi*. This Midrash is the Akivan complement to *Mekhilta de-Rabbi Yishmael* on Exodus, as Rabbi Shimon bar Yohai (Hebrew acronym: Rashbi) was one of Rabbi Akiva's principal students. Israel

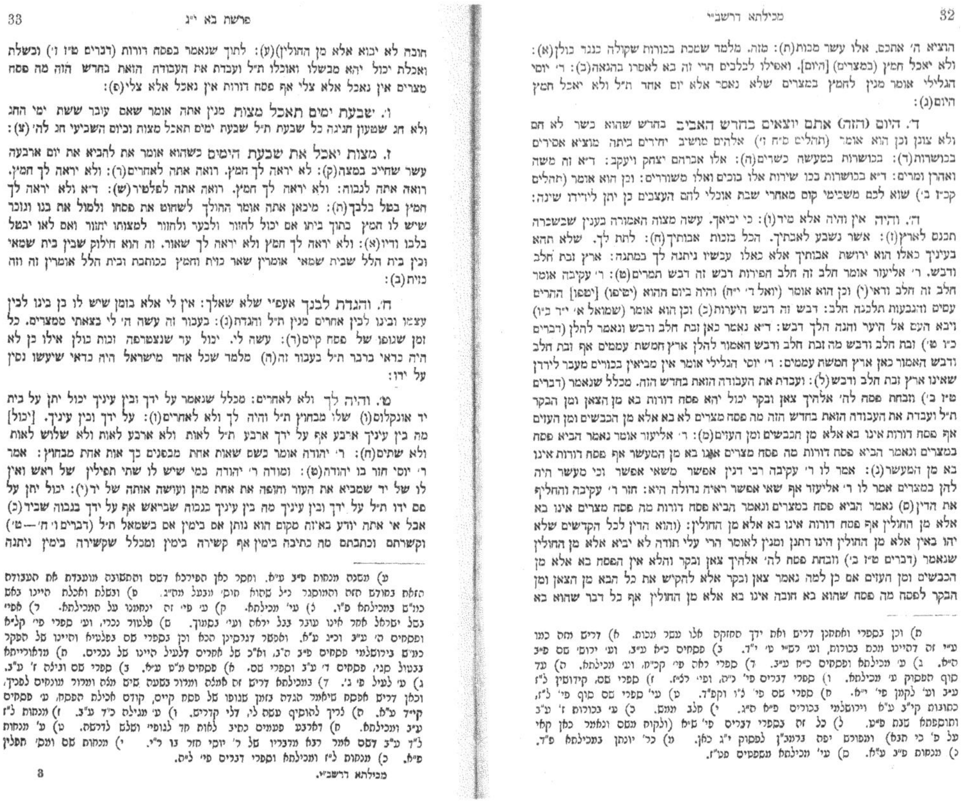

FIGURE 6. A picture from *Mekhilta RSBI*, Hofman's edition, Frankfurt 1865.

Lewy of the Breslau rabbinical seminary was the first to realize that large portions of *Mekhilta de-Rashbi* were included in *Midrash ha-Gadol*, a compendium of derashot edited by Rabbi David Adani in fourteenth-century Yemen.[11]

These contributions formed the basis for the Midrash's reconstruction by David Zvi Hoffmann. Hoffmann also recovered a Midrash on Deuteronomy from the school of Rabbi Yishmael. He labored to reconstruct these two Midrashim from medieval citations, especially from *Midrash ha-Gadol*. The result is necessarily tentative. *Midrash ha-Gadol* does not cite its sources explicitly, and so what looks like an ancient derashah may actually derive from the writings of much later authorities like Moses Maimonides, whose works were treated as canonical in Yemen.[12] Nevertheless, Hoffmann persevered. He published editions of *Mekhilta de-Rashbi* on Exodus (see figure 6) and *Mekhilta de-Rabbi Yishmael* on Deuteronomy (which he named *Midrash Tanna'im*).[13]

A true breakthrough occurred in recovering these lost Midrashim with the discovery of the Cairo Genizah, which preserves intact pages from actual medieval copies of these Midrashim.[14] In the 1940s, Jacob Nahum Epstein and his student Ezra Zion Melamed published a new edition of *Mekhilta de-Rashbi*, of which two-thirds is straight from the Genizah (see

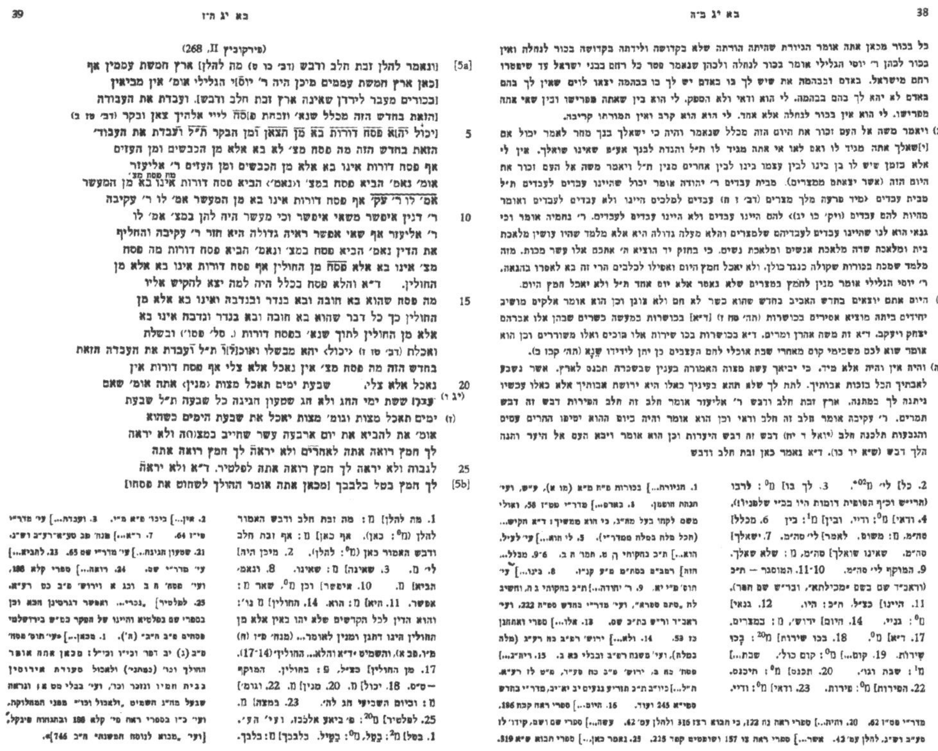

FIGURE 7. A picture from *Mekhilta RSBI*, Epstein-Melamed's edition, Jerusalem, 1956.

figure 7).[15] The Genizah also contains some fragments of the *Mekhilta de-Rabbi Yishmael* on Deuteronomy (from both its halakhic and aggadic parts).[16] Menahem Kahana has collected all the Genizah fragments of these Midrashim (aside from the *Sifra*) in a single volume.[17]

Medieval halakhists mentioned another Midrash on the book of Numbers called *Sifrei Zuta* (meaning the "minor" or "lesser" *Sifrei*, to distinguish it from the much better known *Sifrei*). Scholars noted that the citations from this Midrash display similarities to the ones known from Rabbi Akiva's school but are also dissimilar from them in certain respects, including its roster of rabbis and terminology. It was therefore attributed to a different school of Rabbi Akiva's disciples. Saul Horovitz, a student of Israel Lewy, appended an edition of *Sifrei Zuta Numbers*, recovered from medieval anthologies and some Genizah fragments, to his edition of *Sifrei Numbers*.

Menahem Kahana reconstructed another Midrash on Deuteronomy based on a single, surprising medieval source: the writings of the eleventh-century Karaite scholar Yeshuah ben Yehudah. His citations yield a Midrash quite similar in its cast of rabbinic figures and terminology to *Sifrei Zuta Numbers*, the Midrash that Horovitz cobbled together from Rabbanite excerpts. Neither seems familiar with our edition of the Mishnah.[18] On the strength of these affinities,

TABLE 3 The existing Midrashic compositions

Biblical Book	Rabbi Yishmael's School	Rabbi Akiva's School	Rabbi Akiva's School *Sifrei Zuta*
Exodus	<u>*Mekhilta de-Rabbi Yishmael*</u>	*Mekhilta de-Rashbi* (ed. Hoffmann and ed. Epstein-Melamed)	ø
Leviticus	[Excerpts appear in the *Sifra*]	<u>*Sifra*</u>	ø
Numbers	<u>*Sifrei Numbers*</u>	ø[a]	*Sifrei Zuta* (ed. Horovitz)
Deuteronomy	*Mekhilta Deuteronomy* (*Midrash Tanna'im*, ed. Hoffmann)	<u>*Sifrei Deuteronomy*</u>	*Sifrei Zuta* (ed. Kahana)

[a] There is no evidence of a Midrash on Numbers from the "standard" school of R. Akiva. If it ever existed, it was already lost by the medieval period.

Kahana has titled it *Sifrei Zuta Deuteronomy* and proposed that the academy of Rabbi Akiva had not one but (at least) two series of Midrashim.[19] *Mekhilta de-Rashbi*, *Sifra*, and *Sifrei Deuteronomy* represent one series; *Sifrei Zuta Numbers* and *Sifrei Zuta Deuteronomy* are what remain of a second series that presumably also included Midrashim on Exodus and Leviticus.[20]

What about the book of Leviticus? Presently, it is the only book of the Torah that does not have more than one extant Midrash. But although the Cairo Genizah and medieval works do not seem to preserve a Midrash from Rabbi Yishmael's academy on Leviticus, scholars have identified material in the *Sifra* of Rabbi Akiva's school that originated elsewhere. The theory is that some of it belongs to a lost Midrash of Rabbi Yishmael's school.[21]

Table 3 shows the current state of affairs, with the main Midrashim underlined and the speculative reconstructions not underlined.[22]

B. HERMENEUTIC DIFFERENCES BETWEEN THE SCHOOLS

To learn more about the differences between schools, the founding fathers are a good place to start. A number of disputes between Rabbi Akiva and Rabbi Yishmael themselves highlight their differences in approach to biblical interpretation, which would come to define the schools they each headed.[23] These cluster around the phenomenon of biblical doubling, in which a regular conjugated verb is preceded by what is known in Hebrew grammar as an infinitive absolute (the typical translation of this phrase is emphatic: "shall surely").

In the first example, the Torah delineates the severe biblical punishment of *karet* (pl. *keritot*), being "cut off" from the community, with the doubled *hikkaret tikkaret*. How is one to understand this?

> "That soul shall surely be cut off (*hikkaret tikkaret*)" (Num. 15:31): *hikkaret*—in this world; *tikkaret*—in the World to Come—the words of Rabbi Akiva.

Rabbi Yishmael said to him, Since it says, "that soul shall be cut off *(ve-nikhretah)*" (Num. 15:30), do I hear *(shomea' ani)* three *keritot* in three worlds? What, then, does "that soul shall surely be cut off" teach? The Torah spoke in human language. (*Sifrei Numbers*, §112, p. 121)

"הִכָּרֵת תִּכָּרֵת הַנֶּפֶשׁ הַהִוא" (במדבר טו, לא)—הִכָּרֵת—בעולם הזה, תִּכָּרֵת– לעולם הבא—דברי ר' עקיבה.

אמר לו ר' ישמעאל: לפי שהוא אומר "וְנִכְרְתָה הַנֶּפֶשׁ הַהִוא" (שם ל), שומע אני שלש כריתות בשלשה עולמות? מה תלמוד לומר "הִכָּרֵת תִּכָּרֵת הַנֶּפֶשׁ הַהִוא"? דברה תורה כלשון בני אדם.

Rabbi Akiva believes that every single word in the Torah carries halakhic meaning that the exegete must unpack. Theoretically, the verb *tikkaret*, "shall be cut off," could have sufficed on its own, so why the addition of *hikkaret*? It cannot be just for emphasis, because rhetoric for the sake of rhetoric is an unsatisfactory explanation for Rabbi Akiva. To find the additional meaning the interpreter must be hyperfocused on the precise language of the divine text, and to extract it one can atomize the text, and even read it against the rules of normative grammar, as Rabbi Akiva does here. He separates *hikkaret* from *tikkaret*, even though these function together as a verbal phrase, and expounds them individually. In this case, *hikkaret* teaches that the offender is "cut off" from this world by not having progeny to carry on their legacy, and *tikkaret* teaches that they are "cut off" from the next world through future judgment. A similar hyperliteral reading of *hikkaret tikkaret* appears in Philo and the Targums.[24]

Rabbi Yishmael challenges this on the grounds that there are other mentions of *karet* in this very context. If every mention must refer to a separate punishment, what other states of existence exist beyond this world and the next that one can possibly be "cut off" from? Beyond this "technical" rebuttal there is a fundamental hermeneutical disagreement. For Rabbi Yishmael not every word has independent halakhic meaning. The doubling here is a regular expression in biblical Hebrew indicating emphasis—"shall *surely* be cut off." Instead of grasping for hidden meanings, one ought to listen to the Torah's tone of voice and pay attention to context.

Modern scholarship often presents "the Torah spoke in human language" as Rabbi Yishmael's official motto.[25] But this is the only place it appears in all of tannaitic Midrash. It appears in several additional *baraitot* in the two Talmuds,[26] but there too the contexts are limited to nominal repetitions of the exact same word (e.g., *ish ish*) or to the verbal phrases (technically called: paronomastic infinitive) encountered above (e.g., *hikkaret tikkaret*). Note also that while Rabbi Yishmael himself rejects these techniques, the Midrashim from his school do contain quite a few of them.[27] Apparently, not every member of his school shared his reservations, and certainly the editors of its Midrashim did not. It is indeed a bold hermeneutical assumption of Rabbi Yishmael but its application is pretty limited and confined.

In another case of doubling, the disagreement between the two rabbis is solely exegetical, having no halakhic ramification. The relevant verse states, "You shall surely destroy *(abbed te'abbedun)* all of the places where the nations worshipped . . . their gods" (Deut. 12:2).

Whence that even if one destroyed them[a] once, one must destroy them many times?[b] It therefore teaches, "You shall surely destroy *(abbed te'abbedun)*" (Deut. 12:2)—the words of Rabbi Akiva. [. . .]

Rabbi Yishmael says, "All the days that you live on the earth / you[c] shall surely destroy" (Deut. 12:1–2). (*Mekhilta Deuteronomy*, 12:2)

ומניין אפילו אבדם פעם אחת יאבדם פעמים הרבה? תלמוד לומר "אַבֵּד תְּאַבְּדוּן" (דברים יב, ב)—כדברי ר׳ עקיבה. [. . .] ר׳ ישמעאל אומר: "כָּל הַיָּמִים אֲשֶׁר אַתֶּם חַיִּים עַל הָאֲדָמָה / אַבֵּד תְּאַבְּדוּן" (דברים יב, א–ב).

Since both Sages maintain the same halakhic conclusion, that idol worship must be eradicated however many times it reconstitutes itself, this is a specimen of pure methodological disagreement. Rabbi Akiva zeroes in on the repetition, while Rabbi Yishmael locates the verse in its larger context. Take note, though, that Rabbi Yishmael's reading is not simple either. On a straight reading, the final words of the previous verse belong to that verse and finish its idea: "These are the statutes and the ordinances that you must observe . . . all the days that you live on the earth" (Deut. 12:1). "You shall surely" destroy begins the next verse and clause. Admittedly, Rabbi Yishmael is not chopping up a phrase that grammar glues together, but by severing the end of a verse from what precedes it and ignoring the break between sentences, he is also not reading the Torah as he would a conventional human text.

A third case where Rabbi Akiva learns a halakhah from doubling and Rabbi Yishmael must find another way to derive the law is the cooking of the paschal sacrifice. The Torah commands: "Do not eat from it raw, nor in any way cooked in water, but fire-roasted" (Ex. 12:9). The Midrash states:

"In any way cooked *(u-vashel mevushal)* in water" (Ex. 12:9). I only have water, whence all other liquids? Rabbi Yishmael would say, Say it is an a fortiori: If water, which does not dilute their taste,[d] may not be used for cooking, it is logical that all other liquids, which do dilute their taste, may not be used for cooking.

Rabbi Akiva says, I only have water, whence all other liquids? It therefore teaches, "in any way cooked *(bashel mevushal)*"—to include all other liquids. (*Mekhilta de-Rabbi Yishmael, Pasḥa*, §6, pp. 20–21)

"ובשל מבושל במים" (שמות יב, ט). אין לי אלא מים, שאר כל המשקין מנין? היה ר׳ ישמעאל אומר: אמרת קל וחומר היא: ומה אם מים שאינן מפיגין את טעמן הרי הן אסורין בבישול, שאר המשקין שהן מפיגין את טעמן דין הוא שיהיו אסורין בבישול.

  a The idols.
  b If they are rebuilt after each round of destruction.
  c The slash indicates where verse 1 ends and verse 2 begins, to highlight how Rabbi Yishmael ignores the boundary between verses.
  d Of the sacrifices.

ר' עקיבה אומר: אין לי אלא מים, שאר כל המשקין מנין? תלמוד לומר "ובשל מבושל"—להביא שאר המשקין.

Rabbi Yishmael uses logical reasoning to prohibit the use of other liquids, whereas Rabbi Akiva treats the doubling as inclusive. Previously, we saw Rabbi Yishmael formulate a textual principle. This case adds his reliance on the logical principles of human reasoning.

How to treat doublings and repetitions, as a normal linguistic phenomenon or as a cue for deduction, is emblematic of how the two darshanim and their schools treat the biblical text. Their principled approaches can be seen in other examples as well. Consider the Torah's prohibition against oppressing widows and orphans:

> "[Do not oppress a] widow or orphan" (Ex. 22:21). I only have a widow and orphan, whence all other people? It therefore teaches, "Do not oppress anyone (*kol*)"[a] (Ex. 22:21)—the words of Rabbi Akiva.
>
> Rabbi Yishmael says, "Any *(kol)* widow or orphan"—Scripture spoke about those who are generally oppressed. (*Mekhilta de-Rabbi Yishmael, Nezikin*, §18, p. 313)[28]

"אַלְמָנָה וְיָתוֹם [לֹא תְעַנּוּן]" (שמות כב, כא). אין לי אלא אלמנה ויתום, שאר כל אדם מנין? תלמוד לומר "כָּל לֹא תְעַנּוּן"—דברי ר' עקיבה. . . .

ר' ישמעאל אומר: "כָּל אַלְמָנָה וְיָתוֹם"—שדרכן ליענות, בהן דיבר הכתוב.

Here, too, the two midrashic figureheads are in agreement that no one should be mistreated, but they disagree about where to find this in the biblical text. In Rabbi Akiva's view, the Torah is precise in its language: "widow or orphan" means widow and orphan. By the same token, the word *kol* is not strictly necessary. If so, its insertion must have a purpose: to include everyone else and thus universalize this law. This entails rereading the Torah in a way that allows the exegete to break syntactic bonds and form new clauses or sub-clauses.[29] Rabbi Yishmael, by contrast, reads the verse conventionally and explains these specific individuals as examples. The verse singles out the widow and orphan because they are especially vulnerable to abuse, but that does not imply that one may oppress anyone else. Rabbi Yishmael is sensitive to the Torah's casuistic nature, presenting prevalent cases without intending them to be exclusive.[30]

So far, we have seen how Rabbi Akiva looks at the immediate text, while Rabbi Yishmael incorporates broader considerations like context and rational inferences. Rabbi Yishmael's school also tends to engage more in comparative analyses.[31] The midrash below from *Sifrei Numbers* showcases this. Although Rabbi Akiva is the only named Tanna, the other, unat-

---

a This word, inserted here in the middle to make sense in English, appears at the beginning of the verse. Rabbi Akiva reads it as a noun, where in the original context it is an adjective: "any (*kol*) widow or orphan."

tributed opinion most probably belongs to his regular interlocutor, the founder of the school that produced this Midrash—Rabbi Yishmael.

"The Lord spoke to Moses saying *(lemor)*: Speak to the Children of Israel, When a man or woman commits any sin etc."[a] (Num. 5:5–6).

Why was this passage said?[b] Since it says, "When a person sins and betrays the Lord's trust etc. or finds a lost object etc." (Lev. 5:21–22), yet we do not hear about stealing from a convert anywhere in the Torah. It therefore teaches, "Speak to the Children of Israel, When a man or woman commits any human sin, to betray the Lord's trust"— Scripture comes to teach that someone who steals from a convert[c] and swears to him must pay the principal and a fifth to the priests[d] and a guilt-offering to the altar.

This is a principle (middah)[e] *of the Torah:* Any passage that is stated in one place with a missing detail is repeated elsewhere only for that missing detail.

Rabbi Akiva says, Wherever it says "saying" *(lemor)*[f] it must be expounded.[g] (*Sifrei Numbers*, §2, p. 4)

"וַיְדַבֵּר ה' אֶל מֹשֶׁה לֵּאמֹר: דַּבֵּר אֶל בְּנֵי יִשְׂרָאֵל אִישׁ אוֹ אִשָּׁה כִּי יַעֲשׂוּ מִכָּל חַטֹּאת הָאָדָם וגו'" (במדבר ה, ה-ו).

למה נאמרה פרשה זו? לפי שהוא אמר "נֶפֶשׁ כִּי תֶחֱטָא וּמָעֲלָה מַעַל בַּה'" וגו' "אוֹ מָצָא אֲבֵדָה וגו'" (ויקרא ה, כא-כב). אבל בגוזל הגר לא שמענו בכל התורה. תלמוד לומר "דַּבֵּר אֶל בְּנֵי יִשְׂרָאֵל אִישׁ אוֹ אִשָּׁה כִּי יַעֲשׂוּ מִכָּל חַטֹּאת הָאָדָם לִמְעֹל מַעַל בַּה'"—בא הכתוב ולימד על גוזל הגר ונשבע לו, שישלם קרן וחומש לכהנים ואשם למזבח.

זו מידה בתורה: כל פרשה שנאמרה במקום אחד וחסר בה דבר אחד וחזר ושנאה במקום אחד, לא שנאה אלא על שחיסר בה דבר אחד.

ר' עקיבא אומר: כל מקום שנאמר "לאמר" צריך לידרש.

a This passage states that if a person wrongs their fellow man, say by stealing, the penalty is to repay the principal plus a fifth.

b This penalty is already explicitly stated in Leviticus 5:24, about a slew of cases in which one financially wrongs their fellow man and denies it under oath.

c The reiterated law of Numbers 5:5–7 is only necessary for a new case mentioned in Numbers 5:8: the wronged individual who the Torah says has no "redeemer," which the Sages take to be the convert, since in rabbinic Halakhah such a person is disconnected from their biological family.

d If the convert has no children who were born after his conversion, there is no one else to whom the inheritance passes, so restitution is brought to the priests.

e Literally, "a measure," encapsulating the notion that it is a fixed rule by which to compare or contrast verses.

f See first line: "The Lord spoke to Moses saying *(lemor)*."

g For its own sake; one may not presume that it is simply here to fill out a discussion elsewhere. On the word *lemor* here, see Kahana, *Sifre on Numbers*, 35.

The lengthy derashah of Rabbi Yishmael compares two legal passages, Leviticus 5 and Numbers 5, regarding the restitution made and guilt-offering brought for various financial offenses against one's fellow man.[32] According to Rabbi Yishmael, the passage in Numbers looks like a repetition of Leviticus, but its addition of a legal novelty justifies its entire existence.[33] Since the Torah contains manifold legal repetitions, this tenet, characterized here as a *middah* or hermeneutic principle, has immense explanatory power. It instructs the exegete not to spend too much time pondering all the implications of a repeated passage; one can rest after discovering even a single new legal detail.[34]

For Rabbi Akiva, in contrast, every scriptural utterance brims with meaning, so one must delve into every word of the repeated passage. He is less interested in how to square the two passages in Leviticus and Numbers. And so, while *Sifrei Numbers* from Rabbi Yishmael's school on Numbers 5 compares the pieces in five separate derashot, the *Sifra* from Rabbi Akiva's school on the parallel in Leviticus 5 makes no such comparisons.[35]

In Midrashim from Rabbi Yishmael's school, comparisons and contrasts take on varied dimensions. One type of comparison uses an explicit statement or qualification in one place to shine light on a general, unqualified expression in another. Enshrined in the Ten Commandments is the prohibition not to steal, *lo tignov*. But does this refer to the kidnapping of people or to the theft of property?

> Three mitzvot are said about this matter: two are explicit[a] and one is unspecified.[b] Let us learn about the unspecified one from the explicit one: Just as the explicit one is a commandment for which one is liable for death by the court, so the unspecified one is a commandment for which one is liable for death by the court. (*Mekhilta de-Rabbi Yishmael, Ba-Ḥodesh*, §8, p. 233 = *Nezikin*, §5, p. 267)

> שלוש מצות נאמרו בעניין, שתים מפורשות ואחת סתומה. נלמד סתומה ממפורשת: מה מפורשת מצוה שחייבין עליה מיתת בית דין, אף סתומה מצוה שחייבין עליה מיתת בית דין.

In two places, the Torah explicitly talks about the abduction of human beings and sentences the perpetrator to death. Rabbi Yishmael's academy thinks that one can define the eighth of the Ten Commandments on their basis, so that it, too, refers not to the stealing of property but of human beings. What is the advantage of triplicating this prohibition? First, the two unequivocal verses are casuistic in nature; they don't outlaw kidnapping so much as state the penalty for it. This third verse is apodictic, so this derashah establishes an outright biblical prohibition. Second, it avoids overlap with a similarly worded prohibition in Leviticus 19:11, *lo tignovu*, which is unmistakably about theft and not kidnapping. Rabbi Yishmael's

---

a Exodus 21:16 and Deuteronomy 24:7 both specify kidnapping and capital punishment for the crime.

b Exodus 20:13, part of the Decalogue, does not specify the type of stealing or the punishment.

school views the entire Torah as an intertextual unit, allowing the interpreter to contextualize a verse based on verses in other books of the Torah.

Rabbi Yishmael's preference for rule-based interpretation is enshrined in a *baraita* (a tannaitic teaching not included in the Mishnah) that attributes thirteen interpretive *middot* to him.[36] Only seven, less-sophisticated principles are attributed to Hillel the Elder, who was active in the first century CE.[37] Rabbinic tradition considers the *middot* of Rabbi Yishmael's school to be the pinnacle of exegetical evolution, although in practice their status in and relationship with the Midrashim of Rabbi Yishmael's school is complicated.[38] Some of these *middot* bear on parallel but distant passages through techniques like a fortiori reasoning and the *gezerah shavah*, a verbal equivalence. About half deal with the possible relationships of elements in closer proximity, involving a generality *(kelal)* and a particular *(perat)*.[39]

The most general comparative *middah* on the list is the *binyan av*, a paradigm set up in a single verse. This principle holds that one verse is primary and its halakhic data illuminate all other scriptural manifestations of the same idea or law. Here is a classic example regarding the exemption of women from living in the sukkah (the booth for the holiday of Sukkot):

> Do I hear that even women are implied? It therefore teaches, "the native *(ezraḥ)* of Israel [shall dwell in sukkot]" (Lev. 23:42)—it created a paradigm *(banah av)*: Wherever it says "native" *(ezraḥ)*, Scripture is speaking of males. (*Sifrei Numbers*, §112, p. 119)

> שומע אני אף הנשים במשמע? תלמוד לומר "הָאֶזְרָח בְּיִשְׂרָאֵל" (ויקרא כג, מב) – בנה אב: בכל מקום שנאמר "אזרח", בזכרין הכתוב מדבר.

For Rabbi Yishmael, the meaning of a word in one verse blooms outward, because the entire Torah is interconnected. That is why comparative analysis of parallels is characteristic of his school's Midrashim.

In another area of Halakhah, a *binyan av* includes women even when only men are mentioned:

> "When men quarrel etc." (Ex. 21:18). I only have men, whence women? Rabbi Yishmael would say, Since it did not specify regarding all damages in the Torah, but it did specify regarding one of them that men are like women, I can specify that in all damages in the Torah men are like women. (*Mekhilta de-Rabbi Yishmael, Nezikin*, §6, p. 269)

> "וְכִי יְרִיבֻן אֲנָשִׁים" וג' (שמות כא, יח). אין לי אלא אנשים, נשים מנין? היה ר' ישמעאל אומר: הואיל וכל הנזקין שבתורה סתם, ופרט באחד מהן שעשה בו נשים כאנשים, פורט אני כל הנזקין שבתורה לעשות בהן נשים כאנשים.

Where is the one place that the Torah specifies that "men are like women"? If a bull has violent tendencies of which the owner has been apprised and it kills "a man or a woman," the

Torah rules that it must be stoned and the owner executed (Ex. 21:29).[40] Rabbi Yishmael globalizes this explicit equivalency to every area of tort law, even where it is not indicated. In the continuation of the midrash, Rabbi Yoshiyah says outright: "'A man or woman'—Scripture comes to make women like men in all damages in the Torah."[41]

At the other end of the spectrum are highly detailed principles that apply to specific sequences. One principle that appears ten times in tannaitic Midrash states, "A generality, a particular, and a generality you treat only like the particular."[42] Here is an example: The Torah rules that if an unpaid watchman, say a friend, is given something to watch and it is stolen or lost, they must swear that they weren't involved or responsible. The Torah's formulation is long-winded:

> In every matter of misappropriation, whether for an ox, for a donkey, for a sheep, for a garment, for every loss about which one says, "This is it," the matter of both shall come before the judges. Whomever the judges find guilty shall pay double to his fellow. (Exodus 22:8)

What is one to make of all this, the broad categories and specific animals and items? The *Mekhilta* expounds:

> "In every matter of misappropriation"—it generalized.
>
> "Whether for an ox, for a donkey, for a sheep, for a garment"—it particularized.
>
> [. . .] And when it says "for every loss"—it generalized again. [. . .]
>
> A generality, a particular, and a generality you treat only like the particular: Just as the particular is explicitly movable property that does not serve as a guarantee, so I only have movable property that does not serve as a guarantee. (*Mekhilta de-Rabbi Yishmael, Nezikin,* §15, pp. 300–301)

"עַל כָּל דְּבַר פֶּשַׁע" (שמות כב, ח)—כלל. "עַל שׁוֹר עַל חֲמוֹר עַל שֶׂה עַל שַׂלְמָה"—פרט. [. . .] וכשהוא אומר "עַל כָּל אֲבֵדָה"—חזר וכלל. [. . .] כלל ופרט וכלל אין את דן אלא כעין הפרט: מה הפרט מפורש בנכסים מטלטלין שאין להם אחריות, אף אין לי אלא נכסין מטלטלין שאין להן אחריות.

According to the school of Rabbi Yishmael, the categories and specifications of the verse are arranged in a halakhically meaningful sequence of generality-particular-generality. The *middah* governing this dictates that the sandwiched particular controls the applicability of the general rule.[43] In the law of the unpaid watchman, the fact that oxen, donkeys, sheep, and clothing are specified indicates its application to movable property, or "property that does not serve as a guarantee."

If Rabbi Yishmael's tendency is to look at the broader picture, to detect patterns in the way the Torah communicates, Rabbi Akiva scrutinizes Scripture through a macro lens, inspecting individual words and letters. The two Talmuds report that Rabbi Akiva had an exegetical rule about the function of certain Hebrew grammatical particles, a rule that he obeyed methodically, even when context seemed to preclude its usage. Here is the version in the Palestinian Talmud:

> Nehemiah Imsuni[a] attended to Rabbi Akiva for twenty-two years, and he taught him that *et*[b] and *gam*[c] are inclusive, *akh* and *rak*[d] are exclusive.
>
> He said to him,[e] "What is that which is written, '*et* the Lord your God you[f] shall fear' (Deut. 6:13)?"
>
> He said to him,[g] "Him and His Torah."[h] (Palestinian Talmud, *Berakhot*, 9:5, 13b)

נחמיה עימסוני שימש את ר' עקיבה עשרים ושתים שנה, ולמדו אתים וגמים ריבויין, אכין ורקין מיעוטין.

אמר ליה: מה הוא ההן דכתיב "אֶת ה' אֱלֹהֶיךָ תִּירָא" (דברים ו, יג)?

אמר ליה: אותו ואת תורתו.

Words like "also" and "but" are critical for anyone to express themselves fully. They are to be expected in a text that conveys meaningful information. Rabbi Akiva, though, regularly extended the inclusive or exclusive force of *gam*, *akh*, and *rak* beyond the immediate context to the plane of Halakhah, where they exert legal force. He further endowed *et*, a function word solely necessitated by grammar that has no lexical meaning, with an inclusive implication. Rabbi Nehemiah, his senior student, was perplexed: How could Rabbi Akiva interpret the *et* in this specific verse as halakhically inclusive without veering into some kind of dualistic theology? What entity could possibly be bundled with God in the command to fear Him? Likely to Nehemiah's surprise, Rabbi Akiva daringly answered that the Torah has a similar status to God in this regard. The *et* has to include something, and sometimes that inclusion can be quite radical.[44]

The Midrashim of Rabbi Akiva's school often relate to words in a verse by isolating them successively from one another. These derashot chop up the verse and interpret each element.[45] Under Torah law, a newlywed husband is released from military service for his first year of marriage: "he shall be free for his household and gladden the wife whom he has

---

a Possibly indicating affiliation with the village of Emmaus near Jerusalem.
b A grammatically necessary particle that marks the direct object of a clause but that is homonymous with a preposition meaning "with"; it has no English equivalent.
c A connector meaning "also" or "even."
d Connectors meaning "but" or "only."
e Nehemiah to Rabbi Akiva.
f *et* isn't translated into English because it just marks "the Lord your God" as the direct object.
g Rabbi Akiva to Nehemiah.
h Shall you fear.

taken" (Deut. 24:5). The Torah says elsewhere that the officers turn away from the front line those who have just finished building a house, planting a vineyard, or marrying a wife (Deut. 20:5–7). The following midrash reads the latter into the former:

> "He shall be free for his household" (Deut. 24:5)—this is his house.
>
> "He shall be"—this is his vineyard.
>
> "And gladden the wife"—this is his wife.
>
> "Whom he has taken"—this is his levirate wife. (*Sifrei Deuteronomy*, §271, p. 292)

> "נָקִי יִהְיֶה לְבֵיתוֹ" (דברים כד, ה)—זה ביתו; "יִהְיֶה"—זה כרמו; "וְשִׂמַּח אֶת אִשְׁתּוֹ"—זו אשתו; "אֲשֶׁר לָקָח"—להביא את יבימתו.

In this deconstructed sentence, each word conveys a halakhic datum. Some adhere to the literal meaning ("wife—this is his wife"), and others leave it entirely behind. What is important is that each biblical phrase teaches something new.

Rabbi Akiva even isolates prefixes from the words they front.[46] He magnifies the import of another innocuous connector, the conjunctive *vav*, a move with a potentially grave halakhic consequence, as can be seen in a debate with R. Yishmael preserved in the Babylonian Talmud:

> For it is learned:[a]
>
> "And if the daughter (*u-vat*)[b] of a priest profanes herself"[c] (Lev. 21:9)—the verse is talking about a *na'arah*[d] who is betrothed. [. . .]—the words of Rabbi Yishmael.
>
> Rabbi Akiva says, Both the betrothed and the married go out for burning.[e] [. . .]
>
> Rabbi Akiva said to him, "Yishmael, my brother, I expound *bat u-vat*."[f]
>
> He said to him, "Because you expound *bat u-vat* you will take her out for burning?" (Babylonian Talmud, *Sanhedrin* 51b)

---

a In a baraita.
b The conjunctive vav here loses its consonantal quality here to become the vowel u.
c Through harlotry, the penalty is death by burning.
d A young woman in the intermediate halakhic stage between minority and majority.
e The penalty for adultery is usually strangulation, which is considered the least severe form of execution in Halakhah; see *Mekhilta de-Rabbi Yishmael*, Nezikin, §5, p. 266.
f The fact that there is a conjunctive *vav* meaning "and" before the word bat endows it with inclusive force, so that the word *bat* alone refers to a betrothed girl, and the vav includes a married one in the same punishment.

דתניא: "וּבַת אִישׁ כֹּהֵן כִּי תֵחֵל" (ויקרא כא, ט)—בנערה והיא ארוסה הכתוב מדבר. [. . .]—דברי ר' ישמעאל.

ר' עקיבה אומר: אחת ארוסה ואחת נשואה יוצאת לשריפה. [. . .]

אמר לו ר' עקיבא: ישמעאל אחי, "בַת" "וּבַת" אני דורש.

אמר לו: וכי מפני שאתה דורש "בַת" "וּבַת" אתה מוציא זו לשריפה?

The various derashot above typify Rabbi Akiva's exegetical methodology. His halakhic interpretation occurs at the smallest level, releasing textual molecules from their bonds so that they can form inclusions (ribbuyyim) and exclusions (mi'utim).[47] "Each and every one is included (mitrabbeh) from its place," by which Rabbi Akiva intends that every inclusion and exclusion must be local.[48] Unlike Rabbi Yishmael's generalization and particularization, *Kelal uFerat*, which follow the grammar of the verse, Rabbi Akiva's inclusion (ribbuy) and exclusion (mi'ut) are wholly technical and atomistic. For Rabbi Akiva, the Torah is a string of isolatable utterances, in which meanings are confined to their point of origin. There is no place in his hermeneutic scheme for a *binyan av* that can hold true across the entire Torah, nor does he usually see the need to compare passages. Instead, Rabbi Akiva's darshan is supposed to peer ever deeper into the verse at hand.

It is hard to view Rabbi Akiva's approach as genuine interpretation, at least in the way we generally use the word, since it does not focus on the meaning of the words per se. It is almost as if words are portals to the halakhic plane, which is how a *vav* can join words, phrases, or clauses in context, and can also be used independently for deducing new ideas and categories. Rabbi Akiva's belief in the divinity of the Torah and the absolute necessity of every word drive him to seize upon on every last letter to expand or restrict the Halakhah.

Rabbi Yishmael, on the other hand, uses sophisticated exegetical principles. Only in the Midrashim of his school do we find the statement "This is a hermeneutic principle (middah) of the Torah."[49] Even in their most minute applications, these principles still deal with whole phrases and not words or letters, and Rabbi Yishmael regularly searches for patterns in the text, like sequences of generalities (kelalim) and particulars (peratim).[50] His attitude is more interpretive, as it delves into the logical, syntactic, and semantic relationships between categories and their members.

An important caveat must be made here. Each school's methodology described here does not filter down into their respective Midrashim in pure form. No bet midrash is consistent all the time; it is a matter of emphasis and frequency. The scholastic characterizations are generalizations.

The novel radicality of Rabbi Akiva's approach, which broke with all antecedents, understandably generated rabbinic opposition. The source above records Rabbi Yishmael's shock at Rabbi Akiva's exegetical confidence to send a woman to her death. He was not the only one to challenge Rabbi Akiva to his face:

"He shall offer[a] with the thanksgiving sacrifice [flatcakes mixed in oil *(ba-shemen)* and flatcake wafers spread with oil *(ba-shamen)*]" (Lev. 7:12). What does *ba-shemen ba-shamen* twice teach? [. . .]

Rabbi Akiva said, Had it said *ba-shemen* once, I would have said it is like any other meal offering for purposes of a *log*.[b] When it says *ba-shemen ba-shemen twice*, and an inclusion after an inclusion in the Torah serves only to exclude *(lema'et)*.[c]

Its reduction *(mi'utah)* is to half a *log*. Could it be that one divides the half-*log* into three for the three types—the flatcakes, flatcake wafers, and cakes of choice flour?[d] It therefore teaches, "and cakes of choice flour mixed with oil *(ba-shamen)*, soaked through" (Lev. 7:12)—it has included, and an inclusion after an exclusion serves only to include. [. . .]

Rabbi Elazar ben Azariah said to Rabbi Akiva, "Even if you say '*ba-shemen* is to exclude,' '*ba-shemen* is to include' all day long, I won't listen to you. The half-*log* of oil for the thanksgiving offering is . . . a halakhah of Moses from Sinai."[e] (*Sifra, Tzav*, 6:2, 34d)

"וְהִקְרִיב עַל זֶבַח הַתּוֹדָה וגו'" (ויקרא ז, יב). מה תלמוד לומר "בַּשֶּׁמֶן" "בַּשָּׁמֶן" שני פעמים? [. .].

אמר ר' עקיבה: אילו נאמר "בַּשֶּׁמֶן" אחד הייתי אומר, הרי הוא ככל המנחות ללוג. כשהוא אומר "בַּשֶּׁמֶן" "בַּשָּׁמֶן" שני פעמים—אין ריבוי אחר ריבוי בתורה אלא למעט. מיעוטה לחצי לוג. יכול ישתליש חצי לוג זה לשלוש המינים הללו, לחלות ולרקיקין ולרבוכה? תלמוד לומר "וְסֹלֶת מֻרְבֶּכֶת, חַלֹּת בְּלוּלֹת בַּשָּׁמֶן"—ריבה, ואין ריבוי אחר מיעוט בתורה אלא לרבות. [. .].

אמר לו ר' אלעזר בן עזריה לר' עקיבה: אפילו אתה מרבה כל היום כולו "בַּשֶּׁמֶן" ו"בַּשָּׁמֶן" לרבות ו"בַּשֶּׁמֶן" למעט, איני שומע לך. אלא חצי לוג שמן לתודה . . . הלכה למשה מסיני.

Through the tripling of *ba-shemen*, Rabbi Akiva uses exclusions and inclusions to support the halakhah that the thanksgiving meal offering only receives a half-*log* of oil, contrary to all other sacrifices. Rabbi Elazar ben Azariah is having none of it, even if it means forfeiting all scriptural support for this law. Better to leave it out of the Torah and attribute it to tradition than to forcefully, unconvincingly cram it in there. Rabbi Yishmael is also forced to concede that "in three places tradition circumvents Scripture,"[51] because his interpretive principles have their limits and he is unwilling to adopt Rabbi Akiva's techniques.

    a The meal offering that accompanies the thanksgiving sacrifice.
    b Meal offerings are usually mixed with a *log* of oil. Approximately a third of a liter.
    c Hebrew *lema'et*, which in this context means to reduce the oil brought with the meal offering.
    d These are the third component mentioned in the continuation of the verse, quoted immediately below.
    e An ancient extrascriptural tradition.

Part of the objection to Akivan exegesis is its apparent arbitrariness. It seems almost as if he pulls halakhot out of words like rabbits out of hats. Another prefix his approach considers pregnant with meaning is the definite article represented by the single letter *he*.[52] The Torah states that the Israelite native, the *ezrah*, must dwell in the sukkah on Sukkot. The school of Rabbi Akiva learns:

ezrah (Lev. 23:42)—this is the native; *ha-ezrah*—to exclude women. (*Sifra, Emor*, 17:9, 103a)

"אֶזְרָח" (ויקרא כג, מב)—זה אזרח, "הָאֶזְרָח"—להוציא את הנשים.

What indicates to the interpreter that women should be excluded? Clearly, the halakhic end. The ability to ground the tradition of female exemption from the sukkah in the Torah justifies the wild interpretive means.[53] Recall that the school of Rabbi Yishmael maintains this same halakhic tradition but uses a *binyan av*, a principled comparison to another verse, to root it in the Torah. The glaring weakness of Rabbi Akiva's exegetical technique is also its strength. One of Midrash's main motivations, to be detailed in the next chapter, is to anchor halakhot of the Oral Torah in the Written Torah. The fungibility of Rabbi Akiva's techniques facilitates this goal.[54]

But even as it supports tradition, it simultaneously poses a serious threat to it. Radical exegesis can produce halakhot that conflict with it and permit what is prohibited. Rabbi Akiva uses his unprecedentedly strong exegetical tool in support of tradition, but like any tool it has the potential to be wielded differently. That could explain why Rabbi Akiva's school instituted a prohibition against expounding the sexual relationships forbidden by the Torah in Leviticus 18 and 20.[55] One can imagine how *mi'utim* excluding certain relations from the biblical prohibitions would compromise the rabbinic legal system.

In taking up the subject of Midrash, scholarship has tended to focus on Rabbi Akiva's methodology, because its extreme character accentuates Midrash's major features. In recent years, though, scholars have devoted more attention to Rabbi Yishmael's school. Azzan Yadin-Israel has proposed that this bet midrash uses *middot* because they help the darshan locate signposts embedded within the Torah, which point the way to its interpretation. Torah is conceived by him as both code and cipher. The way the Midrashim of this school talk about Scripture indicate that it is an active partner in interpretation: "Scripture comes to distinguish," "Scripture comes to teach," "until Scripture expressly decides," and so on. The darshan is the apt pupil, who expectantly looks for a sign from Scripture to know how to proceed.[56]

In Yadin-Israel's account, Rabbi Akiva's school is trying to hitch tradition to Scripture by any suitable device. Its primary motivation is the desire to fuse the Written and Oral Torahs into a single system.[57] In the coming chapters, we will try to define more precisely Rabbi Akiva's perception of the biblical text that permits him to handle it with a certain playfulness.[58]

Yakir Paz has also studied the distinctive approaches of the schools. He compares the Midrash to scholia, brief marginal notations made by Hellenistic scholars on the Homeric corpus. He perceives a likeness between the hermeneutic activity of the darshanim, especially in the simpler exegetical techniques of Rabbi Yishmael's school, and the work of ancient commentators on Homer. The idea that one can resolve a local ambiguity from express statements elsewhere, the principle that also underlies the *binyan av*, bears an unmistakable resemblance to a principle in Homeric interpretation, "to clarify Homer from Homer."[59] Paz further claims that the idea that "the Torah spoke in human language" is not, as the simple reading has it, that the Torah is written in spoken language. What it really means is that it is a literary work of the kind produced by human beings, so it should be interpreted according to literary rules. That is exactly why the darshanim of Rabbi Yishmael's school rely on exegetical principles developed by the Alexandrian scholars of Homer, Homeric Greek being the model for high literature in Hellenistic culture.[60]

C. DIFFERENT WORLDVIEWS AND SHARED TEXTS OUTSIDE OF HALAKHAH

Since interpretation and application go hand in hand, one can draw a line from hermeneutics to Halakhah. Scholars have identified systematic differences between each school's treatment of halakhic areas concerning slaves, converts, idol worship, mitzvot pertaining to the Land of Israel, the attitude toward Gentiles, and many more.[61] For example, Rabbi Yishmael has a stricter approach toward idolatry, while Rabbi Akiva reinterprets the verses preaching annihilation of idols (Deut. 12:2) as a mere prohibition to derive benefit from them.[62]

Aside from these halakhic disagreements, which stem from the interpretation of specific legal passages, there has also been an attempt to find more general philosophical, ethical, and even metaphysical differences between schools, ones that that are not necessarily products of local exegetical disagreements. Since the thrust of our discussion is hermeneutical, only a brief survey of some of the key points is possible.

Abraham Joshua Heschel, who was the first to break new ground on this issue, argued that the two schools were divided on fundamental questions of theology.[63] Rabbi Yishmael was more rationalistic and held a transcendent conception of God, erecting a barrier between heaven and earth, God and man. Rabbi Akiva adopted a more mystical approach that blurred these lines. He believed in an immanent God; there can be heaven on earth. He considered the entire Torah—both the Written and the Oral—as wholly divine. Rabbi Yishmael, on the other hand, limited the place of Sinai and revelation in the development of the Oral Torah. Heschel cast a very wide net, and scholars have substantiated certain aspects of his account[64] while criticizing others.[65] The main critique is methodological: Heschel did not sufficiently distinguish between Midrashim originating in one or the other school, or between source material from earlier and later eras.[66]

Mindful of these pitfalls, Menahem Hirshman has undertaken a more cautious study based solely on the tannaitic Midrashim of the two schools. He argues that Rabbi Yishmael's Midrashim exhibit a universalistic conception of the Torah, according to which it is aimed toward everyone and not only the Jewish people. This would explain that school's positive attitude toward conversion and its encouragement of missionizing. If the Torah is for everyone, Jews have the obligation to get it out there. Rabbi Akiva's school, on the other hand, was populated by isolationists. Hirshman's evidence is more persuasive than Heschel's, but it is limited to the sphere of Aggadah. Tracking systematic halakhic expressions of these orientations is a lot more difficult.[67]

I have also attempted to characterize a systematic disagreement between the two schools regarding the evil inclination. The idea of the evil inclination as a demonic entity that besets man is found only in the Midrashim of Rabbi Yishmael's school. The other school treats it as a natural, fundamentally neutral drive of man and never uses the adjective "evil."[68]

Isolating differences in worldview is naturally limited by the nature of the available material. The tannaitic Midrashim focus primarily on Halakhah. *Mekhilta de-Rabbi Yishmael* deliberately does not begin with the history of Israelite slavery in Exodus 1, but with the very first divine legislation in Exodus 12, the offering of the paschal sacrifice. The book of Leviticus is almost entirely law, so legal coverage is to be expected. *Sifrei Numbers* skips the first four chapters of the book's narrative about the Israelite encampment and begins with the first mitzvah of that book in Numbers 5: banishing the ritually impure from the camp. The Midrashim of Rabbi Akiva's academy include more biblical narrative. *Sifrei Deuteronomy* begins with some passages on Moshe's recounting of Israelite history, and *Mekhilta de-Rashbi* has an entire section devoted to Moses's encounter with the burning bush, before turning to the commandments of Pesach (Passover). Quantitatively, both schools deal with all legal passages in the Torah and only a small number of biblical stories. Even so, the narrative sections that are covered are treated relatively extensively. All in all, approximately 30 percent of the Tannitic Midrashim discuss aggadic matters.

And what a surprise these aggadic portions contain. The kinship between the two schools in these areas is far greater than what we find in halakhic ones. Much of the time, the only thing that separates them is terminology. In exploring *Mekhilta de-Rabbi Yishmael* and *Mekhilta de-Rashbi* on Exodus, Menahem Kahana dissected the derashot in Tractate 'Amalek, and found that taxonomically the source material is the same, except that *Mekhilta de-Rashbi* (a Midrash that was edited later than others) reworks it more. He explains this curiosity by positing that the aggadic material was not composed in either school. It originated with anonymous aggadists,[69] and then the schools incorporated it into their collections.[70]

The verse says, "Moses said to Joshua, 'Choose men for us and go out to do battle against Amalek. Tomorrow, I will station myself on top of the hill, with the staff of God in my hand'" (Ex. 17:9). Here (table 4) are the two Midrashim side by side for ease of comparison. Kahana observes that the two texts are identical aside from the omission of a single word: *ki-shemu'o* ("as it sounds"). The omission in *Mekhilta de-Rashbi* changes the entire structure of the derashah, because it conflates the two derashot. With this, the latter derashah disappears. This is a clear example of both the commonality of midrashic material and the derivative text of *Mekhilta de-Rashbi*.

TABLE 4   A comparison of the aggadic part of the two Mekhiltot

Mekhilta de-Rabbi Yishmael, 'Amalek, §1, p. 179	Mekhilta de-Rashbi, 17:9, p. 121
"Tomorrow, I will station myself on top of the hill" (Ex. 17:9).	"Tomorrow, I will station myself etc." (Ex. 17:9).
Tomorrow, we will stand ready.	Tomorrow, we will stand ready on top of the hill.
"On top of the hill"—as it sounds *(ki-shemu'o)*.	
"מָחָר אָנֹכִי נִצָּב עַל רֹאשׁ הַגִּבְעָה" (שמות יז, ט) — מחר נהא מעותדין ועומדין. על ראש הגבעה — כשמועו.	"מָחָר אָנֹכִי נִצָּב וג'" (שמות יז, ט) — מחר נהיה מעותדין ועומדין על ראש הגבעה.

One should not conclude that the two schools outsourced all aggadic exegesis. The shared source material is the basis for the extended aggadic tracts in the Midrashim, which are independent units that expound biblical stories from beginning to end. For example, the major aggadic portion of the *Mekhilta* covers the narrative of the Israelites from the exodus from Egypt to the Sinai, Exodus 14–19. This is full-blown aggadic Midrash. But there is other aggadic Midrash interspersed within the halakhic portions that are creations of the two schools, which will be discussed in chapter 14 below.

ELEVEN

The Motivations of Midrash

Midrash regularly deviates from what most sensible people would agree is the plain meaning of the verse. Yet, occasionally it does focus on the simple, literal-contextual meaning. Thus, "X is nothing but Y" is a definitional gloss that appears about two hundred times in Midrashim from both schools. For example, when the Torah instructs the leadership to caution the Israelites about ritual impurity, it uses the unusual word *hizzartem* (Lev. 15:31) from the root *n-z-r*. The Midrash glosses, "*Nezirah* is nothing but separation,"[1] which is also how modern dictionaries explain this word. If someone were to compile all such derashot, we would have a kind of midrashic dictionary of rare words in Scripture. It has been even argued that the simplicity of these derashot and their existence in the Midrashim of both schools point to them being an early stratum of the Midrash.[2]

Alongside these lexical glosses are other *peshat*-oriented readings, especially in the Midrashim of Rabbi Yishmael's school. One recurring formula is "Scripture comes to teach" followed by a simple extrapolation. When the Torah states that someone who comes into contact with a corpse is impure for seven days, the Midrash comments: "Scripture comes to teach that a corpse transmits seven-day ritual impurity."[3] This is little more than a restatement of the verse using the terminology of rabbinic Halakhah.

But such derashot are the exception, rather than the rule. In its present form, the Midrash is exponentially more ambitious, and it usually sets aside the straightforward sense of Scripture.[4] Both traditional and modern scholars are not quite sure how to define Midrash, but all would concede that its motivation cannot be reduced to a search for the Torah's simple meaning. By the same token, one cannot take seriously the claim that Midrash marches to its own drum and pays no attention to the biblical verse at all. To try to recover some "muddled" or "organic" mode of thinking of the darshanim also seems like the wrong track.[5]

Instead of trying to define Midrash, over the next two chapters we will focus on the problems that the Midrash attempts to solve and the conceptions of the biblical text that allow it to operate the way it does. This chapter focuses on the motivations driving the Midrash, and the next one explores the ways in which it views the hallowed text. Only then can we understand what the darshanim were after and how they found it.

Although it can feel as if the Midrash does what it pleases with the text of the Torah, it actually operates on a set of assumptions and constraints that stimulate as well as limit its interpretation. The darshan in antiquity did not just look at the text in front of him and free associate. When he had a Torah scroll open to concentrate on a specific passage, he had to be aware of the thousands of other verses rolled up in this and other parchments that constitute the Torah, verses that can generate contradictions or superfluities. He had also to be mindful of the authoritative oral traditions that existed independently of the physical Torah that he grasped and handled. The darshan acted like a juggler who had to keep his eye on all the balls in order to keep them moving, and if he was really talented he could add memorable flourishes here and there.

This metaphor only works for those things of which the darshanim were conscious, however. They were also undoubtedly guided by the contemporary values of rabbinic society, which itself was shaped by the wider cultural landscape. This chapter examines all these different elements that together constituted the broader framework of midrashic activity. It begins with exegetical considerations (sections A–B) and then moves to juristic ones (sections C–E).

While the previous chapter dwelled on the differences between the midrashic schools, here we will concentrate on their common assumptions and address differences only when they are significant. Scholars have emphasized the hermeneutic gap between the schools, as we have seen in detail above, but it is no less important to acknowledge the shared foundations of midrashic thinking in all its branches.

A. JUSTIFYING SCRIPTURE

Modern Bible scholars all grapple, in one way or another, with a basic question: What does the text say? They draw from a variety of disciplines and apply an array of techniques to produce their answers. Thematic comparison with ancient Near Eastern material, contextualization of verses, linguistic parsing of words, literary analysis of pericopes—these and more constitute the work of scholars.

Midrash, on the other hand, is preoccupied first and foremost with a categorically different question: Why does the text say what it does? The question flows from the conception of the Torah as a divine, perfect text, in which every word is absolutely necessary. A superfluous word, a phrase out of place, or a trivial verse must be an illusion. If the reason it exists is not immediately obvious, one must dig deeper with a midrashic spade. Exegesis that proves the necessity of everything in the Torah is fundamentally, then, an act of justification.

Here is a classic example of a justificatory derashah:

"Do not sow your vineyard with *kil'ayim*"[a] (Deut. 22:9). Why do I need it? Does it not already say, "Do not sow your field with *kil'ayim*" (Lev. 19:19)? It teaches that whoever preserves[b] *kil'ayim* in a vineyard violates two negative commandments. (*Sifrei Deuteronomy*, §230, p. 262)

"לֹא תִזְרַע כַּרְמְךָ כִּלְאָיִם" (דברים כב, ט). מה אני צריך? והלא כבר נאמר "שָׂדְךָ לֹא תִזְרַע כִּלְאָיִם" (ויקרא יט, יט)? מלמד שכל המקיים כלאים בכרם עובר בשני לוויין.

Since the prohibition against sowing *kil'ayim* is already on record in the book of Leviticus, for what purpose does the book of Deuteronomy repeat it? The Midrash explains that the later verse adds a narrower prohibition against planting *kil'ayim* in a vineyard specifically. Anyone who mixes species in a vineyard now simultaneously violates the global prohibition and the specific one.

As will become evident throughout the chapter, it can be difficult to disentangle legal motivations from textual ones. As divine legislation, the Torah is perceived by the rabbinic darshanim as a work of perfection in form and content. In this example, though, form rather than content seems to be the primary driver. It is difficult to see why a vineyard would require its own prohibition to augment the transgression's severity. When placed in the larger context of derashot from Rabbi Akiva's school, it becomes obvious that the notion of double proscription in *Sifrei Deuteronomy* is intended to solve the problem of redundancy. This school regularly dispenses with redundancy by turning a phrase or clause into some form of prohibition, phrased negatively or even positively, with the simple aim of multiplying infractions. If two prohibitions are worse than one, then the verse is making a necessary halakhic contribution and is consequently not redundant.

The repetitiveness of the two verses above is plain enough. But the Midrash holds the Torah to such a lofty standard that it takes it upon itself to resolve what we would not even consider a repetition. Since, for the darshan, the Torah can be atomized for meaning, repetitions threaten to occur on a scale far smaller than that of the verse. A single verse can be laden with its own internal redundancies. Take the following midrash from Rabbi Yishmael's school about someone who contracted ritual impurity from a corpse and failed to attain purification, by being sprinkled with water containing ashes of the red heifer, before entering the holy precincts:

"And does not cleanse himself" (Num. 19:13).

---

a Two (or more) different species that may not be planted in close proximity in a field or vineyard, the laws of which can be found in Tractate *Kil'ayim* of the Mishnah.
b And does not uproot the forbidden mixture.

Rabbi says,[a] "Does not cleanse himself"—with blood.[b] Do you say "does not cleanse himself" with blood, or "does not cleanse himself" with water? When it says, "the water of sprinkling was not dashed on him" (Num. 19:13), water has been said. What, then, does "and does not cleanse himself" teach? Does not cleanse himself with blood, to include someone lacking atonement.[c] (*Sifrei Numbers*, §125, pp. 160–161)

"וְלֹא יִתְחַטָּא" (במדבר יט, יג). רבי אומר: לא יתחטא בדמים. אתה אומר לא יתחטא בדמים, או לא יתחטא במים? כשהוא אומר "מֵי נִדָּה לֹא זֹרַק עָלָיו" (שם)—הרי מים אמורין. הא מה תלמוד לומר "וְלֹא יִתְחַטָּא"? לא יתחטא בדמים, להביא את מחוסר כפרה.

The meaning of "does not cleanse himself" *(ve-lo yitḥatta)*, the verse fragment that opens this derashah, is not self-evident when deprived of context. But one need look no further than to the continuation of the very same verse to gain insight: "the water of sprinkling was not dashed on him." We know Rabbi Yehudah ha-Nasi is well aware of this simple reading, as he himself mentions it. But this later clarification is actually a problem that drives him in the opposite direction. If "the water of the sprinkling was not dashed on him" is the explanation of "does not cleanse himself," then the latter is superfluous. Since Holy Writ has no need to repeat itself, the darshan must search out the novelty. Since "water has been said," Rabbi Yehudah ha-Nasi contorts the cleansing to refer to the sprinkling of the blood on the altar and generates a new law. The fact that this interpretation does not accord with Halakhah as we know it (in which corpse impurity does not require a sacrifice) corroborates how forced this is.[6]

This represents another common type of justificatory derashah, which derives an additional law or detail thereof in order to banish the specter of repetition. It often has a formal structure: "When it says X [then the relevant law] has been [already] said. What, then, does Y teach?" Importantly, this formula is completely transparent. The darshan does not try to hide what he is doing; he willingly shows his hand by presenting and rejecting the literal-contextual meaning of the verse. Unlike earlier biblical interpretation, Midrash discloses its hermeneutical considerations so that it can be emulated by students in the study hall.

In the name of redundancy prevention, Midrashim from both schools must, at times, resort to restricting a phrase to a remote case that is far removed from the world of the verse. The two *Mekhiltot* on Exodus do this when expounding the law of the killer ox:

---

a Rabbi Yehudah ha-Nasi.

b The blood of the animal sacrifice that must be offered on the altar to complete the purification process, after the water has been sprinkled.

c The person has been ritually purified of the corpse impurity and has waited the requisite amount of time, but because they haven't yet offered the sacrifice, they still may not enter the Temple.

"It shall surely be stoned and its flesh shall not be eaten" (Ex. 21:28). Why is it said? By implication, when it says "it shall surely be stoned" we have learned that the meat may not be eaten.[a] What, then, does "its flesh shall not be eaten" teach? Rather,[b] the meat of an ox that is going out to be stoned and the owner has preemptively slaughtered is prohibited. It therefore says, "its flesh shall not be eaten." (*Mekhilta de-Rabbi Yishmael*, Nezikin, §10, pp. 281–282)

"סָקוֹל יִסָּקֵל הַשּׁוֹר וְלֹא יֵאָכֵל אֶת בְּשָׂרוֹ" (שמות כא, כח)—למה נאמר? ממשמע שנאמר "סָקוֹל יִסָּקֵל", הא למדנו שבשרו אסור באכילה, ומה תלמוד לומר "לֹא יֵאָכֵל אֶת בְּשָׂרוֹ"? אלא שור שהוא יוצא ליסקל וקדמו בעלים ושחטוהו—בשרו אסור באכילה. לכך נאמר "לֹא יֵאָכֵל אֶת בְּשָׂרוֹ".

"Its flesh shall not be eaten" (Ex. 21:28). Why do I need it? Do we not know that it is an unslaughtered animal and that an unslaughtered animal may not be eaten? What, then, does "its flesh shall not be eaten" teach? It tells us that if one slaughters it after its verdict has been handed down, the meat may not be eaten. (*Mekhilta de-Rashbi*, 21:28, pp. 178–179)

"וְלֹא יֵאָכֵל אֶת בְּשָׂרוֹ" (שמות כא, כח)—מה אני צריך? וכי אין אנו יודעין שהיא נבלה ונבלה אסורה באכילה? מה תלמוד לומר "וְלֹא יֵאָכֵל אֶת בְּשָׂרוֹ"? מגיד שאם שחטו משנגמר דינו, בשרו אסור באכילה.

The two midrashim, in almost identical language, assign "its flesh shall not be eaten" to a farfetched scenario devised to solve the problem of implicit redundancy. While the verse is prohibiting the flesh after the ox has been stoned, the Midrash moves it back to the brief duration between sentencing and stoning. If it did not make this imaginative reassignment, the phrase in question would be superfluous, because—and here's the important point—its legal content can be derived from the fact that it is stoned and not slaughtered. In this verse, the redundancy is only evident if one places it in the full context of Halakhah, which requires ritual slaughtering to make meat kosher. The Torah must convey new information, and whatever the text already logically entails is not truly new.

The justificatory derashah is often produced by textual rather than halakhic pressures. The pursuit of meaning can therefore lead to the phenomenon of contradictory halakhic derivations from a single phrase. For example, when the Torah thrice warns in identical language not to cook a kid in its mother's milk, the Midrash is troubled by the excessive repetition and offers over five distinct explanations.[7] Rabbi Yonatan answers that the three separate mentions *include* domesticated animals, wild animals, and fowl in the prohibition, whereas Rabbi Akiva says that they *exclude* precisely the same three categories.[8] Contradictory legal opinions can be cited as long as they solve the textual repetition.

---

a Because the animal has not been ritually slaughtered, which is necessary to render it kosher.
b The verse must be referring to a very narrow case.

Given that the text is the primary driver of the justificatory derashah, it fittingly exists for Aggadah, too. The Torah warns not to oppress the orphan or widow; otherwise, God says, "My wrath shall flare up and I will kill you by the sword, and your wives shall become widows and your children orphans" (Ex. 22:23). The Midrash unsurprisingly considers the second half of the verse superfluous:

> "And your wives shall become widows etc." (Ex. 22:33). By implication, when it says "My wrath shall flare up and I will kill," don't I know that your wives shall become widows and your children orphans? What, then, does "your wives shall become widows and your children orphans" teach? Rather, they shall be quasi-widows,[a] along the lines of "and they were bound until the day they died, in living widowhood" (2 Sam. 20:3); and your children shall be quasi-orphans, for no court will allow them to sell their fathers' property, under the presumption that they are alive. (*Mekhilta de-Rabbi Yishmael, Nezikin*, §18, p. 314)

"וְהָיוּ נְשֵׁיכֶם אַלְמָנוֹת" וג' (שמות כב, כג). ממשמע שנאמר "וְחָרָה אַפִּי וְהָרַגְתִּי", איני יודע שנשיכם אלמנות ובניכם יתומים? ומה תלמוד לומר "וְהָיוּ נְשֵׁיכֶם אַלְמָנוֹת וּבְנֵיכֶם יְתֹמִים"? אלא אלמנות ולא אלמנות, כעינין שנאמר "וַתִּהְיֶינָה צְרֻרוֹת עַד יוֹם מֻתָן אַלְמְנוּת חַיּוּת" (שמואל ב כ, ג); ובניכם יתומים ולא יתומים, שאין בית דין מניחין אותן למכור מנכסי אביהן, בחזקת שהן קיימין.

Necessity is the mother of invention. To uphold the need for the verse's continuation, this midrash creates liminal states in which the words "widows" and "orphans" do not mean what they say.

We have seen how the Midrash rushes to defend the Torah even when the redundancy only exists in the eye of the darshan and on a microscopic level. Still, in such instances the challenge emerges from the text itself. But the Midrash also concerns itself with the charge of triviality made by human reason. If exegesis or logical reasoning yields the same information as contained in the verse, why does the Torah have to state it? The Midrash therefore labors to demonstrate that reason is fallible and that the Torah's pronouncement is necessary and justified. To this end, it offers a potential rational line of thinking—"for it would have been logical" *(she-hayah be-din)*—that would have led to the opposite of Torah law.[9] The Midrash valiantly vindicates the Torah in the court of human reason by pointing out the latter's deficiencies.

In Numbers 15, for example, the Torah enumerates the meal offering and wine libation that are to accompany each of the types of animal sacrifice. After this detailed directive comes a general one: "Thus shall be done with each ox, with each ram, and with any sheep or goat" (Num. 15:11). Why is this necessary?

---

a   Literally, "widows and not widows" and "orphans and not orphans." Since the fathers and husbands are killed but there is no evidence of their death, the wives and children are widowed and orphaned but do not have the formal halakhic status of the widow and the orphan.

The Motivations of Midrash   243

"Thus shall be done with each ox" (Num. 15:11). Thus does it relate that the Torah does not distinguish between the libations of a calf and those of an ox. For it would have been logical: A youngling of small cattle[a] and a youngling of large cattle[b] require libations; if I have learned that[c] the Torah distinguishes between the libations of a lamb and those of a ram, so should you distinguish between the libations of a calf and those of an ox. It therefore teaches, "thus shall be done with each ox"—thus does it relate that the Torah does not distinguish between the libations of a calf and those of an ox. (*Sifrei Numbers*, §107, p. 110)

"כָּכָה יֵעָשֶׂה לַשּׁוֹר" (במדבר טו, יא)—הא מגיד שלא חלקה תורה בין נסכי עגל לנסכי שור. שהיה בדין: בן הצאן טעון נסכין ובן הבקר טעון נסכין. אם למדתי שחלקה תורה בין נסכי כבש לנסכי איל, כך תחלוק בין נסכי עגל לנסכי שור. תלמוד לומר "כָּכָה יֵעָשֶׂה לַשּׁוֹר"—הא מגיד שלא חלקה תורה בין נסכי עגל לנסכי שור.

The midrashic interpretation essentially restates the simple meaning of the verse.[10] According to it, the Torah is extending the libation for the young calf mentioned in the preceding verses to the full-grown ox, because "the Torah does not distinguish between the libations of a calf and those of an ox." Why must it make this extension? Because of the dangers of unfettered human reason. Since the Torah distinguishes between immature and mature sheep, one might have thought to distinguish between bullock and bull. It is up to the Midrash to set forth the Torah's subtle contribution of preventing logical reasoning from making incorrect deductions. The goal is clear: no detail in this verse is trivial.

Notably, when the *dersahah* uses the verse to reject the logical possibility, it does not advance a counterargument to make Scripture accord with reason in the end. Its aim is only to justify the need for the Torah to say what it says, which it achieves by showing that scriptural fiat trumps logic. It sets out to establish the Torah's non-triviality, not its rationality.

Human reason loomed large for the exegetes of the Midrash. One side of the coin, seen in the previous example, is that the Torah must block certain lines of incorrect reasoning. The other side of the coin is that the Torah should not duplicate correct reasoning. "If I have it from reason, what does X teach?" is a commonplace in the Midrashim of Rabbi Yishmael's school. If the content of a verse can be deduced from something else, the verse is redundant. The Midrash then must reveal human reason to be unreliable: "lest one say, I have it from reason."[11] This accounts for the typical structure of a midrash, which begins with some possible logical inference—an analogy, an a fortiori argument—and ends with its being cut down by Scripture: "it therefore teaches" *(talmud lomar)*. Such derashot often take the form of a rhetorical conversation, so that the language can be couched in the first person addressing someone in the second or third person.

a A lamb or kid.
b A bullock.
c The Torah specifies the different amounts for the two immediately above in verses 4–7.

Justificatory derashot that deal with logical reasoning can be more elaborate. Instead of a simple raise-and-reject, a darshan might propose multiple logical possibilities. If all are plausible, the darshan is claiming, the verse is needed to give its stamp of approval to one of them.[12] In Rabbi Yishmael's school, this type of midrash has a consistent form: "I have reasoned the alternative, voiding 'or the opposite,' so I have reinstated the original reasoning."[13] Rabbi Akiva's Midrashim proceed in the same fashion without any fixed terminology.

In light of this, one can suggest that the enterprise of justification underlies the entire midrashic project. Simpler derashot that do not appear on their surface as concerned with superfluousness and never pose the question of "why" may also in fact be justificatory. When the Midrash asks, regularly enough, "Do you say X or is it instead Y?" and ends with "It therefore teaches . . .," we might be looking at covert justification.

This basic function of Midrash can illuminate a recurring, curious gloss found in the Midrashim of Rabbi Akiva's school, the *Sifra* and *Sifrei Deuteronomy*: "to relate what caused it." Leviticus 17, for example, establishes the prohibition against consuming blood and then gives the reason, namely, that the life-force (or soul according to the Sages) of the living creature is in the blood (Lev. 17:11). The Midrash comments briefly: "to relate what caused it."[14] Anyone who can read biblical Hebrew knows that this verse provides the reason for the prohibition. What is the Midrash's point? It conveys that the verse may not introduce new legal information, but its explication of the mitzvah's rationale is necessary. In short, its existence is justified.

Why does the Midrash consider justification of the Torah so important? Any text that does not adopt the rigors of formal logic contains repetition and verbosity, and the Torah is certainly no exception. This is clear in its narrative, like when the story of Abraham's servant meeting Rebecca and her family is repeated three times in the very long chapter of Genesis 24. But it is also true of Torah law, which is rendered in high definition, especially in its casuistic presentation. The Torah is a work of foundational stories and laws intended to teach and edify its readers, and it relies on various rhetorical devices to drive home this instruction. We find nothing amiss in the verse discussed above, "My wrath shall flare up and I will kill you by the sword, and your wives shall become widows and your children orphans" (Ex. 22:23). The same holds for almost every verse in the Torah, which is addressed to human beings in their own messy language. Yet to the Midrash, God's locution is exact; He does not cover the same ground without cause. This is why the question of why—and not what—is the most basic one, the first one asked before anything else. It also explains why there is Midrash on virtually every phrase. This focus on the minutest of textual details will be detailed in the next chapter, as part of the Sages' exhaustive search for meaning—an endless endeavor—in the divine text. In a sense, then, the Midrash cuts out its own work for itself.

In this theological and exegetical mission to account for every single word in the Torah, the Midrash has the entire Torah unrolled before it. In the first derashah of the chapter, the Midrash questions the need for the prohibition against *kil'ayim* in Deuteronomy, given that it is already stated in Leviticus. This setting of similar verses side by side is relatively insubstantial; in other derashot the comparisons between parallel passages are much meatier. The drive to justify the biblical text therefore opens the door to serious comparative legal analysis.

The Motivations of Midrash   245

Let us consider the laws governing the Israelite slave, which appear in three places in the Torah. Both *Mekhiltot* on Exodus begin their treatment as follows:

"When you acquire a Hebrew slave" (Ex. 21:2)—this is someone who sells himself.[a] And there it says, "When your Hebrew brother or sister is sold to you" (Deut. 15:12)—this is someone whom the court sells[b] to you. (*Mekhilta de-Rashbi*, 21:2, p. 159)

"כִּי תִקְנֶה עֶבֶד עִבְרִי" (שמות כא, ב)—זה שהוא מוכר את עצמו. ולהלן הוא אומר "כִּי יִמָּכֵר לְךָ אָחִיךָ הָעִבְרִי אוֹ הָעִבְרִיָּה" (דברים טו, יב)—זה שבית דין מוכרים אותו לך.

"When you acquire a Hebrew slave" (Ex. 21:2)—the verse is speaking about someone sold by the court for his theft, so that he shall serve him and serve the son. Do you say the verse is speaking about someone sold by the court for his theft, so that he shall serve him and serve the son, or is it instead about someone who sells himself? When it says, "And should your brother become impoverished under you and be sold to you" (Lev. 25:39), someone who sells himself is mentioned. What, then, does "when you acquire a Hebrew slave" teach? The verse is speaking about someone sold by the court for his theft, so that he shall serve him and serve the son. (*Mekhilta de-Rabbi Yishmael*, Nezikin, §1, p. 247)

"כִּי תִקְנֶה עֶבֶד עִבְרִי" (שמות כא, ב)—בנימכר בבית דין על גניבתו הכתוב מדבר, שיהיה עובדו ועובד את הבן. אתה אומר בנימכר בבית דין על גניבתו הכתוב מדבר, שיהיה עובדו ועובד את הבן, או אינו מדבר אלא במוכר עצמו? כשהוא אומר "וְכִי יָמוּךְ אָחִיךָ עִמָּךְ וְנִמְכַּר לָךְ" (ויקרא כה, יט)—הרי מוכר עצמו אמור. ומה תלמוד לומר "כִּי תִקְנֶה עֶבֶד עִבְרִי"? בנימכר בבית דין על גניבתו הכתוב מדבר, שיהיה עובדו ועובד את הבן.

The two *Mekhiltot* agree that the Israelite has been enslaved as a result of poverty. What they dispute is the proximate cause: Did he sell himself because he had no money to live, or was he sold by the court because he had no money to repay a theft? *Mekhilta de-Rashbi* argues that the case in Exodus is self-sale and the one in Deuteronomy is court-ordered, since the latter uses a passive construction, "is sold to you." *Mekhilta de-Rabbi Yishmael* compares it instead to a case in Leviticus, and asserts that Exodus is the court sale and Leviticus the self-sale. Both Midrashim assume two circumstances of sale, and by comparing the relevant texts elsewhere they arrive at opposite conclusions. But both justify the relevant biblical passages while also engaging in comparative analysis.

In the Midrashim of Rabbi Yishmael's school, this comparative-justificatory derashah often has a fixed format: "Why is it said? Because it says [elsewhere]." The darshan has the entire Torah in mind, so if in one place the Torah's phraseology is lacking or liable to create

---

a To make a living.
b Because he stole and cannot repay it; cf. Exodus 22:2.

a potential misunderstanding, the Torah must rectify this elsewhere. Slave law furnishes another fine illustration:

> "He shall go free" (Ex. 21:2). Why is it said? Because it says, "And when you set him free etc." (Deut. 15:13). Do I hear that he should write him[a] a writ of emancipation?[b] It therefore teaches, "[he shall go] free"[c] (Ex. 21:2).
>
> Or perhaps he must give him money[d] in order to go? It therefore teaches, "He shall go free, for nothing" (Ex. 21:2) (*Mekhilta de-Rabbi Yishmael, Nezikin*, §1, p. 249)

> "יֵצֵא לַחָפְשִׁי" (שמות כא, ב)—למה נאמר? לפי שהוא אומר "וְכִי תְשַׁלְּחֶנּוּ חָפְשִׁי" וג' (דברים טו, יג). שומע אני יכתוב לו גט שחרור? תלמוד לומר "[יֵצֵא] לַחָפְשִׁי". או יתן לו מעות ויצא? תלמוד לומר "יֵצֵא לַחָפְשִׁי חִנָּם."

Deuteronomy makes it sound as if the master must actively send out the slave, which could be construed as a requirement for a formal written document. The verse in Exodus excludes this possibility by stating that the slave leaves, implying that he does so of his own accord. Perhaps, then, it is the slave who dictates the terms of his release, and he can buy his early freedom? The verse in Exodus adds a qualification that does not appear in Deuteronomy—"for nothing." By illumining the discrepancies between the passages, the derashah justifies the necessity of both verses. They complement each other in legal content.

Here is a similarly structured midrash from the academy of Rabbi Akiva on the very same verse:

> "When you acquire a Hebrew slave" (Ex. 21:2). Whence that when you acquire, you should only acquire a Hebrew slave?[e] It therefore teaches, "When you acquire a Hebrew slave." And whence that when he is sold,[f] he should be sold only to you?[g] It therefore teaches, "And should your brother become impoverished under you and be sold to you" (Lev. 25:39). And whence that when the court sells him, they should sell him only to you? It therefore teaches, "When your Hebrew brother . . . is sold to you" (Deut. 15:12). (*Mekhilta de-Rashbi*, 21:2, p. 159)

---

    a The master for the slave, since the active party in the verse in Deuteronomy seems to be the master.
    b A document releasing him from his service.
    c He leaves of his own accord and does not need anything from the master to formalize his emancipation.
    d The slave must indemnify the master.
    e And not a Canaanite slave.
    f When he sells himself due to his impoverishment, as the prooftext from Leviticus indicates.
    g And not to a Gentile.

"כִּי תִקְנֶה עֶבֶד עִבְרִי" (שמות כא, ב). מניין כשתהא קונה לא תהא קונה אלא עבד עברי? תלמוד לומר "כִּי תִקְנֶה עֶבֶד עִבְרִי" (שמות כא, ב). ומניין כשיהא נימכר לא יהא נמכר אלא לך? תלמוד לומר "וְנִמְכַּר לָךְ" (ויקרא כה, יט). ומניין שיהוא בית דין מוכרים אותו לא יהא מוכרין אותו אלא לך? תלמוד לומר "כִּי יִמָּכֵר לְךָ אָחִיךָ הָעִבְרִי" (דברים טו, יב).

This midrash creates a composite set of laws by analyzing the three passages side by side, thereby also justifying the necessity of all of them.

At one and the same time, the Midrash explicates the reason for all the verses and derives halakhic data from them. Does the Midrash primarily seek textual justification or legal derivation? Most of the time, one cannot tell. A data set that allows us to probe the range of possibilities comprises those derashot of Rabbi Yishmael's school that begin with the phrase "[Do] I hear . . . ?" *(shomea' ani)*, by which a legal possibility is raised and then rejected.[15] When it reflects a real halakhic doubt, the Midrash's eye seems to be on Halakhah; when it does not, the possible redundancy of the text is the primary concern.

The Torah begins its first real legal passage by declaring the month in which Pesach (Passover) falls, called Nisan in the rabbinic calendar, as the first month of the year. The *Mekhilta* expounds:

> "[This month shall be for you] the beginning of months" (Ex. 12:2). I hear *(shomea' ani)* a minimum of "months"[a] is two, whence the other months? It therefore teaches, "of the months of the year" (Ex. 12:2). (*Mekhilta de-Rabbi Yishmael, Pasḥa*, §2, p. 8)

"רֹאשׁ חֳדָשִׁים" (שמות יב,ב)—שומע אני מיעוט "חדשים"—שנים. מנין לשאר חדשים? תלמוד לומר "לְחָדְשֵׁי הַשָּׁנָה".

Is the Midrash seriously entertaining the possibility that the Torah means to say that Nisan is the "beginning" of only two months, that it is only referring to a slice of the year? Such a proposition sounds nonsensical.[16] It seems as but an artificial construct to justify the ostensible repetitiveness of the verse: "This month shall be for you the beginning of months; it shall be the first of the months of the year for you" (Ex. 12:2). Halakhic inquiry in the service of textual justification.

At the other extreme is the derashah that sounds genuinely uncertain about the law, like this one about someone who rents an item that something unfortunate happens to while in his possession:

---

[a] Since "months" is plural, it has to be more than one but not necessarily more than two.

"If he is hired, he gets his wages" (Ex. 22:14). Do I hear (*shomea' ani*) that one can swear and be exempt?[a] You can reason:[b] The wage earner[c] benefits [the owner][d] and the renter benefits [the owner].[e] Since you have learned that the wage earner swears about force majeure[f] and pays for theft or loss, so the renter pays for theft or loss. (*Mekhilta de-Rabbi Yishmael, Nezikin*, §16, p. 307)

"אִם שָׂכִיר הוּא בָּא בִּשְׂכָרוֹ" (שמות כב, יד)—שומע אני ישבע ויהיה פטור? הרי את דן: הואיל ונושא שכר מהנה ושכיר מהנה, אם למדתה על נושא שכר שהוא נשבע על האונסין ומשלם את הגניבה ואת האבידה, אף שוכר ישלם הגנבה והאבדה.

The Torah never states the law regarding someone who rents an object or animal. The Sages therefore have to analogize from cases it does discuss: those of the unpaid watchman, the paid watchman, and the borrower.[17] The midrash begins by supposing that the renter would not have to pay so long as he takes an oath, but then rejects this by logical argument: the renter is more analogous to the paid watchman, who is obviously on the hook for theft or loss, than to the unpaid watchman, who is doing his friend a favor. The midrash is not interested in textual justification here, as there isn't any textual problem. The rejection comes not from Scripture but from logic. The content, rather than the form, is the concern here.

Most derashot lie somewhere between the two extremes, where textual justification and legal derivation may both be motivating factors:

"Seven days shall you eat unleavened bread" (Ex. 12:15). I hear all unleavened bread[g] implied; it therefore teaches, "You shall not eat leavened bread with it" (Deut. 16:3). I only said it about something that can be unleavened or leavened.[h] (*Mekhilta de-Rabbi Yishmael, Pasḥa*, §8, p. 26)

"שִׁבְעַת יָמִים מַצּוֹת תֹּאכֵלוּ" (שמות יב, טו)—שומע אני כל מצה במשמע, תלמוד לומר "לֹא תֹאכַל עָלָיו חָמֵץ" (דברים טז, ג). לא אמרתי אלא דבר שהוא בא לידי מצה וחמץ.

There is an element of justification here, as the unquoted continuation of the verse in Deuteronomy has a clause nearly identical to that of Exodus: "seven days shall you eat unleavened bread with it." Deuteronomy's inclusion of the prohibition against eating hametz is

  a From restitution for the stolen or lost item.
  b From the explicit Torah law regarding the paid watchman; see Exodus 22:9–11.
  c The paid watchman.
  d By being a watchman.
  e By paying for his rent. Later the midrash adds that these two types of bailees also profit (*nehene*) from the object they keep.
  f Accidents that cannot be foreseen and for which one cannot be considered negligent.
  g Matza made from any kind of flour, even one that doesn't have potential to rise and become hametz.
  h That the dough will inevitably rise given enough time.

what distinguishes the two verses from each other. The halakhic problem, though, is also not contrived. The original deduction is totally reasonable, because nothing in Exodus indicates that only some grains can produce valid matza. To reject this possible understanding, the Midrash looks to Deuteronomy, which links the leavened and unleaved breads, hametz and matza. The Midrash does both simultaneously.

The strong rabbinic desire to explain the existence of every word in the Torah exists with regard to other corpora too. The canonical text of the Oral Torah, the Mishnah, is subjected to a similarly searching exegesis in the two Talmuds. To rescue the Mishnah from repugnant repetitions and trivialities, the talmudic Sages force interpretations on it that, like the Midrash's, cannot be the simple meaning of the text. This interpretive trend peaks in the later strata of the Babylonian Talmud, which assume that every word of the Mishnah has been deliberately placed.[18] In one midrash examined above, biblical "widows" and "orphans" are reinterpreted as quasi-widows and quasi-orphans. Witness the exact same phenomenon in an interpretation of a mishnah. It states that an object found by a wife belongs to her husband, whereas one found by a divorcee belongs to her alone.[19] The Talmud is bewildered: "A divorcee? That's obvious!" If they're no longer married, why would something she finds belong to her ex-husband? It answers: "With what are we dealing with here? A quasi-divorcee."[20] The Mishnah is dealing with a case where there is doubt about the validity of the divorce. The woman is in limbo, so the Mishnah has to spell out the law.[21] Structurally, the Talmud's quasi-divorcee is exactly like the Midrash's quasi-widow and quasi-orphan, and they are brought into existence solely so that the canonical text can dodge the charge of triviality. In rabbinic eyes, a text cannot be venerated as canonical if it states the obvious.

B. HARMONIZING SCRIPTURE

In its pursuit to reveal the necessity of the Torah's every utterance, the Midrash addresses the Torah as a totality, comparing and contrasting parallel passages from its constituent books. This comparative analysis is also integral to a second fundamental goal of the Midrash: harmonization.

The Torah is rife with contradictions. Scholars today assume that these arose from its inclusion of disparate legal collections: the laws of Leviticus are attributed to a "Priestly" source, those of Deuteronomy to a second source, and those in Exodus 21–23 to yet a third source that might have preceded the other two.[22] For readers in antiquity, however, such a position was untenable. It was all one, the word of the living God.[23]

The tendency to harmonize the Torah, which would fully flower in the rabbinic period, may have roots in the Bible itself. For instance, the original laws dictating the preparation and consumption of the paschal lamb require it to be roasted rather than boiled or otherwise cooked in liquid: "Do not eat from it raw, nor in any way cooked *(u-vashel mevushal)* in water, but fire-roasted" (Ex. 12:9). Three books later, though, the Torah uses a verb generally reserved for cooking in a liquid medium: "you shall cook *(u-vishalta)* and eat it" (Deut. 16:7). Take note that Exodus employs the very same verbal root *(b-sh-l)* for the *prohibited* type of cooking. Much later, the second book of Chronicles states: "They cooked *(vayvashelu)* the paschal sacrifice in the fire, according to its law" (2 Chr. 35:13). Again the verb reserved for cooking with liquid is used, yet the sacrifice is also somehow being roasted in a fire. This linguistic oddity was probably created to harmonize the two conflicting biblical accounts.[24]

Second Temple literature, including the book of Jubilees, the Temple Scroll, and the works of Philo and Josephus, deals with many such contradictions.[25] Like Chronicles, though, its peacemaking efforts generally take place behind the scenes. If rewriting Scripture is an option, the reader doesn't even need to be informed of the problem.[26]

The Midrash is heir to this interpretive endeavor of eliminating contradictions. Where it breaks new ground is in its willingness to explicitly state the contradiction, offer a solution, and show how to get from point A to point B. In other words, the Midrash walks the student through its hermeneutical method. Contrast this with Qumranic literature, where the answer is communicated from heaven to the authorized exegete in a kind of revelation.[27] Rather than keep the keys of interpretation out of the hands of others, the Midrash allows learners to make copies of the master key. Midrashic exegesis also differs from its forerunners in that its conflict resolution is systematic and well developed. The Midrash has forged a complete set of tools and coined a terminology to solve this precise problem.[28]

The severity of the disharmony dictates how much work the Midrash must do. In some cases, the biblical passages are utterly divergent but not necessarily contradictory. Regarding the sabbatical year, Leviticus 25 details laws against working the land, while Deuteronomy 15 talks about loan forgiveness. What is the relationship between these two and the seventh year? This is a soft, indirect contradiction, which the Midrash can easily solve by combining the two instructions.[29] Direct contradictions require no mental processing to see: Does the Hebrew slave work for six years (Ex. 21:2, Deut. 15:17) or until the Jubilee year (Lev. 25:40)? These require more creativity to solve.

The derashah below explicitly addresses a contradiction about the number of sacrifices offered on the festivals:

> "You shall bring a fire offering, a pleasing aroma for the Lord" (Num. 28:27)—these you are to bring, beyond what is stated in *Torat Kohanim*.[a] Or are these the same ones stated in *Torat Kohanim*? But are they equivalent?! Then you should not say the second option but the first one: these you are to bring, beyond what is stated in *Torat Kohanim*. (*Sifrei Numbers*, §149, p. 195)

> "וְהִקְרַבְתֶּם עוֹלָה לְרֵיחַ נִיחֹחַ לַה'" (במדבר כח, כז)—אלו אתה מקריב, חוץ מן האמור בתורת כהנים. או הן הן האמורים בתורת כהנים? וכי שוין הן?! הא אין עליך לומר כלשון אחרון אלא כלשון ראשון: אלו אתה מקריב, חוץ מן האמור בתורת כהנים.

---

a The rabbinic name for the book of Leviticus, since it primarily consists of ritual laws concerning the Kohanim (priests).

The numbers and types of sacrifices in the two accounts offer no leeway for reinterpretation. Neither Leviticus 23 nor Numbers 28 can be established as the rule and the other coerced through exegesis to match it. Since both passages must remain in force, the Midrash has no choice but to add up the number of sacrifices in both texts.[30] In this case, the Midrash was preceded by Josephus, who also joined the two passages, albeit without formulating the problem explicitly.[31]

The Midrashim of Rabbi Yishmael's school sometimes set up the conundrum in plain, consistent terms: "One verse says X, and another verse says Y. How can the two verses be maintained?" Regarding contradictory verses about the sabbatical year, the *Mekhilta* says:

> One verse says, "so that the poor of your people may eat" (Ex. 23:11), but another verse says, "for you, and for your male and female slaves" (Lev. 25:6). *How can both be maintained?* When the fruit is plenty, everyone eats; when the fruit is poor, it is "for you, and for your male and female slaves." (*Mekhilta de-Rabbi Yishmael, Pasḥa*, §3, p. 330)

> כתוב אחד אומר "וְאָכְלוּ אֶבְיֹנֵי עַמֶּךָ" (שמות כג, יא), וכתוב אחר אומר "לְךָ וּלְעַבְדְּךָ וְלַאֲמָתֶךָ" (ויקרא כה, ו).
> כיצד יתקיימו שני כתובין? כשהספירות מרובין—הכל אוכלין, וכשהספירות מעוטין—"לְךָ וּלְעַבְדְּךָ וְלַאֲמָתֶךָ".

Who eats the fruit, the Midrash explains, depends on whether the harvest yields a cornucopia or barely enough for subsistence. This presentation of two conflicting verses followed by the question of their coexistence appears no fewer than thirty times in Midrashim of Rabbi Yishmael's academy. Similar homilies appear in Rabbi Akiva's school, which first present the contradiction and then the compromise:

> "And on the seventh day[a] shall be a convocation (*'atzeret*) for the Lord your God"[b] (Deut. 16:8).

> Rabbi says, Could it be that a person is confined (*'atzur*) in the bet midrash[c] all day long? It therefore teaches, "[a convocation] for you"[d] (Num. 29:35). Could it be that a person should eat and drink all day long? It therefore teaches, "for the Lord your God" (Deut. 16:8). *How so?*[e] Devote a portion to the bet midrash and a portion to eating and drinking. (*Sifrei Deuteornomy*, §135, p. 191)

---

  a Of Pesach.
  b Presumably meaning it should be spent at the Temple.
  c According to the rabbinic ethos the study hall is where God is served after the destruction of the Temple, through Torah study.
  d For your pleasure, such as feasting.
  e How can the two be maintained simultaneously.

"וּבַיּוֹם הַשְּׁבִיעִי עֲצֶרֶת לַה' אֱלֹהֶיךָ" (דברים טז, ח). רבי אומר: יכול יהא אדם עצור בבית המדרש כל היום כולו? תלמוד לומר "לָכֶם" (במדבר כט, לה). יכול יהא אדם אוכל ושותה כל היום כולו? תלמוד לומר "לַה' אֱלֹהֶיךָ". הא כיצד? תן חלק לבית המדרש ותן חלק לאכילה ושתיה.

The ostensible contradiction does not jump out at the reader of the Torah. The verse in Deuteronomy is speaking of the seventh day of Pesach, whereas the verse in Numbers is describing the eighth day of Sukkot. The only connection between them is that the Torah refers to them both with the word "convocation" (*'atzeret*). It is the Midrash, then, that sharpens the dialectic for its ultimate synthesis. It is appropriate that this is the product of Rabbi Akiva's school, which makes mountains out of textual molehills.

Most legal contradictions, however, are solved without explicit notification, through a dialectical move in which one verse "corrects" what can be learned from the other.[32] Here is an example:

> "And he shall serve him forever" (Ex. 21:6)—until the Jubilee. [. . .] Or is "and he shall serve him forever" as it sounds? It therefore teaches, "[It shall be a Jubilee for you,] and each man shall go back to his ancestral holding" (Lev. 25:10). (*Mekhilta de-Rabbi Yishmael, Nezikin*, §2, p. 254)

"וַעֲבָדוֹ לְעֹלָם" (שמות כא, ו): [. .] —עד היובל. [. .] או "וַעֲבָדוֹ לְעֹלָם" כשמועו? תלמוד לומר "[יוֹבֵל הִוא תִּהְיֶה לָכֶם] וְשַׁבְתֶּם אִישׁ אֶל אֲחֻזָּתוֹ" (ויקרא כה, י).

The Midrash does not pose the problem of contradiction outright, but it also does not conceal that it refuses to read one of the verses "as it sounds" in order to bring the two into alignment.

In the above derashot, the meaning of each contradictory verse was maintained somehow and interpreted as components of a larger system (sacrifices), thematic aspects of a single entity (the holiday), or changing conditions of an event (the sabbatical year). In this instance, there is no compromise. Instead, the verse in Leviticus "wins" and the verse in Exodus is reinterpreted in its light (probably because "forever" is easier to reinterpret figuratively than the explicit reference to the "Jubilee year").

The harmonizing derashah can generate law, or, in the other direction, preexisting law can be used to make peace between verses. Below, the Midrash compares the stonings of the man who gathered wood on Shabbat and the man who cursed God:

> "And they pelted him with stones (*ba-avanim*)" (Num. 15:36). Here you say, "and they pelted him with stones," and here you say,[a] "and they pelted him with a stone (*aven*)" (Lev. 24:23). *How can both be maintained?* The stoning site was two floors

---

a A variation of "One verse says X and another verse says Y."

The Motivations of Midrash   253

high. . . .[a] He would take the stone and place it on his chest. If he died from it, he fulfilled his obligation, and if not, all Israel would participate in his stoning. (*Sifrei Numbers*, §114, p. 123)

"וַיִּרְגְּמוּ אֹתוֹ בָּאֲבָנִים" (במדבר טו, לו). כן (= כאן) אתה אומר "וַיִּרְגְּמוּ אֹתוֹ בָּאֲבָנִים" וכן אתה אומר "וַיִּרְגְּמוּ אֹתוֹ אָבֶן" (ויקרא כד, כג). כיצד יתקיימו שני כתובין? בית הסקילה היה גבוה שתי קומות . . . נוטל את האבן ונותנה על לבו. אם מת בה—יצא; ואם לאו—רגימתו בכל ישראל.

The Midrash resolves the contradiction with an exact quote of mishnaic law. The singular stone of Leviticus is the initial large stone, heaved by one of the witnesses to crush the offender, while the multiple stones of Numbers are cast by the people if the first one does not do the job.

A parallel midrash from Rabbi Akiva's school reads:

"And you shall pelt them with stones" (Deut. 17:5). Could it be with many stones? It therefore teaches, "with a stone" (Lev. 20:2). Or could it be that "with a stone" is even one stone? It therefore teaches, "with stones." Say, therefore: One who is not dead from the first one will die from the second. (*Sifrei Deuteronomy*, §149, p. 204, with many parallels)

"וּסְקַלְתָּם בָּאֲבָנִים" (דברים יז, ה). יכול באבנים מרובות? תלמוד לומר "בָּאֶבֶן" (ויקרא כ, ב). או "בָּאֶבֶן" יכול אפילו באבן אחת? תלמוד לומר "בָּאֲבָנִים". אמור מעתה: לא מת בראשונה ימות בשנייה.

In comparison to the Midrash of Rabbi Yishmael's school, this one has less sophisticated language and uses different verses. Nevertheless, the problem and solution are fundamentally identical, as both draw on the mishnaic ritual.[33] The different midrashim are not clones, but they are certainly kin.

As is the case with repetitions—apparent or real—so with contradictions. Even when a conflict between verses has no halakhic ramification, it remains an irritant in the Midrash's eye that cannot be ignored and must be removed.

"Yet, there will be no pauper among you" (Deut. 15:4). But there it says, "For the pauper will not cease from the midst of the land" (Deut. 15:11). When you do the will of the Omnipresent, the paupers are among others, but when you do not do the will of the Omnipresent, the paupers are among you. (*Sifrei Deuteronomy*, §114, p. 174)

"אֶפֶס כִּי לֹא יִהְיֶה בְּךָ אֶבְיוֹן" (דברים טו, ד). ולהלן הוא אומר "כִּי לֹא יֶחְדַּל אֶבְיוֹן מִקֶּרֶב הָאָרֶץ" (דברים טו, יא). בזמן שאתם עושים רצונו של מקום, אביונים באחרים; וכשאין אתם עושים רצונו של מקום, אביונים בכם.

---

a   A quotation from Mishnah, *Sanhedrin*, 6:4.

This circumstantial solution resembles the one proposed by the Midrash for those who should eat the produce during the sabbatical year. Halakha and Aggada receive similar exegetical treatment.

This derashah concerns non-halakhic elements within a legal passage, but other aggadic derashot are more properly situated in the narrative portion of the Torah. In Numbers 12, Aaron and Miriam slander their brother Moses regarding his marriage to a Cushite woman. As a result, God rebukes them and also physically afflicts Miriam. Who is this Cushite woman? The Midrash identifies her as Zipporah, the only named wife of Moses.[34] The trouble is that she hailed from Midian rather than Cush, which is identified by the rabbis with the area of modern-day Ethiopia. How does the Midrash resolve this?

> "A Cushite woman" (Num. 12:1). But was she a Cushite? Was she not a Midianite, as it says, "and the priest of Midian [had seven daughters]" (Ex. 2:16)? What, then, does "Cushite" teach? Rather, just as a Cushite has striking skin, so Zipporah was strikingly more beautiful than all other women. (*Sifrei Numbers*, §99, p. 98)

> "אִשָּׁה כֻשִׁית" (במדבר יב, א)—וכי כושית היתה? והלא מדיינית היתה, שנאמר "וּלְכֹהֵן מִדְיָן [שֶׁבַע בָּנוֹת]" (שמות ב, טז). מה תלמוד לומר "כֻשִׁית"? אלא מה כושי זה משונה בעורו, כך ציפורה היתה משונה בנוייה יותר מכל הנשים.

"Cushite" cannot be a demonym, denoting Zipporah's birthplace, because she is not from Cush. Instead, Zipporah must resemble a Cushite in some respect. The Midrash decides that in the same way very dark skin stands out, so she was a standout beauty.[35]

Other aggadic contradictions regarding Moses touch on graver matters of theology. In one place, Moses is described as speaking to God face to face and beholding an image of the Lord. How can Moses see God when God Himself attests that no living human can see Him?

> "A vision" (Num. 12:8)—this is a vision of speech. Do you say this is a vision of speech, or is it instead a vision of the countenance?[a] It therefore teaches, "You will not be able to see My countenance, for no man can see Me and live" (Ex. 33:20). (*Sifrei Numbers*, §103, p. 101)[36]

> "בְּמַרְאֶה" (במדבר יב, ח)—זה מראה דיבור. אתה אומר זה מראה דיבור או אינו אלא מראה פנים? תלמוד לומר "לֹא תוּכַל לִרְאֹת אֶת פָּנָי כִּי לֹא יִרְאַנִי הָאָדָם וָחָי" (שמות לג, כ).

What is a "vision of speech"? Does it mean visually beholding the words? Perhaps it is a super-sensory experience that is solely auditory or synaesthetic? Since this term appears

---

a Since Moses is described as speaking to God "mouth to mouth," one would think he was gazing upon God's face.

only here and seems like an ad hoc solution, preserving the word "vision" while uprooting its normal meaning, there is no simple way to know what the darshan intended.

The numerous biblical contradictions sampled here, whether imagined or real, do not alone contain sufficient growth hormone to sustain the fecundity of the Midrash's solutions. It is the rabbinic commitment to harmonize the entire Torah—both Written and Oral—that further nourishes and drives this interpretive growth.

C. ANCHORING TRADITION

Textual anomalies attract a darshan like an oil seep beckons to a prospector, in the knowledge that there is something of great value to be extracted. But sometimes the impetus to expound the Torah comes not from within but from without.[37] Some of the well-developed halakhic traditions possessed by the Tannaim were the product of scriptural exegesis,[38] but the rest were developed independently of the Bible in antiquity.[39] Since the Tannaim considered both the Torah and tradition as authoritative bodies of law, they needed to unify them as much as they could. An interpretation that fastens an extra-biblical tradition to the text of the Torah is called an *asmakhta*, a scriptural "support," in the two Talmuds.[40] Many scholars in fact consider the primary legal function of Midrash to be the fusion of extra-biblical halakhic traditions with the Torah rather than the generation of new laws.[41]

Midrash as *asmakhta* is associated in the tannaitic sources first and foremost with Rabbi Akiva, the darshan par excellence. According to the Mishnah, Rabban Yohanan ben Zakkai worriedly predicted that an ancient law declaring something ritually impure would become defunct, since it lacked support from Scripture. When his disciple Rabbi Akiva discovered a textual basis for it—however tenuous—Rabbi Yehoshua was so ecstatic that he lamented that their mentor and teacher Rabban Yohanan was no longer alive to witness it: "If only you could see this!"[42] Backed by Scripture, the law could no longer be discarded or ignored.

Along similar lines, two midrashim have Rabbi Tarfon praising Rabbi Akiva for restoring lost Temple traditions: "Tarfon observed and forgot; Akiva has expounded it of his own accord and agrees with the tradition"; "I myself heard it but couldn't explain it; you have expounded it and agree with the tradition."[43] Although the specifics must be left for another discussion, the general point is that Rabbi Akiva's exegetical genius found a way for the biblical text to embrace rabbinic tradition. Finding supports that could hold up the weight of tradition was surely no easy feat, but Rabbi Akiva was considered equal to the task and was celebrated for his achievement.[44]

Rabbi Akiva's extraordinary knack for gluing any tradition to the Torah, though, is in fact a virtuosic expression of a regular, widespread trend common to both midrashic schools. A derashah about tefillin (phylacteries) that appears in collections from each school demonstrates this:

"And it shall be a sign for you on your hand" (Ex. 13:9). This is a single scroll of four passages. And logic dictates: Since the Torah says, Place tefillin on your arm and place tefillin on your head, just as the head has four *totafot*,ᵃ shouldn't the arm have four *totafot*? It therefore teaches, "and it shall be a sign *(le-ot)* for you on your hand"—a single scrollᵇ of four passages.

Could it be that just as the arm has a single scroll, so the head has a single scroll? And logic dictates: Since the Torah says, Place tefillin on your arm and place tefillin on your head, just as the arm has a single scroll, shouldn't the head have a single scroll? It therefore teaches, *"le-totaf{o}t"* (Ex. 13:16), *"le-totaf{o}t"* (Deut. 6:8), *"le-totafot"* (Deut. 11:18)—four *totafot*ᶜ are mentioned.

Or should one make them four receptacles of four passages? It therefore teaches, "and as a reminder *(u-le-zikkaron)* between your eyes" (Ex. 13:9)—one receptacleᵈ of four passages.ᵉ (*Mekhilta de-Rabbi Yishmael, Pasḥa*, §17, p. 66; *Sifrei Deuteronomy*, §35, p. 63)

"וְהָיָה לְךָ לְאוֹת עַל יָדְךָ" (שמות יג, ט)—זה כרך אחד של ארבע פרשיות. והדין נותן: הואיל ואמרה תורה, תן תפילין ביד תן תפילין בראש, מה בראש ארבע טוטפות אף ביד ארבע טוטפות? תלמוד לומר "וְהָיָה לְךָ לְאוֹת עַל יָדְךָ"—כרך אחד של ארבע פרשות. יכול כשם שביד כרך אחד, כך בראש כרך אחד? והדין נותן: הואיל ואמרה תורה תן תפילין ביד תן תפילין בראש מה ביד כרך אחד אף בראש כרך אחד? תלמוד לומר "לטטפת", "לטטפת", "לטוטפות"—הרי ארבע טוטפות אמורות. או יעשם ארבע כיסין של ארבע פרשות? תלמוד לומר "וּלְזִכָּרוֹן בֵּין עֵינֶיךָ" (שמות יג, ט)—כיס אחד של ארבע פרשות.

One could reasonably assume that the tefillin wrapped on the arm and the tefillin donned on the head should be identical, but the Torah describes them slightly differently. The former is to be a singular "sign," and the latter involves plural *totafot*. From this the darshan derives that the arm tefillin should be on one slip of parchment and the head tefillin on four separate ones within a single compartment.

On closer examination, a problem emerges from this derashah. How exactly does the darshan derive from the words "a sign . . . on your hand" so that it refers to scrolls and compartments? Nothing in the verse indicates this. It must be that the tefillin exist outside the biblical text, and the Midrash does the work of binding them to the Torah. The multiple

---

a A biblical word (see ll. 9–10) referring to frontlets, but reread by ancient interpreters to refer to tefillin.

b Since the word for "sign," ot, is in the singular, it indicates that all of the passages must be written on a single writing support.

c In the first two instances, the word *totafot* is written defectively, meaning that it is a plural without a typical component of the feminine plural marker, a *vav* (represented by the vowel "o" here). The Midrash counts each of these as singular for exegetical purposes. The third instance has the plural marker, and the Midrash considers any plural to be a minimum of two.

d Since the word for "reminder," zikkaron, is in the singular, it indicates that all of the passages must be contained within a single receptacle.

e One plus one plus two is four. The four passages of the head tefillin must therefore be written on four separate parchments.

appearances of *totafot* are not the true source for the requirement to have four compartments in the head tefillin either. Indeed, the form of the tefillin is no innovation of the Midrash, or even of the Tannaim. Archeological finds from Qumran show such ritual objects in use there already in the time of the Second Temple.[45] What we have here is an *asmakhta*, tying an extra-biblical tradition to the text of the Torah.

An *asmakhta* from a completely different area of Halakhah reflects how complicated midrashic anchorage can be:

> "He may give him forty lashes" (Deut. 25:3). Could it be forty full lashes? It therefore teaches, "forty in number"[a] (Deut. 25:2–3)—a count that is almost forty.[b] (*Sifrei Deuteronomy*, §286, p. 303)

"אַרְבָּעִים יַכֶּנּוּ" (דברים כה, ג). יכול ארבעים שלימות? תלמוד לומר "ארבעים במספר"—מניין שסמוך לארבעים.

This derashah looks like it is generating law, but a source from the end of the Second Temple era already attests that thirty-nine was the upper limit in practice.[46] The complication is that the driving force behind that older tradition is undoubtedly our verse, which continues with a prohibition against administering more than forty lashes: "he shall not give more; lest he go on to give him many more, and your brother be degraded in your eyes" (Deut. 25:3). In order to prevent the transgression of this explicit scriptural prohibition, the old halakhists subtracted one lash from the forty. In this reconstruction, this derashah is an *asmakhta* rooting an extra-biblical practice to the very spot in the Torah from which it was earlier derived. Back and forth![47]

This fact, that the Midrash often paints the bullseye around the arrow, can explain the near arbitrariness of some midrashic interpretations. In expounding the same word, the Midrash can choose to take notice of context or ignore it, to be inclusive or exclusive, yielding contrary interpretations. The word *ezraḥ*, meaning "native" or "citizen," in Leviticus is a case in point: the *Sifra* uses it both to exempt women from certain mitzvot and to obligate them in others. The end determines the means.[48]

The goal of anchoring tradition to Scripture can dovetail with the search for justification detailed above in section A. By weaving every last detail of a tradition through the Torah's threads, the interstices of the Torah are completely filled. The *Mekhilta* on the obligation to make a pilgrimage to the Temple for the festivals is a perfect example of this. The verse states, "Three times a year all your males shall be seen in the presence of the Master, the Lord" (Ex. 23:17). The Midrash atomizes the verse:

a The Midrash reads our verse in conjunction with the final word *be-mispar*, "in number," of the previous verse. This term is understood to convey that it is not actually forty but a proximate number.

b i.e., thirty-nine.

"Three times (pe'amim)"[a] (Ex. 23:17)—those who walk on their own feet;

"shall be seen"—to exclude the blind;

"your males"—to exclude women;

"all your males"[b]—to exclude the lame, the *tumtum*,[c] and the androgynous.[d]

"You shall read this Torah"[e] (Deut. 31:11)—to exclude the convert[f] and the slave;

"within their earshot"—to exclude the deaf-mute.

"You shall rejoice"[g] (Deut. 16:11)—to exclude the sick and the minor.[h]

"before the Lord your God"—to exclude the ritually impure.

Hence they said: All are obligated in appearing, except for the deaf-mute, the mentally incompetent, and the minor; the *tumtum* and the androgynous; the lame and the blind; the ill and the elderly.[i] (*Mekhilta de-Rabbi Yishmael*, Kaspa, §4, p. 333)

"שָׁלֹשׁ רְגָלִים" (שמות כג, יז)—המהלכין ברגליהן; "יֵרָאֶה"—להוציא את הסומין; "זְכוּרְךָ"—להוציא את הנשים; "כָּל זְכוּרְךָ"—להוציא חגרים, טומטום ואנדרוגינוס.

"תִּקְרָא אֶת הַתּוֹרָה הַזֹּאת" וג' (דברים לא, יא)—להוציא גרים ועבדים; "בְּאָזְנֵיהֶם"—להוציא חרשים.

"וְשָׂמַחְתָּ" (דברים טז, יא)—להוציא את החולה ואת הקטן; "לִפְנֵי ה' אֱלֹהֶיךָ"—להוציא את הטמא.

מיכן אמרו: הכל חייבין בראייה חוץ מחרש שוטה וקטן טומטום ואנדרוגינוס, החגר והסומא החולה והזקן.

---

a The Hebrew word for "times" in this verse, *pe'amim*, can also mean "footfalls," excluding those who cannot make the ascent unassisted.

b The derivation is from the word *kol*, "all."

c Someone with no distinguishable genitalia.

d Someone with both male and female genitalia.

e The full verse discusses the convening of the entire nation every seven years at the site of the Temple during the festival of Sukkot: "when all Israel comes to appear before the Lord your God, in the place that He chooses, you shall read this Torah to all Israel, within their earshot."

f The convert is included explicitly in the next verse (Deut 31:12). This is probably a scribal error due to the regular appearance of the convert next to the slave. See Rosen-Zvi, "Text, Redaction, and Hermeneutics," 144n46.

g This is a third verse that discusses appearing "before the Lord," which is understood to mean at the Temple, on a festival, this time Shavuot: "You shall rejoice before the Lord your God: you, your son, your daughter, your male and female slave, the Levite within your gates, the stranger/sojourner, the orphan, and the widow in your midst, in the place where the Lord your God chooses to make His name dwell."

h Since rejoicing is understood as feasting and drinking wine.

i A quotation of Mishnah, Ḥagigah, 1:1.

This midrash puts together the verses on ascending to the Temple on festivals, and it uses nearly every expression to exclude some group of people from the obligation. This manifestly serves the purpose of justification, yet it also generates a biblical basis for those exclusions enumerated in the opening mishnah of Tractate *Ḥagigah*. One can tell that the entire midrash is building toward its concluding sentence, the legal tradition prefaced by "Hence they said, ..." by its exegesis of multiple verses to arrive at all the details. The darshan engages in eisegesis rather than exegesis. He collects and arranges the verses so that they pave the way to the familiar tradition, instead of letting those verses guide him wherever they may.[49]

D. ELABORATING THE LAW

Breaking with biblical and ancient Near Eastern codes, the Tannaim grounded justice on the rule of law.[50] Accordingly, halakha must be totalizing, all-encompassing, and elaborate.[51] The Torah, being a combination of casuistic and apodictic law, is anything but. To build a legal system of the kind represented in the Mishnah requires the translation and elaboration of Torah law.[52] Casuistic law has to be generalized,[53] and apodictic law specified. One of the aims of Midrash is to work this thorough transformation.

To see how the change occurs, let us begin with a verse: "He who strikes a man so that he dies shall surely die" (Ex. 21:12). This is not very specific, so the Midrash wrings out the text of the Torah for details:

> "He who strikes a man" (Ex. 21:12). I only have[a] a man who struck a man, whence one who struck a woman or minor? "Any man who strikes any human being [shall surely die]" (Lev. 24:17)—to include one who struck a woman or minor.
>
> Whence a woman who killed her fellow woman or a minor? It therefore teaches,[b] "[the one who struck down shall surely die,] he is a murderer" (Num. 35:21)—it comes to teach this. (*Mekhilta de-Rabbi Yishmael, Nezikin*, §4, p. 261)

"מַכֵּה אִישׁ" (שמות כא, יב)—אין לי אלא איש שהכה את האיש, הכה את האשה ואת הקטן מנין? תלמוד לומר "וְאִישׁ כִּי יַכֶּה כָּל נֶפֶשׁ אָדָם" וגו' (ויקרא כד, יז)—להביא את שהכה האשה ואת הקטן. האשה שהרגה את חבירתה ואת הקטן מנין? תלמוד לומר "רֹצֵחַ הוּא" (במדבר לה, כא)—לתלמודו הוא בא.

The comparative methodology of this midrash should be familiar by now. In bringing together these passages about intentional murder to justify the necessity of all three, it also

---

a The death penalty is only spelled out for killing a man.

b The words "he is a murderer" seem redundant, and thus are read as conveying an additional law: anyone who kills any human being is a murderer. The principle that the Torah repeats an entire legal passage in order to teach one new detail is unique to the school of R. Yishmael. See chapter 10, section B.

adds substantive legal content to the general law on homicide. The verse never spells out the kinds of perpetrator and victim that trigger the death penalty, so rabbinic exegesis fills in those details.[54]

Other verses in the same legal passage present the opposite problem, that is, wordiness in place of terseness:

> If men quarrel and one strikes the other with stone or fist, and he does not die but is bedridden—then if he gets up and walks outside on his staff, the assailant shall be clear; he must only pay for his idleness and cure. (Exodus 21:18–19)

Here, the Torah presents a very specific set of circumstances and then states the law. The reader, and certainly the jurist, is left wondering which elements are essential to the case. Is this the law if and only if a stone or fist is used, but not a farming implement or kitchen utensil? Must the victim be bedridden, or does this simply measure the strength of the blow?

> "With stone or fist" (Ex. 21:18)—telling us that the stone and fist are indicators of deadliness. Do you say that it comes for this,[a] or does it instead come to teach that if he struck him with a stone or fist he is liable, but with anything else he is exempt? It therefore teaches,[b] "and [he struck him] with a hand stone" (Num. 35:17)—telling us that one is not liable unless he strikes with something that can be deadly. (*Mekhilta de-Rabbi Yishmael*, Nezikin, §6, p. 269)

"בְּאֶבֶן אוֹ בְאֶגְרֹף" (שמות כא, יח)—מגיד שאבן ואגרף סימני מיתה הן. אתה אומר לכך בא, או לא בא אלא ללמד שאם הכהו באבן או באגרף יהא חייב, ובשאר כל דבר יהא פטור? תלמוד לומר "וְאִם בְּאֶבֶן יָד" (במדבר לה, יז)—מגיד שאינו חייב עד שיכהו בדבר שיהיה בו כדי להמית.

The darshan looks to a parallel in the book of Numbers to establish that stone and fist are only handy examples of something that can deliver a fatal blow. The Midrash frequently makes this interpretive move of construing a limited number of objects or circumstances as members of a much broader set or category. The Torah states the penalty for putting out a slave's eye or knocking out their tooth, and the Midrash expands it to other parts of the body that also fail to heal or grow back.[55] While the Torah discusses an ox that gores someone to death, the Sages claim that it applies to any dangerous animal.[56] The Torah encases its law in real-world situations in lieu of expressing it through abstract rules.

One can put it this way. Our analysis of the Mishnah's style in part 1 showed that it often adopts the Torah's casuistic presentation. In its legal ideology, though, mishnaic law is

---

a To teach about deadliness.
b The continuation of the verse specifies that it must be able to deliver a mortal blow: "by which a man may die."

The Motivations of Midrash   261

utterly different, because its ambition is to encompass the entirety of the human experience. A full-fledged legal system must be wrangled from a welter of detail.

In drawing generalizations from the cases given in the Torah, a phrase recurs dozens of times in the Midrashim of Rabbi Akiva's school: "I only have X, whence to include Y?" After these words, there is an expansion from certain details of the verse. In some midrashim, that extension is then constricted by some element of the verse. For example:

> "Do not muzzle an ox during its threshing" (Deut. 25:4). I only have the ox, whence to treat every other domesticated animal, undomesticated animal, and fowl like the ox? It therefore teaches, "Do not muzzle"—under any circumstances. If so, why does it say "ox"?[a] You may not muzzle an ox, but you may muzzle a person.[b] (*Sifrei Deuteronomy*, §287, p. 305)

> "לֹא תַחְסֹם שׁוֹר בְּדִישׁוֹ" (דברים כה, ד). אין לי אלא שור, מנין לעשות שאר בהמה חיה ועוף כיוצא בשור? תלמוד לומר "לֹא תַחְסֹם"—מכל מקום. אם כן למה נאמר "שׁוֹר"? את השור אי אתה חוסם, אתה חוסם את האדם.

The ox of the verse is interpreted as standing in for the category of animals, which by definition excludes human beings. This conceptualization generalizes the law while also justifying Scripture's specific reference.

In the preceding example, the simple reading of the verse accords with the rabbis'. Modern biblical scholars agree that this law would apply equally to other beasts of burden like the donkey. This isn't always the case, though. Consider the law of giving a gift to one's slave upon emancipation:

> "You shall surely furnish him[c] from the flock, threshing floor, and vat" (Deut. 15:14). Could it be that one only furnishes from the flock, threshing floor, and vat which are specified? Whence to include everything? It therefore teaches, "You shall surely furnish him"—to include everything.[d] If so, why does it say, "from the flock, threshing floor, and vat"? The flock, threshing floor, and vat are specified because of their capacity for blessing,[e] to the exclusion of money, which has no capacity for blessing—the words of Rabbi Shimon.
>
> Rabbi Eliezer ben Yaakov says, It excludes mules, which are sterile. (*Sifrei Deuteronomy*, §119, p. 178)

---

a Since the darshan has just established that the law is the same for all other animals.
b The worker, who may not eat boundlessly while working; cf. Deuteronomy, 23:25–26.
c For the laws of furnishing a freed slave, see Babylonian Talmud, *Kiddushin* 17a.
d The doubled language of the Hebrew, *ha'anek ta'anik*, indicates expansiveness.
e They can yield a little or an abundance of produce.

"[הַעֲנֵיק תַּעֲנִיק לוֹ] מִצֹּאנְךָ וּמִגָּרְנְךָ וּמִיִּקְבֶךָ" (דברים טו, יד). יכול אין מעניקין אלא מצאן ומגרן ומיקב מיוחדין? מנין לרבות כל דבר? תלמוד לומר "הַעֲנֵיק תַּעֲנִיק"—לרבות כל דבר. אם כן למה נאמר "מִצֹּאנְךָ וּמִגָּרְנְךָ וּמִיִּקְבֶךָ"? מה צאן, גרן, ויקב מיוחדים שהם ראוים לברכה, יצאו כספים שאינם ראוים לברכה— דברי רבי שמעון.

רבי אליעזר בן יעקב אומר: יצאו פרדות שאינן יולדות.

In this instance, it is hard to say if the Torah intended only those foodstuffs or would itself allow for gifts of other kinds. The same is true of the law of withholding wages:

> "Do not oppress a poor and needy laborer" (Deut. 24:14). I only have the "poor and needy," whence to include everyone? It therefore teaches, "Do not oppress"—under any circumstances. If so, why does it say "poor and needy"? I am quicker[a] to exact vengeance for the poor and needy than for anyone else. (*Sifrei Deuteronomy*, §278, p. 296)

"לֹא תַעֲשֹׁק שָׂכִיר עָנִי וְאֶבְיוֹן" (דברים כד, יד). אין לי אלא "עָנִי וְאֶבְיוֹן", מנין לרבות כל אדם [שאסור לעושקו]? תלמוד לומר "לֹא תַעֲשֹׁק"—מכל מקום. אם כן למה נאמר "עָנִי וְאֶבְיוֹן"? ממהר אני ליפרע על ידי עני ואביון יותר מכל אדם.

Is the verse relating only to the egregious act of financially abusing someone who really needs their money, or does it use this as an example for workers in general?

Whatever the case, the application of midrashic techniques to the biblical text produces a robust and comprehensive legal system. We should not overlook the revolutionary nature of this practice: for the first time, the laws of the Torah are transformed into more than just halakhot to be followed (a practice we traced back to Ezra-Nehemiah). They now constitute an integrated halakhic system that complements and reinforces the Mishnahic framework.[57]

E. BRIDGING CONCEPTUAL WORLDS

The darshanim undertook the exegetical-theological project of justifying and harmonizing the divine text, and committed themselves to the juristic endeavor of anchoring oral tradition and developing a complete legal system. But we must not forget that they were products of their time and place. The need for an interpreter to bring a text into consonance with the world he or she inhabits, with its ideas, judgments, mores, and practices, is not a rabbinic phenomenon. When an interpreter of any canonical text of instruction is bound to a set of norms and conceptions other than the text's, they necessarily mediate between the canon and the norm.[58]

---

a God is the speaker.

Take the biblical *ger*. In the original biblical contexts, the *ger* is a "sojourner" or "foreigner" who lives among the Israelites, and he is frequently contrasted with the Israelite *ezraḥ*, the "native born." The Midrash, however, systematically recasts this category in halakhic terms: the *ger* is a convert who has formally joined the nation of Israel. Practically every appearance of the *ger* in the Torah is glossed with "a convert" in the Midrash. Why? Because the Sages wore polarizing lenses that divided the world into Jew and Gentile. To allow for a foreigner to reside among Jews would break down this binary and create a liminal space. The rabbinic worldview is what shaped the interpretation, and thus resident alien became righteous Jew.[59]

Another type of adjustment pertains to a core legal-ethical principle of rabbinic law. When the Torah describes the wayward city that worships foreign gods, it says that the citizens are "saying *(lemor)*" to others to join in this worship. Although this word simply introduces a quote of direct speech, the Midrash glosses it: "having been warned."[60] What is the point of this derashah, beyond basic justification of the word's necessity? A foundation of rabbinic penology is that an offender can only be punished if they were warned prior to committing their transgression. If they willfully ignored the warning, it proves that they committed the offense with full awareness and intentionality. The Midrash, especially in collections from Rabbi Yishmael's school, frequently asks: "We have heard the punishment, whence the warning?" The darshan must find some allusion to this, as farfetched as it may be, in the verses.[61] Being absolutely certain of intent before administering punishment may be a legal concern, stemming from the rabbinic view of an ideal legal system, or a moral one, flowing from the rabbinic conception of justice.[62]

Testimony is another area of Torah law that the Sages bend to match their conception of justice. In the Torah, certain types of evidence fall short of what the Sages consider probative. When a new husband defames his bride as having not been the virgin she claimed, the Torah says that they "spread out of the sheet" to check for hymenal blood (Deut. 22:17). The Midrash, however, requires real testimony. The nuptial bedding is not actually held up tautly for all to see, says Rabbi Yishmael's bet midrash, but "the matters are brightened like a sheet."[63] In fact, this biblical law "is one of three Torah statements that Rabbi Yishmael would expound parabolically."[64] Rabbi Akiva's academy in contrast reads the witnesses into the verse: "Let the witnesses of this one and the witnesses of that one come and say what they have to say before the city elders."[65] Both schools share the assumption that a sheet is insufficient evidence to corroborate the husband's complaint.[66]

The necessity of formal witnessing is introduced into every nook of Halakhah by the Midrash. When the Torah states a murderer "shall surely die" (Ex. 21:12), the Midrash adds: "with the warning of witnesses."[67] If someone kidnaps and sells another person and the victim is "discovered" in their possession (Ex. 21:16), the Torah clarifies that "discovery is only with witnesses."[68]

The most famous reinterpretation of biblical law concerns fairness in punishment. Where the Torah demands "an eye for an eye" (Ex. 21:22), the principle of lex talionis, the Midrash explains that it is a reference to "money."[69] No eyes are put out as a penalty. Instead, the victim must be paid the value of their eye. The Sages could not morally stomach the biblical command.[70]

The darshanim are aware of the gap between Scripture and Halakhah. Around one hundred times the Midrashim wonder: How are they to "maintain" (*mekayem*) a verse when its straightforward meaning is unconscionable or otherwise untenable? The solution they propose is usually to forcibly restrict or reconstrue the biblical phrase.[71] For example, tradition dictates that the count of the Omer from Pesach to Shavuot commences after the first day of Pesach, yet the verse says that the count is to begin "from the morrow of the Shabbat" (Lev. 23:15). "How, then, am I to maintain 'from the morrow of the Shabbat'? From the morrow of the holiday."[72] The darshan is trying to bridge Torah law with contemporary practice and explicitly acknowledges the valley separating them.

The Midrash does the same in aggadic contexts. In the midrash below, the darshan overlays the rabbinic perception of divine recompense and the afterlife onto the Torah.[73] The Torah promises: "And you shall keep My statutes and My laws which a person shall do and live through them" (Lev. 18:5). Regarding this promise of "life" for fulfilling the mitzvot, the Midrash has this to say:

> "And live through them" (Lev. 18:5)—in the World to Come.[a] If you say in this world, doesn't one ultimately die? How then do I maintain, "and live through them"? In the World to Come. (*Sifra, Aḥarei Mot*, 8:1, 85d)

> "וָחַי בָּהֶם" (ויקרא יח, ה)—לעולם הבא. אם תאמר בעולם הזה, והלוא סופו מת הוא? הא מה אני מקיים "וָחַי בָּהֶם"? לעולם הבא.

In another instance, the Midrash rejects the notion that non-Jews can have genuine prophets, despite overwhelming scriptural evidence to the contrary.[74] Moses promises: "The Lord your God shall establish for you a prophet from your midst, from your brethren, like me" (Deut. 18:15). The Midrash interprets:

> "The Lord your God shall establish for you" (Deut. 18:15)—but not from the Gentiles.[b] How am I to maintain, "I have made you a prophet for the Gentiles" (Jer. 1:5)? For those who act like Gentiles.[c] (*Sifrei Deuteronomy*, §175, p. 221)

> "יָקִים לְךָ ה' אֱלֹהֶיךָ" (דברים יח, טו)—ולא מן הגוים. מה אני מקיים "נָבִיא לַגּוֹיִם נְתַתִּיךָ" (ירמיהו א, ה)? בנוהג מנהג גוים.

---

a The eschatological era.
b A different version reads, "not for the Gentiles," meaning that they shouldn't have a prophet.
c Jews who act like Gentiles in that they are sinful.

The Midrash works rabbinic beliefs or convictions into the text of the Torah, while being aware that this is not what the text plainly says.

We have seen that the Midrash is prompted to do its work by the text of the Torah itself, such as contradictions and superfluities, as well as by exegetical pressures that exist outside the text, like tradition and rabbinic sensibilities. Although these all fire the imagination of the darshan, there is a fundamental distinction between them. The internal issues are more or less transparent, whereas the external ones are buried in the same terminology. In other words, the Midrash speaks in the language of textual problems and solutions, even when its chief consideration is ethics or tradition. It is left to the careful analyst to identify the latter. This concludes our analysis of the primary drivers behind midrashic exegesis, and we now turn our attention to the Midrash's assumptions about the nature of the biblical text.

TWELVE

Midrash's Conception of the Biblical Text

The characteristically colorful and surprising interpretations of the biblical text found in the Midrash are the product of a series of hermeneutic principles and textual motivations discussed in the previous chapter. But these principles and motivations do not tell the whole story. The darshanim unwaveringly interpreted the Torah according to them because they had a particular conception of the biblical text to which the modern reader generally does not subscribe. While we can conceive of the Torah as an archaic work belonging to the world of antiquity, the darshan felt required to make the Torah fit his present worldview. While we can classify the Torah as a literary work with its own rhetorical figures, the darshan had to justify every repetition or instance of wordiness. While we can consider the Torah to be a composite text of multiple authors, the darshan worked to eliminate every contradiction and generate a single halakhic system.

The preceding chapter concentrated on the hermeneutic motivations of the tannaitic Midrashim, and this chapter complements it by unpacking the textual conceptions behind them. Together, the two chapters endeavor to explicate what makes the midrashic moves both possible and necessary for the Tannaim.

From examples of midrashim from the schools of Rabbi Akiva and Rabbi Yishmael analyzed in the preceding chapters, the reader should by now have a sense that they look and feel different. But these can be likened to variable surface formations pushing up from chemically identical bedrock. They are both engaged in the exegetical enterprise called Midrash, and they share the same assumptions about the text. What are they?

James Kugel has articulated a set of beliefs that ancient interpreters evidently held about the Torah.[1] This comprehensive list has profoundly influenced academic discourse for good cause, but it also has its shortcomings. Two primary critiques are that it is too broad, resulting in the inclusion of works that are fundamentally different, and that it is anachronistic, pegging certain works as "Bible interpretation" when the Torah (let alone the Tanakh) had yet to be canonized.[2] Since the focus of this book is on Midrash specifically, the accuracy of Kugel's list will be assessed only on its applicability to that genre. I believe that Kugel's insights can fit Midrash, with a few fundamental changes.[3] Since they were not cut to the measure of Midrash, they need to be tailored further. The discussion below is arranged around each of Kugel's assumptions.

1. *The Torah is a cryptic text whose meaning is not readily apparent, so exegetical tools must be used to draw out its meaning.* This perfectly characterizes the *pesher* literature at Qumran, which relates to the Torah's text as enigmatic, and Philo's allegorical exegesis, which assumes that the Torah says one thing while gesturing at another. But it only half suits Midrash. While it agrees that the Torah deserves comprehensive interpretation, it does not regard the text as cryptic. Furthermore, the question at the heart of Midrash is not what is being said but why it is being said.[4]

2. *The Torah is fundamentally didactic and relevant to readers of every generation, even in its narrative portions.* Unlike the previous tenet, this one is upheld fully in the Midrash. The Torah is the Sages' ultimate roadmap. From it they learn how to navigate life according to God's will, as embodied in Halakhah and Aggadah. But Midrash shares this umbrella with other forms of biblical interpretation,[5] and here is one of the weaknesses of Kugel's definition. The *pesher* literature expects the words of the Torah to be fulfilled in real time. Philo elevates the Patriarchs to moral exemplars.[6] Does Midrash agree with them or does it extract meaning from the Torah in other ways? Fine-tuning is needed here.[7]

3. *The Torah is a perfect work without contradictions, mistakes, or superfluities.* Midrash is arguably the most extreme instantiation of this principle in ancient Jewish exegesis. The Torah's perfection entails that every single textual detail yields meaning when prodded, even though in practice some escape the Midrash's attention. Sentences, clauses, words, letters—all of them are islanded in the gaze of the darshan, with a stare so intense that surrounding context fades indistinctly into the periphery. But note that although the darshan is allowed to undo the syntactic snaps holding phrases together to allow additional meaning to be released, his attitude toward the biblical text is toward that of human language. The Torah is semantically intelligible to the reader. The darshan is there to extract further meaning or correct mistakes, not to mediate what is actually written. Even the letter-splitting midrashim of Rabbi Akiva do not assume that the Torah is composed in a cryptic divine code. This contrasts with the approach of Jewish kabbalists in

the Middle Ages, who used various ciphers to decode the Torah's symbolic language.[8]

4. *The Torah is a divine text.* The Sages undoubtedly believed this, but again this is a belief so broad that it can lead in many—even opposite—directions. According to Midrash, the divine text is polysemous, that is, it is capable of bearing many meanings simultaneously that do not exclude one another.[9] But the number of valid interpretations is not endless. Some interpretations can be downright wrong, which is why Sages sometimes tussle over the text's meaning. Additionally, the interpretations are not ordered hierarchically, from surface to profound meaning, as is typical of allegorical and mystical interpretation. Midrash's conception of semantic multiplicity is distinct from what we find elsewhere.

Kugel's enumeration of ancient interpretive assumptions provides context for and gives us insight into the mindset of the darshanim. His analysis, however, is only a starting point. The four general beliefs about the nature of the Torah need to be tweaked and narrowed down for Midrash, and there are other distinctive ones that set Midrash apart. For example, Midrash acknowledges an inviolable boundary between the biblical text and its interpretation. The Torah is a discrete, hallowed, and complete textual object that the darshan can handle but cannot tamper with. He cannot insinuate himself into the text, emending it with reed and ink, as other ancient readers did. Midrash is not rewritten Scripture but interpreted Scripture. It systematically separates biblical quotation from midrashic elaboration.

The practitioners of Midrash never state programmatically their views on the Torah. The only way to learn more is to dig deep into the derashot and find the textual assumptions that control them. Distinctions will be drawn between the two schools where warranted, but in this chapter too the schools will be revealed to hold fundamentally very similar positions, even if they apply them in different ways and with dissimilar intensity.

This chapter, and the entire book for that matter, takes Midrash to be at root an interpretive endeavor with specific controlling assumptions. Not all scholars agree with this. Some argue that Midrash is but a post-facto attempt to anchor, in whatever manner possible, extra-biblical ideas in the Bible.[10] But this cannot explain the numerous cases where all the darshanim agree about the pertinent law or moral and debate only how it ought to be arrived at through the text.[11] Midrash is a genuine interpretive endeavor whose operative assumptions await discovery.

The discussion in the first section homes in on one essential assumption of Midrash that distinguishes it from other ancient types of interpretation: every element of the Torah's text is swollen with meaning that must be extracted to the very last drop. Midrash has many techniques at its disposal for doing this, one of which is chopping up clauses or phrases into asyntactic bits. The second section therefore looks at the dialectic attitude toward context in midrashic practice. The chapter ends with a typology of midrashic constructions discussed in this and preceding chapters.

Before we proceed, it is essential to recognize a crucial point: these expectations are neither "obvious" nor natural, nor are they an inevitable universal outcome of canonization. Rather, they are shaped within a specific interpretive community and emerge as part of its distinctive reading practices.[12] What we are tracing here is the co-construction of a particular text alongside its unique modes of exegesis, interpretive practices, and expectations—all of which are deeply interconnected

A. MAXIMAL EXTRACTION OF MEANING

Our reading of a text is always shaped by our expectations. Genre dictates what we should anticipate from the text, from its literary structure to its word choice. We don't read the daily news so much as scan it, whereas we relish the diction of poetry and devote time to unpacking its possible meanings.[13] The Sages revered the Torah as a sacred, divine text—Kugel's fourth assumption—and accordingly treated its every word as embracing many meanings. The sheer volume of information the interpreter expected to find goes beyond anything we are used to as consumers of modern texts.

Previous chapters have demonstrated that the Midrash assumes that the Torah includes no unnecessary words. Halakhic passages encode halakhic data, and narrative ones contain moral religious instruction. The idea that part of a text is there solely to set a scene, to add a dose of realism, or to introduce the circumstances is not accepted by the Midrash as applicable to the Torah. The drive to justify repetitive or superfluous material, documented extensively in the previous chapter, derives from this conception of the biblical text.[14]

Everything in the Torah is subject to exegesis, even when there is nothing inherently problematic—no repetition, no superfluity, no contradiction. Casuistic presentations of Torah law, such as the law on the administration of corrective lashes, showcase this. The relevant verses state:

> When there is a dispute between men, they shall approach the court of justice, and they shall judge them: they shall find for the one in the right and against the one in the wrong. If it turns out that the one in the wrong is to be lashed, the judge shall make him lie down and have him struck before him, according to his wrongdoing in number. He may give him forty lashes, he shall not give more; lest he go on to give him many more, and your brother be degraded in your eyes. (Deuteronomy 25:1–3)

This is a classic casuistic presentation of Halakhah in the Torah. The passage begins with a description ("When there is a dispute . . ."), gives the general law ("the judge shall . . ."), and then adds specifics about implementation ("He may give . . . he shall not give . . ."). The progression is logical, yet the Midrash interprets each element independently, isolating it from the larger framework and treating law and setup as equally rich with meaning. On this reading, every piece of the text generates a new norm:

"When there is a dispute between men" (Deut. 25:1). What caused this one to be lashed?[a] Say it is the dispute.

"Between men" (Deut. 25:1). I only have men, whence a man and a woman, a woman and a man, or two women with each other? It therefore says, "they shall approach[b] the court of justice"—under all circumstances. (*Sifrei Deuteronomy*, §286, pp. 302)

"כִּי יִהְיֶה רִיב בֵּין אֲנָשִׁים" (דברים כה, א). מי גרם לזה ללקות? הוי אומר זו מריבה.

"בֵּין אֲנָשִׁים" (שם). אין לי אלא אנשים, איש עם אשה, ואשה עם איש, ושתי נשים זו עם זו מנין? תלמוד לומר "וְנִגְּשׁוּ אֶל הַמִּשְׁפָּט"—מכל מקום.

The first derashah teaches a moral lesson: avoid quarrels because they can have serious consequences. The second derashah learns a fine point of law, that women can also be lashed by a bet din (rabbinic court). Both interpretations take the background to the statement of the law as grist for the midrashic mill. Every word of divine Scripture has a relevant and binding message.

Since the casuistic elements framing Torah law are a kind of short narrative, they lend themselves more to aggadic derashot than to halakhic ones. *Sifrei Deuteronomy* in particular develops special techniques to transform case descriptions into moral lessons. Here are two examples from the halakhah of the beautiful captive woman in Deuteronomy 21. The Torah opens the passage by describing a successful sortie and the spoils of war: "If you go out to do battle against your enemy and the Lord your God delivers him into your hand, and you take captives from him" (Deut. 21:10). Only then does it proceed to dictate how the soldier is to treat the miserable female captive (Deut. 21:11–15). The Midrash, however, extracts meaning even from the initial stage-setting verse:

"And the Lord your God delivers him into your hand" (Deut. 21:10). If you have done everything said in the passage,[c] the Lord your God ultimately delivers him into your hand. (*Sifrei Deuteronomy*, §211, p. 245)

"וּנְתָנוֹ ה' אֱלֹהֶיךָ בְּיָדֶךָ" (דברים כא, י). אם עשית כל האמור בענין, סוף שה' אלהיך נותנו בידך.

The backdrop becomes its own lesson. The *Sifrei* begins many derashot with this direct address, "If you have done . . .," and they always signal that the setting is the lecture.

---

a Since lashes are usually reserved for sins, the darshan looks for the sin at hand.
b The subject of the verb is unspecified and can therefore include men and women.
c The laws of war detailed immediately above in Deuteronomy 20:1—21:9; the law of the captive woman concludes the whole unit of the laws of war.

After laying out the procedure for keeping this captive woman, the Torah addresses the possibility that the re-socialized soldier will not want to keep her after the war ends. In that event, it rules that he must set her free and not try to sell or otherwise exploit her. The *Sifrei* comments:

> "If it turns out that you do not want her" (Deut. 21:14). Scripture informs you that you will ultimately detest her. (*Sifrei Deuteronomy*, §214, p. 247)

"וְהָיָה אִם לֹא חָפַצְתָּ בָּהּ" (דברים כא, יד). הכתוב מבשרך שאתה עתיד לשנאה.

According to the Midrash, the Torah's very mention of the possibility prophetically hardens it into an eventuality. The circumstantial phrase crucial to the full presentation of the law is reconfigured into a general warning about falling prey to impulsive desires during wartime. It won't end well. Here, too, the Midrash uses an idiom—"Scripture informs you"—that propels phrases that play second fiddle to the law into their own aggadic stardom.

Innocent and informative statements are regularly upgraded into moral or legal instruction. For instance, Deuteronomy 25 establishes the obligation of a brother-in-law to perform *yibbum* or *ḥalitzah* with the wife of a deceased and childless brother.[15] The latter ritual of rejection takes place in public: "His sister-in-law shall go up to the gate, to the judges" (Deut. 25:7). In the biblical period, this is where the judges held court, so by default the ceremony would occur there. The Midrash elevates this description into a prescription: "It is a mitzvah for the court to be at a high point in the city."[16] The action of "going up" that is there to move the case forward produces a new rule that is applied to all courts. The court's station is to be reflected by its literally superior location.

These examples are all drawn from *Sifrei Deuteronomy*, a work by the school of Rabbi Akiva, whose darshanim are unsatisfied with anything less than drawing out all potential meaning from the biblical text. The Midrashim of Rabbi Akiva's bet midrash scrutinize and magnify textual minutiae, a tendency that has been well covered by this point. Deriving meaning from the presence of a single *vav* shows that nothing is beneath interpretation for them. Rabbi Yishmael and his school are more reserved.[17]

Another display of semantic differential lies in whether to treat non-imperative phrasing as norm-producing. For example, a priest is forbidden from coming into contact with a corpse because it makes him ritually impure. The Torah lists immediate family members for whom this prohibition is lifted and it includes an unmarried sister (Lev. 21:3). Is the priest only allowed to help handle her body or must he do so? Rabbi Yishmael reads it as a license to pay his last respects to his sister; Rabbi Akiva construes it as an obligation that he may not opt out of in order to preserve his purity. Where the former's school sees "may," the latter's systematically sees "must." This is not a linguistic semantic debate, but rather one of intensification and magnification.

Along similar lines, the two disagree whether the narrative mortar cementing the halakhic bricks together are of equal importance to the structure they create. The casuistic formulations of Torah law often begin with *im* ("if"), setting up an if-then clause: If X happens (the protasis), then Y is the halakhah (the apodosis). Rabbi Yishmael strongly argues for the normative irrelevance of the protasis: "Every single *im* in the Torah is optional except for three."[18] *Im* signifies a conditional statement that provides the conditions for the ensuing law. The center of gravity lies in the halakhic apodosis. For Rabbi Akiva, however, everything is equally weighted. In the search for religious moral meaning every word is a potential vehicle for it. *Im* is thus not "if" but "when." It represents an absolute obligation and therefore inevitable reality.[19]

In summary, Rabbi Akiva's academy is consistent in applying pressure to every word of the Torah in order to maximally extract its normative meaning. The words of the Torah cannot just function as introductions or mise-en-scène; they also must signify their own meaning. We will reencounter this phenomenon below on a smaller scale with "islanding derashot."

Rabbi Yishmael and his school don't see normativity implied everywhere, nor do they load any innocuous word with normative weight. And yet, they too are trying to maximize meaning. Instead of breaking up every word of the Torah like Rabbi Akiva, they look for telltale veins of meaning and strike where they expect to find a lode. We thus must be careful not to overstate the differences between academies. Their conceptual agreement about the perfection of the biblical text and all its implications massively overshadows their disagreements about the degree of extractable meaning and the proper techniques of its extraction.[20]

The Midrashim of Rabbi Yishmael's school also read the casuistic descriptions of the Torah as teaching independent laws. Recall these verses from the previous chapter:

> If men quarrel and one strikes the other with stone or fist, and he does not die but is bedridden—then if he gets up and walks outside on his staff, the assailant shall be clear; he must only pay for his idleness and cure. (Exodus 21:18–19)

The phrase "one strikes the other with stone or fist" is a fact of the case. The stone and fist are examples of typically nonlethal weapons. But Rabbi Yishmael's Midrash doesn't see things this way:

> "And one strikes the other with stone or fist" (Ex. 21:18)—to obligate him for this independently and for that[a] independently. (*Mekhilta de-Rabbi Yishmael*, Nezikin, §6, p. 269)

"וְהִכָּה אִישׁ אֶת רֵעֵהוּ [בְּאֶבֶן אוֹ בְאֶגְרֹף]" (שמות כא, יח)—לחייב על זה בפני עצמו ועל זה בפני עצמו.

From these two methods of causing injury the Midrash learns a new law: each mode of striking creates a separate liability. "To obligate him for this independently and for that

---

a For striking with a stone and striking with a fist.

independently" occurs eight more times in the *Mekhilta*, each of which likewise derives a new law from a fact of the case. This midrashic reading ignores the internal literary logic of the verse and isolates the phrase to extract the maximum normative meaning. The Midrashim of Rabbi Yishmael's school also search for meaning against the literary grain. This hermeneutic approach of wringing out all normative and edificatory meaning from the Torah is the foundation of all Midrash and lends it its unique character.

What distinguishes the two schools? In a word, intensity. The Midrashim of Rabbi Akiva's school are more dogged in their search and leave no word unturned. The most intense application of this tenet is reflected in what can be called "islanding derashot," on account of the fact that they break up a sentence into tiny islands of independent meaning. In these, Rabbi Akiva's Midrash breaks down the syntactic connections in a verse, fragments the verse into phrases that form sentences or clauses, and interprets each one sequentially. The result is an island chain of text, in which words and phrases are independent, detached, and self-sufficient units of meaning. One finds a good example of this type in the midrashic interpretation of the command to keep one's vows. The verse reads: "The utterance of your lips you shall keep and fulfill, as you have vowed to the Lord your God a freewill gift, the promise that you made with your mouth" (Deut. 23:24). Notice how the midrash below ignores the strictures of grammar:

> "The utterance of your lips" (Deut. 23:24)—a positive commandment.
>
> "You shall keep"—a negative commandment.[a]
>
> "And fulfill"—this is a warning to the court to make you do it.
>
> "As you have vowed *(nadarta)*"—this is a vow *(neder)*.[b]
>
> "To the Lord your God"—these are *'arakhin*[c], *ḥaramin*,[d] and *hekdeshot*.[e]
>
> "A freewill gift *(nedavah)*"—this is a freewill gift *(nedavah)*.[f]
>
> "The promise that you made"—this is a consecration for the upkeep of the Temple.
>
> "With your mouth"—this is *tzedakah*. (*Sifrei Deuteronomy*, §265, p. 286)

---

a To keep and not to violate one's vow.

b A halakhic category that refers to a vow to bring a sacrifice; see Mishnah, *'Arakhin*, 1:1.

c Donations that correspond to the value assigned to a human being of a certain age; see Leviticus 27 and Mishnah, Tractate *'Arakhin*.

d A consecration using the term *ḥerem* that is given to the priests; see Mishnah, *'Arakhin*, 8:4–8.

e Anything dedicated to the Temple.

f A halakhic category that refers to a vow to bring a specific animal as a sacrifice and has lesser liability should something happen to the animal to disqualify it; see Mishnah, *Megillah*, 1:6.

"מוֹצָא שְׂפָתֶיךָ" (דברים כג, כד)—מצות עשה. "תִּשְׁמֹר"—מצות לא תעשה. "וְעָשִׂיתָ"—הרי זו אזהרה לבית דין שיעשוך. "כַּאֲשֶׁר נָדַרְתָּ"—זה נדר. "לַה' אֱלֹהֶיךָ"—אילו ערכין, וחרמין, והקדשות. "נְדָבָה"—זו נדבה "אֲשֶׁר דִּבַּרְתָּ"—זו הקדש בדק הבית. "בְּפִיךָ"—זו צדקה.

The verse is repetitive because it is an extended exhortation. This midrash's first move is to break down the verse into its constituent parts, liberating the words and phrases from their stiff matrix. This creates little islands at which every ritual financial commitment recognized by rabbinic Halakhah can find anchorage. At the same time, maximum meaning is extracted from the verse.

The islanding derashah is common in *Sifrei Deuteronomy* not only because the composition is a product of Rabbi Akiva's academy, but also because the book of Deuteronomy is an exhortative work of oratory rather than a compendium of law or a report of historical-mythical episodes.[21] Since Midrash does not think that rhetoric alone justifies repetition in a divine text, it must translate the seemingly superfluous exhortations into new teachings. Two examples follow, one from a halakhic context and the other from an aggadic one.

After warning the people about false prophets, the Torah commands the correct course of action: "You shall follow the Lord your God and you shall fear Him. You shall keep His commandments, and you shall listen to His voice. You shall worship Him and cleave to Him" (Deut. 13:5). Here is the midrashic breakdown:

"You shall follow the Lord your God" (Deut. 13:5)—this is the cloud.[a]

"And you shall fear Him"—so that the dread of Him is upon them.

"You shall keep His commandments"—a positive commandment.

"And you shall listen to His voice"—to apply a negative commandment.[b] The voice of His prophets.[c]

"You shall serve Him"—through the Torah. Serve Him in the Temple.[d]

"And cleave to Him"—separate from idol worship and cleave to the Omnipresent. (*Sifrei Deuteronomy*, §85, p. 150)

"אַחֲרֵי ה' אֱלֹהֵיכֶם תֵּלֵכוּ" (דברים יג, ה)—זה ענן. "וְאֹתוֹ תִירָאוּ"—שיהא מוראו עליהם. "וְאֶת מִצְוֹתָיו תִּשְׁמֹרוּ"—מצוות עשה. "וּבְקֹלוֹ תִשְׁמָעוּ"—ליתן לא תעשה. בקול נביאיו. "תַעֲבֹדוּ"—בתורה. עיבדו במקדשו. "וּבוֹ תִדְבָּקוּן"—הפרישו מעבודה זרה ודבקו במקום.

---

a The pillar of cloud that guided the Israelites in the desert.
b It's not clear how the Midrash understands that a negative commandment is implied. See the emendation of Finkelstein, *Sifra*, ad loc. with the note in the critical apparatus on line 5.
c This is a second, additional interpretation of "His voice."
d This is an additional interpretation of "You shall serve Him."

The verse is hammering in the same point with diverse language, so the Midrash feels impelled to assign significance to each and every imperative. Some derashot simply repeat the verse in other words, as with the fear of God. Others deviate drastically, so that following God refers to following around His earthly manifestation in the supernatural cloud. The commands to listen to God's voice and serve Him both receive more than one interpretation. All this is to say that the derashot here have no internal consistency, wandering as they do across Jewish geography and history, from the Sinai desert to the Temple grounds to the post-destruction study hall. The primary motivation is justification of the repetitiveness.

The midrashic catalyst above was a thick concentration of sequential imperatives. In this next example, the subject is the setup that leads to the statement of the law. It describes a case touched on in the previous chapter, namely, a city that has strayed after idol worship and must be destroyed. We have already seen multiple examples of the facts of a case being interpreted to learn law or ethics. The novelty here is the fragmenting treatment to which the narrative is subjected. The verse reads: "Men of *beliya'al* have gone out from your midst and have drawn away the inhabitants of their town, saying: 'Let us go and worship other gods,' which you do not know" (Deut. 13:14).

> "Men . . . have gone out" (Deut. 13:14)—but not women; "men"—but not minors; "men"—not fewer than two.
>
> "Men of *beliya'al*"[a]—wrongdoers *(benei 'avel)*; men who have thrown off the yoke *('ol)* of God.
>
> "From your midst"—but not from the frontier.
>
> "And have drawn away the inhabitants of their town"—but not the inhabitants of another town.
>
> "Saying *(lemor)*"—having been warned.[b]
>
> "'Let us go and worship other gods,' which you do not know." (*Sifrei Deuteronomy*, §93, p. 154)

"יָצְאוּ אֲנָשִׁים" (דברים יג, יד)—ולא נשים; "אֲנָשִׁים"—ולא קטנים; "אֲנָשִׁים"—אין פחות משנים. "בְּנֵי בְלִיַּעַל"—בני עוול, בני אדם שפרקו עולו של מקום. "מִקִּרְבֶּךָ"—ולא מן הספר. "וַיַּדִּיחוּ אֶת יֹשְׁבֵי עִירָם"—ולא ישבי עיר אחרת. "לֵאמֹר"—בהתראה. "נֵלְכָה וְנַעַבְדָה אֱלֹהִים אֲחֵרִים אֲשֶׁר לֹא יְדַעְתֶּם".

---

a The derashah uses words from the root '-w-l to interpret *beliya'al* as to be without a yoke, *beli 'ol*.

b Literally, "with a warning," meaning that the Midrash hears in the word "saying" bystanders cautioning the wrongdoers that they are violating a prohibition; otherwise, they would not be punishable according to rabbinic law.

As in the previous example, here too there are straightforward interpretations, like the etymological ones for *beliya'al*, and contorted ones, like "saying" indicating a warning by others. Furthermore, the same word, "men," is the subject of multiple derashot. Note that most of the derashot are exclusionary, requiring very specific—and likely unrealistic—conditions to be met in order for the city to be sentenced to destruction. The people involved must be adult men only, they must be locals, they must be trying to persuade their fellow townsfolk, they must be warned by witnesses. The Midrash in effect renders this law obsolete.[22]

But beyond the normative implications of this midrash, there is also a hermeneutic side to it. Each term is read separately, making the story much more exhaustive. This could explain the presence of the final line, a direct quote from the verse with no midrashic interpretation: "'Let us go and worship other gods,' which you do not know." Apparently, the Midrash wants to integrate its fleshed-out account into the biblical text to form a complete narrative.

The islanding midrash, therefore, fulfills the cardinal tenet of maximal extraction of meaning. That pursuit gives the midrash its basic slotted form, and then the blanks are filled in with halakhic and aggadic particulars based on context. Since Rabbi Yishmael's school has the same interpretive agenda, the islanding derashah occurs in its Midrashim too. As with many phenomena discussed throughout these chapters, the difference between schools is less fundamentals and more degree, emphasis, and frequency.

Mekhilta de-Rabbi Yishmael contains islanding derashot on the biblical law about taking a lender's garment as collateral for a loan. The Torah says that the garment must be returned by sunset, "for it is his sole covering, it is his garment for his skin—in what will he sleep?" (Ex. 22:26). The Midrash breaks up the verse:

> "For it is his sole covering" (Ex. 22:26)—this is a cloak.
>
> "It is his garment for his skin"—this is a shirt.
>
> "In what will he sleep"—to include a leather mat. (*Mekhilta de-Rabbi Yishmael, Kaspa*, §2, p. 317)

> "כִּי הִוא כְסוּתוֹ לְבַדָּהּ" (שמות כב, כו)—זו טלית. ו"הִוא שִׂמְלָתוֹ לְעֹרוֹ"—זו חלוק. "בַּמֶּה יִשְׁכָּב"—להביא עור מצע.

The first two derashot expound synonymous phrases that describe a physical object. The midrash justifies the repetition by showing that not one but two types of clothing are intended. The third derashah, though, pulls a third type of object out of a clause that is entirely rhetorical and has no ostensible legal function. It ignores its grammatical role in the verse to maximize the text's meaning and justify every element of the text.

To conclude, both schools follow the principle of maximum extraction of meaning from the Torah's text. They detect extra meaning that exists outside the strict semantics of the verse. Rabbi Akiva's school views every word as a carbon atom open for bonding to form new molecules of meaning. Rabbi Yishmael's school, in contrast, considers some words to be nonreactive; they are what they are and cannot be induced to become something else. The islanding derashah, an extreme form of meaning maximization, features prominently in the Midrashim of Rabbi Akiva's school, but it also plays some role in those of Rabbi Yishmael's.

B. THE RELEVANCE OF CONTEXT

Midrash often ignores or minimizes the Torah's literariness—narrative flow, lead-in versus law—and the islanding derashah splits verses down to textual quanta. Can we expect it to care at all about the even broader framework of context?

Midrashim from the school of Rabbi Yishmael tend to respect the natural use of language and are less atomistic, so they serve as a logical point of departure for assessing the role of context in midrashic interpretation. About ten times these Midrashim ask the question, "About what is the *'inyan* speaking?" The manner in which the question is raised and answered indicates that *'inyan* here means "context" or "subject." It has a parallel formulation in one of the *middot* (hermeneutic principles) attributed to Rabbi Yishmael: "something learned from its context *('inyano)*."[23]

Consider the brief derashah on the prohibition for a Nazirite to contract corpse impurity in the book of Numbers:

> "He shall not come to a dead *nefesh*"[a] (Num. 6:6). Do I hear even the *nefashot* of domesticated animals[b] implied? It therefore teaches, "He shall not become impure for his father and mother . . ." (Num. 6:7). About what is the context *('inyan)* speaking? Human *nefashot*. (*Sifrei Numbers*, §26, p. 32)

> "עַל נֶפֶשׁ מֵת לֹא יָבֹא" (במדבר ו, ו). שומע אני נפשות בהמה במשמע? תלמוד לומר "לְאָבִיו וּלְאִמּוֹ . . . לֹא יִטַּמָּא" (שם, ז). במה עניין מדבר? בנפשות אדם.

The Midrash determines that "dead *nefesh*" refers only to human beings from the *'inyan*, the context, of the very next verse.[24]

Rabbi Akiva's bet midrash has no parallel term for *'inyan*. As shown in previous chapters, his school relies less on principles and has a less developed terminology, so the absence of a parallel fits the pattern.

It bears noting that for Rabbi Yishmael's academy context is not always a deciding factor. The following exegetical principle encapsulates this: "If it is not a subject *('inyan)* of X, make it a subject *('inyan)* of Y." If the immediate context doesn't make sense for an element of a verse, it gives the darshan a license, or even a mandate, to find another suitable context where it does.[25]

---

a Can mean "life," "living thing," and, in rabbinic psychology, "soul."
b Is coming into contact with an animal carcass also forbidden for a Nazirite?

Let us examine an application of this principle. In Numbers 10, Moses tries to convince his father-in-law Jethro to join him and his nation on their journey to the promised land. A midrash of Rabbi Yishmael's school interprets his words in the following manner:

> "To the place that the Lord said, 'That I shall give to you'" (Num. 10:29)—but converts *(gerim)* have no portion in it.[a] How, then, am I to fulfill, "It shall be that the tribe that the convert *(ha-ger)*[b] resides with[, there shall you give him his portion]" (Ezek. 47:23)? If it is not a subject *('inyan)* of inheritance, make it a subject *('inyan)* of atonement.[c] If he was in the tribe of Judah, he receives atonement through the tribe of Judah; if in the tribe of Benjamin, he receives atonement through the tribe of Benjamin.
>
> Another matter:
>
> If it is not a subject *('inyan)* of inheritance, make it a subject *('inyan)* of burial: converts are granted burial in the Land of Israel. (*Sifrei Numbers*, §78, p. 75)

"אֶל הַמָּקוֹם אֲשֶׁר אָמַר ה' אֹתוֹ אֶתֵּן לָכֶם" (במדבר י, כט)—ואין לגרים בו חלק. ומה אני מקיים "וְהָיָה בַשֵּׁבֶט אֲשֶׁר גָּר הַגֵּר [אִתּוֹ שָׁם תִּתְּנוּ נַחֲלָתוֹ]" (יחזקאל מז, כג)? אם אינו ענין לירושה, תנהו ענין לכפרה. שאם היה בשבט יהודה—מתכפר לו בשבט יהודה, בשבט בנימין—מתכפר לו בשבט בנימין.

דבר אחר: אם אינו ענין לירושה, תניהו ענין לקבורה. ניתן לגרים קבורה בארץ ישראל.

The Midrash views Moses's father-in-law as a convert, and it glosses God's promise to give the land "to you," addressing the Israelites, as excluding converts.[26] The halakhah observed by the darshan disallows inheritance of the land by converts. How does the darshan get around the verse in Ezekiel, which states outright that a convert is to receive an inheritance within the tribe he has chosen? By reinterpreting the verse's "portion" to mean a burial plot or atonement. The darshan is fully cognizant of the context and subject matter of the verse in Ezekiel, but he is forced to uproot the verse from there and give it a new halakhic home. In this case, it can be potentially rehomed in two unrelated areas of Halakhah.[27]

Context does not only show up on the midrashic radar when it competes with received tradition. In fact, the way that the Midrash explicates entire passages often shows respect for the text's continuity and integrity.[28] This especially stands out when there is a running debate between named Sages over the course of an entire pericope. Two prominent examples, which are too complicated to examine here, are Rabbi Yehoshua versus Rabbi Elazar ha-Moda'i in the aggadic portions of Tractates *Vayyassa'* and *'Amalek* in *Mekhilta de-Rabbi Yishmael,* and Rabbi Eliezer versus Rabbi Akiva on the law of the captive woman in *Sifrei*

---

a The Land of Israel; see Mishnah, *Ma'aser Sheni,* 5:14.
b This is the rabbinic understanding of the biblical word *ger.*
c If an entire tribe transgresses Torah law unintentionally, it must bring a sacrifice as atonement; see Mishnah, *Horayot,* 1:5.

Deuteronomy.²⁹ Another example of an *explication de texte* that builds on itself as it proceeds and picks up on broader themes woven throughout the entire biblical passage will be discussed in chapter 14.³⁰

How can it be that darshanim, especially those of Rabbi Yishmael's school, let context inform some of their interpretations, while they utterly ignored or flat out rejected it in others? How did their conception of the biblical text allow them to do this? It must be that the sequential reading of the Torah verse after verse was only one option among others for them, because the number of meanings it can produce is limited. The principle of maximal extraction of meaning, evidenced in the previous section, pushed them to approach the text from other directions. That is why Midrash is defined by intertextuality, the view in which all of Scripture can be the appropriate context for any one of its parts. The text surrounding a given phrase in a column of the Torah scroll imbues it with one meaning, but many others can emerge if the same phrase is overlain on the text of other columns.

The same logic frees Midrash from the shackles of syntax, so that it can atomize the text. Grammar reigns supreme only in the circumscribed fiefdom of human language. The divine text may speak in "human language," but its repository of meaning is not fully emptied by grammatical conventions. This atomization is far more extreme than de- or re-contextualization, because, instead of rearranging or moving the furniture, it dismantles it. Although such atomistic readings are more extreme in the Midrashim of Rabbi Akiva's school, they are also present in those of Rabbi Yishmael's school. Yet again, the differences are of degree and not of kind.

An example of atomization underscores how a darshan can manipulate context. The Torah orders the Israelites to be sure to offer God's daily offering at the appropriate time: "Command the Israelites and say to them, 'My sacrifice, My bread . . . you shall keep *(tishmeru)*, to offer up to Me at its fixed time'" (Num 28:2). Here is a midrash from Rabbi Yishmael's school:

"You shall take care *(tishmeru)*" (Num. 28:2)—so that you bring it only from what has been kept^a *(shamur)*. [. . .]

"You shall take care *(tishmeru)*"—so that the priests, Levites, and Israelites stand over it.^b (*Sifrei Numbers*, §142, p. 188)

"תִּשְׁמְרוּ" (במדבר כח, ב)—שלא יביא אלא מן השמור. [. . .]

"תִּשְׁמְרוּ"—שיהיו כהנים ולוים וישראל עומדים על גביו.

a Aside under protection so that it doesn't contract a blemish; see further Noam, *Megillat Ta'anit*, 170–172.
b Representatives of all three classes must be present in the Temple when the daily offering is brought, demonstrating that it is on behalf of the entire nation; see Mishnah, *Ta'anit*, 4:1.

In its original context, *tishmeru* means "you shall keep" and has an infinitive complement, "to offer up." In the Midrash, *tishmeru* is interpreted independently from "to offer up," and so acquires another shade of meaning: "you shall take care."[31] One cannot possibly attribute these two derashot to a misunderstanding or lack of syntactical knowledge, because the very next derashah is contextual: "'You shall keep, to offer up to Me at its fixed time'—why is it said?" The semi-syntactical reading is deliberate. The Midrash deems it equally legitimate to read the verse within the boundaries of syntax, straddling them, or outside of them.

The fact that Midrash is not restrained by strict word order fosters interpretive ingenuity. The most extreme examples of this can be found, as expected, in the Midrashim of Rabbi Akiva's school. The Torah orders the establishment of a judicial system and law enforcement: "Judges and officers you shall set for yourself in all your gates, which the Lord your God gives you according to your tribes, and they shall judge the people with righteous judgment" (Deut. 16:18). This translation of the verse follows the original Hebrew word order, so that the reader can see how the Midrash operates:

> Whence that a court is appointed for all Israel?[a] It therefore teaches, "Judges . . . you shall set for yourself" (Deut. 16:18).
>
> And whence that officers are appointed for all Israel? It therefore teaches, "[and] officers you shall set for yourself." [. . .]
>
> And whence that a court is appointed for every city? It therefore teaches, "Judges . . . [in all] your gates."
>
> And whence that officers are appointed for every city? It therefore teaches, "and officers . . . [in all] your gates."
>
> And whence that a court is appointed for every tribe? It therefore teaches, "Judges . . . according to your tribes."
>
> And whence that officers are appointed for every tribe? It therefore teaches, "and officers . . . according to your tribes."
>
> Rabbi Shimon ben Gamliel says, "according to your tribes, and they shall judge"—it is a mitzvah for every tribe to judge itself. (*Sifrei Deuteronomy*, §144, p. 197)

מנין שממנין בית דין לכל ישראל? תלמוד לומר "שֹׁפְטִים" "תִּתֶּן לְךָ" (דברים טז, יח). ומנין שממנין שוטרים לכל ישראל? תלמוד לומר "שֹׁטְרִים תִּתֶּן לְךָ". [. . .] ומנין שממנין בית דין לכל עיר ועיר? תלמוד לומר "שֹׁפְטִים" "שְׁעָרֶיךָ". ומנין שממנין שטרים לכל עיר ועיר? תלמוד לומר "וְשֹׁטְרִים" "שְׁעָרֶיךָ". ומנין שממנין בית דין לכל שבט? תלמוד לומר "שֹׁפְטִים" "לִשְׁבָטֶיךָ". ומנין שממנין שטרים לכל שבט ושבט? תלמוד לומר "וְשֹׁטְרִים" "לִשְׁבָטֶיךָ".

רבן שמעון בן גמליאל אומר "לִשְׁבָטֶיךָ וְשָׁפְטוּ"—מצוה על כל שבט ושבט להיות דן את שבטו.

---

a Referring to the Great Court in Jerusalem; see Mishnah, *Sanhedrin*, 11:2. The Babylonian Talmud (Sanhedrin 16b) indeed cites this derasha as a source for the mishnaic laws of Sanhedrin.

At first glance, this midrash derives the necessary details from the verse in classic fashion: "Whence . . . ? It therefore teaches. . . ." But one can readily see from the points of ellipsis that the biblical prooftexts are not your typical quotes; they skip intervening words at will. The derashot are alternately connecting one of its first two words, "judges" and "officers," with words that appear much later.[32]

Behind this type of derashah stands a conception of the Torah as a string of utterances that can be mixed and matched to produce new meanings. The anonymous darshan can join "judges/officers" with "according to your tribes," while Rabbi Shimon ben Gamaliel can link "according to your tribes" with the next verb "and they shall judge," thus running roughshod over the natural break. In this midrash, the derashot contract space to bring distant words together, and new legal details are thereby learned or traditions anchored. Note, though, that all these combinations obey a rule: they all respect the word order of the verse even when skipping words.[33]

Another noteworthy point about this midrash is its interspersion of contemporary realities with long-gone ones. The "judges" of the biblical era are translated into the rabbinical court of the tannaitic period.[34] The "officers," on the other hand, remain officers, despite the fact that none existed to enforce Halakhah in the rabbinic era. The two exist side by side, the one real and the other not. This pattern repeats with "every city" and "every tribe," the first being realistic and the second historical or utopian.[35] Whatever is learned from the Torah has equal status, whether it is pertinent to the current state or not. Recall that the Mishnah also equates the real and the imagined, since both are subsumed under a single body of oral law.[36]

In the above midrash, the unconventional readings do not expressly contradict the overall thrust or tenor of the verse. A more extreme derashah already encountered in chapter 10, however, does gainsay the meaning of the verse:

> "[Do not oppress] widow or orphan" (Ex. 22:21). I only have a widow and orphan, whence all other people? It therefore teaches, "Do not oppress anyone *(kol)*" (Ex. 22:21)—the words of Rabbi Akiva. (*Mekhilta de-Rabbi Yishmael, Nezikin*, §18, p. 313)[37]

> "אַלְמָנָה וְיָתוֹם [לֹא תְעַנּוּן]" (שמות כב, כא). אין לי אלא אלמנה ויתום, שאר כל אדם מנין? תלמוד לומר "כָּל לֹא תְעַנּוּן"—דברי ר' עקיבה.

The verse does not say: "Do not oppress anyone." To the contrary, it is pointedly about not kicking the downtrodden. The darshan selectively omits words so that he can universalize what is otherwise a narrowly conceived prohibition.[38]

This textual flexibility, of which there are numerous examples, could be classified merely as a rhetorical artifice, a way for the darshan to highlight certain parts of the text while dimming others. But it seems far more likely, given the preceding, that the Midrash considers this a completely valid form of reading based on its understanding of the divine nature of the Torah.

This section has explained how context is one factor, and not an overriding one, in rabbinic interpretation. Sometimes, it can be partly acknowledged and partly ignored, as if the words in question exist on two separate planes. The darshan can dance over words extraneous to the point he wants to make or couple words or phrases at a remove from each other. When necessary, he can construe words as belonging to subject matter outside the immediate verse. It is the midrashic conceptualization of the Torah as an iridescent text, glittering with new shades of meaning when viewed from shifting angles, that encourages this textual manipulation.

Still, the midrashic sandbox has ground rules. Verses can be atomized, but the meaning of words cannot be denied. The Torah's word order leaves indelible impressions even when words are left out. Midrash cannot rewrite the Torah and must respect its basic integrity.

C. A TYPOLOGY OF MIDRASHIC CONSTRUCTIONS

This and the preceding chapter have covered a lot of ground and much of the discussion has been nuanced and complex. This concluding section lays out the fundamental structures and some of the key points about them. Midrash presents the reader with chaotic variations, but these exist only on the surface. If we can understand the currents underneath, we can efficiently navigate the sea of Midrash.

Deductions

Chapter 10 discussed principles of interpretation, like *kelal u-ferat* (generality and particular) and *binyan av* (paradigmatic verse). Since much of Torah law is casuistic, these guide the interpreter in determining the scope of a particular halakhah. Additionally, because the traditions inherited by the Tannaim did not always match biblical law, these principles acted as tools to harmonize them.

The most common type of derashah takes the form "Just as X, so too Y." The Torah explicitly states the rule with regard to one person, object, or situation, and the darshan extends it to others. Ambiguous terminology or subject matter is clarified by qualifications found elsewhere. When this derashah goes through thousands of iterations across Torah law, a complete legal system is the output. It is one of the most basic interpretive moves of Midrash, and in chapter 15 we will see a derashah like this attributed to the early Sage known as Hillel the Elder.

We saw this type of derashah in our comparison of the sectarian exegesis at Qumran with rabbinic interpretation of two similar halakhic passages, one about a seducer and the other about a rapist:

> "He must weigh out silver" (Ex. 22:16)—but we have not heard how much. So I reason: It says "silver" here and it says "silver" there (Deut. 22:29). Just as there it's "fifty [shekels of] silver," so too here it's fifty [shekels of] silver. (*Mekhilta de-Rabbi Yishmael*, Nezikin, §17, p. 309)

In Deuteronomy 22, the Torah sets the amount of silver the rapist must pay at fifty shekels, but in Exodus 22 the fine levied on the seducer is unquantified. The Midrash decides the sum based on the more explicit source.

The borrowing of details through analogy occurs with aggadic material as well. The Torah says about the crossing of the Sea of Reeds that God "cast horse and rider into the sea" (Ex. 15:1). The Midrash wants a more dramatic fate for the Egyptians, one that is worthy of the poetic song.

> Rabbi Assi ben Shammai says, It says "horse" (Ex. 15:1) here ambiguously,[a] and it says "horse" there explicitly, as it says, "On that day, says the Lord, I will strike every horse with confusion etc." (Zech. 12:4). And it says, "And this shall be the plague etc." (Zech. 14:12), and it says, "And so shall there be a plague against horse etc. [like this plague]" (14:15). The explicit one comes to teach about the ambiguous one: Just as the explicit one is with fifty plagues, so the ambiguous one is with fifty plagues. (*Mekhilta de-Rabbi Yishmael, Shirata*, §2, p. 125)

ר' אסי בן שמאי אומר: נאמר כאן "סוּס" (שמות טו, א) סתום, ונאמר להלן סוס מפורש, שנאמר "בַּיּוֹם הַהוּא נְאֻם ה' אַכֶּה כָל סוּס בַּתִּמָּהוֹן" וג' (זכריה יב, ד). ואומר "וְזֹאת תִּהְיֶה הַמַּגֵּפָה" וג' (שם יד, יב), ואומר "וְכֵן תִּהְיֶה מַגֵּפַת הַסּוּס" וג' (שם, יד, טו). בא מפורש ולימד על הסתום: מה מפורש בחמשים מכה, אף סתום בחמשים מכה.

The Midrash is unsatisfied with God casting the chariots into the roiling waters. Perhaps that death is too mercifully quick to fit the crime? It therefore looks to Zechariah, where warhorses are also brought down with their riders. While the prophecy has more than enough gory details to spare for the Song of the Sea (Ex. 15), the translation does not fully work. One can envision "confusion" at the sea, but unless the water is caustic, why would the eyes of the horses melt in their sockets, as described in Zechariah? However we to envision it, the idea that God struck the Egyptians with additional plagues at the sea is recorded elsewhere in the *Mekhilta* and the Passover Haggadah. One can further suggest that the darshan intends to show that there is a pattern in history: God avenged His people in Egypt and will do so again, quite mercilessly, at the end of time. The midrashic principle of biblical intertextuality allows non-legal passages from the ends of the Bible to illuminate one another.

Inclusions and Exclusions

Chapter 10 demonstrated that localized inclusions and exclusions dot every page of the Midrashim of Rabbi Akiva's school, but they are not altogether absent from the Midrashim of Rabbi Yishmael's school. Their purpose is simultaneously to sharpen the boundaries of the

---

[a] Meaning that its precise fate is uncertain, even though the reader understands implicitly that by being cast into the sea it drowned.

law and to justify ostensible textual superfluities. To round out that discussion, let us consider one final example, this time from a Midrash of Rabbi Yishmael's school.

Exodus 12 sets forth the laws of the paschal lamb that was sacrificed by the Israelites in Egypt. These laws are numerous, so the Midrash spends time determining what is limited to that initial sacrifice and what endures for the sacrifice to be brought annually on Pesach. For instance, does the requirement that the sacrifice be an unblemished, male, and yearling lamb or kid apply for all time?

> "It shall be *(yihyeh)* for you" (Ex. 12:5)—to include the paschal sacrifice for generations,[a] so that one may bring it only from sheep or from goats—the words of Rabbi Eliezer. (*Mekhilta de-Rabbi Yishmael, Pasha,* §4, p. 13)

> "יִהְיֶה לָכֶם" (שמות יב, ה)—להביא פסח דורות, שלא יביא אלא מן הכשבים ומן העזים—דברי ר' אליעזר.

"It shall be for you" could be omitted and the rest of the verse would read fine. Its presence, as well as the potentially future orientation of the imperfect *yihyeh* form, suggests to Rabbi Eliezer that the law is for all generations.

While this looks like a derashah that is generating new law or elaborating Halakhah, the fact that Rabbi Yoshiyah and Rabbi Yonatan in the continuation learn the very same legal expansion from other phrases indicates that this is a retrospective, anchoring derashah using an opportune turn of phrase. This is buttressed by another derashah from the same Midrash that this time excludes, rather than includes, the post-Egypt sacrifice from another law:

> "On the tenth of this month" (Ex. 12:3)—to exclude the paschal sacrifice for generations. For the taking of the paschal sacrifice in Egypt was on the tenth, and the taking of the paschal sacrifice for generations is at any time. (*Mekhilta de-Rabbi Yishmael, Pasha,* §4, pp. 10–11)

> "בֶּעָשֹׂר לַחֹדֶשׁ הַזֶּה" (שמות יב, ג)—להוציא פסח דורות. שפסח מצרים מקחו מבעשור, ופסח דורות מקחו בכל זמן.

Only the one sacrifice in Egypt had to be taken on the tenth of Nisan. This derashah, too, aligns biblical law with rabbinic tradition, according to which there is no set time for purchasing a sacrifice. The darshanim of Rabbi Yishmael's school, like those of Rabbi Akiva's, included and excluded, expanded and contracted biblical law according to the received

---

a This is the sacrifice to be brought in subsequent years, called "Pesach for generations" after the language of the verse (Ex. 12:17). See further Rosen-Zvi snd Kroizer, "'Throughout Your Generations.'"

rabbinic tradition. They, too, anchored the accepted law in the Torah while justifying the perfect precision of its text.

Hypotheticals

Chapter 11 dwelled on the prevalent construction "Could it be / Do I hear . . .? It therefore says. . . ." Justification of the text mainly motivates this type of derashah. By inventing a hypothetical alternative reading, the darshan reveals the Torah's words as crucial to correct one's thinking. While most hypotheticals in the Midrash serve as a pretext for this justification, scholars have discovered that some potential interpretations were actually espoused by people, and the derashot were intended to disqualify them as legitimate readings.

For example, the Torah allows a father to annul the vows of his daughter for as long as she is "in her father's household, in her youth" (Num 30:4). What are the precise parameters of "youth"?

> "And if a woman [takes a vow]" (Num. 30:4). Do I hear once she has reached majority? It therefore teaches, "in her youth *(bi-ne'ureha).*"[a] Alternatively, do I hear even a minor from "in her youth"? It therefore teaches, "And if a woman." How so? She has left the category of the minor and has yet to enter the category of majority.
>
> Hence they said:[b] "At twelve years and one day, her vows are effective."[c] (*Sifrei Numbers*, §153, p. 200)

"וְאִשָּׁה" (במדבר ל, ד). שומע אני משתבגור? תלמוד לומר "בִנְעֻרֶיהָ". או "בִנְעֻרֶיהָ" שומע ואפילו קטנה? תלמוד לומר "אִשָּׁה". הא כיצד? יצאת מכלל קטנה ולכלל בגרות לא באת. מיכן אמרו: "בת י"ב שנה ויום אחד נדריה קיימין".

As Moshe Halbertal argues, the Midrash is in the thick of a controversy surrounding a father's authority over his daughters. Tannaitic Halakhah sought to reduce his reach, but it couldn't limit the verse's annulment to a very young age, because vow-taking in Halakhah requires sufficient intellectual maturity. The Sages had no choice but to posit an intermediate stage of female development, in which a young woman has the presence of mind to make a vow but her father is allowed to annul it.[39] The initial position of the Midrash, that the father can annul his daughter's vow while she is still under his roof, is not a mere theoretical option to be rejected by the verse; it is the simple reading of the Torah and was likely the

---

a In biblical Hebrew *ne'urim* is an abstract noun meaning "youth," but in the rabbinic understanding it refers to the *na'arah*, a young woman in the intermediate halakhic stage between minority and majority. For the precise duration of this period, see BT *Ketubbot* 39a with parallels.

b Mishnah, *Niddah*, 5:6. On the use of "hence they said" in the Midrash, see chapter 15, section B.

c For at that age she is considered mentally mature; see the above mishnah.

strongly enforced cultural norm. Until marriage, the father had the final say.⁴⁰ It is this long-standing conception that our derashah strives to oppose.

Logical Reasoning

Chapter 11 documented how Midrash uses legal reasoning as a justificatory tool. If reason can lead the student of the Torah astray, the Torah must dedicate some words to shutting down that intellectual avenue.

> "An Ammonite or a Moabite shall not enter the assembly of the Lord"[a] (Deut. 23:4)—the verse speaks of males and not females.[b]
>
> Another matter:
>
> "An Ammonite"—but not an Ammonitess; "a Moabite"—but not a Moabitess—the words of Rabbi Yehudah.
>
> But the Sages say,[c] "because they did not greet you with bread and water" (Deut. 23:5). Who generally does the greeting? Men and not women.
>
> For it would have been logical: If it equates women with men regarding a *mamzer*,[d] about whom "forever" is not said,[e] then isn't it logical to equate women with men regarding Ammonites and Moabites, about whom "forever" is said? [. . .] It therefore teaches, "An Ammonite"—but not a Ammonitess—the words of Rabbi Yehudah. (*Sifrei Deuteronomy*, §249, p. 277)

"לֹא יָבֹא עַמּוֹנִי וּמוֹאָבִי" (דברים כג, ד)—בזכרים הכתוב מדבר ולא בנקיבות.

דבר אחר: "עַמּוֹנִי"—ולא עמונית; "מוֹאָבִי" ולא מואבית—דברי ר' יהודה.

וחכמים אומרים: "עַל דְּבַר אֲשֶׁר לֹא קִדְּמוּ אֶתְכֶם בַּלֶּחֶם וּבַמַּיִם" (דברים כג, ה). מי דרכן לקדם? אנשים ולא נשים.

שהיה בדין: ומה ממזר שלא נאמר בו "עַד עוֹלָם"' עשה בו נשים כאנשים, עמנים ומאבים שנאמר בהן "עַד עוֹלָם" אינו דין שנעשה בהם נשים כאנשים? [. . .] תלמוד לומר "עַמּוֹנִי" ולא עמונית—דברי ר' יהודה.

The exclusion of women from the prohibition against marrying Ammonites and Moabites is a rabbinic innovation. It might be motivated by a desire to account for King David being

---

   a This refers to marriage in the rabbinic understanding; see Mishnah, *Kiddushin*, 4:3 and *Yadayim*, 4:4.
   b Female converts from these nations may halakhically marry Jewish men; see Mishnah, *Yevamot*, 8:3 and *Yadayim*, 4:4.
   c They disagree not with the halakhah but rather with Rabbi Yehudah's reasoning.
   d The progeny of first-degree incest or adultery; see Mishnah, *Yevamot*, 4:13.
   e In the previous verse, Deuteronomy 23:3, which prohibits a *mamzer* from ever entering "the assembly of the Lord."

the progeny of Ruth, a Moabitess, as recorded in the genealogical list at the end of the book of Ruth.[41] The Midrash stresses the legal novelty by explaining how logical reasoning would lead to the opposite conclusion. It argues that if we take the law about the *mamzer* as a template, neither the men nor the women of Ammon and Moab would be admitted into the Jewish collective.

This deployment of logical reasoning justifies the need for words in a verse and marks the derashah as unobvious. The "failure" of pure reason to arrive at the Halakhah on its own underscores both the necessity of the verse and the innovativeness of the midrash.

Identifications and Translations

Derashot with the least complex structure are identifications: "X is nothing but Y." When bound together, these derashot form a kind of lexicon. Translating biblical Hebrew into mishnaic Hebrew or choosing among possible meanings does not exhaust their function, though. They operate on words that do not require semantic translation so much as conceptual translation. Two examples, one from the domain of Halakhah and the other from the world of Aggadah, make plain what I mean.

The halakhic derashah concerns the laws of Shabbat. Moses instructs the people not to go out and collect manna on Shabbat, and some fail to obey. God is frustrated at this disobedience and says that the Israelites will be given a double portion on Friday, lessening the urge to go out and collect it on Shabbat. The *Mekhilta* expounds:

> "Every man should sit where he is" (Ex. 16:29)—these are four cubits.[a]
>
> "No man shall leave his place"—these are two thousand cubits.[b] (*Mekhilta de-Rabbi Yishmael*, Vayyassa', §5, p. 170)

> "שְׁבוּ אִישׁ תַּחְתָּיו" (שמות טז, כט)—אלו ארבע אמות. "אַל יֵצֵא אִישׁ מִמְּקֹמוֹ"—אלו אלפים אמה.

The identificatory derashot justify God's repeated commands to stay put by anchoring halakhic traditions about Shabbat observance in them. Biblical commands are translated into concrete and well-defined concepts in rabbinic Halakhah.[42]

The aggadic example, also from the *Mekhilta*, makes identifications in the Song of the Sea (Ex. 15):

---

a One may not move an object more than four cubits in the public domain on Shabbat; see Tractates *Shabbat* and *'Eruvin*.

b At the onset of Shabbat one's "place" is fixed, from which may not travel more than two thousand cubits in any direction.

"[Your right hand] smashes the enemy" (Ex. 15:6)—this is Pharaoh, as it says, "The enemy said etc."ᵃ (Ex. 15:9).

Another interpretation: This is Esau, as it says, "Because the enemy has said against you etc."ᵇ (Ezek. 36:2). (*Mekhilta de-Rabbi Yishmael, Shirata*, §5, p. 134)

"תִּרְעַץ אוֹיֵב" (שמות טו, ו)—זה פרעה, שנאמר "אָמַר אוֹיֵב וגו'" (שמות טו, ט).

דבר אחר: זה עשו, שנאמר "יַעַן אָמַר הָאוֹיֵב עֲלֵיכֶם הֶאָח וגו'" (יחזקאל לו, ב).

Most derashot that consist of nothing but a simple identification are aggadic in nature, like this one. Chapter 9 contrasted this type of derashah with the exegesis of the *pesher* literature from Qumran, which spells out how the Torah was being realized in the interpreter's own time. Unlike *pesher*, the first derashah here confines itself to biblical time. "The enemy" is Egypt personified, and it is only natural for Pharaoh to be its inimical embodiment. The second derashah, however, moves closer to *pesher*. Since the Sages identified Edom with the Roman Empire, suddenly the biblical song spoke to the present condition of the Jewish people. Still, this midrash differs from *pesher* by not being specific, and not privileging the second interpretation over the first one. In this way, Midrash is both similar to and different from its interpretive precedents. The uniqueness of Midrash is explored further in the next chapter.

---

a The quote from the enemy is in the first-personal singular, so it could reasonably refer to the leader of the Egyptians, Pharaoh.

b In Ezekiel the foe is Edom, who is identified in the Bible with Esau. The rabbis identify Esau/Edom with Rome.

THIRTEEN

The Self-Awareness and Didacticism of Midrash

To what extent is Midrash reflexive and are its practitioners aware of exactly what they are doing? Early scholars of rabbinics believed that, like a shy person at a dance, the darshanim could only let loose textually because they lacked self-awareness. Isaac Heinemann forcefully argued for Midrash as an "organic" outgrowth of the text, with no sharp line defining where the Torah ends and interpretation begins.[1] More recently, scholars have tried to restore interpretive autonomy, in a sense, to the darshanim. Moshe Halbertal, for example, has argued that the very structure of comparative Midrash, which sifts through interpretations to isolate the best of them, perforce generates awareness of a gap between text and exposition, and that this is its purpose.[2]

The question of reflexiveness is knotty, and two analyses will help us cut to the heart of it. The first (sections A–B) focus on the relationship between the language of the Torah and that of the Midrash, and on the explicit midrashic markers that call attention to their differences. The second (sections C–D) examines specific terms that express consciousness on the part of the darshan: *ki-shemu'o* and *eino tzarikh*. By the end of the chapter, we will have seen that Midrash definitely operates with full knowledge of its being an entity distinct from the biblical text.

A. BIBLICAL HEBREW VERSUS MISHNAIC HEBREW

One innovative feature of Midrash is that it neatly separates biblical quotation from exegetical interpretation. This starkly contrasts with the genre of rewritten Scripture, which rewrites the original in line with its own interpretation.[3] A similar phenomenon occurs in setting off biblical Hebrew from the Hebrew of the Midrash's day. Some derashot are brief glosses that simply translate biblical Hebrew words and phrases into mishnaic Hebrew equivalents. The meaning of outdated biblical idioms, curious usages, or rare words would not have been evident to the average student. Below is a sample of this regarding a verbal phrase:

"The Lord heard and His anger flared *(vayyiḥar appo)*" (Num. 11:1)—the Omnipresent heard and became filled with anger *(nitmalle ḥeimah)* on their account. *(Sifrei Numbers, §85, p. 85)*

"וַיִּשְׁמַע ה' וַיִּחַר אַפּוֹ" (במדבר יא, א)—שמע המקום ונתמלא עליהן חימה.

A certain preposition could sound off, the same way those from Old or Middle English would grate on our modern ears, and needed to be replaced with the one in current use.[4] Or a phrase might seem circumlocutory, since Mishnaic Hebrew could express the same idea succinctly or more precisely:

"That it is not a tree for food *('etz ma'akhal)*" (Deut. 20:20)—this is a barren tree *(illan serak)*. *(Sifrei Deuteronomy, §204, p. 239)*

"כִּי לֹא עֵץ מַאֲכָל הוּא" (דברים כ, כ)—זה אילן סרק.

Mishnaic Hebrew uses *illan* instead of biblical Hebrew *'etz* for "tree," and it also has a category for non-food trees: *illan serak*. Biblical Hebrew, like English, has no such precise classification.

Words also undergo changes in meaning over time. By the time of the Sages, the root *y-sh-b* was no longer typically used to mean "dwell" or "live" and was used more narrowly to mean "sit." This necessitated a gloss, using the more common word from the root *d-w-r*:

"You shall live *(teshvu)* in sukkot for seven days" (Lev. 23:42)—*teshvu* is nothing but *taduru*. *(Sifra, Emor, 17:5, 103a)*

"בַּסֻּכֹּת תֵּשְׁבוּ שִׁבְעַת יָמִים" (ויקרא כג, מב)—אין תשבו אלא תדורו.

Sitting down and having a meal isn't the only activity that must take place in the special booth for Sukkot, the Midrash conveys. One must live in the sukkah. Biblical Hebrew *y-sh-b* overlapped semantically with mishnaic Hebrew *d-w-r* (the equivalent of biblical *g-w-r*)[5] and the Midrash points this out.

When a language changes or where different dialects are involved, a word may shed meanings or acquire new ones. Regarding dwelling in the sukkah, the meaning of *y-sh-b* was narrower in mishnaic Hebrew than in biblical Hebrew, so the Midrash supplied the mishnaic Hebrew verb that best captured the Torah's original intent. In many other

Self-Awareness and Didacticism

derashot, however, the Midrash reinterprets biblical Hebrew words in light of additional meanings that they take in mishnaic Hebrew.[6] In biblical Hebrew, *l-k-ḥ* has the general meaning of "to take," but in mishnaic Hebrew it means a specific taking in exchange for money: "to buy." To interpret the former in light of the latter has halakhic ramifications:

> "And take *(ve-yikḥu)* for yourselves a red heifer" (Num. 19:2)—from the Temple fund.[a] (*Sifrei Numbers*, §123, p. 151)

"וְיִקְחוּ אֵלֶיךָ פָרָה אֲדֻמָּה" (במדבר יט, ב)—מתרומת הלשכה.

The Torah intends that the nation should take a red heifer to perform the ritual. But the fact that *l-k-ḥ* has the specific meaning of acquisition in mishnaic Hebrew allows the Sages to solve a problem: Who should put up the funds for this ultra-rare animal? The answer is the entire people through the communal fund.

> "When a man takes *(yikkaḥ)* a wife and marries her" (Deut. 24:1). It teaches that a wife can be acquired with money. (*Sifrei Deuteronomy*, §268, p. 287)

"כִּי יִקַּח אִישׁ אִשָּׁה וּבְעָלָהּ" (דברים כד, א)—מלמד שהאשה נקנית בכסף.

If *l-k-ḥ* means "buy," and things are bought with money, then the verse is saying that a man can acquire a wife with cash, as rabbinic Halakhah states.[7] What these two derashot, so dissimilar in content, share is their reinterpretation of a biblical word in light of what was the current usage.

In these derashot, the line between the biblical quotation and the rabbinic translation is clearly drawn, but this is not always so. At times, the Midrash may say, "The Torah said," and then proceed to paraphrase the verses in mishnaic Hebrew. The paraphrase is not always a simple restatement in other words but can include rabbinic exegesis. Our earlier discussion of the anchoring derashah included such an example: "Since the Torah said, Place tefillin (phylacteries) on your arm and place tefillin on your head."[8] Search all you will, no such verse can be found in the Torah. The Torah does say, "And it shall be a sign for you on your hand, and as a reminder between your eyes" (Ex. 13:9), which the Sages reinterpret as the tefillin of the arm and of the head. The Sages are paraphrasing the Torah according to their own halakhic interpretation and ascribing it to Scripture itself.[9]

At times, derashot will even speak for the Torah or even God in first person, extending what the verse says:

---

a A communal account for Temple activities funded by the half-shekel tax; see Mishnah, *Shekalim*, ch. 3.

Rabbi Shimon says, Since we find that a domesticated animal which actively or passively copulated[a] with a person is invalid,[b] could it also be for the person?[c] It therefore teaches, "it is [an abomination[d] to the Lord your God]" (Deut. 17:1)—I spoke about the sacrifice, but I did not speak about the one sacrificing it. (*Sifrei Deuteronomy*, §147, p. 202)

ר׳ שמעון אומר: לפי שמצינו ברובע ובנרבע שהן פסולין בבהמה, יכול אף באדם? תלמוד לומר "[תּוֹעֲבַת ה׳ אֱלֹהֶיךָ] הוּא" (דברים יז, א)—בזבח דיברתי, ולא דיברתי בזובח.

Who is speaking in the first person at the end of the derashah? In context, it is either the Torah or God (who are anyway equated in the rabbinic mind). The Midrash speaks in its or His name.[10]

We also encounter derashot that mimic the second-person address used in the verse:[11]

"I am your[e] portion and your inheritance" (Num. 18:20). At My table do you eat,[f] and at My table do you drink. (*Sifrei Numbers*, §119, p. 142)

"אֲנִי חֶלְקְךָ וְנַחֲלָתְךָ" (במדבר יח, כ)—על שולחני אתה אוכל, ועל שולחני אתה שותה.

Even where there is no paraphrase of the verse or conscious imitation of it, the language of the Torah exerts influence over the Midrash:[12]

"The Lord your God shall establish for you a prophet like me from your midst, from your brothers" (Deut. 18:15).

"A prophet . . . from your midst"—but not from outside the Land.

"From your brothers"—but not from others.

"The Lord your God shall establish for you"—but not for the Gentiles.[13]

How am I to maintain, "I have made you a prophet for the Gentiles" (Jer. 1:5)? For those who act like Gentiles. (*Sifrei Deuteronomy*, §175, p. 221)

"נָבִיא מִקִּרְבְּךָ מֵאַחֶיךָ כָּמֹנִי יָקִים לְךָ ה׳ אֱלֹהֶיךָ" (דברים יח, טו).

"נָבִיא מִקִּרְבְּךָ"—ולא מחוצה לארץ. "מֵאַחֶיךָ"—ולא מאחרים. "יָקִים לְךָ ה׳"—ולא לגוים. מה אני מקיים "נָבִיא לַגּוֹיִם נְתַתִּיךָ" (ירמיה א, ה)? בנוהג מנהג גוים.

a A male animal that penetrated a woman, or a female animal penetrated by a man.
b As a sacrifice.
c Someone who copulated with an animal may not bring a sacrifice?
d This is being read as an exclusion: the animal is an abomination but not the person.
e The verse is addressed to Aaron, a Kohen (priest).
f Meaning that, from the altar, the showbread table, etc. the priests receive a portion to eat.

Consider the lack of linguistic coherence here. At first it speaks of "others," and then it mentions "Gentiles." Why the shift when it is talking about the same group—non-Jews? "Others" is the Midrash's term; it switches to "Gentiles" in anticipation of the verse in Jeremiah that immediately follows. The interlacing of biblical language in derashot leans toward rewritten Scripture, although they remain distinct literary forms.[14]

On the one hand, Midrash differentiates between the biblical text it interprets and its own exegesis. On the other hand, it is influenced by Scripture and even speaks in its name. It has not quite cut the umbilical cord to earlier forms of interpretation. This tension uniquely characterizes the new rabbinic genre of Midrash.

B. DIFFERENTIATING MARKERS

In some derashot, the Midrash explicitly distinguishes between itself and the Torah, which is a clear break from earlier interpretive trends. A good example is a derashah on a verse about the offering of the firstborn domesticated kosher animal as a sacrifice. It uses a plural form, "they are holy," which is appropriate in context, but which the Midrash understands to include other sacrifices:

> Rabbi Yoshiyah says, "They are holy" (Num. 18:17)—why is it said? To include the tithe[a] and paschal sacrifice in requiring one pouring,[b] for we hear nothing about them[c] in the entire Torah. (*Sifrei Numbers*, §118, p. 139)

> ר' יאשיה אומר: "קֹדֶשׁ הֵם" (במדבר יח, יז)—למה נאמר? להביא את המעשר והפסח שיטענו שפיכה אחת, שלא שמענו להן בכל התורה.

The plural language is a springboard for Rabbi Yoshiyah to extrapolate the law regarding other sacrifices, whose precise procedure is unstated in the Torah. Of interest in this context is the demarcation between the Torah's contents and the Midrash's interpretive move. The Midrashim of Rabbi Yishmael's school declare about biblical laws here and elsewhere, "for we hear nothing about them in the entire Torah," a declaration that deepens the furrow between what the Torah says—or rather doesn't say—and what the Midrash includes. Since the Midrash learns these laws from the text of the Torah itself, it could have formulated them as Torah law or as an unquestionable, natural corollary of the Torah law. Instead, it distinguishes between what the Torah says explicitly and what the Midrash makes it say. It presents the Torah as a kind of inert material that the midrashic chemist coaxes into reacting.

---

    a Not an agricultural tithe but the annual obligation to offer one out of every ten domesticated kosher animals as a sacrifice.
    b Of their blood on the altar.
    c About what is to be done with their blood.

Chapter 10 discussed Rabbi Yishmael and his school's exegetical principles, which are candidly described as operations of the interpreter. Here is an example:

"When men quarrel etc." (Ex. 21:18). I only have men, whence women? Rabbi Yishmael would say, Since it did not specify regarding all damages in the Torah, but it did specify regarding one of them that men are like women, I can specify that in all damages in the Torah men are like women. (*Mekhilta de-Rabbi Yishmael, Nezikin*, §6, p. 269)

"וְכִי יְרִיבֻן אֲנָשִׁים" וג' (שמות כא, יח). אין לי אלא אנשים, נשים מנין? היה ר' ישמעאל אומר: הואיל וכל הנזקין שבתורה סתם, ופרט באחד מהן שעשה בו נשים כאנשים, פורט אני כל הנזקין שבתורה לעשות בהן נשים כאנשים.

The Torah only specifies in one place, but "I"—says the darshan—can specify for all of them. The darshan is explicit about his role as interpreter and about how his legal extension goes beyond what the Torah contains.

In the same way that there is a range with language, as observed in the previous section, so too there is a spectrum of self-reflection. There are cases where the darshan of Rabbi Yishmael's school steps out of the frame and attributes the interpretation to Scripture itself.[15] Thus, on the very same issue, not long after Rabbi Yishmael's pronouncement, Rabbi Yoshiyah says:

"A man or woman" (Ex. 21:29)—Scripture comes to make women like men in all damages in the Torah. (*Mekhilta de-Rabbi Yishmael, Nezikin*, §6, p. 269)

"אִישׁ אוֹ אִשָּׁה" (שמות כא, כט) – בא הכתוב והשווה אשה לאיש בכל הנזקין שבתורה.

According to this formulation, the Torah itself, and not a later darshan, makes the legal equation.

This dialectic is also present, albeit differently, in the Midrashim of Rabbi Akiva's school. That school tends to pick apart every word, balancing reams of derashot, like an inverted pyramid, on the tip of a *yod*. Pulling in the other direction is the terminology that distinguishes between verses and the convoluted midrashic processes imposed on them. Let us examine a derashah on the obligation to remove agricultural tithes from one's home:

I only have *ma'aser 'ani*,[a] about which Scripture is speaking. Whence to include all other tithes?[b] It therefore teaches, "the tithe of your produce" (Deut. 14:28)—it included *(ribbah)*. (*Sifrei Deuteronomy*, §109, p. 170)

---

a During years three and six of the sabbatical cycle, a 10-percent tithe for the poor is separated instead of *ma'aser sheni*. For more on the various tithes, see part 1, chapter 2, section E.

b In the requirement to remove them from one's house on Pesach (Passover) of the third and sixth years; see Mishnah, *Ma'aser Sheni*, 5:10.

אין לי אלא מעשר עני, שבו דיבר הכתוב, מנין לרבות שאר מעשרות? תלמוד לומר "מַעְשַׂר תְּבוּאָתְךָ" (דברים יד, כח)—ריבה.

The prepositional phrase "about which Scripture is speaking" *(she-bo dibber ha-katuv)* occurs a few more times in *Sifrei Deuteronomy*, where it always spotlights the gulf separating explicit Scripture and midrashic inclusion.

The Midrashim of Rabbi Akiva's academy regularly discuss inclusions and their limits.[16] The basic format establishes the Torah law and then sets out to expand it: "I only have X. Whence Y?" Sometimes there are limits on this expansion, resulting in a lengthier formula: "I only have X. Whence even Y? It therefore teaches. . . . Could it be that even Z? It therefore teaches. . . ." The inclusions and exclusions characteristic of this school maintain awareness of the distinction between verse and Midrash.

Another example of preserving this distinction involves a verse that sends the would-be soldier home from the front line if he has only just planted a vineyard and not managed to enjoy its fruits:

"A vineyard" (Deut. 20:6). I only have a vineyard, whence someone who plants five fruit trees and even of the five species?[a] It therefore teaches, "who has planted."[b] Could it be even someone who plants four fruit trees or five barren trees? It therefore teaches, "a vineyard."

Rabbi Eliezer ben Yaakov says, Only the vineyard is included *(be-mashma')*. (*Sifrei Deuteronomy*, §195, p. 235)

"כֶּרֶם"—אין לי אלא כרם, מנין לנוטע ה אילני מאכל ואפילו מחמשת המינין? תלמוד לומר "אֲשֶׁר נָטַע". יכול אף הנוטע ד אילני מאכל וה אילני סרק? תלמוד לומר "כֶּרֶם".

ר' אליעזר בן יעקב אומר: אין לי במשמע אלא כרם.

Both Tannaim acknowledge that there is only a vineyard in the verse. They wonder if this narrow case serves as an example so that the law should apply to other similar cases. What if someone plants an orchard of pomegranates? Would not getting to enjoy the tangy arils be less of a disappointment? The anonymous *tanna kamma* endeavors to expand the verse's scope, while Rabbi Eliezer ben Yaakov limits it to its explicit meaning. A vineyard is a vineyard. The Midrash first recognizes what is explicit in the text and only then considers whether to expand upon it midrashically.

The *Sifra* seeks to justify the Torah's repetition of the laws of the four non-kosher mammals that bear only one of the two required signs to be considered kosher:

a Grape, fig, pomegranate, olive, and date.
b The darshan cuts off the verb from its specific direct object, "a vineyard."

"The camel because it chews its cud. . . ; the hyrax because it chews its cud. . . ; the hare because it chews its cud . . ."[a] (Lev. 11:4–6). What does this teach? If it is to complete Scripture,[b] but it already says, "the camel, the hare, and the hyrax because they chew their cud . . . do not eat of their flesh" (Deut. 14:7–8)! For what do they come?[c] To include the inclusions *(ribbuyyim)* that they said.[d] (*Sifra, Sheratzim*, 2:3, 48d)

"אֶת הַגָּמָל כִּי מַעֲלֵה גֵרָה . . . ; אֶת הַשָּׁפָן כִּי מַעֲלֵה גֵרָה . . . ; אֶת הָאַרְנֶבֶת כִּי מַעֲלַת גֵּרָה" (ויקרא יא, ד-ו). מה תלמוד לומר? אם לתיקון המקרא, והלא כבר נאמר "אֶת הַגָּמָל וְאֶת הָאַרְנֶבֶת וְאֶת הַשָּׁפָן כִּי מַעֲלֵה גֵרָה הֵמָּה . . . מִבְּשָׂרָם לֹא תֹאכֵלוּ" (דברים יד, ז-ח)! ולמה באו? לרבות את הריבויים שאמרו.

The Midrash is comfortable saying that the Torah repeated its laws for the purposes of midrashic exegesis (contrast with Rabbi Yishmael's principle, discussed in chapter 10: "Any passage that is stated in one place with a missing detail is repeated elsewhere only for that missing detail"). In terms of its aims, this derashah simultaneously fulfills the overarching midrashic goals of justifying superfluities and of anchoring extra-biblical legal details. But in the course of doing so it explicitly distinguishes between the completion of Scripture and "the inclusions that they said," namely, the additions of the Midrash. Sometimes the verse is there to express new law, and sometimes it is there to provide the midrashic additions something to hang on to. The distinction between the two is stated here outright.

Prominent in this connection is a midrashic construction prevalent especially in *Sifrei Deuteronomy*: "If we ultimately include X, what then does Y teach?" In one verse (Deut. 20:19), the Torah forbids cutting down trees used for food in order to provision a siege, and in the very next verse it permits felling trees that one knows are not used for food. The Midrash then expands the scope of this permissive verse to include even fruit trees, leaving it to wonder why the Torah makes any distinction in how the trees are used:

"Only a tree which you know" (Deut. 20:20)—this is a tree for food.

"That it is not a tree for food"—this is a barren tree.

If we ultimately include barren trees, what then does "a tree for food" teach? It teaches that a barren tree takes precedence to a tree for food. (*Sifrei Deuteronomy*, §204, p. 239)

"רַק עֵץ אֲשֶׁר תֵּדַע" (דברים כ, כ)—זה אילן מאכל.

a Each chews their cud, a kosher sign, but the points of ellipsis stand in for the omitted non-kosher sign: their hooves are split.
b To make the biblical law complete, without lacunas.
c What do they teach?
d The midrashic inclusions articulated by the Sages in the *Sifra*.

"כִּי לֹא עֵץ מַאֲכָל הוּא" (דברים כ, כ)—זה אילן סרק.

אם סופנו לרבות אילן סרק, מה תלמוד לומר "עֵץ מַאֲכָל"? מלמד שאילן סרק קודם לאילן מאכל.

The Midrash answers that although cutting down any tree can be permitted, the specification adds a legal detail, an order of operations: cut down the cedar before taking an ax to the olive. For our purposes, the structure rather than the substance commands our attention. The Midrash explicitly and knowingly distinguishes between the explicit wording of the Torah and the midrashic derivation. Moreover, the first-person plural in "we ultimately include" indicates that the inclusion is the product of the darshanim. We have already seen use of the first-person in Rabbi Yishmael's own statement, and there are others like these. In general, after a derashah the Midrashim of Rabbi Akiva will ask, "If so, why does it say X?" This again demonstrates awareness of the discrepancy between the expanded Midrash and narrower Scripture.

The Midrashim of Rabbi Akiva frequently attribute the inclusion or exclusion to Scripture itself: "After the verse included, it excluded."[17] But it is the darshan who determines *what* to include or exclude ("I include x"), as we have seen.

The Midrashim of this school fence off Scripture from Midrash when it comes to the use of reason as well. The Torah rules that if any of Aaron's offspring, the priests, have the skin affliction known as *tzara'at* or a genital discharge, they may not consume consecrated food until they have been ritually purified. The Midrash probes the exact nature of the food that may not be eaten:

> "Who has *tzara'at* or an emission may not eat sacred food until he is purified" (Lev. 22:4). The Israelites may eat[a] *ma'aser*[b] as *tevulei yom*.[c] Whence Aaron and his sons? It is logical: If the Israelites, who may not eat *terumah*[d] when the sun sets, may eat *ma'aser* as *tevulei yom*, then doesn't it stand to reason that Aaron and his sons, who may eat *terumah* when the sun goes down, may also eat *ma'aser* as *tevulei yom*? The Israelites are derived from the verse, and Aaron and his sons through an a fortiori inference. (*Sifra, Emor*, 4:2, 96c)

"וְהוּא צָרוּעַ אוֹ זָב בַּקֳּדָשִׁים לֹא יֹאכַל עַד אֲשֶׁר יִטְהָר" (ויקרא כב, ד). אוכלין הן ישראל במעשר טבולי יום. אהרן ובניו מנין? ודין הוא: מה אם ישראל שאינן אוכלין בתרומה במערבי שמש, הרי הן אוכלין במעשר טבולי יום, אהרן ובניו שהן אוכלין בתרומה במערבי שמש, אינו דין שיאכלו במעשר טבולי יום? יצאו ישראל מן הכתוב, אהרן ובניו מקול וחומר.

   a The Torah only forbids Kohanim from eating holy foodstuffs before full purification; there is no parallel verse restricting Israelites in this manner.
   b This refers to *ma'aser sheni*, the second 10-percent tithe that is consumed by its owner in a state of ritual purity in Jerusalem.
   c A *tevul yom* is someone ritually impure who immersed in a *mikveh* but must wait until nightfall for full purity to set in; see Mishnah, *Nega'im*, 14:3.
   d Only Kohanim may eat *terumah*.

Scripture on its own excludes one group and human reason excludes another, and the Midrash considers it important to score a groove between them.

The foregoing demonstrates that the Midrashim of both schools belong to a single genre that possesses essential features—irrespective of any school-specific methodologies. The fancy structures above are but the most explicit manifestations of a much larger phenomenon omnipresent in the Midrash. The fundamental distinction between source text and interpretation is marked everywhere by setting off biblical citations from midrashic discourse. Midrash continuously maintains self-awareness of its essentially interpretive character by articulating textual problems in the Torah, using a fixed set of formulae and operators, and explicitly reflecting on its own exegetical methodology. Practitioners of Midrash from both schools explicate what they are doing.[18] Why? The reason seems didactic: so that students in the study hall can learn not only the Halakhah, but also how to arrive at it on their own.[19]

This phenomenon is unprecedented. Midrash is worlds apart from rewritten Scripture, which remolds the text to fit its interpretations. It goes beyond the *pesher* literature and Philonic exegesis, which do respect the Torah's textual boundaries, but do not lay emphasis on the line between interpretation and Scripture and are not transparent about their methodology. Thus, while scholarship tries to delineate the independent character of each midrashic school, this study shows that they share much more than initially meets the eye. Their interpretations fundamentally belong to a single, distinct, and new genre within Jewish literature.

C. *KI-SHEMU'O:* SCRIPTURE "AS IT SOUNDS"

Tannaitic Midrash is a formulaic and stylized genre, so a proper understanding of its largely invariable terminology affords better insight into its ancient texts. Because there are hundreds of terms that deserve their own analysis, the best I can do is point the reader to the major midrashic dictionaries. First and foremost is Wilhelm Bacher's groundbreaking *Die exegetische Terminologie der jüdischen Tradition-Literatur*, the first volume of which treats tannaitic Midrash.[20] Being over a century old, it is marred by deficiencies that were unavoidable at the time. It does not distinguish between halakhic and aggadic Midrashim, or between tannaitic terms and amoraic ones. It incorporates terminology from the much later Babylonian Talmud. Since its publication, scholars have shied away from trying to compile a single definitive dictionary and have focused their efforts, to great effect, on volumes dedicated to individual Midrashim.[21]

Systematic analysis of midrashic terminology yields a different result than individual treatments of select derashot. Derashot appear to take an unpredictable, freewheeling flight path through the Torah, but after watching repeated performances, one finds patterns in the loops and chandelles, a limited number of exegetical maneuvers that repeat in variable but predictable sequences. A microanalysis of two key terms will shed new light on midrashic consciousness and reflexivity.

The Hebrew term *ki-shemu'o* and its variations, which all mean "as it sounds," appear a little over sixty times in tannaitic literature, mostly in the Midrashim of Rabbi Yishmael's school.[22] Let us examine a few of the term's classic appearances in *Mekhilta de-Rabbi Yishmael*, the first being about placement of the tefillin on the head:

> "Between your eyes" (Ex. 13:9)—on the high point of the head.[a] Do you say on the high point of the head or instead on [the place] "between your eyes" as it sounds *(ki-shemu'o)*? It therefore teaches, "You are children of the Lord, your God: Do not gash yourselves nor put a bald spot between your eyes"[b] (Deut. 14:1). Just as "[between] your eyes" stated there is on the high point of the head, so "between your eyes" stated here is on the high point of the head. (*Mekhilta de-Rabbi Yishmael*, Pasḥa, §17, p. 67)

> "בֵּין עֵינֶיךָ" (שמות יג, ט)—על גובה של ראש. אתה אומר על גובה של ראש או על "בֵּין עֵינֶיךָ" כשמועו? תלמוד לומר "בָּנִים אַתֶּם לַה' אֱלֹהֵיכֶם לֹא תִתְגֹּדְדוּ [וְלֹא תָשִׂימוּ קָרְחָה בֵּין עֵינֵיכֶם]" (דברים יד, א). מה "עֵינֵיכֶם" האמור להלן על גובה של ראש, אף "בֵּין עֵינֶיךָ" האמור כן על גובה של ראש.

Ki-shemu'o indicates the literal interpretation of the phrase "between your eyes," a possible reading that is rejected. Since the Sages interpret this verse as the mitzvah of laying tefillin, the placement of the leather container housing the parchment cannot be literally between the eyes, on the bridge of the nose. Note how this midrash does not reject the literal reading by appealing to tradition or to halakhic practice (which is the real basis for the reading, as we saw in chapter 11) but by invoking another verse. Only Scripture itself is a legitimate source for rejecting a reading.

The next midrash interprets a biblical list of responsibilities that an Israelite may not shirk when taking another wife:

> "Her *she'er*" (Ex. 21:10)—this is her sustenance,[c] as it says, "Who devour my people's flesh *(she'er)*" (Mic. 3:3), and it is written, "He rained flesh[d] *(she'er)* on them like dust" (Ps. 78:27).

> "Her clothing *(kesut)*" (Ps. 78:27)—as it sounds *(ke-mashma'o)*.

---

a The top of the forehead.
b These were forbidden pagan practices of mourning.
c The husband has an obligation to sustain his wife; see Mishnah, *Ketubbot*, 4:4.
d A reference to the abundant quail God provided in the wilderness.

"Her *'onah*" (Ps. 78:27)—this is the way of the world.[a] As it says, "and he lay with her and abused her *(vay'anneha)*"[b] (Gen. 34:2). (*Mekhilta de-Rabbi Yishmael, Nezikin,* §3, p. 258)

"שְׁאֵרָהּ" (שמות כא, י)—אילו מזונותיה, שנאמר "וַאֲשֶׁר אָכְלוּ שְׁאֵר עַמִּי" (מיכה ג, ג), וכתוב "וַיַּמְטֵר עֲלֵיהֶם כֶּעָפָר שְׁאֵר" (תהלים עח, כז).

"כְּסוּתָהּ"—כמשמעו.

"עֹנָתָהּ"—זו דרך ארץ, שנאמר "וַיִּשְׁכַּב אֹתָהּ וַיְעַנֶּהָ" (בראשית לד, ב).

This midrash takes this verse as a template for every husband's responsibilities to his wife. The middle derashah uses *ki-shemu'o* to signify that, unlike the other two terms, the Hebrew needs no exegetical work. Why didn't the darshan feel the need to explain *kesut*, the word for clothing? Because unlike *she'er* and *'onah*, which were not used in mishnaic Hebrew and required explanation, the word *kesut* still had currency in the tannaitic era.

Another example of this very same phenomenon, where the term indicates that a gloss is unnecessary, concerns a verse recited in the Shema. It promises that God will bring rain so that the Jewish people will gather in the following foodstuffs:

"Your grain *(dagan)*" (Deut. 11:14)—as it sounds *(ke-mashma'o)*.

"Your *tirosh*" (Deut. 11:14)—this is wine, like the usage in the following context, "Thus said the Lord: As when wine *(tirosh)* is present etc." (Isa. 65:8).

"Your *yitzhar*" (Deut. 11:14)—this is oil, like the usage in the following context, "and the vats shall overflow with wine and oil" (Joel 2:24). (*Sifrei Deuteronomy,* §42, p. 91)

"דְּגָנֶךָ" (דברים יא, יד)—כמשמעו.

"תִּירֹשְׁךָ"—זה היין, כעניין שנאמר [. . .]

"יִצְהָרֶךָ"—זה השמן, כעניין שנאמר [. . .]

Only the first word in this list, *dagan*, enjoyed continuous use from the biblical period into the rabbinic one. Here again the term *ki-shemu'o* is used when a rabbinic exegete believes that the text is intelligible as is.

Whether *ki-shemu'o* will be appended to a word or phrase does not always depend on the expectation of unintelligibility. It can be an executive decision by the darshan not to gloss a term for some reason or other. Consider how the Midrash glosses God's promise to Moses,

---

a Sexual relations. The husband has an obligation to have marital relations with his wife; see Mishnah, *Ketubbot,* 5:6.

b The description of Shechem having his way with Dinah uses the root *'-n-h*, which underlies *'onah*, to refer to sexual relations.

which contains a doubled expression for emphasis: "I shall surely blot out *(maḥoh emḥeh)* the remembrance of Amalek" (Ex. 17:14):

> *Maḥoh* (Ex. 17:14)—in this world; *emḥeh*—in the World to Come.
>
> "Remembrance"—this is Haman.
>
> "Amalek"—as it sounds *(ke-shom'o)*. (*Mekhilta de-Rabbi Yishmael*, '*Amalek*, §2, p. 185)

"מָחֹה" (שמות יז, יד)—בעולם הזה; "אֶמְחֶה"—לעולם הבא.

"זֵכֶר"—זה המן.

"עֲמָלֵק"—כשמעו.

The first derashah is the classic exegesis of a doubled phrase.[23] The second derashah on "remembrance" does not define the Hebrew word but gives its historical realization. The third phrase, "Amalek," is an equally good candidate for such an interpretation. By not supplying one and insisting that the word is *ki-shemu'o*, the darshan signals that he has deliberately chosen *not* to identify Amalek with a nation of his own time, such as the Romans.

In some places, the term *ki-shemu'o* factors into a dispute:

> "They went three days in the wilderness [and they did not find water]" (Ex. 15:22).
>
> Rabbi Yehoshua says, As it sounds *(ki-shemu'o)*.
>
> Rabbi Eliezer says, But wasn't water beneath the feet of the Israelites, for the land floats on water, as it says, "who spread out the earth on the water" (Ps. 136:6)? What, then, does "they did not find water" teach?[a] Rather *(ella)*, it was to tire them out.[b]
>
> Others say, Water that the Israelites took from between the parted waters was finished at that time. What, then, does "they did not find" teach?[c] Like the usage in the following context,[d] "And their nobles sent their lads for water. [They came to the cisterns and did not find water; their vessels returned empty]" (Jer. 14:3).
>
> The expounders of difficult verses *(dorshei reshumot)*[e] said, "They did not find water"—words of Torah that are compared to water. (*Mekhilta de-Rabbi Yishmael*, *Vayyassa'*, §1, p. 154)

a How is it possible that they didn't find water if it's everywhere?
b God purposely sabotaged their efforts; there was water but they were not allowed to find it.
c Why does it mention finding if the source of their water was waterskins they carried with them?
d In this usage, not finding water is associated with vessels being empty.
e For reshumot (sg. rashum) difficult or unintelligible, see Boyarin, "Dorshe Reshumot." These interpreters have been identified as some kind of allegorists; see Lauterbach, "Ancient Jewish Allegorists."

"וַיֵּלְכוּ שְׁלֹשֶׁת יָמִים בַּמִּדְבָּר [וְלֹא מָצְאוּ מָיִם] וגו'" (שמות טו, כב).

ר' יהושע אומר: כשמועו.

ר' אליעזר אומר: והלא המים תחת רגלי ישראל היו, והארץ אינה צפה אלא על המים, שנאמר "לְרֹקַע הָאָרֶץ עַל הַמָּיִם" (תהלים קלו, ו)! הא מה תלמוד "לֹא מָצְאוּ מָיִם"? אלא כדי ליגען.

אחרים אומרים: מים שנטלו ישראל מבין הגזרים שלמו מהן באותה שעה. הא מה תלמוד לומר "לֹא מָצְאוּ"? כעינין שנאמר "וְאַדִּירֵיהֶם שָׁלְחוּ צְעִירֵיהֶם לַמָּיִם [בָּאוּ עַל גֵּבִים לֹא מָצְאוּ מַיִם שָׁבוּ כְלֵיהֶם רֵיקָם]" (ירמיה יד, ג).

דורשי רשומות אמרו: "לֹא מָצְאוּ מָיִם"—דברי תורה שנמשלו במים.

The verse under debate describes the trying beginning of the Israelites' travels in the desert. They do not locate any water and begin complaining to Moses. The first opinion of Rabbi Yehoshua declares that the verse is "as it sounds." This adds nothing to the verse, and that is precisely the point: Rabbi Yehoshua disagrees with all the interpretations that make it about anything other than the failure to find an oasis. Rabbi Eliezer views the disappointment as divinely orchestrated. The anonymous opinion ("others") uses the only other verse in Scripture to include the verbatim clause "and they did not find water," in order to complete the picture of empty flagons here. The "expounders of difficult verses" characteristically explain that the Israelites' thirst is not physical but spiritual. Rabbi Yehoshua stands against all of them, proclaiming that sometimes water is just water.

It pays to dwell on Rabbi Eliezer's position for a moment. His presumption that a person can find water anywhere is contradicted not only by the experience of any agrarian society but also by other narratives in which searches for water by biblical protagonists come up dry. His actual argument, though, is not realistic but textual. The verse does not say that there was no water, but rather that the Israelites did not find it. God, deduces the darshan, concealed the water purposely, to test the resolve of the Israelites. This textual clue is enough to support his claim that God was testing the newborn nation, turning the episode into a divine trial and loading it with moral significance from the very outset. The use of "rather (ella)" supports this, as it indicates a shift from the straightforward sense to a midrashic one.[24] Philo, and Christian allegorists like Origen whom he influenced, commonly would challenge the basic meaning of a verse with mild objections as a pretext to endow the text with new meaning.[25]

In the usages of *ki-shemu'o* exemplified thus far, one can see that it comes after a biblical citation and is nearly never followed by any explanation. Its point is to highlight the self-evidence of the Torah's words, to negate interpretations that do not fit the simple reading. All occurrences of the term in tannaitic Midrash fit the three types seen above: to mark a literal reading that is ultimately rejected (about half of occurrences); to indicate a word that is left uninterpreted (most of the other half); to oppose other opinions (a few percent). It is used contrastively against the final reading of the conclusion, other terms that are glossed, or other interpretive opinions.

It sounds as if *ki-shemu'o* is there to preserve the *peshat*, the literal-contextual meaning, but that is not accurate. It is true that overlap frequently occurs between *peshat* and *ki-shemu'o*, but the latter can be hyperliteral and yield a reading that no medieval proponent of *peshat* would support as reasonable. The expositor of *peshat* looks to context and recognizes certain expressions as idioms instead of interpreting them literally. To accentuate points of divergence between *ki-shemu'o* glosses and *peshat*, take the derashah on the verse that instructs someone to wait eight days before offering a baby animal as a sacrifice. The Torah says that for seven days it must remain "*taḥat* its mother" (Lev. 22:27). The *Mekhilta* raises the possibility that *taḥat* is intended literally, that the baby should be "underneath" its mother for that period of time. The Midrash rightfully rejects this by the end, since clearly the Torah means the baby should be left in its mother's care, and the phrase means "with its mother." A biblical exegete of the medieval *peshat* school would not even entertain the rejected reading.[26]

A profounder distinction between *ki-shemu'o* and *peshat* is the fact that the former, unlike the latter, does not represent an actual interpretive method. It is not an alternative to other interpretations that the Midrash might introduce with "another thing" *(davar aḥer)*. To put it in everyday terms, *ki-shemu'o* is a traffic cone that prevents any interpretation from being parked next to the verse. The option that *ki-shemu'o* presents is binary: leave the text as is, or apply Midrash. If interpretation explains one thing in terms of another, *ki-shemu'o* is the contentless opposition to interpretation.[27] Furthermore, if *ki-shemu'o* were used to label every literal interpretation, it would be everywhere in the Midrash. The low number of its occurrences proves that it is deployed only in circumstances where a special reason exists to underline the literal meaning: either to reject that meaning or to resist interpretation altogether.[28]

What are the implications for the larger issue this chapter tackles, Midrash's degree of self-awareness? It is abundantly clear that Midrash is the product of active exegesis, since prior to any such interpretation the text is "as it sounds." The darshan is cognizant of the biblical text's lexical meaning, and usually finds it unsatisfying in some legal or other respect. This means that *ki-shemu'o* is essentially a reflexive term, as it marks all other interpretations as the product of midrashic tools (often intertextual ones) that deviate from this primary meaning.[29]

But *ki-shemu'o* does more than instruct us implicitly that Midrash is self-reflective interpretation; it is the Midrash actively announcing such exegetical activity. Since it does not advance a specific interpretation, it exists only to call attention to the literal reading, and by automatic extension to call out all other readings as deviating from it. The term, then, is by its very nature about the midrashic act and its relation to the literal sense. *Ki-shemu'o* is a rhetorical device that proclaims its self-awareness, since it offers nothing substantive with which to confront other interpretations.

Fittingly, *ki-shemu'o* belongs to the Midrashim of Rabbi Yishmael's school, because awareness of interpretive possibilities and distinguishing between them is characteristic of this school. Where these Midrashim have *ki-shemu'o*, parallel passages in the Midrashim of

Rabbi Akiva's school usually lack any term and either paraphrase or repeat the biblical language. Compare the following midrashic glosses, one of which is a repeat from above:

> "Her clothing" (Ex. 21:10)—as it sounds *(ke-mashma'o)*. (*Mekhilta de-Rabbi Yishmael, Nezikin*, §3, p. 258)
>
> "Her clothing *(kesutah)*" (Ex. 21:10)—this is clothing *(kesut)*. (*Mekhilta de-Rashbi*, 21:10, p. 167)[30]

And again:

> Do you say on the high point of the head or on [the place] "between your eyes" as it sounds *(ki-shemu'o)*? (*Mekhilta de-Rabbi Yishmael, Pasḥa*, §17, p. 67)
>
> Could it be *(yakhol)* that one places it on the forehead? (*Mekhilta de-Rashbi*, 13:9, p. 41)

Elsewhere, the Midrashim of Rabbi Akiva's school omit these derashot entirely, while preserving all of the surrounding derashot.[31] This accords with what we know about Rabbi Yishmael's school, namely, it has a better-developed terminology that reflects its concerted effort to order and level the many kinds of interpretation and stages thereof.

Tellingly, whenever *ki-shemu'o* has a polemical purpose, it almost always comes before the interpretation it excludes.[32] This editorial choice appears to privilege the exegesis that follows, by giving the impression that the uninterpreted text is insufficient. Regarding the Israelite failure to find water quoted above, the editor placed the opinion of Rabbi Yehoshua, who insists on the simple meaning, first. When the readers then encounter all the other interpretations afterward, they pick up on the dissatisfaction. Rabbi Yehoshua's offering did not slake the interpretive thirst of his colleagues. Not only the meaning of the term but also its placement announce the Midrash's awareness of the dictionary definition of biblical Hebrew as well as the necessity of midrashic interpretation. The meaning of Scripture exactly "as it sounds" precedes interpretive activity, but it does not preclude it.

Why not? Why do the darshanim reject the simple meaning of the Torah? One can give contextualized answers—here it's too literal, there it doesn't fit the context, elsewhere it contradicts tradition—but there is a bigger issue at play. Beyond the fact that without a midrashic coating the contents of the Torah may prove too bitter to swallow,[33] to leave the Torah "as it sounds" means overlooking or embracing the repetitions, superfluities, and contradictions that for the rabbis sully the divine text. Midrash is the Torah's proverbial white knight, coming to rescue it from itself.

Of course, the Midrash never says any of this. This sort of self-reflection isn't discoverable within midrashic praxis. It is the stuff of programmatic meta-statements about hermeneutics, ruminations of the kind found in the writings of Philo and Origen, but a rarity in rabbinic literature.[34] We have no choice but to be satisfied with the partial reflexivity reflected in parts of the Midrash, like the particular applications of *ki-shemu'o*.

D. *EINO TZARIKH:* MIDRASHIC OPTIMIZATION

At times, the Midrash presents multiple interpretations of a single verse or phrase, which it usually separates with attributions to named Sages (Rabbi X says ... Rabbi Y says) or the separator *davar aḥer* (another thing), without stating a preference for any of them. Does that mean that it considers any derashah legitimate and correct, so long as it fulfills a core midrashic goal or arrives at the right result?[35]

This brings us to the second midrashic term analyzed in this chapter, which is part not of the interpretive machinery but of quality assurance. The term *eino tzarikh*, "it is unnecessary," appears fifty-five times in tannaitic Midrash. Like *ki-shemu'o*, it is most closely associated with the school of Rabbi Yishmael. The term is placed after a derashah to convey that the derashah (or rather its verse)[36] is unnecessary, because a better way to learn the same halakhah exists.[37] The format in which it appears is pretty rigid. It opens with a halakhic derivation, most often based on scriptural exegesis. A named Sage then comments *eino tzarikh*, rejecting the initial derivation in favor of a simpler alternative grounded in exegesis, logic, or an express verse.[38]

Eino tzarikh can reject the interpretation due to the existence of an express verse. For example, when the Midrash tries to establish that priests must have their genitalia covered based on the prohibition against having a stepped altar (Ex. 20:23), Rabbi Yishmael rejects it on the grounds that it is explicit in another verse, which states that the pants worn by the priests cover their private parts (Ex. 28:42). Why work at extrapolating something that is stated outright? Or consider the continuation of a midrash cited above in the chapter:

> Rabbi Yoshiyah says, "They are holy" (Num. 18:17)—why is it said? To include the tithe and paschal sacrifice in requiring one pouring, for we hear nothing about them in the entire Torah.
>
> Rabbi Yitzhak says, It is unnecessary *(eino tzarikh)*, for it already says, "and the blood of your sacrifices shall be poured on the altar of the Lord your God" (Deut. 12:27). (*Sifrei Numbers*, §118, p. 139)

ר' יאשיה אומר: "קֹדֶשׁ הֵם" (במדבר יח, יז)—למה נאמר? להביא את המעשר והפסח שיטענו שפיכה אחת, שלא שמענו להן בכל התורה.

ר' יצחק אומר: אינו צריך, שהרי כבר נאמר "וְדַם זְבָחֶיךָ יִשָּׁפֵךְ עַל מִזְבַּח ה' אֱלֹהֶיךָ" (דברים יב, כז).

Rabbi Yitzhak's reservation about Rabbi Yoshiyah's derivation is that the Torah unambiguously expresses in another verse the selfsame law teased out through exegesis. The derashah is superfluous.

More often, though, *eino tzarikh* introduces another, ostensibly better derashah. Here is a midrash containing two derashot about the obligation to get rid of hametz (leavened bread) prior to the onset of Passover:

"Only *(akh)* on the first day [you shall eliminate leaven from your households]" (Ex. 12:15)—from the eve of the festival.[a] Do you say from the eve of the festival, or is it instead on the festival itself? It therefore teaches, "You shall not slaughter the blood of My sacrifice with hametz" (Ex. 34:25)—do not slaughter[b] the paschal sacrifice while hametz is present—the words of Rabbi Yishmael.

Rabbi Yonatan says, It is unnecessary *(eino tzarikh)*. Does it not already say, "No labor may be performed on them" (Ex. 12:16)? Burning[c] is a kind of labor.[d] What, then, does "eliminate leaven from your households" teach? From the eve of the festival. (*Mekhilta de-Rabbi Yishmael*, *Pasḥa*, §8, p. 28)

"אַךְ בַּיּוֹם הָרִאשׁוֹן [תַּשְׁבִּיתוּ שְּׂאֹר מִבָּתֵּיכֶם]" (שמות יב, טו)—מערב יום טוב. אתה אומר מערב יום טוב, או אינו אלא ביום טוב עצמו? תלמוד לומר "לֹא תִשְׁחַט עַל חָמֵץ דַּם זִבְחִי" (שמות לד, כה)—לא תשחט את הפסח וחמץ קיים—דברי ר' ישמעאל.

ר' יונתן אומר: אינו צריך, והלא כבר נאמר "כָּל מְלָאכָה לֹא יֵעָשֶׂה בָהֶם" (שמות יב, טז)—שריפה מעין מלאכה היא. מה תלמוד לומר "תַּשְׁבִּיתוּ שְּׂאֹר מִבָּתֵּיכֶם"? מערב יום טוב.

A second example focuses on the requirement for priests to recite the priestly blessing while standing:

"Thus shall you bless the Children of Israel" (Num. 6:23)—while standing. Do you say while standing, or is it instead while standing or not standing?[e] It therefore teaches, "These shall stand to bless the people on Mount Gerizim"[f] (Deut. 27:12). It says "blessing" here and it says "blessing" there." Just as the blessing said there is while standing, so the blessing said here is while standing.

Rabbi Natan says, It is unnecessary *(eino tzarikh)*. For it already says, "and the priests, the sons of Levi, shall come forward etc.[g] in the name of the Lord" (Deut.

---

a The word *akh* is interpreted in such a way to mean that by the first day of Pesach, before the holiday commences, one must get rid of the hametz.

b The slaughtering is performed on the Fourteenth of Nisan, before the festival begins, and at that point the hametz must already be disposed of.

c Burning hametz is understood to be the optimal way for fulfilling the mandate to eliminate it; see Mishnah, *Pesaḥim*, 2:1.

d There are thirty-nine prohibited categories of labor, which include kindling a fire.

e Either option is permissible, so blessing while seated would be valid.

f This refers to the national blessing pronounced after entry into the land, and although those standing are six tribes of Israelites and not the Kohanim, the Torah associates blessing with standing here.

g The abbreviated portion says that God chose the Kohanim "to serve Him and bless in His name."

21:5), juxtaposing blessing to service. Just as service is while standing, so blessing is while standing. (*Sifrei Numbers*, §68, p. 63)

"כֹּה תְבָרֲכוּ אֶת בְּנֵי יִשְׂרָאֵל" (במדבר ו, כג)—בעמידה. אתה אומר בעמידה, או בעמידה ושלא בעמידה? תלמוד לומר "אֵלֶּה יַעַמְדוּ לְבָרֵךְ אֶת הָעָם עַל הַר גְּרִזִים" (דברים כז, יב). נאמר כאן "ברכה" ונאמר להלן "ברכה", מה "ברכה" האמור להלן בעמידה, אף "ברכה" האמורה כאן בעמידה.

ר' נתן אומר: אינו צריך, שכבר נאמר "וְנִגְּשׁוּ הַכֹּהֲנִים בְּנֵי לֵוִי וְגֹ' בְּשֵׁם ה'" (דברים כא, ה)—מקיש ברכה לשירות, מה שירות בעמידה אף ברכה בעמידה.

The two midrashim about the removal of hametz and the priestly blessing share the same format. They each begin with an exegetically derived halakhah, the first attributed and the second unattributed. Along comes a Sage who declares it unnecessary and provides an alternative derivation of the same law. In what way is the alternative superior to the original? The Midrash never says. The answer must be extrapolated inductively from the individual midrashim. In these two, one can see that the original derashah is narrow and limited, and the improved one is conceptually broader. In the first midrash, a derashah specifically about hametz is replaced by one about the general categories of labor prohibited for all festivals. In the second, instead of a specific analogy, Rabbi Natan offers a general inference that blessings are to be said while standing. A comprehensive analysis of the occurrences of *eino tzarikh* shows that having a wider compass is only one of three reasons the alternative is "superior." The second reason is that it is based on a more direct verse. The third is that it entails fewer midrashic moves than the rejected derashah. Although the rejected derashah doesn't possess a fixed form, it exhibits a strong tendency toward complex structures. These are replaced by a simple exegesis or logical argument in the substitute derashah.[39]

The judgment of *eino tzarikh* is original to the Midrash. It can't be an editorial phenomenon, whereby some anonymous editors put derashot together and linked them with the evaluative, pivotal term *eino tzarikh*. The improved derashah is always attributed to an actual rabbinic authority, which wouldn't be the case if it were the product of editors. The usual anonymity of the initial, rejected derashah likely indicates that these midrashim reflect the study method of Rabbi Yishmael's bet midrash.[40] One possibility is that novices would try their hand at anchoring the law, and the masters evaluated and refined their derivations in real time. Another possibility is that later generations of darshanim proposed more streamlined and elegant alternatives for derashot that were so well known that they weren't attached to any particular rabbinic figure.[41]

The originality of the *eino tzarikh* derashah also explains why some midrashim contain multiple derashot yet only one utterance of *eino tzarikh*. Only one of the derashot was actually said in response to a previous one, and the others were collated by an editor.[42]

If my reading of this phenomenon is correct, it adds a deep wrinkle to the conventional account of the Midrash's anchoring of extra-biblical law in the Torah. The typical directionality proposed in scholarship is toward increasing complexity and sophistication.[43] While it is true that over time darshanim forged more effective tools and developed new techniques that allowed them to craft more sophisticated midrashic arguments, they concurrently honed their skills to the point that they could eliminate waste and bloat. Even if caution is warranted in drawing a paradigm-shaking conclusion from a patchwork of data, it seems that optimization for simplicity was pursued in Rabbi Yishmael's bet midrash.

The two key terms explored in this and the previous section reveal the inner workings of Midrash. *Ki-shemu'o* is a window to the Midrash's consciousness, which enable us to decide the question of its reflexiveness. *Eino tzarikh* takes us into the midrashic workshop, where we can see the quality control of midrashic output. The use of the two terms or lack thereof yields results at variance with the conventional scholarly account. First, Rabbi Yishmael's school coined a term whose entire purpose is to show that Midrash is a deliberate interpretive activity. Second, the same bet midrash had a protocol for deciding between derashot based on their simplicity and elegance. These two findings contradict the bird's-eye view of the batei midrash, in which darshanim appear to go about their activities because that is just what they do and in which all are more or less equals. A view from the ground shows considerable reflection about their own work as well as judgment about the work of peers or predecessors.

The first and second sections of this chapter documented acknowledged gaps between biblical and mishnaic Hebrew and between the Torah and Midrash. Combining the findings of all the sections proves that Midrash is aware of exegetical operations and even accentuates the discontinuity between itself and the Torah. It thereby teaches its students both the contents of the Halakhah and the methodology that establishes it. It lays no claim to being the word of God, nor does it portray itself as the natural outgrowth of Scripture. It is the product of exegetical activity, a technique that can be learned in the study hall. This didacticism is unprecedented in the history of Jewish Bible interpretation.

FOURTEEN

Aggadah in the Midrash

The tannaitic Midrashim focus primarily on the legal portions of the Torah, and only secondarily do they expound some of its narratives aggadically.[1] The amount of Aggadah varies from Midrash to Midrash. It depends on the nature of the biblical book being explicated and the preferences of the Midrash's editors. Exodus and Deuteronomy have a lot of narrative, so *Mekhilta de-Rabbi Yishmael* and *Sifrei Deuteronomy* have a correspondingly high amount of Aggadah. Leviticus, by contrast, is the biblical book with the fewest stories, and *Sifra* follows suit. Numbers has a considerable number of stories yet *Sifrei Numbers* does not have a corresponding amount of Aggadah, because of editorial policies. All told, about 30 percent of all tannaitic Midrash is aggadic.

The examples presented in the previous chapters clearly demonstrate that aggada is more flexible in style compared to halakha, with fewer established rules and conventions. However, this does not mean that it is entirely without structure or guiding principles. The goal of this chapter is thus to characterize aggadic Midrash and compare it to the halakhic Midrash as discussed in the previous chapters. It will cover everything from brief aggadic derashot to extended sequences to see how aggadic Midrash operates hermeneutically and how it generates meaning.

Most of the examples analyzed in this chapter have been taken from *Mekhilta de-Rabbi Yishmael*, because around 40 percent of it is aggadic Midrash. It is divided into nine tractates with mainly Aramaic titles that follow the sequence of events in the book of Exodus, beginning with Tractate *Pasḥa* on the laws of the paschal sacrifice (Ex. 12–13).[2] Tractates *Be-Shalaḥ*, *Shirata*, *Vayyassa'*, and *'Amalek* are all aggadic, and they stretch from the exit from Egypt in Exodus 14 through the Israelite sojourn through the Sinai Desert in Exodus 19. Tractates *Nezikin* and *Kaspa*, on the various laws from Exodus 21 to 23, are purely halakhic, while Tractates *Pasḥa, Ba-Ḥodesh,* and *Shabbeta* interleave Aggadah with Halakhah. The *Mekhilta* conveniently contains all the possible types of derashot: pure halakhic, pure aggadic, and a combination of the two.

The end of the chapter shifts briefly to *Sifrei Deuteronomy,* in which Halakhah and Aggadah interact in singularly surprising ways.

A. INTERPRETATION FOR ITS OWN SAKE

The first characteristic that sets apart the aggadic derashah is its interest in textual interpretation for its own sake. The way the Midrash uses the term *maggid,* "it relates/teaches," in halakhic and aggadic derashot bears this out.[3] This term appears approximately ninety times in *Mekhilta de-Rabbi Yishmael,* half of them in aggadic contexts. Here are two examples, the first halakhic and the second aggadic:

> "[They shall eat the meat] roasted with fire and matzot (unleavened bread); [they shall eat it with bitter herbs]" (Ex. 12:8). Scripture relates *(maggid)* that the mitzvah of the paschal sacrifice is matzah, roasted meat, and bitter herbs. (*Mekhilta de-Rabbi Yishmael, Pasḥa,* §6, pp. 19–20)

"צלי אש ומצות [על מרורים יאכלוהו]" (שמות יב, ח)—מגיד הכתוב שמצוַת פסח מצה צלי ומרור.

> "[Pharaoh rose at night—]he, and all his servants, and all of Egypt" (Ex. 12:30). Scripture relates *(maggid)* that Pharaoh was going door to door, to all his servants and to all the Egyptians, and rousing each and every one from their place. (*Mekhilta de-Rabbi Yishmael, Pasḥa,* §13, p. 44)

"[ויקם פרעה לילה] הוא וכל עבדיו וכל מצרים" (שמות יב, ל)—מגיד שהיה פרעה מחזיר על בתי כל עבדיו ועל בתי כל מצרים ומעמידן כל אחד ואחד ממקומו.

Each derashah homes in on the specific wording of its verse. The halakhic derashah understands the mitzvah of eating the paschal sacrifice to be a reenactment of its original consumption, roasted and accompanied by matzah and bitter herbs. The aggadic derashah uses the widening circles, from Pharaoh to the servants to all Egyptians, as a springboard for ridicule. The ruler of a mighty empire is reduced to frantically running around pounding on doors, shaking footmen and peasants awake, all in order to save his own skin.[4]

The methodology is similar, but is the goal? The halakhic derashah gives applicable instruction, but the expected practical lesson or moral guidance is missing from the aggadic derashah. It remains in the realm of the narrative, belonging to the world of Moses and Pharaoh. It expands upon and enriches the biblical text.[5]

Of course, there are places where aggadic Midrash is explicitly or implicitly didactic. When the Torah says that Moses "drew near" the dark, thick cloud on Mount Sinai (Ex.

20:17), the Midrash explains that his humility brought him there. It then draws a lesson from this: "Scripture relates that whoever is humble will ultimately cause the divine presence to dwell with man on the earth."[6] The Midrash encourages the cultivation of humility with the promise of spiritual reward.

In another instance, the Midrash is less forthcoming about its underlying motivation, but one need not look very hard to find it. The Torah says that Moses came forward and called to the elders (Ex. 19:7), on which the *Mekhilta* has this to say: "It relates that Moses accorded honor to the elders."[7] The moral is evident: If the greatest prophet, who enjoyed a personal relationship with God, could show respect to his elders, you can too.

In some places, the Midrash develops a general religious principle or theological idea from the text: "It relates that the exodus from Egypt was equivalent to all of the miracles and wonders."[8] On rare occasions, aggadic interpretation can even have a halakhic application. The Midrash understands that the pillar of fire, which guided the Israelites at night, would begin rising before the pillar of cloud, which led the way by day, had dissipated. It learns from this that one must light the Shabbat candles before sunset on Friday.[9]

But the places in which one tries in vain to identify some goal beyond interpretation of the text itself are numerous.[10] This is in contrast to the halakhic derashot on the legal portions of the Torah, which almost always end with a halakhic ruling. In the aggadic derashot that focus on biblical narrative, there is more room for pure exegesis. While lessons are important, they are not all-consuming, the way halakhic implications are in the legal sections. In aggadic contexts, the Midrash devotes more space to plumbing the meaning of the text, while in legal areas, it concentrates on extracting halakhic information from it.

B. AFFECTIVE EXEGESIS

The darshanim were not only interpreters but preachers. At least some of the aggadic derashot seem to have come from an actual synagogue setting in which they were delivered to a live audience.[11] To appreciate this, we need to analyze a longer, self-contained passage. A derashah on a verse from the Song of the Sea (Ex. 15) is a fine specimen of aggadic interpretative technique, which also showcases how a darshan could powerfully move his audience:

> "The Lord is a man of war, the Lord is His name" (Ex. 15:3).
>
> Rabbi Yehudah says, This verse is enriched[a] from many places. It relates that He revealed Himself to them with every weapon of war. He revealed Himself to them like a champion girded with a sword, as it says, "Gird your sword etc." (Ps. 45:4). He revealed Himself to them with a coat of mail and helmet, as it says, "And He donned righteousness like a coat of mail" (Isa. 59:17). He revealed Himself to them

---

a Because it is poor in detail here.

with a spear, as it says, "by the radiance of the gleam of Your spear" (Hab. 3:11), and it is written, "Unsheathe the spear and close" (Ps. 35:3). He revealed Himself to them with bow and arrows, as it says, "Your bow is laid bare etc." (Hab. 3:9), "And He sent forth arrows and scattered them etc." (2 Sam. 22:15). He revealed Himself to them with shield and buckler, as it says, "His truth is a shield and buckler" (Ps. 91:4), "Take up shield and buckler" (Ps. 35:2).

Or do I hear that He has some need of one of these measures?[a] It therefore teaches, "The Lord is a man of war, the Lord is His name"[b] (Ex. 15:3)—He fights with His name[c] and has no need of any of these measures. Why, then, does Scripture need to specify each and every one? Rather, if Israel has a need for any of them, the Omnipresent does battle for them.

Woe to the nations of the world for what they hear in their ears, for the One who spoke the world into being will fight against them. (*Mekhilta de-Rabbi Yishmael, Shirata*, §4, p. 129)

"ה' אִישׁ מִלְחָמָה ה' שְׁמוֹ" (שמות טו, ג). ר' יהודה אומר: הרי זה מקרא עשיר במקומות הרבה. מגיד שנגלה עליו בכל כלי זיין. נגלה עליהם כגבור חגור חרב, שנאמר "חֲגוֹר חַרְבְּךָ וגו'" (תהלים מה, ד). נגלה עליו בשירין וכובע, שנאמר "וַיִּלְבַּשׁ צְדָקָה כַּשִּׁרְיָן" (ישעיה נט, יז). נגלה עליו בחנית שנאמר, "לְנֹגַהּ בְּרַק חֲנִיתֶךָ" (חבקוק ג, יא), וכתוב "וְהָרֵק חֲנִית וּסְגֹר" (תהלים לה, ג). נגלה עליו בקשת ובחיצים, שנאמר "עֶרְיָה תֵעוֹר קַשְׁתֶּךָ וגו'", (חבקוק ג, ט), "וַיִּשְׁלַח חִצִּים וַיְפִיצֵם וגו'" (שמואל ב כב, טו). נגלה עליהם בצינה ובמגן, שנאמר "צִנָּה וְסֹחֵרָה אֲמִתּוֹ" (תהלים צא, ד), "הַחֲזֵק מָגֵן וְצִנָּה וגו'" (שם לה, ב).

או שומע אני שהוא צריך לאחת ממידות הללו? תלמוד לומר "ה' אִישׁ מִלְחָמָה ה' שְׁמוֹ"—בשמו הוא נלחם ואינו צריך לאחת מכל מידות הללו. ואם כן למה צריך הכתוב לפרט כל אחד ואחד בפני עצמו? אלא שאם צרכו להן לישראל, המקום עושה להם מלחמה. אי להם לאומות העולם מה הם שומעים באזניהם, שהרי מי שאמר והיה העולם עתיד להלחם בם.

The first point of analysis is the technique. Previous chapters have detailed at length how the Midrash regularly puts together a pastiche of verses to engage in parallel analysis or to justify the need for all the verses.[12] In this midrash, the darshan adopts this method to interpret a laconic phrase in the light of more detailed verses.[13] He begins with a bare sketch of God as "a man of war," and dips his brush into the rest of the Tanakh, which is "richer" in its descriptions, to apply thick layers of colorful paint to the canvas. The resulting portrait is no mere soldier but a bonafide one-man-army; God is the infantry, the archery, the cavalry. In modern terms, He is like the action hero who can adroitly wield any weapon and take the pilot's seat of any vehicle of war.

  a The weapons and armor just detailed.
  b The preceding passage focuses on God as armed and armored, now it shifts to the second half of the verse regarding God's name.
  c See 1 Samuel 17:45.

Beyond injecting color and adding layers to the monochromatic verse in Exodus, this compilation of verses builds up the divine persona and reveals a pattern of behavior. Time and time again, God "revealed Himself" to the Israelites of antiquity in the guise of a warrior. God is indeed a "man of war," says the Midrash.

But what about the present day of the Midrash? Is He still a "man of war" for the Jewish people? The Song of the Sea revels in God's destruction of the Israelites' enslavers, the mighty empire of Egypt, but can the downtrodden people under Roman imperial rule identify with its contents? Throughout its interpretation of this poem, the Midrash posits that past events in fact predict future outcomes: "He became my deliverance" (Ex. 15:2). He was such for me in the past and will be in the future"; "Worker of wonders" (Ex. 15:11). He has worked wonders for the forefathers and will work them for their progeny. (*Mekhilta de-Rabbi Yishmael, Shirata*, §3, p. 126, and §8, p. 144). In our derashah, too, the darshan promises his audience that they can rely on God winning a final showdown with their world-spanning oppressors. Be patient, he encourages, because God will return to bring down the mighty and arrogant Roman Empire.

The midrash then goes a step further. There is one verb in the derashah that appears neither in the past tense ("revealed") nor in the future ("will fight"), but refers to the present of the audience: "they hear." The darshan claims that the biblical verses, which the enemy "hears with its own ears," put the fear of God into them. This is likely hyperbole intended to lift the spirits of those present during the reading of the Torah in the synagogue. The darshan equips the well-attested divine arsenal in the fight against his enemies, although the actual battle is limited to the plane of morale.[14]

The darshan brings the Torah to life. He expands the snapshot of a "man of war" into a movie. He brings past to meet the present with a promise for the future. God will eventually reveal His omnipotence and redeem His people. Right now, they can catch a glimpse of Him through the biblical snippets furnished by the darshan. Through his interpretation, the Song of the Sea can continue to resound even after the destruction of the Temple and the seeming abandonment of the Jewish people by their God. The Midrash is affective, in the sense that it brings consolation and inspires hope. In this way, it is no less relevant to everyday life than a halakhah exegetically extracted from the Torah.[15] This homily can be argued to promote militarism, by entertaining fantasies of revenge, or even nonresistance, by replacing actual weapons with verses, but its consolatory role is undeniable.

In late Antiquity, there were other ways to vivify the Torah, such as allegorical interpretation. While we have briefly looked at Jewish allegory from that period, let us now consider a contemporaneous Christian interpretation.[16]

Origen of Alexandria, who lived at roughly the same time and in the same cultural sphere as the last generation of Tannaim, wrote about the splitting of the sea:

If you flee Egypt, if you leave behind the darkness of ignorance and follow Moses, the Law of God, should the sea hinder you and the waves of contradictions rush

> ORIGEN OF ALEXANDRIA
>
> Origen lived from circa 185 to 255 CE. He was raised a Christian in Alexandria, where he spent the first half of his life and received a comprehensive classical education. In the 230s, he came into conflict with the local bishop and relocated to Caesarea. He wrote prolifically in Greek, and his writings included homilies and exegesis of the Old and New Testaments, and philosophical and polemical works. His interpretations harmonize Platonic philosophy with Christian belief.
>
> Only a small percentage of his voluminous writings survives because the fourth and fifth centuries saw controversies over them. Due to his Platonic inclinations, Origen was declared a heretic and many of his works were destroyed. Those that remain were preserved in Latin translations done by Jerome and Rufinus in the same period.
>
> He compiled the Hexapla (literally "sixfold"), the first critical edition of the Bible that included the Hebrew text, four Greek translations (including the Septuagint), and a Greek transliteration. He was also quite familiar with Jewish traditions and maintained contacts among the Sages of Caesarea. See further de Lange, *Origen and the Jews*.

against you, strike the opposing waves with the rod of Moses, that is the word of the Law and by vigilance in the Scriptures open a way for yourself by disputing with the adversaries. Immediately the waves will yield and the floods which surmounted will give place to the conquerors. [. . .] In this way, therefore, we can "see" even today (*etiam hodie*) "the Egyptians dead and lying on the shore," their four-horse chariots and cavalry drowned. [. . .] And therefore, if you cross the Red Sea, if you see the Egyptians drowned and Pharaoh destroyed and cast headlong into the depth of the abyss, you can "sing a hymn to God."[17]

For Origen, Scripture is realized in the here and now. He does not need to follow the darshan's gaze into the future. The splitting of the sea is interpreted on the psychological plane, which calls to mind Philo's approach.[18] The journey to and through the sea symbolizes the soul's striving toward perfection and its struggle to overcome the obstacles on that path. Egypt is Satan's works, the sea's waves are challenges to one's faith, and Moses represents the spiritualized path of the Torah that contends with the body's baser drives.

The Midrash, in contrast, avoids reducing the Torah's relevance to the psyche of the individual.[19] The national story of yore continues to bear meaning for the nation—even if it potentially concerns only the distant future.[20] The Midrash also eschews the approach taken in Qumranic writings, in which every element of the verses speaks directly to present-day events.[21] The most the darshan can do is extend his fistful of verses as consolation. In this, though, lies its potency. Midrash might be an intellectual endeavor, but it also has tremendous affective power to reconfigure the way its addressees feel about their own religious identity and relationship with God.

C. DEVELOPING A THEME

The single aggadic derashah, brief or long, is the first and smallest unit of analysis for assessing the Midrash's techniques and aims. The next one is the larger sequence of derashot, through which the Midrash regularly develops themes.[22]

The selection chosen for scrutiny is from Tractate *Ba-Ḥodesh* of the *Mekhilta*. It interprets the verses on the lead-up to the giving of the Torah when the Israelites stood at the foot of Mount Sinai. The Torah describes the moments before the divine revelation in these words:

> It happened on the third day, as morning dawned, that there were thunderclaps and lightning-flashes and a heavy cloud on the mountain, and the sound of a shofar, very strong, and all the people who were in the camp trembled. And Moses brought out the people toward God from the camp and they stationed themselves at the bottom of the mountain. (Ex. 19:16–17)

The first derashah states:

> "It happened on the third day, as morning dawned" (Ex. 19:16). It teaches that the Omnipresent preceded them, to fulfill what is said, "While the king sat at his table, my spikenard sent forth its fragrance"[a] (Songs 1:12). (*Mekhilta de-Rabbi Yishmael, Ba-Ḥodesh*, §3, p. 214)

"וַיְהִי בַיּוֹם הַשְּׁלִישִׁי בִּהְיֹת הַבֹּקֶר" (שמות יט, טז)—מלמד שהקדים המקום על ידו, לקיים מה שנאמר, "עַד שֶׁהַמֶּלֶךְ בִּמְסִבּוֹ נִרְדִּי נָתַן רֵיחוֹ" (שיר השירים א, יב).

If the forces of nature herald God's presence, the Torah's observation that they beset the mountain "as morning dawned" conveys that God got there first, before Moses and the rest of the Israelites.

The darshan here uses an exclusively aggadic phrase, "to fulfill what is said." This encapsulates the notion that all of Scripture is a prophecy to be realized. In rabbinic exegesis, as opposed to the *pesher* literature and Christological interpretation,[23] this occurs within the Bible itself.[24] The intertextuality here involves a verse in Song of Songs. The Midrash reads that book generally as a romance between God and the Jewish people. Within that framework, the giving of the Torah at Sinai becomes a metaphysical marriage between God the groom and Israel the bride. Plugging this back into Exodus, when God shows up first thing

---

a The proof from the verse seems to be based on the verse's sequence: God is already at the wedding hall when the scent of the approaching beloved wafts toward Him. Cf. *Songs Rabbah*, 1:12, where God arrives to find the Israelites asleep and jolts them awake with bolts of lightning and claps of thunder.

in the morning with forces of nature as the orchestra and lighting, it signifies His excitement and desire to enter this binding relationship through the wedding.

Through this intertextual interpretation, the ratification of a covenant between an all-powerful sovereign and his subjects morphs into a bond of matrimony between two persons in love. The darshan's simple technique of linking verses, one from Exodus with another from Song of Songs, speaks volumes, with nary a word of exposition.[25] This reading is jarring, as the biblical verses themselves describe not only an atmosphere of utmost gravity, but a people feeling sheer terror. The Midrash is well aware of this tension, as we will soon see.

The next derashah elucidates the natural wonders that signaled the presence of God upon the mount:

> "There were thunderclaps *(kolot)*"[a] (Ex. 19:16)—*kol, kolot;* different, distinct types of thunderclaps.
>
> "And lightning-flashes *(u-verakim)*" (Ex. 19:16)—*barak, berakim;* different, distinct types of lightning. (*Mekhilta de-Rabbi Yishmael, Ba-Ḥodesh,* §3, p. 214)

"וַיְהִי קֹלֹת" (שמות יט, טז)—קוֹל, קוֹלוֹת, וּמִינֵי קוֹלוֹת מְשׁוּנִים זֶה מִזֶּה.

"וּבְרָקִים" (שם)—בָּרָק, בְּרָקִים, וּמִינֵי בְּרָקִים מְשׁוּנִים זֶה מִזֶּה.

According to the Midrash, the verse could have used singular *kol* to denote thunder and singular *barak* for lightning. The fact that it uses the plural is understood to mean that there was unusual variation in the peals of thunders and flashes of lightning. Two elements encountered in halakhic contexts recur here: the exhaustive parsing of words into their constituent parts, and the assumption that a linguistic plural must mirror some multiplicity in reality. Through this technique, the darshan thickens the frightening atmosphere: the lightning and thunder are weird and unsettling. The full meaning of this move, however, only becomes clear as the derashot proceed, which is why taking in the full sweep of derashot is important.

The exegesis of the verses continues:

> "And a heavy cloud *('anan kaved)* on the mountain" (Ex. 19:16). This is the thick cloud *('arafel),* as it says, "and Moses approached the thick cloud *('arafel)*" (Ex. 20:18). (*Mekhilta de-Rabbi Yishmael, Ba-Ḥodesh,* §3, p. 214)

"וְעָנָן כָּבֵד עַל הָהָר" (שמות יט, טז)—זֶה עֲרָפֶל, שֶׁנֶּאֱמַר "וּמֹשֶׁה נִגַּשׁ אֶל הָעֲרָפֶל" (שמות כ, יח).

Why does the Midrash identify the "heavy cloud" with the "thick cloud"? To align two discrepant accounts of the divine revelation, the theophany, at Mount Sinai. Chapter 19 mentions the

---

a The fact that the plural is used instead of the singular indicates not only repetition but variability, and is intended to heighten the drama.

heavy cloud and chapter 20 the thick cloud. While Bible scholars characteristically attribute these discrepancies to divergent sources, the rabbinic exegete ties them together. Recall that harmonization of discrepancies is a basic driver of midrashic activity, and it applies equally to law and narrative.[26]

> "And the sound of a shofar was strengthening greatly *(ḥazak me'od)*" (Ex. 19:16). Normally, the longer it extends the fainter it grows; here, though, the longer it extends the louder it gets.
>
> Why did it begin softly? To accustom the ear to what it can hear. (*Mekhilta de-Rabbi Yishmael, Ba-Ḥodesh*, §3, p. 214)

> "וְקוֹל שֹׁפָר חָזָק מְאֹד" (שמות יט, טז). מנהג הדיוט, כל זמן שהוא הולך, קולו עמום; אבל כאן כל זמן שהוא הולך, קולו מגביר. ולמה רך מבתחלה? לשבר את האוזן מה שהיא יכולה לשמוע.

According to the accepted vocalization of the consonantal biblical text, which was systematized by early medieval Jewish masoretes,[27] the word *ḥazak* is an adjective; the phrase *ḥazak me'od* means "very strong." According to the Midrash, it is a stative verb, so the translation given here is "strengthening greatly."[28] Why does the Midrash deviate from the simple sense? Again, harmonization. The parallel account in the next chapter of Exodus has *ḥazak* as a verb: "The sound of the shofar was getting stronger and stronger *(holekh ve-ḥazak me'od)*" (Ex. 20:19).

While aligning the two descriptions of the revelation at Sinai, the darshan also imparts its uniqueness. As anyone who plays a brass or wind instrument can tell you, the sound begins strong before fading out over time. Here, the shofar blast announcing God's descent on the mountain starts out softly and crescendos. If the volume dial had been turned to the maximum at the outset, the Israelites would have been frightened.

Was this gradual increase in sound effective? If we were to read this derashah in isolation, we might think so. The very next derashah answers in the negative:

> "And all the people who were in the camp trembled *(va-yeḥerad)*" (Ex. 19:16). It teaches that they were shaken up *(nizda'ze'u)*. (*Mekhilta de-Rabbi Yishmael, Ba-Ḥodesh*, §3, p. 214)

> "וַיֶּחֱרַד כָּל הָעָם אֲשֶׁר בַּמַּחֲנֶה" (שמות יט, טז)—מלמד שנזדעזעו.

This derashah seems trivial: it simply translates the biblical Hebrew word (from the root ḥ-r-d) to the corresponding one in mishnaic Hebrew (from the duplicative root z-'-z-'). Nothing appears to be gained since both combine the emotional experience of fear with the physical one of trembling. When viewed in context of the previous derashah, one sees a thematic tension developing. God tries to introduce Himself gently, but He is God after all, and an encounter with a deity is scary. We are witnessing the budding tension between the vision of the giving of the Torah as a blissful marriage and the reality of a bride who is terrified of her husband.

The Midrash moves to the next verse:

> "And Moses brought out the people toward God from the camp" (Ex. 19:17).
>
> Rabbi Yose said: Yehudah would expound, "the Lord came from Sinai *(mi-Sinai)*" (Deut. 33:2)—don't read it this way, but as[a] "the Lord came *to* Sinai *(le-Sinai),*" to give to the Torah to Israel.
>
> Or one should not say thus, rather "the Lord came *from* Sinai *(mi-Sinai),*" to receive Israel, like the groom goes out to greet the bride. (*Mekhilta de-Rabbi Yishmael, Ba-Ḥodesh,* §3, p. 214)

> "וַיּוֹצֵא מֹשֶׁה אֶת הָעָם לִקְרַאת הָאֱלֹהִים מִן הַמַּחֲנֶה" (שמות יט, יז).
>
> אמר ר' יוסי: יהודה היה דורש, "ה' מִסִּינַי בָּא" (דברים לג, ב)—אל תקרא כן, אלא "ה' לסיני בא", ליתן תורה לישראל.
>
> או אינו אומר כן, אלא "ה' מסיני בא", לקבל את ישראל, כחתן זה שהוא יוצא לקראת כלה.

This midrash relates to the opening words of Moses's farewell address at the end of Deuteronomy. The verse there mentions Sinai, so the Midrash assumes that it refers to the giving of the Torah at Sinai. The action described in that verse, however, is perplexing. Why would God be coming *from* Sinai, and if He was, what was His destination?[29] Rabbi Yehudah, as cited by Rabbi Yose, plays with the preposition to change the directionality, so that God is coming *to* Sinai. Rabbi Yose himself reads the text as is, so that God, whom the Midrash has already established arrived bright and early at Sinai, went forth to greet His bride. Although Rabbi Yose does not invoke Song of Songs, the imagery is redolent of it.

This midrash grapples with a difficulty in Deuteronomy, and that is probably its original context.[30] It was moved here given its relevance to our verse in Exodus.[31] While our verse describes Moses as bringing out the people to God, Rabbi Yose understands the other verse to mean that God goes out to greet the people. The composite image, then, is of the two parties moving toward each other in mutual love, with Moses ushering their union.

Yet, here too, this love is adulterated by fear:

> "And they stationed themselves *(vayyityatzevu)*" (Ex. 19:17)—they were huddling together. It teaches that the Israelites were afraid of the successive brilliant lights,

---

a   This is not an emendation of the biblical text but an interpretive rereading.

Aggadah in the Midrash   319

quaking earth, thunderclaps, and lightning flashes.ᵃ (*Mekhilta de-Rabbi Yishmael, Ba-Ḥodesh*, §3, p. 214)

"ויתיצבו"—ניצפפו. מלמד שהיו מתיראין מפני הזיקין ומפני הזועות מפני הרעמים מפני הברקים הבאים.

The word *vayyityatzevu* is regular enough in biblical Hebrew, where it means "to stand or station oneself." The gloss that it means "huddling" must therefore stem from the immediate continuation of the verse, "at the bottom of the mountain." The idea seems to be that the throngs of people all shrank back from fear so that they squeezed into a single space.³² This is a far cry from the picture-perfect moment of the bride meeting her groom. This picks up the earlier midrashic imagery of awe and fright.

The *Mekhilta* offers two conflicting portrayals of the relationship between the Israelites and God at Mount Sinai: fear and trembling, and love and attraction. Studying the derashot sequentially has further uncovered that the two sets of imagery alternate. The Midrash appears to be conveying, as well as it can given the constraints of the literary format, that the sensory synesthesia of hearing lightning and seeing thunder extended into the realm of emotions. The people experienced conflicting emotions simultaneously: love gave way to fear and fear to love.

The Midrash's dialectical account may be incipient in the biblical narrative itself. Exodus 19 begins with God's promise, "you shall be to Me a kingdom of priests and a holy nation" (Ex. 19:6), after which the people passionately accept this charge: "All that the Lord has spoken we will do" (Ex. 19:8).³³ Wedding imagery is absent, but the consensual relationship is there. Then the Torah depicts the pyrotechnics and the waves of fear, accompanied by threats not to touch the mountain on pain of death. The Midrash picks up on this courting and fear and threads them through the entire pericope. It winds the threads so tightly that in one phrase attraction is visible, and in the very next fear is palpable.

This dialectic culminates in the final derashah of the sequence:

"At the bottom *(taḥtit)* of the mountain" (Ex. 19:17). It teaches that the mountain was uprooted and they drew near and stood under *(taḥat)* the mountain, as it says, "and they drew near and stood under *(taḥat)* the mountain" (Deut. 4:11). Regarding them there is an explicit tradition,ᵇ "My dove in the rock's crevices, in the hollow of the cliff, let me see your looks, let me hear your voice, for your voice is sweet, and your appearance desirable" (Songs 2:14).

---

a This list is taken verbatim from Mishnah, *Berakhot*, 9:2: "On shooting stars, earthquakes, lightning, and thunder one says, 'Blessed be He whose power fills the world.'" On the relationship between the Midrash and the Mishnah, see chapter 15.

b Heb. *kabbalah* here refers to all of Scripture àthat postdates the Torah, meaning the Writings and the Prophets, rather than oral tradition.

"Let me see your looks"—these are the twelve pillars[a] for the twelve tribes of Israel.

"Let me hear your voice"—this is the Decalogue.

"For your voice is sweet"—after the Decalogue.

"And your appearance desirable"—"The entire assembly drew near and stood before *(lifnei)* the Lord"[b] (Lev. 9:5). (*Mekhilta de-Rabbi Yishmael, Ba-Ḥodesh*, §3, pp. 214–215)

"בְּתַחְתִּית הָהָר" (שמות יט, יז)—מלמד שנתלש ההר ממקומו, וקרבו ועמדו תחת ההר, שנאמר "וַתִּקְרְבוּן וַתַּעַמְדוּן תַּחַת הָהָר" (דברים ד, יא). עליהם מפורש בקבלה, "יוֹנָתִי בְּחַגְוֵי הַסֶּלַע בְּסֵתֶר הַמַּדְרֵגָה הַרְאִינִי אֶת מַרְאַיִךְ הַשְׁמִיעִנִי אֶת קוֹלֵךְ כִּי קוֹלֵךְ עָרֵב וּמַרְאֵיךְ נָאוֶה" (שיר השירים ב, יד). "הַרְאִינִי אֶת מַרְאַיִךְ"—אלו שתים עשרה מצבה לשנים עשר שבטי ישראל; "הַשְׁמִיעִנִי אֶת קוֹלֵךְ"—אלו עשרת הדברות; "כִּי קוֹלֵךְ עָרֵב"—לאחר הדברות; "וּמַרְאֵיךְ נָאוֶה"—"וַיִּקְרְבוּ כָּל הָעֵדָה וַיַּעַמְדוּ לִפְנֵי ה'" (ויקרא ט, ה).

In context, singular *taḥtit* refers to the foot of the mountain. Everywhere else in Scripture, though, the singular form is an adjective, often referring to Sheol, the place under the earth where the dead are said to go. Only here does it appear to be a noun. This is the first curiosity that tingles the darshan's homiletical sense. Second, if *taḥtit* refers to the lowest part of something, in this case the mountain, how are we to resolve the Israelites standing at the bottom with the express prohibition not to touch the mountain (Ex. 19:12)? The darshan therefore construes *taḥtit* as a preposition meaning "underneath," which matches the description in Song of Songs of the "dove" in or under the rock. The result is a fantastic image of a mountain suspended in the air, hovering over the people, so that they are literally at the bottom of—underneath—it.[34]

A much later derashah preserved in the Babylonian Talmud stresses the fear induced by a mountain held over the Israelites' heads:

"And they stationed themselves at the bottom of the mountain" (Ex. 19:17). Rav Avdimi bar Hamma bar Hassa said, It teaches that the Holy One inverted the mountain over them like a tub, and said to them: "If you accept the Torah—good, but if not, there will be your grave." (Babylonian Talmud, *Shabbat*, 88a)

The mountain is like a knife held at the throat; the covenant is accepted under duress.[35]

But the *Mekhilta* does not have to be read that way.[36] Perhaps the mountain on which God has descended is borne aloft so that the people can come as close as possible to Him. Since it is forbidden to ascend the mountain, they can huddle together underneath it. The reference to Song of Songs supports this, since attraction is the central emotion there. Nevertheless, one cannot discount the reading of the Talmud. Both are equally valid, especially

---

a Visible from afar; see Exodus 24:4.

b The darshan may read "*lifnei* the Lord" to mean "toward the countenance of the Lord," which explicitly connects to the phrase in the next verse: "the glory of the Lord will appear to you."

because the *Mekhilta* itself, as we have seen throughout, toggles between love and fear. This ambiguity might even be the point of the editor placing this derashah here, after the back and forth attested above. The preceding derashot switch off between one and the other, and here both are possible at once.[37]

Analysis of these derashot yields insights into aggadic Midrash that can be arranged in three concentric circles: the individual derashah, the series of derashot, and the tractate. Regarding the individual derashah, we can glean from this group of exegetical comments that aggadic derashot are less standardized and terminologically formulaic than halakhic ones. The derashot anchoring halakha have much less freedom of movement, because they must affix oral legal traditions to some unsuspecting phrases at all costs. The aggadic derashot, by contrast, even when they develop a theme in a certain direction, have more room to maneuver. Unencumbered by the weight of tradition, the aggadic darshan has freer rein, and can dwell more on the meaning of the local verse.

Next, we have seen how a series of derashot develops a complex theme. Here, it elaborates the dialectical experience of the Israelites' encounter with God at the giving of the Torah. To do so, the Midrash employs many forms of derashot, from short glosses to lengthy intertextual interpretations, and uses multiple midrashic tools, including linguistic atomization and symbolic explication. Only when reading these derashot in sequence does one discover the alternation that communicates the unique interplay of emotions that the Midrash imagines to have occurred with the touching of the earthly and divine planes at Sinai.

The lesson to be learned is that the Midrash can exhibit thematic interest in longer biblical passages. In this passage of the *Mekhilta*, thematic development is the product of editorial work, but scholars have identified other places where identifiable darshanim carry on systematic disputes in their interpretation of longer tracts.[38] This lines up with what we have seen in halakhic midrashim, where darshanim also demonstrate awareness of the larger context.[39]

Finally, the widest circle of all is the tractate. The thematic coherence of these derashot in Tractate *Ba-Ḥodesh* exposes a larger phenomenon in the *Mekhilta:* some of its tractates have a special character produced by editing. Tractate *Shirata*, scholars have shown, has certain tendencies, such as the heavy use of the measure-for-measure principle of retributive justice, and the reading of past events as promises for the future.[40] Ideas animate aggadic Midrash as much as textual issues, so one must keep one's eye on both when reading any derashah.

D. COMPLEMENT TO HALAKHAH

Aggadic Midrash comes in two flavors: pure and mixed. The former exists in its own self-contained midrashic collections. The pure aggadic Midrash from the *Mekhilta* discussed above (as well as in the *Be-Ha'alotekha* sections of *Sifrei Numbers* and *Ha'azinu* in *Sifrei Deuteronomy*) does not belong to any single school.[41] The mixed aggadic Midrash, in contrast, runs like a band, thinner in some places and thicker in others, through the halakhic Midrash of the two major schools. It interprets the non-legal verses interspersed within Torah law, or adds aggadic dimensions to the legal verses themselves. This commingling of material informs us of a significant historical reality: Aggadah had a place in the same bet midrash where Halakhah was studied and taught. The same Sages who pored over the halakhic portions of the Torah also devoted (at least some of) their energies to aggadic interpretation.

When the Torah rules that the firstborn son receives a double portion of inheritance, *Sifrei Deuteronomy* expounds the legal details from the verses. Sandwiched between those halakhic derashot is an aggadic comment:

> "[And the firstborn son is] the despised one's" (Deut. 21:15). Scripture apprises *(mevasser)* you that [if you marry two women] the firstborn son will belong to the despised one. (*Sifrei Deuteronomy*, §215, p. 249)

> ״[וְהָיָה הַבֵּן הַבְּכֹר] לַשְּׂנִיאָה״ (דברים כא, טו)—הכתוב מבשרך שהבן הבכור לשניאה.

In the Torah, the clause assigning the firstborn son to the despised wife is part of the setup for the ultimate ruling that the firstborn son receives a double portion. But the Midrash lets no detail go to waste. The background details of the legal case, therefore, become a lesson themselves. Embedded in inheritance law is the Torah's attitude—according to the rabbis—toward maintaining the integrity of the family. Through this aggadic reading, the darshan expresses his disapproval of polygamy.[42] The Midrash softens the edges between Halakhah and Aggadah in a kind of literary sfumato.

Some Torah passages are subject to a mix of halakhic and aggadic treatment because they straddle the fence between narrative and law. Chapters 12 and 13 of the book of Exodus are a case in point: they are filled with law but also form part of the narrative of the exodus from Egypt. Tractate *Pasḥa* of the *Mekhilta* accordingly integrates Aggadah with Halakhah:

> "And you shall keep watch over it[a] [until the fourteenth day of this month]" (Ex. 12:6). Why did Scripture precede the taking of the paschal sacrifice to its slaughter by four days? Rabbi Matteyah ben Harash would say:

> Well it says, "When I passed by you and saw you, behold, your time was the time of love"[b] (Ezek. 16:8). The oath that the Holy One swore to Abraham,[c] that He would redeem his progeny, was being fulfilled, but they had no mitzvot to perform in order to be redeemed.[d] As it says, "Your breasts were ripe and your hair sprouted

---

a The paschal lamb.
b Sexual maturity and marriageability.
c See Genesis 15:14.
d They needed to merit redemption. On the tension between the merit of the Patriarchs and the need for action by their progeny, see Urbach, *The Sages*, 483–511.

[but you were naked and bare]" (Ezek. 16:7)—bare of mitzvot. The Holy One gave them two mitzvot—the mitzvah of the paschal sacrifice and the mitzvah of circumcision[a]—to perform in order to be redeemed. As it says, "And I passed by you [and saw you wallowing in your blood. I said to you: in your blood, live]" (Ex. 16:6), and it says, "As for you, too, for the sake of the blood of your covenant [I have sent out your prisoners, from the pit that has no water]" (Zech. 9:11). Therefore, Scripture preceded the taking of the paschal sacrifice to its slaughter by four days, for one receives reward only for action. (*Mekhilta de-Rabbi Yishmael, Pasḥa*, §5, p. 14)

"וְהָיָה לָכֶם לְמִשְׁמֶרֶת [עַד אַרְבָּעָה עָשָׂר יוֹם לַחֹדֶשׁ הַזֶּה] וגו'" (שמות יב, ו). מפני מה הקדים הכתוב לקיחתו של פסח לשחיטתו ארבעה ימים? היה רבי מתיא בן חרש אומר: הרי הוא אומר, "וָאֶעֱבֹר עָלַיִךְ וָאֶרְאֵךְ [וְהִנֵּה עִתֵּךְ עֵת דֹּדִים]" (יחזקאל טז, ח). הגיע שבועתו שנשבע הקב"ה לאברהם שהוא גואל את בניו, ולא היה בידם מצות שיתעסקו בהם כדי שיגאלו, שנאמר "שָׁדַיִם נָכֹנוּ וּשְׂעָרֵךְ צִמֵּחַ [וְאַתְּ עֵרֹם וְעֶרְיָה]" (שם ז)—"עריה מן המצות. נתן להם הקודש שתי מצות: מצות פסח ומצות מילה, שיתעסקו בהן כדי שיגאלו, שנאמר "וָאֶעֱבֹר עָלַיִךְ וָאֶרְאֵךְ מִתְבּוֹסֶסֶת בְּדָמָיִךְ]" (שם ו), ואומר "גַּם אַתְּ בְּדַם בְּרִיתֵךְ [שִׁלַּחְתִּי אֲסִירַיִךְ מִבּוֹר אֵין מַיִם בּוֹ]" (זכריה ט, יא). לכך הקדים הכתוב לקיחתו של פסח לשחיטתו ד' ימים, שאין נוטלין שכר אלא על המעשה.

The Torah requires the Israelites in Egypt to take the paschal lamb on the tenth of Nisan, even though it is only to be sacrificed on the fourteenth. This puzzling requirement is not found elsewhere. The darshan addresses this lag by adducing two verses from the Prophets that he reads as being about the Exodus.[43] The Prophets and Writings yet again act as a thickening agent when the Torah is too thin for the darshan's taste.

Ezekiel 16 is interpreted here as a poetic description of the nation's spiritual state at the time of the Exodus. This has some textual basis, since the chapter is manifestly an allegory about the relationship between the people and God. It depicts the Israelite nation as a foundling that God took in and eventually married, only to have the favor repaid with infidelity. What is striking is how the Midrash turns this posterchild of wretchedness, an infant abandoned while still wallowing in the blood of its birth, into a nation on the cusp of redemption.[44] To accomplish this, the darshan reverses the flow of the verses, making verse 6 ("in your blood, live") the response to verse 7 ("you were naked"). The verse from Zechariah serves as the linchpin: it explicitly connects covenantal blood with freedom from imprisonment. The blood of circumcision accrues merit for redemption.

This looks like a real stretch, but it is actually grounded in Exodus 12 as a whole. There, the Torah underscores the centrality of the sacrificial blood, which is to be smeared on the doorpost (v. 22), and it also requires circumcision in order for the Israelites to partake of the sacrifice (v. 48). In fact, it is the only mitzvah in the Torah that explicitly requires circumcision as a prerequisite for its performance. In a way, the chapter begins with the blood of the paschal lamb and ends with the blood of circumcision, practically crying out to the darshan

---

a See Exodus 12:48 and Joshua 5:5.

to be connected. The intertextuality of the derashah is surprising, but its contextual basis is quite sound.

The message in all this is clear: the merit of the forefathers isn't enough for God to redeem them, but they must themselves be worthy: "one receives reward only for action."[45] The story of the exodus from Egypt can thus serve as a template for the future redemption.

This example is everything we have seen so far wrapped in one. There is midrashic ingenuity in the intricate intertextual linkages. Minute details and the much broader context all factor into the exegesis. Religious lessons flow effortlessly, as if naturally, from their textual source.

Another specimen of sophisticated aggadic Midrash centers on the very next verse in Exodus 12:

> "They shall put it[a] on the two doorposts" (Ex. 12:7)—on the inside. Do you say on the inside, or instead on the outside? It therefore teaches, "and I will see the blood" (Ex. 12:13)—visible to Me and not to others[b]—the words of Rabbi Yishmael.
>
> Rabbi Yonatan says, On the inside. Do you say on the inside, or instead on the outside? It therefore teaches, "And the blood will be a sign for you" (Ex. 12:13)—a sign for you and not a sign for others.
>
> Rabbi Yitzhak says, It is actually on the outside, so that the Egyptians see and their insides churn. (*Mekhilta de-Rabbi Yishmael, Pasḥa*, §6, p. 18)

"וְנָתְנוּ עַל שְׁתֵּי הַמְּזוּזֹת" (שמות יב, ז) וגו'—מבפנים. אתה אומר מבפנים או אינו אלא מבחוץ? ת"ל "וְרָאִיתִי אֶת הַדָּם" (שמות יב, יג)—הנראה לי ולא לאחרים—דברי רבי ישמעאל.

ר' יונתן אומר: מבפנים. אתה אומר מבפנים או אינו אלא מבחוץ? ת"ל "וְהָיָה הַדָּם לָכֶם לְאֹת" (שמות יב, יג)—לכם לאות ולא לאחרים לאות.

ר' יצחק אומר: לעולם מבחוץ, כדי שיהיו המצריים רואים ומעיהם מתחתכין.

This midrash records three approaches to the placement of the blood of the paschal lamb, since the verse does not specify where to smear it. The first two agree that it is put inside while disagreeing about the exact textual source. The third argues for external placement without any source beyond a reasonable suggestion.

The commonality of these three opinions, though, overshadows these differences. By placing them together, the editor of this midrash emphasizes that they all partake in the othering of the Egyptians: the threshold of the Israelite house keeps the Egyptians outside, apart from God and the Israelites inside. Notably, all three also ignore the Torah's own explanation of the

---

a The blood of the paschal sacrifice.
b The Egyptians.

blood's purpose in verse 23, that God needs the visible sign to know which Israelite homes to save from the "destroyer" during the plague of the firstborn. Even Rabbi Yitzhak, who argues for external placement, theorizes that its purpose is to unsettle the Egyptians, acting as an ominous sign of things to come. Why not follow the simple reading? In all likelihood, it would have been considered theologically objectionable for God to require an external sign to identify friend from foe. Once again, halakhic exegesis and aggadic ideas feed into each other.

The interface of Halakahah and Aggadah does not only happen when the biblical text itself mixes narrative and law. It occurs in many other contexts in Midrashim of both schools. In the Mishnah, tractates often end with Aggadah, and the same is true for the Midrash.[46] The end of a biblical legal passage, especially one that ends with some non-legal declaration like "I am the Lord your God who took you out of Egypt," is a good place to find aggadic passages.[47] For instance, after outlawing various idolatrous practices, the Torah states its attitude toward their practitioners:

> "For whoever does these is abhorrent to the Lord, and because of these abhorrent things the Lord your God dispossesses them before you" (Deut. 18:12).

> When Rabbi Eliezer would reach this verse he would say, Woe unto us! If an impure spirit dwells on someone who adheres to impurity, it follows logically that the Holy Spirit dwells on someone who adheres to the divine presence. [So] what caused [our fallen condition]? "It is your iniquities that have separated between you and your God" (Isa. 59:2). (*Sifrei Deuteronomy*, §173, p. 220)

> "כִּי תוֹעֲבַת ה' כָּל עֹשֵׂה אֵלֶּה וּבִגְלַל הַתּוֹעֵבֹת הָאֵלֶּה ה' אֱלֹהֶיךָ מוֹרִישׁ אוֹתָם מִפָּנֶיךָ" (דברים יח, יב). כשהיה רבי אליעזר מגיע לפסוק זה, היה אומר: חבל עלינו! מי שמדבק בטומאה—רוח טומאה שורה עליו, המידבק בשכינה—דין הוא שתשרה עליו רוח הקודש. ומי גרם? "כִּי אִם עֲוֺנֹתֵיכֶם הָיוּ מַבְדִּלִים בֵּינֵכֶם לְבֵין אֱלֹהֵיכֶם" (ישעיה נט, ב).

At times, the Torah itself adds some non-halakhic dimension at the end of a set of laws. After it sets forth the prohibition on eating tree fruit within the first three years of planting, and the requirement to treat the fruit of the fourth year with sanctity, it promises: "But in the fifth year you may eat its fruit, to increase *(lehosif)* its produce for you" (Lev. 19:25). The final words add no new halakhic information, so what do they mean?

> Rabbi Yose ha-Gelili says, It is as if you are adding *(mosif)*[a] the produce of the fifth to the produce of the fourth.[b] Just as the produce of the fifth is the owner's, so too the produce of the fourth is the owner's.[c]

a The word *lehosif* in context means "to increase," but it can also mean "to add onto."
b Years since planting.
c And does not belong to the priest, as the ancient tradition had it. See Werman and Shemesh, *Revealing the Hidden*, 216–221; and Kister, "Some Aspects," esp. 576–581.

Rabbi Akiva says, The Torah was speaking regarding the inclination.[a] So that a person does not say, "I have suffered needlessly for four years," it therefore says, "to increase[b] its produce for you." (Sifra, Kedoshim, 4:1, 90b)

רבי יוסי הגלילי אומר: הרי אתה כמוסיף פירות חמישית על פירות רביעית, מה פירות חמישית לבעלים אף פירות רביעית לבעלים.

רבי עקיבא אומר: דברה תורה כנגד היצר, שלא יהיה אדם אומר הרי ארבע שנים אני מיצטער בו חינם, לכך נאמר "לְהוֹסִיף לָכֶם תְּבוּאָתוֹ" (ויקרא יט, כה).

According to Rabbi Yose ha-Gelili, our assumption was wrong. There *is* new halakhic information to discover: the fruit of the fourth year belongs to the owner and not to the priests, against the ancient tradition. Rabbi Akiva, on the other hand, accepts the non-halakhic verse for what it is and engages in aggadic exegesis. The Torah, in his opinion, addresses our tendency to grumble.[48] Humans are too impatient to wait three years for fruit and then to have its consumption strictly regulated for another year. The Torah guarantees that God will reward the believer's patience and compliance and compensate them for the lost produce with a bumper crop.

Similarly, Deuteronomy's command to give tithes ends with a goal, which the Midrash expounds aggadically:

"In order that you learn to fear the Lord your God" (Deut. 14:23). It relates that the tithe brings a person to Torah study. (*Sifrei Deuteronomy*, §106, p. 167)

"לְמַעַן תִּלְמַד לְיִרְאָה אֶת ה' אֱלֹהֶיךָ" (דברים יד, כג)—מגיד שהמעשר מביא את האדם לידי תלמוד תורה.

After comprehensively expounding the halakhot of tithing, the *Sifrei* interprets the ultimate goal of the mitzvah. In the Torah, the intent is for the tither to come to the Temple as part of the very fulfillment of the mitzvah, which is supposed to instill fear of God's palpable presence. In the hands of the darshan, the Torah's words are malleable: "you learn to fear" (*tilmad le-yir'ah*) becomes "Torah study" (*talmud Torah*). The reconfiguration of a visceral reaction into an intellectual endeavor translates the biblical ideal into the rabbinic one.[49] In this example, the Midrash does not try to squeeze any halakhah from this patently non-halakhic statement.

One final derashah reveals how a single verse can be the subject of both halakhic and aggadic interpretation. The verse states: "Observe the month of Aviv and make the paschal sacrifice to the Lord your God, because in the month of Aviv the Lord your God took you out of Egypt at night" (Deut. 16:1). The command in the first half of the verse to celebrate the

---

a A human being's baser drives.
b And make up for the discarded fruit of the previous years.

holiday in the spring is interpreted halakhically, while the reasoning ("because . . . ") provided in the second half receives aggadic commentary:

> "Because in the month of Aviv" (Deut. 16:1)—a month that is suitable, neither hot nor cold. (*Sifrei Deuteronomy*, §128, p. 186)

> "כִּי בְּחֹדֶשׁ הָאָבִיב" (דברים טז, א)—חדש שהוא כשר, ולא חם ולא צונן.

This derashah does two things at once: it praises God for taking out the slaves during a season of fair weather, and it explains why the Torah supplies this information. The aggadic derashah shares the same justificatory aim as the halakhic derashah.

Some of the derashot examined above reflect a pattern: halakhic Midrash teaches what the Torah demands of humans, and aggadic Midrash accounts for divine behavior. This is borne out nicely by a derashah on the halakhic requirement to ascend to the Temple thrice yearly: "Three times a year all your males shall be seen in the presence of the Lord your God" (Deut. 16:16):

> "The presence of the Lord your God" (Deut. 16:16). If you do everything said about it, I shall put aside all of My dealings and preoccupy Myself only with you. (*Sifrei Deuteronomy*, §143, p. 196)

> "אֶת פְּנֵי ה' אֱלֹהֶיךָ" (דברים טז, טז)—אם עושה אתה כל האמור בעינין, מניח אני מכל עסקי ואיני עוסק אלא בך.

The aggadic interpretation brings in the theological angle, the divine recompense for fulfilling the mitzvot. The Midrash thus acts as an extension of the biblical book of Deuteronomy. More than any other book of the Torah, Deuteronomy is brimming with exhortations to observe Torah law and promises of reward and punishment.[50] These motifs elicit a response from the Midrash. This last derashah is a perfect instance of the Midrash picking up the biblical signal and amplifying it.

E. HALAKHIC GARB

Another kind of aggadic derashah, which also reflects the unique nature of the book of Deuteronomy, is one that has the semblance of Halakhah. Look carefully at this derashah:

> "Only to the place that the Lord your God will choose from among all your tribes" (Deut. 12:5)—seek it out *(derosh)*[a] from the mouth of a prophet. Could it be that you should wait until a prophet says it to you? It therefore teaches, "seek out His

a The future site of the Temple.

dwelling place" (Deut. 12:5)—seek it out and find it, and afterward the prophet will tell it to you.ª (*Sifrei Deuteronomy*, §62, pp. 127–128)

"כִּי אִם אֶל הַמָּקוֹם אֲשֶׁר יִבְחַר ה' אֱלֹהֵיכֶם מִכָּל שִׁבְטֵיכֶם" (דברים יב, ה)—דרוש על פי נביא. יכול תמתין עד שיומר לך נביא? תלמוד לומר, "לְשִׁכְנוֹ תִדְרְשׁוּ וּבָאתָ שָׁמָּה" (דברים יב, ה)—דרוש ומצוא ואחר כך יאמר לך נביא.

The derashah solves a textual problem. In the first half of the verse the site is chosen by God, and in the second half man is bidden to seek it out. The resolution is to flip the order: first man finds it, and then God confirms that this was His choice.

Now, this derashah has all the trappings of a halakhic derashah, couched as it is in the singular imperative, "seek it out" *(derosh)*. But by the darshan's time this directive would have been wholly obsolete, for Jerusalem had already been chosen. It is a "historical," exegetical halakhah pertinent to the biblical narrative of King David settling on Jerusalem as the site of the Temple. David planned the Temple's construction in Jerusalem ("seek it out and find it") and his plans were later approved by the seer Gad ("afterward the prophet will tell it to you").[51] This derashah teaches us not to be distracted by a derashah's form. The halakhic garb may clothe an idea that more properly belongs to the world of Aggadah.

This derashah thus reveals that, like the Mishnah, the Midrash also can also be interested in biblical stories for their own sake, without any possibility of application. If anything, this is easier to see in the Midrash, which follows the sequence of the verses, than in the independent halakhic treatments that comprise the Mishnah.

The schools of Rabbi Akiva and Rabbi Yishmael disagree about mitzvot that the Torah introduces with "When you enter into the land." Do they mean immediately upon entry, or only after the conquest and settlement? This is a running dispute, yet the stakes, at least as measured from the vantage point of halakhic practice, are very low.[52] The Torah study has no goal other than the study itself.

Another midrash contains two aggadic derashot, one in halakhic format and the other in aggadic:

"Only be strong in order not to eat the blood, because the blood is the life" (Deut. 12:23).

Rabbi Yehudah says, It relates that Israel were steeped in blood[b] before the giving of the Torah. Could it be even after they accepted it joyously at Mount Sinai? It therefore teaches, "Only."[c]

a Confirm it.
b In its consumption.
c Exegetically, the Hebrew word *rak* is used to minimize the scope of what precedes it.

Rabbi Shimon ben Azzai says, Are there not three positive mitzvot[a] in the Torah like this one?[b] It is to teach you that if Scripture cautions you about the blood, the easiest mitzvah of all,[c] then it is all the more true regarding all other positive mitzvot. (*Sifrei Deuteronomy*, §76, p. 141)

"רַק חֲזַק לְבִלְתִּי אֲכֹל הַדָּם" (דברים יב, כג).

ר' יהודה אומר: מגיד שישראל שטופין בדם קודם למתן תורה. יכול אף משקיבלו אותם בשמחה בהר סיני? תלמוד לומר "רק".

אמר ר' שמעון בן עזיי: והלא שלוש מצות עשה בתורה כיוצא בזה? ללמד מה הדם, שאין בכל מצוות קל ממנו, הזהירך הכתוב עליו, שאר כל מצוות עשה, על אחת כמה וכמה.

Why does the Torah encourage its adherents to "only be strong" not to eat the blood? Rabbi Yehudah winds back the clock to the biblical era when, he contends, the Israelites had an addiction to blood. His derashah has the structure of many halakhic ones: "It relates *(maggid)* . . . Could it be *(yakhol)*. . . ? It therefore teaches *(talmud lomar)* . . ." Nevertheless, the content belongs to the era of Moses. Rabbi Shimon ben Azzai, by contrast, assumes that one can easily stop consuming blood. The Torah repeatedly issues warnings about "the easiest mitzvah of all" to combat overconfidence. His derashah advances a type of a fortiori argument ("it is all the more true") that is standard in aggadic Midrash.

A third and final halakhic-looking derashah about the consequences of not giving tzedakah to the poor:

"So that you look meanly at your destitute brother and you do not give, and he calls out to the Lord against you, and it will be a sin in you" (Deut. 15:9).

Could it be that it is a mitzvah to call out? It therefore teaches, "but he does not call out[d] [and it will be a sin in you]" (Deut. 24:15).

Could it be that if he calls out against you, there will be a sin in you, but if he does not, then there is no sin in you? It therefore teaches, "and it will be a sin in you"— under all circumstances.

If so, why does it say, "and he calls out to the Lord against you"? I am quick to exact punishment on the one who calls out than on the one who does not call out. (*Sifrei Deuteronomy*, §117, p. 176)

---

a Mitzvot phrased positively that state what to do rather than what not to do.
b See Genesis 9:4 and Leviticus 17:12, 14.
c There is no strong drive to consume blood that must be overcome; see Mishnah, *Makkot*, 3:15.
d This refers to the indigent laborer whose wages are withheld. In context the phrase means "lest he call out"; see Deuteronomy 24:15.

"וְרָעָה עֵינְךָ בְּאָחִיךָ הָאֶבְיוֹן וְלֹא תִתֵּן לוֹ וְקָרָא עָלֶיךָ אֶל ה' וְהָיָה בְךָ חֵטְא" (דברים טו, ט). יכול מצוה שלא לקרות? תלמוד לומר "קְרָא". יכול מצוה לקרות? תלמוד לומר "וְלֹא יִקְרָא" (שם כד, טו). יכול אם קרא עליך יהיה בך חט ואם לאו לא יהא בך חט? תלמוד לומר "וְהָיָה בְךָ חֵטְא"—מכל מקום. אם כן למה נאמר "וְקָרָא עָלֶיךָ אֶל ה'"? ממהרני ליפרע על ידי קורא יתיר משאינו קורא.

In the beginning, this midrash discusses the pauper's potential halakhic obligation to complain to God about the improper treatment, which violates God's laws in the Torah. The phraseology used to raise and reject the possibilities is that of halakhic Midrash. The continuation clarifies that the midrash actually intends to give a stern warning to the rich, rather than to give a command to the pauper. It once again feels like Halakhah, but the voice is Aggadah.

Aggadic Midrash that could pass for Halakhah only appears in the halakhic sections of the Midrash and not in the independent aggadic portions on Torah narrative discussed above. This can be explained perfectly by returning to the question of origins shunted aside at the beginning of the chapter. Aggadic tracts were probably gathered by professional aggadic circles who were not aligned with either of the major midrashic powerhouses. In contrast, the nuggets of Aggadah served on the table of Halakhah originated in the academies of Rabbi Akiva and Rabbi Yishmael. They give the impression of being halakhic because the same study houses generated them. In attempting to characterize the relationship between halakhic and aggadic Midrash, we must remember this mixing that occurred at the source.

In the Mishnah, Aggadah almost always exists to complement Halakhah. In the tannaitic Midrash, though, Aggadah enjoys an independent existence in dedicated tractates or sections. This largely occurs when the base text, the Torah, has a narrative that is (relatively) uninterrupted by law. Elsewhere in the Midrash, Aggadah is incorporated into the legal exegesis, where it enters into a complex relationship with Halakhah that ranges from complementarity to imitation. In the world of the Tannaim, Aggadah lived in an environment mostly dominated by halakhic concerns, whether in the Mishnah or the halakhic Midrashim. It was only in the amoraic period that Aggadah became a completely independent domain with exclusively aggadic Midrashim, such as *Genesis Rabbah*, and thrived.

FIFTEEN

The Midrash and the Mishnah

After learning separately about the Mishnah and the Midrash, the time has come to tackle the looming question: What is the relationship between these two massive bodies of rabbinic literature?

The Mishnah, you will recall, contains entire tracts of law that have no biblical basis.[1] In those that do trace their roots to the Torah, the presentation does not resemble that of the Midrash. The mitzvah to take four species on Sukkot is a fine topic for comparison:

> Rabbi Yishmael says, Three myrtles, two willows, one lulav, and one etrog. Even if two[a] are topped,[b] and one is not topped.
>
> Rabbi Tarfon says, Even if three of them are topped.
>
> Rabbi Akiva says, Just as it is one lulav and one etrog, so it is one myrtle and one willow. (Mishnah, *Sukkah*, 3:4)

> רבי ישמעאל אומר: שלושה הדסים ושתי ערבות ולולב אחד ואתרוג אחד. אפילו שניים קטומין, ואחד שאינו קטום.
>
> רבי טרפון אומר: אפילו שלושתן קטומין.
>
> רבי עקיבה אומר: כשם שלולב אחד ואתרוג אחד, כך הדס אחד וערבה אחת.

a Referring to the myrtles.
b The tip of the myrtle branch is removed.

Compare this to the same exact law recorded in the *Sifra*:

> Rabbi Yishmael says, "The fruit *(peri)*[a] of beautiful trees" (Lev. 23:40)—one; "branches *(kapp{o}t)* of palm trees"—one;[b] "boughs of leafy trees"—three;[c] "willows of the brook"—two.[d] Even if two branches [are topped], and one is not topped.
>
> Rabbi Tarfon says, Even if three of them are topped.
>
> Rabbi Akiva says, "The fruit of beautiful trees"—one; "branches of palm trees"—one; "boughs of leafy trees"—one; "willows of the brook"—one. So just as[e] it is one lulav and one etrog, thus is it one myrtle and one willow. (*Sifra, Emor*, 12:3, 102d)
>
> ר׳ ישמעאל אומר: "פְּרִי עֵץ הָדָר" (ויקרא כג, מ)—אחד; "כַּפֹּת תְּמָרִים"—אחד; "עֲנַף עֵץ עָבֹת"—שלושה; "וְעַרְבֵי נָחַל"—שתים. ושתי דליות ואחת שאינה קטומה.
>
> ר׳ טרפון אומר: אפילו שלושתן קטומין.
>
> ר׳ עקיבה אומר: "פְּרִי עֵץ הָדָר"—אחד; "כַּפֹּת תְּמָרִים"—אחד; "וַעֲנַף עֵץ עָבֹת"—אחד; "וְעַרְבֵי נָחַל"—אחד. הא כשם שלולב אחד ואתרוג אחד, כך הדס אחד וערבה אחת.

The two sources stylize the debate each in their own way. The mishnah has no biblical references, while the midrash is laden with them. The mishnah uses the contemporary terms for the four species (e.g., lulav), based on a long-standing tradition, while the midrash uses the original names in quotation (e.g., branches of palm trees), thus anchoring the mishnaic tradition in Scripture.[2]

However, the relationship is not one-sided. For even if tradition furnished the identity of the species to be taken on Sukkot, it is likely that the number of each species to be taken is indeed based on derashot. Otherwise, one would be hard-pressed to explain why Rabbi Yishmael requires specifically three myrtles, two willows, one lulav, and one etrog.[3] The derashot in the *Sifra*, or similar ones, are the most plausible source for the opinions of these Sages.[4]

Placing the Mishnah and Midrash next to each other is revealing. From afar, the two presentations of the law look parallel; from closer up, one discerns multiple intersections. The minimalism of the Mishnah obscures its reliance on derashot of the Midrash for some legal details. The Midrash explicitly cites the Mishnah, a regular occurrence in the *Sifra*,[5] because it seeks to anchor its traditions to the Torah.[6] The relationship between the corpora is both reciprocal and multilayered.

---

a Since *peri* is singular, only one etrog need be taken.
b *Kappot* is traditionally read as a plural, but it is written defectively without the vowel of the plural marker, so it can be read as *kappat*, indicating that only one lulav need be taken.
c Three corresponding to the number of Hebrew words, *'anaf 'etz 'avot*.
d Two corresponding to the number of Hebrew words, *'arvei naḥal*.
e A citation of the above mishnah, *Sukkah*, 3:4.

But despite these intersections, the Midrash and the Mishnah are distinct, independent works. Although they deal with many of the same areas of law, their treatments can have little overlap. For instance, Numbers 30 states the laws regarding vows, which is treated in *Sifrei Numbers* (§153–§156) and Tractate *Nedarim* of the Mishnah. Nearly the entire discussion in the Midrash revolves around the possibility of a woman's vows being annulled by her father or husband. In the Mishnah this aspect of the law of vows is only discussed in the final chapters of the tractate (chs. 10–11). The bulk of the tractate covers the formulae that are effective in generating a vow and the social repercussions of certain vows. It also dedicates a chapter to the release of vows by a Sage, which, by the Mishnah's own admission, has no biblical basis: "the dissolution of vows hovers in the air and has nothing on which to rely."[7] Why are the treatments of the Midrash and the Mishnah, both produced by the Sages, so divergent?

When we look at the compositions as a whole, the answer becomes obvious. The Midrash follows the order of the verses and focuses on matters of concern to the Torah. The Mishnah, as an independent composition, is free to develop its own approach to this area of law. It begins by clarifying the type of language that effects a vow, moves on to the social and interpersonal consequences of taking such a vow, and codifies a method of taking back a vow. Only then does it examine the specific cases discussed in biblical law. But the disconnect is far from total. The Mishnah chooses to place this tractate on vows in *Seder Nashim*, because the original context in the Torah is vows made by girls and women. The Midrash, for its part, does not limit itself to biblical law alone and includes extra-biblical institutions like the release of a vow by a Sage.[8]

The laws of the Nazirite exhibit a similar pattern. In *Sifrei Numbers* (§22–§38), the prohibitions and the rituals are front and center, as they are in the Torah (Num. 6). The Mishnah, by contrast, dedicates the first half of Tractate *Nazir* to the expressions that invoke the Nazirite vow, which parallels its sister tractate, *Nedarim*. Stylistically and substantively, the Mishnah does its own thing. The two rabbinic legal projects, the Mishnah and the Midrash, are kin, but they are far from being twins.

This chapter is an attempt to sort out the complex interrelationship between the Mishnah and the Midrash. The first section examines the Midrash's attitude toward extra-biblical tradition, and the second investigates its manifold connections to the Mishnah. There are places where derashot are based on laws codified in the Mishnah, and places where the Mishnah bases itself on prior midrashic derashot. The end of the chapter addresses the conceptual implications of the tangled lines crisscrossing the two corpuses. Synthesizing much of parts 1 and 2 of this book, the discussion here forms the coda to this study.

A. MIDRASH AND EXTRA-BIBLICAL TRADITION

The Mishnah and the tannaitic Midrashim are not compositions of late, nameless editors, who artificially attributed them to Sages of the tannaitic period.[9] They are the organic literary outgrowth of the learning that took place in the study halls of the Tannaim.[10] As such, they document Torah study in Judea and the Galilee over the entire tannaitic period, from the end of the first century CE through the entirety of the second century and the beginning of the third. The Sages who engaged in this learning were both jurists and exegetes, and their intensive labors respectively produced two corpora: the Mishnah and the Midrash.[11] By and large, I believe that most of the debates preserved in tannaitic literature actually happened. To be sure, the debates have been stylized and cannot be taken as actual minutes.[12] But one can still learn from them about the nature of the bet midrash (study hall) and its scholarly activities.[13] Both Midrash and Halakhah were intellectual-religious pursuits of scholars studying in the same institutions of learning.[14]

The dialectics of the Midrash ("Do you say X or instead Y?") is patterned on the push-and-pull of real-life dialogue, but any actual conversations were adapted according to rhetorical rules.[15] The tannaitic sources preserve two types of give and take: midrashic dialogue involving biblical verses, and juristic and Bible-less debates. Presumably, some of the actual discussions in the study hall made reference to the Torah, while others developed halakhic themes independently of Scripture. The extent of editorial intervention, however, prevents us from knowing exactly what the original discussion was like.

Here is a narration of an early halakhic discussion about the paschal sacrifice that the Tosefta attributes to a time when the Temple was still standing:[16]

Once the fourteenth[a] occurred on Shabbat. They asked Hillel the Elder: Does the paschal sacrifice override Shabbat?[b] [. . .]

He said to them, The daily sacrifice is a public sacrifice and the paschal sacrifice is a public sacrifice. Just as the daily sacrifice is a public sacrifice and overrides Shabbat, so the paschal sacrifice is a public sacrifice and overrides Shabbat.

Another thing:

Regarding the daily sacrifice it says, "its appointed time" (Num. 28:2), and regarding the paschal sacrifice it says, "its appointed time" (Num. 9:3). Just as the daily sacrifice, about which it says, "its appointed time," overrides Shabbat, so too the paschal sacrifice, about which it says "its appointed time," overrides Shabbat. (Tosefta, *Pasha*, 4:13)

פעם אחת חל ארבעה-עשר להיות בשבת. שאלו את הלל הזקן: פסח מהו שידחה את השבת? [. . .] אמר להם: תמיד קרבן צבור ופסח קרבן צבור, מה תמיד קרבן צבור ודוחה את השבת, אף פסח קרבן צבור דוחה את השבת.

דבר אחר: נאמר בתמיד "מוֹעֲדוֹ" (במדבר כח, ב) ונאמר בפסח "מוֹעֲדוֹ" (במדבר ט, ג). מה תמיד שנאמר בו "מוֹעֲדוֹ" דוחה את השבת, אף פסח שנאמר בו "מוֹעֲדוֹ" דוחה את השבת.

a Of Nisan, when the paschal sacrifice is to be offered at the Temple.
b Since offering a sacrifice is considered prohibited labor on Shabbat.

According to the Tosefta, in the early first century CE Hillel presented two arguments permitting the offering of the paschal sacrifice on Shabbat. The first drew an analogy from the daily sacrifice and brought no prooftext; the second focused exclusively on biblical language. Daniel Schwartz has argued that the first is the original argument and the second (appearing after the divider "another thing") is a later addition. It follows that in the time of Hillel the basic legal inference was juristic rather than midrashic.[17] This cannot be more than an informed speculation, though, since the Tosefta is not an eyewitness account but a much later literary presentation. The only information that can be deduced with certainty is that by the second century, mishnaic and midrashic modes of discussion could be found in the bet midrash and its literature.[18]

The fact that the Mishnah and the Midrash coexisted in the study hall does not mean that they enjoyed equal status. In general, Midrash was the handmaiden of extra-biblical law.[19] Scholars conventionally set up a binary of creative Midrash versus preservative Midrash, that is, Midrash as generating new laws versus Midrash as reinforcing old ones.[20] But the relationship of Midrash to extra-biblical tradition is more nuanced than that. First of all, that relationship undoubtedly evolved over time.[21] Second, the nature of Midrash changes depending on the specific legal area involved. Practical law differs from theoretical law, as does robust pre-rabbinic Halakhah from thinly elaborated tradition. Third, there is a kind of feedback loop between extra-biblical traditions and Midrash, in which the Midrash rests on those laws while changing them as it carries out its mission.[22] Despite this variability, the general assumption is that the substantive law was already known, and the Midrash was largely trying to tack it onto the Torah.

One way to probe the nature of the Midrash's relationship to extra-biblical tradition is to see what happens when a derashah does *not* accord with it. One tradition from the Second Temple period required the separation of *ma'aser sheni*, the second tithe that is to be eaten in a state of ritual purity by it owners in Jerusalem, from all produce.[23] When the darshan questions the scope of this law, he is really seeking a biblical source for it:

Since it says, "And you shall eat before the Lord your God, in the place that He chooses to make His name dwell [the tithe of your grain, wine, and oil]" (Deut. 14:23), could it be that I have it that only grain, wine, and oil are obligated in tithes? Whence to include all other produce? It therefore teaches, "the produce of your seed" (Deut. 14:22). (*Sifrei Deuteronomy*, §106, p. 164)

מכלל שנאמר "וְאָכַלְתָּ לִפְנֵי ה' אֱלֹהֶיךָ בַּמָּקוֹם אֲשֶׁר יִבְחַר . . . [מַעְשַׂר דְּגָנְךָ תִּירֹשְׁךָ וְיִצְהָרֶךָ וּבְכֹרֹת בְּקָרְךָ וְצֹאנֶךָ]" (דברים יד, כג)—יכול אין לי חייב במעשרות אלא דגן תירוש ויצהר, מנין לרבות שאר פירות? תלמוד לומר "תְּבוּאַת זַרְעֶךָ" (דברים יד, כב).

The darshan knows that *ma'aser sheni* is not limited to the staples derived from grain, grapes, and olives. His goal is to bring this tradition back to the Torah. This derashah is followed by another that the Midrash condemns harshly:

They said, The stores of the Hananites were destroyed three years before the Land of Israel,[a] because they would exclude their fruit from tithing. For they would expound, "You shall surely tithe. . . . And you shall eat"[b] (Deut. 14:22–23)—but not sell.[c] (*Sifrei Deuteronomy*, §106, p. 165)

אמרו: חרבו חנויות [של] בני חנן שלש שנים קודם לארץ ישראל, שהיו מוציאים פירותיהם מידי מעשרות, שהיו דורשין לומר "עַשֵּׂר תְּעַשֵּׂר . . . וְאָכַלְתָּ" (דברים יד, כב–כג)—ולא מוכר.

The exegetical technique of the Hananites is flawless and virtually indistinguishable from accepted, normative derashot. The problem is that its conclusion, serving the interest of wholesalers moving a lot of produce, contradicts the accepted extra-biblical tradition.[24] Sound methodology isn't enough for the Midrash; the derashah's bottom line must uphold the tradition.

B. SUBSTANTIATION OF MISHNAIC LAW

In its service of extra-biblical tradition, the Midrash is occupied with finding scriptural foundations for the laws codified in the Mishnah. Menahem Kahana has observed that the Mishnah features a far greater number of early Tannaim (first Yavneh generation) than the Midrash does.[25] This is a good indicator that the Midrash in large part serves to further ground the earlier mishnaic laws. The Mishnah presents itself as an independent work, relying only sporadically on biblical prooftexts.[26] Part of the task that the Midrash takes upon itself is to connect the dots between the canonical text and the body of extra-biblical law contained in the Mishnah.

The Torah declares that the Ammonites and Moabites may never enter "the assembly of the Lord" (Deut. 23:4), yet it admits entry to Egyptians and Edomites after three generations (Deut. 23:9). The Sages interpret this to be talking about marrying a convert from one of these nations. The Mishnah records a dispute about the status of female converts of Egyptian and Edomite origin. Since the Torah's prohibition refers to the Egyptian and Edomite in the masculine, perhaps Israelite men may marry such female converts without waiting three generations?

> The Ammonite and the Moabite are forbidden and their prohibition is forever, but their women are permitted immediately.

---

a Before the Romans destroyed the Second Temple.
b The Torah connects tithing with eating, so the Hananites understood that the obligation applies to retailers and not to wholesalers. For the requirement to tithe in the context of commerce, see Mishnah, *Demai*, 2:2.
c The tithe is only taken when the produce is going to be eaten and not resold.

The Egyptian and the Edomite are forbidden only for three generations—both men and women.

Rabbi Shimon says, It is an a fortiori: If when the prohibition on males is everlasting, it permitted the females immediately, then when the men are only prohibited for three generations, isn't it logical that the females be permitted immediately?

They said to him, "If it is a traditional law *(halakhah)*, we will accept it; if it is a logical deduction, there is a response."

He said to them, "Not so, I am stating a traditional law *(halakhah)*." (Mishnah, Yevamot, 8:3)

עמוני ומואבי אסורין ואיסורן אסור עולם, אבל נקיבותיהם מותרות מיד. מצרי ואדומי אינן אסורין אלא עד שלושה דורות, אחד זכרים ואחד נקיבות.

אמר ר׳ שמעון: קל וחומר הדברים: ומה אם במקום שאסר את הזכרים אסור עולם התיר את הנקיבות מיד, מקום שלא אסר את הזכרים אלא עד שלושה דורות—אינו דין שנתיר את הנקיבות מיד?

אמרו לו: אם הלכה נקבל ואם לדין יש תשובה.

אמר להן: לא כי, אלא הלכה אני אומר.

Rabbi Shimon allows one to marry Edomite and Egyptian female converts, instead of having to wait for their granddaughters, using a logical argument from the law about Ammonites and Moabites. The Sages have either devised a counterargument or identified some flaw in Rabbi Shimon's logical reasoning, so they question its provenance. Rabbi Shimon retorts that there is a *halakhah*, an extra-biblical traditional law, behind the analogical reasoning, putting it beyond the reach of human reason. The Mishnah here is clearly working with the verses quoted above, yet it never raises the option of an exegetical solution. The only authoritative sources in play are long-held tradition or valid legal reasoning.

Compare this to the midrash on this law. It cites the above mishnah verbatim, but appends a line of its own:

He said to them,[a] "Not so, I am stating a traditional law *(halakhah)*, and Scripture supports me: 'sons *(banim)*'[b] (Deut. 23:9)—but not daughters." (*Sifrei Deuteronomy*, §253, p. 279)

---

a Rabbi Shimon to the Sages.
b The full verse reads: "*Banim* that will be born to them, a third generation, may enter the assembly of the Lord." In context *banim* has the broader meaning of "descendants," but Rabbi Shimon reads it more narrowly as male descendants.

In addition to the extra-biblical tradition and reason of the Mishnah, the Midrash has Rabbi Shimon invoke scriptural exegesis. Scripture, logical reasoning, and tradition come together in the Midrash, which connects the law of the Mishnah to its biblical roots.[27]

The Midrash announces its self-conception as a bridge between mishnaic law and the Torah through a certain key phrase: "Hence they said . . ." *(mi-kan ameru)*. "Hence" means from Scripture, and "they" most often refers to the Sages of the Mishnah.[28] Over one hundred times, after presenting a verse from the Torah the Midrash uses this phrase and then cites a mishnaic law.[29] Yakir Paz calls this "editorial re-scripturizing," which is especially necessary for the many extra-biblical laws in the Mishnah.[30]

Let us examine the phrase in context:

> "This is the statement *(devar)*[a] of the remission *(shemittah)*" (Deut. 15:2). <u>Hence they said</u>:[b] To someone repaying a debt in the seventh year one should say,[c] "I am remitting it." And if he says to him, "Even so,"[d] he may accept it[e] from him. For it says, "This is the statement of the remission." (*Sifrei Deuteronomy*, §112, p. 172)

> "וְזֶה דְּבַר הַשְּׁמִטָּה" (דברים טו, ב). מיכן אמרו: המחזיר חוב בשביעית יאמר להם "משמט אני". ואם אמר לו "אף על פי כן", יקבל ממנו, משום שנאמר "וְזֶה דְּבַר הַשְּׁמִטָּה".

Immediately after the initial quotation, the Midrash uses the key phrase to justify the mishnaic ruling in Tractate *Shevi'it*. It "re-scripturizes" this extra-biblical halakhic requirement of verbalizing the forgiveness of the debt. But why is the initial verse repeated at the end? It is actually part of the mishnah being quoted. The Mishnah sometimes concludes its statement of the law with a scriptural prooftext. What we have here, then, is a midrash that cites a Mishnah ("Hence they said"), which in turn cites a derashah ("For it says").

Most of the time, "Hence they said" does not immediately follow the initial quote from the Torah, as it does above.[31] Mishnaic law typically does not flow seamlessly from the simple reading of the Torah's words and midrashic exposition is necessary. Let us revisit, with greater insight, a midrash and a mishnah partly discussed in part 1 of this book.[32] The Mishnah states regarding the obligation to make a pilgrimage to the Temple and bring an offering on the festivals: "All are obligated in appearing, except . . . minors." It subsequently brings a dispute between Bet Hillel and Bet Shammai about how to define the excluded minor. Now for the Midrash:

---

a Hebrew *devar* is typically translated as "matter," but it also can have the meaning "word" or "statement," which the Midrash seizes upon to require the verbal remission.

b In Mishnah, *Shevi'it*, 10:8.

c The lender should say to the borrower.

d i.e., the borrower insists on repaying the debt.

e Since all loans are to be canceled, one might have thought that accepting repayment would effectively be a failure to cancel the debt and therefore prohibited.

"Your males" (Deut. 16:16)—to exclude women; "all your males"—to include male minors.

Hence they said:[a]

Who is a minor? Whoever cannot ride on his father's shoulders and ascend from Jerusalem to the Temple Mount—so the words of Bet Shammai, <u>as it says</u>, "your males."

But Bet Hillel say, Whoever cannot hold his father's hand and ascend from Jerusalem to the Temple Mount, <u>as it says</u>, "three times *(regalim)*" (Ex. 23:14). (*Sifrei Deuteronomy*, §143, p. 196)

"זְכוּרְךָ" (דברים טז, טז)—להוציא את הנשים; "כָּל זְכוּרְךָ"– להביא את הקטנים.

<u>מיכן אמרו</u>: אי זה הוא קטן? כל שאינו יכול לרכוב על כתפי אביו לעלות מירושלים להר הבית—דברי בית שמאי, <u>שנאמר</u> "זְכוּרְךָ". ובית הלל אומרים: כל שאין יכול לאחוז בידו שלאביו לעלות מירושלים להר הבית, <u>שנאמר</u> "שָׁלֹשׁ רְגָלִים" (שמות כג, יד).

The initial derashah begins by including male minors. Thematically, this fits with the Mishnah, which is also discussing minors. Stylistically, however, there is a prominent incongruity: the derashah obligates minors, while the cited mishnah details which minors are *not* obligated. The underlying cause is no mystery. The Midrash's quotation of the Mishnah ("Hence they said") begins in the middle of the mishnah, which is preceded by the following rule: "All are obligated in appearing, *except for* the deaf-mute, the mentally incompetent, and minors." The Midrash thus switches between a derashah that deals with minors who *are* obligated and a mishnah that discusses those who are *not*.

The Midrash also does not cite the Mishnah exactly as we have it. In the Mishnah, Bet Hillel bring scriptural support, while Bet Shammai offer no source. Bet Shammai's definition of the exempt minor is an extra-biblical tradition or based on actual practice, and Bet Hillel dispute it on scriptural grounds.[33] The Midrash, however, cannot abide this asymmetry, because it seeks to link every opinion in the Mishnah to the Written Torah. It achieves this goal by awkwardly tacking Deuteronomy 16:16 onto the tail of Bet Shammai's opinion (underlined above). "The words of Bet Shammai" marks the end of their opinion, yet a verse follows: "as it says, 'your males.'"

Much less frequently, "Hence they said" returns us to the starting verse, bookending the derashah.[34] One can see this visually in this midrash:

"Wherever [I mention[b] My name, I shall come to you and bless you]" (Ex. 20:21).

---

a In Mishnah, Ḥagigah, 1:1.
b This is the reading of the Masoretic Text, but it would seem that the Midrash's text read, "Wherever you mention My name."

Rabbi Yoshiyah says, This verse is reversed.[a] It should have said, Wherever I reveal Myself to you, there should you mention My name. And where do I reveal Myself to you? In the Temple. So, too, should you mention My name only in the Temple.

Hence they said:[b] It is prohibited to pronounce the Tetragrammaton[c] in the countryside.[d]

Rabbi Eliezer ben Yaakov says,[e] If you come to My house, I shall come to yours; if you do not come to My house, so too I will not come to yours. My legs carry Me to the place I love.

Hence they said:[f] Any quorum of ten men who gather at a synagogue have the divine presence with them. As it says, "God stands in the congregation of God" (Ps. 82:1). And whence even three who are adjudicating?[g] As it says, "He judges in the midst of the judges" (Ps. 82:1). And whence even two?[h] As it says, "Then they who feared the Lord spoke with one another" (Mal. 3:16). And whence even one? As it says, "Wherever I mention My name etc." (Ex. 20:21). (*Mekhilta de-Rabbi Yishmael, Ba-Ḥodesh*, §11, p. 243)

"בְּכָל הַמָּקוֹם [אֲשֶׁר אַזְכִּיר אֶת שְׁמִי אָבוֹא אֵלֶיךָ וּבֵרַכְתִּיךָ]" (שמות כ, כא).

ר' יאשיה אומר: זה מקרא מסורס. היה צריך לאמר, בכל מקום שאני נגלה עליך, שם תהי מזכיר את שמי. והיכן אני נגלה עליך? בבית הבירה. אף אתה לא תהא מזכיר את שמי אלא בבית הבירה.

מיכן אמרו: שם מפורש אסור להאמר בגבולין.

ר' אליעזר בן יעקב אומר: אם תבא לביתי—אבא לביתך, ואם לא תבא לביתי—ואף אני לביתך איני בא. מקום שלבי אוהב שם רגלי מוליכות אותי.

מיכן אמרו: כל עשרה בני אדם שנכנסין לבית הכנסת שכינה עמהן, שנאמר "אֱלֹהִים נִצָּב בַּעֲדַת אֵל" וג' (תהלים פב, א). ומנין אפילו שלשה שדנין? שנאמר "בְּקֶרֶב אֱלֹהִים יִשְׁפֹּט" (שם). ומנין אפילו שנים? שנאמר "אָז נִדְבְּרוּ יִרְאֵי ה'" וג' (מלאכי ג, טז). ומנין אפילו אחד? שנאמר "בְּכָל הַמָּקוֹם אֲשֶׁר אַזְכִּיר אֶת שְׁמִי" וג'.

---

a For rhetorical or literary reasons, and to be properly understood, it must be read in the correct order. See Paz, *Scribes to Scholars*, 269–274.

b See Mishnah, *Sotah*, 7:6.

c The four-letter name of God, YHWH, uttered according to its original pronunciation, rather than according to the vocalization *adonai*.

d Outside the Temple.

e Similar statements appear in Tosefta, *Sukkah*, 4:3, about the Temple celebration of the drawing of the water on Sukkot, and were likely taken by the Midrash from a similar collection. Note also the clear linguistic and thematic connections between R. Eliezer ben Yaakov's derashah and the preceding one of R. Yoshiyah, both speaking about the "house," i.e., the Temple.

f Mishnah, Avot 3:6.

g A bet din.

h Discussing Torah.

In this midrash, "Hence they said" appears twice with distinct functions. The first flows from the derashah that precedes it. That derashah and the mishnah in Tractate *Sotah* both say that God's name, the Tetragrammaton, may be enunciated as it is written only in the Temple. The second "Hence they said" has no direct connection to any of the preceding material.[35] The mishnah in Tractate *Avot* is cited in order to allow the midrash to conclude with the verse with which it started. If God goes wherever someone mentions Him, as the verse says, that should be true even if one person is learning Torah.

In the Midrashim of Rabbi Akiva's school, "Hence they said" introducing a mishnaic quote is encountered regularly. This is to be expected. The dependency of these Midrashim on the Mishnah of Rabbi Yehudah ha-Nasi, which is based on the "Mishnah of Rabbi Akiva," runs very deep. Looking at *Sifrei Deuteronomy*, one sees this in many ways. The Midrash will sometimes refer to a line in the Mishnah and add an "etc.," as if the learner ought to know the rest.[36] When an entire biblical passage has a dedicated treatment in the Mishnah, the Midrash will incorporate that very long tract, even if it spans multiple mishnayot.[37] For example, regarding the remission of debts during the sabbatical year, the Midrash cites the first three mishnayot of the tenth chapter of Tractate *Shevi'it*.[38] The same happens with the *Sifrei* on the *'eglah 'arufah*, the heifer whose neck is broken, which quotes much of the ninth chapter of Tractate *Sotah*.[39]

The *Sifra* is exceptional in its tendency to cite mishnaic material at length, and it frequently forgoes "Hence they said." The hundreds of quotations coalesce into a mission statement: this Midrash, more than any other, strives to the utmost to find scriptural sources for mishnaic law.[40] The material it quotes is almost always identical to the language of our Mishnah.[41] Let us see how an unmarked citation of the Mishnah functions in the context of the mitzvah to sit in a sukkah (booth) on the holiday of Sukkot:

"In sukkot" (Lev. 23:42). Not in a sukkah inside the house, nor in a sukkah under a tree, nor in a sukkah on top of a sukkah.

Rabbi Yehudah says, If there are no residents in the upper one, the lower one is valid. (*Sifra, Emor*, 12:4, 102d–103a)

"בַּסֻּכֹּת" (ויקרא כג, מב)—לא בסוכה בתוך הבית, לא בסוכה תחת האילן, לא בסוכה על גבי סוכה.

ר' יהודה אומר: אם אין דיורין בעליונה, התחתונה כשרה.

This midrash is riddled with oddities. Why does it put on the same list of invalid sukkot ones that are *under* some problematic covering (a roof and a tree) and one that is under the dome of heaven but happens to be *on top of* another sukkah? If the focus is on the upper of the two sukkot, why does Rabbi Yehudah discuss the validity of the bottom one? It sounds like he is expressing dissent—with whom or what opinion? How does any of this emerge from "in sukkot," the header quote from the Torah? Yonatan Sagiv has shown that the disjointedness of this midrash is readily understood if we view the *Sifra* as adapting the pertinent mishnah:

If one makes his sukkah under a tree, it is as if he made it inside the house.

Regarding a sukkah that is on top of another sukkah, the upper one is valid and the lower one is invalid.

Rabbi Yehudah says, If there are no residents in the upper one, the lower one is valid. (Mishnah, *Sukkah*, 1:2)

העושה סוכתו תחת האילן, כאילו עשאה בתוך הבית.

סוכה על גבי סוכה—העליונה כשירה והתחתונה פסולה.

ר' יהודה אומר: אם אין דיורים בעליונה, התחתונה כשרה.

The *Sifra*, in Sagiv's reconstruction, reorganizes the information in this mishnah into a list. This adaptation puts like and unlike together, and also orphans Rabbi Yehudah's opinion of its preceding contrast.[42]

The Mishnah undoubtedly plays an outsized role in the Midrashim of Rabbi Akiva's school. Nevertheless, some also draw from other tannaitic collections of Halakhah, or even select them as the primary source. For *Mekhilta de-Rashbi*, the Tosefta is the main authoritative body of law, at least when it comes to torts.[43] For instance, the Torah says that if someone opens a pit and doesn't cover it, they must pay for any damages incurred when an animal falls into it (Ex. 21:33–34). The Midrash expounds:

"A man *(ish)*" (Ex. 21:33)—to include that of two.[a]

Regarding a pit[b] of two: if one covers and the other uncovers, the uncoverer is liable. If one covered it and it became uncovered, and he saw it but did not cover it, he is liable.[c] If he covered it and went on his way, even though it later became uncovered, he is exempt. (*Mekhilta de-Rashbi*, 21:33, p. 185)

"איש" (שמות כא, לג)—להביא את השנים. בור של שנים, אחד מכסה ואחד מגלה—המגלה חייב. כיסהו עד שעמד ונתגלה, ראהו ולא כיסהו—הרי זה חייב. כיסהו והלך לו—אף על פי שנתגלה לאחר כן, פטור.

How does the Midrash unpack all of this from one word, *ish*? It doesn't. The halakhic passage about the jointly owned pit is taken verbatim from the Tosefta. The actual derashah at the beginning is just a hook to connect the law of the Tosefta to a small eyelet in the Torah.[44]

So far, we have learned that the Midrashim of the school of Rabbi Akiva do not adopt a uniform approach to our Mishnah. The *Sifra* and *Sifrei Deuteronomy* exclusively base

a People; i.e., a pit for which there is joint responsibility.
b This is from Tosefta, *Bava Kamma*, 6:10.
c This refers to whichever of the responsible parties saw it uncovered and failed to recover it. See Lieberman, *Tosefta ki-Feshutah*, vol. 9–10, p. 53.

themselves on the Mishnah, while *Mekhilta de-Rashbi* does not privilege it above the Tosefta. The *Sifrei Zuta* Midrashim, in contrast, rely on neither the Mishnah nor the Tosefta. Rather they cite a completely different set of mishnayot, whose divergence from our Mishnah ranges from slight to extreme.[45]

How can this variability within a single school be explained? Chronology cannot account for the differences, since the editing of both the *Sifra* and *Mekhilta de-Rashbi* postdate that of the Mishnah by one to two generations.[46] Since the change cannot be accounted for diachronically, we must explain it synchronically. Even though the Mishnah was edited before the core Midrashim, there was a lag between its completion and its canonization. Some study halls were slow to recognize the Mishnah as *the* corpus of Oral Law, while others never did. At one pole is the *Sifra*, which employs midrashic techniques to connect the Mishnah to the Torah. At the other are the *Sifrei Zuta* Midrashim, which apparently do not recognize Rabbi Yehudah ha-Nasi's Mishnah as authoritative.[47] All the other Midrashim lie somewhere in between.

If this is the state of the Midrashim of the academy of Rabbi Akiva, whose Mishnah formed the basis for Rabbi Yehudah ha-Nasi's, one can imagine that the Midrashim of Rabbi Yishmael's school paint a poorer picture. Indeed, in them, the Hebrew word *mishnah* never appears, even when parallel midrashim of Rabbi Akiva's school have it.[48] "Hence they said," the lead-in to mishnaic quotations discussed extensively above, is uncommon in these Midrashim.[49] And when it does appear, the cited halakhot are almost always those that circulated in the bet midrash of Rabbi Yishmael.[50]

A Genizah fragment of *Mekhilta Deuteronomy* showcases this. The scriptural verse interpreted there orders the complete destruction of various types of idols:

> "You shall break their altars [dash their pillars to pieces, burn down their Asherah trees, chop up the images of their gods, and obliterate[a] their name from that place]" (Deut. 12:3). I hear that one may break them and leave them;[b] it therefore says, "dash their pillars to pieces." I hear that one may dash them to pieces and leave them; it therefore says, "burn down their Asherah trees." I hear that one may burn them and leave them; it therefore says, "chop up the images of their gods." I hear that one may chop them up and leave them; it therefore says, "and obliterate their name from that place"—utter obliteration. Finish off, destroy, burn, obliterate, and remove them from this world.
>
> Hence they said: Burn whatever is fit to be burnt, and whatever is not fit to be burnt[c] grind down and cast it in the wind, fling it into the sea, or crush it into the ground until it is gone. (*Mekhilta Deuteronomy* 12:3)

a The biblical Hebrew action verbs denote various types of destruction, some of which are specific and others not. Their translation has been made to accord with the midrashic reading below, so that they can be plausibly understood as the progressive destruction of a single object.
b As is, in their broken condition.
c Wooden or metal objects of idolatry.

"וְנִתַּצְתֶּם אֶת מִזְבְּחֹתָם [וְשִׁבַּרְתֶּם אֶת מַצֵּבֹתָם וַאֲשֵׁרֵיהֶם תִּשְׂרְפוּן בָּאֵשׁ וּפְסִילֵי אֱלֹהֵיהֶם תְּגַדֵּעוּן וְאִבַּדְתֶּם אֶת שְׁמָם מִן הַמָּקוֹם הַהוּא" (דברים יב, ג). שומע אני יתצם ויניחם, תלמוד לומר "וְשִׁבַּרְתֶּם אֶת מַצֵּבֹתָם" (שם). שומעני ישברם ויניחם, תלמוד לומר "וַאֲשֵׁרֵיהֶם תִּשְׂרְפוּן בָּאֵשׁ" (שם). שומע אני ישרפם ויניחם, תלמוד לומר "וּפְסִילֵי אֱלֹהֵיהֶם תְּגַדֵּעוּן" (שם). שומע אני יגדעם ויניחם, תלמוד לומר "וְאִבַּדְתֶּם אֶת שְׁמָם מִן הַמָּקוֹם הַהוּא" (שם)—אבידת כלאה. כלה והשחת ושרוף ואבד והעבירן מן העולם.

מיכן אמרו: הראוי לשריפה—שרוף, ואת שאינו ראוי לשריפה—שוחק וזורה לרוח או מטיל לים או שף בארץ עד שתכלה.

Not only is the closing halakhah not drawn from our Mishnah, but it contradicts the Mishnah's lenient approach. The Mishnah only requires a person to deface an idol, in the literal sense of removing the tip of its nose.[51] It need not be smashed to smithereens. This minimized destruction also appears in *Sifrei Deuteronomy*, of Rabbi Akiva's bet midrash, which seems to polemicize against the aforecited derashah in *Mekhilta Deuteronomy*:

"You shall break their altars [dash their pillars to pieces]" (Deut. 12:3). If you have broken the altar, leave it! And if you have dashed the pillar to pieces, leave it! (*Sifrei Deuteronomy*, §61, p. 127)

"וְנִתַּצְתֶּם אֶת מִזְבְּחֹתָם" (דברים יב, ג). נתצת את המזבח—הנח לו, ושברת את המצבה—הנח לה.

The language of the two Midrashim is way too close for coincidence. Each expresses the halakhic tradition of its own school. *Mekhilta Deuteronomy* may preserve a quotation for us from the "Mishnah of Rabbi Yishmael," which rivaled the "Mishnah of Rabbi Akiva" that underlies Rabbi Yehudah ha-Nasi's final edition.[52]

C. THE INTERRELATIONSHIP BETWEEN THE MIDRASH AND THE MISHNAH

The Midrash pulls quotes from and provides a scriptural foundation for the Mishnah, and it usually is working with something close to Rabbi Yehudah ha-Nasi's edited edition. The Midrash-Mishnah relationship, however, is not a one-way street, as we have seen. Although the Mishnah is not working with the edited Midrashim as we know them, it does integrate earlier midrashim into its laws.[53] This generates a feedback loop between the Mishnah and the Midrash:

"The entire assembly of the congregation of Israel *(kehal 'adat Yisra'el)* slaughtered it" (Ex. 12:6). *Hence they said*,[a] The paschal sacrifice is slaughtered in three groups: assembly *(kehal)*, congregation *('edah)*, and Israel *(Yisra'el)*. (*Mekhilta de-Rabbi Yishmael, Pasḥa*, §5, p. 17)

a In Mishnah, *Pesaḥim*, 5:5.

"וְשָׁחֲטוּ אֹתוֹ כֹּל קְהַל עֲדַת יִשְׂרָאֵל" (שמות יב, ו). מיכן אמרו: הפסח נשחט בשלש כיתות: קהל ועדה וישראל.

The Midrash restates the law of the Mishnah, which is nothing but a midrashic reading of the verse. Wheels within wheels.

It was noted above in passing that *Sifrei Deuteronomy* cites considerably from the second chapter of Tractate *Bava Metzi'a* on the laws of lost objects. A deeper look complicates this directionality, since the Mishnah's laws themselves are produced by midrashic exegesis. In three places the Mishnah calls explicit attention to this with "as it says," but the rest of the time it does not.[54] The fifth mishnah in this chapter illustrates this:

> The garment *(simla)* was included in all of these, why was it singled out? To draw an analogy from it: Just as a garment is singular in that it has identifying signs and claimants, so too anything that has identifying signs and claimants must be announced. (Mishnah, *Bava Metzi'a*, 2:5)

אף השימלה היתה בכלל כל אילו. ולמה יצאת? להקיש אליה: אלא מה השימלה מיוחדת שיש בה סימנין ויש לה תובעין, אף כל דבר שיש בו סימנין ויש לו תובעין חייב להכריז.

Why does the Mishnah fixate on a garment of all lost objects? Undeniably, the law here is derived exegetically from the relevant verses. The Torah states the law regarding oxen and sheep, and then applies it specifically to donkeys, garments *(simlato)*, and "any lost object of your brother" (Deut. 22:3). This derashah teases out the unique legal status of the garment that merits its being singled out by the Torah. The general question and answer given in the Mishnah is characteristic of the Midrashim of Rabbi Akiva's school, and, indeed, a parallel derashah exists in *Sifrei Deuteronomy* for this verse.[55] Back and forth and back again; the derashah in the *Sifrei* cites this mishnah, and this mishnah relies on an earlier derashah.

As intimated throughout, one can conceive of the mutual relationship between the Mishnah and the Midrash diachronically. Much of the Second Temple Halakhah was rooted in extra-biblical traditions, and the desire to affix it to the Torah grew until it become an exigent need.[56] This midrashic process would eventually climax in the two Talmuds, which furnish verses for nearly every single mishnah.[57] But one can also formulate the relationship in synchronic terms, as an irreducible, ever-present tension within the rabbinic study hall, between the Oral Torah and the Written Torah, between jurists and exegetes.

Although there is truth to the historical model, the continuous tension is apparent, even in the final form of the midrashic collections. The Midrash wants to present traditions passed down orally as if they originated from Scripture, while the Mishnah presents halakhot undoubtedly derived from the Torah as if they are its own. These are two different, sometimes oppositional agendas. Thus, the same material is often codified both in the form of the Mishnah and in the form of the Midrash.[58]

But the conceptualization of an inner tension is not enough. It fails to account for the fact that the very same people produced these works. Both the Mishnah and many Midrashim were born in the study halls of Rabbi Akiva and his disciples. How can works that treat Scripture so differently have been produced by a tightly knit group of scholars? One possibility is that the two works were intentionally created to complement each other, as part of a unified vision. A second possibility is that the passage of time resulted in a shift in orientation, since the editing of the Midrashim postdated that of the Mishnah. A third, complementary possibility is that the answer lies somewhere in the murky editorial stages, as reflected by the variability in the treatment of the Mishnah in the Midrashim of Rabbi Akiva's school. Unfortunately, we do not know who was involved in the editorial processes or how they envisioned the relationship between these two genres.

This chapter has attempted to map out the relationship between the Mishnah and the Midrash on a number of levels. The final editions of these works allow us to analyze with relative ease the editorial phenomena that characterize the distinct schools, and to identify shifts in emphasis and methodology over time. But beyond that, everything becomes obscure. These multilayered works are like an oral version of a palimpsest, paper on which earlier versions have been erased to make room for the final one. In the end, we are left with more questions than answers, but one thing is sure: only an integrative study of the two major literary preoccupations of the tannaitic study hall can begin to do justice to the very complex relationship between them.

However, we must not allow this complexity to obscure one fundamental fact: As demonstrated in the opening of tractate *Avot*, the early rabbis maintained a sense of continuity with "the tradition of the fathers," much like Josephus's depiction of the Pharisees. This commitment is evident in their insistence on preserving the independent study of halakha, which later developed into the Mishnah, rather than subordinating everything to Midrash. Although they could, and often did, find scriptural foundations for their halakhot through Midrash, they deliberately upheld the coexistence of these two distinct genres instead of merging them. However, this sense of independence was not destined to endure. By the time of the Tannaitic Midrashim—and even more so in the Talmudim—the Mishnah would be re-integrated with scripture and subjected to Midrashic interpretation.

SIXTEEN

The Editing and Transmission of the Midrash

The Midrash is not a detailed record of the activities of the rabbinic study hall. It is a literary creation produced by anonymous editors from their source material. The Midrashim that we possess today vary in style and language, repetitiveness, and juxtaposed contradictions, all of which point to their historically complex formation and editing. Our crisp printed editions belie the messy transmission history behind them, the unwitting corruptions and intentional emendations of the long oral and written existence of the midrashic collections. Accordingly, scholars of Midrash look at midrashic texts through a set of scholarly bifocals, so to speak. They scrutinize the final version in front of them from up close, but they also peer far "behind" the text to catch sight of the sources that gave rise to it and to try to sketch its early form.

Philologists refer to this sort of critical work as higher (or source) criticism and lower (or textual) criticism. This chapter begins with the former, moves to the latter, and concludes with the modern reconstruction of lost Midrashim.

Before we begin, a word on method and on the limitations of the analysis. This chapter focuses on the redactional techniques that can be extracted from the sources. It ought to begin with a discussion of the source material that the editors had before them, the identity of the editors themselves, their goals and ideologies. It does not, for the simple reason that we know almost nothing about any of this. In fact, we know much less about the Midrashim than we do about the Mishnah. We can name the Mishnah's final editor and identify some of his editorial techniques thanks to the enlightening discussions of the Amoraim.[1] Unfortunately for us, the Talmudim devoted much less attention to the Midrashim than to the Mishnah, regarding the former as merely ancillary to the latter. The sources that would

> **HIGHER AND LOWER CRITICISM**
>
> These terms were coined in the nineteenth century to represent two scholarly branches of philology. Higher criticism tries to recover the earlier stages or sources of a text, prior to its ultimate editing, by paying close attention to relevant indicators. For this reason, it is also referred to as source criticism or redaction criticism. The goal of lower criticism is to reconstruct the original form of a text as it was when it was created or formally edited, by comparing printed editions and manuscripts.
>
> The two are connected. In order to get at the earlier material underlying a text through the text itself, one must make sure that the starting point is as close to the original text as possible. (See the example regarding Leviticus 22 below in section B.)
>
> Since rabbinic literature was preserved, partially or exclusively, in oral form for many centuries, its textual criticism—already a thorny enterprise—becomes even more complicated and tentative.

answer our questions do not exist. We cannot even tell for sure whether the Midrashim were transmitted orally or in writing.[2]

Due to these inherent limitations, the best we can do is draw inferences regarding the Midrash's editorial policies from the text as it is in front of us. The most effective tool here is comparative analysis of derashot from different Midrashic compilations, which exposes how the source material was transferred, adapted, and edited to create the final composition. Any conclusions drawn in this chapter are necessarily tentative and partial.

A. EDITORIAL PHENOMENA

Our Midrashim consist of sequences of derashot that adhere to the order of verses in the relevant books of the Torah. But behind the rigorous arrangement of this final product stands a vast number of sources that were collected and combined. Scholars have tried to reconstruct the origins of particular derashot or infer certain editorial policies. For example, Saul Lieberman suggested that the simple identity derashah, "X is nothing but Y," belongs to an earlier stage of Midrash.[3] If correct, this could help map the chronological layers within the Midrash. Yakir Paz has argued that the Midrash contains differentiated instruction: elementary instruction for novices and advanced halakhic reasoning for more seasoned Torah scholars. For him, the recurring statement that "the Torah teaches you *derekh eretz*," in the sense of normative behavior, is an example of the former.[4] This would tell us about the different types of traditions from which the Midrashim were edited. These are, however, conjectures, based on textual cues and clues, about the editing and collation that went into producing the polished, orderly text. Higher criticism is by definition an uncertain exercise. With this in mind, we shall dwell on some of the more remarkable phenomena in the Midrash, from which we can glimpse editorial practices.

Transfer of Material

In midrashic collections, the same derashot recur in distinct contexts. It is reasonable to assume that there was a single original context in which the exegetical comment was made, after which editors from both schools transferred it to other relevant places in their collections.[5] In this, the Midrash is no different from other genres and works of rabbinic literature.[6] Challengingly, only in a minority of cases is there textual signage regarding the transfer, with an explicit reference such as "That is what we have said . . ." *(ze hu she-amarnu)*. Most of the time, it is not evident which is the birthplace of the derashah. In some cases, no viable candidate can be found in the extant Midrashim, and it seems as though the transplants have outlasted their parent.[7]

Sometimes, the relocated derashah is reworked into its new context, as is the case with so-called mirror image derashot. Here is an example involving apparently contradictory statements of fact by the Torah:

> "Yet, there will be no pauper among you" (Deut. 15:4). But there it says, "For the pauper will not cease from the midst of the land" (Deut. 15:11). When you do the will of the Omnipresent, the paupers are among others, but when you do not do the will of the Omnipresent, the paupers are among you. (*Sifrei Deuteronomy*, §114, p. 174)

> "אֶפֶס כִּי לֹא יִהְיֶה בְּךָ אֶבְיוֹן" (דברים טו, ד). והלן הוא אומר "כִּי לֹא יֶחְדַּל אֶבְיוֹן מִקֶּרֶב הָאָרֶץ" (דברים טו, יא). בזמן שאתם עושים רצונו של מקום, אביונים באחרים; וכשאין אתם עושים רצונו של מקום, אביונים בכם.

> "For the pauper will not cease from the midst of the land" (Deut. 15:11). But there it says, "Yet, there will be no pauper among you" (Deut. 15:4). How can the two verses be reconciled? When you do the will of the Omnipresent, the paupers are among others, but when you do not do the will of the Omnipresent, the paupers are among you. (*Sifrei Deuteronomy*, §118, p. 177)

> "כִּי לֹא יֶחְדַּל אֶבְיוֹן מִקֶּרֶב הָאָרֶץ" (דברים טו, יא). והלן הוא אומר "אֶפֶס כִּי לֹא יִהְיֶה בְּךָ אֶבְיוֹן" (דברים טו, ד). כיצד נתקיימו שני כתובים הללו? בזמן שאתם עושים רצונו של מקום, אביונים באחרים; וכשאין אתם עושים רצונו של מקום, אביונים בכם.

The derashah resolves the contradiction through an *okimta*, that is, by placing a limitation on the verses so that they refer to the specific circumstance of heeding or not heeding God. The derashah appears in connection with both verses, and each time the relevant verse appears first. It seems reasonable to posit that the original context was the first verse, Deuteronomy 15:4, which explains why both derashot give the limitation on that verse first: "when you do the will of the Omnipresent." Of interest here is the slight accommodation the editors made for the derashah to make it comfortable in its new home.

Derashot often repeat whenever their biblical subject matter reappears, and this is unquestionably the handiwork of editors. *Sifrei Deuteronomy* offers many good illustrations of this, since the book of Deuteronomy contains scores of repetitive phrases. Here is a partial list:

1. In several places in Deuteronomy, a passage concludes with the phrase "you shall eliminate the evil from your midst." Every single time the *Sifrei* glosses "eliminate the evildoers from Israel" to clarify that that the evil spoken of resides in human beings. All the Midrash does is translate "the evil" with "evildoers" and "your midst" with "Israel."[8]

2. In a few places, Deuteronomy uses the infinitive absolute with an imperative, which is generally translated emphatically ("shall surely").[9] Each time this grammatical construction appears, the *Sifrei* comments: "even one hundred times."[10]

3. Deuteronomy frequently refers to "the place where the Lord shall choose to make His name dwell." For this or similar phrases, the *Sifrei* often concretizes the location: "this is Shiloh (where a temporary tabernacle was standing) and the eternal Temple (in Jerusalem)."[11] The Midrash is addressing the glaring absence of Jerusalem—later so central to the Israelite religion—from the book of Deuteronomy.

4. When the beginning of Deuteronomy recounts the history of the young Israelite nation, Moses speaks in the first person. Since the language of "I said to you" (Deut. 1:9) and the like sounds like Moses is speaking on his own authority, the *Sifrei* occasionally sees fit to append a clarification: "I say this not of my own accord; rather, it is from the mouth of the Holy that I say this to you."[12]

5. When delineating the parameters of a particular mitzvah, Deuteronomy at times will enumerate those obligated in list form: "you, your sons, your daughters. . . ." The *Sifrei* explains the order: "the most beloved come first."[13]

Sifrei Deuteronomy is richest in these repetitions, but other Midrashim contain them as well. The book of Leviticus says dozens of times that a sacrificial act must take place "*etzel* the altar," meaning near it, and the *Sifra* consistently glosses this with the word *samukh*, the mishnaic Hebrew equivalent of *etzel*.[14] The editors adopt the same approach to Aggadah. The book of Leviticus states about a number of mitzvot "and you shall fear your God," and the *Sifra* comments that this is because their fulfillment depends on motivations or feelings that are inscrutable to observers.[15]

The same is true of Midrashim from the school of R. Yishmael. For example, whenever the book of Numbers says that a sacrifice is "a pleasing aroma *(reah nihoah)*, a fire offering for the Lord," *Sifrei Numbers* explicates: "it is pleasing *(nahat ruah)* to Me, for I have spoken and My will was done."[16] In all these examples, the duplication of derashot is the product of systematic editing.

Editing and Transmission

Combining Derashot

Perhaps the hallmark of midrashic literature is its multivocality. A single biblical phrase can inspire manifold derashot that take the text in utterly different directions. This sets it apart from the various kinds of biblical interpretation that were current in the Second Temple era. When a few derashot on the same text are attributed to specific Sages, they are generally presented as a disagreement. The Midrash introduces the latter, "dissenting" Sage formulaically, "Rabbi Y says," with an implied contrast. Recall the example discussed in chapter 14 about applying the blood of the paschal lamb:

> "They shall put it on the two doorposts" (Ex. 12:7)—on the inside. Do you say on the inside, but instead on the outside? It therefore teaches, "and I will see the blood" (Ex. 12:13)—visible to Me and not to others—the words of Rabbi Yishmael.
>
> Rabbi Yonatan says, On the inside. Do you say on the inside, or instead on the outside? It therefore teaches, "And the blood will be a sign for you" (Ex. 12:13)—"a sign for you" and not a sign for others.
>
> R. Yitzhak says, It is actually (le-'olam) on the outside, so that the Egyptians see and their insides churn. (*Mekhilta de-Rabbi Yishmael, Pasḥa*, §6, p. 18)

"וְנָתְנוּ עַל שְׁתֵּי הַמְזוּזֹת" (שמות יב, ז) וגו'—מבפנים. אתה אומר מבפנים או אינו אלא מבחוץ? ת"ל "וְרָאִיתִי אֶת הַדָּם" (שמות יב, יג)—הנראה לי ולא לאחרים—דברי רבי ישמעאל.

ר' יונתן אומר: מבפנים. אתה אומר מבפנים או אינו אלא מבחוץ? ת"ל "וְהָיָה הַדָּם לָכֶם לְאֹת" (שמות יב, יג)—"לכם לאות" ולא לאחרים לאות.

ר' יצחק אומר: לעולם מבחוץ, כדי שיישהו המצריים רואים ומעיהם מתחתכין.

This midrash cites three approaches to the same verse: one of Rabbi Yishmael the teacher, and two of his disciples. The final opinion of Rabbi Yitzchak declares its disagreement with the preceding ones through the contrastive term *le-'olam*. But even the middle opinion of Rabbi Yonatan, which agrees with Rabbi Yishmael about the application of the blood inside, disagrees about the precise proof for it. Since the rabbinic figures in question were master and pupils, one could imagine the three being aware of one another's opinions and debating them in real life. In many other midrashim, though, there is no mutual awareness of opinion, and the collation of various exegeses must be the product of editing.

Here is an example of such an editorial adjoining of various opinions. When the Torah rules that the owner of a generally tame ox that kills a human being is "clear," four Tannaim offer their legal interpretations:

> "The ox's owner is clear" (Ex. 21:28). Rabbi Yehudah ben Betera says, Clear of the hands of Heaven.[a] [. . .]

---

[a] A death penalty imposed by Heaven, like the one applied to the owner of a violent ox that kills a human being; see Exodus 21:29.

Shimon ben Azzai says, "The ox's owner is clear"—clear of half damages.[a] [. . .]

Rabban Gamaliel says, "The ox's owner is clear"—clear of the slave's value.[b] [. . .]

Rabbi Akiva says, "The ox's owner is clear"—clear of the offspring's value.[c] [. . .]
(*Mekhilta de-Rabbi Yishmael*, Nezikin, §10, p. 283)

"וּבַעַל הַשּׁוֹר נָקִי" (שמות כא, כח). ר' יהודה בן בתירה אומר: נקי מידי שמיים. [. . .]

שמעון בן עזאי אומר: "בַּעַל הַשּׁוֹר נָקִי"—נקי מחצי נזק. [. . .]

רבן גמליאל אומר: "וּבַעַל הַשּׁוֹר נָקִי"—נקי מדמי עבד. [. . .]

רבי עקיבא אומר: "וּבַעַל הַשּׁוֹר נָקִי"—נקי מדמי ולדות. [. . .]

This sequence of derashot comes from the Sages of Yavneh, but nothing in the midrash gestures toward verbal disagreement or even mutual acknowledgment. The Midrash simply collects these opinions and presents them all as viable alternatives.

It is important to note that the editors of the Midrash usually allot equal space to all its voices and do not promote any one of them. While the Mishnah shares a similar editorial policy, it is one thing not to take a halakhic stand, and quite another to maintain as a matter of hermeneutics that all interpretations of the Torah are of equal validity.

In the preceding example, one could affirm all the legal opinions without getting entangled in a halakhic contradiction. But even in midrashim where Sages explicitly relate to and disagree with one another's derashot, the Midrash does not try to settle the dispute. The Midrash stands out in embracing both contradictory and complementary derashot, in stark contrast to all preceding scriptural exegesis that dogmatically holds that a verse has one authoritative explanation.[17] I am reiterating this point here because this phenomenon is the product of purposive editing. Nowhere do we find in tannaitic Midrash (as opposed to later, amoraic Midrash) a single Sage giving multiple explanations, in succession, for a single verse. It is the editors who collect these opinions and string them together, thereby fashioning a remarkable work of interpretation. While the ideology of interpretive multivocality appears in the name of Tannaim, the practice of citing multiple—even contradictory—interpretations side by side, without deciding between them, is editorial.[18]

In most instances, the editors do not attribute derashot to particular Sages and just juxtapose them. They may modestly link them with the phrase "another matter" or a new *sub verbo*, or not. One example, selected at random, concerns the postmortem hanging of someone executed for a capital crime:

"If a man is guilty of a capital offense and is put to death, and you hang him on a tree" (Deut. 21:22).

a Paid by the owner of a tame ox that gores another ox; see Exodus 21:35.
b The payment for killing a slave; see Exodus 21:32.
c The payment for the killing of a fetus in its mother's womb; see Exodus 21:22.

"Him"—but neither his clothing[a] nor his witnesses.[b]

"Him"—but not his conspiring witnesses.[c]

"Him"—it teaches that two are not sentenced on the same day.[d] (*Sifrei Deuteronomy*, §221, p. 254)

"וְכִי יִהְיֶה בְאִישׁ חֵטְא מִשְׁפַּט מָוֶת וְהוּמָת וְתָלִיתָ אֹתוֹ עַל עֵץ" (דברים כא, כב).

"אֹתוֹ"—ולא את כליו, ולא את עדיו.

"אֹתוֹ"—ולא את זוממיו.

"אֹתוֹ"—מלמד שאין דנין שנים ביום אחד.

A second midrash concerns the prohibition against seeing forbidden leaven on Pesach (Passover) recorded in Deuteronomy 16:4:

"No leaven of yours shall be seen"—you may see that of others.

"No leaven of yours shall be seen"—you may see that of the Most High.[e]

"No leaven of yours shall be seen"—you may see that of the *pattir*.[f]

"No leaven of yours shall be seen"—annul it in your heart. (*Sifrei Deuteronomy*, §131, p. 188)

"וְלֹא יֵרָאֶה לְךָ שְׂאֹר" (דברים טז, ד)—רואה אתה לאחרים.

"וְלֹא יֵרָאֶה לְךָ שְׂאֹר"—רואה את לגבוה.

"וְלֹא יֵרָאֶה לְךָ שְׂאֹר"—רואה את לפטיר.

"וְלֹא יֵרָאֶה לְךָ שְׂאֹר"—בטיל בליבך.

Both midrashim offer a string of exclusionary inferences that repeat the same language, and then conclude with a final derashah that breaks the pattern (possibly in order to mark its exceptionality). Notably, none of the derashot in either midrash exclude one another. The assumption guiding the editors is that there isn't a one-to-one correspondence between a legal phrase

---

a He is to be hanged naked.

b This refers to false witnesses. If people falsely testify that they saw him commit a capital crime and he is executed, then their punishment is execution.

c This refers to another type of false witnesses. If people falsely testify that witnesses of capital crime are lying, since they were with them in another place and so could not see what they testified to have seen, then their punishment too is execution.

d To death; see Mishnah, *Sanhedrin*, 6:4.

e Meaning, it has been consecrated and belongs to the communal Temple fund.

f Probably a corruption (or a variant) of *palter*, the seller of baked goods, but see the editions of Hoffmann and Finkelstein ad loc., which emend the text to read *pelatya*, "the street."

in the Torah and its halakhic application;[19] the divine word is sturdy enough to bear many interpretations, and these can be juxtaposed without any need to decide between them.

These two latter midrashim exemplify another phenomenon: tannaitic Midrashim regularly present their derashot anonymously. Generally, a Sage is only named when a dissenting opinion is noted.[20] One can reasonably conclude that including or omitting an attribution is an editorial decision. There is no reason to assume that anonymous derashot are necessarily late or the creations of the editors themselves.

Furthermore, we saw in chapter 10 that occasionally identical derashot appear in Midrashim of both academies and are contradictorily attributed to interpreters from each school. Similarly, a derashah attributed to Rabbi Yishmael in the Midrashim of Rabbi Akiva's school can appear anonymously in the Midrashim of Rabbi Yishmael's school, and vice versa. This is reminiscent of the editing of the Mishnah, which anonymizes rulings and opinions that are preserved with attribution in the Tosefta,[21] although the aim in our case is less obvious. As of this writing, no systematic study of this phenomenon has been undertaken, and it may vary across Midrashim.[22]

The connections between the exegetes of the tannaitic academies and their editors is poorly understood. On the one hand, the latter had their own rules; on the other hand, their vision was rooted in the ethos of the study halls, which made room for debate and extended legitimacy to a plurality of opinion. Many of the issues pertaining to editorial policies and practices of the various Midrashim await systemic study.

Derashot of Different Schools

The editing of the Midrash did not function like a machine that extruded a smooth, homogenous product from heterogenous inputs. It bears a resemblance to the editing of the Mishnah, which was not totalizing and produced a work of uneven style and occasionally contradictory content. Such contradictions can coexist in close proximity, that is, not only within a midrashic collection associated with a single school, but on the very same verse therein. Nothing in the text suggests that the authors of these derashot are aware of what the others are doing. It is the editors who combine them.

As an example, let us examine the Torah's law about a woman who gets involved in a fight to save her husband.

> If two men get into a fight with each other, and the wife of one comes forward to save her husband from the hand of the one striking him, and she reaches out her hand and seizes him by his genitals, you shall cut off her hand—show no pity. (Deut. 25:11–12)

The *Sifrei* has two radically different readings of this, the first with attribution and the second anonymous:

> "To save her husband" (Deut. 25:11).
>
> Rabbi [Yehudah Ha-Nasi] says, Since we find that the Torah considers some who cause damage unintentionally as acting intentionally, perhaps here too? It therefore

teaches, "by his pudenda *(bi-mevushav),*" telling us that one is not obligated for humiliation *(ha-boshet)* unless one intended it.

"[By] his pudenda" (Deut. 25:11). I only know about his pudenda, whence do I include anything that poses a threat to life? It therefore teaches, "and seizes"—anything. Why, then, does it say, "his pudenda"? Just as "his pudenda" specifically constitutes a threat to life and entrains "you shall cut off her hand," so anything that constitutes a threat to life entrains "you shall cut off her hand." (*Sifrei Deuteronomy,* §292, p. 311)

"לְהַצִּיל אֶת אִישָׁהּ" (דברים כה, יא). רבי אומר: לפי שמצינו שיש מזיקין בתורה שעשת בהן שאין מתכוין כמתכוין, יכול אף כן? תלמוד לומר "בִּמְבֻשָׁיו"—מגיד שאין חייב על הבושת עד שהוא מתכוין.

"מְבֻשָׁיו" (שם). אין לי אלא מבושיו, מנין לרבות דבר שיש בו סכנת נפשות? תלמוד לומר "וְהֶחֱזִיקָה"—מכל מקום. אם כן למה נאמר "מְבֻשָׁיו"? מה "מְבֻשָׁיו" מיוחד דבר שיש בו סכנת נפשות והרי הוא ב"קַצֹּתָה אֶת כַּפָּהּ", כך כל דבר שהו בסכנת נפשות הרי הוא ב"קַצֹּתָה אֶת כַּפָּהּ".

Rabbi Yehudah Ha-Nasi's derashah assumes that the biblical passage is discussing the offense of public humiliation and its restitution. According to the Mishnah, someone who injures someone else has to pay up to five different kinds of damages, one of which is for the humiliation *(boshet)* they suffered. The Mishnah actually cites the same verse as the Midrash:

> If someone fell from the roof and injured and humiliated someone, they are obligated for the injury and exempt from the humiliation. As it says, "and she reaches out her hand and seizes him by his genitals" (Deut. 25:11)—one is not obligated for humiliation unless one has intention. (Mishnah, *Bava Kamma,* 8:1)

This mishnah and the first derashah in the *Sifrei* understand the Torah's specification of the genitalia as the target as underscoring the public humiliation involved. Perhaps nothing is more mortifying for a man than public emasculation (or the real threat thereof). Since the Sages categorize humiliation as one of the five kinds of damages for which one must pay restitution, nobody's hands are severed as punishment. The phrase "you shall cut off her hand" is construed metaphorically to mean that the penalty for a low blow is stiff, although it concerns pockets rather than hands. The continuation in the *Sifrei* spells this out:

> Rabbi Yehudah says, It says here "show no pity" (Deut. 25:12), and it says there "show no pity" (Deut. 19:21). Just as "show no pity" stated there refers to monetary payment, so "show no pity" stated here refers to monetary payment. (*Sifrei Deuteronomy,* §293, p. 312)

רבי יהודה אומר: נאמר כן "לֹא תָחוֹס עֵינֶךָ" (דברים כה, יב) ונאמר להלן "לֹא תָחוֹס עֵינֶךָ" (דברים יט, כא). מה "לֹא תָחוֹס עֵינֶךָ" האמור להלן ממון, אף "לֹא תָחוֹס עֵינֶךָ" האמור כן ממון.

The rabbinic understanding of "an eye for an eye" is a monetary, rather than physical, equation, and the same is true here.

The second derashah makes no mention of humiliation or money and focuses instead on the danger posed by harming the genitalia. It is part of a series of derashot that deal with the law of the pursuer, under which someone who is out for blood may be killed before they take their victim's life. The *Sifrei* reads:

> "You shall cut off her hand" (Deut. 25:12). It teaches that you are obligated to save her [from sin][23] by [cutting off] her hand. Whence save her [from sin] by her life? It therefore teaches, "show no pity" (Deut. 25:12). (*Sifrei Deuteronomy*, §293, p. 312)

> "וְקַצֹּתָה אֶת כַּפָּהּ" (דברים כה, יב)—מלמד שחייב אתה להצילה בכפה. הצילה בנפשה מניין? תלמוד לומר "לֹא תָחוֹס".

This isn't about lawsuits after the damage has been done, but action to be undertaken so that the perpetrator is stopped and the victim comes to no harm. If the wife's life-threatening assault can be stopped by severing her hand, that is the legal measure to take. If it would prove insufficient, she may be killed. The phrase "you shall cut off her hand" means exactly what it says.

Amit Gvaryahu demonstrates that although the two derashot appear right next to each other in the *Sifrei*, conceptually they could not be further apart. The two midrashic schools take distinct approaches to damages more globally, yet they are presented side by side even within the Midrashim of Rabbi Akiva's school *(Sifrei Deuteronomy* and *Mekhilta de-Rashbi)*.[24] Vicinity is not a sufficient indicator of affinity.

This editorial tendency is even more noticeable in the Midrashim of Rabbi Yishmael's school. Above, we saw that a midrash in the *Sifrei* aligns with a ruling in the Mishnah, which is logical since both draw on the same traditions. The halakhic traditions of Rabbi Yishmael's school, by contrast, do not accord with those that gave rise to the Mishnah. Therefore, its Midrashim are sometimes the only source to preserve ancient traditions that were gradually lost to history, due to rejection by the Mishnah and by the Midrashim it influenced. Scholars interested in reconstructing the full sweep of ancient Halakhah often rely heavily on the Midrashim from this school.[25] The case below exemplifies how this reconstruction can proceed.

The Torah requires a person to give their firstborn kosher animals to a priest, and to redeem their firstborn non-kosher animals and sons. In the book of Exodus, this command is couched in rather narrow terms, "and every donkey's breach you shall redeem with a lamb" (Ex. 13:13), whereas in the book of Numbers the same mitzvah is broader, "and the firstborn of the unclean animal you shall redeem" (Num. 18:15). One could have said that the first verse is merely casuistic so that the law isn't limited to redeeming a donkey specifically. But the Mishnah rejects this possibility and rules that the law of redeeming a firstborn non-kosher animal applies only to a donkey.[26] A midrashic reconciliation of these two verses in *Sifrei Numbers* gives the exegesis codified in the Mishnah:

Editing and Transmission   357

"But you shall surely redeem . . . and the firstborn of unclean animals" (Num. 18:15). I hear all other unclear animals implied; it therefore teaches, "and every donkey's breach you shall redeem with a lamb" (Ex. 13:13)—a "donkey's breach" you redeem, but you do not redeem the firstling of any other unclean animal. (*Sifrei Numbers*, §118, p. 138)

"אַךְ פָּדֹה תִפְדֶּה [. . .] וְאֵת בְּכוֹר הַבְּהֵמָה הַטְּמֵאָה" (במדבר יח, טו). שומע אני אף שאר בהמה טמאה במשמע, תלמוד לומר "וְכָל פֶּטֶר חֲמֹר תִּפְדֶּה בְשֶׂה" (שמות יג, יג)—"פֶּטֶר חֲמֹר" אתה פודה, ואי אתה פודה בכור שאר בהמה טמאה.

The verse in Exodus restricts the implied universality of the verse in Numbers, so only the donkey's firstborn is redeemed.

Mekhilta de-Rabbi Yishmael on Exodus, however, flips the relationship between verses and comes to the opposite conclusion:

Another thing:

"[Every] donkey's breach you shall redeem with a lamb" (Ex. 13:13)—but every other unclean animal with clothing or vessels. (*Mekhilta de-Rabbi Yishmael, Pasḥa* §18, p. 71)

דבר אחר: "פֶּטֶר חֲמֹר תִּפְדֶּה בְשֶׂה" (שמות יג, יג)—ושאר בהמה טמאה [תפדה] בכסות וכלים.

According to this midrash, all non-kosher animals must be redeemed, and the reason it only mentions the donkey in Exodus is that only it is redeemed specifically with a lamb. Other animals can be redeemed with any other possessions. Menahem Kahana has shown that this derashah reflects an ancient law that was rejected by mainstream rabbinic literature, so it only survives here and there in rabbinic literature.[27]

Note the term "another thing" *(davar aḥer)* here. Indeed, Abraham Goldberg argued that when a midrash contains one derashah and then introduces another with "another matter," it can signify a shift in source material from one school to the other. Editors, in other words, used this term to combine derashot with distinct origins.[28]

Editors could work adroitly and ensure consistency, but they could also be clumsy or less heavy-handed. The latter have left us textual gaps by which we can sneak into the text and see the editors at their workstations.

B. TEXTUAL TRANSMISSION

Carrying out lower, textual criticism is no easier going. The first part of this book described how the Mishnah's exclusively oral existence for many centuries gave rise to all sorts of complications.[29] Since there is some evidence that the Midrash was already, at least partly, written down in the third century CE,[30] one might surmise that it would facilitate textual criticism. However, since it also enjoyed a long oral transmission until it was transcribed in manuscripts in the Middle Ages, and eventually printed in the sixteenth century, its simultaneous "coexistence" in both oral and written forms actually makes reconstructing the original more challenging.[31]

All midrashic quotations in the preceding chapters have been taken from the most complete manuscript witnesses of each Midrash, as selected for the Ma'agarim database of the Academy of the Hebrew Language (see figure 8). The critical editions of the various Midrashim prepared in the first half of the twentieth century are usually not based on such manuscripts.[32] For his edition of *Mekhilta de-Rabbi Yishmael*, Saul Horovitz used the printed editions, with some of his emendations, as the base text. Louis Finkelstein created an eclectic text for his edition of *Sifrei Deuteronomy:* he based it primarily on a single manuscript he deemed superior, but picked and chose what he thought were the best readings. Both included in their scholarly apparatus variant readings from whatever manuscripts were available to them. Today, scholars preparing a critical edition typically use the best manuscript witness as the base text. Menahem Kahana's edition of *Sifrei Numbers* is such an exemplar. Caution is still warranted when using such an edition, though. Even superior manuscripts contain a text that underwent many changes during the hundreds of years of oral recitation and experienced even more alterations as it was repeatedly transcribed by fallible copyists, until it finally came to rest in its unique parchment preserved in a monastery, library, or private collection.

One corruption encountered everywhere is the introduction of corrections and explanations into the body of the text by later scribes and printers. Regarding the psalmist's description of the making of the golden calf, the Midrash says:

Rabbi Papyas expounded *(darash)*: "They exchanged their Glory for the likeness of an ox that eats grass" (Ps. 106:20). Do I hear *(shomea' ani)* that it is about the supernal ox? It therefore teaches *(talmud lomar)*, "that eats grass."

Rabbi Akiva said to him, "That's enough out of you, Papyas." (*Mekhilta de-Rabbi Yishmael*, Vayhi, §7, p. 112)

דרש ר' פפיס: "וַיָּמִירוּ אֶת כְּבוֹדָם בְּתַבְנִית שׁוֹר אֹכֵל עֵשֶׂב" (תהלים קו, כ). שומע אני בשור של מעלה? תלמוד לומר "אֹכֵל עֵשֶׂב".

אמר לו ר' עקיבא: דייך פפיס.

Rabbi Papyas wondered if the Israelites intended to fashion an image in the likeness of a supernal ox.[33] He concluded that the verse teaches that they were so debased that they made it in the mold of an ordinary beast of burden. This derashah incensed Rabbi Akiva, but why? After all, Rabbi Papyas ended up rejecting this reading!

Menahem Kahana has found that the concluding negation is an invention of the printed editions and does not appear in any of the manuscripts. Knowing that the typical midrashic formula is "Do I hear X? It therefore teaches Y," some learned editor appended the second half. This is indeed the typical formula, but there are atypical cases in which *shomea' ani* is

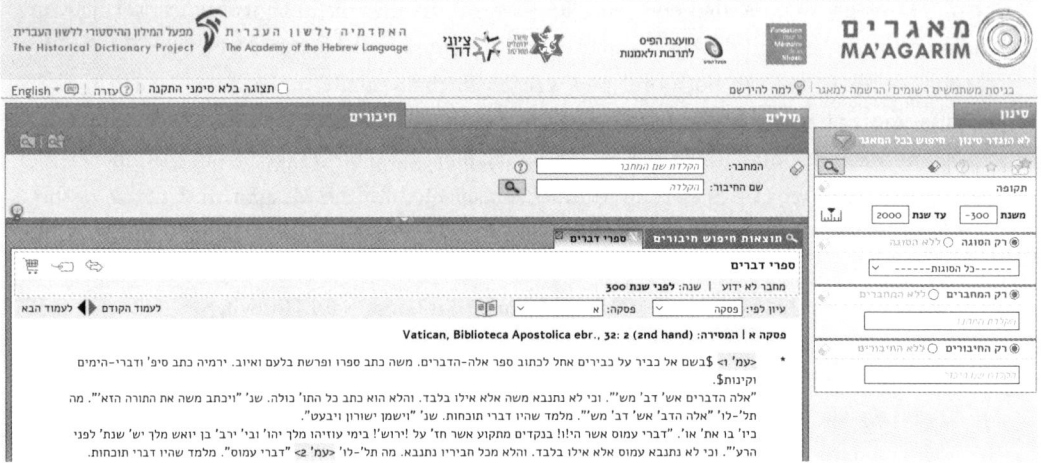

FIGURE 8. Screenshot from "Ma'agarim" website, the beginning of the Midrash *Sifrei Devarim*.

a declarative ("I hear X!") rather than an interrogative ("Do I hear X?"). In this unusual usage, *shomea' ani* does not anticipate a *talmud lomar* rejection.[34] In our case, Rabbi Papyas was indeed reading the verse as referring to "the supernal ox." This would be an assertion that the Israelites intended to worship the mythological ox on high, which caused Rabbi Akiva to silence him. His anger is now theologically understandable, because Rabbi Papyas would have been making room in heaven for other powers beyond God.

This midrash illuminates the way in which editors hired by the printing presses would normalize and standardize derashot to match their typical, expected forms, especially when they preserved rarer forms that broke the mold. The manuscripts in these cases may tell a more original story.

The above corruption occurs in an aggadic context and so has no practical ramifications. Elsewhere, alterations of the text can have real halakhic consequences. For instance, Leviticus 22 says that one may not accept blemished animal sacrifices from a non-Jew, and the Midrash, in Horovitz's edition relying on the regular printing, comments: "you may not accept these from them, but you may accept unblemished ones *(temimim)*."[35] The inference seems sound enough and is in keeping with midrashic exegesis, but this might not be the original reading. The best manuscript witness of *Sifrei Numbers*, has one letter change: "but you may accept daily sacrifices *(temidim)*."[36] A tiny stroke separates the two words, yet the halakhic gulf between them is vast. But in this situation matters are less certain. One cannot say definitively that this reading, not attested in any other manuscript, is more original. As noted above, even the best manuscripts are not perfect, and the reading of the standard edition better fits the context of disqualifying blemishes. But if the manuscript is right that a non-Jew can contribute the daily sacrifice, what is the halakhic significance? According to the rabbinic understanding, the daily burnt offering is a communal sacrifice that is paid for from communal funds. To say that the daily sacrifice is accepted from non-Jews would mean that they can voluntarily pay the half-shekel Temple tax that raises funds for such sacrifices. Problematically, the Mishnah forcefully excludes the gentile from contributing to this head tax:

> If a gentile or a Cuthean paid the half-shekel, it is not accepted from them. [. . .] Ezra made this explicit, as it says, "You have nothing to do with us to build a house for our God" (Ezra 4:3). (Mishnah, *Shekalim*, 1:5)

This means that *Sifrei Numbers* preserves an opinion rejected by canonical rabbinic literature, nearly all vestiges of which were subsequently erased by copyists, editors, or rabbis who wanted to support the accepted Halakhah. If not for the painstaking research of a modern philologist, they would have succeeded.[37]

This is a prime example of where higher criticism depends on lower criticism. As noted in the previous section, Midrashim from Rabbi Yishmael's academy are full of fascinating halakhot that normative Halakhah swept away, and deep philological work is crucial to recovery efforts.

Critical editions are gamechangers for scholarly pursuits, but, as with any tool, one must know how to use them properly. A brief comparison between the editions of Horovitz (figure 9) and Kahana (figure 10) on *Sifrei Numbers* drives this home. In the Torah, God commands Aaron, the High Priest:

> And your brothers, too, the tribe of Levi, your father's tribe, bring forward with you, so that they may be joined to you and serve you, and you and your sons with you are to be before the Tent of Testimony. (Numbers 18:2)

Here is the comment of *Sifrei Numbers* according to the two principal editions:

> "And your brothers, too" (Num. 18:2). [. . .] Do I hear *(shomea' ani)* even women implied? It therefore teaches *(talmud lomar)* "your father's tribe." Amram merited having a tribe called after him. (*Sifrei Numbers*, §116, ed. Horovitz, p. 131)

> "וְגַם אֶת אַחֶיךָ" (במדבר יח, ב). [. . .] שומע אני אף הנשים במשמע? תלמוד לומר "שֵׁבֶט אָבִיךָ". זכה עמרם שיקרא שבט על שמו.

> "And your brothers, too" (Num. 18:2). [. . .] I hear *(shomea' ani)* that even women are implied.
>
> "Levi, your father's tribe." Amram merited having a tribe called after him. (*Sifrei Numbers*, §116, ed. Kahana, 333–334)

> "וְגַם אֶת אַחֶיךָ" (במדבר יח, ב). [. . .] שומע אף הנשים במשמע.
>
> "לֵוִי שֵׁבֶט אָבִיךָ". זכה עמרם שיקרא שבט על שמו.

ספרי   פיסקא קטז   **קרח**   131

אמור הא מה ת"ל תשאו את עון כהונתכם זה עון דבר המסור לכהונה. אמרת ישראל
לא ישאו עון כהנים אבל לוים ישאו עון כהנים ת"ל ועבר הלוי הוא את עבדת אהל
מועד והם ישאו עונם (במדבר יח כג).

וגם את אחיך, שומע אני אף ישראל במשמע ת"ל מטה לוי שומע אני אף
5   הנשים במשמע ת"ל <שבט אביך זכה עמרם שיקרא שבט על שמו. רבי אומר מטה לוי
שומע אני אף הנשים במטמע ת"ל> את אחיך להוציא את הנשים: הקרב אתך רבי
עקיבא אומר נאמר כאן אתך ונאמר להלן אתך מה אתך האמור להלן בלוים הכתוב
מדבר אף אתך האמור כאן בלוים הכתוב מדבר להזהיר את הלוים בשיר על דוכנם:
וילוו עליך וישרתוך, בעבודתם ומנה מהם גזברים ואמרכלים אתה אומר ישרתוך
10   בעבודתם ומנה מהם גזברים ואמרכלים או ישרתוך בעבודתך ת"ל ושמרו משמרתך
ומשמרת כל האהל. עדיין אני אומר ישרתוך בעבודתך ישרתוך בעבודתם ת"ל ואני
הנה לקחתי את אחיכם הלוים מתוך בני ישראל לכם מתנה נתונים לה' לשם הם
מסורים ולא לכהנים הא אין עליך לומר כלשון אחרון אלא כלשון ראשון ישרתוך
בעבודתם ומנה מהם גזברים ואמרכלים: ואתה ובניך אתך לפני אהל העדות,
15   הכהנים מבפנים והלוים מבחוץ אתה אומר הכהנים מבפנים והלוים מבחוץ או אלו ואלו
מבפנים ת"ל ונלוו עליך ושמרו את משמרת אהל מועד הא מה ת"ל ואתה ובניך אתך
לפני אהל העדות הכהנים מבפנים והלוים מבחוץ.

ושמרו משמרתך ומשמרת כל האהל, זו היא שאמרנו ישרתוך בעבודתם
ומנה מהם גזברים ואמרכלים: אך אל כלי הקדש, זה הארון ובה"א ולא יבאו

FIGURE 9. A picture from *Sifre on Numbers*. Horowitz's edition, Leipzig, 1914.

יקטירון את החלב, ויאמר אליו האיש קטר יקטירון וגו', ותהי חטאת הנערים {..}.
וכן {לא} מצינו שלא נתחתם גזר דינן שלאנשי ירושלם אלא על שנהגו בזיון
10   קדשים, שני קדשי בזית וג'.

ואתה ובניך אתך וג' — זה עון דבר המסור לכהונה. אתה או' זה עון המסור
לכהונה או עון דבר המסור לבית דין. כשהוא אמר ואתה ובניך אתך תשאו את עון
כהנתכם לכל דבר המזבח, הרי עון דבר המסור לבית דין אמור. הא מה ת"ל תשאו
את עון כהנת', זה עוון דבר המסור לכהונה. אמרת ישר' לא ישאו את עון כהנים,
15   אבל לוים ישאו עוון כהנים. ת"ל והם ישאו עונם.

וגם את אחיך — שומע אני אף ישר' במשמע, ת"ל { {לוי} } מטה לוי. שומע אף
הנשים במשמע. לוי שבט אביך — זכה עמרם שייקרא שבט על שמו. ר' או' מטה
לוי — שומע אני אף הנשים במשמע, ת"ל אחיך — להוציא את הנשים.
הקרב אתך — ר' עקיבא או' נא' כאן אתך ונא' להלן אתך. מה אתך האמור להלן
20   בלוים הכת' מדבר, אף אתך האמור כאן בלוים הכת' מדבר. להזהיר את הלוים
בשיר על דוכנן.

וילוו עליך וישרתוך — בעבודתם ומני מהן גיזברין ואמרכלין. או ישרתוך
בעבודתך, ת"ל ושמרו משמרתך ומשמ' כל האהל. עדן אני או' ישרתוך בעבודתך,
ישרתוך בעבודתם. ת"ל ואני הנה לקחתי את אחיכם הלוים נתנים ליי, לשם הם

1 אלן ר ק"ה נ': 'משה' (אשגרה בהשראת הפתיחה הרווחת) והסופר מחקה בעזרת נקודות מחיקה
מעל האותיות.   7 קדשים] ר נ': 'קדש'' (הכפלה מוטעית של תחילת המילה?). ההשמטה על פי

FIGURE 10. A picture from Kahana, *Sifre on Numbers*.

This discrepancy echoes the divergence between manuscript and printed edition seen above with Rabbi Papyas's derashah. Horovitz's edition based on earlier printings has the classic question-and-answer formulation of *shomea' ani* followed by *talmud lomar*, while Kahana's edition based on manuscript has only the less common declarative *shomea' ani*. Kahana's text also splits the material into two independent derashot. Given that the biblical phrase "your father's tribe" is rare, it is reasonable that it would warrant its own derashah. Here is the rub: if Kahana's manuscript has it right, it implies that women could serve in the Tabernacle or Temple—a daring supposition in light of the accepted Halakhah. Alas, in a footnote, Kahana himself dismisses this possibility and deems it more likely that the manuscript is corrupt.[38] But if one were to look only at the body of the text in Kahana's edition, one would have no inkling that there is any textual problem.

The type of edition produced by Kahana has unquestionable advantages over an eclectic one like Horovitz's, but anyone consulting it must not let their guard down by mistakenly thinking that its base text always offers superior readings. By choosing one manuscript tradition, the modern editor makes the conscious decision to leave mistakes and other errors as they are and to note any potential problems in the technical, scholarly, and occasionally formidable apparatus. It is absolutely necessary, therefore, to use the edition in the manner intended, by consulting the apparatus in conjunction with the body of the text. Otherwise, one might come away with fanciful ideas, alluring but sadly probably groundless in the case, about the stirrings of proto-feminist sentiment among the Midrashic rabbis.

Beyond additions and alterations, other prevalent and intentional scribal practices degrade the text. An alert scribe might recall that he had recently copied an identical derashah a few folios before and abbreviate the repeated material. More frequently, he would truncate scriptural quotes, leaving only the first few words and replacing the rest with the Hebrew equivalent of "etc." In many cases, the removed clause or phrase was actually the one relevant to the derashah. His operative assumption was that people know their Bible. Why did scribes do this? As always, time and money: they saved themselves time and the person commissioning the text money. The production of parchment was labor-intensive and expensive. By truncating the biblical quotations that crowd every recto and verso of the written Midrash, precious space was saved.[39]

When a midrashic text bears evidence of being cut short in some way, one might find the unabbreviated original text in parallel Midrashim, in some of the extant manuscripts, or in Genizah fragments. For example, *Mekhilta de-Rabbi Yishmael* contains a dialogue between the nations of the world and the Jewish people, which is based on an exchange between the female lover and the daughters of Jerusalem in Song of Songs. When the lover is asked what makes her beloved different, Rabbi Akiva, author of this midrash, glosses: "so that you die for Him and are killed for Him." In other words, why do the Jews die for their God? Why do they not come to their senses and join the Romans?[40] Here is the answer given in the midrash:

> **THE CAIRO GENIZAH**
>
> For centuries, Jews in Fustat (Old Cairo), Egypt, disposed of material written in Hebrew, Aramaic, and Judeo-Arabic using Hebrew script by respectfully depositing it in a dedicated storeroom or *genizah* of the local, ancient Ben-Ezra synagogue. Beginning in the late nineteenth century, European scholars of Jewish Studies discovered this dusty, fragmentary treasure trove, from which one could reconstruct Jewish (and to some extent also Islamic) history.
>
> All genres of Jewish writing are represented in the Genizah: Torah scrolls, Midrashim, copies of the Mishnah and Talmud, as well as magical recipes, contracts, personal letters, tax receipts, and more. Autographs of great Jewish leaders and philosophers, like Moses Maimonides and Judah Halevi, were also discovered among its crumbling leaves. For the story of the Genizah and its discovery, see Hoffman and Cole, *Sacred Trash*.

Israel says to the nations of the world, Do you know Him? Let us relate some of His praise: "My lover is shining white and ruddy etc." (Songs 5:10). (*Mekhilta de-Rabbi Yishmael, Shirata,* §3, p. 127)

ישראל אומרין להן לאומות העולם: מכירין אתם אותו? ונאמר לכם מקצת שבחו, "דודי צח ואדום" (שיר השירים ה, י) וגומ׳.

Rabbi Akiva applies the physical depiction of the lover to God. In the continuation of the midrash, the nations are so taken by this description of God that they ask to join the Jewish people. They are rebuffed; lover and Beloved share a special bond that is theirs alone to enjoy.

This derashah has been the subject of much scholarship, particularly from the angles of martyrology and the Jewish attitude toward missionizing.[41] The final lines could indicate that not only did some Jews of antiquity not actively missionize, but they refused those interested in converting. In this context, though, the text is our principal concern. A version of this midrash preserved in the Genizah reads:

> Let us relate some of His praise: "My lover is shining white and ruddy etc. His head is purest gold etc. His eyes are like doves etc. His cheeks are like beds of spices etc. His arms are coils of gold etc. His thighs are ivory pillars etc. His mouth is sweetest drink etc. O daughters of Jerusalem" (Songs 5:10–16).

Each "etc." stands in for the rest of the verse, and the subsequent text begins the next verse. This makes for a total of seven verses cited. As Liora Elias Bar-Levav pointed out, if we didn't have this version we would assume that Rabbi Akiva only intended to cite one verse (Songs 5:10). What is lost without the full quotation? First there is the artistry of the exegete, who uses exactly seven verses, a typological number in ancient sources.[42] On a deeper level, the cutting away of these verses also severs possible connections between this midrash and the *Shi'ur Komah* literature. This corpus speculates on God's unfathomably massive dimensions in the physical universe, and it uses precisely these verses as its scriptural basis.[43] Additionally, according to a tannaitic tradition, the author of our midrash, Rabbi Akiva, participated in a mystical ascent to heaven where he beheld God and returned unscathed.[44] Perhaps some learned person, who considered this material detestable or heretical, preferred to downplay it. By heavily truncating this quote, he would have eliminated this concern. In this case, a Genizah fragment reveals how a midrash can be in conversation with other Jewish literature, whether from its own time or from a later date.

With the modern discovery of the Cairo Genizah, dozens of fragments of tannaitic Midrashim have been identified, which preserve original readings like this one.

Menahem Kahana has published a comprehensive edition of midrashic Genizah fragments aside from those of the *Sifra*.[45] The *Sifra* has more Genizah fragments than any other Midrash, because the Midrash was the most popular of them all. Traditionally, schoolchildren would begin their biblical studies with the book of Leviticus, so naturally the accompanying Midrash was learned. Furthermore, there is no dedicated talmudic commentary on *Seder Teharot*, so the enterprising student needs the Midrash on Leviticus alongside the Mishnah. A separate volume on the Genizah fragments of the *Sifra* has been promised for future publication.

C. MIDRASHIC RECONSTRUCTION

Higher and lower criticism start with a text and then interrogate it from multiple critical perspectives. What about when there is no text? Scattered references indicate that the midrashic landscape of two millennia ago was far more populated than it is today. As described in chapter 10, each of the pentateuchal books from Exodus to Deuteronomy had Midrashim from both schools that were lost over time. Beginning at the end of the nineteenth century, David Zvi Hoffmann spearheaded the scholarly project of reconstructing these lost Midrashim based on secondary citations from medieval anthologies, particularly the fourteenth-century Yemenite collected titled *Midrash ha-Gadol*. With the discovery of the Cairo Genizah at the fin de siècle, this scholarly project received a boost of good fortune. Fragments of lost Midrashim were identified among the heaps of Genizah scraps, providing textual confirmation for speculative reconstructions. About 70 percent of *Mekhilta de-Rashbi* was found in the Genizah, enough for Jacob Nahum Epstein and Ezra Zion Melamed to put out a new edition of this Midrash in 1955.

Not all Midrashim are well represented in the Genizah. Little remains of *Mekhilta Deuteronomy*, for example, and what there is comes for the most part from its aggadic sections. Any reconstructed parts of lost Midrashim that have no corroborating Genizah fragments must be treated as highly speculative. For instance, in his edition of *Mekhilta Deuteronomy*, Hoffmann includes a derashah about the "beautiful woman" that the Israelite soldier may take as a wife after a protracted process:

> Scripture was only speaking to the evil inclination. Better that Israel eat the meat of a dying animal that has been ritually slaughtered than the meat of a dying animal that has not been ritually slaughtered. (*Midrash Tanna'im*, 127)

לא דבר הכתוב אלא כנגד יצר רע. מוטב שיאכלו ישראל בשר המתות שחוט, ואל יאכלו בשר המתות נבלות.

Hoffmann found this derashah in *Midrash ha-Gadol*, and since it doesn't appear in *Sifrei Deuteronomy*, he attributed it to the lost *Mekhilta Deuteronomy*. This derashah boldly suggests that the law of the beautiful captive wife exists as a concession to human nature, or rather to the warrior's lust in wartime. It is a compromise with reality rather than an ideal. Slaughtering a dying animal does not render it halakhically fit for human consumption, but the gesture counts for something. Surely it is better than utterly flouting Halakhah by eating an unslaughtered carcass.

The textual complication here is the existence of a nearly identical *baraita* (a tannaitic teaching not included in the Mishnah) in the Babylonian Talmud.[46] Remember that *Midrash ha-Gadol* dates from the fourteenth century. Could its Yemenite compiler have been merely quoting the Talmud? On what basis can Hoffmann justify attributing this derashah to the lost *Mekhilta*?

The answer may lie in the slight terminological discrepancy between the two versions. Where the *baraita* in the Talmud reads "the Torah was . . . speaking," the version in *Midrash ha-Gadol* is "Scripture was . . . speaking" (*dibber ha-katuv*), a phrase that is actually characteristic of Rabbi Yishmael's bet midrash. Another clue comes from mention of the "evil inclination," which makes frequent appearances in the Midrashim of Rabbi Yishmael's academy.[47] It therefore seems—emphasis on seems—more likely that *Midrash ha-Gadol* is indeed citing the lost *Mekhilta* rather than the Talmud.[48]

Any and every midrashic reconstruction must be inspected closely, and a shadow of doubt hangs over our usage of the reconstructed Midrashim, including *Mekhilta de-Rashbi*, *Sifrei Zuta Numbers*, and *Mekhilta Deuteronomy*. Those derashot that withstand scrutiny can be fruitfully compared to other derashot of both schools, allowing us to see long-forgotten exegetical minds at work.

To get as close as possible to the original text of the standard Midrashim, as well as the "lost-and-found" ones, one must apply the questions and tools of higher and lower criticism. The student or scholar of Midrash must also bear in mind that the printed editions in front of them, and even the manuscripts that are increasingly accessible over the internet, have undergone long processes of beneficial and detrimental editing. Nor are critical editions infallible. The ranking of texts as base and supplemental in each edition relies on the assessment of the editor. To avoid the pitfalls inherent in a critically edited text, one must learn to navigate the scholarly apparatus that accompanies this, as boring or daunting as it may be. Only once the most accurate text has been determined, with more or less certainty, can one begin the exciting intellectual enterprise of mining the exegetical richness of the Midrash.

Epilogue

The Midrash and Future Scholarship

In our analysis of midrashic terminology, we have identified two major characteristics that distinguish Tannaitic Midrash from other ancient modes of exegesis:

a. All ancient Jewish and Christian readers of the Bible sought instruction within its texts. The key question, however, is: instruction for what? Unlike Philo, who looked for guidance on the soul's spiritual journey, or the authors of the Dead Sea Scrolls, who sought direction for the end of days, the early rabbis turned to the Torah for practical, mundane instruction. Their focus was on halakha, daily teachings, and the aggadic lessons embedded in everyday life of piety.

b. The novelty of Midrash lies as much in its form as in its content. Its explicit use of set terminology—much like the use of Lema, which distinguishes between the quoted verse and its interpretation—sets it apart as an unprecedented mode of study. No prior tradition systematically laid out both the procedure and the technique of interpretation as the Midrashic method did. Students were not merely given fish; they were taught how to fish for themselves.

However, what we do not know about Midrash far outweighs what we do. This fact informed the tentativeness of many conclusions drawn throughout this volume, as duly noted. The burden on future scholars is therefore immense, but the opportunities for genuine discovery are commensurately tremendous. There are three major active areas in Midrash research in which scholarly digging has only scratched the surface. Deeper probing will undoubtedly yield rich rewards.

The first is the application of literary analysis to tannaitic Midrash. Literary readings of midrashic units are prevalent in the aggadic sections of Midrash but not in the halakhic ones. Yet, halakhic derashot of a dialogic nature are plentiful and should be amenable to rhetorical and literary analyses. After all, rabbinic narratives also mostly consist of dialogues between Sages.[1] One profound difference between the two is that halakhic dialogues are mostly schematic and are formed out of repetitive, set structures. Can specific literary devices be identified in them too? Only a few studies exist and this seems a promising avenue for future scholars.[2]

The second area of research looks at the Hellenistic and Roman contexts. The epilogue to part 1 on the Mishnah noted that rabbinics has recently witnessed a trend towards thematic comparison between tannaitic and Roman law. But forms and structures are no less important than themes. Pre-rabbinic literature exhibits no real precedent for the dialectical forms replete in tannaitic Midrash, so naturally one looks to the broader context, to Hellenistic and Roman techniques, to explain this novelty. Early studies on this issue concentrated on exegetical principles and specific common techniques.[3] Yakir Paz recently made more headway on this front with the discovery of a series of midrashic terms, techniques, and interpretive assumptions that are also found in the Homeric scholia. He contends that there was both direct and indirect borrowing from Hellenistic exegetical methods in tannaitic Midrash. Rhetorical devices, however, remain understudied. Rabbinic dialectics seems closer to the Hellenistic field of rhetoric than to that of pure logic,[4] but much more needs to be done in order to substantiate this.[5]

Finally, the Christian connection ought to be investigated more intensively. Paul's letters are filled with citations, allusions, and implicit and explicit homilies. His debt to ancient Jewish interpretive techniques has been the topic of much discussion in the past few decades, as part of a trend that emphasizes Paul's Jewish context.[6] These studies tend to go in one of two directions. Either they attempt to reconstruct early Midrash based on Pauline statements (assuming he studied midrashic techniques as part of his Pharisaic upbringing), or they view Midrash as a reaction to and polemic against Pauline ideas.[7] These are not mutually exclusive, but they do stem from different scholarly sensitivities and orientations, and they reflect how little we know about the early roots of Midrash. To begin to pin this down demands a great deal more work.

I leave the reader with these questions and a map of promising, if challenging, routes to answers, in the hopes that he or she will continue the work of generations of scholars. "The day is short and the work plentiful. . . . It is not your duty to finish the work, but neither are you at liberty to neglect it."[8]

NOTES

PART I. INTRODUCTION: THE EMERGENCE OF HALAKHIC LITERATURE

1. The original Hebrew text of translated rabbinic sources is supplied in accompanying footnotes throughout the book. The Hebrew text is based on the superior manuscripts chosen for the Ma'agarim database of the Academy of the Hebrew Language (https://maagarim.hebrew-academy.org.il/Pages/PMain.aspx). In the case of the Mishnah, this is MS Kaufmann A 50 (for more on this special manuscript, see chapter 7). Note that, for ease of reading, no distinction has been made between the original scribal hand and later additions, and punctuation has been added.

2. When capitalized, "the Mishnah" refers to the entire corpus as a whole; when uncapitalized, "the mishnah" refers to a specific textual unit within the larger corpus. A mishnah is referred to by tractate, chapter number, and unit number, in this case *Sukkah*, 1:1.

3. The relationship between the Mishnah and other bodies of Jewish law is treated in chapter 3.

4. The Mishnah's style is discussed in chapter 1, section C. On the centrality of measures that already existed in the laws of Bet Shammai and Bet Hillel, two major tannaitic houses of learning, see Kahana, "Fixed Measure Policy."

5. This reflects the Mishnah's editing, the subject of chapter 4.

6. On the meaning of the word "Halakhah," see Urbach, *The Halakhah*, 8. Capitalized "Halakhah" refers to the entire corpus of Jewish law and "halakhah" to a specific law.

7. On this development, see Collins, *Invention of Judaism;* Satlow, *How the Bible Became Holy*. On the development of the concept of "Torah" as a binding law in the Persian and Hellenistic periods, see Honigman and Ben Zvi, "Spread of the Ideological Concept."

8. See also Deut. 33:10; Hos. 4:6; Jer. 18:18; Ezek. 7:26; etc. For more on the continuation of the attitude toward priests as the teachers of wisdom in the postbiblical world, see Mason, "Priesthood in Josephus."

9. The fact that *torah* is missing a definite article and that it participates in a parallelism (a common biblical structure indicating synonymy) with *da'at* bears this out.

10. See Friedman, "Holy Scriptures."

11. See I Macc. 2:40, and Josephus, *Antiquities of the Jews*, 12:276. For more on this episode and the role of priestly legislation in it, see Rappaport, *First Book of Maccabees*, 130–132.

12. See Baumgarten, "Invented Traditions."

13. On the relationship between the rabbis, the priests, and Halakhah, see Rosen-Zvi, "Bodies and Temple."

14. See Urbach, "Homiletical Interpretations"; and Urbach, *The Halakhah*, 7–29.

15. There is a similar, albeit more sophisticated, interpretive move in Ezra 9 that adumbrates what would come to be called midrash: see Kaufmann, *History of the Israelite Religion*, 8:293; Fishbane, *Biblical Interpretation*, 114–129; and below, part 2, chapter 9.

16. Note that the species enumerated in Nehemiah are not identical to those in Leviticus. See Milgrom, *Leviticus 23–27*, 2041–2042, 2064–2065; and Rubenstein, *History of Sukkot*, 31–45.

17. See Grabbe, *Judaism from Cyrus to Hadrian*, 488–491, with works cited.

18. See Josephus, *Antiquities of the Jews*, 18:11–22; Josephus, *The Jewish War*, 2:119–166. Josephus also wrote about a fourth group, the Zealots, but they did not actively contribute to this broader halakhic discourse. For more on these sects, see Grabbe, *Judaism from Cyrus to Hadrian*, and for their disappearance after the destruction of the Second Temple, see Cohen, "The Significance of Yavneh."

19. See Nakman, "Josephus and Halacha."

20. For a basic introduction to Qumran, see Vermes, *Dead Sea Scrolls*, and for the identification with the Essenes, see García Martínez, "Origins of the Essene Movement."

21. This reading is not undisputed. See Adamczewski, "Are the Dead Sea Scrolls Pharisaic?"

22. Dead Sea Scrolls have a particular form of reference that follows an increasing order of specificity: cave of discovery, scroll number, fragment number (if applicable), and line number(s). This quotation is from Cave 4 at Qumran, scroll 394, fragment 8, lines 5 through 8. For the Hebrew original, see Qimron, *Dead Sea Scrolls*, 2:204–211.

23. For debates on purity matters with origins in the Second Temple period versus those stemming from later halakhic developments attested in the Mishnah, see Noam, *From Qumran to the Rabbinic Revolution*.

24. For more on the impurity of liquids and their influence on everyday life, see Furstenberg, *Purity and Community*.

25. See Schwartz, "From Priests at Their Right."

26. See VanderKam, "Origin and Purposes."

27. On the dating of Jubilees, see Segal, *Book of Jubilees*, 28–31. On the proximity to sectarian literature, see Kister, "History of the Essenes."

28. VanderKam, *Jubilees*, 506–507.

29. See Schmid, "Judean Identity."

30. See Segal, *Book of Jubilees*, 243.

31. Martínez and Tigchelaar, *Dead Sea Scrolls Study Edition*, 569.

32. See Schiffman, *Halakhah at Qumran*. On Halakhah at Qumran in general, see Baumgarten, *Studies in Qumran Law*; Sussman, "History of Halakhah"; Werman and Shemesh, *Revealing the Hidden*.

33. See, respectively, Belkin, *Philo and the Oral Law*; Jackson, *Essays on Halakhah*; and Nakman, "Halakhah in the Writings of Josephus."

34. The six major divisions *(sedarim)* of the Mishnah and their subject matter are discussed at the beginning of chapter 1.

35. See Adler, "Priestly Cult and Common Culture."

36. See Schwartz, *Imperialism and Jewish Society*, 122ff.

37. See Schremer, "Religious Orientation."

38. For the gradual demise of the ethos of uniformity, see Furstenberg, "From Tradition to Controversy."

39. On the Great Court, which should not be confused with the Sanhedrin (the court of the Second Temple period), see Rosen-Zvi, "Protocol of the Court."

CHAPTER 1. THE FORM OF THE MISHNAH

1. The former is given in BT *Shabbat* 31a; the latter in *Midrash Shoher Tov*, Ps. 19:14.

2. Kahana, "Arrangement of the Orders."

3. Modern printed editions of the Mishnah contain sixty-three tractates due to additional subdivisions within *Seder Nezikin*. Tractates *Bava Kamma*, *Bava Metzi'a*, and *Bava Batra* were originally all subsumed under Tractate *Nezikin*, and Tractates *Sanhedrin* and *Makkot* were united in a single tractate.

4. For more on the Torah's influence on the Mishnah, especially in terms of organization, see chapter 3, section A.

5. The principle of arrangement by length was first discovered in the nineteenth century by Abraham Geiger ("Plan und Anordnung"). This arrangement was common in classical canons; Paul's letters, for instance, were also organized by length, with Romans—the longest—placed first and Philemon—the shortest—last. Unaware of this phenomenon, medieval commentators on the Mishnah like Sherira Gaon (Lewin, *Iggeret Rav Sherira Ga'on*, 33) and Moses Maimonides devised various thematic explanations for the order of the tractates in each *seder*. For attempts to understand the peculiar order of *Seder Zera'im*, see Strack and Stemberger, *Introduction to the Talmud and Midrash*, 135. For an original suggestion, see Cherlow, "The Division of Tractates Nezikin and Kelim," 175n1. See, however, Epstein, *Introduction to the Mishnaic Text*, 981, who argued from BT *Bava Kama* 102a ("the Mishnah has no order") that in the days of the Amoraim there was still no fixed order to the tractates.

6. The logic and editing of this chapter is discussed in chapter 4.

7. For more on this ritual, see chapter 8, section A.

8. See the further discussion of the arrangement of Tractate *Sotah* in chapter 4, section A.

9. The term is italicized because it is a technical term to be distinguished from the same Hebrew term used for "laws." An example of the technical usage is: "Whoever recites *halakhot* every day can be certain that he will reach the World to Come" (BT *Niddah* 73a).

10. The role of the end of tractates will be discussed further in chapter 6, end of section C.

11. For more on the oral learning and transmission of the Mishnah, see chapter 7.

12. For the punishment known as *karet*, commonly translated as "spiritual excision," see chapter 5, section C.

13. The editing of the Mishnah is the subject of chapter 4.

14. Naeh, "Craft of Memory," 567. In his study, Naeh comprehensively analyzes the mnemotechnics of the Sages.

15. Doering, *Ancient Jewish Letters*, 65.

16. According to formal grammar these should be *et ha-shayamim* and *et ha-kevalim*. In spoken language, however, it was shortened: *et ha-shamayim* > *ta-shamayim*. The same phenomenon is observed among speakers of Modern Hebrew today.

17. See Kutscher, *Hebrew and Aramaic* Studies, 73–107; and Talshir, "Ha-'Ivrit ba-Me'ah ha-Sheniyyah." For a lexicon of the Hebrew of the documents found in the Judaean Desert, see Mor, *Judean Hebrew*, 376–394 (and see esp. 385).

18. Mor, *Judean Hebrew*, 375.

19. Naveh, *Sherd and Papyrus*, 110–111; Cotton, "Languages," 225.

20. See, e.g., *Megillah*, 2:1 and 4:10, and *Yadayim*, 4:5. For the practice of translation in the synagogue, see Shinan, *Biblical Story*, and a shorter English treatment in Shinan, "Live Translation."

21. See Mor, *Judean Hebrew*, 17–19.

22. On R. Yehudah ha-Nasi's special attitude toward Hebrew, see Oppenheimer, *Rabbi Yehuda ha-Nasi*, 208–214.

23. The singular and plural participles are both translated throughout the book using the gender-neutral, indefinite pronoun "one," except in cases where translating this way would be unidiomatic and a passive construction is instead used. There are also instances where the plural is not used generically but refers to a somewhat defined group; see chapter 5, section A.

24. For evidence in Jewish, Pagan, and Christian sources of the prevalence of lighting Shabbat candles, see Cohen, "Crossing the Boundary," 20–21.

25. See Novick, *What Is Good*.

26. BT *Pesaḥim* 86b and PT *Pesaḥim* 7:13 (35c).

27. It is difficult to accept the contention of Daube (*New Testament and Rabbinic Judaism*, 90–97) that the Tannaim chose the ambiguous participle to make clear that their normative authority is less binding than that of the Torah. For other explanations, see Novick, *What Is Good*, 110n3.

28. For more on the chronological layers of the Mishnah, see chapter 2.

29. Of course, this rhetoric does not mean that the Mishnah itself is describing events that its Sages actually witnessed; see chapter 2, section B.

30. For these two forms see Hezser, *Rabbinic Scholarship*, 183.

31. Tosefta, *Berakhot*, 2:2 and BT *Berakhot* 13b.

32. On the appearance of two styles in Roman law from the same period, see Babusiaux, "Legal Writing," 178–180. Interestingly, unlike Roman law, the Mishnah does not use stock names. See the immediate example from *Bava Metzi'a* below: "this one says . . . and that one says . . ." Apparently, the Mishnah does not want the details to obscure the principles it seeks to present, albeit casuistically, and so it makes everything generic. Contrast this with the two Talmuds, where the use of generic names like Reuven and Shimon is widespread.

33. In the second case there is no claim and counterclaim of "I found it." There is also no option of an uneven split, which the Mishnah gives for the first case; see chapter 5, section B.

34. Like the Talmuds, halakhic Midrash, as we will see in the second half of this volume, is faced with the challenge of delimiting the scope of the law from specific cases.

35. On the rhetorical use of anonymity in the Mishnah, in the guise of the *tanna kamma* and "the Sages" (*ḥakhamim*), see chapter 4, section A.

36. *Mishneh Torah*, "Hilkhot Shabbat," 13:1.

37. BT *Shabbat* 18a.

38. Moscovitz, *Talmudic Reasoning*, 47–97.

39. See Lorberbaum, "Rules and Reasons," 63–66. Lorberbaum attributes the scarcity of explicit reasons to the Mishnah's nature as an obligatory codex. The problem with this characterization is that, as we have seen, the Mishnah hardly decides the law. Perhaps we should connect this instead to the objective to form the Mishnah as a canon—short, laconic, and easy to memorize.

40. See chapter 8 for the relationship between the Mishnah and the Tosefta.

41. See Rosen-Zvi, *Mishnaic Sotah Ritual*, 67–100.

42. *Gittin* 2:5, *Ḥagigah* 1:1, *Megillah* 2:4, *Menaḥot* 9:8, *Parah* 5:4, and *Ḥullin* 1:1, the last of which includes the cited rationale.

43. On the exegesis of this mishnah and its purpose, see Halbertal, *Interpretative Revolutions*, 42–68.

CHAPTER 2. THE MISHNAH'S SOURCES AND LAYERS

1. See *Avot*, 1:1 and the discussion below in chapter 3, section B.

2. On this type of Mishnah, see Simon-Shoshan, *Stories of the Law*, 194–219.

3. Blau and Yahalom, *Sefer ha-Galui*, 119; Albeck, *Introduction to the Mishna*, 65–66. Compare this to the request for information about the Mishnah's composition sent by the Jewish commu-

nity of Qayrawan (Kairouan) in North Africa to Sherira Gaon, as reformulated by the latter: "As for what you have asked, How was the Mishnah written? Did the Men of the Great Assembly begin writing [it down] and the Sages of every generation wrote some of it until Rabbi came and sealed it?" (Lewin, *Iggeret Rav Sherira Ga'on*, 5). B. M. Lewin, who edited and published the two major recensions of Sherira's epistolary response, claimed that this query was prompted by Saadia Gaon's historical account. Sherira himself affirmed the antiquity of the Mishnah and explained that later Sages based themselves on traditions they had received (Lewin, 7, 17, 31).

    4. See Lewin's remarks in the introduction to his edition of *Iggeret Rav Sherira Ga'on*, v.

    5. See Harris, *Nachman Krochmal*, 206–273.

    6. For more on this, see the introduction to this volume.

    7. See the various approaches in Strack and Stemberger, *Introduction to the Talmud and Midrash*, 142–143. The chronological precedence of midrash is argued by Weiss Halivni, *Midrash, Mishnah, and Gemara*.

    8. Urbach, "The Derashah as the Basis for the Halakhah." The precise nature of the relationship between the Sages and Pharisees is difficult to pin down. While the Sages never expressly identified themselves as Pharisees, descriptions of the latter in Josephus and the New Testament do align with what we know about the Sages. Furthermore, when it comes to sectarian polemics, the Mishnah seems to identify its own position with that of the Pharisees (e.g., *Yadayim*, 4:6–7). Shaye Cohen has offered that the Sages were the Pharisees' successors, but they purposely obscured this continuity in attempt to make room for people of all camps. See Cohen, "The Significance of Yavneh." For the tendency of early Christian writers to avoid identifying the rabbis with the Pharisees of the New Testament, see Reed, "When Did the Rabbis Become Pharisees?" See further Lauterbach, *Rabbinic Essays*, 163–258.

    9. For the scribes as the first darshanim, see Epstein, *Introduction to Tannaitic Literature*, 503–504; Lieberman, *Hellenism*, 37. Those who argue for continuity between the scribes and the Sages consider the latter to be the successors of the secondary elite and not the primary elite like the priests. Seth Schwartz has compared this to the Industrial Revolution, which was driven by the innovations of technologists in local factories and not by leading scientists in the major academies of the day. See Schwartz, "Law in Jewish Society," 55n13.

    10. See Herr, "Continuum in the Chain of Torah Transmission"; Kister, "History of the Essenes"; Schremer, "'[T]he[y] Did Not Read in the Sealed Book.'" But see the criticism of Fraade, "'Comparative Midrash' Revisited." On the development of midrashic methodology at Qumran, see Noam, "Early Signs," and Shemesh, "4Q251." On the relationship between tradition and Scripture in early Christianity, see Mitchell, "Footsteps of Paul."

    11. On the cause for this change see Schremer, *Male and Female*, 329–333.

    12. Sometimes the *mishnah rishonah* is changed by an anonymous "succeeding bet din" (*Ketubbot* 5:3 and *Gittin* 5:6), but at other times it is superseded by a ruling of R. Akiva (*Nazir* 6:1 and *Sanhedrin* 3:4).

    13. For this new usage, see Hoffmann, *The First Mishna*, 65. For Geonic precedent for this usage, see Lewin, *Iggeret Rav Sherira Ga'on*, 25; and Gafni, *Mishna's Plain Sense*, 262.

    14. Krochmal, *Writings*, 161–204; Hoffmann, *The First Mishna*; Epstein, *Introduction to Tannaitic Literature*, 15–58. On this approach, see also Lewy, *Fragmente*, and Frankel, *Darkhei ha-Mishnah*. On the Mishnah and *Wissenschaft*, see Harris, *Nachman Krochmal*, 250–257; Gafni, *Mishna's Plain Sense*.

    15. Albeck, *Introduction to the Mishna*, 63–87.

    16. Although three Sages are named in all, they all appear in later additions (3:8, 5:2, and 7:2). See Ginzberg, "Tractate *Tamid*."

17. For Tractate *Middot*, see Walfish, "Conceptual Ramifications"; for Tractate *Yoma*, see Glasner, "Use of Mishnayot." See also Goldberg, "Tosefta to Tractate *Tamid*."

18. Ginzberg, "Tractate *Tamid*." For a recent defense of Ginzberg's claim and a rebuttal of various critiques, see Mali, "*Mi-Miqdash le-Midrash*," 133–152.

19. For examples that point to early material, see Bar-Asher, *Studies in Mishnaic Hebrew*, 1:125–126, 303–304.

20. See Rosen-Zvi, *Mishnaic Sotah Ritual*, 161–164, 239–247.

21. Philo, *On Laws*, 2:215–222; Josephus, *Antiquities of the Jews*, 4:240–243.

22. On the one hand, archaic usages in the Mishnah can in some cases point to an early literary stratum dating from the Second Temple period, because such usages are quite uncommon among the post-Destruction Sages (see Noam, "Story of King Janneus.") On the other hand, the higher incidence of archaic language precisely when it comes to the Temple makes one suspect that it was deliberately chosen; see Rosen-Zvi, *Mishnaic Sotah Ritual*, 239–254. Deciding whether archaic language is genuine or affected must thus be done on a case-by-case basis. In our example, the continuation of 3:6 is attributed to R. Yehudah of the generation of Usha (see below, section D), and his wording is quite similar to that of the supposedly archaic mishnah. See further Henshke, "Strata in the Passover Haggadah."

23. Lieberman, *Hellenism in Jewish Palestine*, 144–146.

24. The *gizbar* is a treasurer in the Bible (Ezra 8:8) and the term persists into Second Temple times where it has a similar meaning (*Shekalim*, 5:2, *Menaḥot*, 8:7, etc.). The *paḥot* and *seganim* are kinds of officials with authority in the Bible (Est. 3:12 and Neh. 3:12 respectively, and together in Jer. 51:23 and Ezek. 23:6.) While the *segen* also appears as a Second Temple official, in one case as someone who oversaw the priests and was the Kohen Gadol's second (see *Avot*, 3:1), the term *paḥot* (or sg. *paḥah*) does not appear at all after the Persian period.

25. The anthropologist Victor Turner called this sort of atmosphere *communitas*; see Turner, *Ritual Process*, 131–165. Cf. Cohn, *Memory of the Temple*, which construes the Mishnah's *bikkurim* ceremony as part of a broader process of reimagining Temple ceremonies as spectacular communal events.

26. See Breuer, "Perfect and Participle," and Cohn, *Memory of the Temple*, 1–16. See also the end of chapter 5, section C.

27. For the radical claim that all attributions are late and unreliable, see Green, "What's in a Name?"

28. For a similarly structured mishnah, in which Bet Shammai and Bet Hillel debate an earlier law about checking two rows in a cellar for hametz before Pesach, see *Pesaḥim*, 1:1.

29. For more on the Tosefta see below, chapter 8.

30. This chapter includes interpretations from various generations: R. Eliezer and R. Yehoshua, R. Akiva's disciples, and all the way to the Mishnah's editor. See Sabato, "Teachings of Rabbi Joshua," 137–142.

31. See Slotnick, "Tzibburei Ma'ot."

32. After the Bar Kokhba Revolt was crushed and Judaea was laid waste, the rabbinic leadership moved to the Galilee. Yavneh was the rabbinic nerve center before the revolt, and Usha took its place afterward. The Babylonian Talmud says laconically, "From Jerusalem to Yavneh and from Yavneh to Usha" (BT *Rosh ha-Shanah* 31a), and another source reports, "At the end of the persecution our rabbis convened in Usha" (*Songs Rabbah*, 2).

33. This is true for almost a quarter of the Mishnah's tractates: *'Eruvin, Shevi'it, Pesaḥim, Sukkah, Betzah, Rosh ha-Shanah, Ḥagigah, Yevamot, Kiddushin, Ḥullin, Niddah, Zavim, Makhshirin*, and *Tevul Yom*. The beginning of Tosefta *'Eduyyot* says: "When the Sages entered Kerem be-Yavneh, they said . . . 'Let us begin from Hillel and Shammai.'" For halakhic collections of Bet

Shammai and Bet Hillel see: *Berakhot*, ch. 8; *Shabbat*, 1:2–8; *Betzah*, 1:1–2, 5; *'Eduyyot*, chs. 1, 4–5. At times, the Mishnah distinguishes between the opinions of Hillel and Shammai the individuals and those of their academies, see, e.g., *'Orlah*, 2:4–5, *Ma'aser Sheni*, 2:4. Take note that Bet Hillel and Bet Shammai appear occasionally in relation to laws that postdated the destruction of the Temple, such as *Ma'aser Sheni*, 5:7 (cf. Tosefta, *Ma'aser Sheni*, 3:14) and Tosefta, *Ahilot*, 5:11.

34. A description of the generations in the Palestinian Talmud stresses the continuity between them: "R. [Ab]ba said, Originally, each one would ordain his disciples. For example, Rabban Yohanan ben Zakkai ordained R. [E]liezer and R. Yehoshua, and R. Yehoshua [ordained] R. Akiva, and R. Akiva [ordained] R. Meir and R. Shimon" (PT *Sanhedrin* 1:3 [19a]). For a comprehensive list of mishnaic Sages by generation, see *Iggeret Rav Sherira Ga'on* and Albeck's *Introduction to the Mishna*.

35. See Epstein, *Introduction to Tannaitic Literature*, 251–252. About twenty times in the Mishnah the attribution "Rabbi says" is followed by a citation of Rabbi Yehudah ha-Nasi's opinion. It usually appears at the end of a discussion and is considered a later addition.

36. See Kazhdan and Kay, "Unlocking Ancient Texts," 28. See also the exception they note there: R. Akiva does argue with his masters and students. This is understandable in light of his centrality to the tannaitic bet midrash, both as a student and as a rabbi. See Kahana, "On the Fashioning and Aims of the Mishnaic Controversy," 74.

37. This is not a circular argument. Although the very assignment of Sages to different generations comes from tannaitic literature, the agreement across tannaitic corpora despite the lack of an overarching editorial program points to the general reliability of the attributions.

38. See *Sifrei Numbers*, §142, 188; *Sifrei Zuta Numbers*, 15:2, 280; *Megillat Ta'anit*, 1 Nisan (Noam, *Megillat Ta'anit*, 164). See also Safrai and Safrai, *Mishnat Eretz Israel: Shekalim*, 157–158; Kahana, *Sifre on Numbers*, 4:730.

39. According to the *mishnah rishonah*, Bet Hillel appear to say that the buildings are not only part of Jerusalem but part of the Temple, "like the chambers." However, this is likely an addition of the Tosefta; see Furstenberg, "History of the Temple Mishnayot," 507n134.

40. See Furstenberg, "History of the Temple Mishnayot."

41. The strongest proof is the complete absence of R. Yishmael's chief disciples (R. Yoshiyah, R. Yonatan, and R. Natan) from R. Yehuda ha-Nasi's Mishnah. See further Zlotnick, *Iron Pillar*, 24–32.

42. See De Vries, *General Introduction*, 32–33, where multiple additional examples are cited.

43. Lewin, *Iggeret Rav Sherira Ga'on*, 12.

44. See above, section A.

45. Albeck, *Introduction to the Mishna*, 82. His proposal relies on an interpretation of the beginning of Tosefta *'Eduyyot*; for alternative interpretations of this source, see Furstenburg, "From Tradition to Controversy."

46. Kramer, "The Mishnah," 313.

47. Neusner, *Ancient Israel after Catastrophe*.

48. See Goldberg, "The Mishnah," 211–215, as well as Cohen, "The Significance of Yavneh." Cf. Noam, "Beit Shammai," 46n7.

49. Yuval, "Orality of Jewish Law."

50. See Dohrmann, "Law and Imperial Idioms," and Furstenberg, "Imperialism." On the rise of legal culture in the eastern provinces in the second century based on the papyrological evidence, see Bryen, "Judging Empire." On comparisons between the editing of the Mishnah and the editing of Roman legal compositions, see chapter 4 below.

51. Naeh, "Craft of Memory."

CHAPTER 3. THE MISHNAH'S LEGAL SOURCES

1. Cohen, "Judaean Legal Tradition." Such legal contributions and contexts have been the subject of recent reevaluation in Cohen, *What Is the Mishnah?*

2. The important and knotty question of the Mesopotamian sources of mishnaic law cannot be done justice here. For two fascinating case studies, see Milgram, *From Mesopotamia to the Mishnah*, on inheritance law, and Ayali-Darshan, "Origin and Meaning," on Yom Kippur rituals.

3. See esp. chapter 1, section A.

4. See Satlow, *Jewish Marriage*, 199–224. On possible ancient precursors of the ketubah, see Schremer, *Male and Female*, 228–240.

5. For the ways in which the laws of ritual purity reflect developments from the late Second Temple era and the tannaitic period, see Furstenberg, *Purity and Community*.

6. Benovitz, "Approaching a Sage."

7. For a brief example from *Sanhedrin* 8:1, see chapter 1, section C.

8. The Mishnah contains 286 scriptural exegeses; see Kahana, "Relations between Exegeses," esp. 49–58. The imbalance across tractates is likely attributable to the different academies and editorial processes involved. See Samely, *Rabbinic Interpretation*.

9. See also Ex. 34:23 and Deut. 16:16.

10. See part 2, chapter 15, section B.

11. *Sifrei Deuteronomy*, §143, p. 196.

12. See the discussion in Henshke, *Original Mishna*, 7 and 27.

13. This combination of paraphrase and partial translation into mishnaic Hebrew is especially common in the early chapters of Tractate *Bava Kamma*; compare also *Bava Kamma*, 5:5, with Ex. 21:33–34.

14. Only in rare instances does a mishnah disclose the fact that it is paraphrasing the Torah. For example, after paraphrasing, *Pesaḥim*, 9:1 asks: "If so, why does [the verse] say . . . ?"

15. Based on, respectively, Deut. 21:1–9, Deut. 18:4–5, Joel 2:17, Deut. 22:23–29, and Ex. 21:28. See Albeck, *Introduction to the Mishna*, 129–130; Haneman, "Biblical Loanwords"; Bar-Asher, *Studies in Mishnaic Hebrew*, 125, 301–311; Braverman, "Biblical Calques."

16. See Daube, "Civil Law," and Zohar, "Scripture, Mishnah, and Ideas."

17. See Balberg, "Rabbinic Authority," 326n18.

18. See also chapter 1, section A, for the biblically inspired placement of Tractate *Nedarim* in *Seder Nashim*.

19. The mishnaic designations of the species were the widespread contemporary names for them, as attested in a letter sent by Bar Kokhba to his soldiers to procure the four species for him. See Yadin et al., *Documents from the Bar Kokhba Period*, 326–328.

20. See Rubenstein, *History of Sukkot*, 191–197. See further part 2, chapter 15, section B.

21. See, e.g., *Berakhot*, ch. 1 and ch. 9; *Bava Metziʿa*, ch. 5; *ʿAvodah Zarah*, ch. 1.

22. BT *Berakhot* 2a.

23. See Benovitz, *BT Berakhot*, 6.

24. This does not necessarily mean that the Mishnah reads the Torah straightforwardly. The plain meaning of "in your lying down and your getting up" is every waking moment, whereas the Mishnah takes it to mean two specific times of day. The rabbinic reading of Scripture will be addressed in Part 2.

25. PT *Ḥagigah* 1:8 (76c), BT *Ḥagiga* 10a. See Henshke, *Festival Joy*, 9.

26. For explicit emphases of a gap between the Oral Torah and Scripture in the Mishnah, see also *ʿOrlah*, 3:9, *Bava Metziʿa*, 7:8, and *Ḥullin* 8:4.

27. For a similar case, see the testimony of the two weavers in the name of the *Zugot* in *ʿEduyyot*, 3:1.

28. On *Avot* see further chapter 6, section D.

29. Chapter 2, section A.

30. *'Eduyyot*, 8:7 and *Yadayim*, 4:3.

31. Cf. *Yevamot*, 8:3. On R. Akiva's attitude toward tradition, see Rosen-Zvi, "'Who Will Uncover the Dust from Your Eyes?'"

32. Josephus, *Antiquities of the Jews*, 13:297, p. 377. Cf. 18:9, and Josephus, *The Jewish War*, 2:119. See also the charge in Mark 7:8. On this see Baumgarten, "Pharisaic Paradosis."

33. This will change in the two Talmuds, where long chains of tradents are commonly cited for legal traditions; see Vidas, "What Is a *Tannay*?"

34. See Albeck, *Introduction to the Mishna*, 82–84. That Tractate *'Eduyyot* was formed before the others can be demonstrated from the fact that some tractates contain *'Eduyyot* material that does not fit the thematic context. It is reasonable to assume that material was moved from *'Eduyyot* in chunks, so that not everything aligns with the subject matter of the destination tractate. Compare, e.g., *Pe'ah*, 6:1–2, with *'Eduyyot* 4:3–4, and see Sabato, "Teachings of Rabbi Joshua," 128.

35. Tosefta, *'Eduyyot*, 1:3. See Shapira, "The Court in Yavne."

36. See Furstenberg, "From Tradition to Controversy"; Sabato, *The Sages of Yavne*, 159–162.

37. Here, too, it's possible that the generalized ruling at the beginning of the mishnah was taken from the words of Rabban Gamaliel's disciples, to which was added, "through Saturday night if he has not done the deed." For Rabban Gamaliel's self-imposed stringencies, cf. *Bava Metzi'a*, 5:8.

38. See *Ta'anit*, 3:8. The story of Honi is analyzed in depth in chapter 6, section B.

39. For additional examples, see *'Eruvin*, 6:2, 8:7, and 10:9; *Ta'anit*, 3:6; *Yevamot*, 16:7; *Bava Batra*, 9:7; *Sanhedrin*, 6:4 and 7:2; *'Eduyyot*, 3:10 and 5:6.

40. The literature on this is enormous. For a recent state-of-the-art anthology, see Czajkowski, Eckhardt, and Strothmann, *Law in the Roman Provinces*. On the court system see Bryen, "Judging Empire."

41. See chapter 2, beginning of section C.

42. Gordon and Robinson, *Institutes of Gaius*, 75 (bk. 1, §110). Gaius elaborates on these means in the continuation, on which, see De Zulueta, *Institutes of Gaius*, 34–36.

43. While this mishnah lists *bi'ah* (intercourse) as a method of acquisition, a nearby, structurally parallel mishnah (1:3) about the acquisition of slaves and land reads: "money, a contract, or possession *(ḥazakah)*. This indicates that intercourse was viewed as a type of acquisition by possession, and Hebrew *ḥazakah* is the equivalent of Latin *usus*. See Furstenberg, "Acquisition and Possession."

44. See Cohen, *Jewish and Roman Law*, 290–291.

45. See the references below and Dohrmann, "Law and Imperial Idioms." For a fuller accounting of purported parallels (up to 2016), see Rosen-Zvi, "Is the Mishnah a Roman Composition?"

46. See, respectively, Tosefta, *Kiddushin*, 5:2 and Mishnah, *Kiddushin*, 3:12. Both laws are discussed in Furstenberg, "Rabbis and the Roman Citizenship Model."

47. Moscovitz, "Legal Fictions." Compare Stein Hain, *Circumventing the Law*, 53–64.

48. Hannah Cotton observes that Jews went to Roman courts voluntarily: "Without coercion or attempts to impose uniformity, the simple presence of the Romans as the supreme authority in the province invited appeals to their authority, to their courts as well as to their laws. [. . .] [T]he documents from the Judaean Desert reveal to us a facet of the Roman-Jewish relationship not often in evidence . . . a day-to-day routine of good working relations" (Cotton, "Impact of the Documentary Papyri," 234–235). Ze'ev Safrai, on the other hand, views the phenomenon of Jews in Roman courts as the product of necessity: "Since there was no nearby Jewish court, how could the

rabbis complain if the residents of Zoar were compelled to turn to non-Jewish courts? [. . .] If a Jew wanted a document between him and his fellow to have legal validity, he was forced to write the document in Greek, and in a manner that would meet the requirements of the court in Petra or in Rabbah" (Safrai, "Halakhic Observance," 225).

49. See Elman, "Order, Sequence, and Selection" and below chapter 4, section A.

50. For a comparison of the Mishnah to Roman writing on religion (Varro, Cicero, etc.), see MacRae, *Legible Religion*, 79–100. For a wholly different comparison of the same mishnaic material with the Greek *oeconomika*, house-keeping literature, see Amsler, *The Babylonian Talmud and Late Antique Book Culture*, 40. The sheer fact that the Mishnah has been compared to such diverse Hellenistic and Roman genres testifies to its unique characteristics. For the limitations of the legal perspective see also Neis, "Seduction of Law."

51. See Hezser, "The Mishnah and Roman Law."

52. See further Rosen-Zvi, "Is the Mishnah a Roman Composition?," and Rosen-Zvi, "Rabbis as *Nomikoi*?"

53. See Benovitz, *BT Berakhot, Chapter 1*, 65–79.

54. See Zadok et al., "Comparative Network Analysis," 9. See the list in Albeck, *Introduction to the Mishna*, 223–234. Of the 160, some are earlier figures in whose name teachings are reported, and who were not members of the tannaitic academies. On the difficulty of extracting an accurate number of Tannaim from such lists, see Lapin, *Rabbis as Romans*, 66–67.

55. See Kahana, "On the Fashioning and Aims of the Mishnaic Controversy."

56. For the Tosefta, see chapter 8; for the Midrash see part 2, chapter 15.

57. See Hezser, *Jewish Travel*, 441–462. For the corporate characteristic of the Palestinian rabbis, as opposed to the more individualistic nature of their Babylonian counterparts, see Kalmin, *The Sage in Jewish Society*.

58. See Tosefta, *Sanhedrin*, 7:6, as well as *Yadayim*, 4:3, together with Rosen-Zvi, "Protocol of the Court."

59. See Jubilees, 2:26–30 and 50:6–10; and CD 10:14–11:18. On the laws of Shabbat at Qumran, see Noam and Qimron, "Qumran Composition."

CHAPTER 4. THE EDITING OF THE MISHNAH

1. For the talmudic evidence that R. Yehudah ha-Nasi was the editor, see Zlotnick, *Iron Pillar*, 19–21. For Christian evidence of the Mishnah's canonization, see Fonrobert, "*Didascalia Apostolorum*."

2. *The Institutes of Justinian*, 1. For the purpose of this editing, see Harries, *Law and Empire*, 19–31.

3. For more on the Mishnah of R. Akiva, see chapter 2, section E.

4. R. Yehudah ha-Nasi's inclusive tendency is preserved in statements attributed to him throughout the Tosefta, in which he decides the law among various rabbinic opinions: "The words of X are correct about A, and the words of Y are correct about B." On this, see Albeck, *Introduction to the Mishna*, 110. Cf. R. Yehudah ha-Nasi's report: "When I went to learn Torah from R. Elazar ben Shamua' . . . they only let me learn one thing in our Mishnah" (BT *Yevamot* 84a, and cf. PT *Yevamot* 9:6 [8d]). It would seem that he went around collecting laws and versions thereof from R. Akiva's students (one of whom is R. Elazar ben Shamua') and then inserted them into his Mishnah; see Lieberman, *Hellenism*, 96. This policy is responsible for the notorious difficulty one encounters in trying to identify sources of specific mishnaic laws. See further Baumgarten, "Politics of Reconciliation."

5. See Weiss Halivni, "Reception."

6. For a comparison of the minimalist editing of the Mishnah with the maximalist editing of the *Corpus Juris Civilis*, see Zlotnick, *Iron Pillar*, 33–38. For a general comparison between the editing of the Mishnah with contemporary codification of Roman law in the second century, see

Elman, "Order, Sequence, and Selection," 65–70. For the editing of the Mishnah in the context of late antique Roman encyclopedism, see Hezser, "Rabbis as Intellectuals," 177–181; and Stern, "Publication and Early Transmission," 462.

7. For duplicate and triplicate mishnayot, see Zlotnick, *Iron Pillar*, 73–79; for variations in formulation, see Epstein, *Introduction to Tannaitic Literature*, 234–240.

8. Respectively, *Menaḥot*, 10:5, and *Sukkah*, 3:12/*Rosh ha-Shanah*, 4:3. In Tosefta, *Megillah*, 2:10, it further appears in the context of prohibitions that last an entire day.

9. Seven: *Middot*, 1:4 and 2:3; thirteen: *Middot*, 2:6 and *Shekalim*, 6:3. See the list of contradictions between the traditions underlying Tractate *Tamid* and Tractates *Middot* and *Yoma* in Ginzberg, "Tractate *Tamid*," 44–45. On the various sources of the tractates related to the Temple, which combine scriptural exegesis and priestly traditions, see Mali, "Mi-Miqdash le-Midrash."

10. Cf. BT *Berakhot* 35a. On the implications of these sources, see Epstein, *Introduction to the Mishnaic Text*, 13–16.

11. See Albeck's commentary in *Shishah Sidrei Mishnah, Seder Zera'im*, 404.

12. Lewin, *Iggeret Rav Sherira Ga'on*, 30.

13. See Zohar, *Secrets of the Rabbinic Workshop*, 9–32.

14. See chapter 1, section A.

15. See Rosen-Zvi, "'Who Will Uncover the Dust from Your Eyes?'"

16. This is the manuscript reading; the printed editions have "in any language." Landau, "The Editing of Tractate Sotah," suggests that one reason for including these rituals in the tractate is to encourage comparison between the Sotah ritual and the ritual of the broken-necked heifer, which is also discussed in these chapters and exhibits notable parallels to the Sotah procedure.

17. The endings of tractates are discussed further in chapter 6, section C.

18. For a series of such examples, see Weinberg, "Sources of the Mishnah."

19. For the antiquity of Tractate *Tamid*, see chapter 2, section B.

20. Similarly, *Tamid*, 3:1–2 was moved to *Yoma*, 2:2 and 3:1 (with the addition of etiological backstories), and in between them the order of the lotteries and the time for bringing the daily *'olah* sacrifice were added.

21. See Walfish, "Conceptual Ramifications."

22. One sees the same editorial move in *Sukkah*, ch. 4; see Henshke, *Festival Joy*, 90.

23. Another example: In the second chapter of Tractate *Pesaḥim* the Sages reject R. Yehudah assertion that "the only [valid] removal of hametz is by burning." Nevertheless, in the first chapter of the tractate, the Mishnah talks about the removal of hametz through burning, indicating that R. Yehudah ha-Nasi adopted R. Yehudah's opinion as normative. This technique is evident when comparing the Mishnah with the more inclusive approach of the Tosefta, which cites named sages much more frequently. See Zadok, "Comparative Network Analysis," 9, and see ch. 8 below.

24. See esp. Frankel, *Darkhei ha-Mishnah*, 282–321.

25. See PT *Yevamot* 4:10 (6b). Compare: "Rabbi stated anonymously here according to R. Meir and stated anonymously here according to R. Yehudah" (BT *Ketubbot* 95b). Rav Nahman also ruled like a certain opinion in the Mishnah "since the Tanna has stated it anonymously according to him" (BT *Yevamot* 101b and *Kiddushin* 54b). See Goldberg, "Purpose and Method"; and Goldberg, "All Base Themselves."

26. For examples of ruling through anonymization, see Rosenthal, "Mishnah *Ta'anit*"; and Kahana, *Sifre on Numbers*, 3:60–61.

27. Twersky, *Introduction*, 34, with slight stylistic modifications.

28. This is the version that the R. Yohanan had before him, as we shall see below. In MS Kaufmann, the text does not mention "the Sages." Instead, one reads: רבי מאיר אומר מחייב ורבי שמעון פוטר. On this version see Epstein, *Introduction to the Mishnaic Text*, 1144.

29. R. Yohanan used the same working methods to turn the Mishnah into a halakhic code (Brandes, "The Canonization of the Mishnah"). In light of talmudic dicta like the one above, one can see that the Amoraim were relying on editorial interventions they discerned in the Mishnah itself. See also Weiss Halivni, *Sources and Traditions: Baba Kama*, 356–374.

30. See chapter 3, beginning of section C.

31. Interestingly, the parallel tosefta (*Berakhot*, 1:1) cites the anonymous position as that of "the Sages." In other words, the Tosefta adopted the other editorial technique in presenting this law.

32. For our mishnah, see BT *Bava Metzi'a* 92a.

33. For examples of each formula, see *Kelim*, 15:1 and *Kil'ayim*, 2:6. See Weinberg, "Sources of the Mishnah."

34. For a discussion of this mishnah's structure, see chapter 3, section A.

35. See chapter 2, section C.

36. See Friedman, *Talmud Arukh*, 1:247.

37. Henshke, *Original Mishna*, 5–59. According to him, the fourfold scheme is from no earlier than the generation of Rabbi Akiva's disciples.

38. For a comparison between the editing of the Mishnah and the editing of the Torah, see Berman, *Inconsistency in the Torah*, 192–198.

39. See *Sotah*, 7:1, and Tosefta, *Sotah*, 7:7, with Epstein, *Introduction to Tannaitic Literature*, 200–201.

40. Lewin, *Iggeret Rav Sherira Ga'on*, 21–22.

41. Blau and Yahalom, *Sefer ha-Galuy*, 117.

42. "Introduction to Maimonides's *Mishneh Torah*," in *Mishneh Torah* (ed. Kafah), 1:40–41. For Maimonides's view of the Mishnah's editing as a precedent for his *Mishneh Torah* and crisis as catalyst in both works, see Halbertal, *Maimonides*, 99; Michaelis, "Crisis Discourse."

43. On the difference between Sherira Gaon and Saadia Gaon on the writing of the Mishnah, see chapter 7 below.

44. For a synthesis of both explanations, see Rashi on BT *Bava Metzi'a* 33b, s.v. *bi-yemei Rabbi nishnet mishnah zo*.

45. But see Goldberg, "Purpose and Method," and Goldberg, "All Base Themselves," who identifies some didactic tendencies in the Mishnah.

46. *Mishneh Torah*, "Hilkhot Gittin," 1:1.

47. Tractate *Rosh ha-Shana* is an exception, as it begins by listing the four New Years of the Jewish calendar.

48. See chapter 1, section A.

49. In the Mishnah, respectively, *Nazir*, 6:2, 6:3, and chs. 7–9, corresponding to Num. 6:3–4, 6:5, and 6:6–7.

50. See Walfish, "Literary Method of Redaction"; Zohar, *Secrets of the Rabbinic Workshop*; Zohar, "Partitions"; and Zohar, "Scripture, Mishnah, and Ideas."

51. For a detailed survey and criticism of these proposals, see Elman, "Order, Sequence, and Selection."

52. As a result, when the opinion of an Amora clashes with the Mishnah, the Talmuds are forced to reinterpret the sources so that the contradiction disappears. For the gradual acceptance of the Mishnah as binding, see Weiss Halivni, "Reception."

53. Krochmal, *Writings*, 231–232; Frankel, *Darkhei ha-Mishnah*, 224–227, 284; Epstein, *Introduction to Tannaitic Literature*, 212–226; Elon, *Jewish Law*, 1057–1058.

54. Epstein, *Introduction to the Mishnaic Text*, 212.

55. Epstein, 201.

56. See also Weiss, *Dor Dor ve-Doreshav*, 2:39–48. For a rebuttal, see Weinberg, "Sources of the Mishnah." Cf. Elman, *Authority and Tradition*.

57. Albeck, *Introduction to the Mishna*, 102, 108. Cf. Albeck, *Studies*, 172–184.

58. Zlotnick, *Iron Pillar*, 226.

59. Elman, "Order, Sequence, and Selection," 75; Strack and Stemberger, *Introduction*, 154.

60. For Rabbi Yose, see PT *Terumot* 3:1 (42a), and for Rabbi Akiva see BT *'Eruvin* 46b.

61. Brandes, "Canonization of the Mishnah." It is interesting to compare this to a similar transformation in the status of the Roman jurists. See Elman, "Order, Sequence, and Selection," 58.

62. This perspective aligns with how Maimonides understood—and emulated—the project of the Mishnah, which explains why his commentary focused on the Mishnah rather than the Talmud. See Fuchs, "Reception of the Mishnah," 478–481.

63. Further substantiation to this thesis appears in chapter 3, section B above, in the context of our discussion of the chain of transmission in the beginning of tractate *Avot*. It outlines a list of transmitters of the Torah, passed from Moses in Sinai through the generations until it reaches the study house of Rabbi Yoḥanan ben Zakkai and his students (Avot 2:8–16)—the forebears of the Mishnah. As its conclusion shows, this chain serves to authorize the Mishnah itself, presenting it as the embodiment of the orally transmitted Torah.

CHAPTER 5. THE MISHNAH AS A COMPOSITION

1. See Rosen-Zvi, "Responsive Blessings."

2. For advice on protecting oneself from harm, see, e.g. *Terumot*, 8:5; for ethical evaluations see *Pe'ah*, 8:9, and *Bava Metzi'a*, 4:2,6 and 7:5; for laws with no practical application, see Guttmann, "Some Aspects."

3. For the former see *Pesaḥim*, 4:1–5; for the latter see *Sukkah*, 3:11, *Ketubbot*, 6:4, and *Bava Metzi'a*, 7:1.

4. On the Mishnah's attitude toward custom, see Miller, "All Law."

5. BT *Sukkah* 9b.

6. The same enforcing body might be referred to in *Kil'ayim*, 2:5. Compare this to the enforcement of Temple obligations: "he is coerced until he says 'I want to'" (*'Arakhin*, 5:6).

7. Recall from chapter 1 that I usually translate the participles placed in parentheses here with the gender-neutral, indefinite pronoun "one" or with a passive construction. In this context, though, neither seems appropriate.

8. See, e.g., *Shevi'it*, 3:1 and 4:1, *Ma'aser Sheni*, 1:4.

9. The phenomenon of counting the number of violations in a single act is only a rhetorical strategy to emphasize its severity (e.g., *Bava Metzi'a*, 5:11).

10. See also *Ḥallah*, 1:9.

11. Similarly: "If one has rolled with wheat [flour]. . ., whoever eats from it is liable for death" (*Ḥallah*, 3:1). Said with respect to untithed dough, this is not an admonition but a measure of the point at which the dough must be tithed. The punishment is not at all the focus of this mishnah or of the rest of the chapter that follows.

12. On the judicial system in Tractate *Sanhedrin* and its literary, synthetic character, see Shapira, "Courts in the Mishnah."

13. See Lorberbaum, "Theory of Action," and Levinson, "Narrative Practice."

14. See also *Ḥullin*, 12:2 and *Shevi'it*, 10:9. On Aggadah at the end of tractates, see chapter 6, section C.

15. See Blidstein, "Rabbinic Legislation on Idolatry."

16. See Zohar, "Sin Offering."

17. Moscovitz, *Talmudic Reasoning*, 47–97.

18. For a parallel chronological development in the conceptualization of Zoroastrian law among its interpreters, see Elman and Moazami, "Scholasticization of Religion."

19. Another example is discussed in Cherlow, "Development of Tannaitic Laws." Recall that Tractates *Bava Kamma*, *Bava Metzi'a*, and *Bava Batra* were all originally part of one tractate. The last two chapters of *Bava Kamma* are about stolen goods and the first two of *Bava Metzi'a* are about lost property. Why were the latter placed right after the former? Because they both bear on the conceptual question of when and how one acquires another's goods without permission.

20. See Moscovitz, Talmudic Reasoning, 84–90. His treatment of implicit principles, however, is not entirely convincing. The evidence he cites there (esp. 68–72) for the uniqueness of such principles in the Mishnah proves the opposite of what he intends: they show that the Mishnah found inconsistency to be worthy of note and therefore not the norm. See also R. Akiva's preference for R. Eliezer's view over R. Yehoshua's, because the former was consistent (*Shekalim*, 4:7).

21. It has been suggested, for example, that legal analysis of concrete cases (rather than abstract rules) served to prepare students for the intellectual jousting of the bet midrash; see Shanks-Alexander, *Transmitting Mishnah*; Wimpfheimer, "The Mishnah's Reader."

22. See chapter 2.

23. See Rosen-Zvi, *Mishnaic Sotah Ritual*, 239–254. Ben-Shahar ("Biblical and Post-Biblical History," 51–54) argues that the Mishnah systematically obscures the religious significance of the Temple's destruction. The Tosefta, which was edited later than the Mishnah, is more conscious of the destruction as a watershed moment.

24. See, e.g., *Shekalim*, 8:8 and *Bikkurim*, 2:3–4, which compare commandments that are and are not applicable in the present. If the Mishnah had not raised this point explicitly, it would be impossible to infer any difference in applicability based on the presentation of these mitzvot in their respective tractates.

25. *Pesaḥim*, 9:5.

26. *Sotah*, 7:5.

27. *Zevaḥim*, 14:9.

28. *Nega'im*, 7:1.

29. *Menaḥot*, 13:10.

30. See Fonrobert, "Semiotics of the Sexed Body."

31. There are sixty-six appearances of some form of the verb *nit'arev*, "was mixed in." Many of the tractates on sacred foods (e.g., *Terumot*, *Ḥallah*, *'Orlah*) and ritual purity (e.g., *Teharot*, *Mikva'ot*, *Makhshirin*) deal with mixtures. Tractate *Kinnin* is entirely dedicated to mixtures. On the central place of doubt in the Mishnah, which has no precedent in extant halakhic writings from the Second Temple period, see Halbertal, *Birth of Doubt*.

32. See chapter 3, section E.

33. For the evidence these *ma'asim* present for actual halakhic practice and the relationship between the Sages and the people, see Cohen, "The Rabbi."

34. Respectively: *Pesaḥim*, 4:1–5 and elsewhere; *Shabbat*, 5:4, *Pesaḥim*, 5:8, and *Menaḥot*, 10:5; and *Pesaḥim*, 4:8, *Ketubbot*, 1:5, and *Menaḥot*, 10:8. Many of the case story type of *ma'asim* involve practical difficulties in practicing the law and the Sages' response to them.

35. Recall the mishnaic description of the *bikkurim* ceremony, which also seems to call forth an ideal reality; see chapter 2, end of section B.

36. See Lieberman, *Greek in Jewish Palestine*, 115–143. On the ancient roots of the halakhic conception of vows and their development in second Temple period, see Benovitz, *Kol Nidre*.

37. On these mishnaic units, see Koren, "Foreskinned Jew."

38. See above, chapter 3.

39. See Halbertal, "History of Halakhah."

CHAPTER 6. AGGADAH AND HALAKHAH IN THE MISHNAH

1. Aramaic *aggadah* is the equivalent of Hebrew *haggadah*, "statement" or "saying," and more broadly "maxim," "lesson," etc.

2. On the various disciplines of Torah in tannaitic literature, see Rosenthal, "Oral Torah"; and Kister, *Studies*, 42–44.

3. For a bold, speculative attempt to pin it down, see Lifshitz, "Aggadah and Its Role."

4. Fraenkel, "Aggadah in the Mishnah," 657.

5. Fraenkel, 662.

6. BT *Sukkah* 29a.

7. Tosefta, *Sukkah*, 2:6. For this version of the text, see Lieberman, *Tosefta ki-Feshutah*, ad loc.

8. This stance is articulated in Tosefta, *Sukkah*, 2:4.

9. Another example: *Sukkah* 2:4 rules "One may take a casual meal of food and drink outside the sukkah. It once happened *(ma'aseh)* that they brought a dish before Rabban Yohanan ben Zakkai to taste it and [they brought] two dates and a bucket of water before Rabban Gamaliel. They said, 'Bring them up to the sukkah.'" The rabbis' unwillingness to eat or drink even a miniscule amount outside the sukkah reflects a stricter ideal than the preceding halakhah.

10. Fraenkel, "Aggadah in the Mishnah," 668, 678, and 679, respectively.

11. See chapter 3, section C.

12. Fraenkel, "Aggadah in the Mishnah," 660. He brings two proofs for his reading: (1) R. Yohanan ben Matteyah doesn't appear anywhere else in rabbinic literature, supporting the contention that he is a *ḥasid* and not a Sage, similar to Honi the Circle-Maker and R. Hanina ben Dosa (on whom see immediately below). This is pure speculation. (2) The language of "not fulfilling one's obligation" generally only appears in conjunction with mitzvot between man and God. This proof is severely weakened by the indirect object that makes it clearly about people and an interpersonal mitzvah: "you will not have fulfilled your obligation *to them*." For a comprehensive study of this mishnah, which posits tension between Aggadah and Halakhah yet does not dichotomize them, see Marienberg-Milikowsky, "Employer-Worker Dynamics."

13. PT *Bava Metzi'a* 7:1 (11b).

14. In the same vein, there is no cause for reading *Berakhot*, 9:5, *Pe'ah*, 1:1, or *Yoma*, 8:8 as cases where non-halakhic thinking intrudes on halakhic logic. For a thorough critique of Fraenkel's approach, see Lorberbaum, *In God's Image*, 61–88.

15. The preceding mishnah (*Ḥagigah*, 1:5) also ends with a verse introduced by this phrase, and there, too, one strains to see any purported transition from Halakhah to Aggadah.

16. Simon-Shoshan, *Stories of the Law*.

17. See Sarfatti, "Pious Men"; Safrai, "Tales of the Sages"; Green, "Holy Men." For the holy man in late Antiquity, see Brown, *Society and the* Holy; for Jesus as a wonderworker, see Smith, *Jesus the Magician*.

18. Although the Babylonian Talmud (*Berakhot* 33a) argues that the snake here cannot be venomous, that is not the straightforward reading.

19. See, e.g., *Mekhilta de-Rabbi Yishmael, Nezikin*, §4, p. 264, and BT *Sanhedrin* 74a.

20. Its flight and retreat to a hole indicate that it is probably a snake, and the Palestinian Talmud (5:1) explicitly identifies it thus (compare *Genesis Rabbah* 82:15). In this version, Hanina ben Dosa does not even feel its bite due to his intense concentration. In the Babylonian Talmud (*Berakhot* 33a) the story becomes one about the relationship between sin and death rather than about prayer.

21. Based on Naeh, "'Creates the Fruit of Lips.'"

22. The Shema may be recited so long as one's genitalia are covered, whereas the Amidah requires covering the heart as well (*Berakhot*, 2:14). See Halbertal, "David Hartman," esp. 25–26.

23. See *Berakhot*, 5:3 and 2:3, respectively. It is difficult to believe that the prayer leader could not be reminded of the mistaken words. It seems that there is a practical concern that the hazzan's mistakes reflect an association with anti-rabbinic groups, in which case he cannot be allowed to continue to represent a congregation of those faithful to rabbinic Judaism. The preceding mishnah (*Berakhot*, 5:2), which notes outlawed liturgical alternatives, points in this direction.

24. Tosefta, *Berakhot*, 3:3.

25. MS Kaufmann has על instead of עד. If it is not a simple scribal error, it can be rendered: *so that* you will have mercy.

26. Simon-Shoshan, "Story of Honi." See there for references to earlier scholarship.

27. Isaiah Ben-Pazi ("Honi the Circle Drawer") argues that "member of the household" should be construed in its legal sense, i.e., a slave empowered by his master to run the affairs of the household (see Tosefta, *Ketubbot*, 9:3). On this reading, Honi is claiming that he has real power over God, and Shimon ben Shetah counters that Honi possesses no such thing, and that God acquiesces only to appease his whiny son. Compare Hirshman, "Loci of Holiness," 111.

28. The two Talmuds do mention other *yeḥidim* who act outside of the rabbinically mandated set of fasts. See Levine, "Who Participated," esp. 48–52.

29. On this see Ilan and Noam, *Josephus and the Rabbis*, 318–340.

30. Heinemann, *Methods of the Aggadah*, ch. 7.

31. Yerushalmi, *Zakhor*, 21–22. James Kugel similarly writes: "Here then is the crucial factor in the mentality of all early exegesis: for when what *happened* in Scripture happens again and again, unfolds over and over, it is because the Bible is not 'the past' at all [. . .] [T]he Bible's time is important, while the present is not; and so it invites the reader to cross over into the enterable world of Scripture" (Kugel, "Two Introductions," 89–90).

32. For a fuller elaboration, see Rosen-Zvi, *Mishnaic Sotah Ritual*.

33. Note that in the Babylonian Talmud this chapter has been moved to the end of the tractate and is therefore chapter 11.

34. Similar to how lashes save the sinner from the punishment of *karet*; see the treatment of the end of Tractate *Makkot* below.

35. Epstein, *Introduction to the Mishnaic Text*, 428.

36. See Weiss, "Chapters of the Mishnah."

37. For more on this, see below, chapter 7, section C.

38. For a development of this explanation, see Slotnick, "Call to Order."

39. Notably, the distinction between interpersonal mitzvot and those between man and God only arises in the context of repentance in rabbinic literature.

40. See Levinger, "Repentance Atones."

41. A more audacious reading would consider God Himself a metaphysical *mikveh* in which the Jewish people are purified. Metaphors involving ritual immersion also play a central role in Christianity; see 1 Corinthians 10:2. For the complex interrelationship between Jewish and Christian symbolic understandings of immersion, see Furstenberg, "Christianization of Proselyte Baptism."

42. The scholarship is vast. See the bibliography in Lerner, "Tractate Avot," 275–276; and Tropper, *Wisdom, Politics, and Historiography*, 1–16.

43. See Kister, *Studies*, and above, chapter 1, end of section A.

44. The hundreds upon hundreds of printings of Jewish prayerbooks contributed to divergent versions of the tractate; see Sharvit, *Tractate Avoth*.

45. On this dictum see Goldin, *Studies*, 27–37.

46. For more on this and other methods of formal organization in the Mishnah, see chapter 1, section A.

47. For an elaboration of this reading of Tractate *Avot*, see Rosen-Zvi, "Wisdom Tradition." For a different reading, see Schremer, "Avot Reconsidered." On the history of the concept of two Torahs, biblical and non-biblical, side by side, see Fisch, "The Origins of Oral Torah." For the Christian adaptation of this concept, see Bergmeier, "The *Traditio Legis*."

48. Accordingly, this is a rare, if implicit, self-reference within the Mishnah. In *Sifrei Deuteronomy* (§335, p. 385), there is an explicit comparison between preserving the Written and Oral Torahs. Since it is cited in the name of R. Yehudah ha-Nasi, who compares himself to Moses, there is little doubt that he is referring to the Mishnah itself as the counterpart to the Written Torah. On this exceptionally bold homily, see Kahana, *Derash Hamazhir*, 88.

49. This mishnah does not appear in MS Kaufmann. On this unit see further Elitzur, "Middah."

50. In a fourth-century Jewish-Christian text known as the *Pseudo-Clementine Homilies*, the *Written Torah* is said to have been transmitted orally from Moses to the elders and only much later written down (Hom. 3:47). This serves its argument that the Torah contains later additions and "false pericopes." A chain of oral transition can thus serve different, even opposite, goals. For the connection between this composition and rabbinic literature, see A. I. Baumgarten, "Literary Evidence," 42–43. On the general conception of tradition in the *Pseudo-Clementine Homilies*, see Reed, "Jewish Christianity as Counter History?" For an interesting version of the mishnaic chain of tradition, in the Quran (5:44), see Zellentin, "What Is within Judaism," 285.

51. Tropper, *Wisdom, Politics, and Historiography*, 50, 58–59.

CHAPTER 7. THE TRANSMISSION AND TEXTUAL HISTORY OF THE MISHNAH

1. See above, chapter 4.

2. Epstein, *Introduction to the Mishnaic Text*, 703.

3. Confusingly, in rabbinic literature this figure is called a *tanna* since he memorized material produced by the Tannaim. He should not be confused with the Tanna whose opinions he preserved.

4. Lieberman, *Hellenism*, 89–93 (italics and Greek omitted).

5. The Tosefta and other tannaitic literature were not circulated orally with the same precision and authority, resulting in far more divergent versions. On the question of the writing of tannaitic Midrashim, see part 2, chapter 16.

6. Lieberman, *Hellenism*, 87 (italics and Greek omitted).

7. Sussman, "Oral Law," 347 (emphasis in the original).

8. Sussman, 228–233. On the Karaite position regarding the Oral Torah and Islamic influences, see Polliack, "Karaite Inversion."

9. Sussman, "Oral Law," 225 (emphasis in the original).

10. Sussman, 249.

11. BT *Megillah* 28b.

12. Sussman, "Oral Law," 318–319.

13. See Vidas, "What Is a *Tannay*?"

14. See Fuchs, "Review of Yaacov Sussmann."

15. On many of the current theories, see Dohrmann, "Can 'Law' Be Private?," 195–198; for those proposed throughout history and through the nineteenth century, see Gafni, *Conceptions of the Oral Law*. For possible precedents to the concept of Oral Torah in the Second Temple period, see Fraade, *Legal Fictions*, 370–378.

16. Jaffee, *Torah in the Mouth*, 142–152. See also Hezser, "Bookish Circles?," 71.

17. Preference for oral instruction is attested already in Plato's *Phaedrus*. Prophyry's *Life of Plotinus* surveys the reluctance of the philosophers to write down their teachings (see esp. sec. 20). At the very same time, this work shows that reading philosophical works and writing commentaries were integral to a philosophical education (e.g., secs. 15 and 18). For this tension, see Grafton and Williams, *Christianity and the Transformation of the Book*, 29–36. On the combination of oral and written instruction in Roman law, see Harries, "Legal Education," 157. For discussions of orality in ancient Greek literature through the lens of Orality Studies, see Nagy, "Orality and Literacy." He emphasizes that "it is pointless to insist on any universalizing definitions for the 'oral' of 'oral tradition.'"

18. See Yuval, "Orality of Jewish Oral Law."

19. Bregman, "Mishna and LXX." See also Gafni, *Conceptions of the Oral Law*, 25 with lit. cited.

20. Amos Geula argued that this homily reflects a genuine debate occurring during the time and place of the redactor of this Midrash, specifically in ninth-century Southern Italy. See Geula, "The Status of the Mishnah in Byzantium," 278, 281.

21. The Hebrew verb also means "recited," underscoring the orality of it. The same occurs in BT *Berakhot* 18a: "If you have read, you have not repeated *(shanita);* if you have repeated, you have not done it three times." Here, as well, the idea is not only to do it a second time, but to recite the Oral Torah. That is, the basic level of study is reading Scripture, and the next level is reciting the relevant Oral Torah.

22. Cf. *Mekhilta de-Rashbi*, 15:2, p. 80.

23. Linder, *Jews in Legislation*, 25.

24. The halakhic texts at Qumran are obviously written down. See also *Sotah*, 7:5 and Tosefta, *Sotah*, 8:6–7 about the stones on which the Torah was written in seventy languages. Interestingly, these sources seem to have no qualms about written halakhic publication, although one could counter that it is because in this context the writing is directed externally to the nations of the world. See further Fraade, *Multilingualism*, 48–81.

25. Stern, "Publication and Early Transmission," 467–468. On nineteenth-century precedents for this position, see Gafni, *Conceptions of the Oral Law*, 129.

26. Sussmann, "Oral Law," 353–354.

27. We will see in part 2, chapter 9, that for the Sages the Tanakh was not a single book in the physical sense but a collection of scrolls (see Stern, "The First Jewish Books"; and b. Baba Batra 13b). Still, they viewed it as a unified work for purposes of study and exegesis.

28. Prayers were also recited from memory. The first prayerbook did not appear until the Geonic period. Even the Targumim, translations of the Torah into Aramaic, were initially oral. In this way, the reading of the written Torah in the synagogue was kept separated from all other liturgical practices, which were oral in nature. See Satlow, *How the Bible Became Holy*, 270 and 275.

29. One who reads "external books" has no place in the World to Come, according to *Sanhedrin*, 10:1. These books belonged to different genres and covered a wide array of subject matter; their only common denominator was their written form, which necessarily placed them in competition with Scripture. In part 2, chapter 9, we will encounter reworkings and retellings of Scripture, many of which were read as a version of the Torah. This is precisely the sort of blurring that distressed the rabbis.

30. Even the writings of Jews from the Second Temple period, like Philo of Alexandria, were preserved exclusively by Christians. See Milikowsky, "Jewish Historiography."

31. All the fragments and manuscripts are catalogued in Sussmann, *Thesaurus*, and are viewable and searchable on the website of the Friedberg Genizah Project.

32. See Sussmann, "Oral Law," 338 with note 37.

33. A copy of the manuscript has been published (*Mishnah: Kaufmann Manuscript*) and it is also available online (http://kaufmann.mtak.hu/hu/ms50/ms50-coll1.htm). Other manuscripts that are quite close to MS Kaufmann in time and place, and so reflect the same base text, include MS Parma De Rossi 138 and MS Cambridge MS Add. 470.1, which has also been transcribed in Lowe, *Mishnah*. These three will be treated as a unit below, representative of the Palestinian version of the Mishnah.

34. See Albeck's commentary in *Shishah Sidrei Mishnah, Nashim*, 345, and Lieberman, *Tosefta ki-Feshutah, Yevamot-Nezirut*, 185. For the relationship between the Tosefta and the Mishnah see below, chapter 8.

35. In an odd feedback loop, this glossed mishnah ended up back in the Babylonian Talmud in its new form (see BT *Ketubbot* 2a). This can be accounted for by the fact that the opening discourse of many tractates often comes from later in the talmudic period, at which point the mishnah would have been circulating with its incorporated gloss. See Brody, *Mishnah and Tosefta Ketubbot*, 5–6. On the penetration of glosses and interpretive statements into the Mishnah and *baraitot* more generally, see D. Rosenthal, "The Talmudists Jumped."

36. Such reconstruction is one of the principal goals of Epstein's monumental *Introduction to the Mishnaic Text*.

37. See above, note 33 in this chapter.

38. Cf. BT *'Avodah Zarah*, 52b.

39. Rosenthal, "Mishna Aboda Zara," 1:177–178. For a summary of his position, see Rosenthal, "History of the Mishnaic Text."

40. For another example see PT *Bava Metzi'a* 4:1 (9c), and BT *Bava Metzi'a* 44a, with Epstein, *Introduction the Mishnaic Text*, 19–22, and Lieberman, *Tosefta ki-Feshutah*, 9–10:176. For the legal background of this mishnah and its Roman context, see Sperber, *Roman Palestine*, 69–90.

41. In one place (BT *Bava Kamma* 11b), Rabbi taught his son the correct *interpretation* (rather than text) of a mishnah. The fact that he quoted it as a set text points to the canonization of the Mishnah within his lifetime. See Epstein, *Introduction to the Mishnaic Text*, 389–390; and Weiss, "Presentation of Material," 130.

42. This had implications for how the Mishnah was received. The Babylonian Talmud considers mishnaic law to possess supreme authority, while the Palestinian Talmud is willing to also rely on the Tosefta and parallel *baraitot*. See, e.g., Friedman, *Tosefta Atiqta*, 78.

43. Thus in MS Kaufmann and MS Cambridge; in MS Parma the line does appear but without the scriptural quotation.

44. For a highly speculative suggestion, see Finkelstein, *Introduction to the Treatise Abot*, 106.

45. See Rosen-Zvi, *Body and Soul*, 79–88.

46. For the modest beginnings of this exegetical endeavor in tannaitic literature, see *Mekhilta de-Rabbi Yishmael, 'Amalek*, §1, p. 179.

47. Sussmann attributes this to a Palestinian tradition of learning the Mishnah without talmudic commentary ("Manuscripts and Text Traditions," 234). Italy and Byzantium were in many respects preservers and purveyors of the religious culture of the Land of Israel. See further the appendix to this chapter.

48. See further Sussmann, "Manuscripts and Text Traditions," 220–221 with n. 36. For the three complete manuscripts see above, note 33. There is another important manuscript that covers only *Seder Teharot*: MS Parma De Rossi 497, also known as MS Parma B to distinguish it from the complete MS Parma. For this MS, see the introduction to *Mishna Codex Parma "B."* On the Genizah fragments, see Katsh, *Ginze Mishna*, and Yeivin, *Mishnaic Geniza Fragments*.

49. See Weiss Halivni, *Baba Metzia*, 41.

50. See Fuchs, "Reception of the Mishnah"; Landes, "Piyyut, Mishnah, and Rabbinization"; Chwat, "Mishna Study"; and Olman, "Weekly Learning," 179.

51. See Ahrend, "Mishnah Study."

52. Ahrend, 23.

53. See Idel, "Some Concepts"; Werblowsky, *Joseph Karo*, chap. 5.

54. See Urbach, *World of the Sages*, 274–278.

55. See Roth, "Doing Things with Mishna."

56. Raz-Krakotzkin, "Burning and Printing," 30–32.

CHAPTER 8. THE TOSEFTA AND THE MISHNAH

1. When capitalized, "the Tosefta" refers to the entire corpus as a whole; when uncapitalized, "the tosefta" (pl. toseftaot) refers to a specific textual unit within the larger corpus. A tosefta is referred to by tractate, chapter number, and unit number.

2. For a fuller treatment of the issues covered in this chapter, see Hayes, "Intertextuality," esp. 165–196.

3. See above chapter 6, section D.

4. This is the suggestion of Brody (*Mishnah and Tosefta Ketubbot*, 46). If the Tosefta's goal was to gather material that predated the Mishnah (see below, section B), in the case of these three ancient tractates there wouldn't have been any earlier material, thus explaining their absence.

5. Albeck, *Studies*, 88, tries to prove a late dating from the fact that parts of the two Talmuds do not seem familiar with laws in the Tosefta. For a critique of this approach, see Kahana, "Halakhic Midrashim," 60–61n260; Brody, *A Commentary on Bavli Ketubbot*, 21–23. See also note 25 below. Note, however, that the Tannaitic origins of the Tosefta do not preclude the possibility that its primary channel of transmission was Babylonian. This may account for the presence of Babylonian features in the Tosefta that cannot be fully explained as scribal emendations. See Elitzur, "Language and Reality."

6. The style of the Tosefta is far from the dialectics of the Palestinian Talmud and even further from that of the Babylonian Talmud. To take one specific example, the Mishnah uses a participial construction to universalize the applicability of its law, which has generally been translated in this book with the pronoun "one." The Babylonian and Palestinian Talmuds instead employ stock names like Reuven and Shimon to similar effect. If the Tosefta were contemporary with or posterior to the Talmuds, one would expect at least one occurrence of it in the Tosefta, but one searches for it in vain.

7. See Goldberg, *Tosefta Bava Kamma*, 28–31.

8. Lewin, *Iggeret Rav Sherira Ga'on*, 6. Recall that many medievals thought that R. Yehudah ha-Nasi committed the Mishnah to writing; see chapter 7, section A.

9. Lewin, *Iggeret Rav Sherira Ga'on*, 6 and 36. Cf. Maimonides's introduction to his *Mishneh Torah*: "Rabbi Hiyya compiled the Tosefta in order to clarify matters in the Mishnah." On this see Friedman, *Tosefta Atiqta*, 15.

10. Most toseftan parallels to the Mishnah are more or less two times longer, but they can exceed that ratio greatly. For example, chapter 5 of Tractate *Bava Metzi'a* in the Mishnah has eleven mishnayot, whereas the parallel Tosefta (chs. 4–6) stretches to sixty-nine *halakhot*, almost seven times more material. These cover the laws of usury, which, as a practical issue, exercised the Sages greatly. Both Talmuds contain many stories about actual rulings ad loc. The Mishnah's laconic treatment was deemed too brief.

11. The tannaitic Midrashim discussed in part 2 also contain lengthy collections of Aggadah. Seemingly, over time there was a growing consensus regarding the Aggadah's independence of Halakhah, which, at the end of the Amoraic period, culminated in the editing of independent works of Aggadah, like *Genesis Rabbah*.

12. Compare *Sotah* 1:8–9 with Tosefta, *Sotah*, 3:6–4:19. On this see Rosen-Zvi, "Sin of Concealment."

13. MS Vienna hebr. 20. An additional manuscript, MS Erfurt (now Berlin State Library, Or. fol. 1220), contains only the first four *sedarim* and likely dates to the eleventh century, originating in Italy. See Shmidman, Binder, and Rabin, "Margin Notes of Tosefta MS Erfurt." On this manuscript, whose readings are in many cases superior to those of MS Vienna, see further Brody, *Mishnah and Tosefta Ketubbot* and the literature cited therein. Another manuscript (London—British Library, 445) covers only one order (*Seder Mo'ed*). Additionally, there are several Cairo Genizah fragments.

14. Saul Lieberman prepared a critical edition of the Tosefta based on MS Vienna and wrote an important commentary on it titled *Tosefta ki-Feshutah*, although it only reaches *Bava Batra*. For basic introductions to the Tosefta, see Mandel, "The Tosefta," and Fox, Meacham, and Kriger, *Introducing Tosefta*.

15. Scholars have proposed many theories, of which I will mention two. Jacob Nahum Epstein theorized that R. Akiva and his disciples already had collections of toseftaot alongside their collections of mishnayot (see Friedman, *Tosefta Atiqta*, 18–19), but this seems impossible to prove. Paul Mandel sees the origin of the name "Tosefta" in the phrase "they added (*hosifu*) onto them," which recurs in the Tosefta (Mandel, "The Tosefta," 316). It is true that the additional material denoted by this term generally takes the form of new details, but this is only one type of addition found in the Tosefta, along with alternative opinions, legal rationales, and more.

16. See Goldberg, *Tosefta Bava Kamma*, 8 and 38.

17. See chapter 5, section B; and Lorberbaum, "Rejection of Reasons."

18. See Albeck, *Studies*, 150.

19. In *Sifrei Deuteronomy*, §188, pp. 228–229, this mishnaic unit is indeed attached to mishnah 1:1.

20. For a different interpretation of the Hebrew, see Lieberman, *Tosefta ki-Feshutah*, 8:610.

21. Shemesh-Raiskin, *Give-and-Take Conversations*, identified 190 conversations in the Mishnah among the thousands of debates, and they typically only have a single stage.

22. Rosen-Zvi, *Mishnaic Sotah Ritual*.

23. It is unclear if the Tosefta has a different perspective on the ritual or simply wants to present the entire picture, as above.

24. In Kulp and Rogoff's formulation (*Reconstructing the Talmud*, 2:134), the Tosefta sacrifices brevity for clarity and vice versa for the Mishnah.

25. The fact that the Tosefta occupies an intermediate position in the process of canonization is a proof against Albeck's claim that it was edited only toward the end of the amoraic period. See above, note 5. On the question of changes to the Mishnah during the amoraic period, see Henshke, "Abbaye and Rava."

26. See the discussion in chapter 2, section E.

27. Cf. Mishnah, *'Avodah Zarah*, 4:7.

28. The Babylonian Talmud identifies Beruriah as R. Meir's wife, but if R. Yehoshua, a first-generation Sage of Yavneh, knew her, she could not have been the wife of R. Meir, a Sage from the much later generation of Usha. Another law is cited in the Tosefta (*Kelim, Bava Kamma*, 4:17) in the name of R. Hanina ben Teradyon's daughter, who was also later identified with Beruriah. In the Babylonian Talmud, Beruriah becomes a heroine and various traditions are attributed to her. See Boyarin, *Carnal Israel*, 181–196.

29. Sabato, "Teachings of Rabbi Joshua," 76.

30. Lichtenstein, "Towards a History," 65.

31. See chapter 2, section C.

32. See, e.g., Mishnah, *Pesaḥim* 1:1, with Epstein, *Introduction to the Mishnaic Text*, 610, and Sabato, "Why Did They Say?"

33. Respectively, chapter 2, section E; and chapter 7, section C.

34. Lieberman, *Tosefta ki-Feshutah*, 1:5.

35. See Friedman, *Tosefta Atiqta*, 37n90. On Lieberman's different approach and what it can tell us about his interpretation of the Mishnah-Tosefta relationship, see Friedman, 36–38.

36. Cf. Albeck, *Studies*, 144.

37. See Lieberman, *Tosefta ki-Feshutah*, vol. 1, p. 5.

38. Friedman, *Tosefta Atiqta*, 49. See also Friedman, "Primacy of Tosefta."

39. Friedman, *Tosefta Atiqta*, 39.

40. It is difficult to assign chronology based on an explanatory conjunction like "because," for it can be similarly added in one source or extracted from another. Compare this with questions like "How so?" or "Why did they say?" which are clearly additions, bringing the chronology and layering to the fore. In general, Friedman's approach works better where there are parallels and is less effective where there is undeniable literary dependency.

41. Hauptman, *Rereading the Mishnah*. For critique see Brody, *Mishnah and Tosefta Ketubbot*, 44–45.

42. See Walfish, "Unifying Halakhah and Aggadah."

43. See Rosen-Zvi, "Blessing as Mapping."

44. See Deuteronomy 4:19.

45. See *Mekhilta de-Rabbi Yishmael*, *Pisḥa*, §16, pp. 60–61.

46. See Epstein, *Introduction to Tannaitic Literature*, 258. Regarding Tractate *Berakhot* specifically, see Houtman, *Mishnah and Tosefta*.

PART I. EPILOGUE: THE MISHNAH AND FUTURE SCHOLARSHIP

1. For example, Hanukkah is scanted while Purim receives an entire tractate, *Megillah*. The reasons for such imbalances can be various and demand case-by-case examination.

2. Elman, "Order, Sequence, and Selection," 54.

3. On readings of the Mishnah in the context of the codificatory enterprises of the ancient world, see Elman, "Order, Sequence, and Selection." On such projects in late Antique Rome specifically, see Harries, "Roman Law Codes"; and Liebs, "Code System."

4. See Rosen-Zvi, "Orality, Narrative, Rhetoric."

5. See Schmid, *The Scribes of the Torah*, 49–62.

6. See the programmatic article of Furstenberg, "Literary Evolution."

7. For the debate see Rosen-Zvi, "Rabbis as *Nomikoi*?"

8. See the recent volume Berthelot, Dohrmann, and Nemo-Pekelman, *Legal Engagement*, and in particular the following contributions: Berthelot, "Not Like Our Rock"; Dohrmann, *"Ad Similitudinem Arbitrorum"*; Furstenberg, "Imperialism"; Hezser, "Did Palestinian Rabbis Know Roman Law?"; and Wilfand, "Proselyte."

9. Two important new books explore this phenomenon from the dual perspectives of reception history and early modern history, and importantly cover the Levant in addition to Europe. See Raz-Krakotzkin, *Mishna Consciousness*; and Van Boxel, Macfarlane, and Weinberg, "Mishnah between Jews and Christians."

PART II. INTRODUCTION: UNDERSTANDING MIDRASH

1. Without the definite article but with capitalization, "Midrash" refers to the technique or methodology characterized in this chapter. With the definite article and with capitalization, "the Midrash" refers to the entire corpus of midrashic literature or to a discrete work within it (e.g.,

Sifra). Without capitalization, "a/the midrash" refers to a single textual unit within a work of Midrash that typically includes more than one derashah, the basic unit of exegesis.

2. Unless otherwise noted, all midrashic citations are taken from manuscripts selected by the Ma'agarim database of the Academy of the Hebrew Language (https://maagarim.hebrew-academy.org.il/Pages/PMain.aspx), with my punctuation. The page numbers are according to the following scholarly editions: Mekhilta RI, Howowitz's edition, Frankfurt 1931; Mekhilta RSBI, Epstein-Melamed's edition, Jerusalem, 1956; Sifra, Weiss's edition, Vienna 1862; Sifre on and Sifre Zutta on Numbers, Horowitz's edition, Leipzig, 1914; Sifre on Deuteronomy, Finkelstein's edition, New York 1969. When the Midrash cites only the beginning of the verse (a commonplace because the reader is assumed to know their Bible) but the rest of the verse is important for comprehending the derashah, it is added in square brackets. Interlinear explanations appear in regular brackets. For ease of reading, the unique (and estranging) spellings preserved in these manuscripts are not always presented, nor are textual variants noted. These issues are discussed further in chapter 16.

3. On the question of the social setting of Midrash, and its possible connection with the synagogue, see Heinemann, *Public Homilies*.

4. For Aggadah in the Mishnah, see part 1, chapter 6.

5. This discussion draws on the works of Porton, "Defining Midrash"; Teugels, *Bible and Midrash*, ch. 8; and Ben-Yashar, Gottlieb, and Penkower, *The Bible in Rabbinic Interpretation*.

6. When placed in italics, the word *midrash* indicates the linguistic usage of the Hebrew term.

7. Cf. Exodus 18:16 and Deuteronomy 17:9.

8. Psalm 119, probably also from the Persian period, may be a witness to an intermediate stage in the development of the new meaning. Several of its verses include verbal forms in which God's laws, rather than God Himself, are the direct object of the seeking (vv. 45 and 94, and see also vv. 2, 10, and 155). This may be a step toward the Torah, which contains the divine law, becoming the object of one's religious search. See Klein, "Half Way."

9. See Curtis and Madsen, *Chronicles*, 23, for the view that *midrash* here refers to an actual book. Seeligmann (*Studies*, 464n29) argues that the use of the term *midrash* in a book that is itself a sort of Midrash on other biblical books cannot be a coincidence, and points toward *midrash* as a work of interpretation.

10. For more on the semantic development of *d-r-sh*, see I. Heinemann, "Development of Technical Terms"; Gertner, "Terms of Scriptural Interpretation"; and Hurvitz, "Continuity and Innovation." Heinemann claims that the new usage appears first at Qumran, whereas Gertner and Hurvitz identify it already in later books of the Bible (Ezra, Chronicles, and the later psalms).

11. For the Dead Sea Scrolls and Qurman see part 1, introduction, section C.

12. See Baumgarten, "Unwritten Law." On the relationship between Qumran texts and Scripture, see Vermes, "Bible Interpretation."

13. See Joshua 1:8; Psalms 1:2. For a cosmic interpretation of these verses here, portraying them as an imitation of the ceaseless movements of stars and angels, see Becker, *The Secret of Time*, 58–82.

14. García Martínez and Tigchelaar, *Dead Sea Scrolls Study Edition*, 83.

15. In light of Ezra 7:10, Michael Fishbane ("Use, Authority and Interpretation") connects the interpretation to the reading of the Torah. Lawrence Schiffman (*Reclaiming the Dead Sea Scrolls*, 42–47) proposes that the reading is intended to anchor certain sectarian laws in the Torah. Others believe that the reading from a book and the textless study of laws are two separate practices. See further Fraade, "Looking for Legal Midrash," note 29.

16. See Fraade, "Interpretive Authority."

17. Paul Mandel argues in his *Origins of Midrash* that *d-r-sh* at Qumran means "instruction" or "teaching" and not "textual interpretation," which is an invention of the Tannaim (especially of R. Akiva's generation). I believe his reading of the Qumran material is too minimalist. See, e.g.,

4Q174 (Florilegium), frag. 1–2, col. I, 1.14: "Midrash of 'Blessed be the man who does not walk in the counsel of the wicked' (Ps. 1:1)" (García Martínez and Tigchelaar, *Dead Sea Scrolls Study Edition*, 353). The continuation indeed consists of interpretations of the initial chapters of Psalms. See also Shemesh, "Biblical Exegesis"; Ben-Dov and Stökl Ben Ezra, "4Q429," and below chapter 9, section F.

18. See Fraade, "'Comparative Midrash' Revisited," 5.

19. García Martínez and Tigchelaar, *Dead Sea Scrolls Study Edition*, 81. For the "hidden matters," see Werman and Shemesh, *Revealing the Hidden;* and Fishbane, "Use, Authority and Interpretation," 364–365.

20. Mishnah, *Nedarim*, 4:3.

21. On the rabbinic disciplines of Torah study, see Finkelstein, *Sifra*, 5:100–119; Rosenthal, "Oral Torah," 455; Kister, *Studies*, 42–44. See also *Mekhilta de-Rabbi Yishmael*, 'Amalek, §4, pp. 196–197: "'Statutes' (Ex. 18:16)—these are *midrashot;* 'instructions'—these are teachings." This midrash distinguishes *midrashoth* from teachings, which are extra-scriptural laws like the Mishnah. On the nominalization of verbs like *midrash* in mishnaic Hebrew, and what they can tell us about institutionalized Torah study after the destruction of the Temple, see Fraade, "Innovation of Nominalized Verbs."

22. See esp. Bakhos, "Method(ological) Matters," 162n2.

23. See, for example, Gesundheit, *Three Times a Year*, in which interpretive additions to the (reconstructed) original Priestly text in the Pentateuch are called "Midrashic Expansions." See his methodological discussion of "inner biblical midrashim" in pp. 232–234 and n. 10 for references to earlier studies which use similar terminology.

24. See below, chapter 9 for the various approaches. For the claim of rabbinic exclusiveness, see Teugels, *Bible and Midrash*, 161–162.

25. See Bakhos, "Method(ological) Matters."

26. This is the approach of Neusner, *Midrash as Literature*.

27. Formal, instead of substantive, definitions are also proposed for the *pesher* literature; see Brooke, "Qumran Pesher."

28. See Teugels, *Bible and Midrash*, 157–161.

29. See chapter 1, section D.

30. Examples of such definitions can be found in Fraenkel, *Methods of Aggadah;* Stern, *Parables in Midrash;* Weiss Halivni, *Peshat and Derash*.

31. See further the beginning of chapter 12.

32. On the theological assumptions of Midrash, see Hartman and Budick, *Midrash and Literature*.

33. Geiger, "Das Verhältniß des natürlichen Schriftsinnes," 81. On the general attitude of *Wissenschaft* scholars toward Midrash, see Harris, *How Do We Know This?*

34. Frankel, *Darkhei ha-Mishnah*, 17.

35. Weiss, *Sifra*, III.

36. Various rabbinic Bible commentators advanced this argument in the nineteenth century. First and foremost among them was R. Meir Leibush Wisser, the Malbim.

37. Some twentieth-century scholars maintained variations of this regarding aggadic derashot, including Joseph Heinemann, Efraim E. Urbach, and Jonah Fraenkel. They emphasized the polemical, ideological, and literary contexts, respectively. On the larger position regarding halakhic derashot, see Urbach, "The *Derashah*."

38. See Boyarin, *Intertextuality*, 9.

39. Dan, *History of Jewish Mysticism*, 1:253–287 (especially 261). For a more nuanced perspective on the relationship between Midrash and mysticism, see Gruenwald, "Talmudic to Zoharic

Homiletics"; Gruenwald, "Midrash and the Midrashic Condition." For a contemporary interpretation of Midrash as pseudo-reading, see Wollenberg, *The Closed Book*, 103 ("early rabbinic disinterest in the workings of textual meaning-making"). For a (pointed, to my mind) critique of this approach to Midrashic practice, see Fisch, "Book Review."

40. Raviv, "Nature of Biblical Exegesis," argues that even what seem to be anchoring derashot (on which see chapter 11, section C) are resolving local interpretive problems.

41. See my afterword to Boyarin, *Midrash Tanna'im* (pp. 273–286). A similar trend exists in the scholarship of early Christian exegesis; see Young, *Biblical Exegesis*.

42. Boyarin, *Intertextuality*, 16.

43. See "this verse is enriched from many places" (*Mekhilta de-Rabbi Yishmael*, Shirata, §4, p. 129) discussed in chapter 14, section B.

44. See Boyarin, *Intertextuality*, 25–26.

45. Kahana, *Sifre on Numbers*, 1115–1116.

46. Mishnah, *Pesaḥim*, 10:4.

47. Henshke, "Mah Nishtannah," 483–488.

48. The term "as it says" (כמה שנאמר) is extremely rare in our Midrashim (much more common is the term כענין שנאמר), but does appear in a fifth-century-CE Jewish Aramaic amulet (Kotansky, Naveh, and Shaked, "A Greek-Aramaic Silver Amulet"), a fact that may testify to its popular, non-rabbinic origin.

49. While there is no explicit tannaitic derashah on this verse (the Tannaim generally avoided interpreting these verses, see Kahana, "Six Interwoven"), there is circumstantial evidence that makes this reading likely. The sexual reading is implicit in the biblical context itself (the nudity in v. 7) and is explicated by various Second Temple readers. See Anderson, "Celibacy or Consummation." Compare the position of the early third-century Sage R. Yohanan recorded in BT *Yevamot* 103b.

50. Hezser, "Bookish Circles?," 82. For the thesis that the rabbis engage with Scripture chiefly as a memorized, oral text, see Stern, "The First Jewish Books," 181; Wollenberg, *The Closed Book*, 122 and passim. For the rabbis' use of scrolls rather than codices, which can hold multiple books together and are easy to handle, see further part 1, chap. 7, above.

CHAPTER 9. BIBLICAL INTERPRETATION IN SECOND TEMPLE LITERATURE

1. On the gradual processes of the Bible's canonization and the uses of Scripture in the Second Temple period, see Satlow, *How the Bible Became Holy*; Collins, *Invention of Judaism*; and Mroczek, *Literary Imagination*. See also the beginning of chapter 4. For a critique of the development narrative, seeking instead "to narrate the history of the Bible as an ongoing series of assemblages," see Lambert, "Multiplicity and the Idea of Scripture" (citation from p. 24).

2. See Kaufmann, *History of the Israelite Religion*, 8:293; Fishbane, *Biblical Interpretation*, 114–129. For another famous biblical midrash, see Balberg, *Gateway*, 20–21.

3. See vv. 2, 11, 17, 18, and Hayes, *Gentile Impurities*, 19–34. Note that the rabbis are aware that this prohibition does not appear in the Pentateuch. Thus, when a sage cites Ezra 10:3 as a source for excluding a child of intermarriage, he is met with the objection that this is merely *kabbala*, i.e., a non-scriptural tradition. See PT Kidushin 3:12, 64d.

4. VanderKam, *Jubilees*, 1166. On the passage see Balberg and Chavel, "The Polymorphous Pesaḥ," 323–324.

5. For the necessity of following the solar calendar, see Jubilees 6:32–37.

6. Vermès, *Scripture and Tradition*, 95. On the term, see Fraade, *From Tradition to Commentary*, 2–3, Bernstein, "'Rewritten Bible.'" For criticism of the term, see Najman, *Seconding Sinai*; and Mroczek, *Literary Imagination*, 118–119n15. Rewriting of canonical texts also occurred with

Greek classics. A clear example is the rewriting of Aristotle by Themistius in the fourth century CE; see Blumenthal, "Themistius."

7. For an enumeration of the techniques, see Fishbane, "Use, Authority and Interpretation"; and Bernstein and Koyfman, "Interpretation of Biblical Law." See further the pioneering studies of Baumgarten, *Studies in Qumran Law;* Milgrom, "Qumran Cult"; and Schiffman, *Reclaiming the Dead Sea Scrolls.* For specific examples, see Noam, "Early Signs"; and Werman and Shemesh, *Revealing the Hidden,* 51–71. On biblical exegesis at Qumran in general, see Mandel, "Midrashic Exegesis," with lit. cited in note 3.

8. García Martínez and Tigchelaar, *Dead Sea Scrolls Study Edition,* 569.

9. In a parallel preserved in *Mekhilta de-Rashbi,* 20:8, 148, this exegesis is attributed to Shammai the Elder. On the connection between Shammaite Halakhah and that of the Qumran sect, see Noam, "Beit Shammai."

10. The former style is also present in the Mishnah, as noted in part 1, chapter 1, section C.

11. García Martínez and Tigchelaar, *Dead Sea Scrolls Study Edition,* 81.

12. Fraade, "'Comparative Midrash,'" 7, 9, 10 respectively. See also Bernstein, "Midrash Halakhah at Qumran?"

13. Kister, "Common Heritage."

14. See part 1, chapter 3, section A.

15. See Shemesh, *Halakhah in the Making,* 72–106, and Shemesh, "Biblical Exegesis and Interpretations."

16. Fraade, "'Comparative Midrash,'" 12.

17. For a different take on this scroll, see Bernstein, "Scripture in 4QMMT."

18. See Shemesh, "Biblical Exegesis and Interpretations."

19. García Martínez and Tigchelaar, *Dead Sea Scrolls Study Edition,* 1289, with modifications.

20. For example, according to the Midrash, only the rapist may not "send her away all his days." This rule is not carried over to the seducer. For an explicit comparison between the cases in rabbinic literature, see Mishnah, *Ketubbot,* 3:5.

21. On this fusion and its implications, see Yadin, *Temple Scroll,* 1:368–371; Weiss Halivni, *Midrash, Mishnah and Gemara,* 30–34. See also Heger, "The Seducer and the Rapist."

22. See Noam, "Divorce in Qumran."

23. VanderKam, *Jubileees,* 566.

24. Hebrew *mastema* literally means "hatred," so that the "prince of Mastema" is the figure responsible for all evil in the world. This personification of evil is typical of Second Temple literature. Satan, originally just an "adversary" in the Torah, became *the* Devil who opposes God.

25. Cf. *Biblical Antiquities,* 32:2, where it is the jealousy of angels that leads to the Binding of Isaac.

26. See above, section B.

27. VanderKam, *Jubilees,* 566.

28. See VanderKam, 576–582.

29. Segal, *Book of Jubilees,* 45–46.

30. On Greek allegory and its Jewish and Christian adaptations, see Dawson, *Allegorical Readers and Cultural Revision.* On Hellenistic Jewish allegorical exegeses before Philo, see Niehoff, *Jewish Exegesis and Homeric Scholarship.*

31. *On Flight and Finding,* §54–§55 (ed. Loeb, p. 39).

32. *Sifrei Numbers,* §112, p. 121.

33. See Rosen-Zvi, *Body and Soul,* 79–88.

34. The Aramaic Targums bear out the same assumption. For example, Targum Pseudo-Jonathan on *ish ish* (e.g., Lev. 15:2 and 17:3), usually understood idiomatically to mean "whoever,"

parses the two words to refer to young and old men. On this, see Paz, *Scribes to Scholars*, 104–106.

35. Philo himself attributes the allegorical approach to an ascetic Jewish sect known as the Therapeutae: "They read the Holy Scriptures and seek wisdom from their ancestral philosophy by taking it as an allegory, since they think that the words of the literal text are symbols of something whose hidden nature is revealed by studying the underlying meaning" (*On the Contemplative Life*, §28 [ed. Loeb, p. 129]).

36. *On the Creation*, §157–§158 (ed. Loeb, p. 125).

37. Another prominent example is Moses at the burning bush; see *On the Life of Moses I*, §65–§70. On Philo's hermeneutic principles see Kamesar, "Biblical Interpretation."

38. On the Migration of Abraham, §89 and §93 (ed. Loeb, pp. 183 and 185).

39. For further analysis of this allegory, see Boyarin, *Radical Jew*, 32–36; and Fisch, *Written for Us*, 78–130.

40. See Romans 6:17; 1 Corinthians 10:6, 11.

41. For the different types of allegorical interpretation adopted by Jews and Christians in antiquity, see Hanson, *Allegory and Event*.

42. See Dawson, *Allegorical Readers*.

43. On "expounders of difficult verses" (*doreshei reshumot*) as allegorists, see the literature cited below in chapter 13. The Midrash states: "This is one of three things that R. Yishmael would expound as a kind of parable" (*Mekhilta de-Rabbi Yishmael*, Nezikin, §6, p. 270). This indicates that he only interpreted three things in this way, and, indeed, there is little allegory in rabbinic literature. On this phenomenon, see Kister, "Allegorical Interpretations." A comparison of mosaics and other artwork from late antiquity also reveals an absence of allegorical interpretation in synagogues and its presence in churches; see Talgam, "Similarities and Differences." In the Byzantine period, when Christianity was the imperial religion, biblical interpretation became the subject of imperial legislation. Justinian issued the following law in 553 CE: "It was right and proper that the Hebrews, when listening to the Holy Books, should not adhere to the literal writings but look for the prophecies contained in them, through which they announce the Great God and the Saviour of the human race, Jesus Christ. [. . .] Let them read the holy words themselves, therefore, in unfolding these Holy Books for reading, but without hiding what is said in them, on the one hand, and without accepting extraneous and unwritten nonsense they themselves had contrived to the perdition of the more simple minded, on the other hand" (Novella 146; Linder, *Jews in Roman Imperial Legislation*, 408–409). The beginning of the edict places allegory and typology in opposition to the literal-contextual meaning, but then it also rejects the "extraneous and unwritten nonsense," referring to the Oral Torah. In the Christian Emperor's mind, allegory and Midrash could not be further apart; one recovers the truth, the other conveys nonsense. For the development of the Orthodox Christian epistemology in the fourth and fifth centuries, see Letteney, *Christianization of Knowledge*.

44. A *pesher* already appears in the Bible itself, but is probably a later addition. See Isaiah 9:13-14 with Goshen-Gottstein, "Hebrew Syntax."

45. For the different kinds of *pesharim*, see Nitzan, "*Pesher* Scrolls."

46. For the Aramaic origin of the term, in the context of dream interpretation, see Daniel 2:4 and passim. Sometimes the technique appears without the term, and at other times the term does not designate this specific kind of interpretation. See Kaduri, "Biblical Interpretation at Qumran," and Bernstein, "'Rewritten Bible.'"

47. See Nitzan, *Pesher Habakkuk*; Eshel, "Two Historical Layers."

48. Qumran literature includes a whole scroll titled *War of the Sons of Light against the Sons of Darkness*. See Werman, "End of Days."

49. García Martínez and Tigchelaar, *Dead Sea Scrolls Study Edition*, 17, with slight modifications.

50. Note that Pesher Habakkuk interprets the biblical text as if it says *ha-kore* (הקורא) with the definite article, whereas the Masoretic Text only has *kore* (קורא). The former allows for a very specific reader to be intended. Still, a careful reading reveals that the *pesher* distinguishes the Teacher of Righteousness from "His servants, the prophets," and refrains from calling him a prophet. For the historical worldview and notion of gradual revelation that undergirds the *pesher* literature, see Dimant, "Exegesis and Time."

51. Similar to the previous footnote, Pesher Habakkuk apparently had a text that varied from the Masoretic Text. In place of *va-goyim* (בגוים) in the verse, it reads *bogedim* (בגדים).

52. García Martínez and Tigchelaar, *Dead Sea Scrolls Study Edition*, 13 [modified].

53. The Hebrew term that the Pesher translates as "traitors" is *'aritzei ha-berit*. Since *'aritz* in biblical Hebrew is typically a tyrant, it seems that this group persecuted the sect. Their designation as "traitors" may indicate that they were members of the sect that broke off from it. See Goldman, *Those Who Hold Fast*, 216, which claims that sectarian works indeed considered the Pharisees a splinter group.

54. Note that here too the biblical base text diverges from the Masoretic text.

55. García Martínez and Tigchelaar, *Dead Sea Scrolls Study Edition*, 21.

56. García Martínez and Tigchelaar, 13.

57. García Martínez and Tigchelaar, 331.

58. The *pesharim* mention details selectively. With regard to places, they explicitly refer to Jerusalem and other cities of Judea. When it comes to specific individuals, it never goes beyond allusion. Accordingly, the "Chaldaeans" of the original prophecy are replaced with the murky referent "Kittim." The Wicked Priest and Teacher of Righteousness are never named. The reason for this vagueness is that the interpretation is supposed to be a secret to which only members of the sect are privy, after its revelation by the Teacher of Righteousness. Outsiders will only understand the prophecy when the eschatological events actually unfold.

59. Bilhah Nitzan claims that Pesher Habakkuk on Habakkuk 2 offers three interpretations of the word *bogedim*, but these are actually three manifestations of betrayal in distinct historical periods. Menahem Kister (*Dynamics of Midrashic Traditions*, 203) argues that there are multiple successive interpretations in the Community Rule (and possibly in additional scrolls) but these are hidden interpretations that do not demand an explicit acknowledgment of interpretive pluralism, which is the core of rabbinic Midrash. See further below on "another matter" *(davar aḥer)* in the Midrashim. Note that in the final days of the Second Temple the (proto-)rabbis offered alternative *pesharim* to those of the Zealots regarding the Temple. This interpretive conflict could signify different things to different groups. There is good reason to think that, for the rabbis, it entailed a questioning of the pesher method and, more broadly, of the very conception of prophetic interpretation. For this reading see Kister, *Dynamics of Midrashic Traditions*, 224–226, and Ilan and Noam, *Josephus and the Rabbis*, 637.

60. See Nitzan, *Pesher Habakkuk*, 4–34.

61. See the introduction to part 2, note 17. The *pesharim* sometimes demonstrate a sophisticated method of extracting meaning from scripture, akin to what we will observe below in rabbinic Midrash. For instance, they interpret the two stanzas of biblical poetic parallelism as conveying distinct messages. See, for example, the Damascus document (CD 6:3–7.)

62. See Stern, "Midrash and Indeterminacy."

63. See Lieberman, "On Persecution."

64. Kugel, *Traditions of the Bible*, 15–19; and Kugel, *How to Read the Bible*, 14–16. See also Kugel, "Two Introductions."

65. For possible Greek influence on the development of dialogical rhetoric in Midrash, see Brodsky, "From Disagreement to Talmudic Discourse," 182; and Hidary, *Rabbis and Classical Rhetoric*, 137–139.

66. Steven Fraade shows that various ancient works which scholars associate with distinct genres actually share this combination of biblical exegesis with thematic organization; see Fraade, "Temple Scroll," 139–143.

67. Historical explanations can be found in Schremer, "'[T]he[y] Did Not Read in the Sealed Book'"; Kister, "Common Heritage"; and Mandel, "Midrashic Exegesis."

68. See Fraade, "'Comparative Midrash' Revisited," 12. Both Steven Fraade and Menahem Kister ("Common Heritage") account for the lack of running sectarian commentaries on legal parts of the Torah, given their existence for the prophetic books. Kister attributes this to the more traditional form of legal codes that predated the sectarian schism and was adopted by them. Fraade explains it as ideologically motivated: a running commentary would expose the exegetical basis of sectarian law.

69. "It is [the] ability to read a work analytically and decode it—be it Virgil, the Bible, or 'scientific' texts—that presents a characteristic of Late Antiquity: the texture of the tradition is used as the template for new creations that would be inconceivable without that form" (Formisano, "Toward an Aesthetic Paradigm," 283). Cf. Hadot, *What Is Ancient Philosophy*, 169–170. On rabbinic study house and literature as part and parcel of this general scholastic context, see Hezser, *Rabbinic Scholarship in the Context of Late Antique Scholasticism*. On Late Antiquity as the age of interpretation in the sciences too, see Netz, "Deuteronomic Texts."

70. In a lecture, Yakir Paz claimed that tannaitic literature contains the first instances of the Torah as a speaker independent of God or Moses. Phrases such as "the Torah said" and "the verse speaks" recur throughout the Midrash. While in the writings of Philo and the Qumran sect verses are attributed to Moses, in rabbinic literature the Torah has become an autonomous text, independent of an author, human or divine.

CHAPTER 10. THE SCHOOLS OF RABBI AKIVA AND RABBI YISHMAEL

1. Note that *Sifra* is the Babylonian name for this Midrash. In the Land of Israel, it was called *Torat Kohanim*, identical to the traditional name for the book of Leviticus itself.

2. See Lauterbach, "Name of the Mekilta." Lauterbach discusses the possibility that *mekhilta* is similar to *midda*, a hermeneutic principle, but he judiciously prefers the redactional meaning.

3. *Sifra* means "**the** book," because the study of Leviticus was of great importance in the rabbinic curriculum. In fact, in the Babylonian Talmud, the other Midrashim are called "the rest of the books *(sifrei)* of the study hall" *(Bava Batra* 124b), which originally included the *Mekhilta* on Exodus, before it received a separate name sometime in the Geonic period. See Lauterbach, "Name of the Mekilta," 171–173.

4. These names seem to indicate written compositions copied in "books," unlike the name "Mishnah," which refers to an oral recitation. Shlomo Naeh ("Torat Kohanim (A)") indeed argues that, unlike the Mishnah, the Midrashim were written down already in the rabbinic period. Since they were not viewed as competing with the Written Torah, they did not have to be kept solely oral. On the question of the writing down of the Midrashim, see below, chapter 16, section B, with note 30.

5. Hoffmann, *Zur Einleitung*. See section B below for scholarly antecedents.

6. See the table of terms unique to each bet midrash in Kahana, "Halakhic Midrashim," 27. It is important to note that although each school has its own mode of expression, most of the terminology is shared.

7. For a full list of Sages see Kahana, "Halakhic Midrashim," 30–31.

8. Hoffmann showed that unattributed derashot in these Midrashim are identical to *baraitot* attributed to R. Yishmael in the two Talmuds. The claim that R. Yishmael's school had a special connection with Babylonia is unsubstantiated; see Kahana, "The Importance," 512–513; Cohen, *Out of Babylonia*, 3–4.

9. These differences are accepted by most scholars today. For a dissenting position that claims that they did not characterize the midrashic schools but emerged much later, see Albeck, *Introduction to the Talmud*, 130–133; Harris, *How Do We Know This?*

10. *Sifra, Nega'im*, 8:1, 68b. The target of this specific barb is R. Eliezer, not R. Akiva.

11. See Lewy, *Mechilta des R. Simon*.

12. For novel ways of tackling this problem of anachronism with advanced computing, see Bar-Asher Siegal and Shmidman, "Reconstruction of Mekhilta Deuteronomy."

13. He called the latter by the generic title *Midrash Tanna'im*, because the textual reconstruction was so conjectural that he did not want to commit himself to the claim that the reconstructed text was identical with the lost *Mekhilta*.

14. On the Cairo Genizah, see below, chapter 16, end of section B.

15. The text reconstructed from secondary sources is set in a smaller font.

16. One Genizah fragment of *Mekhilta Deuteronomy* was incorporated into Hoffmann's *Midrash Tanna'im* (pp. 58–62), and several more were identified by Menahem Kahana; see Kahana, "Importance of Dwelling in the Land of Israel."

17. Kahana, *Genizah Fragments*.

18. Yitz Landes ("Rise of the Jewish Patriarchate") has proposed a connection between the loss of the *Sifrei Zuta* Midrashim and their ostensible refusal to accept the authority of R. Yehudah ha-Nasi (i.e., the absence of the Mishnah from these specific Midrashim). According to him, the patriarchate might have had a hand in determining what was studied and preserved.

19. Kahana's work relies heavily on the groundbreaking scholarship of Lieberman, *Siphre Zutta*.

20. See Kahana, *Sifre Zuta on Deuteronomy*, 99–102. This claim rests mainly on derashot that seem to be transferred from their original contexts in Exodus and Leviticus. See also Baitner, "Sifre Zuta Numbers," 59.

21. Support for this comes from derashot in other Midrashim of R. Yishmael's school, which indicate their transfer from a Midrash on Leviticus. See Epstein, *Introduction to Tannaitic Literature*, 634–643. On the origin of the sections known as *Mekhilta de-'Arayot* and *Mekhilta de-Millu'im*, see Shammah, "Mekhiltot That Are Appended."

22. For introductions to these Midrashim and their editions, see Balberg, *Gateway*, 106–113; Reizel, *Introduction*, 25–95; Kahana, "The Halakhic Midrashim." For more on the textual transmission and scholarly editions, see chapter 8, section B.

23. Note that these disputes are recorded in the Midrashim of R. Yishmael, which tend to be more inclusive than those of R. Akiva.

24. See chapter 1, section E.

25. For a comparison of this idiom with similar ones in the Hellenistic world, see below, note 60.

26. *Baraitot* (lit. "external ones") are tannaitic traditions studied in the bet midrash that were not incorporated into the Mishnah. For a list of the relevant verses and derashot, see BT *Bava Metzi'a*, 31a–b. Menahem Kahana theorizes that this maxim was deliberately erased from those derashot of R. Yishmael's school cited in the Midrashim of R. Akiva's school, and thus only survives in citations of these derashot in *baraitot*. See Kahana, "Halakhic Midrashim," 36.

27. See, e.g., *Mekhilta de-Rabbi Yishmael, Nezikin*, §1, p. 252, and the related analysis of Yehuda, "The Two Mekhiltot," 314–317. For a full list, see Glatzer, "The Linguistic Background," 127, 238.

28. This version is taken from the Cairo Genizah; see Kahana, *Genizah Fragments*, 127; and Boyarin, "From the Hidden Light."

29. See further below, chapter 12, section B.

30. For this principle and its applications, see *Mekhilta de-Rabbi Yishmael, Kaspa*, §20, p. 321.

31. See Kahana, *Sifre on Numbers*, 35–36.

32. On the two passages themselves, see Knohl, "Guilt Offering."

33. See Mishnah, *Bava Kamma*, 9:11; and Kahana, *Sifre on Numbers*, 33 and 51.

34. This does not mean that R. Yishmael's Midrashim rest on their laurels after finding a novelty. Counterexamples abound. Perhaps, as Menahem Kahana has suggested, this midrash belongs to an earlier, more extreme vision of his school's approach, which was later moderated. At any rate, it shows that R. Yishmael sees no need to go to R. Akiva's exegetical extremes.

35. Kahana, *Sifre on Numbers*, 35–36. See also Kahana, *Sifre Zuta on Deuteronomy*, 83; and Kahana, "Halakhic Midrashim," 27.

36. It appears at the beginning of the *Sifra*, probably because that was the student's first encounter with Midrash, given that Leviticus was the first book traditionally studied. On the *middot*, see Balberg, *Gateway*, 97–101, with lit. cited.

37. For an enumeration of them, see *Sifra*, *Nedavah*, 1:2, and Tosefta, *Sanhedrin*, 7:11. On the development of the *middot*, see Finkelstein, *Sifra on Leviticus*, 1:191–120; Kahana, "Halakhic Midrashim," 13–17.

38. See Kahana, "Kelal uFerat," 204; and Yadin-Israel, *Scripture as Logos*, 99–106. Note that the list is partial and omits several principles of Rabbi Yishmael's school that only appear in one or two places in the Midrash, as seen above with "the Torah spoke in human language."

39. For the enumeration of the *middot*, see Kahana, "Kelal uFerat." He concludes (p. 211) that the *baraita*'s main innovation, when contrasted with the *middot* attributed to Hillel, is the six *middot* regarding generalities and particulars.

40. This paradigm, though, is about victims and not offenders. See the bold proposal that the intended verse is Numbers 5:6, in Kahana, "Kelal uFerat," 37.

41. *Mekhilta de-Rabbi Yishmael*, Nezikin, §6 p. 269.

42. See Kahana, "Kelal uFerat," 186 and 204.

43. See Kahana, 188.

44. The Babylonian Talmud (*Pesaḥim* 22b) takes this a step further to include Torah scholars, thus making the homily self-reflective. R. Akiva equates Torah scholars with God, and his very own homily reveals the power of the darshan to add to the Torah's precepts.

45. These are most popular in *Sifrei Deuteronomy*, although they do appear in other Midrashim, even those of R. Yishmael's school. See chapter 12, section A.

46. It bears noting that for R. Akiva only elements that are not part of the conjugation or declension can be separated out.

47. Inclusions and exclusions are five times more prevalent in the Midrashim of R. Akiva's school than in those of R. Yishmael's.

48. See Tosefta, *Bava Kamma*, 6:18; *Mekhilta de-Rashbi*, 21:1, with the editor's note ad loc.

49. See Kahana, *Sifre on Numbers*, 33.

50. The order of these sequences is important for R. Yishmael's generalities *(kelalim)* and particulars *(peratim)*. For R. Akiva's inclusions *(ribbuyyim)* and exclusions *(mi'utim)*, in contrast, the order doesn't matter. Again, R. Yishmael cares more about the text's linguistic integrity. See further chapter 12.

51. *Sifrei Deuteronomy*, §122, p. 180.

52. On such derashot, see Baitner, "*Sifre Zuta Numbers*," 77.

53. See Tosefta, *Kiddushin*, 1:10.

54. See chapter 11, section C.

55. See Mishnah, *Ḥagigah*, 2:1.

56. See Yadin-Israel, *Scripture as Logos*. It is difficult to know, however, how much weight to give this midrashic rhetoric. Was it intended literally? See Rosen-Zvi, "Joining the Club."

57. In *Sifra*, *Beḥukkotai*, 8:12, R. Akiva argues against the notion of two Torahs.

58. Yadin-Israel argues that there is no underlying hermeneutical conception of the biblical text, because there is no real interpretation going on. Eisegesis masquerades as exegesis. See Yadin-Israel, *Scripture and Tradition*. For a critique of this thesis, see Gvaryahu, "Review."

59. Paz, *Scribes to Scholars*, 43–54. This principle is also employed in aggadic exegesis; see chapter 14, section B.

60. Paz, *Scribes to Scholars*, 105–127. Paz demonstrates that the debate between R. Akiva and R. Yishmael about doubling (e.g., *hikkaret tikkaret*) echoes Philo's debates with the Jewish Alexandrian literalists. The Greek translations of the Torah that Philo used preserved the doubled forms, and in the Greek translation they are far more grating than in the original Hebrew. Paz claims that Alexandrian Jewish exegetes were thus the ones who adapted Homeric interpretation to Bible interpretation, which were then taken up by the two midrashic academies, each in their own way. For Hellenistic Jewish Bible interpretation, see Niehoff, *Jewish Exegesis and Homeric Scholarship*.

61. See, e.g., Yehuda, "The Two Mekhiltot"; Shemesh, "'Mitzvah Ha-Teluyah Ba-Aretz'"; Kahana, "Importance of Dwelling in the Land"; Kahana, "Attitude towards Gentiles"; Kulp, "History, Exegesis, or Doctrine."

62. Rosen-Zvi, "Rereading *Herem*."

63. Heschel, *Heavenly Torah*.

64. Regarding divine transcendence vs. immanence, see Henshke, "Rabbis' Approach." On anthropomorphism, see Kahana, *Sifre on Numbers*, 676 with note 64, and 718 with note 153.

65. Arguing against the view of R. Yishmael the rationalist, Menahem Kahana has demonstrated that it was specifically he who mystically expounded the divine account of creation (*ma'aseh Bereshit*), while R. Akiva refused. See Kahana, "Six Interwoven."

66. See Hirshman, *Torah for the Entire World*, 13; Kahana, "Halakhic Midrashim, 26."

67. Kahana, *Sifre on Numbers*, 940. See also Kahana, 731n251. Kahana claims that the Midrashim of R. Yishmael's school include more varied source material, and one finds both universalist and particularist positions in them.

68. Rosen-Zvi, *Demonic Desires*.

69. On these aggadists, see Hirshman, "What Is the Place of Aggada."

70. Similar adaptations appear in other parts of the *Mekhilta* that do not stem from the shared aggadic source material. See Friedman, "Clouds of Glory," 282.

CHAPTER 11. THE MOTIVATIONS OF MIDRASH

1. *Sifra, Metzora'*, 9:6, 79b.

2. See Lieberman, *Hellenism*, 49–51; and Gottlieb, "Midrash as Biblical Philology." For less straightforward uses of this structure in polemical contexts in tannaitic literature, see Sagiv, "When 'Slaughtering' Means 'Pulling.'"

3. *Sifrei Numbers*, §125, p. 160.

4. Only in about sixty places does the Midrash state that the verse is to be left *ki-shemu'o*, "as it sounds"; see below, chapter 13, section C.

5. All of this is discussed in the introduction to part 2.

6. See Kahana, *Sifre on Numbers*, 1033.

7. Exodus 23:19 and 24:26, and Deuteronomy 14:21, and see *Mekhilta de-Rabbi Yishmael, Kaspa*, §20, p. 335.

8. Cf. Mishnah, *Ḥullin*, 8:4.

9. For conceptual differences regarding *din* in the two schools, see Rosen-Zvi, "Hermeneutic Lexicon."

10. Pace Kahana, *Sifre on Numbers*, 716.

11. For a parallel formulation in *Sifrei Zuta*, see Kahana, *Sifre Zuta*, 47–48.

12. Note that in other contexts logical inference is a legitimate tool for legal deduction, especially in the school of Rabbi Yishmael (usually with the term "you can reason" *[harei atta dan]*). It is only rejected when there is a need to negate redundancy and justify the necessity of Scripture.

13. See Kahana, *Sifre on Numbers*, 729n238 and 1258n45.

14. *Sifra, Aharei Mot*, 7:1, 84c; cf. *Sifrei Deuteronomy*, §76.

15. This appears about 110 times in the *Mekhilta*. It is mostly unattributed but a few times it's attributed to "the Sages." About 80 percent of occurrences are in a halakhic context. Rabbi Akiva's school uses "Could it be . . . ?" *(yakhol)*; see chapter 10, section A.

16. See Menahem Kahana's (*Sifre on Numbers*, p. 1198) fancy suggestion that it is actually a polemic against the four different New Years in the Book of Jubilees.

17. See how the Mishnah deals with this in part 1, chapter 4, section A.

18. See Cohen, "Halakhic Criticism vs. Literary Criticism." This phenomenon is especially prominent in the opening *sugyot* of various tractates, which are generally late; see Elman, "World of the Sabboraim."

19. Mishnah, *Bava Metzi'a*, 1:5.

20. Babylonian Talmud, *Bava Metzi'a* 12b. Literally, "a woman who is divorced and not divorced." For this category see Mishnah, *Gittin*, 7:4 and 8:2.

21. The parallel in the Yerushalmi (*Bava Metzi'a* 1:5 [8a]) offers a simpler explanation; see Weiss Halivni, *Sources and Traditions: Bava Metzia*, 37–38.

22. See Friedman, *Who Wrote the Bible*.

23. This is therefore a matter not just of canonicty but of theology. The Talmuds pursue coherence in the Mishnah too, but they sometimes admit that a mishnah should be split into different sources ("whoever recited this did not recite that"). The Written Torah presents a bigger problem because it is held to be all the word of God. *Mekhilta de-Rabbi Yishmael* indeed advances a theological explanation for the phenomenon of explicit intra-biblical contradiction. It compiles a list of such occurrences and asserts that "both of them were said in a single utterance . . . which flesh-and-blood cannot do" (*Ba-Hodesh*, §7, p. 229). Only the divine mind can comprehend—and therefore express—the contradiction as a unified whole. On this solution, see Henshke, "Rabbis' Approach."

24. See Seeligmann, "Beginnings of Midrash."

25. A Greek tradition maintaining that contradictions are illusory was adopted by Philo as well as Christian writers regarding Scripture (e.g., Justin Martyr, *Dialogue with Trypho*, 65:2). See Paz, *Scribes to Scholars*.

26. See, e.g., Endres, *Biblical Interpretation*.

27. See chapter 9, section C.

28. An exceptional external testimony to the rabbinic approach to resolving biblical contradictions and to their use of exegetical principles is preserved in a contemporary Jewish-Christian text, *Kerygmata Petrou*. See Baumgarten, "Literary Evidence."

29. For example: "'And this is the manner of the abrogation: He shall abrogate' (Deut. 15:2). The verse speaks of two types of abrogation: one is the release of land, and one is the abrogation of monetary debts" (BT *Kiddushin* 38b).

30. See also *Sifra, Emor*, 13:6, 101b.

31. Josephus, *Antiquities of the Jews*, 3:252–253. See Kahana, *Sifre on Numbers*, 1208.

32. The explicit exposure of contradictions is far more prevalent in aggadic contexts, apparently because there was less sensitivity outside of Halakhah. See Rosen-Zvi and Rosen-Zvi, "Halakhic and Aggadic Methodology."

33. The execution procedure of the Mishnah does not reflect any historical practice and is a theoretical construct. The contradiction noted in these midrashim does not seem to be a pretext to anchor

the mishnaic ritual to the text, but a real exegetical problem that stimulates the creation of the ritual to solve it. The strange idea of dropping a large stone on the person seems to come directly from Leviticus 20:2. For a possible ethical motivation behind the creation of the ritual, see Lorberbaum, *In God's Image*. On the complex, reciprocal relationship between Midrash and Mishnah, see below, chapter 15.

34. See Exodus 2:1 and 18:2.

35. For *meshunnah be-noyah* as "especially beautiful," see Kahana, *Sifre on Numbers*, 655. Contrast the preceding derashot, which interpret "Cushite" derogatorily. Cf. Tosefta, *Berakhot*, 6:3. Note that in the plain sense of scripture "Cushite" could simply be a different designation for "Midianite." But the Midrash dwells on the naming inconsistency, as is its wont.

36. For other versions see Kahana, *Sifre on Numbers*, 672–673. Kahana (*Sifre on Numbers*, 676n64) links this derashah to Rabbi Yishmael's anti-anthropomorphic bent.

37. Distinguishing between them is not always easy, because the very detection of textual problems depends on one's preconceptions and expectations, which are dynamic. On this see Levinson, *Twice-Told Tale*, 48–53.

38. For pre-rabbinic halakhic exegesis, see chapter 9.

39. On the traditions passed down among the Pharisees, see part 1, chapter 3, section B.

40. Patently rabbinic enactments, like washing the hands before bread, are tied to the Torah in tannaitic Midrash. The Talmuds differentiated between *asmakhtot* and institutions with genuine biblical roots, but the Tannaim themselves did not systematically do so. See De Vries, *General Introduction*, 69–95. On the gradual development of the concept of *asmakhta*, see Kahana, "Kelal uFerat," 214–215.

41. On this scholarly debate, see Yadin-Israel, *Scripture and Tradition*, 186–189 and 200. See further below, chapter 15, on the relationship between the Midrash and the Mishnah.

42. Mishnah, *Sotah*, 5:2. On this see Rosen-Zvi, "'Who Will Uncover the Dust,'" 95–128.

43. *Sifrei Numbers*, §75, p. 70, and *Sifra*, *Nedavah*, 4:5, 6b, respectively.

44. See Yadin-Israel, *Scripture and Tradition*.

45. See Nakman, "Tefillin and Mezuzot," 146; Cohn, *Tangled Up in Text*, 128.

46. See 2 Corinthians 11:24. But see also the dissenting view in Mishnah *Makkot*, 3:10.

47. We will return to the complex relationship between tradition and Midrash in chapter 15. Christian thinkers from the same period also assumed that scripture and tradition cannot contradict each other. See Letteney, *Christianization of Knowledge*, 48.

48. See Kahana, *Sifre on Numbers*, 796.

49. See Rosen-Zvi, "Text, Redaction, and Hermeneutics," 142–145, who argues that the exegetical list of exemptions is based on the Mishnah of Rabbi Yishmael. See further chapter 15, especially section B.

50. See Flatto, *Crown and Courts*, 164 and passim. Flatto discusses there also precedents in the legal traditions of the late Second Temple period. In contrast, ancient Near Eastern codes did not serve as binding laws, but rather as illustrative guidelines to aid the judge in reaching a just ruling. See Westbrook, "Introduction." Note that this is a distinct issue from the question of judicial discretion in the rabbinic system; on the latter, see Ben-Menahem, *Judicial Deviation*.

51. For the Roman context of this new conception of law, see Dohrmann, "Law and Imperial Idioms."

52. See Halbertal, "History of Halakhah."

53. When the Midrash wants to resist generalizing a law, it may describe it as a "decree of the King" (*gezerat melekh*), as if to say it must be left untouched. See Lorberbaum, "Gezereat Melekh," 24.

54. In a few places, the *Mekhilta* formulates general principles, such as, "Scripture equated men and women for all torts in the Torah." In other places, like here, there are independent derashot for specific laws. This lack of consistency may be attributed to different Sages or generations. On the use of general rules versus local exegeses, see chapter 10, section B.

55. See Exodus 21:26–27 with *Mekhilta de-Rabbi Yishmael*, Nezikin, §9, p. 279.
56. See Exodus 21:28 with *Mekhilta de-Rabbi Yishmael*, Nezikin, §10, p. 280.
57. See further below, chapter 15.
58. See Halbertal, *People of the Book*.
59. See Ophir and Rosen-Zvi, *Goy*.
60. *Sifrei Deuteronomy*, §93, p. 154.
61. See Rosen-Zvi, *Mishnaic Sotah Ritual*, 22–23.
62. For ethics as the basis for midrashic processes, see Halbertal, *Interpretative Revolutions*.
63. *Mekhilta de-Rabbi Yishmael*, Nezikin, §6, p. 270.
64. BT *Sotah* 17a.
65. *Sifrei Deuteronomy*, §227, p. 270.
66. On this derashah and the dissenting opinion of R. Eliezer ben Yaakov, see Noam, *Megillat Ta'anit*, 206.
67. *Mekhilta de-Rabbi Yishmael*, Nezikin, §4, p. 261.
68. *Mekhilta de-Rabbi Yishmael*, Nezikin, §5, p. 267 and §13, p. 294.
69. *Mekhilta de-Rabbi Yishmael*, Nezikin, §8, p. 277.
70. See Rosen-Zvi, "Measure for Measure." On the dissenting opinion of R. Eliezer, see BT *Bava Kamma* 84a; and Gilat, *Eliezer ben Hyrcanus*, 70.
71. See Zohar, "Reason and Justification."
72. *Sifra, Emor*, 10:2, 100d.
73. On the next world in rabbinic thought and belief, see Rosen-Zvi, *Body and Soul*.
74. On prophecy among the nations, see Rosen-Zvi, "Like a Priest Exposing His Own Wayward Mother."

CHAPTER 12. MIDRASH'S CONCEPTION OF THE BIBLICAL TEXT

1. See further chapter 9, section G.
2. See, e.g., Reeves, "Problematizing the Bible"; Lambert, "Torah of Moses"; Mroczek, *Literary Imagination*, 135–138. For the different meanings of "torah" in the Hebrew bible as testimony for processes of canonization see Schneidewind, "Diversity and Development."
3. On the application of these criteria to Midrash specifically, see Sommer, "Concepts of Scriptural Language." For a transhistorical application, see Viezel, *The Intention of the Torah*.
4. See chapter 11, section A.
5. For the assumption that every detail in the Bible is meaningful and instructive ("pan-didacticism") as a uniquely Jewish idea not shared by the Greek interpreters of Homer, see Kamesar, "Biblical Interpretation," 82.
6. See Najman, "Law of Nature."
7. On the exemplarity of the Torah in tannaitic literature, see Novick, *What Is Good*, 181–210.
8. See Dan, *Sanctity*, 108–130.
9. On whether the ideology of polysemy is explicit in tannaitic sources, see Yadin-Israel, "Rabbinic Polysemy," and Fraade, "Heart of Many Chambers." Either way, there is no doubt that in practice a plurality of opinions exist side by side in the Midrash. In tannaitic Midrashim this is an effect created by editors who juxtaposed multiple interpretations of the same text. Nowhere are multiple interpretations attributed to a single named darshan like they are in amoraic Midrashim. Monosemy becomes an identifying feature of Jewish medieval exegesis, both Rabbanite and Karaite, likely due to Muslim influence; see Frank, *Search Scripture Well*, 31–32.
10. See chapter 9, section G.
11. This point is emphasized in Yadin-Israel, *Scripture as Logos*, 2.
12. For this concept, see Fish, *Is There a Text in This Class?*

13. See Iser, *Act of Reading*.

14. See at length in chapter 11, section A.

15. For a description of these rituals, see part 1, chapter 5, section A.

16. *Sifrei Deuteronomy*, §289, p. 308. Yadin, *The Temple Scroll*, compares this to the Temple Scroll's systematic transformation of Deuteronomy's third-person narration into the first person.

17. See above, chapter 10, section B.

18. *Mekhilta de-Rabbi Yishmael*, Ba-Ḥodesh, §11, p. 243, with parallels.

19. See Epstein, *Introduction to Tannaitic Literature*, 233 and 534.

20. Azzan Yadin-Israel correctly writes that Midrashim of R. Yishmael's school assume that some verses aren't meant to be interpreted. I disagree with his further contention, though, that a verse must be somehow marked into order to be interpreted by this school; see Yadin-Israel, *Scripture as Logos*, 48–79. The vast majority of the midrashim of Rabbi Yishmael school consist of exposition of verses without any kind of marking. Yadin-Israel's discovery belongs more to the realm of rhetorical strategy rather than to hermeneutics. My emphasis on maximal extraction of meaning also differs from Yakir Paz's claim that the Sages adopted the literary approach of Homer's commentators, which takes into account aesthetics, rhetoric, syntax, context, and so on; see Paz, *Scribes to Scholars*, 307. This expansive approach can be found in some, mainly aggadic, derashot, but a staggering number of them ignore all of the above.

21. See Bartor, *Reading Law as Narrative*, 23–84. For the history of scholarship see Brettler, "Literary Sermon."

22. Cf. Tosefta, *Sanhedrin*, 14:1, and see Halbertal, *Interpretative Revolutions*, 122–144.

23. See Kahana, *Sifre on Numbers*, 793n2. On the *middot* see above, chapter 2, section B. On the variable weight assigned to context in Christian exegesis, see Young, *Biblical Exegesis*, 161–185. Note that the context under discussion refers to thematic portions of texts rather than entire books. Early rabbinic literature rarely discusses complete biblical books (see, e.g., m. Yadayim, 3:5) and never in interpretive context. It is only in Amoraic sources that we find evidence of systematic study of individual biblical books. See PT Horayot 3:7 (48b); BT Berakhot 17a; Avoda Zara 19a. See Vidas, *The Rise of Talmud*, 24–26.

24. Note that Rabbi Yishmael's Midrashim can include a contextual derivation even when the word *'inyan* does not appear. One idiom that reflects this: "Do I hear X? It therefore teaches. . ., Scripture is speaking about Y." On context in Medieval interpretation see Viezel, *The Intention of the Torah*, 201–205.

25. The principle also appears in R. Akiva's Midrashim, but Yonatan Sagiv argues that at least in the *Sifra*, which contains most instances of this principle, it belongs to a secondary layer; see Sagiv, "Studies in Early Rabbinic Hermeneutics," 120–126.

26. See *Sifrei Numbers*, §80, p. 76.

27. This phenomenon ought to moderate Kugel's claim ("Two Introductions," 92) that the Midrash is "versocentric," that it has only the present verse in its field of view. For more on this phenomenon and how it relates to the orality of rabbinic Torah study, see Stern, "First Jewish Books," 181; Wollenberg, *The Closed Book*, 163–192.

28. Derashot based on the juxtaposition of biblical passages also reflect contextual sensitivity.

29. For the first debate, see Boyarin, "Thoughts on Midrashic Hermeneutics," and Kahana, "On the Fashioning and Aims of the Mishnaic Controversy," with works cited. For the second debate see Stern, "Captive Woman," and Rosen-Zvi, *Mishnaic Sotah Ritual*, 232–234.

30. See chapter 14, section C.

31. Note, however, that it is read as a semantic continuation of the beginning of the verse, "Command the Israelites." This type of derashah acknowledges what precedes it and ignores what succeeds it. See Kahana, *Sifre on Numbers*, 1176.

32. For another example of this technique, see *Mekhilta de-Rashbi*, 21:8, p. 166, ll. 7–10.

33. A similar conception was discussed (introduction to part 2, section C) on a macro scale in connection with Daniel Boyarin's intertextual approach to Midrash. There, however, the recombinations do occur "backward" involving earlier biblical books, under the assumption that there is no binding order to the biblical books. One limitation that we have seen, though, is that the Torah is ranked hierarchically in its normativity above the Prophets and the Writings. See Rosen-Zvi, "Even Though There Is No Proof."

34. See Rosen-Zvi, "Protocol of the Court."

35. The Midrash also mingles King David with Agrippa; see *Sifrei Deuteronomy*, §157, p. 209, and cf. §162, p. 212.

36. See part 1, chapter 5, section C.

37. Cf. *Mekhilta de-Rashbi*, 22:21, p. 210, and on this midrash see further chapter 10, section B.

38. For this type of midrashic technique, see Rosen-Zvi, "Text, Redaction, and Hermeneutics," 109–115.

39. Halbertal, *Interpretative Revolutions*, 71.

40. See Kahana, *Sifre on Numbers*, 1230. There are indeed statements in rabbinic literature that seem to reflect such an opinion; see, e.g., Mishnah, *Ketubbot*, 4:5: "She is always under the authority of her father until she enters the huppah."

41. See Babylonian Talmud, *Yevamot* 76b.

42. The Mishnah itself states that the laws of Shabbat "are like mountains suspended by a hair" (*Ḥagigah*, 1:8). On the laws of moving objects on Shabbat as extra-biblical traditions, see Mishnah, *Sotah*, 5:3; and Rosen-Zvi, "Who Will Uncover the Dust."

CHAPTER 13. THE SELF-AWARENESS AND DIDACTICISM OF MIDRASH

1. See the introduction to part 2, section C.

2. Halbertal, *Interpretative Revolutions*, 177, distinguishes between first-order awareness, which recognizes various options that the interpreter must decide between, and second-order awareness, which theorizes about this selection. He only ascribes the first type to the darshan.

3. See chapter 9, section B.

4. See, e.g., *Sifrei Deuteronomy*, §190, p. 232, which swaps *'al* with *ke-negged*.

5. See Genesis 26:3, 6.

6. The discussion here concerns the Hebrew lexicon, but the Midrash also applies the tense system of mishnaic Hebrew to biblical Hebrew, thus using the biblical forms creatively. See Rosen-Zvi, "Can the Homilists Cross the Sea Again?"

7. See Mishnah, *Kiddushin*, 1:1.

8. *Mekhilta de-Rabbi Yishmael, Pasḥa*, §17, p. 66; *Sifrei Deuteronomy*, §35, p. 63. See chapter 11, section C.

9. See Kahana, *Sifre on Numbers*, 836n126.

10. See chapter 11, end of section D, for an example that clearly quotes God.

11. For further details see Rosen-Zvi, "Text, Redaction, and Hermeneutics," 84.

12. For the rabbinic ideology behind this midrash, see chapter 11, section E.

13. A different version reads, "but not from the Gentiles."

14. On the complex relationship between Midrash and rewritten Scripture, see Fraade, "Moses and the Commandments."

15. See Yadin-Israel, *Scripture as Logos*, ch. 1. For this example, see Yadin-Israel, 29–30.

16. See chapter 10, section B.

17. On this term see Baitner, "Sifre Zuta Numbers," 23–26.

18. See above, note 2 of this chapter.

19. In the Midrash from the Geonic period, Sader Eliyahu Rabba (chap. 15), there is an interesting theological reflection on the rabbinic insistence to distinguish between what is biblical and what is midrashic: "we have many things of grave importance, and (yet) scripture did not see it necessary to explicate them. Instead, it put them upon Israel, saying: they will make these distinctions in order to increase their merits."

20. This volume was published in Leipzig in 1899, and was subsequently translated by A. S. Rabinowitz into Hebrew as 'Erkhei Midrash (Tel-Aviv, 1922/1923). On the importance of this work, see Fraenkel, *Methods of Aggadah and Midrash*, 551–553.

21. See, e.g., Bar-Levav, *Mekhilta de-Rabbi Shimeon Ben Yohai*, 62–139; Kahana, *Sifre on Numbers*.

22. It has several variations, including *ke-mashma'o* and *ke-shom'o*, which seem interchangeable. The term also appears in the Mishnah and Tosefta, but its purpose there is different.

23. For a similar derashah see chapter 10, section B (beg.).

24. See Rosen-Zvi, "Midrash and/as Allegory."

25. See chapter 9, section E.

26. *Mekhilta de-Rabbi Yishmael*, Kaspa, §1, p. 319. See Sagiv, "When 'Slaughtering' Means 'Pulling,'" esp. 15.

27. A much later iteration of *ki-shemu'o* used by Saadia Gaon, *masmū'*, adds further clarity. In Saadia's usages, a translation or interpretation always follows the term, which tracks the Judeo-Arabic usage of *ẓāhīr*. See Ben-Shammai, "Tension," 45–46n33. One must therefore differentiate between the Midrash's use of *ki-shemu'o* and other and later ones. See further Cohen, *Rule of Peshat*.

28. For a different analysis of the term's function, see Yadin-Israel, *Scripture as Logos*, 38–41, 61–68.

29. The reliance on scriptural intertextuality allows the derashah to justify the necessity of the text while rejecting its basic meaning.

30. For another example, see *Sifrei Numbers*, §77, p. 71, and compare with *Sifrei Zuta Numbers*, 10:10, p. 262.

31. Compare *Mekhilta Deuteronomy* 12:6 with *Sifrei Deuteronomy*, §63, p. 130, and *Sifrei Numbers*, §103, p. 101, with *Sifra*, Nedavah, 2:2, 4a.

32. The only two exceptions involve derashot attributed to R. Eliezer; see *Mekhilta Deuteronomy*, 23:9, and *Sifrei Deuteronomy*, §213, p. 246 (see the editor's note to the latter, in which he theorizes that this derashah is from *Mekhilta Deuteronomy*!). It is interesting to compare this to the term *devarim ki-khetavam* ("words are as they are written"), which occurs twice in *Sifrei Deuteronomy*, both times in a polemical context and *after* the derashah they exclude (§104, p. 163, in the name of R. Yehoshua, and §237, p. 269, in the name of R. Eliezer). On the rarity of this term in tannaitic Midrashim, see Sussman, "History of Halakha," 57–58n185.

33. See Halbertal, *Interpretative Revolutions;* and Henshke, "Rabbis' Approach."

34. For Origen's justification of exegesis on similar grounds, see Visotzky, *Fathers of the World*, 28–40. For more on Origen and Midrash, see chapter 14, section B.

35. Certainly, each midrashic school regularly rejects opinions of the other school; see Yadin-Israel, *Scripture as Logos*, 1–3. The question here pertains to derashot produced by a single school.

36. So far as one can tell, the subject of *eino tzarikh* is generally the verse used by the derashah. Three pieces of evidence support this. (1) The prevalent continuation is "for it says," which is followed by a verse. (2) There is frequently a third stage (see immediately below) in which the Midrash asks, after a better derashah has been proposed, "What, then, does X [= the initial verse] teach?" Since the initial derashah has been discarded, the biblical words become superfluous again, and the darshan must justify them. (3) The verse is certainly the implied subject or

object of similar midrashic phrases that include a word from the root *tz-r-k*. All that said, in some cases the subject is undeniably the derashah itself. A clear example is when *eino tzarikh* decides between logical arguments without any reference to verses. But this distinction should not be overstated. Since the derashah is the main unit of discourse that cites the verse, no hard distinction between the two is maintained.

37. For the possibly exceptional usage of *eino tzarikh* as an alternative to the substance (and not only the method) of the derashah, see Kahana, *Sifre on Numbers*, 9n54 and 11n62.

38. In aggadic Midrash, this term has broader usage, rejecting both the source and the content of the derashah.

39. It is impossible to reduce simplicity to a single criterion, but there are identifiable trends. (1) An explicit statement or deduction from a biblical narrative > a derashah of a superfluity (e.g., *Sifrei Numbers*, §118, p. 139). (2) A derashah on a verse that explicitly deals with the subject matter > a derashah on a verse that doesn't (e.g., *Sifrei Numbers*, §25, p. 31, and §116, p. 132). (3) A derashah on the pericope under discussion > a derashah on a different passage (e.g., *Mekhilta de-Rabbi Yishmael*, Nezikin, §7, p. 271 [and many parallels]; *Sifrei Numbers*, §26, p. 33, and §70, p. 66). (4) A derashah on a single verse > a derashah that involves two verses, and it follows that a *hekesh* (analogy) from one verse > a *gezerah shavah* (verbal equivalence) from two (e.g., *Sifrei Numbers*, §39, p. 42; §64, p. 61; and §77, p. 71). (5) Exegesis, however farfetched > an inverted reading or other textual distortion of the verse (*Sifrei Numbers*, §98, p. 97). Despite the complexity of this calculus, I have not found any blatant inconsistencies, where a certain type of derashah is privileged in one instance and rejected in another.

40. While these are not minutes recording the discussions between Sages, they do preserve the scholarly practice of supplanting inferior derashot with superior ones. If it were the work of editors alone, one would be hard-pressed to explain why they always preferred derashot linked with named Sages (or consistently attributed them to them) and rejected derashot that were anonymous (or from which they had removed the attributions). Note that there is no reason to think that the various Midrashim of Rabbi Yishmael's school were edited by a single unifying hand; thus, this cannot account for the phenomenon in question. See further the next note.

41. The technique was probably then adopted and developed by editors, who arranged originally independent derashot hierarchically. The aggadic material shared by *Mekhilta de-Rabbi Yishmael* and *Mekhilta de-Rashbi* may bear a trace of this editorial handiwork. *Eino tzarikh* appears in *Mekhilta de-Rabbi Yishmael* ('Amalek, §2, p. 183) but not in the parallel in *Mekhilta de-Rashbi* (17:14, p. 124). On this see Kahana, *Two Mekhiltot*, 209–211.

42. For examples see *Mekhilta de-Rabbi Yishmael*, Pasha, §8, p. 28, and 'Amalek, §2, p. 183; *Sifrei Numbers*, §39, p. 42, and §134, p. 179.

43. See, e.g., Finkelstein, *Sifra*, 1:120–126; Lieberman, *Hellenism*, 185–201; Urbach, "The Derashah," 166–182; Goldberg, "Early and Late *Midrash*"; Kahana, "Kelal uFerat." For an analysis of this scholarly trend, see Mandel, "Midrashic Exegesis."

CHAPTER 14. AGGADAH IN THE MIDRASH

1. The centrality of Halakhah can be seen also from a comparison of the number of occurrences of the word *halakhah* (115 times) and *aggadah* (22 times). See Fraade and Simon Shoshan, "Halakha and Aggada," 464.

2. On the dating of the division of the *Mekhilta* into tractates and numbered *parashot*, see Kahana, "Halakahic Midrashim," 69n301. It is noteworthy that the *Sifra* is also divided into nine tractates. Shlomo Naeh has argued that this shows that the tannaitic Midrashim, unlike the Mishnah, were written down early: this division is known already from the third century CE, and

its breakdown into nine parts of nearly identical length only makes sense in a written document. See below, chapter 16, section B, with note 30.

3. The parallel term in Midrashim of Rabbi Akiva's school is "it teaches" *(melammed)*.

4. Nearby derashot, using the same *maggid* term, depict Pharaoh desperately trying to find Moses and Aaron in the middle of the night and the Egyptian people pressuring the Israelites to leave.

5. This is supported by the fact that in aggadic derashot *maggid* comes immediately after the biblical quotation, whereas in half of the halakhic derashot *maggid* relates to the midrashic exposition of the verse. See, e.g., *Mekhilta de-Rabbi Yishmael, Nezikin*, §17, p. 308.

6. *Mekhilta de-Rabbi Yishmael, Ba-Ḥodesh*, §9, p. 238.

7. *Mekhilta de-Rabbi Yishmael, Ba-Ḥodesh*, §2, p. 209.

8. *Mekhilta de-Rabbi Yishmael, 'Amalek*, §1, p. 190.

9. *Mekhilta de-Rabbi Yishmael, Be-Shallaḥ*, §1, p. 82.

10. See, e.g., *Mekhilta de-Rabbi Yishmael, Pasḥa*, §1, p. 1; *Shirata*, §1, p. 116; *'Amalek*, §2, p. 182; *Ba-Ḥodesh*, §2, p. 207. Note that, broadly speaking, the same Sages who appear in the halakhic sections also appear in the aggadic ones. (For a more nuanced picture, see Rosen-Zvi and Rosen-Zvi, "Tannaitic Halakhic and Aggadic Methodology," 813n121.) The distinction is therefore mainly one of genre and conventions. For distinctions based on different editing of the halakhic and aggadic segments, see further section E below.

11. For the thesis about the origin of aggadic derashot in the synagogue, see Heinemann, "Nature of the Aggadah." Other scholars (most famously Jonah Fraenkel in his *Midrash and Aggadah*) distinguish sharply between Midrash, part of the learned rabbinic activity in the bet midrash, and the synagogue service. For the difficulty in extracting data about the original setting from the edited derashot, see Stemberger, "The Derasha in Rabbinic Times." While Stemberger is right to encourage cautiousness in moving from literary products to social reality, some derashot do manifest characteristics of an actual sermon.

12. See above, chapter 11, sections A and B.

13. On this midrashic method, see Boyarin, *Intertextuality*, 27. Reading one verse in light of others echoes a method attributed to Aristarchus, "to clarify Homer from Homer"; see Paz, *Scribes to Scholars*, 43 and passim.

14. Interestingly, in Rabbi Yehudah's time Gnostic Christianity claimed that the Jewish God was a warrior god and that the Christian God was a peacemaker. The failure of the Jewish rebellions therefore reflected the impotence of their God. See den Dulk, *Between Jews and Heretics*, 82. Rabbi Yehudah would have been "responding" to this blasphemous accusation by delaying the display of God's heroism and power to a future that will come to pass. In his own time, this aspect of God could only be glimpsed textually.

15. For further explication of this derashah, see Rosen-Zvi, "Can the Homilists Cross the Sea Again?" See also Mintz, "Song at the Sea."

16. On the former, see above, chapter 9, section E.

17. Origen of Alexandria, *Homilies on Exodus*, V–VI, 284–285. For the Latin (the Greek original is lost), see *Patrologia Graeca*, 12:331.

18. For Origen's hermeneutics, see Torjesen, *Hermeneutical Procedure*.

19. On Origen's allegory and Midrash, see Boyarin, "Allegory and Midrash in Origen." On the thematic relationship between Origen's interpretations and the midrashic ones, see Urbach, "Homiletical Interpretations." There are few allegories in the Midrash, and they are often ascribed to the anonymous "expounders of difficult verses" *(doreshei reshumot)*. See above, chapter 13, section C.

20. Eschatological interpretation was by no means exclusive to Jewish darshanim. Origen's own hermeneutics admitted three levels of interpretation: the literal-physical, which deals with

the history of the Israelite nation; the psychic (discussed here), about the journey of the soul to perfection; and the mystical-spiritual, which is about the history of the Church and eschatology (see Hanson, *Allegory and Event*, 235–258; and Dively Lauro, *Soul and Spirit of Scripture*.) On the very first verse, Exodus 15:1, he comments on the emphatic doubling *ga'o ga'ah*: "He shall show us the second coming in glory, then the Lord is not only glorified, but his is also 'glorified magnificently'" (Origen of Alexandria, *Homilies on Exodus*, VI, 286–287). The Midrash also interprets this doubling as a reference to the past and to the future: "He was glorified and will be glorified" (*Mekhilta de-Rabbi Yishmael*, Shirata, §2, p. 121). For a comparative analysis, see Castori, "'Israel and the Nations,'" 122–124.

21. See above, chapter 9, section C.

22. While this presentation is a product of editing, my contention is that the editing was rooted in the practice of the bet midrash itself, because the darshanim read the contiguous verses in consistent fashion. See the recurring debates between Rabbi Yehoshua and Rabbi Elazar ha-Moda'i in tractates *Vayyassa'* and *'Amalek*, which represent consistent positions throughout a Torah passage.

23. The Gospels use a similar term, "to fulfill what had been spoken by the Lord through the prophet," to convey the realization of the prophesies through Jesus. See Matthew 1:22–23 on Isaiah 7:14.

24. Compare *Mekhilta de-Rabbi Yishmael*, Pasḥa, §14, p. 48.

25. This exegetical technique of linking verses from the Torah with those of the Prophets or Writings is commonplace in the Midrash. See the introduction to part 2, section C.

26. See above, chapter 11, section B.

27. On whom see Stern, "The First Jewish Books."

28. A similar verbal usage of *ḥazak* can be seen in Genesis 41:57 and 47:20, although there the vocalization supports reading it as a verb.

29. Some modern scholars claim that Sinai was in fact God's abode in Israelite belief; see Knohl, *The Bible's Genetic Code*.

30. *Sifrei Deuteronomy*, §343, cites many derashot on our verse but does not discuss the anomaly of "The Lord came from Sinai." *Midrash Tanna'im* ad loc. does discuss it but offers a different solution: "'The Lord came from Sinai' (Deut. 33:2). It should have said 'came to Sinai,' so why did it say, 'from Sinai'? Rabbi Shimon ben Yohai said, He came from Sinai to judge the nations of the world, who heard the Torah but did not accept it. As it says, 'I shall take revenge on the nations with anger and fury' (Mic. 5:14)."

31. The transfer of material from its original context to other places is a common feature of Midrash; see below, chapter 16, section A.

32. Alternatively, the derashah is based on the shift from singular *ha-'am* (the people) to the plural subject of *vayyityatzevu*.

33. The Midrash amplifies the enthusiasm by pointing to the parallel "we will do and we will obey" (Ex. 24:7) as evidence of blind acceptance of whatever God says.

34. The fact that *taḥtit* is usually associated with Sheol or the netherworld may deepen the sense of danger and threat.

35. The parallel in *Mekhilta de-Rashbi* takes the same position, but it has been reconstructed and probably integrates the Talmud's late derashah.

36. While Amram Tropper ("A Tale of Two Sinais," 153) contends that no fear or coercion is evident in the *Mekhilta* and is introduced only by the Talmud, I believe the *Mekhilta* is open to that interpretation. The reference to Songs of Songs 2:14 supports this interpretive possibility. While the biblical context calls to mind love imagery, the specific derashot that follow do not. "For your voice is sweet" is assigned to the period after the Decalogue, yet that period in the Torah (Ex.

20:14–16) witnesses the Israelites retreating out of mortal fear. The final reference to Leviticus 9:5, about the inauguration of the Tabernacle, may also point in this direction, because God's revelation there includes the immolation of Nadab and Abihu, who die trying to get too close to God. Desire and dread run through all of this like an alternating current.

37. The dialectic nature of Midrash is articulated by Handelman, *Slayers of Moses*.

38. See Boyarin, "Midrashic Hermeneutics," and Kahana, "Torah Study, Labor, Piety, and Realism."

39. Christian exegesis of the time also displays this dual approach of preserving the context and original sequence, and chunking and decontextualization. See Shuve, *Song of Songs*, 9. See further chapter 12, section B.

40. See Goldin, *Song at the Sea*, and Mintz, "Song at the Sea."

41. See above, chapter 10, section C.

42. See Schremer, *Male and Female*, 186–191.

43. Philo interprets this allegorically as the need to prepare the soul ahead of time for its redemption. The Midrash, for its part, is averse to stripping the verses of their historical sense.

44. It is even more striking because there is no reference to the Exodus at all in that chapter; see Hoffman, *Doctrine of the Exodus*, 55. The Midrash makes the connection based on the mention of blood. Modern scholars would not necessarily find the blood to be meaningful, because they assume that the allegory has an independent literary integrity. See further Rosen-Zvi, *Mishnaic Sotah Ritual*, 188–189.

45. One could read this as an anti-Christian polemic establishing the necessity of mitzvah performance for redemption. After all, Rabbi Matteyah ben Harash, according to tradition, was active in Rome (see *Sifrei Deuteronomy*, §80, p. 146; BT *Sanhedrin* 32b). However, on closer inspection the introductory question and conclusion are revealed to be the editor's additions. The original derashah ends with the quote from Zechariah. Rabbi Matteyah was discussing the mitzvah of the lamb's slaughter, and the editor made it about the commandment to take the lamb early.

46. See part 1, chapter 6, section C.

47. See, e.g., the extensive aggadah at the end of the laws of tzitzit in *Sifrei Numbers*, §115, pp. 127–129.

48. See Rosen-Zvi, "School of R. Ishmael."

49. The midrashic logic may be that the need to tithe properly will bring one to study.

50. See von Rad, *Studies in Deuteronomy*, 11–23.

51. See 2 Samuel 7 and 24:18. The parallel derasha in the Mekhilta to Deuteronomy includes an additional message about the obligation to seek out the Temple in the sages' own time—that is, after its destruction—a passage absent from the Sifrei. See Kahana, "When You Enter the Land," 151.

52. For examples, see *Sifrei Numbers*, §107 and §109, pp. 699 and 743, with Kahana's commentary. On this topic, see Shemesh, "Mitzvah Ha-Teluyah Ba-Aretz"; Kahana, "When You Enter"; and Rosen-Zvi, "You Shall Destroy."

CHAPTER 15. THE MIDRASH AND THE MISHNAH

1. See part 1, chapter 3.

2. See Sagiv, "Studies in Early Rabbinic Hermeneutics," 141–149.

3. Ancient coins and synagogue mosaics do not preserve any image that reflects R. Yishmael's opinion. On the connection between the Bar Kokhba coins and R. Akiva's opinion, see Katzoff, "*P. Yadin* 21," 569; and Sperber, "Bar Kokhba Coins."

4. For example, R. Yishmael's opinion could be based on the fact that *'arvei* is plural, and the minimum plural is two. No such derashah is attested, but it seems very reasonable and is in line with midrashic methodology.

5. See below, section B.

6. On the quotation of the Mishnah and the textual incongruities it creates here, see Baitner, "Studies," 93–96.

7. Mishnah, Ḥagigah, 1:8.

8. See, e.g., *Sifrei Numbers*, §153, p. 199.

9. *Pace* Jacob Neusner. See Cohen, "Jacob Neusner, Mishna, and Counter-Rabbinics."

10. For the scholarly debate over which of the two corpora is older, see the summaries in Strack and Stemberger, *Introduction*, 142–143, and Yadin-Israel, *Scripture and Tradition*, 188–189.

11. Chaim Milikowsky has found this division of labor in the writings of Josephus: "For our people [. . .] give credit for wisdom to those alone who have an exact knowledge of the law and who have the capability of interpreting the holy writings" (cited in Milikowsky, "Josephus," 160; see there, note 3). Adiel Schremer ("The Sages," 578n69) adds that it is reasonable that this description, penned in the 90s CE, refers to the Sages. These two fields of activity were also ascribed to the Sages by the Church Fathers. Eusebius, who lived in the fourth century, spoke of Tannaim as expositors of Holy Writ, and his contemporary Epiphanius described mishnayot as collections of "the traditions of the elders." See Newman, "Patristic Perspective," esp. 688 and 690. The Pseudo-Clementine Homilies, composed in the fourth century but incorporating earlier sources, also attest to this. In a letter included therein, Peter praises the Jews to James for their traditions dating back to Moses (see Mishnah, *Avot*, 1:1) and for their scriptural exegesis, especially the resolution of contradictions (on which see above, chapter 11, section B). See Baumgarten, "Literary Evidence."

12. See Kahana, "Mishnaic Controversy."

13. For example, disputation follows the rules of debate set forth in Yavneh; see Rosen-Zvi, "Protocol of the Court."

14. See Rosenthal, "Oral Torah." For firsthand descriptions, we must wait until the amoraic period; see PT *Horayot*, 3:7 (48b): "I expounded for him every aggadah aside from that of Proverbs and Ecclesiastes." See also BT *'Avodah Zarah*, 19a, which relates how Levi and R. Shimon the son of Rabbi Yehudah ha-Nasi were studying Scripture with Rabbi Yehuda ha-Nasi, interpreting it verse by verse.

15. A good example is the midrashic discussion of the red heifer in *Sifrei Numbers*, §123, p. 154 and *Sifrei Zuta*, 19:4, 302. The former presents a formulaic debate, "You reason . . . But I reason. . .," while the latter names R. Yose ha-Gelili and R. Shimon ben Hananiah as the debaters. Obviously, both versions were edited, so that even the one with names is no stenographic account. See further Rosen-Zvi, "Rhetorical Self." For further examples of this difference between these midrashic schools, see Baitner, *"Sifre Zuta,"* 130–135.

16. Cf. PT *Pesaḥim*, 1:5 (33a), and BT *Pesaḥim* 66a. For a comparative analysis of all these sources, see Fraenkel, *Aggadic Narrative*, 22–32.

17. Schwartz, "Hillel and Scripture," is based on the broader claim of Saul Lieberman (*Hellenism*, 59–60) that the verbal analogy *(gezerah shavah)* was initially a type of legal reasoning and only later developed into an exegetical principle. Schwartz also shows how later versions in the two Talmuds blur the lines between the juristic and midrashic bases for this halakhah. On the absence of Scripture from Hillel's rulings, see Gafni, *Jews of Babylonia*, 68–76; and Schremer, "'[T]he[y] Did Not Read in the Sealed Book.'"

18. A sample of the mishnaic style of debate is preserved in Mishnah, *Yadayim*, 4:3–4. The arguments are logical analogies advanced by jurists to determine the status of the lands of Ammon and Moab during the sabbatical year. The only verse included there is a threat, not an exegetical derivation. See Kahana, "Mishnaic Controversy." For the midrashic style of debate, in contrast, see *Sifrei Numbers*, §118 (pp. 923–924), where each Sage tries his hand at establishing

from the Torah that the firstborn domesticated animal sacrifice has the status of a peace-offering. The arguments and counterarguments are entirely based on Scripture.

19. This is the position taken by medieval Torah scholars. Sherira Gaon writes: "The *Sifra* and *Sifrei* are derashot of the verses, [demonstrating] where the halakhot are alluded to in the verses" (Lewin, *Iggeret Rav Sherira Ga'on*, 39). In a similar vein, Moses Maimonides writes in the introduction to his *Mishneh Torah:* "Rav composed the *Sifra* and *Sifrei* to clarify and make known the foundations of the Mishnah." This, however, does not exclude the possibility that in certain cases the version preserved in the Midrash is earlier, and that appearing in the Mishnah is secondary or adapted. See Friedman, *Tosefta Atiqta*, 75–77; Henshke, *Original Mishna*, 147–177.

20. On the history of these categories, see Halbertal, *Interpretative Revolutions*, 13–15. For a summary of scholarly positions from *Wissenschaft des Judentums* to today, see Hayes, "Intertextuality and Tannaitic Literature," 103–124.

21. See Urbach, "The *Derashah*." For an attempt to identify creative and conservative midrashim in Second Temple literature, see Nitzan, "Pesher and Midrash."

22. For an exemplification of this feedback loop in the laws of torts, see Westreich, *Four Archetypes of Damages*, and in the laws of Shabbat see Kister, *Dynamics of Midrashic Traditions*, 97–107 (summary on p. 106). For the earlier existence of this tension in Qumran, see Noam, "Creative Interpretation and Inetgrative Interpretation." For more on the anchoring function of Midrash, see above, chapter 11, section C.

23. See Werman and Shemesh, *Revealing the Hidden*, 192–193.

24. See Safrai, *Mishnat Eretz Israel: Tractate Ma'asrot*, 25–27, which claims that this derashah was maintained by the Sadducees to cozy up to wealthy merchants. The Hananites were a family of High Priests (Josephus, *Jewish Antiquities* 20:198) that included the very last one to hold that office before the Temple's destruction (Josephus, *The Jewish War*, 4:318–325).

25. Kahana, "Halakhic Midrashim," 34–35.

26. See part 1, chapter 3, sec. A.

27. The phrase "I am stating a traditional law, and Scripture supports me" occurs nowhere else in tannaitic literature. This seems to be an ad hoc formulation wedding Torah and tradition.

28. Although "Hence they said" is never attributed to a specific Sage, it is not necessarily the addition of the anonymous editors. Connections between derashot and halakhot existed long before the Mishnah was edited, and sometimes even in the mishnaic collections that preceded it. See Kahana, "Relations between Exegeses," 38, for two derashot in the Mishnah (*Ma'aser Sheni*, 5:13, and *Sanhedrin*, 10:4) that include the phrase "Hence they said." Yakir Paz discusses a similarity between this midrashic term and one used in Homeric scholarship of the time, which increases the likelihood that this is grounded in the study practices of the Sages. See Paz, *Scribes to Scholars*, 99–101.

29. The discussion here relies on the systematic work of Kahana, "Relations between Exegeses," which includes statistical data. For a collection and analysis of the sources, see also Melamed, *The Relationship*. This term has broader non-halakhic uses that will not be discussed here; for those see Paz, *Scribes to Scholars*, 80–97.

30. Paz, *Scribes to Scholars*, 99. Cf. Yadin-Israel, *Scripture and Tradition*, ch. 4.

31. For exact percentages see Kahana, "Relations between Exegeses," 33.

32. See chapter 3, section A.

33. Note that while Hillel based himself on juristic arguments only, as seen above, his disciples were already challenging a tradition based on scriptural exegesis.

34. See Kahana, "Relations between Exegeses," especially notes 97–99.

35. If anything, it stands in tension with it. The preceding establishes that the Temple alone is the locus of the divine presence and the sole place where the Tetragrammaton may be pronounced

as written. God being present in the synagogue, at the court, and anywhere someone learns Torah is the opposite of this.

36. See, e.g., *Sifrei Deuteronomy*, §181, p. 223, and §189, p. 229.

37. In its treatment of the cities of refuge, *Sifrei Deuteronomy* (§181–187, pp. 224–226) quotes the second chapter of Tractate *Makkot*. However, the language is slightly different and the mishnayot are being cited out of order. It seems like the editor tried to incorporate the mishnaic material into the derashot as best he could.

38. The first citation introduces the material with no marker; the second uses "Hence you say"; and the third "Hence they said." See *Sifrei Deuteronomy*, §112–§113, p. 173.

39. *Sifrei Deuteronomy*, §205–§210, pp. 240–244. Bear in mind that "Hence they said" is neither a guarantee of nor a condition for mishnaic citation. *Sifrei Deuteronomy* can cite a mishnah without the term or can use the term for sources other than the Mishnah. See Baitner, "Studies," ch. 2.

40. See Naeh, "Polishing Measures"; Paz, *Scribes to Scholars*, 83.

41. See Sagiv, "Studies in Early Rabbinic Hermeneutics," 33.

42. Sagiv, 22–24.

43. When the same halakhot are preserved in variant versions in the Mishnah and the Tosefta, *Mekhilta de-Rashbi* prefers the latter. When it does cite the Mishnah, it usually shortens and adapts the material. See Elias Bar-Levav, *Mekhilta de-Rabbi Shimeon Ben Yohai*, 243. She proposes that this Midrash uses the Tosefta because it wasn't as well known, and so the editor could more easily conceal his extra-biblical sources.

44. Elias Bar-Levav, *Mekhilta de-Rabbi Shimeon Ben Yohai*, 184–186.

45. See Epstein, *Introduction to the Mishnaic Text*, 746; Lieberman, *Siphre Zutta*, 11; Kahana, *Sifre Zuta*, 86. As these scholars show, the divergence between these and our mishnayot is very valuable for reconstructing the sources of the Mishnah and for comprehending its editing.

46. This is evidenced by the names of later Sages in those Midrashim and the fact that they are familiar with the final, edited version of the Mishnah. See Kahana, "Halakhic Midrashim."

47. See Baitner, "Studies." The authoritativeness of the Mishnah in some of the Midrashim of Rabbi Akiva's school comes across through abbreviated quotations. *Sifrei Deuteronomy* has forty-nine abbreviated citations of the Mishnah, and thus Menahem Kahana concludes: "The Mishnah was already well and widely known by the time *Sifrei Deuteronomy* was edited. The editors' intended audience was an elite class of exceptional scholars, who had absolute command of the Mishnah and recognized its authority" (Kahana, *"Ve-Khullah Matnitin,"* 26).

48. See Kahana, "Notes to the *Mekhilta*."

49. See the breakdown by Midrash in the second appendix of Kahana, "Relations between Exegeses."

50. Kahana ("Relations between Exegeses," 41) infers this from the fact that the halakhot primarily name Sages of R. Yishmael's school, whom the Mishnah never mentions. He suggests that at least some of this material is taken from the so-called Mishnah of Rabbi Yishmael. I find this thesis more convincing than Weiss Halivni's (*Midrash, Mishnah, and Gemara*) suggestion that R. Ishmael possessed no Mishnah and relied solely on midrashic technique. This would require assuming that all instances of *mi-kan amru* in R. Ishmael's midrashim are later additions—an unlikely scenario, as Kahana has shown.

51. Mishnah, *'Avodah Zarah*, 4:5.

52. See Kahana, "Relations between Exegeses," 42–43. On the larger topic, see Rosen-Zvi, "Rereading *Herem*."

53. These could have been other collections altogether or earlier editions of our Midrashim. See Ginzberg, "On the Relationship."

54. See Albeck's introduction to his commentary on *Bava Metzi'a* in *Shishah Sidrei Mishnah*, 4:59; Rosen-Zvi, "Text, Redaction, and Hermeneutics," 188–190.

55. *Sifrei Deuteronomy*, §224, p. 257.

56. Satlow (*How the Bible*, 267 and 275) presents it as a shift from Pharisaic traditions of their own authority to the exclusive authority of the Torah. As we saw in part 1, however, the Mishnah does *not* present extra-biblical traditions as a source of Halakhah outside of Tractate 'Eduyyot.

57. The midrashic link between the Oral and Written Torahs, which merged them, is what raised the ire of the early Karaites; see Erder and Polliack, *Golden Age of Karaism*, 75 and passim.

58. For the multiform nature of rabbinic oral texts, existing in several collections at once, none of them identical, see Cohen, *Synoptic Problem*; Shanks-Alexander, "The Rhetoric of Pedagogy."

CHAPTER 16. THE EDITING AND TRANSMISSION OF THE MIDRASH

1. See part 1, chapter 4.
2. See below, footnote 30.
3. See the beginning of chapter 3.
4. Paz, *Scribes to Scholars*, 66–67.
5. For example, Numbers 30 discusses the annulment of a young girl's vow by her father and the same for a wife by her husband, and many derashot in *Sifrei Numbers* (§153) are transferred from one context to the other. Another example is Deuteronomy 22, which sets forth the law on returning a lost object and on helping load and unload someone's animal. *Sifrei Deuteronomy* (§222–§225) freely transfers material between them.
6. Parallels in rabbinic literature were generated by transfer and integration at every stage of literary production: study, editing, and transmission. On this widespread phenomenon see Cohen, *Synoptic Problem*; Sussmann, "Parallels," esp. 12 with works cited.
7. On this general occurrence, see Kugel, "Mobile Midrash." Many derashot have the following structure: "X—why is it said? Because it says [elsewhere] y" *(lamah ne'emar? Le-fi she-hu omer)*. The Y verse is often the original context, which editors copied to the X verse. In many cases, however, the derashah cannot be found on the Y verse, where it probably originated.
8. *Sifrei Deuteronomy*, §151, p. 205; §155, p. 208; §187, p. 227; §210, p. 244; §220, p. 253; §240, p. 271; §241, p. 272; §273, p. 293.
9. For example, the NRSV translates *abbed te'abbedun* (Deut. 12:2) as "you must demolish completely," and Robert Alter translates as "you shall utterly destroy."
10. *Sifrei Deuteronomy*, §60, p. 125; §116, p. 175; §119, p. 178.
11. *Sifrei Deuteronomy*, §74, p. 139; §107, p. 168; §129, p. 187; §198, p. 317. Cf. §62, p. 128, and §66, p. 132.
12. *Sifrei Deuteronomy*, §5, p. 13; §9, p. 16; §12, p. 19; §19, p. 31. Cf. the Temple Scroll's systematic conversion of Deuteronomy from third-person to first-person divine speech.
13. *Sifrei Deuteronomy*, §69, p. 133; §74, p. 139; §138, p. 193; §141, p. 195.
14. *Sifra*, *Nedavah*, 9:3; *Tzav*, 2:4; *Shemini*, 1:5.
15. *Sifra*, *Kedoshim*, 2:1 and 4:3; *Behar*, 3:2 and 5:3.
16. On this derashah, see Kahana, *Sifre on Numbers*, 717; Kister, *Dynamics of Midrashic Traditions*, 58.
17. Although Philo allows for the validity of multiple interpretations, these still are placed within a hierarchy. See chapter 9, sec. E.
18. See Fraade, "Rabbinic Polysemy." This is not merely a technical matter, or solely an issue of ideological interpretation. Rather, the coexistence of multiple readings enables the editors to explore the various semantic fields of biblical terms and idioms. For example, consider the diverse

interpretations of Exodus 15:2, "My Strength (Ozi)": "Ozi is nothing but Torah . . . royalty . . . stronghold" (*Mekhilta de-Rabbi Yishmael*, Shirta §3, p. 126).

19. The opposite is also true: a single law can be derived from more than one verse. See Kahana, *Sifre on Numbers*, 916, and chapter 12 above. This assumption changes in the Babylonian Talmud, which assumes that every law is deduced from one verse, and every verse is a source of one law.

20. See Fraade, "Anonymity and Redaction."

21. See part 1, chapter 4, sec. A.

22. For the *Sifra*, Yonatan Sagiv, "Studies in Early Rabbinic Hermeneutics," has convincingly shown that most of the anonymous derashot post-date those to which a name is attached. The later anonymous exegeses tend to explicate every verse in order and provide literal definitions, whereas those attributed to specific Tannaim only deal with verses that raise some kind of problem. Of the 240 derashot in the *Sifra* that have parallels in other Midrashim, only twenty-one (~9 percent) contain a divergence regarding attribution. No generalization should be extrapolated from this to other Midrashim, because the schools and their editors might have operated differently. A thorough comparison of attributed and unattributed derashot remains a scholarly desideratum.

23. See Mishnah, *Sanhedrin*, 8:7, and BT *Sanhedrin* 73a.

24. Gvaryhau, "Tannaitic Laws of Battery."

25. For halakhic reconstructions of this nature, see Shemesh, *Punishments and Sins*, and Noam, *From Qumran to the Rabbinic Revolution*.

26. See Mishnah, *Bekhorot*, ch. 1.

27. See Kahana, *Sifre on Numbers*, 912–913.

28. Goldberg, "Davar Aher."

29. See part 1, chapter 7.

30. On the evidence for written transmission in the Midrash, see Naeh, "Torat Kohanim (A)," esp. 494–512. Naeh offers that the Midrashim were written down because, unlike the Mishnah, their explicit reliance on Scripture meant that they weren't perceived as a threat to the unique status of the Written Torah. Yair Furstenberg argues that a total, comprehensive prohibition on writing the Oral Torah appears only in the Babylonian Talmud and suits Sasanian culture, which, unlike Roman culture, was oral in nature; see Furstenberg, "Invention of the Ban." On the scholarly debate regarding the writing down of the Midrashim, see Kahana, *"Ve-Khullah Matnitin,"* 28n120; Kahana, "Halakhic Midrashim," 79n368; Rosenthal, "Devarim She-Al Pe," 709–724; Cherlow, "The Division of Tractates Nezikin and Kelim," 190n56 with lit. cited. The whole issue requires further study.

31. On the phenomenon of "coexistence" and its bearing on rabbinics scholarship, see Shanks-Alexander, *Transmitting Mishnah*.

32. On these editions, see chapter 10.

33. Menahem Kahana suggests that it is the ox on the divine chariot described by the prophet Ezekiel. See Kahana, "Editions of the Mekhilta," 502 with note 73.

34. This is quite close to *ki-shemu'o* and its allied forms, which have a common root, discussed in chapter 13, section C. On the declarative *shomea' ani*, see Kahana, *Sifre on Numbers*, 762, and Baitner, "Sifre Zuta," 21–22.

35. *Sifrei Numbers*, §107, ed. Horovitz, p. 111.

36. *Sifrei Numbers*, §107, ed. Kahana, p. 283.

37. For the rabbinic controversy over the bringing of sacrifices by non-Jews and its origins in the Second Temple period, see Knohl, "Acceptance of Sacrifices."

38. Kahana, *Sifre on Numbers*, 867. One can reconstruct the corruption as follows. The word *lomar* (לומר) is often abbreviated to *lamed vav* (לו׳), and this was misread as *levi* (לוי). With the word *talmud* severed from its natural *lomar* counterpart, it was dropped entirely, and a new derashah,

starting with the newly invented *levi*, was born. In the original, then, the first derashah ended with a negation of female service: "It therefore teaches *(talmud lomar)*, 'your father's tribe.'" A second derashah about "your father's tribe" and Amram came after it. The corruption spread because "your father's tribe" were both the final words of the first derashah and the initial words of the second derashah.

39. See Rosenthal, "Scribal Notations."

40. This argument was frequently advanced by Roman writers of Rabbi Akiva's era. See Ophir and Rosen-Zvi, "Separation, Judeophobia, and the Birth of the 'Goy.'"

41. On martyrology, see Boyarin, "Midrash and Practice"; on missionizing in ideology and practice, see Hirshman, *Torah for the Entire World*, 61–71.

42. Elias (Bar-Levav), *"Mekhilta de-Rabbi Yishmael,"* 123.

43. Lieberman, "Mishnat Shir ha-Shirim," 119.

44. See Tosefta, Ḥagigah, 2:2.

45. Kahana, *Genizah Fragments*.

46. See BT *Kiddushin* 21b–22a.

47. See Rosen-Zvi, "School of R. Ishmael," 47n25.

48. For a new computational technique for reconstructing *Mekhilta Deuteronomy* from *Midrash ha-Gadol*, see Bar-Asher Siegal and Shmidman, "Reconstruction." Recently, Menahem Kahana published another Yemenite collection of Midrashim from which lost segments of *Mekhilta Deuteronomy* can be reconstructed; see Kahana, *Derash Hamazhir*.

PART II. EPILOGUE: THE MIDRASH AND FUTURE SCHOLARSHIP

1. Rubenstein, *Talmudic Stories*, 249–250.

2. I have elaborated on this in Rosen-Zvi, "Rhetorical Self."

3. Lieberman, *Greek in Jewish Palestine*, and Daube, "Rabbinic Methods." See further Hidary, *Rabbis and Classical Rhetoric*, 175–182.

4. See Hidary, *Rabbis and Classical Rhetoric*, 197–198. See also Fischel, "Story and History."

5. See, e.g., Kahana, *Sifre on Numbers*, 997n153.

6. For a review see Fisch, "Written for Us," 13–16.

7. See further Rosen-Zvi, "Pauline Traditions."

8. Mishnah, *Avot*, 2:15–16.

BIBLIOGRAPHY

Adamczewski, Bartosz. "Are the Dead Sea Scrolls Pharisaic?" In *Sacred Texts and Disparate Interpretations: Qumran Manuscripts Seventy Years Later: Proceedings of the International Conference Held at the John Paul II Catholic University of Lublin, 24–26 October 2017*, red. H. Drawnel, 69–92. Leiden: Brill, 2020.

Adler, Yonatan. "Between Priestly Cult and Common Culture: The Material Evidence of Ritual Purity Observance in Early Roman Jerusalem Reassessed." *Journal of Ancient Judaism* 7 (2016): 228–248.

Ahrend, Aaron. "Mishnah Study and Study Groups in Modern Times." [In Hebrew.] *Jewish Studies, an Internet Journal* 3 (2004): 19–53.

Albeck, Hanoch. *Introduction to the Mishna*. [In Hebrew.] Jerusalem: Bialik Institute, 1959.

———. *Introduction to the Talmud, Babli and Yerushalmi*. [In Hebrew.] Tel Aviv: Devir, 1969.

———. *Shishah Sidrei Mishnah*. 6 vols. Jerusalem: Bialik Institute, 1952–1958.

———. *Studies in the Baraita and the Tosefta and Their Relationship to the Talmud*. Jerusalem: Mossad Harav Kook, 1943/1944.

Amsler, Monika. *The Babylonian Talmud and Late Antique Book Culture*. Cambridge: Cambridge University Press, 2023.

Anderson, Gary. "Celibacy or Consummation in the Garden? Reflections on Early Jewish and Christian Interpretations of the Garden of Eden." *Harvard Theological Review* 82 (1989): 121–148.

Ayali-Darshan, Noga. "The Origin and Meaning of the Crimson Thread in the Second Temple Period Scapegoat Ritual in Light of an Ancient Syro-Anatolian Custom." *Journal for the Study of Judaism in the Persian, Hellenistic, and Roman Periods* 44 (2013): 530–552.

Babusiaux, Ulrike. "Legal Writing and Legal Reasoning." In *The Oxford Handbook of Roman Law and Society*, edited by Paul J. du Plessis, Clifford Ando, and Kaius Tuori, 176–187. Oxford: Oxford University Press, 2016.

Baitner, Hallel. "*Sifre Zuta Numbers* on *Parashat Parah*: Studies in Language, Interpretation, Language, and Editing." [In Hebrew.] MA thesis. Hebrew University, 2011.

———. "Studies in the Mishnah of Sifre Zuta and Its Integration into the Midrash." [In Hebrew.] PhD diss., Hebrew University, 2018.

Bakhos, Carol. "Method(ological) Matters in the Study of Midrash." In *Current Trends in the Study of Midrash*, edited by Carol Bakhos, 161–187. Leiden: Brill, 2006.

Balberg, Mira. *Gateway to Rabbinic Literature*. [In Hebrew.] Raanana: Open University, 2013.

———. "Rabbinic Authority, Medical Rhetoric, and Body Hermeneutics in Mishnah Nega'im." *AJS Review* 35.2 (November 2011): 323–346.

Balberg, Mira, and Simeon Chavel. "The Polymorphous Pesaḥ: Ritual between Origins and Reenactment." *Journal of Ancient Judaism* 8 (2017): 292–343.

Bar-Asher, Moshe. *Studies in Mishnaic Hebrew.* [In Hebrew.] 3 vols. Jerusalem: Bialik Institute, 2009–2019.

Bar-Asher Siegal, Michal, and Avi Shmidman. "Reconstruction of the Mekhilta Deuteronomy Using Philological and Computational Tools." *Journal of Ancient Judaism* 9 (2018): 2–25.

Bar-Kochva, Bezalel. "On the History of the Judaean Desert Sect: Relations with the Hasmonean Rulers from Simeon to Jannaeus (143–76 BCE)." *Zion* 84.1 (2019): 5–57.

Bar-Levav, Avriel. "Libraries and Cultural Memory." *Henoch* 40.1 (2018): 95–102.

Bartor, Assnat. *Reading Law as Narrative: A Study in the Casuistic Laws of the Pentateuch.* Atlanta: Society of Biblical Literature, 2010.

Baumgarten, Albert I. "Invented Traditions of the Maccabean Era." In *Geschichte-Tradition-Reflexion: Festschrift für Martin Hengel zum 70. Geburtstag*, vol. 1, edited by Hubert Cancik, Hermann Lichtenberger, and Peter Schäfer, 197–210. Tübingen: Mohr Siebeck, 1996.

———. "Literary Evidence of Jewish Christianity in the Galilee." In *The Galilee in Late Antiquity*, edited by Lee I. Levine, 39–50. New York: JTS, 1992.

———. "The Pharisaic Paradosis." *Harvard Theological Review* 80 (1987): 63–77.

———. "The Politics of Reconciliation: The Education of R. Judah the Prince." In *Jewish and Christian Self-Definition*, edited by E. P. Sanders, vol. 2, 213–225. Philadelphia: Fortress, 1981.

Baumgarten, Joseph M. *Studies in Qumran Law.* Leiden: Brill, 1977.

———. "The Unwritten Law in the Pre-Rabbinic Period." *Journal for the Study of Judaism in the Persian, Hellenistic, and Roman Period* 3 (1972): 7–29.

Becker, Arjen. *The Secret of Time: Reconfiguring Wisdom in the Dead Sea Scrolls.* Leiden: Brill, 2023.

Belkin, Samuel. *Philo and the Oral Law: The Philonic Interpretation of Biblical Law in Relation to the Palestinian Halakah.* Cambridge, MA: Harvard University Press, 1940.

Ben-Dov, Jonathan, and Daniel Stökl Ben Ezra. "4Q249 Midrash Moshe: A New Reading and Some Implications." *Dead Sea Discoveries* 21 (2014): 131–149.

Ben-Eliyahu, Eyal. *Identity and Territory: Jewish Perceptions of Space in Antiquity.* Oakland: University of California Press, 2019.

Ben-Menahem, Hanina. *Judicial Deviation in Talmudic Law: Governed by Men, Not by Rules.* Reading: Harwood Academic, 1991.

Ben-Pazi, Isaiah. "Honi the Circle Drawer: 'A Member of the Household' or 'A Son Who Implores His Father'?" *Journal for the Study of Judaism* 48 (2017): 1–13.

Ben-Shahar, Meir. "Biblical and Post-Biblical History in Rabbinic Literature: Between the First and Second Destruction." [In Hebrew.] PhD diss., Hebrew University, 2012.

Ben-Shammai, Haggai. "The Tension between Literal Interpretation and Exegetical Freedom: Comparative Observations on Saadia's Method." In *With Reverence for the Word: Medieval Scriptural Exegesis in Judaism, Christianity, and Islam*, edited by Jane Dammen McAuliffe, Barry D. Walfish, and Joseph W. Goering, 33–50. Oxford: Oxford University Press, 2003.

Ben-Yashar, Menahem, Isaac Gottlieb, and Jordan S. Penkower, eds. *The Bible in Rabbinic Interpretation.* [In Hebrew.] 3 vols. Ramat-Gan: Bar-Ilan University, 2003–2021.

Benovitz, Moshe. "'Approaching a Sage': Dissolution of Vows and Dissolution of Commandments." [In Hebrew.] *Sidra* 24–25 (2010): 49–69.

———. *BT Berakhot, Chapter 1.* [In Hebrew.] Jerusalem: Ha-Iggud le-Farshant ha-Talmud, 2006.

———. *Kol Nidre: Studies in the Development of Rabbinic Votive Institutions.* Atlanta: Scholars, 1998.

Bergmeier, Aemin F. "The *Traditio Legis* in Late Antiquity and Its Afterlives in the Middle Ages." *Gesta* 56 (2017): 27–52.

Berman, Joshua. *BT Berakhot, Chapter 1.* [In Hebrew.] Jerusalem: Ha-Iggud le-Farshanut ha-Talmud, 2006.

———. *Inconsistency in the Torah: Ancient Literary Convention and the Limits of Source Criticism.* New York: Oxford University Press, 2017.

Bernstein, Moshe J. "4Q252: From Re-Written Bible to Biblical Commentary." *Journal of Jewish Studies* 45 (1994): 1–27.

———. "The Employment and Interpretation of Scripture in 4QMMT." In *Reading 4QMMT: New Perspectives on Qumran Law and History*, edited by John Kampen and Moshe J. Bernstein, 29–51. Atlanta: Scholars, 1996.

———. "Midrash Halakhah at Qumran?" *Gesher* 7 (1979): 145–166.

———. "'Rewritten Bible': A Generic Category Which Has Outlived Its Usefulness?" *Textus* 22 (2005): 169–196.

Bernstein, Moshe J., and Shlomo A. Koyfman. "The Interpretation of Biblical Law in the Dead Sea Scrolls: Forms and Methods." In *Biblical Interpretation at Qurman*, edited by Matthias Henze, 61–87. Grand Rapids, MI: William B. Eerdmans, 2005.

Berthelot, Katell. "'Not Like Our Rock Is Their Rock' (Deut 23:21): Rabbinic Perceptions of Roman Courts and Jurisdiction." In *Legal Engagement: The Reception of Roman Law and Tribunals by Jews and Other Inhabitants of the Empire*, edited by Katell Berthelot, Natalie Dohrmann, and Capucine Nemo-Pekelman, 389–408. Rome: Publications de l'École française de Rome, 2021.

Berthelot, Katell, Natalie Dohrmann, and Capucine Nemo-Pekelman, eds. *Legal Engagement: The Reception of Roman Law and Tribunals by Jews and Other Inhabitants of the Empire.* Rome: Publications de l'École française de Rome, 2021.

Blau, Joshua, and Yosef Yahalom, eds. *Rav Sa'adya Ga'on in the Focus of Controversies in Baghdad: Sa'adya's Sefer ha-Galuy and Mevasser's Two Books of Critiques on Him, a Critical Edition.* [In Hebrew.] Jerusalem: Ben-Zvi Institute, 2019.

Blidstein, Gerald J. "Rabbinic Legislation on Idolatry: Tractate Abodah Zarach, Chapter 1." [In Hebrew.] PhD diss., Yeshiva University, 1968.

Blumenthal, Henry J. "Themistius, the Last Peripatetic Commentator on Aristotle?" In *Aristotle Transformed: The Ancient Commentators and Their Influence*, edited by Richard Sorabji, 113–123. Ithaca, NY: Cornell University Press, 1990.

Boyarin, Daniel. "Allegory and Midrash in Origen." In *The Oxford Handbook of Origen*, edited by Ronald E. Heine and Karen Jo Torjesen, 100–117. Oxford: Oxford University Press, 2022.

———. *Carnal Israel: Reading Sex in Talmudic Culture.* Berkeley: University of California Press, 1993.

———. "*Dorshe Reshumot* Have Said." [In Hebrew.] *Beer-Sheva* 3 (1988): 23–37.

———. "From the Hidden Light of the *Geniza*: Towards the Original Text of the *Mekhilta d'Rabbi Ishmael*." [In Hebrew.] *Sidra* 2 (1986): 5–13.

———. *Intertextuality and the Reading of Midrash.* Bloomington: Indiana University Press, 1990.

———. "Midrash and Practice: On the Historical Study of Rabbinic Literature." [In Hebrew.] In *Saul Lieberman Memorial Volume*, edited by Shamma Friedman, 105–117. New York: Jewish Theological Seminary of America, 1993.

———. *Midrash Tann'aim: Intertekstualiyyut u-Keri'at Mekhilta.* Translated by David Louvish. Jerusalem: Shlaom Hartman Institute, 2011.

———. *A Radical Jew: Paul and the Politics of Identity*. Berkeley: University of California Press, 1994.

———. "Thoughts on Midrashic Hermeneutics: The Pericope of the Manna and Quail in the Mechilta." [In Hebrew.] In *Studies in Bible and Exegesis*, vol. 3, *Moshe Goshen-Gottstein—in Memoriam* [in Hebrew], edited by Moshe Bar-Asher et al., 41–52. Ramat Gan: Bar-Ilan University Press, 1993.

Brandes, Yehuda. "The Canonization of the Mishnah." *Journal of Ancient Judaism* 10 (2019): 145–180.

———. "The Sages as Bible Critics." In *The Believer and the Modern Study of the Bible*, edited by Tova Ganzel, Yehudah Brandes, and Chayuta Deutsch, translated by Avi Staiman, 207–227. Boston: Academic Studies, 2019.

Braverman, Nathan. "Biblical Calques in the Mishnah." [In Hebrew.] *Netu'im* 10 (2003): 9–17.

Bregman, Marc. "Mishna and LXX as Mystery: An Example of Jewish-Christian Polemic in the Byzantine Period." In *Continuity and Renewal: Jews and Judaism in Byzantine-Christian Palestine* [in Hebrew], edited by Lee I. Levine, 333–342. Jerusalem: Ben-Zvi Institute, 2004.

Brettler, Marc Z. "A 'Literary Sermon' in Deuteronomy 4." In *"A Wise a Discerning Mind": Essays in Honor of Burke O. Long*, edited by Saul M. Olyan and Robert C. Culley, 33–50. Providence, RI: Brown Judaic Studies, 2000.

Breuer, Yochanan. "Perfect and Participle in Description of Ritual in the Mishnah." [In Hebrew.] *Tarbiẓ* 56 (1987): 299–326.

Brin, Gershon. "The Firstling of Unclean Animals." *Jewish Quarterly Review* 68 (1977): 1–15.

Brodsky, David. "From Disagreement to Talmudic Discourse: Progymnasmata and the Evolution of a Rabbinic Genre." In *Rabbinic Tradition between Palestine and Babylonia*, edited by Ronit Nikolsky and Tal Ilan, 173–231. Leiden: Brill, 2014.

Brody, Robert. *A Commentary on Bavli Ketubbot*. [In Hebrew.] 3 vols. Jerusalem: Yad Harav Nissim, 2021.

———. *Mishnah and Tosefta Ketubbot: Text, Exegesis, and Redaction*. [In Hebrew.] Jerusalem: Magnes, 2015.

Brooke, George. "Qumran Pesher: Towards the Redefinition of a Genre." *Revue de Qumrân* 10 (1981): 483–503.

Brown, Peter. *Society and the Holy in Late Antiquity*. Berkeley: University of California Press, 1982.

Brownlee, William H. *The Midrash Pesher of Habakkuk: Text, Translation, Exposition*. Missoula, MT: Scholars, 1979.

Bryen, Ari Z. "Judging Empire: Courts and Culture in Rome's Eastern Provinces." *Law and History Review* 30.3 (2012): 771–811.

Castori, Michael. "'Israel and the Nations' in the Mekhilta of Rabbi Ishmael and Origen's Homilies on Exodus: A Study in Biblical Interpretation." PhD diss., UC Berkeley, 2008.

Cherlow, Elyashiv. "The Development of the Tannaitic Laws of Stolen and Lost Property." [In Hebrew.] PhD diss., Hebrew University, 2024.

———. "The Division of Tractates Nezikin and Kelim," [In Hebrew.] *Netu'im* 24–25 (2024): 175–191.

Chwat, Ezra. "Mishna Study among the Rishonim as Found in the Alfasi Gloss-Supplements." [In Hebrew.] *Alei Sefer* 19 (2001): 49–67.

Cohen, Avinoam. "Halakhic Criticism vs. Literary Criticism in Talmudic Pericopae." [In Hebrew.] *Asufot* 3 (1989/1990): 331–346.

Cohen, Barak S. *For Out of Babylonia Shall Come Torah and the Word of the Lord from Nehar Peqod: The Quest for Babylonian Tannaitic Traditions*. Leiden: Brill, 2017.

Cohen, Boaz. *Jewish and Roman Law: A Comparative Study*. 2 vols. New York: Jewish Theological Seminary, 1966.
Cohen, Mordechai Z. *The Rule of Peshat: Jewish Constructions of the Plain Sense of Scripture in Their Christian and Muslim Contexts, 900–1270*. Philadelphia: University of Pennsylvania Press, 2020.
Cohen, Shaye J. D. "Crossing the Boundary and Become a Jew." *Harvard Theological Review* 82 (1989): 13–33.
———. "Epigraphical Rabbis." In *The Significance of Yavneh and Other Essays in Jewish Hellenism*, 227–243. Tübingen: Mohr Siebeck, 2010.
———. "Jacob Neusner, Mishna, and Counter-Rabbinics: A Review Essay." *Conservative Judaism* 37 (1983): 48–63.
———. "The Judaean Legal Tradition and the 'Halakhah' of the Mishnah." In *The Cambridge Companion to the Talmud and Rabbinic Literature*, edited by Charlotte Elisheva Fonrobert and Martin S. Jaffee, 121–143. Cambridge: Cambridge University Press, 2007.
———. "The Rabbi in Second-Century Jewish Society." *The Cambridge History of Judaism*, vol. 3, *The Early Roman Period*, edited by William Horbury, W. D. Davies, and J. Sturdy, 922–990. Cambridge: Cambridge University Press, 1999.
———. "The Significance of Yavneh: Pharisees, Rabbis, and the End of Jewish Sectarianism." *Hebrew Union College Annual* 55 (1984): 27–53.
———, ed. *The Synoptic Problem in Rabbinic literature*. Providence, RI: Brown Judaic Studies, 2020.
———, ed. *What Is the Mishnah? The State of the Question*. Boston: Harvard University Press, 2023.
Cohn, Naftali S. *The Memory of the Temple and the Making of the Rabbis*. Philadelphia: University of Pennsylvania Press, 2013.
Cohn, Yehuda. *Tangled Up in Text: Tefillin and the Ancient World*. Providence, RI: Brown University Press, 2008.
Collins, John J. *The Invention of Judaism: Torah and Jewish Identity from Deuteronomy to Paul*. Oakland: University of California Press, 2017.
Cotton, Hannah M. "The Impact of the Documentary Papyri from the Judaean Desert on the Study of Jewish History from 70 to 135 CE." In *Jüdische Geschichte in hellenistisch-römischer Zeit: Wege der Forschung, Vom alten zum neuen Schürer*, edited by Aharon Oppenheimer and Elisabeth Müller-Luckner, 221–236. Munich: Oldenbourg, 1999.
———. "The Languages of the Legal and Administrative Documents from the Judaean Desert." *Zeitschrift für Papyrologie und Epigraphik* 125 (1999): 219–231.
Curtis, Edward L., and Albert A. Madsen. *A Critical and Exegetical Commentary on the Books of Chronicles* (International Critical Commentary). Edinburgh: T. and T. Clark, 1910.
Czajkowski, Kimberley, Benedikt Eckhardt, and Meret Strothmann, eds. *Law in the Roman Provinces*. Oxford: Oxford University Press, 2020.
Dan, Joseph. *History of Jewish Mysticism and Esotericism*. [In Hebrew.] 13 vols. Jerusalem: Zalman Shazar Center, 2008–2014.
———. *On Sanctity: Religion, Ethics, and Mysticism in Judaism and Other Religions*. [In Hebrew.] Jerusalem: Magnes, 1997.
Daube, David. "The Civil Law of the Mishnah: The Arrangement of the Three Gates." In *Collected Works of David Daube*, vol. 1, *Talmudic Law*, edited by Calum M. Carmichael, 257–304. Berkeley: Robbins Collection, 1992.
———. *The New Testament and Rabbinic Judaism*. Eugene: Wipf and Stock, 2011.
———. "Rabbinic Methods of Interpretation and Hellenistic Rhetoric." *Hebrew Union College Annual* 22 (1949): 239–264.

Dawson, David. *Allegorical Readers and Cultural Revision in Ancient Alexandria*. Berkeley: University of California Press, 1991.

De Lange, Nicholas R. M. *Origen and the Jews: Studies in Jewish-Christian Relations in Third-Century Palestine*. Cambridge: Cambridge University Press, 1977.

De Vries, Benjamin. *A General Introduction to Talmudic Literature*. [In Hebrew.] Tel Aviv: Sinai, 1966.

De Zulueta, Francis. *The Institutes of Gaius, Part II Commentary*. Oxford: Oxford University Press, 1953.

Dimant, Devorah. "Exegesis and Time in the Pesharim from Qumran." In *History, Ideology and Bible Interpretation in the Dead Sea Scrolls*, 315–332. Tübingen: Mohr Siebeck, 2014.

Dively Lauro, Elizabeth Ann. *The Soul and Spirit of Scripture within Origen's Exegesis*. Leiden: Brill, 2005.

Doering, Lutz. *Ancient Jewish Letters and the Beginnings of Christian Epistolography*. Tübingen: Mohr Siebeck, 2012.

Dohrmann, Natalie B. "*Ad Similitudinem Arbitrorum:* On the Perils of Commensurability and Comparison in Roman and Rabbinic Law." In *Legal Engagement: The Reception of Roman Law and Tribunals by Jews and Other Inhabitants of the Empire*, edited by Katell Berthelot, Natalie Dohrmann, and Capucine Nemo-Pekelman, 365–386. Rome: Publications de l'École française de Rome, 2021.

———. "Can 'Law' Be Private? The Mixed Message of Rabbinic Oral Law." In *Public and Private in Ancient Mediterranean Law and Religion*, edited by Clifford Ando and Jörg Rüpke, 187–216. Berlin: De Gruyter, 2015.

———. "Law and Imperial Idioms: Rabbinic Legalism in a Roman World." In *Jews, Christians, and the Roman Empire: The Poetics of Power in Late Antiquity*, edited by Natalie B. Dohrmann and Annette Yoshiko Reed, 63–78. Philadelphia: University of Pennsylvania Press, 2013.

Dulk, Matthijs den. *Between Jews and Heretics: Refiguring Justin Martyr's Dialogue with Trypho*. New York: Routledge, 2018.

Eilberg-Schwartz, Howard. *The Human Will in Judaism: The Mishnah's Philosophy of Intention*. Atlanta: Scholars, 1986.

Elias (Bar-Levav), Liora. *Mekhilta de-Rabbi Shimeon Ben Yohai on the Nezikin Portion*. [In Hebrew.] Edited by Menahem Kahana. Jerusalem: Magnes, 2013.

———. "The *Mekhilta de-Rabbi Yishmael* according to a Good Copy from the Genizah." [In Hebrew.] PhD diss., Hebrew University, 1997.

Elitzur, Yoel. "Language and Reality in Rabbinic Language and the Question of the Tosefta's Antiquity." [In Hebrew.] *Linguistic Studies* 5–6 (1992): 109–122.

———. "*Middah* in Mishnaic Hebrew and the Last Passage in the Tractate *Avoth*." [In Hebrew.] In *Sha'arei Lashon: Studies in Hebrew, Aramaic and Jewish Languages, Presented to Moshe Bar-Asher*, edited by Aaron Maman, Steven E. Fassberg, and Yochanan Breuer, Mosad Bialick: Jerusalem, 2007, vol. 2, 19–30.

Elman, Yaakov. *Authority and Tradition: Toseftan Baraitot in Talmudic Babylonia*. Hoboken, NJ: Ktav, 1994.

———. "Order, Sequence, and Selection: The Mishnah's Anthological Choices." In *The Anthology in Jewish Literature*, edited by David Stern, 53–80. New York: Oxford University Press, 2004.

———. "The Rebirth of Omnisignificant Exegesis in the Nineteenth and Twentieth Centuries." *Jewish Studies, an Internet Journal* 2 (2003): 199–249.

———. "The World of the 'Sabboraim': Cultural Aspects of Post-Redactional Additions to the Bavli." In *Creation and Composition: The Contribution of the Bavli Redactors (Stammaim) to the Aggada*, Tubingen: Mohr Siebeck, 2003, 384–415.

Elman, Yaakov, and Mahnaz Moazami. "The Scholasticization of Religion: From Qumran to Ctesiphon." In *From Scrolls to Traditions: A Festschrift Honoring Lawrence H. Schiffman*, edited by Stuart S. Miller et al., 66–98. Leiden: Brill, 2021.

Elon, Menachem. *Jewish Law: History, Sources, Principles*. Translated by Bernard Auerbach and Melvin J. Sykes. 4 vols. Philadelphia: Jewish Publication Society, 1993.

Endres, John C. *Biblical Interpretation in the Book of Jubilees*. Washington, DC: Catholic Biblical Association of America, 1987.

Epstein, Jacob Nahum. *Introduction to Tannaitic Literature*. [In Hebrew.] Edited by Ezra Zion Melamed. Jerusalem: Magnes, 1957.

———. *Introduction to the Mishnaic Text*. [In Hebrew.] 3rd ed. 2 vols. Jerusalem: Magnes, 2000.

———. "Mechilta and Sifre in the Works of Maimonides." [In Hebrew.] *Tarbiẓ* 6 (1935): 343–382, 432.

———. "*Sifre Zuta, Parashat Parah*." [In Hebrew.] *Tarbiẓ* 1 (1929): 46–78.

Erder, Yoram, and Meira Polliack. *The Golden Age of Karaism: A Hebrew Anthology of Karaite Literature from the Ninth to the Twelfth Centuries*. [In Hebrew.] Jerusalem: Karmel, 2022.

Eshel, Hanan. "The Two Historical Layers of Pesher Habakkuk." In *Northern Lights on the Dead Sea Scrolls*, edited by Anders Klostergaard Petersen et al., 107–117. Leiden: Brill, 2009.

Finkelstein, Louis. *Introduction to the Treatise Abot and Abot of Rabbi Nathan*. [In Hebrew.] New York: Jewish Theological Seminary, 1950.

———, ed. *Sifra on Leviticus*. [In Hebrew.] 5 vols. New York: JTS, 1983–1991.

Fisch, Yael. "Book Review: The Closed Book: How the Rabbis Taught the Jews (Not) to Read the Bible, By Rebecca Scharbach Wollenberg." *Journal of the American Academy of Religion* 20 (2024): 1–3.

———. "The Origins of Oral Torah: A New Pauline Perspective." *JSJ* 51 (2020): 43–66.

———. *Written for Us: Paul's Interpretation of Scripture and the History of Midrash*. Brill: Leiden, 2022.

Fischel, Henry. "Story and History: Observations on Greco-Roman Rhetoric and Pharisaism." In *Essays in Greco-Roman and Related Talmudic Literature*, 443–472. New York: Ktav, 1977.

Fish, Stanley. *Is There a Text in This Class? The Authority of Interpretive Communities*. Cambridge, MA: Harvard University Press, 1980.

Fishbane, Michael. *Biblical Interpretation in Ancient Israel*. Oxford: Clarendon, 1985.

———, ed. *The Midrashic Imagination: Jewish Exegesis, Thought, and History*. Albany: SUNY Press, 1993.

———. "Use, Authority and Interpretation of Mikra at Qumran." In *Mikra: Text, Translation, Reading, and Interpretation of the Hebrew Bible in Ancient Judaism and Early Christianity*, edited by Martin Jan Mulder and Harry Sysling, 339–376. Philadelphia: Fortress, 1988.

Flatto, David C. *The Crown and the Courts: Separation of Powers in the Early Jewish Imagination*. Cambridge, MA: Harvard University Press, 2020.

Fonrobert, Charlotte Elisheva. "The *Didascalia Apostolorum*: A Mishnah for the Disciples of Jesus." *Journal of Early Christian Studies* 9 (2001): 483–509.

———. "The Semiotics of the Sexed Body in Early Halakhic Discourse." In *How Should Rabbinic Literature Be Read in the Modern World?*, edited by Matthew Kraus, 79–104. Piscataway, NJ: Gorgias, 2006.

Formisano, Marco. "Toward an Aesthetic Paradigm of Late Antiquity." *Antiquité Tardive* 15 (2007): 277–284.

Fox, Harry, Tirzah Meacham, and Diane Kriger, eds. *Introducing Tosefta: Textual, Intratextual, and Intertextual Studies*. Hoboken, NJ: Ktav, 1999.

Fraade, Steven D. "Anonymity and Redaction in Legal Midrash: A Preliminary Probe." In *Melekhet Mahshevet: Studies in the Redaction and Development of Talmudic Literature*, edited by Aaron Amit and Aharon Shemesh, 9*–29*. Ramat-Gan: Bar-Ilan University Press, 2011.

———. "'Comparative Midrash' Revisited: The Case of the Dead Sea Scrolls and Rabbinic Midrash." In *Agendas for the Study of Midrash in the Twenty-First Century*, edited by Marc Lee Raphael, 4–17. Williamsburg, VA: College of William and Mary, 1999.

———. *From Tradition to Commentary: Torah and Its Interpretation in the Midrash Sifre to Deuteronomy*. Albany: SUNY Press, 1991.

———. "'A Heart of Many Chambers': The Theological Hermeneutics of Legal Multivocality." *Harvard Theological Review* 108 (2015): 113–128.

———. "The Innovation of Nominalized Verbs in Mishnaic Hebrew as Marking an Innovation of Concept." In *Studies in Mishnaic Hebrew and Related Fields*, edited by Elitzur A. Bar-Asher Siegal and Aaron J. Koller, 129–148. Jerusalem: Magnes, 2017.

———. "Interpretive Authority in the Studying Community at Qumran." *Journal of Jewish Studies* 44 (1993): 46–69.

———. *Legal Fictions: Studies of Law and Narrative in the Discursive Worlds of Ancient Jewish Sectarians and Sages*. Leiden: Brill, 2011.

———. "Looking for Legal Midrash at Qumran." In *Biblical Perspectives: Early Use and Interpretation of the Bible in Light of the Dead Sea Scrolls*, edited by Michael E. Stone and Esther G. Chazon, 59–79. Leiden: Brill, 1998.

———. "Moses and the Commandments: Can Hermeneutics, History, And Rhetoric Be Disentangled?" In *The Idea of Biblical Interpretation: Essays in Honor of James L. Kugel*, edited by Hindy Najman and Judith H. Newman, 399–422. Leiden: Brill, 2004.

———. *Multilingualism and Translation in Ancient Judaism: Before and After Babel*. Cambridge: Cambridge University Press, 2023.

———. "Rabbinic Polysemy and Pluralism Revisited: Between Praxis and Thematization." *AJS Review* 31 (2007): 1–40.

———. "The Temple Scroll as Rewritten Bible: When Genres Bend." In *Ha-Ish Moshe: Studies in Scriptural Interpretation in the Dead Sea Scrolls*, 136–154. Leiden: Brill, 2018.

Fraade, Steven D., and Moshe Simon-Shoshan. "Halakha and Aggada in Tannaic Sources." In *The Literature of the Sages: A Re-Visioning*, edited by Christine Hayes, 463–543. Leiden: Brill, 2022.

Fraenkel, Jonah. "The Aggadah in the Mishnah." [In Hebrew.] In *Talmudic Studies* [in Hebrew], vol. 3, edited by Yaacov Sussman and David Rosenthal, 655–683. Jerusalem: Magnes, 2005.

———. *Aggadic Narrative, Harmony of Form and Content*. [In Hebrew.] Tel Aviv: Ha-Kibbutz Ha-Me'uḥad, 2001.

———. *Methods of Aggadah and Midrash*. [In Hebrew.] Masadah: Yad la-Talmud, 1991.

———. *Midrash and Aggadah*. [In Hebrew.] 3 vols. Tel Aviv: Open University, 1996.

Frank, Daniel. *Search Scripture Well: Karaite Exegetes and the Origin of the Jewish Biblical Commentary in the Islamic East*. Leiden: Brill, 2004.

Frankel, Zacharias. *Darkhei ha-Mishnah ve-Darkhei ha-Sefarim ha-Nilvim Eleha, Tosefta, Mekhilta, Sifra, Sifrei, Ḥelek Rishon, Petiḥah le-ha-Mishnah*. Leipzig: H. Hunger 1859–1867.

Friedman, Richard Elliott. *Who Wrote the Bible?* New York: Summit, 1987.

Friedman, Shamma. "Clouds of Glory: Between Rabbi Eliezer and Rabbi Akiva." [In Hebrew.] In *The Wisdom of the Sages: Biblical Commentary in Rabbinic Literature—Presented to Hananel Mack* [in Hebrew], edited by Avigdor Shinan and Israel Jacob Yuval, 269–293. Jerusalem: Carmel, 2019.

———. "The Holy Scriptures Defile the Hands: The Transformation of a Biblical Concept in Rabbinic Theology." In *Minḥah le-Naḥum—Biblical and Other Studies Presented to Nahum M. Sarna in Honour of his 70th Birthday*, edited by Marc Brettler and Michael Fishbane, 117–132. Sheffield, UK: JSOT, 1993.

———. "The Primacy of Tosefta in Mishnah-Tosefta Parallels: Shabbat 16:1." [In Hebrew.] *Tarbiẓ* 62 (1993): 313–338.

———. *Studies in the Language and Terminology of Talmudic Literature*. [In Hebrew.] Jerusalem: Academy of the Hebrew Language, 2014.

———. *Talmud Arukh, BT Bava Meẓi'a VI*. 2 vols. Jerusalem: Jewish Theological Seminary of America, 1990–1996.

———. *Tosefta Atiqta: Pesaḥ Rishon*. Ramat-Gan: Bar-Ilan University, 2002.

Fuchs, Uziel. "The Reception of the Mishnah from the Geonic Period to the Age of Print." In *What Is the Mishnah? The State of the Question*, edited by Shaye J. D. Cohen, 471–488. Boston: Harvard University Press, 2023.

———. "Review of Yaacov Sussmann, *Oral Law Taken Literally: The Power of the Tip of a Yod*, Jerusalem: Magnes, 2019." *Jewish Studies* 55 (2021): 209–229.

Furstenberg, Yair. "Acquisition and Possession (Hazaqah): Tannaitic Law between Changing Legal Contexts." [In Hebrew.] *Shenaton ha-Mishpat ha-Ivri* (forthcoming).

———. "The Christianization of Proselyte Baptism in Rabbinic Tradition." In *Coping with Religious Change in the Late-Antique Eastern Mediterranean*, edited by Eduard Iricinschi and Chrysi Kotsifou. Tübingen: Mohr Siebeck (forthcoming).

———. "Early Redactions of Purities: Re-Examination of Mishnah Source Criticism." *Tarbiẓ* 80 (2022): 507–537.

———. "Eating in a State of Purity during the Tannaitic period: Tractate Teharot and Its Historical and Cultural Contexts." [In Hebrew.] PhD diss., Hebrew University, 2010.

———. "From Tradition to Controversy: New Modes of Transmission in the Teachings of Early Rabbis." [In Hebrew.] *Tarbiẓ* 85 (2018): 587–641.

———. "The History of the Temple Mishnayot: On the Sources of Tractate *Shekalim* 5–8." In *Talmudic Studies* [in Hebrew], vol. 4, edited by Yoav Rosenthal and Shlomo Naeh, 445–518. Jerusalem: Mandel Institute of Jewish Studies, 2024.

———. "Imperialism and the Creation of Local Law: The Case of Rabbinic Law." In *Legal Engagement: The Reception of Roman Law and Tribunals by Jews and Other Inhabitants of the Empire*, edited by Katell Berthelot, Natalie Dohrmann, and Capucine Nemo-Pekelman, 271–300. Rome: Publications de l'École française de Rome, 2021.

———. "The Invention of the Ban against Writing Oral Torah in the Babylonian Talmud." *AJS Review* 46 (2022): 131–150.

———. "The Literary Evolution of the Mishnah." In *What Is the Mishnah? The State of the Question*, edited by Shaye J. D. Cohen, 98–126. Boston: Harvard University Press, 2023.

———. *Purity and Community in Antiquity: Traditions of the Law from Second Temple Judaism to the Mishnah*. [In Hebrew.] Jerusalem: Magnes, 2016.

———. "The Rabbis and the Roman Citizenship Model: The Case of the Samaritans." In *Citizenship(s) and Self-Definition(s) in the Roman Empire: Roman, Greek, Jewish and Christian Perspectives*, edited by Katell Berthelot and Jonathn Price, 181–216. Leuven: Peeters. 2019.

Gafni, Chanan. *Conceptions of the Oral Law in Modern Jewish Scholarship*. [In Hebrew.] Jerusalem: Zalman Shazar Center, 2019.

———. *Mishnah's Plain Sense: A Study in Modern Talmudic Scholarship*. [In Hebrew.] Tel Aviv: Ha-Kibbutz ha-Me'uḥad, 2011.

Gafni, Isaiah. *The Jews of Babylonia in the Talmudic Era*. [In Hebrew.] Jerusalem: Zalman Shazar Center, 1990.

García Martínez, Florentino. "The Origins of the Essene Movement and the Qumran Sect." In *The People of the Dead Sea Scrolls*, Translated by Wilfred G. E. Watson, 77–96. Leiden: Brill, 1995.

García Martínez, Florentino, and Eibert J. C. Tigchelaar, eds. *The Dead Sea Scrolls Study Edition*. Brill: Leiden, 1999.

Geiger, Abraham. "Einiges über Plan und Anordung der Mischnah." *Wissenschaftliche Zeitschrift für jüdische Theologie* 2 (1836): 474–492.

———. "Das Verhältniß des natürlichen Schriftsinnes zur thalmudischen Schriftdeutung." *Wissenschaftliche Zeitschrift für Jüdische Theologie* 5 (1844): 53–81, 234–259.

Gertner, Meir. "Terms of Scriptural Interpretation: A Study in Hebrew Semantics." *Bulletin of the School of Oriental and African Studies* 25 (1962): 1–27.

Gesundheit, Shimon. *Three Times a Year: Studies on Festival Legislation in the Pentateuch*. Tübingen: Mohr Siebeck, 2012.

Geula, Amos. "The Status of the Mishnah in Byzantium." *Netu'im* 24–25 (2023–1024): 209–288.

Gilat, Yitzhak D. *R. Eliezer ben Hyrcanus: A Scholar Outcast*. Ramat-Gan: Bar-Ilan University Press, 1984.

Ginzberg, Louis. "On the Relationship between the Mishnah and the Mekhilta." [In Hebrew.] In *On Halakhah and Aggadah* [in Hebrew], 66–103. Tel Aviv: Dvir, 1960.

———. "Tractate *Tamid*." [In Hebrew.] In *On Halakhah and Aggadah* [in Hebrew], 41–65. Tel Aviv: Dvir, 1960.

Glasner, Yishai. "On the Use of 'Mishnayot' Tamid in Mishnah Yoma." [In Hebrew.] *Netu'im* 19 (2014): 91–106.

Glatzer, Aharon. "The Linguistic Background of Biblical Exegesis in the Tannaitic Midrashim." [In Hebrew.] PhD diss., Hebrew University, 2022.

Goldberg, Abraham. "All Base Themselves upon the Teachings of Rabbi 'Aqiva." [In Hebrew.] *Tarbiẕ* 38 (1969): 231–254.

———. "The Early and Late *Midrash*." [In Hebrew.] *Tarbiẕ* 50 (1980): 94–106.

———. "The Mishnah—A Study Book of Halakha." In *The Literature of the Sages: Part I*, edited by Shmuel Safrai, 211–262. Philadelphia: Fortress, 1987.

———. "The Phrase 'Davar Aher' in the Halakhic Midrashim." [In Hebrew.] In *Studies in Rabbinic Literature, Bible, and Jewish History* [in Hebrew], edited by Itzchak D. Gilath, Howard Levine, and Zvi Meir Rabinowitz, 99–107. Ramat Gan: Bar-Ilan University, 1982.

———. "Purpose and Method in Rabbi Judah Hannasi's Compilation of the Mishna." [In Hebrew.] *Tarbiẕ* 28 (1959): 260–269.

———. *Tosefta Bava Kamma: A Structural and Analytic Commentary with a Mishna-Tosefta Synopsis*. [In Hebrew.] Jerusalem: Magnes, 2001.

———. "Tosefta to Tractate *Tamid*." [In Hebrew.] In *Benjamin de Vries Memorial Volume* [in Hebrew], edited by Ezra Zion Melamed, 18–42. Tel Aviv: Tel Aviv University, 1968.

Goldin, Judah. *The Song at the Sea; Being a Commentary on a Commentary in Two Parts*. New Haven, CT: Yale University Press, 1971.

———. *Studies in Midrash and Related Literature*. Edited by Barry L. Eichler and Jeffrey H. Tigay. Philadelphia: Jewish Publication Society, 1988.

Goldman, Liora. *Those Who Hold Fast to the Ordinances: The Qumran Community and Its Exegesis in Light of the Pesharim in the Damascus Document*. [In Hebrew.] Jerusalem: Bialik Institute, 2019.

Goodblatt, David. *The Monarchic Principle: Studies in Jewish Self-Government in Antiquity.* Tübingen: J. C. B. Mohr, 1994.
Gordon, William M., and O. F. Robinson. *The Institutes of Gaius.* London: Duckworth, 1988.
Goshen-Gottstein, Moshe H. "Hebrew Syntax and the History of the Bible Text: A Pesher in the MT of Isaiah." *Textus* 8 (1973): 100–106.
Gottlieb, Isaac B. "Midrash as Biblical Philology." *Jewish Quarterly Review* 75 (1984): 134–161.
Grabbe, Lester L. *Judaism from Cyrus to Hadrian.* 2 vols. Minneapolis: Fortress, 1992.
Grafton, Anthony, and Megan Williams. *Christianity and the Transformation of the Book: Origen, Eusebius, and the Library of Caesarea.* Cambridge, MA: Belknap Press of Harvard University Press, 2006.
Green, William Scott. "Palestinian Holy Men: Charismatic Leadership and Rabbinic Tradition." *Aufstieg und Niedergang der römischen Welt* 2.19.2 (1979): 619–647.
———. "What's in a Name?—The Problematic of Rabbinic 'Biography.'" In *Approaches to Ancient Judaism: Theory and Practice*, vol. 1, 77–96. Missoula, MT: Scholars, 1978.
Gruenwald, Ithamar. "From Talmudic to Zoharic Homiletics." [In Hebrew.] *Jerusalem Studies in Jewish Thought* 8 (1989): 255–298.
———. "Midrash and the 'Midrashic Condition': Primary Considerations." In *The Midrashic Imagination: Jewish Exegesis, Thought, and History*, edited by Michael Fishbane, 6–22. Albany: SUNY Press, 1993.
Guttmann, Alexander. "Some Aspects of Theoretical Halakhot." [In Hebrew.] *Proceedings of the Fifth World Congress of Jewish Studies*, Jerusalem, 1969: 67–79.
Gvaryhau, Amit. "Review of A. Yadin-Israel's 'Scripture and Tradition: Rabbi Akiva and the Triumph of Midrash.'" *The Talmud Blog*, February 23, 2015.
———. "The Tannaitic Laws of Battery: Scripture and Halakhah." [In Hebrew.] *Tarbiz* 86 (2019): 533–573.
———. "Twisting Words: Does Halakhah Really Circumvent Scripture?" *Journal of Jewish Studies* 68 (2017): 260–283.
Hadot, Pierre. *What Is Ancient Philosophy.* Translated by Michael Chase. Cambridge, MA: Belknap Press of Harvard University Press, 2004.
Halbertal, Moshe. *The Birth of Doubt: Confronting Uncertainty in Early Rabbinic Literature.* Translated by Elli Fischer. Providence, RI: Brown Judaic Studies, 2020.
———. "David Hartman and the Philosophy of Halakhah." [In Hebrew.] In *Renewing Jewish Commitment: The Work and Though of David Hartman*, vol. 1, edited by Avi Sagi and Zvi Zohar, 13–36. Tel Aviv: Kibbutz Hameuhad, 2001.
———. "The History of Halakhah and the Emergence of Halakhah." [In Hebrew.] *Dine Israel* 29 (2013): 1–23.
———. *Interpretative Revolutions in the Making.* [In Hebrew.] Jerusalem: Magnes, 1999.
———. *Maimonides: Life and Thought.* Princeton: Princeton University Press, 2013.
———. *People of the Book: Canon, Meaning and Authority.* Cambridge, MA: Harvard University Press, 1997.
Handelman, Susan A. *The Slayers of Moses: The Emergence of Rabbinic Interpretation in Modern Literary Theory.* Albany: SUNY Press, 1982.
Haneman, Gideon. "Biblical Loanwords in the Mishnah." [In Hebrew.] *Proceedings of the Fourth World Congress of Jewish Studies*, Jerusalem, 1969: 95–96.
Hanson, Richard P. *Allegory and Event: A Study of the Sources and Significance of Origen's Interpretation of Scripture.* Richmond: John Knox, 1959.
Harries, Jill. *Law and Empire in Late Antiquity.* Cambridge: Cambridge University Press, 1999.

———. "Legal Education and Training Lawyers." In *The Oxford Handbook of Roman Law and Society*, edited by Paul J. du Plessis, Clifford Ando, and Kaius Tuori, 151–163. Oxford: Oxford University Press, 2016.

———. "Roman Law Codes and the Roman Legal Tradition." In *Beyond Dogmatics: Law and Society in the Roman World*, edited by John W. Cairns and Paul du Plessis, 85–104. Edinburgh: Edinburgh University Press, 2007.

Harris, Jay M. *How Do We Know This? Midrash and the Fragmentation of Modern Judaism*. Albany: SUNY Press, 1995.

———. *Nachman Krochmal: Guiding the Perplexed of the Modern Age*. New York: New York University Press, 1991.

Hartman, Geoffrey H., and Sanford Budick, eds. *Midrash and Literature*. New Haven, CT: Yale University Press, 1986.

Hauptman, Judith. *Rereading the Mishnah: A New Approach to Ancient Jewish Texts*. Tübingen: Mohr Siebeck, 2005.

Hayes, Christine. *Gentile Impurities and Jewish Identities: Intermarriage and Conversion from the Bible to the Talmud*. Oxford: Oxford University Press, 2002.

———. "Intertextuality and Tannaitic Literature: A History." In *The Literature of the Sages: A Re-Visioning*, edited by Christine Hayes, 95–216. Leiden: Brill, 2022.

Heger, Paul. "The Seducer and the Rapist: Divergent Qumranic and Rabbinic Interpretations of Deut. 22:28–29." *Journal of Ancient Judaism J* 6 (2015): 232–252.

Heijmans, Shai. "Greek and Latin Loanwords in the Mishnah: Lexicon and Phonology." [In Hebrew.] PhD diss., Tel-Aviv University, 2013.

Heinemann, Isaac. *The Methods of the Aggadah*. [In Hebrew.] 3rd ed. Jerusalem: Magnes, 1970.

———. "On the Development of Technical Terms for Biblical Interpretation." [In Hebrew.] *Lěšonénu* 14 (1946): 182–189.

Heinemann, Joseph. "The Nature of the Aggadah." In *Midrash and Literature*, edited by Geoffrey H. Hartman and Sanford Budick, 41–55. New Haven, CT: Yale University Press, 1986.

———. *Public Homilies in the Talmudic Period*. [In Hebrew.] Jerusalem: Bialik Institute, 1970.

Henshke, David. "Abbaye and Rava: Two Approaches to the Mishnah of the Tannaim," Tarbiz 49 (1980): 187–193.

———. *Festival Joy in Tannaitic Discourse*. [In Hebrew.] Jerusalem: Magnes, 2007.

———. *"Mah Nishtannah": The Passover Night in the Sages' Discourse*. [In Hebrew.] Jerusalem: Magnes, 2016.

———. "On the Strata in the Passover Haggadah in the Mishnah." [In Hebrew.] *Tarbiz* 81 (2012): 25–45.

———. *Original Mishna in the Discourse of Later Tanna'im*. [In Hebrew.] Ramat Gan: Bar-Ilan University, 1997.

———. "The Rabbis' Approach to Biblical Self-Contradictions." [In Hebrew.] *Sidra* 10 (1994): 39–55.

Herr, Moshe David. "Continuum in the Chain of Torah Transmission." [In Hebrew.] *Zion* 44 (1979–1980): 43–56.

———. "A Zoroastrian-Sasanian and a Babylonian Talmudic 'Renaissance' at the Beginning of the Third Century: Could This Be a Mere Coincidence?" [In Hebrew.] In *Between Babylonia and the Land of Israel: Studies in Honor of Isaiah M. Gafni* [in Hebrew], edited by Meir Ben Shahar, Geoffrey Herman, and Aharon Oppenheimer, 65–78. Jerusalem: Zalman Shazar Center, 2016.

Heschel, Abraham Joshua. *Heavenly Torah as Refracted through the Generations*. [In Hebrew.] 2 vols. Expanded ed., edited by Dror Bondi. Jerusalem: Maggid, 2021.

Hezser, Catherine. "Bookish Circles? The Move toward the Use of Written Texts in Rabbinic Oral Culture." In *Reading, Writing, and Bookish Circles in the Ancient Mediterranean*, edited by Jonathan D. H. Norton, Lindsey A. Askin, and Garrick Allen, 66–88. London: Bloomsbury, 2022.

———. "Did Palestinian Rabbis Know Roman Law? Methodological Considerations and Case Studies." In *Legal Engagement: The Reception of Roman Law and Tribunals by Jews and Other Inhabitants of the Empire*, edited by Katell Berthelot, Natalie Dohrmann, and Capucine Nemo-Pekelman, 303–322. Rome: Publicatiobookishns de l'École française de Rome, 2021.

———. *Jewish Travel in Antiquity*. Tübingen: Mohr Siebeck, 2011.

———. "The Mishnah and Roman Law: A Rabbinic Compilation of *Ius Civile* for the Jewish *Civitas* of the Land of Israel under Roman Rule." In *What Is the Mishnah? The State of the Question*, edited by Shaye J. D. Cohen, 141–166. Boston: Harvard University Press, 2023.

———. *Rabbinic Scholarship in the Context of Late Antique Scholasticism: The Development of the Talmud Yerushalmi*. London: Bloomsbury, 2024.

———. "Rabbis as Intellectuals in the Context of Graeco-Roman and Byzantine Christian Scholasticism." In *Scholastic Culture in the Hellenistic and Roman Eras: Greek, Latin, and Jewish*, edited by Sean A. Adams, 169–186. Berlin: De Gruyter, 2019.

Hidary, Richard. *Rabbis and Classical Rhetoric: Sophistic Education and Oratory in the Talmud and Midrash*. Cambridge: Cambridge University Press, 2017.

Hirshman, Marc G. "Changing Loci of Holiness: Honi and His Grandchildren." [In Hebrew.] *Tura* 1 (1989): 109–118.

———. *Torah for the Entire World*. [In Hebrew.] Tel Aviv: Ha-Kibbutz ha-Me'uḥad, 1999.

———. "What Is the Place of Aggada and Who Were the Baalei Aggada?" [In Hebrew.] In *Talmudic Studies* [in Hebrew], vol. 3, edited by Yaacov Sussman and David Rosenthal, 190–208. Jerusalem: Magnes, 2005.

Hoffman, Adina, and Peter Cole. *Sacred Trash: The Lost and Found World of the Cairo Geniza*. New York: Schocken, 2011.

Hoffman, Yair. *Doctrine of the Exodus in the Bible*. [In Hebrew.] Tel Aviv: Tel Aviv University, 1983.

Hoffmann, David Zvi. *The First Mishna and the Controversies of the Tannaim: The Highest Court in the City of the Sanctuary*. Translated by Paul Forchheimer. New York: Maurosho Publications of Cong. Kehillath Yaakov, 1977.

———. *Zur Einleitung in die halachischen Midraschim*. Berlin, 1886.

Honigman, Sylvie, and Ehud Ben Zvi. "The Spread of the Ideological Concept of a (Jerusalem-Centred) Tōrâ-Centred Israel beyond Yehud: Observations and Implications." *Hebrew Bible and Ancient Israel* 4 (2021): 370–397.

Houtman, Alberdina. *Mishnah and Tosefta: A Synoptic Comparison of the Tractates Berakhot and Shebiit*. Tübingen: J. C. B. Mohr, 1996.

Hurvitz, Avi. "Continuity and Innovation in Biblical Hebrew." In *Studies in Ancient Hebrew Semantics*, edited by Takmitsu Muraoka, 1–10. Louvain: Peeters, 1995.

Idel, Moshe. "Some Concepts of Mishnah among 16th-Century Safedian Kabbalists." In *The Mishnaic Moment: Jewish Law among Jews and Christians in Early Modern Europe*, edited by Piet van Boxel, Kirsten Macfarlane, and Joanna Weinberg, 68–86. Oxford: New York, 2022.

Ilan, Tal, and Vered Noam. *Josephus and the Rabbis*. [In Hebrew.] 2 vols. Jerusalem: Ben-Zvi Institute, 2017.

Iser, Wolfgang. *The Act of Reading: A Theory of Aesthetic Response*. Baltimore: Johns Hopkins University Press, 1978.

Jackson, Bernard S. *Essays on Halakhah in the New Testament*. Leiden: Brill, 2008.

Jaffee, Martin S. *Torah in the Mouth: Writing and Oral Tradition in Palestinian Judaism, 200 BCE–400 CE*. Oxford: Oxford University Press, 2001.

Kaduri, Yaakov. "Biblical Interpretation at Qumran." [In Hebrew.] In *Qumran Scrolls and Their World* [in Hebrew], edited by Menahem Kister, 405–408. Jerusalem: Ben-Zvi Institute, 2009.

Kahana, Menahem. "The Arrangement of the Orders of the Mishnah." [In Hebrew.] *Tarbiẓ* 76 (2007): 29–40.

———. "The Attitude towards Gentile in the Tannaitic and Amoraic Periods." *'Et ha-Da'at* 3 (2000): 22–36.

———. "Concerning the Historical Development of the Principle of *Kelal uFerat* in the Tannaitic Period." [In Hebrew.] In *Studies in Talmudic and Midrashic Literature in Memory of Tirzah Lifshitz* [in Hebrew], edited by Moshe Bar-Asher, Joshua Levinson, and Berachyahu Lifshitz, 173–216. Jerusalem: Bialik Institute, 2005.

———. *Derash Hamazhir and Its Contribution to the Research of Sifre on Deuteronomy and Mekhilta on Deuteronomy*. [In Hebrew.] Jerusalem: Bialik Institute, 2022.

———. "Editions of the Mekhilta of Rabbi Ishmael to Exodus in View of the Genizah Fragments." [In Hebrew.] *Tarbiẓ* 55 (1986): 489–524.

———. "Fixed Measure Policy in the Teachings of Beit Hillel and Beit Shammai." [In Hebrew.] *Sidra* 35 (2023): 7–35.

———. "Foreign Bodies of the House of Rabbi in the Halakhic Midrashim." [In Hebrew.] In *Studies in Bible and Talmud* [in Hebrew], edited by Sara Japhet, 59–85. Jerusalem: Hebrew University, 1987.

———. *Genizah Fragments of the Halakhic Midrashim*. [In Hebrew.] Jerusalem: Magnes, 2005.

———. "The Halakhic Midrashim." In *The Literature of the Sages: Part II*, edited by Shmuel Safrai, 3–103. Philadelphia: Fortress, 2006.

———. "The Importance of Dwelling in the Land of Israel According to the Deuteronomy Mekhilta." [In Hebrew.] *Tarbiẓ* 62 (1993): 501–513.

———. "Notes to the *Mekhilta*." [In Hebrew.] *Tarbiẓ* 59 (1989): 235–241.

———. "On Halakhic Tolerance as It Evolved: An Early and Forgotten Disagreement between Bet Shammai and Bet Hillel." [In Hebrew.] *Tarbiẓ* 83 (2015): 401–418.

———. "On the Fashioning and Aims of the Mishnaic Controversy." [In Hebrew.] *Tarbiẓ* 73 (2003): 51–81.

———. "The Relations between Exegeses in the Mishnah and *Halakhot* in the Midrash." [In Hebrew.] *Tarbiẓ* 84 (2015): 17–76.

———. *Sifre on Numbers: An Annotated Edition*. [In Hebrew.] 4 vols. Jerusalem: Magnes, 2011.

———. *Sifre Zuta on Deuteronomy: Citations from a New Tannaitic Midrash*. [In Hebrew.] Jerusalem: Magnes, 2002.

———. "Six Interwoven: On the Organization of the Section *Bereshit Bara* in Genesis Rabbah." In *Higayon l'Yona: News Aspects in the Study of Midrash, Aggadah and Piyyut* [in Hebrew], edited by Joshua Levinson, Jacob Elbaum, and Galit Hasan-Rokem, 347–376. Jerusalem: Magnes, 2007.

———. "The Tannaitic Midrashim." In *The Cambridge Genizah Collections: Their Contents and Significance*, edited by Stefan C. Reif, with the assistance of Shulamit Reif, 59–73. Cambridge: Cambridge University Press, 2002.

———. "Torah Study, Labor, Piety, and Realism: The Controversy between R. Joshua and R. Eleazar ha-Moda'i in the Aggadah of the Mekhilta.'" *Sidra* 31 (2016): 73–94.

———. *The Two Mekhiltot on the Amalek Portion: The Originality of the Version of the Mekhilta d'Rabbi Ishma'el with Respect to the Mekhilta of Rabbi Shim'on ben Yohay*. [In Hebrew.] Jerusalem: Magnes, 1999.

———. "'Ve-Khullah Matnitin': Who were the Abbreviators of Mishnayot in the Tannaitic Midrashim?" [In Hebrew.] *Tarbiẓ* 88 (2020): 5–40.

———. "'When You Enter the Land': A Tannaitic Controversy and Its Realistic Meaning." [In Hebrew.] *Tarbiẓ* 81 (2012): 143–164.

Kalmin, Richard. *The Sage in Jewish Society of Late Antiquity*. New York: Routledge, 1999.

Kamesar, Adam. "Biblical Interpretation in Philo." *The Cambridge Companion to Philo*, edited by Adam Kamesar, 65–91. Cambridge: Cambridge University Press 2009.

Katsh, Abraham Isaac, ed. *Ginze Mishna: One Hundred and Fifty-Nine Fragments from the Cairo Geniza in the Saltykv-Shchedrin Library in Leningrad*. [In Hebrew.] Jerusalem: Mossad Harav Kook, 1970.

Katzoff, Ranon. "*P. Yadin* 21 and Rabbinic Law on Widows' Rights." *Jewish Quarterly Review* 97 (2007): 545–575.

———. "Sperber's Dictionary of Greek and Latin Legal Terms in Rabbinic Literature—A Review-Essay." *Journal for the Study of Judaism in the Persian, Hellenistic, and Roman Period* 20.2 (December 1989): 195–206.

Kaufmann, Yehezkel. *History of the Israelite Religion*. [In Hebrew.] 4 vols. in 8. Tel Aviv: Bialik Institute, 1937–1956.

Kazhdan, Daniel, and Benjamin S. Kay. "Unlocking Ancient Texts with New Tools: A Data-Centered Study of the Mishnah." *Jewish Studies, and Internet Journal* 22 (2022): 1–43.

Kister, Menahem. "Allegorical Interpretations of Biblical Narratives in Rabbinic Literature." In *New Approaches to the Study of Biblical Interpretation in Judaism of the Second Temple Period and in Early Christianity*, edited by Gary A. Anderson, Ruth A. Clements, and David Satran, 133–183. Leiden: Brill, 2013.

———. "A Common Heritage: Biblical Interpretation at Qumran and Its Implications." In *Biblical Perspectives: Early Use and Interpretation of the Bible in Light of the Dead Sea Scrolls*, edited by Michael E. Stone and Esther G. Chazon, 101–111. Leiden: Brill, 1998.

———. "Concerning the History of the Essenes." [In Hebrew.] *Tarbiẓ* 56.1 (1986): 1–18.

———. *Dynamics of Midrashic Traditions in Second Temple and Rabbinic Literature*. [In Hebrew.] Jerusalem: Magnes Press, 2024.

———. "Some Aspects of Qumranic Halakhah." In *The Madrid Qumran Congress: Proceedings of the International Congress on the Dead Sea Scrolls, Madrid, 18–21 March, 1991*, edited by Julio Trebolle Barrera and Luis Vegas Montaner, 571–588. Leiden: Brill, 1992.

———. *Studies in Avot de-Rabbi Nathan*. [In Hebrew.] Jerusalem: Hebrew University; Ben-Zvi Institute, 1998.

Klein, Anja. "Half Way between Psalm 119 and Ben Sira: Wisdom and Torah in Psalm 19." In *Wisdom and Torah: The Reception of Torah in the Wisdom Literature of the Second Temple Period*, edited by Bernd U. Schipper and D. Andrew Teeter, 119–136. Leiden: Brill Academic Publishers, 2013.

Knohl, Israel. "The Acceptance of Sacrifices from Gentiles." [In Hebrew.] *Tarbiẓ* 48 (1979): 341–345.

———. *The Bible's Genetic Code* [In Hebrew.] Or Yehudah: Dvir, 2008.

———. "The Guilt Offering of the 'Holiness School.'" [In Hebrew.] *Tarbiẓ* 71 (2002): 327–335.

Koren, Yedidah. "The 'Foreskinned Jew' in Tannaitic Literature: Another Aspect of the Rabbinic (Re)Construction of Judaism." [In Hebrew.] *Zion* 82 (2017): 397–437.

Kotansky, Roy, Joseph Naveh, and Shaul Shaked. "A Greek-Aramaic Silver Amulet from Egypt in the Ashmolean Museum," *Le Muséon* 105 (1992): 5–25.

Kramer, David. "The Mishnah." In *The Cambridge History of Judaism*, vol. 4, *The Late Rabbinic Period*, edited by Steven T. Katz, 299–315. Cambridge: Cambridge University Press, 2006.

Krochmal, Nachman. *Writings of Nachman Krochmal*. [In Hebrew.] Edited with an introduction by Simon Rawidowicz. Rev. 2nd ed. London: Ararat, 1961.

Kugel, James L. *How to Read the Bible: A Guide to Scripture Then and Now.* New York: Free Press, 2007.

———. "Mobile Midrash." *Proceedings of the Israel Academy of Sciences and Humanities* 8 (2000): 49–61.

———. *Traditions of the Bible: A Guide to the Bible as It Was at the Start of the Common Era.* Cambridge, MA: Harvard University Press, 2009.

———. "Two Introductions to Midrash." In *Midrash and Literature*, edited by Geoffrey H. Hartman and Sanford Budick, 77–103. New Haven, CT: Yale University Press, 1986.

Kulp, Joshua. "History, Exegesis or Doctrine: Framing the Tannaitic Debates on the Circumcision of Slaves." *Journal of Jewish Studies* 57 (2006): 56–79.

Kulp, Joshua, and Jason Rogoff. *Reconstructing the Talmud: An Introduction to the Academic Study of Rabbinic Literature.* 2 vols. New York: Mechon Hadar, 2014–2019.

Kutscher, Edward Yechezkel. *Hebrew and Aramaic Studies.* Edited by Zeev Ben-Hayyim, Aharon Dotan, and Gad Sarfatti, with the assistance of Moshe Bar-Asher. Jerusalem: Magnes, 1977.

Lambert, David. "How the 'Torah of Moses' Became Revelation." *Journal for the Study of Judaism* 47 (2016): 22–54.

———. "Multiplicity and the Idea of Scripture." *Journal of Theological Studies* 20 (2025): 1–25.

Landau, Gilad. "The Editing of Tractate Sotah in Light of Its Unique Aggadic Conclusion." [In Hebrew.] *Netuim* 24–25 (2023–2024): 77–105.

Landes, Yitz. "Piyyut, Mishnah and Rabbinization in the Sixth to Eighth Centuries." *Jewish Studies Quarterly* 30 (2023): 28–47.

———. "The Rise of the Jewish Patriarchate and the Dissemination of Rabbinic Literature." Unpublished paper.

Lapin, Hayim. *Rabbis as Romans: The Rabbinic Movement in Palestine, 100–400 CE.* New York: Oxford University Press, 2012.

Lauterbach, Jacob Zallel. "The Ancient Jewish Allegorists in Talmud and Midrash." *Jewish Quarterly Review* 1 (1911): 291–333.

———. "The Name of the Mekilta." *Jewish Quarterly Review* 11 (1920): 169–196.

———. *Rabbinic Essays.* Cincinnati: Hebrew Union College Press, 1951.

Law, Timothy Michael. *When God Spoke Greek: The Septuagint and the Making of the Christian Bible.* Oxford: Oxford University Press, 2013.

Lerner, Myron Bialik. "The Tractate Avot." In *The Literature of the Sages: Part II*, edited by Shmuel Safrai, 263–281. Philadelphia: Fortress, 2006.

Letteney, Mark. *The Christianization of Knowledge in Late Antiquity.* Cambridge: Cambridge University Press. 2023.

Levine, David. "Who Participated in the Fast-Day Ritual in the City Square? Communal Fasts in Third- and Fourth-Century Palestine." [In Hebrew.] *Cathedra* 94 (December 1999): 33–54.

Levinger, Jacob S. "'Repentance Atones': The History of an Idea." [In Hebrew.] In *Repentance and Penitents* [in Hebrew,] 41–51. Jerusalem: Ministry of Education and Culture, 1979/1980.

Levinson, Joshua. "From Narrative Practice to Cultural Poetics: Literary Anthropology and the Rabbinic Sense of Self." In *Homer and the Bible in the Eyes of Ancient Interpreters*, edited by Maren R. Niehoff, 345–367. Leiden: Brill, 2012.

———. *The Twice-Told Tale: A Poetics of the Exegetical Narrative in Rabbinic Midrash.* [In Hebrew.] Jerusalem: Magnes, 2005.

Lewin, Binyamin M., ed. *Iggeret Rav Sherira Ga'on.* Haifa, 1921.

Lewy, Israel. *Über einige Fragmente aus der Mischna des Abba Saul.* Berlin, 1876.

———. *Ein Wort über die Mechilta des R. Simon.* Breslau, 1899.

Lichtenstein, Mayer. "Towards a History of the Blessings Recited before Eating Food in Rabbinic Literature." [In Hebrew.] PhD diss. Bar-Ilan University, 2017.

Lieberman, Saul. *Greek in Jewish Palestine*. New York: Jewish Theological Seminary, 1942.

———. *Hellenism in Jewish Palestine*, 2nd ed. New York: Jewish Theological Seminary of America, 1962.

———. "Mishnat Shir ha-Shirim." In *Jewish Gnosticism, Merkabah Mysticism, and Talmudic Tradition*, edited by Gershom G. Scholem, 118–126. New York: Jewish Theological Seminary, 1965.

———. "On Persecution of the Jewish Religion." [In Hebrew.] In *Salo Wittmayer Baron Jubilee Volume*, edited by Saul Lieberman and Arthur Hyman, 213–246. Jerusalem: AAJR, 1974.

———. *Siphre Zutta (The Midrash of Lydda): Talmud of Caesarea*. [In Hebrew.] New York: JTS, 1968.

———. *Tosefta ki-Feshutah*. 10 vols. New York: Jewish Theological Seminary of America, 1955–1988.

Liebs, Detlef. "The Code System: Reorganizing Roman Law and Legal Literature in the Late Antique Period." In *Jurists and Legal Science in the History of Roman Law*, edited by Fara Nasti and Aldo Schiavone, 261–285. London: Routledge, 2021.

Lifshitz, Berachyahu. "Aggadah and Its Role in the History of the Oral Law." *Diné Israel* 24 (2007): 11–28.

Linder, Amnon, ed. and trans. *The Jews in Roman Imperial Legislation*. Detroit: Wayne State University Press, 1987.

Lipshitz, Yair, and Ishay Rosen-Zvi. "On Talmud as Performance: Reading Bavli Yoma 20b-21a." *Oqimta* 8 (2021): 87–116.

Lorberbaum, Menachem. "Theory of Action in Halakha: Intention in Mitzvoth." [In Hebrew.] MA thesis, Hebrew University, 1989.

Lorberbaum, Yair. "*Gezerat Melekh* (Decree of King) and *Gezerat ha-Katuv* (Decree of Scripture) in Talmudic Literature." [In Hebrew.] *Tarbiẕ* 82 (2014): 5–42.

———. *In God's Image: Myth, Theology, and Law in Classical Judaism*. New York: Cambridge University Press, 2015.

———. "On Rules and Reasons in Legal and Halakhic Reasoning." [In Hebrew.] *Jerusalem Studies in Jewish Thought* 26 (2021): 1–76.

———. "On the Rejection of Reasons in Halakhic Discourse: The Debate on the Reason for the Prohibitions on Marring the Corners of the Head and the Beard." [In Hebrew.] *Jerusalem Studies in Jewish Thought* 25 (2017): 45–102.

———. "Parables and Laws: Maimonides on Allegorical Interpretation of Mitzvot." *REJ* 183 (2024): 125–158.

Lowe, William Henry. *The Mishnah on Which the Palestinian Talmud Rests*. Cambridge, 1883.

MacRae, Duncan. *Legible Religion: Books, Gods, and Rituals in Roman Culture*. Cambridge, MA: Harvard University Press, 2016.

Mali, Hillel. "*Mi-Miqdash le-Midrash*: Descriptions of the Temple in the Mishna: History, Redaction, and Meaning." [In Hebrew.] PhD diss., Bar-Ilan University, 2018.

Malka, Orit, and Yakir Paz. "A Rabbinic *Postliminium*: The Property of Captives in Tannaitic Halakhah in Light of Roman Law." In *Legal Engagement: The Reception of Roman Law and Tribunals by Jews and Other Inhabitants of the Empire*, edited by Katell Berthelot, Natalie Dohrmann, and Capucine Nemo-Pekelman, 323–344. Rome: Publications de l'École française de Rome, 2021.

Mandel, Paul. "Midrashic Exegesis and Its Precedents in the Dead Sea Scrolls." *Dead Sea Discoveries* 8 (2001): 149–168.

———. *The Origins of Midrash: From Teaching to Text*. Leiden: Brill, 2017.

———. "The Tosefta." In *The Cambridge History of Judaism*, vol. 4, *The Late Rabbinic Period*, edited by Steven T. Katz, 316–335. Cambridge: Cambridge University Press, 2006.

Marienberg-Millikowsky, Itay. "A Study of Employer–Worker Dynamics: A Dialogue between *Aggada* and *Halacha*." [In Hebrew.] *Mishlav* 40 (2006): 87–114.

Mason, S. N. "Priesthood in Josephus and the 'Pharisaic Revolution.'" *Journal of Biblical Literature* 107.4 (1988): 657–661.

Melamed, Ezra Zion. *The Relationship between the Halakhic Midrashim and the Mishna and Tosefta*. [In Hebrew.] Jerusalem: Daat, 1967.

Michaelis, Omer. "Crisis Discourse and Framework Transition in Maimonides' Mishneh Torah." *Open Philosophy* 3 (2020): 664–680.

Milgram, Jonathan S. *From Mesopotamia to the Mishnah: Tannaitic Inheritance Law in Its Legal and Social Contexts*. Tübingen: Mohr Siebeck, 2016.

Milgrom, Jacob. *Leviticus 23–27: A New Translation with Introduction and Commentary*. New York: Doubleday, 2001.

———. "The Qumran Cult: Its Exegetical Principles." In *Temple Scroll Studies*, edited by George G. Brooke, 165–180. Sheffield: JSOT, 1989.

Milikowsky, Chaim. "Jewish Historiography in the Days of the Second Temple, Mishnah and Talmud: Its Fading, Its Renewed Efflorescence, and Its Demise." [In Hebrew.] In *The Paths of Daniel: Studies in Judaism and Jewish Culture in Honor of Rabbi Professor Daniel Sperber* [in Hebrew], edited by Adam Ferziger, 473–504. Ramat-Gan: Bar-Ilan University, 2017.

———. "Josephus between Rabbinic Culture and Hellenistic Historiography." In *Shem in the Tents of Japhet: Essays in the Encounter of Judaism and Hellenism*, edited by James L. Kugel, 159–200. Leiden: Brill, 2002.

Miller, Stuart S. "All Law Begins with Costume: Rabbinic Awareness of Popular Practice and Its Implications for the Study of the Jews of Roman Palestine." In *From Scrolls to Traditions: A Festschrift Honoring Lawrence H. Schiffman*, edited by Stuart S. Miller et al., 350–397. Leiden: Brill, 2021.

Mintz, Alan. "The Song at the Sea and the Question of Doubling in Midrash." *Prooftexts* 1 (1981): 185–192.

Mitchell, Matthew. "In The Footsteps of Paul: Scriptural and Apostolic Authority in Ignatius of Antioch." *Journal of Early Christian Studies* 14 (2006): 27–45.

Mor, Uri. *Judean Hebrew: The Language of the Hebrew Documents from Judea between the First and Second Revolts*. [In Hebrew.] Jerusalem: Academy of the Hebrew Language, 2015.

Moscovitz, Leib. "Legal Fictions in Rabbinic Law and Roman Law: Some Comparative Observations." In *Rabbinic Law in Its Roman and Near Eastern Context*, edited by Catherine Hezser, 105–132. Tübingen: Mohr Siebeck, 2003.

———. *Talmudic Reasoning: From Casuistics to Conceptualization*. Tübingen: Mohr Siebeck, 2002.

Mroczek, Eva. *The Literary Imagination in Late Antiquity*. Oxford: Oxford University Press, 2016.

Naeh, Shlomo. "The Craft of Memory: Constructions of Memory and Patterns of Text in Rabbinic Literature." [In Hebrew.] In *Talmudic Studies* [in Hebrew], vol. 3, edited by Yaacov Sussman and David Rosenthal, 543–589. Jerusalem: Magnes, 2005.

———. "'Creates the Fruit of Lips': A Phenomenological Study of Prayer According to Mishnah Berakhot 4:3, 5:5." [In Hebrew.] *Tarbiẓ* 63 (1994): 185–218.

———. "'Polishing Measures and Cleaning Scales': A Chapter from the Tractate of Weights and Measures." [In Hebrew.] *Tarbiẓ* 59 (1990): 379–395.

———. "The Structure and Division of 'Torat Kohanim' (A): Scrolls." [In Hebrew.] *Tarbiẓ* 66 (1997): 483–515.

Nagy, Gregory. "Orality and Literacy." *Classical Continuum*, December 19, 2022.
Najman, Hindy. "The Law of Nature and the Authority of Mosaic Law." *Studia Philonica Annual* 11 (1999): 55–73.
———. *Seconding Sinai: The Development of Mosaic Discourse in Second Temple Judaism*. Leiden: Brill, 2003.
Nakman, David. "Halakhah in the Writings of Josephus." [In Hebrew.] PhD diss., Bar-Ilan University, 2004.
———. "Josephus and Halacha." In *A Companion to Josephus*, edited by Honora Howell Chapman and Zuleika Rodgers, 282–292. Chichster: Wiley-Blackwell, 2016.
———. "Tefillin and Mezuzot at Qumran." [In Hebrew.] In *Qumran Scrolls and Their World* [in Hebrew], edited by Menahem Kister, 143–155. Jerusalem: Ben-Zvi Institute, 2009.
Naveh, Joseph. *On Sherd and Papyrus: Aramaic and Hebrew Inscriptions from the Second Temple, Mishnaic, and Talmudic Periods*. [In Hebrew.] Jerusalem: Magnes, 1992.
Neis, Rafael Rachel. "The Seduction of Law: Rethinking Legal Studies in Jewish Studies." *Jewish Quarterly Review* 109 (2019): 119–138.
Netz, Reviel. "Deuteronomic Texts: Late Antiquity and the History of Mathematics." *Revue d'histoire des mathématiques* 4 (1998): 261–288.
Neusner, Jacob. *Ancient Israel after Catastrophe: The Religious World View of the Mishnah*. Charlottesville: University Press of Virginia, 1983.
———. *Midrash as Literature: The Primacy of Documentary Discourse*. Lanham, MD: University Press of America, 1987.
Newman, Hillel I. "A Patristic Perspective on Rabbinic Literature." [In Hebrew.] In *The Classic Rabbinic Literature of Eretz Israel: Introduction and Studies* [in Hebrew], edited by Menahem Kahana, Vered Noam, Menahem Kister, and David Rosenthal, 681–704. Jerusalem: Ben-Zvi Institute, 2018.
Niehoff, Maren. *Jewish Exegesis and Homeric Scholarship in Alexandria*. Cambridge: Cambridge University Press, 2011.
Nitzan, Bilhah. "Pesher and Midrash in the Qumran Scrolls." [In Hebrew.] *Meghillot* 7 (2009): 99–127.
———, ed. *Pesher Habakkuk: A Scroll from the Wilderness of Judaea (1QpHab)*. [In Hebrew.] Jerusalem: Bialik Institute, 1986.
———. "The *Pesher* Scrolls at Qumran." [In Hebrew.] In *Qumran Scrolls and Their World* [in Hebrew], edited by Menahem Kister, 169–190. Jerusalem: Ben-Zvi Institute, 2009.
Noam, Vered. "Beit Shammai and the Sectarian Halakha." [In Hebrew.] *Jewish Studies* 41 (2002): 45–67.
———. "Creative Interpretation and Integrative Interpretation in Qumran." In *The Dead Sea Scrolls and Contemporary Culture: Proceedings of the International Conference Held at the Israel Museum, Jerusalem (July 6–8, 2008)*, edited by Adolfo D. Roitman, Lawrence H. Schiffman, and Shani Tzoref, 363–376. Leiden: Brill, 2011.
———. "Divorce in Qumran in Light of Early Halakhah." *Journal of Jewish Studies* 56 (2005): 206–223.
———. "Early Signs of Halakhic Midrash at Qumran." [In Hebrew.] *Diné Israel* 26–27 (2009–2010): 3–26.
———. *From Qumran to the Rabbinic Revolution: Conceptions of Impurity*. [In Hebrew.] Jerusalem: Ben-Zvi Institute, 2010.
———. "A Glimpse into the World of a Golanite Tanna: Rabbi Eliezer ha-Kappar." [In Hebrew.] *'Al Atar* 4–5 (Nisan 5759): 59–66.
———. *Megillat Ta'anit: Versions, Interpretation, History*. [In Hebrew.] Jerusalem: Ben-Zvi Institute, 2003.

———. "The Story of King Jannaeus (b. Qiddušin 66a): A Pharisaic Reply to Sectarian Polemic." *Harvard Theological Review* 107.1 (2014): 31–58.

Noam, Vered, and Elisha Qimron. "A Qumran Composition on the Laws of the Sabbath and Its Contribution to Early Halachic History." [In Hebrew.] *Tarbiẓ* 74 (2005): 511–546.

Novick, Tzvi. *What Is Good, and What God Demands: Normative Structures in Tannaitic Literature.* Leiden: Brill, 2010.

Olman, Arye. "Weekly Learning of Mishnah: Evidence from the Cairo Genizah." [In Hebrew.] *Netu'im* 19 (2014): 171–196.

Ophir, Adi, and Ishay Rosen-Zvi. *Goy: Israel's Multiple Others and the Birth of the Gentile.* Oxford: Oxford University Press, 2018.

———. "Separation, Judeophobia and the Birth of the 'Goy': The Chicken and the Egg." In *Antisemitism and the Politics of History*, edited by Scott Ury and Guy Miron (with Adi Ophir), 105–125. Altham: Brandeis University Press, 2024.

Oppenheimer, Aharon. *Rabbi Judah ha-Nasi: Statesman, Reformer, and Redactor of the Mishnah.* Tübingen: Mohr Siebeck, 2017.

Origen of Alexandria. *Homilies on Genesis and Exodus.* Translated by Ronald E. Heine. Washington, DC: Catholic University of America Press, 1982.

Paz, Yakir. *From Scribes to Scholars: Rabbinic Biblical Exegesis in Light of the Homeric Commentaries.* Tübingen: Mohr Siebeck, 2022.

Piotrkowski, Meron M. *Priests in Exile: The History of the Temple of Onias and Its Community in the Hellenistic Period.* Berlin: De Gruyter, 2019.

Polliack, Meira. "The Karaite Inversion of 'Written' and 'Oral' Torah in Relation to the Islamic Arch-Model of Qur'an and Hadith." *Jewish Studies Quarterly* 22.3 (2015): 243–302.

Porton, Gary G. "Defining Midrash." In *The Study of Ancient Judaism*, edited by Jacob Neusner, 55–92. New York: Ktav, 1981.

Qimron, Elisha. *Dead Sea Scrolls: The Hebrew Writings.* [In Hebrew.] Jerusalem: Ben-Zvi Institute, 2010.

Rappaport, Uriel. *First Book of Maccabees: Introduction, Hebrew Translation, and Commentary.* [In Hebrew.] Jerusalem: Ben-Zvi Institute, 2004.

———. *House of the Hasmoneans: The People of Israel in the Land of Israel in Hasmonean Period.* [In Hebrew.] Jerusalem: Ben-Zvi Institute, 2013.

Raviv, Rivka. "On the Nature of the Biblical Exegesis in Rabbinic Literature." [In Hebrew.] *Tarbiẓ* 70 (2001): 177–188.

Raz-Krakotzkin, Amnon. *Mishna Consciousness, Biblical Consciousness: Safed and Zionist Culture.* [In Hebrew.] Jerusalem: Van Leer Institute Press and Hakibbutz Hameuchad, 2022.

———. "On Burning and Printing." *Zmanim* 112 (2010): 30–41.

Reed, Annette Yoshiko. "Jewish Christianity as Counter-History? The Apostolic Past in Eusebius' Ecclesiastical History and the Pseudo-Clementine Homilies." In *Antiquity in Antiquity: Jewish and Christian Pasts in the Greco-Roman World*, edited by Gregg Gardner and Kevin Osterloh, 173–216. Tübingen: Mohr Siebeck, 2008.

———. "When Did Rabbis Become Pharisees?" Reflections on Christian Evidence for Post-70 Judaism." In *Envisioning Judaism: Essays in Honor of Peter Schäfer on the Occasion of His Seventieth Birthday*, edited by Raanan S. Boustan et al., vol. 2, 859–896. Tübingen: Mohr Siebeck, 2013.

Reeves, John C. "Burning and Printing: The Hebrew Book during the Counter-Reformation." [In Hebrew.] *Zmanim* 112 (Fall 2010): 30–41.

———. "Problematizing the Bible . . . Then and Now." *Jewish Quarterly Review* 100 (2010): 139–152.

Regev, Eyal, and David Nakman. "Josephus and the Halakhah of the Pharisees, the Sadducees and Qumran." [In Hebrew.] *Zion* 64.4 (2002): 401–434.

Reichman, Ronen. *Mishna und Sifra: ein literarkritischer Vergleich paralleler Überlieferungen*. Tübingen: Mohr Siebeck, 1998.

Reizel, Anat. *Introduction to Midrashic Literature*. [In Hebrew.] Edited by Amnon Bazak. Alon Shevut: Tevunot, Herzog College, 2010/2011.

Rosen-Zvi, Assaf. "'Even Though There Is No Proof to the Matter, There Is an Indication of the Matter': The Meaning, Character and Significance of the Phrase in the Tannaitic Literature." [In Hebrew.] *Tarbiẓ* 78 (2009): 323–344.

———. "Text, Redaction, and Hermeneutics in *Mekhilta de-Rabbi Ishmael*, Tractate *Kaspa*." [In Hebrew.] PhD diss., Hebrew University, 2017.

Rosen-Zvi, Assaf, and Ishay Rosen-Zvi. "The Hermeneutics of Aggadic Exegesis in Tannaitic Midrashim: A Terminological Survey." [In Hebrew.] In *Talmudic Studies* [in Hebrew], vol. 4, edited by Yoav Rosenthal and Shlomo Naeh, 765–816. Jerusalem: Mandel Institute of Jewish Studies, 2024.

———. "Tannaitic Halakhic and Aggadic Methodology." *Tarbiẓ* 86 (2019): 203–232.

Rosen-Zvi, Ishay. "The Birth of the Gentile in Rabbinic Literature." [In Hebrew.] *Te'udah* 26 (2004): 361–438.

———. "Blessing as Mapping: Reading Mishnah Berakhot, Chapter 9." [In Hebrew.] *Hebrew Union College Annual* 78 (2007): 25–46.

———. "Bodies and Temple: The List of Priestly Bodily in Mishnah Bekhorot, Chapter 7." [In Hebrew.] *Jewish Studies* 43 (2005): 49–87.

———. *Body and Soul in Ancient Jewish Thought*. [In Hebrew.] Moshav Ben-Shemen: Modan, 2012.

———. "Can the Homilists Cross the Sea Again? Time and Revelation in *Mekilta Shirata*." In *The Significance of Sinai: Traditions about Sinai and Divine Revelation in Judaism and Christianity*, edited by George J. Brooke, Hindy Najman, and Loren T. Stuckenbruck, 217–245. Leiden: Brill, 2008.

———. *Demonic Desires: Yetzer Hara and the Problem of Evil in Late Antiquity*. Philadelphia: University of Pennsylvania Press, 2011.

———. "Hermeneutic Lexicon." [In Hebrew.] *Jewish Studies* 48 (2012): 73–93.

———. "Is the Mishnah a Roman Composition?" In *The Faces of Torah: Studies in the Texts and Contexts of Ancient Judaism in Honor of Steven Fraade*, edited by Christine Hayes, Tzvi Novick, and Michal Bar-Asher Siegal, 487–508. Göttingen: Vandenhoek and Ruprecht, 2017.

———. "Joining the Club: Tannaitic Legal Midrash and Ancient Jewish Hermeneutics." *Studia Philonica Annual* 17 (2005): 153–160.

———. "Like a Priest Exposing His Own Wayward Mother: Jeremiah in Rabbinic Literature." In *Jeremiah's Scriptures: Production, Reception, Interaction, and Transformation*, edited by Konrad Schmidt and Hindy Najman, 570–590. Leiden: Brill, 2016.

———. "Measure for Measure as a Hermeneutic Tool in Early Rabbinic Literature." *Journal of Jewish Studies* 57 (2006): 269–286.

———. "Midrash and/as Allegory: The Case of *Ella*." *Oqimta* 10 (2024): 187–209.

———. *The Mishnaic Sotah Ritual: Temple, Gender, and Midrash*. Translated by Orr Scharf. Leiden: Brill, 2012.

———. "Orality, Narrative, Rhetoric: New Directions in Mishnah Research." *AJS Review* 32.2 (November 2008): 235–249.

———. "Pauline Traditions and the Rabbis: Three Case Studies." *Harvard Theological Review* 110 (2017): 169–194.

———. "The Protocol of the Court at Yavne? A New Reading of Tosefta Sanhedrin 7." [In Hebrew.] *Tarbiẓ* 78 (2009): 447–477.

———. "Rabbis as Nomikoi? Some Questions on a New Paradigm." *Journal for the Study of Judaism* 55 (2023): 1–13.

———. "Rereading *Herem*: Destruction of Idolatry in Tannaitic Literature." In *The Gift of the Land and the Fate of the Canaanites in Jewish Thought*, edited by Katell Berthelot, Joseph E. David, and Marc Hirshman, 50–65. Oxford: Oxford University Press, 2014.

———. "Responsive Blessings and the Development of the Tannaitic Liturgical System." [In Hebrew.] *Jewish Studies, an Internet Journal* 7 (2008): 1–29.

———. "The Rhetorical Self in Tannaitic Halakha." *Dead Sea Discoveries* 28 (2021): 341–366.

———. "The School of R. Ishmael and the Origins of the Concept of *Yeṣer Hara'* (the Evil Inclination)." [In Hebrew.] *Tarbiẓ* 76 (2006): 41–79.

———. "The Sin of Concealment of the Suspected Adulteress." [In Hebrew.] *Tarbiẓ* 70 (2001): 367–401.

———. "'Who Will Uncover the Dust from Your Eyes?' Mishnah *Sotah* 5 and R. Akiva's Midrash." [In Hebrew.] *Tarbiẓ* 75 (2005): 95–127.

———. "The Wisdom Tradition in Rabbinic Literature and Mishnah Avot." In *Rethinking Sapiential Traditions in Ancient Judaism*, edited by Jean-Sebastien Rey, Hindy Najman, and Eibert Tigchelaar, 172–190. Leiden: Brill, 2016.

———. "'You Shall Destroy All Places': A Tannaitic Polemic on the Destruction of Idolatry." [In Hebrew.] *Reshit* 1 (2009): 91–115.

Rosen-Zvi, Ishay, and Yaakov Kroizer, "'Throughout Your Generations': Toward Poetics of Tannaitic Midrash," *Prooftexts* (forthcoming).

Rosenthal, Abraham. "Devarim She-al Pe Ie Ata Rashai Leomram Bikhtav." In *Talmudic Studies* [in Hebrew], vol. 4, edited by Yoav Rosenthal and Shlomo Naeh, 645–730. Jerusalem: Mandel Institute of Jewish Studies, 2024.

———. "Oral Torah and Torah from Sinai: Halakhah and Practice." [In Hebrew.] In *Talmudic Studies* [in Hebrew], vol. 2, edited by Moshe Bar-Asher and David Rosenthal, 448–489. Jerusalem: Magnes Press, Hebrew University, 1993.

Rosenthal, David. "History of the Mishnaic Text." [In Hebrew.] In *The Classic Rabbinic Literature of Eretz Israel: Introduction and Studies* [in Hebrew], edited by Menahem Kahana, Vered Noam, Menahem Kister, and David Rosenthal, 65–104. Jerusalem: Ben-Zvi Institute, 2018.

———. "Mishnah Aboda Zara." [In Hebrew.] 2 vols. PhD diss., Hebrew University, 1980.

———. "'The Talmudists Jumped to Raise an Objection into the Baraita': Bavli Ketubbot 77a–b." [In Hebrew.] *Tarbiẓ* 60 (1991): 551–576.

Rosenthal, Eliezer S. "Regarding the Interpretation of Mishnah *Ta'anit* 1:1–2." [In Hebrew.] In *Yad Re'em: Kovetz le-Zekher Eli'ezer Me'ir Lifshitz*, 261–270. Jerusalem: Daf-Ḥen, 1974/1975.

———. "Scribal Notations." [In Hebrew.] In *Yuval Shay: A Jubilee Volume Dedicated to S. Y. Agnon on Occasion of His Seventieth Birthday* [in Hebrew], edited by Baruch Kurzweil, 293–324. Ramat-Gan: Bar-Ilan University Press, 1958.

———. "Tradition and Innovation in the Halakha of the Sages." [In Hebrew.] *Tarbiẓ* 63 (1994): 321–374.

Roth, Pinchas, "Doings Things with Mishna: A Chapter in the Cultural History of Rabbinic Literature." [In Hebrew.] Seminar paper, Hebrew University, 2004.

Rubenstein, Jeffrey L. *The History of Sukkot in the Second Temple and Rabbinic Periods*. Atlanta: Scholars, 1995.

———. *Talmudic Stories: Narrative Art, Composition, and Culture*. Baltimore: Johns Hopkins University Press, 1999.

Sabato, David, "The Teachings of Rabbi Joshua ben Hanania." [In Hebrew.] PhD diss., Hebrew University, 2019.

———. *The Sages of Yavne: A Journey into the Origins of Tannaitic Halakha*, Jerusalem: Magness, 2025.

Sabato, Mordechai. "Why Did They Say Two Rows in the Cellar?" [In Hebrew.] *Sidra* 19 (2004): 101–116.

Safrai, Shmuel. "The Tales of the Sages in Palestinian Tradition and the *Babylonian Talmud*." *Scripta Hierosolymitana* 22 (1971): 209–232.

Safrai, Shmuel, and Ze'ev Safrai. *Mishnat Eretz Israel: Tractate Shekalim*. [In Hebrew.] Jerusalem: E. M. Liphshitz, 2009.

Safrai, Ze'ev. "Halakhic Observance in the Judaean Desert Documents." In *Law in the Documents of the Judaean Desert*, edited by Ranon Katzoff and David Schaps, 205–236. Leiden: Brill, 2005.

———. *Mishnat Eretz Israel: Tractate Ma'asrot*. [In Hebrew.] Jerusalem: Lifshitz College of Education, 2013.

Sagiv, Yonatan. "Studies in Early Rabbinic Hermeneutics as Reflected in Selected Chapters in the *Sifra*." [In Hebrew.] PhD diss., Hebrew University, 2009.

———. "When 'Slaughtering' Means 'Pulling' and 'A Tent' Means 'A Wife': A New Approach to the Literal Interpretation of the Sages and Its Purposes." [In Hebrew.] *Jewish Studies, an Internet Journal* 9 (2010): 1–17.

Samely, Alexander. *Rabbinic Interpretation of Scripture in the Mishnah*. Oxford: Oxford University Press, 2002.

Sanders, Ed P. *Paul and Palestinian Judaism: A Comparison of Patterns of Religion*. Philadelphia: Fortress, 1977.

Sarfatti, Gad B. "Pious Men, Men of Deeds and the Early Prophets." [In Hebrew.] *Tarbiẓ* 26 (1957): 126–153.

Satlow, Michael L. *How the Bible Became Holy*. New Haven: Yale University Press, 2014.

———. *Jewish Marriage in Antiquity*. Princeton, NJ: Princeton University Press, 2001.

Schiffman, Lawrence H. *The Halakhah at Qumran*. Leiden: Brill, 1975.

———. *Reclaiming the Dead Sea Scrolls: The History of Judaism, the Background of Christianity, the Lost Library of Qumran*. Philadelphia: JPS, 1994.

Schmid, Konrad. "Judean Identity and Ecumenicity: The Political Theology of the Priestly Document." In *Judah and the Judeans in the Persian Period*, edited by Oded Lipschits and Manfred Oeming, 3–26. Winona Lake, IN: Eisenbrauns, 2006.

———. *The Scribes of the Torah: The Formation of the Pentateuch in Its Literary and Historical Contexts*. Atlanta: SBL Press, 2023.

Schneidewind, William M. "Diversity and Development of Tora in the Hebrew Bible." In *TORAH: Functions, Meanings, and Diverse Manifestations in Early Judaism and Christianity*, edited by William M. Schneidewind, Jason M. Zurawski, and Gabriele Boccaccini, 17–36. Atlanta: SBL Press, 2021.

Schremer, Adiel. "Avot Reconsidered: Rethinking Rabbinic Judaism." *Jewish Quarterly Review* 105 (2015): 287–311.

———. *Male and Female He Created Them*. [In Hebrew.] Jerusalem: Zalman Shazar Center, 2003.

———. "The Religious Orientation of Non-Rabbis in Second Century Palestine: A Rabbinic Perspective." In *"Follow the Wise": Studies in Jewish History and Culture in Honor of Lee I. Levine*, edited by Oded Irshai, Jodi Magness, Seth Schwartz, and Zeev Weiss, 319–341. Winona Lake, IN: Eisenbrauns, 2010.

———. "The Sages in Palestinian Society of the Mishnah Period: Torah, Prestige, and Social Standing." [In Hebrew.] In *The Classic Rabbinic Literature of Eretz Israel: Introduction and Studies* [in Hebrew], edited by Menahem Kahana, Vered Noam, Menahem Kister, and David Rosenthal, 553–581. Jerusalem: Ben-Zvi Institute, 2018.

———. "'[T]he[y] Did Not Read in the Sealed Book': Qumran Halakhic Revolution and the Emergence of Torah Study in Second Temple Judaism." In *Historical Perspectives; from the Hasmoneans to Bar Kokhba in Light of the Dead Sea Scrolls, Proceedings of the Fourth International Symposium of the Orion Center for the Study of the Dead Sea Scrolls and Associated Literature, 27–31 January, 1999*, edited by David Goodblatt, Avital Pinnick, and Daniel R. Schwartz, 105–126. Leiden: Brill, 2000.

Schürer, Emil. *The History of the Jewish People in the Age of Jesus Christ (175 B.C.–A.D. 135)*. Revised and Edited by Geza Vermes, Fergus Millar, and Matthew Black. 3 vols. Edinburgh: Clark, 1973–1987.

Schwartz, Daniel R. "From Priests at Their Right to Christians at Their Left? On the Interpretation and Development of a Mishnaic Story (M. Rosh HaShanah 2:8–9)." [In Hebrew.] *Tarbiẓ* 74.1 (2004): 21–41.

———. "Hillel and Scripture: From Authority to Exegesis." In *Hillel and Jesus: Comparative Studies of Two Major Religious Leaders*, edited by James H. Charlesworth and Loren L. Johns, 335–362. Minneapolis: Fortress, 1997.

Schwartz, Seth. *Imperialism and Jewish Society, 200 B.C.E. to 640 C.E.* Princeton, NJ: Princeton University Press, 2001.

———. "Law in Jewish Society in the Second Temple Period." In *The Cambridge Companion to Judaism and Law*, edited by Christine Hayes, 48–75. Cambridge: Cambridge University Press, 2017.

Seeligmann, I. L. "The Beginnings of Midrash in the Books of Chronicles." [In Hebrew.] *Tarbiẓ* 49 (1979): 14–32.

———. *Studies in Biblical Literature*. [In Hebrew.] Edited by Avi Hurvitz, Emanuel Tov, and Sara Japhet. Jerusalem: Magnes, 1992.

Segal, Michael. *The Book of Jubilees: Rewritten Bible, Redaction, Ideology and Theology*. Leiden: Brill, 2007.

Shammah, Abraham. "Mekhiltot That Are Appended to the Sifra: Mekhilta De-Miluim and Mekhilta Da-Arayot." [In Hebrew.] PhD diss., Hebrew University, 2008.

Shanks-Alexander, Elizabeth. "The Rhetoric of Pedagogy in Early Rabbinic Literature." In *Cambridge History of Rhetoric*, edited by Harvey Yunis and Henriette van der Blom. Cambridge: Cambridge University Press, forthcoming.

———. *Transmitting Mishnah: The Shaping Influence of Oral Tradition*. Cambridge: Cambridge University Press, 2006.

Shapira, Haim. "The Court in Yavne: Status, Authority and Functions." [In Hebrew.] In *Studies in Jewish Law: Judge and Judging* [in Hebrew], edited by Yaakov Habba and Amihai Radzyner, 305–334. Ramat-Gan: Bar-Ilan University, 2007.

———. "The Courts in the Mishnah: *M. Sanhedrin*, Chapter 1, Revisited." [In Hebrew.] *Tarbiẓ* 88 (2022): 139–182.

Sharvit, Shimon, *Tractate Avoth through the Ages*. [In Hebrew.] Jerusalem: Bialik Institue, 2004.

Shemesh, Aharon. "4Q251: Midrash Mishpatim." *Dead Sea Discoveries* 12.3 (2005): 280–302.

———. "Biblical Exegesis and Interpretations from Qumran to the Rabbis." In *A Companion to Biblical Interpretation in Early Judaism*, edited by Matthias Henze, 467–489. Grand Rapids, MI: Eerdmans, 2012.

———. *Halakhah in the Making: The Development of Jewish Law from Qumran to the Rabbis*. Berkeley: University of California Press, 2009.

———. *Punishments and Sins: From Scripture to the Rabbis*. [In Hebrew.] Jerusalem: Magnes, 2003.

———. "The Term 'Mitzvah Ha-Teluyah Ba-Aretz' Reexamined." [In Hebrew.] *Sidra* 16 (2000): 151–177.

Shemesh-Raiskin, Rivka. *Halakhic Give-and-Take Conversations in the Mishnah.* [in Hebrew.] Jerusalem: Academy of the Hebrew Language, 2022.

Shilat, Yitzhak. *Iggerot ha-Rambam.* 2 vols. Maale Adumim: Ma'aliyyot, 1988.

Shinan, Avigdor. *The Biblical Story as Reflected in Its Aramaic Translations.* [In Hebrew.] Tel Aviv: Hotza'at ha-Kibbutz ha-Me'uḥad, 1993.

———. "Live Translation: On the Nature of the Aramaic Targums to the Pentateuch." *Prooftexts* 3.1 (1983): 41–49.

Shmidman, Shira, Joel Binder, and Ira Rabin. "Margin Notes of Tosefta MS Erfurt," *Journal of Jewish Studies* 76 (2025): 272–300.

Shuve, Karl. *The Song of Songs and the Fashioning of Identity in Early Latin Christianity.* Oxford: Oxford University Press, 2016.

Simon-Shoshan, Moshe. *Stories of the Law: Narrative Discourse and the Construction of Authority in the Mishnah.* New York: Oxford University Press, 2012.

———. "The Story of Honi Hame'agel in Mishnah Ta'anit 3:8: A Case Study in the Art of Mishnaic Narrative." [In Hebrew.] *Jerusalem Studies in Hebrew Literature* 26 (2013): 1–20.

Sirat, Collette. *Hebrew Manuscripts of the Middle Ages.* Edited and Translated by Nicholas de Lange. Cambridge: Cambridge University Press, 2002.

Slotnick, Yosef. "A Call to Order: An Analysis of the Structure and Editing of Chapters *Ha-Neḥenakin* and *Ḥelek* in Tractate *Sanhedrin*." [In Hebrew.] *Asuppot* 5 (2016): 99–118.

———. "Tzibburei Ma'ot: Three Coins Stacked One on Top of the Other." [In Hebrew.] *Ma'agalim* 8 (2013): 43–65.

Smith, Morton. *Jesus the Magician.* New York: Harper & Row, 1978.

Sommer, Benjamin D. "Concepts of Scriptural Language in Midrash." In *Jewish Concepts of Scripture: A Comparative Introduction*, edited by Benjamin D. Sommer, 64–79. New York: NYU Press, 2012.

Sperber, Daniel. *Roman Palestine, 200–400: Money and Prices.* Ramat-Gan: Bar-Ilan University, 1975.

———. "A Study of the Bar Kokhba Coins." [In Hebrew.] *Sinai* 55 (1964): 37–41.

Stein Hain, Elana. *Circumventing the Law.* Philadelphia: University of Pennsylvania Press, 2024.

Steinmetz, Devora. *Punishment and Freedom: The Rabbinic Construction of Criminal Law.* Philadelphia: University of Pennsylvania Press, 2008.

Stemberg, Günter. "The Derasha in Rabbinic Times." In *Preaching in Judaism and Christianity: Encounters and Developments from Biblical Times to Modernity*, edited by Alexander Deeg, Walter Homolka, and Heinz-Günther Schöttler, 7–21. Berlin: De Gruyter, 2008.

Stern, David. "The Captive Woman: Hellenization, Greco-Roman Erotic Narrative, and Rabbinic Literature." *Poetics Today* 19 (1998): 91–127.

———. "The First Jewish Books and the Early History of Jewish Reading." *Jewish Quarterly Review* 98 (2008): 163–202.

———. "Midrash and Indeterminacy." *Critical Inquiry* 15 (1988): 132–161.

———. *Parables in Midrash: Narrative and Exegesis in Rabbinic Literature.* Cambridge, MA: Harvard University Press, 1991.

———. The Publication and Early Transmission of the Mishnah." In *What Is the Mishnah? The State of the Question*, edited by Shaye J. D. Cohen, 444–470. Boston: Harvard University Press, 2023.

Stern, Sacha. "Rabbi and the Origins of the Patriarchate." *Journal of Jewish Studies* 54 (2003): 193–215.

Strack, H. L., and Günter Stemberger. *Introduction to the Talmud and Midrash.* Translated and edited by Markus Bockmuehl. 2nd print. Minneapolis: Fortress, 1996.

Sussman, Yaacov. "The History of Halakha and the Dead Sea Scrolls—Preliminary Observations on Miqṣat Ma'ase Ha-Torah (4QMMT)." [In Hebrew.] *Tarbiẓ* 59.1–2 (1990): 11–76.

———. "Manuscripts and Text Traditions of the Mishnah." [In Hebrew.] *Proceedings of the Seventh World Congress of Jewish Studies: Studies in the Talmud, Halacha and Midrash*. Jerusalem, 1981: 215–250.

———. *Oral Law—Taken Literally: The Power of the Tip of a Yod*. [In Hebrew.] Jerusalem: Hebrew University Magnes, 2019.

———. "'Parallels' in Rabbinic Literature." [In Hebrew.] *Netu'im* 23 (2022): 7–13.

———. *Thesaurus of Talmudic Manuscripts*. [In Hebrew.] With the cooperation of Yoav Rosenthal and Aharon Shweka. 3 vols. Jerusalem: Ben-Zvi Institute, 2012.

Talgam, Rina. "Similarities and Differences between Synagogue and Church Mosaics in Palestine during the Byzantine and Umayyad Periods." In *From Dura to Sepphoris: Studies in Jewish Art and Society in Late Antiquity*, edited by Lee I. Levine and Zeev Weiss, 93–110. Portsmouth, RI: Journal of Roman Archaeology, 2000.

Talshir, David. "Ha-'Ivrit ba-Me'ah ha-Sheniyyah la-Sefirah: Leshon ha-Epigrafiyah be-Hashva'ah li-Leshon ha-Tanna'im." In *'Iyyunim bi-Leshon Ḥakhamim*, edited by Moshe Bar-Asher, 42–49. Jerusalem: Institute for Advanced Studies, Hebrew University, 1996.

Teugels, Lieve M. *Bible and Midrash: The Story of "The Wooing of Rebekah" (Gen. 24)*. Leuven: Peeters, 2004.

Torjesen, Karen Bo. *Hermeneutical Procedure and Theological Structure in Origen's Exegesis*. Berlin: Walter De Gruyter, 1986.

Tropper, Amram. "A Tale of Two Sinais: On the Reception of the Torah according to *bShab* 88a." In *Rabbinic Traditions between Palestine and Babylonia*, edited by Ronit Nikolsky and Tal Ilan, 147–157. Leiden: Brill, 2014.

———. *Wisdom, Politics, and Historiography: Tractate Avot in the Context of the Graeco-Roman Near East*. Oxford: Oxford University Press, 2004.

Turner, Victor W. *The Ritual Process: Structure and Anti-Structure*. Chicago: Aldine, 1969.

Twersky, Isadore. *Introduction to the Code of Maimonides (Mishneh Torah)*. New Haven: Yale University Press, 1980.

Urbach, Efraim E. "The *Derashah* as the Basis for the Halakhah and the Problem of the *Soferim*." Translated by Christine Hayes. In *Classic Essays in Early Rabbinic Culture and History*, edited by Christine Hayse, 281–302. London: Routledge, Taylor & Francis, 2018.

———. *The Halakhah: Its Sources and Development*. Ramat-Gan: Yad la-Talmud, 1986.

———. "The Homiletical Interpretations of the Sages and the Expositions of Origen on Canticles, and the Jewish-Christian Disputation." In *Studies in Aggadah and Folk-Literature* [Scripta Hierosolymitana, vol. 22], edited by Joseph Heinemann and Dov Noy, 247–275. Jerusalem: Magnes, 1971.

———. *The Sages, Their Concepts and Beliefs*. Translated by Israel Abrahams. Jerusalem: Magnes, 1975.

———. *World of the Sages: Collected Studies*. [In Hebrew.] 2nd ed. Jerusalem: Magnes, 2002.

Van Boxel, Piet, Kirsten Macfarlane, and Joanna Weinberg. "The Mishnah between Jews and Christians in Early Modern Europe." In *The Mishnaic Moment: Jewish Law among Jews and Christians in Early Modern Europe*, edited by Piet Van Boxel, Kirsten Macfarlane, and Joanna Weinberg, 3–43. Oxford: Oxford University Press, 2022.

VanderKam, James C. *Jubilees: A Commentary on the Book of Jubilees, Chapters 22–50*. Edited by Sidnie White Crawford. Minneapolis: Fortress, 2018.

———. "The Origin and Purposes of the Book of Jubilees." In *Studies in the Book of Jubilees*, edited by Matthias Albani, Jörg Frey, and Armin Lange, 3–24. Tübingen: Mohr Siebeck, 1997.

Vermes, Geza. "Bible Interpretation at Qurman." *Eretz-Israel* 20 (1989): 184–191.

———. *The Dead Sea Scrolls: Qumran in Perspective*. Rev. 3rd ed. London: SCM, 1994.

———. *Scripture and Tradition in Judaism: Haggadic Studies*. Leiden: Brill, 1961.

Vidas, Moulie. *The Rise of Talmud*. Oxford: Oxford University Press, 2025.

———. "What Is a *Tannay*?" *Oqimta* 7 (2021): 21–96.

Viezel, Eran. *The Intention of the Torah and the Intention of Its Readers: Episodes of Contention*. [In Hebrew.] Jerusalem: Magness, 2021.

Visotzky, Burton L. *Fathers of the World: Essays in Rabbinic and Patristic Literatures*. Tübingen: J. C. B. Mohr, 1995.

von Rad, Gerhard. *Studies in Deuteronomy*. Translated by Davis Stalker. London: SCM Press, 1953.

Walfish, Avraham. "Conceptual Ramifications of Tractates *Tamid* and *Middot*." [In Hebrew.] *Judea and Samaria Research Studies* 7 (1997): 79–92.

———. "The Literary Method of Redaction in Mishnah Based on Tractate Rosh Hashanah." [In Hebrew.] PhD diss., Hebrew University, 2001.

———. "Response: To S. Naeh, 'Creates the Fruit of Lips.'" [In Hebrew.] *Tarbiz* 65 (1996): 301–314.

———. "Unifying Halakhah and Aggadah: A Study of the Editorial Strategies of the Tosefta." [In Hebrew.] In *Higayon l'Yona: News Aspects in the Study of Midrash, Aggadah and Piyyut* [in Hebrew], edited by Joshua Levinson, Jacob Elbaum, and Galit Hasan-Rokem, 309–331. Jerusalem: Magnes, 2007.

Weinberg, Yechiel Yaakov. "The Sources of the Mishnah and the Method of Its Arrangement." [In Hebrew.] *Talpiyyot* 7 (1961): 72–88, 290–316.

Weiss, Abraham. "The Presentation of Material in Tractate *Kiddushin*." [In Hebrew.] *Horeb* 12 (1956): 70–148.

Weiss, Isaac Hirsch. *Dor Dor ve-Doreshav*. 6th ed. 5 vols. Vilna: Y. L. Goldberg, 1911.

———. *Sifra de-Vei Rav*. Vienna, 1882.

Weiss, Moses Isaac. "Chapters of the Mishnah of a Toseftan Character." [In Hebrew.] In *Proceedings of the Eleventh World Congress of Jewish Studies: Jerusalem, 1993*: 55–62.

Weiss Halivni, David. *Midrash, Mishnah, and Gemara: The Jewish Predilection for Justified Law*. Cambridge, MA: Harvard University Press, 1986.

———. *Peshat and Derash: Plain and Applied Meaning in Rabbinic Exegesis*. New York: Oxford University Press, 1991.

———. "The Reception Accorded to Rabbi Judah's Mishnah." In *Jewish and Christian Self-Definition*, edited by E. P. Sanders, vol. 2, 204–212. Philadelphia: Fortress, 1981.

———. *Sources and Traditions: A Source Critical Commentary on the Talmud Tractate Baba Kama*. [In Hebrew.] Jerusalem: Magnes, 1993.

———. *Sources and Traditions: A Source Critical Commentary on the Talmud Tractate Baba Metzia*. [In Hebrew.] Jerusalem: Magnes, 2003.

Werblowsky, R. J. Zwi. *Joseph Karo: Lawyer and Mystic*. Philadelphia: JPS, 1977.

Werman, Cana. "The End of Days in the Thought of the Qumran Sect." [In Hebrew.] In *Qumran Scrolls and Their World* [in Hebrew], edited by Menahem Kister, 529–549. Jerusalem: Ben-Zvi Institute, 2009.

Werman, Cana, and Avraham Shemesh. *Revealing the Hidden: Exegesis and Halakha in the Qumran Scrolls*. [In Hebrew.] Jerusalem: Bialik Institute, 2011.

Westreich, Avishalom. *The Four Archetypes of Damages: Law, Tradition and Interpretation*. [In Hebrew.] Jerusalem: Carmel, 2023.

Westbrook, Raymond. "Introduction: Character of Ancient Near Eastern Law." In *A History of Ancient Near Eastern Law*, edited by Raymond Westbrook, 1–92. Leiden: Brill, 2003.

Wilfand, Yael. "'A Proselyte Whose Sons Converted with Him': Roman Laws on New Citizens' Authority over Their Children and Tannaitic Rulings on Converts to Judaism and Their Offspring." In *Legal Engagement: The Reception of Roman Law and Tribunals by Jews and Other Inhabitants of the Empire*, edited by Katell Berthelot, Natalie Dohrmann, and Capucine Nemo-Pekelman, 345–364. Rome: Publications de l'École française de Rome, 2021.

Wimpfheimer, Barry Scott. "The Mishnah's Reader: Reconsidering Literary Meaning." *Jewish Quarterly Review* 113 (2023): 335–367.

Wollenberg, Rebecca Scharbach. *The Closed Book: How the Rabbis Taught the Jews (Not) to Read the Bible*. Princeton: Princeton University Press, 2023.

Yadin, Yigael. *The Temple Scroll*. 3 vols. Jerusalem: Israel Exploration Society, 1977–1983.

Yadin, Yigael, Jonas C. Greenfield, Ada Yardeni, and Baruch A. Levine, eds. *The Documents from the Bar Kokhba Period in the Cave of Letters: Hebrew, Aramaic, and Nabatean-Aramaic Papyri*. With additional contributions by Hannah M. Cotton and Joseph Naveh. 2 vols. Jerusalem: Israel Exploration Society, Hebrew University, and the Israel Museum, 2002.

Yadin-Israel, Azzan. "Rabbinic Polysemy and Pluralism Revisited: Between Praxis and Thematization." *Association for Jewish Studies Review* 31 (2007): 1–40.

———. *Scripture and Tradition: Rabbi Akiva and the Triumph of Midrash*. Philadelphia: University of Pennsylvania Press, 2015.

———. *Scripture as Logos: Rabbi Ishmael and the Origins of Midrash*. Philadelphia: University of Pennsylvania Press, 2004.

Yehuda, Zvi Arie. "The Two Mekhiltot on the Hebrew Slave." PhD diss., Yeshiva University, 1974.

Yeivin, Israel, ed. *A Collection of Mishnaic Geniza Fragments with Babylonian Vocalization*. [In Hebrew.] Jerusalem: Makor, 1974.

Yerushalmi, Yosef Haim. *Zakhor: Jewish History and Jewish Memory*. Foreword by Harold Bloom. Seattle: University of Washington Press, 1989.

Young, Frances M. *Biblical Exegesis and the Formation of Christian Culture*. Cambridge: Cambridge University Press, 1997.

Yuval, Israel Jacob. "The Orality of Jewish Oral Law: From Pedagogy to Ideology." In *Judaism, Christianity and Islam in the Course of History: Exchange and Conflicts*, edited by Lothar Gall and Dietmar Willoweit, 237–260. München: R. Oldenbourg Verlag, 2011.

Zadok, Avital Maayan, et al. "Comparative Network Analysis as a New Approach to the Editorship Profiling Task: A Case Study of the Mishnah and Tosefta from Rabbinic literature." *Digital Scholarship in the Humanities* (2023): 1–20.

Zellentin, Holger. "What Is 'within Judaism' according to the Quran?" In *Within Judaism? Interpretive Trajectories in Judaism, Christianity, and Islam from the First to the Twenty-First Century*, edited by Anders Runesson and Karin Hedner Zetterholm, 282–308. Lanham, MD: Lexington Books/Fortress Academic, 2023.

Zlotnick, Dov. *The Iron Pillar—Mishnah: Redaction, Form, and Intent*. Jerusalem: Bialik Institute, 1988.

Zohar, Noam. "Partitions around a Common Public Space: Gentiles and Their Statues in Mishnah Avodah Zarah." [In Hebrew.] *Reshit* 1 (2009): 145–163.

———. "Reason and Justification in the Mishnah." *Journal of Law, Religion and State* 2 (2013): 250–262.

———. "Scripture, Mishnah, and Ideas: Redaction and Meaning at the Beginning of Tractate *Nezikin*." In *By The Well: Studies in Jewish Philosophy and Halakhic Thought, Presented to Gerald J. Blidstein* [in Hebrew], edited by Uri Ehrlich, Howard Kreisel, and Daniel Lasker, 195–208. Beersheba: Ben-Gurion University, 2008.

———. *Secrets of the Rabbinic Workshop: Redaction as a Key to Meaning*. [In Hebrew.] Jerusalem: Magnes, 2006/2007.

———. "The Sin Offering in Tannaitic Literature." [In Hebrew.] MA thesis, Hebrew University, 1988.

GENERAL INDEX

Akiva, Rabbi (school of), 73, 76, 218–237, 240, 245, 256, 272–274, 277–278, 296, 298, 305, 329, 342–344, 347
allegorical interpretation, 209–212, 268, 314
Amidah. *See* prayer
ancient Near East, 209, 239, 260
apocalypse, 212, 284
Apocrypha, Jewish, 12–13, 13*box*
apodictic law, 26, 260, 273
asmakhta (anchoring tradition in Scripture), 256, 269, 308, 336–337, 342, 346
ʿAvodah Zarah (tractate), 101, 109
Avot (tractate), 61, 115, 133–135, 155
Avot de-Rabbi Natan, 23*box*, 134

Babatha, archive of, 69*box*
bailees and deposits, 56, 88–89
Bar Kokhba letters, 23–24
Bava Metzi'a (tractate), 88
Berakhot (benedictions), 168–169, 174–175
Berakhot (tractate), 17–18, 90, 94, 118, 125, 168–169, 172–173
Bet Hillel and Bet Shammai, 22*box*, 31, 43, 45, 49, 67
Betzah (tractate), 91
bibleless tractates, 53*box*
biblicisms, 57–59. *See also* mishnaic Hebrew
bikkurim (first fruit ceremony), 39–41

Cairo Genizah, 364*box*
canonization, 165, 217, 250, 263, 344

capital punishment, 33, 100–101, 109–110, 130–132, 177, 208
casuistic law, 26–27, 260–261, 272–273, 283
Christianity, early, 51, 140–141
Chronicles, book of, 186, 205
circumcision, 13–14, 211, 324
codices/codification, 51–52, 59, 70, 76, 78, 89–92, 94–95, 176–177, 260–261
Community Rule, 186*box*
conceptualization, 103–108
Constituo Antoniniana, 70*box*
Corpus Juris Civilis, 76
criticism, higher and lower, 349*box*
customs, 95–96, 110

Dead Sea Scrolls, 10–15, 11*box*, 200–205. *See also pesher;* Second Temple literature
deaf-mutes, 32, 43–44, 53–54, 259–260. *See also* mentally incompetent; minors

ʿEduyyot (tractate), 62–63
eino tzarikh, 306–309
Eliezer, Rabbi, 73
Eliezer ha-Kappar, Rabbi, 134*box*
enforcement, 95–97, 100–101, 264
ʿEruvin (tractate), 74
exogamy (intermarriage), 8–9, 198–199
Ezra the Scribe, 6, 8, 36, 185, 198

findings (laws of), 27–29, 44, 107, 110, 346

Geonim, 35*box*
Gittin (tractate), 90–91
glosses, 145*box*

Haggadah (Passover), 191, 194
Halakhah, 4, 49, 51–52, 59, 69–70, 90–93, 95–98, 100–101, 161, 176–177, 185, 210, 216, 235, 248, 260–261, 347
halakhah le-Moshe mi-Sinai ("halakhah of Moses from Sinai"), 60–61, 233
Halakhic Letter, 203*box*
Ḥallah (tractate), 106
ḥasidim (pietists), 117–118, 125
Hellenistic culture, 140, 235
hermeneutics, 183–184, 184*box*, 219, 222–235, 238–239, 267, 310, 353
ḥol hamo'ed, 100*box*

intertextuality, 189–196, 226–227, 280, 284
'*inyan* (context), 241, 278–283
Ishmael, 13, 211
Ishmael, Rabbi (school of), 218–238, 244–246, 252, 264, 272–274, 277–278, 280, 294–295, 304–305, 309, 329, 344, 357
Israel, land of, 16*box*

Kabbalah, theosophical, 153*box*
Karaites, 35
kavvanah (intention), 27, 101–102, 113, 164
ke-illu ("as if it were"), 68–69
Kelim (tractate), 110
Keritot, 102
ketubah (marriage contract), 53, 68
Ketubbot (tractate), 53
Kiddushin (tractate), 78
kil'ayim (forbidden mixtures), 96, 99
ki-shemu'o, 236–237, 299–305

ma'aseh, 53, 63–67, 70, 110, 115–126
Ma'aser Sheni (tractate), 78
maggid, 219, 311
Maimonides (commentary of the Mishnah), 30–31, 148, 152, 154,
Makkot (tractate), 101
manuscripts, 141–143, 143*box*, 147–152, 359, 363
marriage, 68
martyrdom, 215, 364
measure for measure, 126*box*

memorization, 20–22, 33, 79, 92, 139
Menaḥot (tractate), 91
mentally incompetent, 32–33, 43, 53–54, 259–260. *See also* deaf-mutes; minors
middah, middot (hermeneutic principals), 219, 228, 232, 234–235, 278
Middot (tractate), 80, 155
mi-kan ameru ("hence they said"), 339
minors, 32, 43, 53–55, 57, 62, 259–260, 286, 339–340. *See also* deaf-mutes; mentally incompetent; vows
Mishnah, the six *sedarim* of, 18*box*
"mishnah does not budge," 76, 92
mishnah rishonah, 38–42, 48–49
mishnaic Hebrew, 150–151, 155, 288–94. *See also* biblicisms; participles
Mo'ed (seder), 54
Mo'ed Katan (tractate), 104

Nazir (tractate), 91, 334
Nedarim (tractate), 54, 110–111, 334
Nega'im (tractate), 58
Nezikin (tractate), 54, 58

'*omer*, 77
Onias (Honyo), temple of, 109*box*
Oral Torah, 35*box*
Oral vs. Written Torah, 135, 234–235, 358
Origen of Alexandria, 211–212, 314–315, 315*box*

participles, 62. *See also* mishnaic Hebrew
Passover (*pesaḥ*), 206–207, 250–251
Paul, 210–212, 211*box*, 368
Pe'ah (law), 60
Pesaḥim (tractate), 90
peshat, 238, 304
pesher, 212–215, 268, 289. *See also* Dead Sea Scrolls
Pharisees, 10*box*, 10–15, 36, 62–63
Philo, 208–212, 216, 223, 268, 303, 305, 367
prayer, 118–119, 173–174
Priestly Code, 4, 250
priests, 5–8
print, 152–154, 178–179, 360
punishment. *See* enforcement
purity laws, 5–6, 11, 15, 37, 58, 62, 70, 110, 176–177

Qumran. *See* Dead Sea Scrolls

Rav, 147*box*
rebellious son, 54
Reciters, 138–140
rewritten Bible, 188, 199–200, 202, 205–207, 251, 290, 294
Roman Empire, 51, 102, 215, 289, 314
Roman law, 67–70, 76, 100, 141, 178, 368
Rosh ha-Shanah (tractate), 91

Saadia Gaon, 35, 89
sacrifices, 46–47, 102–103
Sages (*ḥakhamim*, as a collective attribution), 84–85, 87
Sages, 70–73, 81–84, 155–156, 168, 219, 334–335, 337, 355. *See also* vows
Sanhedrin (tractate), 101, 130–132
Scribes, 8–10, 36, 61
scrolls (Torah, biblical), 195
Second Temple literature, 51, 74, 212, 215, 251, 315. *See also* Dead Sea Scrolls; *pesher*; Philo
Second Temple period, 5*box*
sects, 10*box*, 10–15, 36, 51, 176, 186–187, 200–205. *See also pesher*
Septuagint (LXX), 208*box*
Shabbat (tractate), 20, 53, 74, 90–91
Shabbat, 24, 31–32, 102
shemittah, loan forgiveness during, 105*box*
Sherira Gaon, 50, 78, 89, 155
Shevu'ot (tractate), 58
Sotah (tractate), 79, 156
sotah ritual, 32, 79–81, 87, 129–130, 162
structuralism, 191*box*
sukkah (booth), 96
Sukkah (tractate), 90–91

Ta'anit (tractate), 53, 66
Talmuds, 20*box*, 59–60, 66, 145, 147–148, 176, 348
Tamid (tractate), 39, 79–80, 155
tanna kamma (the anonymous opinion), 82–83, 87
Teacher of Righteousness, 212–213, 217. *See also* Dead Sea Scrolls
Teharot (seder), 54
Temple law, 6–7, 39, 62, 66, 77, 108, 110, 256
terminology, 219, 236, 251, 299, 305, 322
testimonies. *See 'Eduyyot* (tractate)
theology in Midrash, 235, 245, 312, 327
tithes, 47*box*, 59, 327
traditions, extrabiblical, 60–63, 233–234, 256–260, 283, 334–338

Usha, 16, 45, 49–50

vows, 60, 286–287, 334

"Why did they say X?," 157, 169
Wissenschaft des Judentums, 36*box*
witnesses (rabbinic law), 264

"X is nothing but Y," 238, 288, 349

Yavneh, 16, 39, 45, 49–50, 61, 337
Yehudah ha-Nasi, Rabbi, 77*box*
Yevamot (tractate), 105–106
yibbum and *ḥalitzah*, 98*box*
Yoma (tractate), 132–133

Zera'im (seder) 19*box*
Zevaḥim (tractate), 101
Zugot, 37*box*

INDEX OF PRIMARY SOURCES

BIBLE

Genesis
    22:10–12   205

Exodus
    19:16–17   316
    21:18–19   261, 273
    21:28–32   57–58
    22:6, 9   28
    22:6, 9–10   56
    22:8   229
    22:15–16   202
    23:17   55

Leviticus
    22:14   59
    22:27   304
    23:40–43   9

Numbers
    18:2   361

Deuteronomy
    16:1   327–328
    22:28–29   202
    25:1–3   270
    25:3   258
    25:11–12   355

Isaiah
    53:12   193

Haggai
    2:11–14   5–6

Malachi
    2:7   5

Ezra
    7:10   185
    9:1–2, 10–12   198

Nehemia
    8:14–17   9
    13:1–3   8–9

APOCRYPHA

Jubilees
    15:25–33   13
    18:8–12   206
    18:17–19   206
    49:7–9   199

DEAD SEA SCROLLS

Community Rule Scroll, 1QS
    5:11   187
    5:16–18   201
    6:6–8   186

Damascus Document   14–15, 200
Halakhic Letter (4QMMT)   11–12

Pesher Habakkuk
    2:5–10   213
    2:10–13   214
    7:1–5   212
    12:6–10   213

Pesher Hosea
    2:8–14   214

Temple Scroll, 11Q19
    66:8–11   203

FIRST CENTURY CE COMPOSITIONS

Josephus
  Antiquities of the Jews, 14:22   124
Paul
  Galatians 4:21–31, NRSVUE   210–211
Philo
  On Flight and Finding,
    §54–§55 (ed. Loeb, p. 39)   208
  On the Creation, §157–
    §158 (ed. Loeb, p. 125)   209
  *On the Migration of
    Abraham*, §89 and §93
    (ed. Loeb, pp. 183 and 185)   210

RABBINIC WORKS

Mishnah

'Arakhin
  3:1   21
'Avodah Zarah
  1:6–8   102
  4:4   145–146
Bava Batra
  2   24–25
Bava Kamma
  1:2   156
  4:5   57–58
  8:1   356
Bava Metzi'a
  1:1–2   27–28, 103
  1:6   151
  2:1   28–29
  2:1–2   107
  2:2   44
  2:5   346
  3:1   55–56, 88
  4:1   157
  4:9   157
  4:12   101
  7:1   116
  7:5   86, 99
  7:8   88
Berakhot
  1:1   60, 63–64, 70, 85–86, 90
  1:2   99
  1:4   169
  2:1   27, 164
  4:2   110
  4:3   158
  5:1   118
  5:2   65
  5:5   119
  6:7   29–30
  9:1   166
  9:1–5   173
  9:3   172
Bikkurim
  2:1   100
  3:2–4, 6   39–41
'Eduyyot
  6:1   62
'Eruvin
  4:3   69
Gittin
  9:1   99
Ḥagigah
  1:1   54–55, 259–260, 339–340
  1:6   114–115
  1:8   54
Ḥallah
  1:8   106
Ḥullin
  2:8–9   26
  3:1   99
  5:3   84
  6:2   84
Kelim
  11:4   167–168
Keritot
  3:4–5   110
  3:7   61, 73
  3:10   102–103
Ketubbot
  1:1   143
  3:5   205
Kiddushin
  1:1   42, 68
Kil'ayim
  1:9   99

Index of Primary Sources   451

Mishnah *(continued)*

Ma'aser Sheni
3:7	48
5	77–78

Ma'asrot
1:8	171

Makkot
3:9	109

Middot
1	80

Mo'ed Katan
2:3	104
2:5	99

Nazir
5:4	108

Niddah
1	43

'Orlah
1:2	108
3:9	61

Pe'ah
2:6	60
4:6	109
8:9	101

Pesaḥim
6:1–2	71–72
7:13	25
10:4	194

Rosh ha-Shanah
3:7–8	113

Sanhedrin
6:2	131
6:3	130
8	54
8:1	32–33
9:3	109
10:1	130–131, 148–150

Shabbat
1:1	21, 30
1:5–8	31
2:1	24–25
16:6	98
19:5	14

Shekalim
1:3	96–97
1:4	7
1:5	361
2:3	83
2:5	83
4:7	46

Shevi'it
8:7	50
10:7	105

Sotah
1:1	162–163
1:2	159–160
1:4	161–162
1:5	32
1:5–7	129
1:8–9	126–128
2:2	87
6:2–3	159
7:2	80–81

Sukkah
1:1	3
1:2	343
1:6	27
2:7	67
2:8	65–66
2:9	114
3:4	332
3:8	66
3:9, 13	95–96

Ta'anit
1:4–7	122–123
2:1	123
3:8	120–121

Tamid
1:1	79–80

Teharot
10:3	99

Temurah
1:1	25

Terumot
1:1–2	43–44
6:1	59

'Uktzin
3:10	105

Yadayim
3:5	73
4:2	73
4:7	11–12

Yevamot
4:4	97–98
8:3	337–338
16:4	64

Yoma
7:2	26
8:9	132
8:8	133

Zavim
4:4, 6–7	110

Tosefta

Bava Kamma
1:1	156
10:25–27	81–82

Bava Metzi'a
1:2	103–104
2:7	44
3:13	157
3:24	157, 171

Berakhot
1:5	169–170
2:2	164
3:1	156
3:3	157
6:1–25	173
6:2	166
6:5	174
6:7	174

Kelim, Bava Metzi'a
1:6	168

Ma'aser Sheni
2:12	48

Ma'asrot
1:11	171

Pasḥa
4:13	335

Ta'anit
2:13	124–125

Sotah
1:1	163
1:2	158–161
1:5	32
1:6	162

Tannaitic Midrashim

Mekhilta de-Rabbi Yishmael

'Amalek
§1, p. 179	237
§1, p. 190	312
§2, p. 185	302

Ba-Ḥodesh
§2, p. 209	312
§3, p. 214	316–320
§3, pp. 214–215	320–321
§6, p. 227	215
§7, p. 229	200
§8, p. 233	227
§9, p. 238	312
§11, p. 243	340–341

Be-Shallaḥ
§1, p. 82	312

Kaspa
§2, p. 317	277
§4, p. 333	259

Nezikin
§1, p. 247	246
§1, p. 249	247
§2, p. 254	253
§3, p. 258	300–301, 305
§4, p. 261	260
§5, p. 267	227
§6, p. 269	228, 261, 273, 295
§10, pp. 281–282	242
§10, p. 283	352–353
§15, pp. 300–301	229
§16, p. 307	249
§17, p. 308	204
§17, p. 309	203–204, 283
§18, p. 313	225, 282
§18, p. 314	243

Pasḥa
§2, p. 8	248
§3, p. 330	252
§4, pp. 10–11	285
§4, p. 13	285
§5, p. 14	323–324
§5, p. 17	345–346
§6, p. 18	325, 352
§6, pp. 19–20	311
§6, pp. 20–21	224–225
§8, p. 26	249
§8, p. 28	307
§13, p. 44	311
§17, p. 66	256–257
§17, p. 67	300, 305
§18, p. 71	358

Tannaitic Midrashim (continued)

Shirata

§2, p. 125	284
§3, p. 126	314
§3, p. 127	364
§4, p. 129	312–313
§5, p. 134	289
§8, p. 144	314

Vayhi

§7, p. 112	359

Vayyassa'

§1, pp. 153–154	191–193
§1, p. 154	302–303
§5, p. 170	288

Mekhilta de-Rashbi

13:9, p. 41	305
17:9, p. 121	237
21:2, p. 159	246–248
21:10, p. 167	305
21:28, pp. 178–179	242
21:33, p. 185	343

Mekhilta Deuteronomy

12:2	224
12:3	345–346

Midrash Tanna'im

127	366

Sifra

  Aḥarei Mot

8:1 [85d]	265

  Emor

4:2 [96c]	298
12:3 [102d]	333
12:4 [102d–103a]	342
17:5 [103a]	291
17:9 [103a]	234

  Kedoshim

4:1 [90b]	326–327

  Sheratzim

2:3 [48d]	297

  Tzav

6:2 [34d]	233

Sifrei Deuteronomy

§35 p. 63	256–257
§42, p. 91	301
§61, p. 127	345
§62, pp. 127–128	328–329
§76, p. 141	329–330
§85, p. 150	275
§93, p. 154	276
§106, p. 164	336
§106, p. 165	337
§106, p. 167	327
§109, p. 170	295–296
§112, p. 172	339
§114, p. 174	254, 350
§117, p. 176	330–331
§118, p. 177	350
§119, p. 178	262–263
§128, p. 186	328
§131, p. 188	354
§135, p. 191	252–253
§143, p. 196	328, 340
§147, p. 202	293
§149, p. 204	254
§173, p. 220	326
§175, p. 221	265, 293
§195, p. 235	296
§204, p. 239	291, 297–298
§211, p. 245	271
§214, p. 247	272
§215, p. 249	323
§221, p. 254	353–354
§230, p. 262	240
§249, p. 277	287
§253, p. 279	338
§265, p. 286	274–275
§268, p. 287	292
§271, pp. 291–292	188
§271, p. 292	231
§278, p. 296	263
§286, pp. 302	271
§286, p. 303	258
§287, p. 305	262
§292, p. 311	356
§293, p. 312	356–357

Sifrei Numbers

§2, p. 4	226
§68, p. 63	307–308
§78, p. 75	279
§85, p. 85	291
§90, p. 91	183–184, 195
§99, p. 98	255
§103, p. 101	255
§107, p. 110	244

§107, p. 111	360
§112, p. 119	228
§112, p. 121	222–223
§114, p. 123	253–254
§116, p. 131	361–362
§118, p. 138	358
§118, p. 139	294, 306
§119, p. 142	293
§123, p. 151	292
§125, pp. 160–161	240–241
§131, p. 173	193
§142, p. 188	280
§144, p. 197	281
§149, p. 195	251
§153, p. 200	286

Palestinian Talmud

'Avodah Zarah	
4:4 [44a]	146
Berakhot	
9:5 [13b]	230
Ma'aser Sheni	
5:5 [55d]	78

Babylonian Talmud

'Avodah Zarah	
42b	146
Bava Metzi'a	
12b	250
Ḥullin	
85a	85
Ketubbot	
2a	143
Sanhedrin	
51b	231–232
99b	207
Shabbat	
88a	321

Aggadic Midrashim

Avot de-Rabbi Natan, version A	
ch. 18	22
Leviticus Rabbah	
1:10	141
Pesikta Rabbati	
§5	140–141

Founded in 1893,
UNIVERSITY OF CALIFORNIA PRESS
publishes bold, progressive books and journals
on topics in the arts, humanities, social sciences,
and natural sciences—with a focus on social
justice issues—that inspire thought and action
among readers worldwide.

The UC PRESS FOUNDATION
raises funds to uphold the press's vital role
as an independent, nonprofit publisher, and
receives philanthropic support from a wide
range of individuals and institutions—and from
committed readers like you. To learn more, visit
ucpress.edu/supportus.